Psychology of Physical Activity
Determinants, well-being and interventions

Stuart J. H. Biddle and Nanette Mutrie

 Routledge
Taylor & Francis Group

LONDON AND NEW YORK

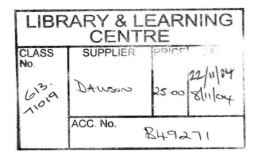
First published 2001
by Routledge
11 New Fetter Lane, London EC4P 4EE

Simultaneously published in the USA and Canada
by Routledge
29 West 35th Street, New York, NY 10001

Reprinted 2002, 2003

Routledge is an imprint of the Taylor & Francis Group

© 1995 Carol Duncan

Typeset in Times
Printed and bound in Great Britain by
TJ International Ltd, Padstow, Cornwall

British Library Cataloguing in Publication Data
A catalogue record for this book is available from the British Library

Library of Congress Cataloging in Publication Data
Biddle, Stuart.
  Psychology of physical activity : determinants, well-being, and interventions / Stuart J. H. Biddle and Nanette Mutrie.
    p. cm
  Includes bibliographical references and index.
    1. Exercise–Psychological aspects. 2. Health psychology. 3. Health promotion. I. Mutrie, Nanette, 1953– II. Title.
  RA781 .B486 2001
  613.7'1'019- -dc21   00–062753

ISBN 0–415–23525–1 (hbk)
ISBN 0–415–23526–X (pbk)

Contents

Figures

Tables

Foreword

Kenneth R. Fox

Exercise psychology emerged from its sport psychology roots and began to establish itself as a serious science as recently as the 1980s. Since that time it has seen exponential growth as a field of study that is reflected in a string of national and international journals and associations adding *exercise* to their titles. The number of exercise psychology research papers presented at international conferences and published in specialist and general psychology journals continues to multiply each year. There is little doubt that exercise psychology as a legitimate area of research is here to stay.

This growth is not simply a response to academic curiosity or whim, but to the synchronous recognition by medical and health authorities world-wide that exercise is critical to health and well-being. Subsequently, national policies and strategies have emerged across the world to promote exercise among the general public. It is not surprising that the prescriptive model of medicine has been applied to exercise and the focus has been on the required dosage of exercise per unit of health benefit. However, there has been an increasing realisation that the key challenge is in the promotion and maintenance of exercise as a health behaviour. This is where exercise psychology comes to the fore. It addresses three key questions that are skilfully woven into the key fabric of this book:

1   Which individual factors cause or prevent physical activity?
2   How does participation influence mental well-being?
3   How are effective activity promotion initiatives designed and delivered for public health?

The choice of physical activity in the book title is no doubt deliberate and wise. In the past five years, there has been a strong shift in perspective to a broader acceptance of the importance of lifestyle activity for health, of which programmed exercise sessions might be just one part.

This is their second book and Stuart Biddle and Nanette Mutrie have once again responded to the demand for answers regarding exercise motivation and mental health outcomes from exercise. They have recognised the need to assimilate the rapidly growing research base in exercise psychology into an up-to-date synthesis and have applied it skilfully to the professional issues facing individual health and exercise specialists and also the purchasers and providers of health services. At the same time through this book, they have produced an essential read for all undergraduates and graduates who intend to develop their research or professional careers in this important and expanding field.

Both are eminently qualified to achieve this formidable task. Stuart Biddle has a record of publishing in the social psychological aspects of exercise that stretches back twenty years.

At the same time he has been at the forefront of developments in the field serving as the Secretary for the British Association of Sport and Exercise Sciences (BASES), and has been responsible for taking European exercise and sport psychology forward in giant leaps during his eight-year presidency of the European Federation of Sport Psychology (FEPSAC). He is now the Editor-in-Chief of *Psychology of Sport and Exercise*. Nanette Mutrie has a similarly strong record in exercise psychology and had been the leading researcher in the UK in clinical aspects of exercise promotion, particularly with special groups. She has served as Chair of the Psychology section of BASES, has worked closely for over ten years with the Health Education Board for Scotland, and is now the UK representative for FEPSAC. Both these widely-known academics have grown with the field and in the process have earned a reputation of high professionalism and integrity. During this period, I have been fortunate to share their friendship and collegiality and can think of no stronger partnership for providing this contemporary overview of this important body of knowledge.

Kenneth R. Fox
Professor of Exercise and Health Sciences
University of Bristol

Foreword

Steven N. Blair

Investigators in exercise science initially focused on biological responses to physical activity, and later progressed to experimental studies of adaptation to exercise. In the latter half of the twentieth century the epidemiology of physical activity and health received attention, and physical inactivity has been identified as an important public health problem in many countries. It is clear that humans evolved to be active animals, and that we are not well equipped to live in a society in which physical activity has largely been engineered out of daily life and where highly palatable food is abundant, cheap, and usually only minutes away. Think about it: how often are you more than about five minutes away from food if you decide that you want something to eat? These living conditions have resulted in a large percentage of the population in industrialised societies becoming sedentary and unfit, and often overweight or obese.

Many individuals are nearly completely sedentary. Over the past several years my research group has conducted a number of large clinical trials of physical activity interventions in order to develop and investigate, and hopefully improve, methods to help sedentary persons be more active. We have recruited almost one thousand adults from our community to participate in these studies. Selection criteria for these studies require that individuals be inactive. After all, we are studying the effect of interventions to increase physical activity, and it would not make sense to recruit marathon runners. We use a structured seven-day physical activity recall as the primary measure of physical activity, and this method provides an estimate of the average total daily caloric intake of study participants. The average energy expenditure in the groups recruited for these studies is about 33 or 34 kcal $\cdot$ kg^{-1} $\cdot$ day^{-1}. To put those numbers in perspective, a score on the seven-day recall of 32 kcal $\cdot$ kg^{-1} $\cdot$ day^{-1} would be obtained by a person who slept for eight hours and spent sixteen hours in activities that did not reach the energy expenditure equivalent of walking at three miles per hour. In other words, the average participants recruited for our studies spend their entire waking hours sitting or in slow moving tasks around the house or office. They have sedentary jobs, do little work around the house or garden, and are largely sedentary in their leisure-time. There is no shortage of eligible participants for our studies, and meeting recruitment goals has not been difficult.

Epidemiological research over the past few decades clearly documents the health hazards of sedentary behavior. Inactive and unfit individuals are much more likely to develop cardiovascular diseases, Type II diabetes, some cancers and obesity. Much of the frailty associated with old age is likely due to decades of inactivity and the progressive loss of muscle tissue and aerobic power. The high prevalence of sedentary and unfit individuals in many countries and the high risk associated with these conditions makes inactivity a major public health problem.

Until quite recently exercise scientists have focused little attention on the principles, concepts and methods from the behavioural and social sciences. It is clear that this must change if we are to apply the findings from exercise biology and physical activity epidemiology to the public health problems faced by an increasingly sedentary society. It does little good to have an understanding of physiological adaptations to exercise or to document the numerous health hazards of a sedentary and unfit way of life unless this information can be applied in effective intervention programmes to help more people be more active.

Fortunately, over the past decade many investigators have turned their attention to behavioural and social aspects of physical activity. We have learned much about the determinants of physical activity (or perhaps of inactivity), how to help sedentary individuals adopt and maintain higher levels of physical activity, and the effects of physical activity on psychosocial outcomes. Much additional work is needed, and this text by Stuart Biddle and Nanette Mutrie will be extremely useful to all health professionals who have an interest in the psycho-social aspects of physical activity.

The authors present an ambitious and broad-ranging review of the current state of our understanding of the psychology of physical activity. The introductory chapter provides an excellent overview of the history of physical activity, health problems caused by inactivity, and physical activity patterns in industrialised countries. Biddle and Mutrie are authorities on physical activity models and theories, motivational and attitudinal aspects of physical activity, and other psychosocial characteristics of physical activity. They present a thorough review of these topics, written in a clear and understandable format. They also review the evidence on the relation of physical activity to mental health and illness, and close with discussions of intervention approaches at the individual and community levels.

This text will be useful for physicians and other healthcare providers, public health professionals, health and fitness leaders, and anyone interested in learning more about the psychology of physical activity from two leaders in the field. It is my hope that many more individuals will become knowledgeable about the issues covered here, and that more effective campaigns will be mounted to address one of our most serious public health problems.

Steven N. Blair
Director of Epidemiology
Cooper Institute, Dallas, Texas

Preface

A book of any length is a big undertaking these days. In the UK, the Research Assessment Exercise, in which university departments are judged on their research standards, focuses on peer reviewed publications as the major outcome on which research is assessed. This means that writing textbooks has become a low priority. Time to write is even harder to find than it used to be. However, we would like to acknowledge our colleagues around the world, but particularly in Europe and in the British Association of Sport and Exercise Sciences (BASES), for encouraging us to re-write and update our 1991 text. When we wrote our first text, *Psychology of Physical Activity and Exercise* (Biddle and Mutrie 1991) our UK association was called BASS (British Association of Sports Sciences) rather than BASES. We hope that our work has played a part in including the area of exercise for health in the work of our national association. Indeed, at the time of the first text being published we were seeing a huge increase in the study of health-related exercise from a psychological point of view. Inevitably this led to the text becoming quickly dated, particularly in areas such as mental health where significant meta-analytic reviews were published from 1990. In addition, sadly, the text was not brought to the attention of the North American market to the extent that a text on exercise psychology published in 1992 was marketed in the USA as the first such text! Overall, therefore, a new book is long overdue. While this current book stems from our first, it is far more than a second edition. We prefer to see it as a completely new text in its own right, although some sections have required only minor updating.

We dedicated our first book to the memory of our mentor and Professor at The Pennsylvania State University: Dr Dorothy V. Harris. Her enthusiasm for the area of exercise and health – well ahead of its time – provided us with the motivation to continue to study that area and we think she would be pleased with our efforts to highlight exercise psychology as a field of study. We therefore acknowledge her teaching and leadership in this area again for this book. In addition, Stuart's mentor in the early part of his career was Dr Basil Ashford. Sadly, Basil passed away within four months of a well-earned retirement. He, too, had the vision to promote and support exercise psychology through his teaching and research and this vision, coupled with his motivational drive, is badly missed. We acknowledge Basil's contributions to the field.

As everyone knows, writing a book expands into all other spheres of life and at crucial moments takes priority over other things. As exercise psychologists, we would like to think that we kept a balance (with the help of the cycle rides, workouts or games of squash) between work and the rest of our lives. We know, however, that those close to us had to put up with a lot to get this book finished. When Stuart's son said to him 'why are you always working?' we knew that the book had to get finished fast! To our families, friends, students and colleagues who supported us in the completion of this work we can certainly say 'we could not have done it without you'. Indeed, special recognition is given to the many outstanding students we have had the privilege of working with over the years.

Nanette Mutrie would like to acknowledge the University of Glasgow for providing sabbatical leave that allowed the final chapters to be completed and her colleagues in the Centre for Exercise Science and Medicine for taking up the extra load that the sabbatical no doubt created. Stuart Biddle acknowledges the University of Exeter for granting a study leave which resulted in the text getting started prior to his departure to Loughborough University. The excellent environment of Loughborough is particularly appreciated.

Gaining insight into exercise and health comes from many sources. We are grateful for the opportunities that have come our way, such as working on projects supported by the Health Education Authority, Somerset Health Authority, Greater Glasgow Health Board, British Heart Foundation, Institute of Youth Sport (Loughborough University), Nike, and the Devon Northcott Medical Foundation. Finally, we thank the excellent work of the staff at Routledge for their support and encouragement.

Stuart Biddle
Loughborough University
Nanette Mutrie
University of Glasgow

Part I
Introduction and rationale

1 Introduction and rationale

We must get serious about improving the health of the nation by affirming our commitment to healthy physical activity.

Acting US Surgeon General, Audrey F. Manley
(Department of Health and Human Services 1996)

Chapter objectives

The purpose of this chapter is to introduce key concepts in the study of physical activity, exercise and health as a prelude to a more extensive discussion in subsequent chapters of physical activity, psychological determinants, psychological well-being, and interventions to promote physical activity. Specifically, in this chapter we aim to:

- To provide a brief synopsis of human evolution and history that is relevant to current physical activity and health behaviours.
- Define key terms.
- Highlight recent policy and position statements on physical activity and exercise.
- Summarise the evidence linking physical activity and exercise with various health outcomes and risks.
- Review the prevalence and trends in physical activity in selected countries.

This book is written in the belief that many forms of physical activity are healthy! As a result we have been interested in the promotion of physical activity for some time now and this represents our second text on the subject (Biddle and Mutrie 1991). However, a great deal of time seems to be spent on identifying the biological mechanisms of the health effects of activity – which is fine, and indeed essential – but rather less energy has been devoted to the issues of why people do or do not exercise much, what the psychological benefits might be, or the best ways of promoting physical activity. But to be fair, times are changing. We have seen a significant increase in interest in 'exercise psychology' and related topics in the past decade, although the 'medical' model of health still has a strong influence. In writing our book in 1991 we had available as a resource the excellent proceedings book of the 1988 *International Conference on Exercise, Fitness and Health* held in Toronto, Canada (Bouchard *et al.* 1990). In the sixty-two chapters (most of which contained parallel 'discussant' chapters), we could locate only six with a clear psychological/behavioural emphasis; in effect, this meant three topics. However, in the proceedings from the second International Conference, held in Toronto in 1992 (Bouchard, Shephard and Stephens 1994), twelve of seventy-one chapters (excluding the consensus statement), were psychological or behavioural in orientation or contained substantial behavioural material. All twelve chapters also addressed a different behavioural issue.

Even within the field of physical activity psychology, there has been a greater recognition of exercise for health whereas in the past the vast majority of the literature focused on competitive sport. For example, one of the key research journals, *Journal of Sport Psychology*, became the *Journal of Sport and Exercise Psychology* (JSEP) in 1988 to better reflect the field. Similarly, in a recent review of trends in sport and exercise psychology (Biddle 1997b), two journals (JSEP and the *International Journal of Sport Psychology*) were analysed for content over the ten-year period 1985–94 and exercise studies were the most popular overall in comparison to sport-related constructs and showed the most significant increase over the time period studied (nearly 250 per cent). Also, Tenenbaum and Bar-Eli (1995), using a computer search of sport/exercise psychology research, found that 'health, physical fitness and wellness' papers increased greatly from 1975 to 1991, for both advanced and all types of papers (see Figure 1.1).

This book, therefore, provides a review of contemporary psychological knowledge in physical activity, with an emphasis on participation and health rather than sport performance. Although usually referred to as 'exercise psychology', we feel that this may reflect only structured bouts of physical activity, as we discuss in the definitions section shortly. We therefore prefer to broaden the discussion to 'physical activity' in its widest sense, at least as far as health is concerned. However, as you will see, a great deal of the literature does actually refer to exercise as this is often an easier behaviour to quantify and study.

In this introductory chapter, we present a rationale for the study of physical activity, outline briefly some of the health benefits of physical activity, and summarise initiatives and statements from key organisations that illustrate the importance of the topic. Finally, we overview the evidence on how active, or inactive, people are in contemporary Western societies. The chapter provides a background on which to judge and assess the role of behavioural and psychological factors in physical activity. Specifically, in this book we address:

- psychological determinants of physical activity
- psychological well-being and physical activity involvement
- interventions to increase physical activity.

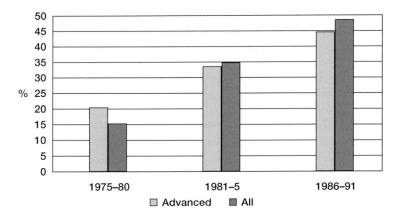

Figure 1.1 Publication trends for 'health, physical fitness and wellness' psychology papers from 1975–91 (data from Tenenbaum and Bar-Eli 1995). Figures show percentage of each category of publication being published across the three time periods.

Finally, let us say that we fully acknowledge that psychological factors are but one set of influences, or potential influences, on physical activity. Our preference, at this stage, however, is to write a review of these issues so as to provide a more focused analysis, while recognising the powerful influence of social, political, economic, environmental and many other factors.

Physical activity, evolution and history

In the wonderful animated film *The Wrong Trousers,* Wallace buys his dog, Grommit, a pair of 'techno-trousers': automatically walking trousers that allow Wallace to sit at home while the techno-trousers take Grommit for a walk. Is this the shape of things to come, seeking ways of allowing our pets to exercise without moving ourselves? As Wallace said, 'I think you will find these a valuable addition to our modern lifestyle'. It is ironic that we wouldn't dream of depriving our dogs of their walk!

From Grommit to Astrand: 'There is virtually no way of reverting to our "natural" way of life, but with insight into our biological heritage we may be able to modify the current, self-destructive, elements of our modern lifestyle' (Astrand 1994: 103). Astrand's fascinating analysis of evolutionary history in relation to current lifestyles highlights the central issue: we are now living our lives, at least in developed countries, in ways that are largely unhealthy and different from what we have done for most of our past. Astrand's analysis of lifestyles of humans since we first appeared on Earth some 4 million years ago led him to conclude 'during more than 99 per cent of our existence we were hunters and food gatherers. Now we are exposed to an enormous experiment – without control groups' (Astrand 1994: 101).

Blair (1988), for example, suggests that four evolutionary periods are important in understanding the relationship between physical activity and health. The pre-agricultural period (up until about 10,000 years ago) was characterised by hunting and gathering activities. Exercise levels were high and diet was low in fat. The agricultural period (from 10,000 years ago until about the beginning of the nineteenth century) was characterised again by reasonably high physical activity levels and relatively low-fat diets, although the fat content probably increased during this time.

The industrial period (1800–1945) saw the development of the 'industrialised society' with the accompanying problems of over-crowding, poor diet, poor public health measures and inadequate medical facilities and care. Infectious diseases were responsible for a high proportion of premature deaths. However, this trend became reversed in the 'nuclear/technological' period, which Blair (1988) identified as from 1945 until the present. The major improvement in public health measures and medical advances meant that infectious diseases were becoming less common in 'advanced' societies. However, health problems were merely shifted in terms of causes and outcomes. The major causes of premature mortality have now become 'lifestyle related', such as coronary heart disease, with risk factors such as cigarette smoking, diet and lack of physical activity (Paffenbarger *et al.* 1994a). As Paffenbarger *et al.* put it, 'both energy intake and energy output are determined primarily by individual behavior' (119).

In short, humans have now adopted lifestyles in industrialised countries that were quite unknown until very recently in terms of human evolution. This is not to say, of course, that 'health' has deteriorated necessarily. Far from it in some cases, although this depends on the definition and measurement of health. Lifespan itself has increased dramatically. In developed Western societies we can expect to live at least until we are 70 years old, whereas average life expectancy was less than 50 only in the middle of the last century (Malina 1988). Similarly, other indicators of physical and mental health have shown improvements, although Malina (1988) says that these are largely restricted to the 'developed' countries. Indeed, it has been an explicit health objective for international (Department of Health 1995) and national (Department of Health 1993b) concerns to increase both longevity and quality of life.

But the change in lifestyle, particularly in the latter part of the twentieth century, has brought its own health problems. Some have referred to a selection of these as 'hypokinetic diseases', or health problems caused by, or related to, a lack of physical activity (Kraus and Raab 1961). Such hypokinetic problems can include poor mental health, coronary heart disease (CHD), obesity, low back pain, osteoporosis, hypertension, diabetes and some cancers. The evidence linking physical activity patterns with such health measures is increasing rapidly and will be reviewed in brief shortly.

Box 1.1 Some do, some don't: observations of physical activity

In addition to analysing the increasing amount of data we have on physical activity in our society, it is informative and certainly interesting to note a few observations of everyday life that relate to physical activity. To support the claims made in this opening chapter that some forms of physical activity have increased over the past decade or so, it is quite obvious that there are more exercise classes available in the community and more joggers on the street in comparison to, say, fifteen years ago. Even the social climate seems to have changed. No longer, or certainly less often, do you get the 'get yer knees up!' 'encouragement' shouted at you as you jog the streets. Even cycling is becoming a fashionable pursuit again. Sports shops are numerous and sports/leisure wear is fashionable, although whether this reflects increased participation, of course, is another matter.

Mass media is content to carry the exercise massage too. The early morning workout 'experts' are now well-known and Britain's 'Mr Motivator' appears to be in big demand for TV, radio, videos and mass participation events. Exercise videos and 'shape up' books, however dubious the content for some, reach the top ten lists of best sellers. Of course, many are bought for Christmas presents and the recipients never get past the first few days of involvement.

On the other hand, we can also observe many people actively pursuing inactivity! Arriving back at London's Heathrow airport one time, Stuart came across the amusing sight of a passenger deciding whether to walk to the *right* about 20 metres in order to get on the moving walkway which was travelling *left* back to the baggage claim area! And surely we have far more labour-saving devices than a few years ago (who needs an electric toothbrush?), and we use motorised transport far more than we need. Yet, at the same time, local planning officers are attempting to integrate more cycle paths into our communities, reduce private car use, and increase public transport. Although these are often for environmental and life quality reasons, rather than to increase physical activity *per se*, they are a move in the right direction.

Defining key terms

With the increasing interest being shown in the exercise and sports sciences, and the links now being made between various medical and non-medical disciplines in relation to physical activity, the terminology adopted in the study of health and physical activity has not always been consistent. This section will give operational definitions and clarifications to key words and terms.

Physical activity

Caspersen, Powell and Christenson (1985) define physical activity in terms of the three following elements:

- Movement of the body produced by the skeletal muscles.
- Resulting energy expenditure which varies from low to high.
- A positive correlation with physical fitness.

As far as health outcomes are concerned, the energy expenditure is usually required to be well above resting levels (Bouchard and Shephard 1994). For example, while I could be classified as being physically active while writing this book (fingers are moving fairly rapidly across the keyboard), this type of physical activity is largely irrelevant for health for most people. However, in special cases such manipulative skills are encouraging the maintenance of functional capacity and life quality, such as in very old or activity-impaired individuals.

Given the decline in the amount of physical activity that most people have to perform in work duties, and the increase in motorised transport, a great deal of physical activity that has become necessary for health must be freely chosen in leisure time or consciously integrated into one's normal daily routine. This, in itself, justifies the increasing importance of studying psychological processes, such as motivation and decision-making, in physical activity.

Exercise

Given that physical activity includes all movement, it is helpful also to recognise sub-components, or elements, of physical activity. Caspersen *et al.* (1985: 127) define exercise with reference to the following factors:

- Body movement produced by skeletal muscles.
- Resulting energy expenditure varying from low to high (so far, these points are the same as for physical activity).
- 'Very positively correlated with physical fitness'.
- 'Planned, structured and repetitive bodily movement'.
- The objective is to maintain or improve physical fitness.

Exercise may also have the objective of health enhancement or improving performance (Bouchard and Shephard 1994). However, the distinction between physical activity and exercise is not always easy and one should recognise an overlap between the two constructs. In this book, exercise will usually refer to more structured leisure-time physical activity, such as participation in jogging, swimming, 'keep-fit' activities and recreational sports.

In the past few years, it has been recognised that, for many, exercise is perceived as being hard-work, vigorous, and possibly unpleasant. Consequently, the need to promote 'active living' (Killoran, Cavill and Walker 1994; Quinney, Gauvin and Wall 1994) or an 'active lifestyle' has been recognised in an effort to produce a more acceptable or palatable message.

Sport

Philosophers have argued long and hard over the word sport, but for our purposes we define it as a sub-component of exercise whereby the activity is rule governed, structured and competitive and involves gross motor movement characterised by physical strategy, prowess and chance (Rejeski and Brawley 1988). The competitive nature of sport has sometimes been difficult to clarify. Indeed, the sports councils in the UK have jurisdiction over activities that are non-competitive (for example, keep-fit and yoga), and 'Sport for All' campaigns have often included a wider range of activities than 'traditional' competitive sports. Indeed, it is common to hear the phrase 'mass sport' or 'health sport' (Nitsch and Seiler 1994) on the European mainland when physical recreation or exercise might be more usual terms for those in North America or the UK.

Health and well-being

Health is multifactorial in nature and includes dimensions of the physical, mental and social, and some might argue the 'spiritual'. It involves enhancement of well-being as well as absence of disease. High positive health is sometimes referred to as 'wellness' or high level well-being. This is positive physical and emotional well-being with a high capacity for enjoying life and challenges, and possessing adequate coping strategies in the face of difficulties. Negative health is characterised by disease, morbidity and possibly premature death (Bouchard and Shephard 1994).

Physical fitness

Broadly speaking, physical fitness refers to the ability of the individual to perform muscular work. Caspersen *et al.* define it as 'a set of attributes that people have or achieve that relates to the ability to perform physical activity' (Caspersen *et al.* 1985: 129). This suggests that physical fitness is partly related to current physical activity levels ('attributes that people *achieve*') and partly a function of heredity ('attributes that people *have*').

In recent years it has become more usual to refer to health-related and performance (skill)-related components of physical fitness (Caspersen *et al.* 1985). The performance-related aspects of fitness are associated with athletic ability and are sometimes referred to as 'motor fitness'. The components include agility, balance, co-ordination, power, reaction time and speed. There is no evidence linking the development of such qualities to 'health' outcomes, such as the reduction of risk for chronic disease. However, they may have more indirect or less tangible health benefits such as through the development of independence for older people. Generally speaking, though, they are separated from health-related components of fitness, and epidemiological evidence supports such a distinction. The skill-related aspects of fitness are important, of course, for sport and other activities relying on motor skills and abilities.

The health-related components of physical fitness have traditionally been identified as cardiovascular fitness, muscular strength and endurance, muscle flexibility and body composition (Caspersen *et al.* 1985). The development of these components of health-related fitness (HRF) has been related to specific 'health' or disease outcomes. Indeed, Pate

(1988) has argued that 'physical fitness' should be defined solely in terms of the health-related aspects by stating that the following criteria should be met in such a definition:

- Fitness should refer to the functional capacities required for comfortable and productive involvement in day-to-day activities.
- It should 'encompass manifestation of the health-related outcomes of high levels of habitual activity' (Pate 1988: 177).

Bouchard and Shephard (1994), however, broaden the definition of HRF by referring to morphological, muscular, motor, cardiovascular and metabolic components. Given the public health perspective adopted in this book, the types and forms of exercise and physical activity that have been reviewed in relation to psychological principles and research are generally health-related. Those interested in the development and control of motor skill activities, and associated psychological aspects, are referred elsewhere (Magill 1989; Schmidt 1982). Similarly, competitive sport, except where it sheds some light on the wider public health aspects of exercise and physical activity, is not covered. Again readers are referred elsewhere (Biddle 1995b; Singer, Murphey, and Tennant 1993).

Determinants

We have used the word 'determinants' to reflect the factors that affect, or are thought to affect, participation in exercise and physical activity. It has become the standard term to use for this in the literature, although it should be recognised that many of the factors discussed under this heading are not, or may not be, true determinants. In other words, data may show associations but information cannot necessarily be gleaned as to causality. Other words, such as antecedents or correlates are appropriate, but the word determinants is widely accepted now.

Policy and position statements on physical activity and exercise

A growing number of organisations are producing position statements and policy documents on health-related behaviours, including physical activity. This reflects the increasing concern regarding the changes in morbidity and premature mortality that face many contemporary societies. Two of the largest projects undertaken in this respect emanate from the World Health Organization and the Department of Health and Human Services in the United States. In addition, many other national organisations have made statements or been involved in substantial promotion of physical activity.

Health for All 2000

The World Health Organization (WHO) published its targets for 'health for all' in their European region in 1985. The 1986 revision of their book *Targets for Health for All* 'set out the fundamental requirements for people to be healthy, to define the improvements in health that can be achieved by the year 2000 for the peoples of the European region of WHO, and to propose action to secure these improvements' (World Health Organization 1986: 1). Broadly, WHO lists four dimensions of health outcomes they wish to achieve. These are equity in health, adding 'life to years', adding 'health to life' and adding years to life.

Specifically, thirty-eight targets have been outlined up until the year 2000. The targets which are of particular interest to exercise researchers are summarised in Table 1.1.

Such broad statements are only likely to be effective when placed in a more specific national and regional context and with more precise goals. Nevertheless, the importance of such statements should be recognised as indicative of a greater role for preventive health practices in the future.

Health of the Nation/Our Healthier Nation in England

The 'Health of the Nation' (HON) initiative in England by the British government of the time (Department of Health 1993b) marked a significant change in approach in health care and promotion in England. This is discussed more fully in Chapter 12 when we consider legislative initiatives in physical activity promotion, but for the sake of continuity we shall outline a few key points here also.

The overall aims of the HON were:

- 'Adding years to life': reduce premature mortality and improve life expectancy.
- 'Adding life to years': improve the quality of life.

Physical activity was identified as an important element to combat coronary heart disease and stroke, one of the five priority areas of the HON initiative. A 'Physical Activity Task Force' (PATF) was established with the remit of recommending targets and strategies for physical activity for the English population. However, later on the Government decided that they did not want targets, leaving the PATF to consider strategies. This led to the Health Education Authority's 'Active for Life' campaign and other local initiatives.

Table 1.1 Selected WHO 'Health for All 2000' targets relevant to physical activity

Target Number	Target
9	Diseases of the Circulation: by the year 2000, mortality in the Region[1] from diseases of the circulatory system in people under 65 years of age should be reduced by at least 15%
13	Healthy Public Policy: by 1990, national policies in all Member States[2] should ensure that legislative, administrative and economic mechanisms provide broad intersectoral support and resources for the promotion of healthy lifestyles and ensure effective participation of the people at all levels of such policy-making.
15	Knowledge and Motivation for Healthy Behaviour: by 1990, educational programmes in all Member States should enhance the knowledge, motivation and skills of people to acquire and maintain health.
16	Positive Health Behaviour: by 1995, in all Member States, there should be significant increases in positive health behaviour, such as balanced nutrition, non-smoking, appropriate physical activity and good stress management.
32	Research Strategies: before 1990, all Member States should have formulated research strategies to stimulate investigations which improve the application and expansion of knowledge needed to support their 'Health for All' developments.

Notes
1 Region: Europe.
2 Member States: the thirty-three European countries who are members of WHO (see World Health Organization 1986).

The new Labour Government developed the HON through the *Our Healthier Nation* discussion paper early in 1998 (Department of Health 1998). This sought to tackle the 'root causes' of ill health and was explicit about the need to address social inequalities as a contributing factor to health and health inequalities.

The American experience: Health Objectives for the Nation and Healthy People 2000

A more specific set of goals was established by the Department of Health and Human Services (DHHS) of the United States' Government (Department of Health and Human Services 1980). Initially, the DHHS set 223 'health objectives for the nation' by the year 1990. As with the WHO targets these included many objectives unrelated to physical activity. However, the DHHS did set eleven objectives for 1990 that were concerned specifically with exercise and physical fitness. A review in 1985 revealed a mixed pattern of success in moving towards the objectives and targets set (Powell *et al.* 1986).

Consequently, a revision of the 1990 objectives was made in a 'midcourse review'. New proposals (Department of Health and Human Services 1986) suggested that thirty-six exercise and fitness objectives be stated for the year 2000. Of particular importance from the point of view of the psychological approach adopted in this book are the following two objectives:

- 'By 2000, the relationship between participation in various types of physical activities during childhood and adolescence and the physical activity practices of adults will be known'.
- 'By 2000, the behavioural skills associated with a high probability of adopting and maintaining a regular exercise programme will be known' (Dishman 1988b: 435).

The American Healthy People 2000 project (Department of Health and Human Services 1991), has rationalised these thirty-six objectives into twelve. These include national objectives for physical activity levels, physical education provision, workplace physical activity promotion, availability of community facilities and primary care interventions to increase physical activity. With the increased recognition of the health benefits of physical activity levels below the threshold thought to be necessary for cardiovascular fitness, the Healthy People 2000 objectives place greater emphasis than the 1990 objectives on reducing inactivity and increasing participation in moderate physical activity.

In addition to the Healthy People 2000 strategy, several of the main American agencies also contributed to the influential Surgeon General's *Report on Physical Activity and Health* (Department of Health and Human Services 1996). Its main purpose was to summarise existing evidence on the benefits of physical activity and to draw conclusions for improving health in Americans. Some of the major conclusions from this report are shown in Table 1.2.

Position statements

A number of position statements have emerged that address the issues of physical activity, exercise and physical fitness. One of the first statements addressed adults. The American College of Sports Medicine (ACSM) (American College of Sports Medicine 1978) produced the standard guidelines for the development of cardiovascular fitness in healthy adults. This has now been revised and extended into a new position paper concerning

Table 1.2 Selected major conclusions from the Surgeon General's *Report on Physical Activity and Health*

- People of all ages benefit from regular physical activity.
- Significant health benefits can be obtained by including moderate amounts of physical activity on most days of the week.
- Physical activity: reduces the risk of premature mortality, improves mental health and is important for the health of muscles, bones and joints.
- More than 60% of American adults are not regularly active; 25% are not active at all.

Source: Department of Health and Human Services 1996.

cardiovascular fitness, as well as muscular strength and endurance and body composition (American College of Sports Medicine 1990). The recommended parameters for cardiovascular fitness are:

- Frequency: 3–5 days per week.
- Intensity: 60–90 per cent of maximum heart rate, or 50–85 per cent $VO_{2\,max}$ or heart rate reserve.
- Duration: 20–60 minutes of continuous aerobic activity.
- Mode: large muscle groups' activities that are continuous, rhythmic and aerobic.

Subsequent research now shows that a graded dose-response relationship exists between physical activity and health, consequently it makes better sense not to 'prescribe' exercise only for the development of cardiovascular fitness but for other health outcomes as well. This can be done through more moderate levels of physical activity and has led to the recent statement by Pate *et al.* (1995) for the Centers for Disease Control and Prevention and ACSM that stated that adults should accumulate thirty minutes or more of moderate intensity physical activity on most, and preferably all, days of the week. This is similar to recommendations in England associated with the 'Active for Life' campaign.

The ACSM has also made a statement about the physical fitness of children and youth (American College of Sports Medicine 1988). They make eight specific recommendations, including the development of appropriate school physical education programmes that emphasise lifetime exercise habits, enhanced knowledge about exercise, and behaviour change; the encouragement of a greater role in the development of children's activity levels from parents, community organisations and healthcare professionals; the adoption of a scientifically sound approach to fitness testing in schools whereby the emphasis is placed on health-related aspects assessed in relation to acceptable criteria rather than normative comparison; and finally award schemes for fitness should encourage individual exercise behaviour and achievement rather than superior athletic ability.

A similar statement on children was issued by the Sports Council, in conjunction with the Health Education Authority, in England, and covered the physical growth and development of the child, promotion of health and prevention of disease, body weight, children with special needs, and ten recommendations for the future (Health Education Authority and Sports Council 1988). From the standpoint of this book, the most important recommendation was that more research was required on the development of effective strategies for promoting exercise habits in children. Despite the date of the statement, we have made slow progress in the intervening years.

The European Federation of Sport Psychology (FEPSAC) has produced a position statement on children in sport and made nine recommendations (FEPSAC 1996). These include:

- Children's sport should be organised with the prime objective of enhancing the well-being of the child.
- A mastery motivational climate should be created for children's sports by emphasising personal and self-improvement goals, and stressing enjoyment, the learning and development of new skills, co-operation and feelings of autonomy.

These recommendations are based on the premise of maximising the quality of the experience for children and also sustaining motivation and involvement in physical activity.

Other comprehensive statements on exercise and health are also available. These include, among others, the 'Workshop on epidemiologic and public health aspects of physical activity and exercise' arranged by the American Centers for Disease Control in 1984 (published as a special issue of *Public Health Reports* (1985) vol. 100, issue 2), a position statement from the American Heart Association (Fletcher *et al.* 1992), and the comprehensive volumes stemming from the 1988 and 1992 physical activity consensus conferences in Toronto, Canada (Bouchard *et al.* 1990; 1994). Readers are strongly encouraged to see the consensus statement in Bouchard *et al.* (1994) which contains nearly 70 topics and 355 'important research topics'.

A statement was also endorsed by the World Health Organization and UNESCO as part of the World Forum on Physical Activity and Sport in Quebec City, in May 1995 (*Research Quarterly for Exercise and Sport* 1995). The statement is a succinct consensus on physical activity, health and well-being. Key extracts are shown in Table 1.3.

Health-related outcomes of physical activity and exercise

To understand psychological determinants, psychological well-being and physical activity interventions, it is important to identify the proposed links between physical activity and health that have emerged over recent years. A comprehensive overview can be found in Bouchard *et al.* (1994).

Physical activity, physical fitness and chronic disease

Much of the literature dealing with the health outcomes of physical activity and exercise has been associated with chronic diseases and health risks such as coronary heart disease (CHD) and obesity. Blair *et al.* (1992) review the evidence for various diseases or conditions and the effect physical activity or fitness may have on them. The strongest evidence appears for all-cause mortality and CHD, evidence they describe as 'excellent'. Evidence is 'good' for hypertension, obesity, colon cancer, non-insulin-dependent diabetes mellitus (NIDDM), osteoporosis and functional capacity.

All-cause mortality

Large studies in Finland (Salonen *et al.* 1983) and the USA (Paffenbarger *et al.* 1986) have shown that those who are physically more active are less likely to suffer premature death and thus have greater longevity. Prospective epidemiological studies have established that

Table 1.3 Summary of consensus statement from International Scientific Consensus Conference on 'Physical Activity, Health and Well-Being', Quebec City, Canada, May 1995

1	Physical activity positively influences physical and psychosocial health: it is important at all stages in the life cycle.
2	A sedentary lifestyle influences a variety of vascular and metabolic disturbances, specifically atherosclerosis, hypertension and adult-onset diabetes mellitus. Regular physical activity decreases the risk.
3	Physical activity benefits most of the structural and functional components of the musculo-skeletal system, increasing functional capacity and hence independence and quality of life. A substantial part of the age-related decline in functional capacity is due to decreased and insufficient physical activity, rather than to ageing *per se*.
4	Physical activity decreases the risk of colon cancer and may reduce the risk of developing breast cancer.
5	Exercise has a consistent beneficial effect on mood and psychological well-being, anxiety, depression and psychosocial stress, and may enhance cognitive functioning.
6	A sizeable portion of the population in industrialised countries is sedentary and unfit. Physical inactivity seems to be less common in developing countries but will become an issue with continued development and urbanisation.
7	Some interventions to increase physical activity through work site, community and primary healthcare settings have been successful, showing a potential for change.
8	Promotion of physical activity for children, adolescents, young adults, the middle-aged and the elderly is one of the most effective means of improving health and enhancing function and quality of life.

Source: *Research Quarterly for Exercise and Sport* 1995.

sedentary living carries at least twice the risk of morbidity and all-cause mortality (Powell and Blair 1994). This is also the case when physical fitness is assessed, rather than just physical activity. For example, Blair *et al.* (1989) split their sample of over 10,000 men and 3,000 women from the Aerobics Center Longitudinal Study in Dallas, into five fitness categories based on scores on a maximal treadmill test. Age-adjusted all-cause death rates showed significantly greater risk for the lower fitness groups. This is illustrated in Figure 1.2 where the highest fitness group (5) is represented by the relative risk of 1.0.

Paffenbarger *et al.* conclude that 'evidence accumulates that risks of premature death as compared with its reciprocal, increased longevity, are related to physical activity expressed by participation or non-participation in moderately vigorous sportsplay and by high or low levels of weekly energy expenditure' (Paffenbarger *et al.* 1994a: 130).

Coronary heart disease and stroke

Most interest, if volume of research is considered, has been focused on the proposed link between CHD risk and physical activity. CHD is known to be a major health problem in many industrialised countries. For example, in England and Wales CHD is the leading cause of mortality in males and females and is the condition leading to the second highest number of hospital admissions after cancers. Cardiovascular disorders rank second in terms of certified days lost at work. Countries of the United Kingdom are very high in the international league table for premature deaths from CHD, with estimates putting the total cost of CHD for the National Health Service in hundreds of millions of pounds annually (Barker and Rose 1990).

EPIDEMIOLOGY AND THE CAUSAL LINK

Powell *et al.* (1987) selected forty-three studies having the criterion of sufficient data to calculate relative risk or 'odds ratio' for CHD at varying levels of physical activity. They concluded that:

> the inverse association between physical activity and incidence of CHD is consistently observed, especially in the better designed studies; this association is appropriately sequenced, biologically graded, plausible and coherent with existing knowledge. Therefore, the observations reported in the literature support the inference that physical activity is inversely and causally related to the incidence of CHD
>
> (Powell *et al.* 1987: 283)

This was the first time that such respected researchers had stated their belief that the relationship is causal. Powell *et al.* (283) went on to say that the 'relative risk of inactivity appears to be similar in magnitude to that of hypertension, hypercholesterolemia, and smoking'.

The bulk of the evidence associating CHD and physical inactivity has been accumulated using epidemiological methods. These involve the quantification of health-related behaviours and disease in the population. Specifically, epidemiology attempts to establish the magnitude of the health problem, the causes and modes of transmission, the scientific base for prevention, and evaluation of the effectiveness of preventive or curative measures (Caspersen 1989). The emergent field of 'physical activity epidemiology' can now be identified (Caspersen 1989; Powell 1988; Walter and Hart 1990).

The initial studies on CHD and physical activity investigated activity at work, with the studies of Morris in Britain and Paffenbarger in the USA forming the basis of a demonstrated link (Morris *et al.* 1953; Morris *et al.* 1966; Paffenbarger, Wing and Hyde 1978; Paffenbarger *et al.* 1986). For reviews, see Blair (1993; 1994), Leon (1997) and Paffenbarger *et al.* (1994a).

Although epidemiologic studies can be criticised for problems of self-selection, as was the case with the early Morris *et al.* (1953) studies, the establishment of a plausible cause–effect relationship is possible but requires a number of criteria to be satisfied first, such as temporal sequencing, consistency, specificity, and a dose-response relationship (see Caspersen 1989). The weight of evidence is now supportive of such a relationship for physical inactivity and CHD risk (Blair 1993; Leon 1997).

VIGOROUS OR MODERATE, FITNESS OR ACTIVITY?

The nature and type of exercise necessary to positively affect CHD risk has also been debated. Morris's work has tended to support the notion that aerobic activity of a relatively 'vigorous' nature is the key to reduced CHD risk (although the activities referred to, such as brisk walking and cycling, are probably 'moderate' level activities). He has suggested that the activity should be of the intensity requiring energy expenditure of 7.5 kcals/min. sustained for three periods of twenty minutes per week. Alternatively, Paffenbarger and his co-workers have stressed total leisure-time energy expenditure rather than exercise intensity *per se*. Paffenbarger's study of Harvard alumni showed that those who expended less than 2,000 kcal per week in leisure time were significantly more at risk of premature mortality from CHD than those who expended more than 2,000 kcal/week (see Paffenbarger *et al.* 1994a).

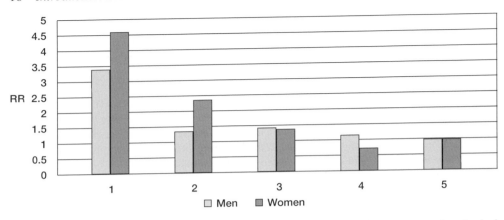

Figure 1.2 Relative risk for age-adjusted all-cause death rates per 10,000 person-years by physical fitness group, indicating the importance of low physical fitness as a risk factor (adapted from Blair *et al.* 1989). Most fit group is the reference category with relative risk (RR) = 1 (1 = low fitness group, 5 = high fitness group).

Whether it is physical fitness or habitual physical activity that is critical in the reduction of CHD risk has remained an issue for discussion for some time now (Blair 1993). In reviewing their own studies, Morris, Everett and Semmence conclude that:

> The main finding in the present studies is that habitual vigorous aerobic exercise for sustained periods, involving the movement of large muscle masses, is the only exercise factor which is consistently and substantially associated with a lower incidence of coronary heart disease. This type of exercise improves 'physical fitness' and its principal components, aerobic power or VO_2 max; and even more, aerobic capacity, stamina and endurance fitness, which means the capacity to function for prolonged periods at a high proportion of VO_2 max whatever the level of that may be.
>
> (Morris *et al.* 1987: 15)

This summary suggests that Morris has some faith in the physical fitness hypothesis for CHD protection. However, his studies provided measures of *activity* rather fitness, so his suggestion that fitness provides the protection for CHD has yet to be substantiated, at least in his research.

Although the epidemiological studies of both work and leisure time activity and CHD tend to support the physical activity hypothesis, a large-scale prospective study of healthy men and women has supported the hypothesis that fitness is related to lowered CHD risk (Blair *et al.* 1989; see Figure 1.2). It appears, therefore, that both physical fitness (at least cardiovascular fitness) and habitual physical activity are both inversely related to CHD risk in adults. Blair (1993) concludes that the physical fitness studies have shown a stronger inverse association with mortality than the physical activity studies, although this may be due to the difficulty of measuring physical activity in contrast to fitness.

Changes in physical activity have also been shown to be associated with reduced risk of CHD. For example, Paffenbarger *et al.*'s (1993) follow-up of men in the Harvard alumni study showed that for those who were sedentary in 1962 or 1966, but later (1977) took up moderate-to-vigorous sports/activities, the health effects were strong. Using 1.0 as the adjusted relative risk index for 1962/66, those active in 1977 had reduced their CHD risk index to less than 0.6, as important to risk reduction as stopping smoking. Similar results were obtained from the Aerobics Center Study, leading Blair to conclude that 'sedentary habits increase the risk of early death and that starting an activity program in middle age can significantly protect against coronary heart disease' (Blair 1993: 371).

Other health outcomes

One of the advantages of physical activity is that it can affect many different health parameters. We shall briefly review the areas of hypertension, obesity, diabetes, immune function, musculo-skeletal health and mental health.

Hypertension

Reviews suggest that favourable effects of exercise can be found for hypertension and that lack of physical activity is a primary risk factor of hypertension (Bouchard and Despres 1995; Fagard and Tipton 1994). Moderate aerobic exercise can reduce systolic/diastolic blood pressures by 3/3 mmHg in normotensives, about 6/7 mmHg in borderline hypertensives, and 10/8 mmHg in hypertensives (Fagard and Tipton 1994). If such reductions were made in large sections of the population, particularly for borderline hypertensives and hypertensives, significant public health benefits would accrue. For example, the English Health of the Nation target for blood pressure for the year 2005 was a reduction of 5 mmHg in systolic blood pressure for adults. If this was achieved, it is estimated that a 10 per cent reduction in CHD and stroke would result (Department of Health 1993b).

Obesity

Based on defining obesity as a Body Mass Index (BMI; weight in kg divided by height in m squared) of thirty or above (British Nutrition Foundation 1999), The Department of Health (1993) has reported that over 10 per cent of the English adult population is obese and that current trends suggest that this is increasing, as shown in Figure 1.3 (Department of Health 1995). Fehily (1999) reports 1996 data showing 16 per cent of men and 18 per cent of women in England are obese. If true, the prevalence of obesity will have more than doubled over sixteen years. The HON target for obesity in England was to reduce obesity levels by the year 2005 by at least 25 per cent in men and 33 per cent in women, leaving only 6 per cent of men and 8 per cent of women classified as obese; figures which equate to obesity levels in 1980. Unfortunately, if current rates continue in the UK, by the year 2005, 24 per cent of women and 18 per cent of men will be clinically obese. With a decline in energy consumption between 1970 and 1990 (Prentice and Jebb 1995), the obesity figures suggest that physical inactivity is a primary cause (Fox 1999a). Increases in overweight and obesity is a world-wide problem for developed countries (Flegal 1999).

Despite physical activity being the principal discretionary component of energy expenditure, the relationship between exercise and body fat is complex (Fox 1999a; Grundy *et al.* 1999; Hill, Drougas and Peters 1994). Nevertheless, the use of exercise in the control of body fat levels is supported despite the small caloric expenditure associated with exercise in comparison with normal dietary intake (Fox 1992; Fox 1999b).

Hill *et al.* (1994) conclude that physical activity helps prevents moderate obesity in some individuals, and inactivity contributes to the development of obesity in some also. However,

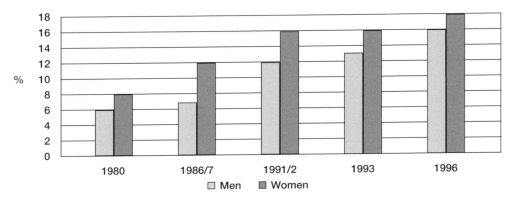

Figure 1.3 Percentage of adult men and women in England classified as obese (BMI>30) across four surveys from 1980–96 (Fehily 1999; Department of Health 1995)

they believe it is erroneous to say that physical inactivity is the sole cause of obesity. Indeed, for severely obese individuals, they are often unable to engage in sufficient physical activity for it to have much effect. Atkinson and Walberg-Rankin conclude that 'the studies evaluating effects of exercise in severely obese subjects on body weight, body composition and metabolic rate are conflicting' (Atkinson and Walberg-Rankin 1994: 709). However, for others, physical activity is the best predictor of successful long-term weight reduction (Bouchard and Despres 1995). Physical activity may be most important in preventing weight increase. Williamson *et al.* (1993), in a large prospective study, calculated the relative risk of moderate (8–13 kg) and large (>13 kg) weight increases over a ten-year period. Men who reported low activity on both occasions had a four-fold chance of moderate weight gain whereas there was a seven-fold chance of a large weight gain for women who were inactive.

Diabetes

Berg (1986) reports that even prior to the discovery of insulin in 1921, exercise was recommended in the treatment of diabetes. Indeed, the 'treatment triad' of diet, insulin and exercise is a frequent term in the control of diabetes (Cantu 1982). The potential positive effects of exercise on diabetes are well documented (Giacca *et al.* 1994), although there are very few experimental studies which use exercise as an independent variable. In addition, the relationship between exercise and metabolic control is complex (Vranic and Wasserman 1990).

Diabetes is a metabolic disorder that may have its origins in childhood or adulthood. Type I (insulin dependent) diabetes is less common than Type II (non-insulin dependent; NIDDM), but exercise has potential benefits for both types. Berg (1986) identifies the following benefits: improved blood sugar control, reduced likelihood of hypoglycaemia during exercise, enhanced efficiency of fat metabolism, reduced requirement for insulin for Type I diabetics and reduced amount or elimination of insulin to control blood sugar in Type II diabetics, and reduced bodyweight. Similarly, Bouchard and Despres (1995) conclude that physical activity and exercise can increase insulin sensitivity, reduce plasma insulin levels, improve glucose tolerance and thus reduce the risk of developing adult-onset diabetes, even for those who are overweight. Glucose tolerance decreases with increased age and obesity, and exercise has been shown to slow this effect (Fentem, Bassey and Turnbull 1988).

Giacca *et al.* (1994) conclude that physical activity has both psychological and physiological benefits for Type I diabetes. Gudat, Berger and Lefebvre (1994) are less optimistic about physical activity in established NIDDM patients, but conclude that exercise seems to have good potential for improving glucose tolerance in patients with already impaired glucose tolerance or in the early stages of NIDDM. Cross-sectional studies have shown that physical activity is inversely related to the prevalence of diabetes (Manson, Rimm and Stampfer 1991), and a fifteen-year prospective study showed that leisure time physical activity was inversely related to the development of NIDDM (Helmrick *et al.* 1991).

Immune function and cancers

The relationship between exercise and all-cause mortality has been demonstrated by Paffenbarger *et al.* (1986). Although the clearest evidence for mortality and low levels of physical activity is for CHD, there is evidence linking exercise levels with some forms of cancer (Lee 1994). However, the complexities of the numerous forms and aetiologies of cancers provides researchers with a difficult problem in identifying links with exercise. Nevertheless, Lee (1995) concludes that there is now good, possibly causal, evidence showing an inverse relationship between physical activity and colon cancer. Physical activity has also been associated with reduced risk of breast cancer in superior research studies (Lee 1995).

In addition to a great deal of interest being shown in cancer and physical activity, the relationship between immune function and physical activity is now also attracting attention (Lee 1995; Mackinnon 1989). It appears that moderate exercise can enhance the immune system, but high levels of training may depress immune function and increase the risk of infection, such as in the upper respiratory tract (Lee 1995; Nieman 1994).

Functional capacity and musculo-skeletal health

Vuori (1995) states that an adequately functioning musculo-skeletal system is very important for functional capacity and quality of life and that a substantial part of the age-related decline in functional capabilities is due to decreased or insufficient physical activity. As the populations of developed countries show extended life expectancies, this aspect of health is likely to become increasingly important over the coming years. For example, 70 per cent of fatal home accidents in England occur in people over 65 years of age. For this age group, 65 per cent of home accidents involve falls (Department of Health 1993b). Maintenance or improvement in functional capacity may be a critical factor in reducing these figures and improving life quality for older adults.

OSTEOPOROSIS

The excessive loss of bone mineral content, often resulting in fractures, is the condition known as osteoporosis. It is common in older people, particularly in women after the menopause. At this time, bone mineral loss increases from about 1 per cent per year to 2–3 per cent (Smith, Smith and Gilligan 1990). Fentem *et al.* (1988) report that physical activity is correlated with bone density and that bone density can be improved with exercise. Weight bearing activities, such as walking, are considered the most appropriate for reducing the risk of osteoporosis, although the optimal frequency and intensity of exercise for the prevention of osteoporotic fractures have not yet been determined (Smith *et al.*

1990). It is possible that severe training loads experienced by athletes may actually increase the likelihood of osteoporosis.

Physical activity does not appear to prevent bone loss post-menopause but it may be effective in maximising and maintaining bone mass in young and more mature adults. There is no evidence suggesting that exercise can be a substitute for hormone replacement therapy (Drinkwater 1994).

LOW BACK PAIN

It has been reported that over 80 per cent of adults will suffer from back pain at some time in their lives, although only about 10 per cent will seek medical attention. Approximately 10 per cent of certified days of absence from work in England and Wales are attributed to back pain.

Despite the widespread recommendation of improving the strength, endurance and flexibility of muscles for the prevention and rehabilitation of low back pain, there is little evidence that muscle fitness prevents this problem (Biering *et al.* 1994; Powell 1988). Nevertheless, there is evidence of a weak relationship between a generally healthy lifestyle, including moderate exercise of the lumbar region of the spine, and low back pain health (Nachemson 1990; Vuori 1995). Physical activity involving a strengthening (Carpenter and Nelson 1999) or lengthening of key muscles of the pelvic girdle is recommended, although more research is required as to their beneficial effect across different conditions of low back pain (Biering-Sorensen *et al.* 1994).

Mental health and psychological well-being

A link between exercise and mental health has been suggested for centuries. Data have now been accumulated on the complex processes involved and we have a much clearer picture than only a few years ago. Although this topic is dealt with specifically in several chapters in this book (see Chapters 8–10), summary statements will be made here also.

Drawing on clinical and epidemiological studies, as well narrative and meta-analytic reviews, it can be concluded that physical activity and/or exercise:

- Has a small-to-moderate beneficial effect on anxiety reduction and stress reactivity.
- Has a moderate to large beneficial effect on mild to moderate depression.
- Has a moderately favourable effect on self-perceptions, mood and psychological well-being.
- Has been associated with positive effects on selected measures of cognitive function and psychological adjustment (Biddle 1995a; Biddle, Fox and Boutcher 2000).

Risks of exercise and physical activity

Although the evidence supports quite clearly the generally beneficial health effects of physical activity, there are some aspects that may be contra-indicated for some groups or situations in which a particular health risk is elevated during exercise.

The most commonly cited risks of exercise are sudden cardiac death and musculo-skeletal injury (Siscovick 1990). Although the risk of sudden cardiac death is elevated with exercise, the balance of cardiac benefit and risk as a result of being an exerciser is positive. Siscovick *et al.* (1984) reported that men who exercised vigorously for more than twenty minutes each week had an overall risk of primary cardiac arrest only 40 per cent of their sedentary counterparts. It appears, therefore, that despite a temporary rise in risk during exercise, this is outweighed by the long-term effects of exercise on cardiac risk.

Knowledge on the musculo-skeletal risks of exercise is not extensive, although clinical studies have been conducted on swimming, running, cycling, callisthenics and racket sports and have identified a number of injuries (Koplan, Siscovick and Goldbaum 1985; Pate and Macera 1994). Epidemiological methods have not generally been employed until more recently. Blair, Kohl and Goodyear (1987) reported three population studies on the rates of running injuries. In their first study, they found that 24 per cent of runners reported an injury during the previous year and the rate increased with body weight and weekly distance run. In their second study, Blair *et al.* (1987) found that when comparing runners with non-runners at a preventive medicine clinic, only knee injuries were significantly higher in runners. Finally, a worksite population study found that risk of injury was associated with a number of factors, including increased age and body mass index.

Some mental health problems have been identified with exercise, such as eating disorders or dependence on exercise. Polivy (1994) located only eleven studies on addiction to exercise and concluded that exercise could indeed be a compulsive behaviour for some individuals. This is likely to be unhealthy due to increased risk of injury, fatigue, illness and psychological ill health. However, the prevalence of exercise dependence is not known and is likely to be very small (Szabo 2000). The issue of negative psychological outcomes from physical activity is discussed more fully in Chapter 9.

Physical activity and its relationship with other health behaviours

A question that has interested physical activity researchers in recent years is whether involvement in physical activity is associated with the adoption of other health behaviours, such as good nutrition and no smoking. In a review of the literature on leisure-time physical activity, Wankel and Sefton (1994) concluded the following:

- There is a small negative association between physical activity and smoking behaviours.
- Moderate increases in physical activity levels of non-obese individuals have been shown to be associated with corresponding increases in caloric intake.
- More active groups tend to have better nutritional habits and this is strongest in most active groups, such as runners.
- No relationship exists between physical activity and alcohol consumption.
- A small positive association exists between physical activity and some preventive health behaviours, such as seat belt use.

A recent large-scale study of 2,400 Belgian adults, however, showed through cluster analysis that physical activity was not associated with other health behaviours (De Bourdeaudhuij and Van Oost 1999).

Patterns of physical activity across developed countries

The proposed health outcomes of physical activity suggest that considerable public health benefits could be achieved through physical activity, although some risks are also evident. However, the impact on public health is dependent on people being physically active. The identification of patterns of physical activity is important in any effort to plan public health initiatives in this field (Caspersen, Merritt and Stephens 1994).

Measurement and surveillance of physical activity

The problems in determining the activity levels of the population should not be under-estimated. The measurement of physical activity becomes less reliable as techniques more suited to large-scale surveys are used (Sallis and Owen 1999). In a review of physical activity assessment in epidemiological research, LaPorte, Montoye and Caspersen (1985) identified over thirty different techniques. For large-scale population-based research, however, the use of some variation on survey recall of activity is inevitable. However, physiological indicators, such as heart rate monitors or movement sensors, are possible in smaller samples, although these also have limitations (Durnin 1990). There is no 'gold standard' technique for assessing physical activity (Ainsworth, Montoye and Leon 1994).

Prevalence of physical activity

The estimates of activity levels of the population will partly be dependent on the method used. Similarly, the criteria defining the quantification of 'activity' will likely be inversely related to the activity levels reported. In other words, the more stringent the criterion adopted for classifying people as 'active', the fewer people will be classified as active. This accounts for why Stephens, Jacobs and White (1985), in their analysis of eight national leisure-time physical activity surveys, found that estimates of population physical activity levels varied from 15 to 78 per cent. They concluded, however, that in North America approximately 20 per cent of the population take part in leisure-time physical activity of sufficient intensity and frequency that cardiovascular benefits are likely to result, while 40 per cent may be considered to be sedentary. The other 40 per cent would appear to be moderately or intermittently active with the possibility of some health benefits.

An international analysis, however, shows that prevalence of 'aerobic activity' across Australia, Canada, England and the USA varies between 5 and 15 per cent, whereas 'moderate activity' varies between 29 and 51 per cent (including data from Finland). Similarly, estimates of sedentary adults in these countries varies from 43 per cent to 15 per cent (Stephens and Caspersen 1994). Surveillance of physical activity patterns usually shows that levels of activity are highest for males, for the young, and for those with higher educational/socio-economic status (Stephens and Caspersen 1994). In a summary of data

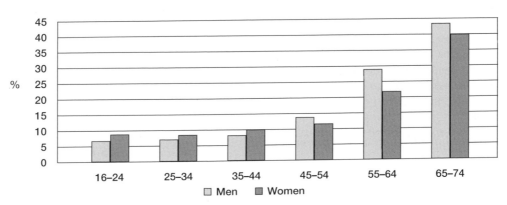

Figure 1.4 Percentage of English adults in different age groups reporting no physical activity in the Allied Dunbar National Fitness Survey

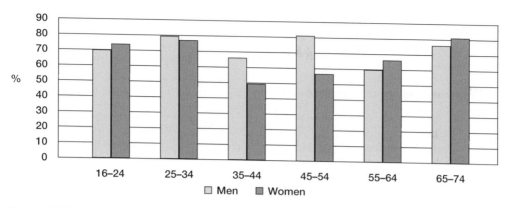

Figure 1.5 Percentage of English men and women in different age groups below an estimated healthy 'physical activity threshold' in the Allied Dunbar National Fitness Survey

from Canada, England, Finland, Germany and Sweden, Oja (1995) concluded that 'health-enhancing physical activity' varied from about 20 per cent in Sweden to nearly 50 per cent in Canada and England, with Finland at about 30 per cent.

Data from the Allied Dunbar National Fitness Survey (ADNFS) in England (The Sports Council and Health Education Authority 1992) shows a dramatic increase in sedentary behaviour with age (see Figure 1.4). Adults below an estimated healthy 'activity threshold' included the majority of men and women (see Figure 1.5).

Temporal trends in physical activity

Stephens (1987) investigated whether North American adults are more active now than in the past. He used three sources of data: national probability surveys, national non-probability surveys, and trend data on leisure-time physical activity indicators, such as the purchase of sports and exercise magazines and sports equipment. In his conclusion, Stephens stated 'that there are no truly satisfactory statistical sources for judging trends in adult leisure-time activity' (Stephens 1987: 102). However, despite the methodological problems encountered, he concluded that there had been an increase in activity during the 1970s and 1980s. In addition, the following factors were identified:

- Women increased activity levels more than men.
- Adults over 50 years of age increased activity more than younger adults.
- The increase in activity is not confined to low or moderately intense activities.

Data from several developed countries show that the prevalence of sedentary behaviour has decreased and that moderate or vigorous activity has increased. Stephens and Caspersen (1994) conclude that the trend is for sedentary people to become involved in moderate activity, and that vigorous activity has not markedly increased over the past decade. However, Caspersen *et al.* (1994) point out that the greatest increases in Australia and Canada have been in vigorous activity. Oja (1995) supports the view that the main increases have been in moderate activities, such as walking, golf, cross-country skiing and swimming. More vigorous pursuits in Finland, for example, have decreased in popularity.

In conclusion, despite favourable trends in the past decade or so, the majority of adults in developed countries appear not to be active enough for optimal health benefits (Oja 1995). In addition, those identified as inactive are more likely to be older, less well-educated and have lower incomes (Owen and Bauman 1992).

Chapter summary and conclusions

Evidence supports the view that appropriate physical activity can have significant health benefits for all sectors of the population. This book, therefore, will consider psychological factors likely to influence the participation of individuals in physical activity, as well as the likely psychological outcomes of such involvement. Through a better understanding of these outcomes, determinants and interventions we should be able to increase participation rates, decrease sedentary behaviour, and bring about significant public health benefits.

In this chapter, as a prelude to a discussion of the psychological issues affecting determinants, well-being and interventions in physical activity, we have introduced key topics associated with physical activity.

Specifically, we have:

- Sketched a brief synopsis of the issues associated with human evolution and history that impact on current physical activity and health behaviours and outcomes.
- Defined key terms, including physical activity, exercise, fitness and health.
- Highlighted key statements on physical activity and exercise.
- Summarised the evidence linking physical activity and exercise with various health outcomes and risks.
- Provided information on the prevalence and trends in physical activity in selected countries.

In summary, therefore, we conclude:

- That humans in developed Western societies have lifestyles quite dissimilar to that which our evolution has prepared us for and that this is likely to be a major factor in modern disease patterns.
- A number of national and international organisations have supported the promotion of physical activity as an important health behaviour through the publication of policy and position statements.
- Physical activity has been shown to be beneficial for many health outcomes, including all-cause mortality, CHD, hypertension, moderate obesity, diabetes, some cancers, immune function, functional capacity and capabilities, musculo-skeletal health and psychological well-being.
- Physical activity in the form of vigorous exercise does have risks, such as injury and occasional sudden cardiac death, but the evidence shows clearly that people are at greater risk if they are inactive.
- Physically active people may be more likely to adopt some other health behaviours, such as non-smoking and healthy nutrition, but evidence is mixed.
- Data from a few developed countries shows that the majority of the adult population is not active enough for health benefits, although the trends over the past ten years or so suggest that physical activity has increased.

Part II

Motivation and psychological determinants

2 Motivation for physical activity
Introduction and overview

Why we do what we do

(Title of book on 'understanding self-motivation' by prominent
motivational researchers Edward L. Deci and R. Flaste (1995))

Chapter objectives

The purpose of this chapter is to introduce key concepts of motivation, including early
research efforts made in an attempt to understand exercise participation. Subsequent chapters will deal with specific motivational theories in more detail. Specifically, we have the
following objectives for this chapter:

- To define motivation and its subcomponents.
- To outline, briefly, historical trends in the study of human motivation, as well as principles for a general theory of motivation so that exercise and physical activity research
  can be better evaluated.
- To discuss the literature dealing with descriptive approaches to motivation, such as that
  addressing children's and adult's participation motives and reasons for ceasing participation, as well as the identification of barriers to physical activity.
- To describe and comment on early approaches to the study of exercise and physical
  activity 'determinants', including the identification of self-motivation, commitment and
  other individual difference variables.

The initiation, maintenance and resumption of many health behaviours, and physical
activity is certainly no exception, are rarely easy. The complex psychological, social,
environmental and biological influences on involvement in physical activity merely highlight the difficulty of singling out one perspective, theory or approach in attempting to
understand the field. Nevertheless, discussion of exercise and physical activity involvement
inevitably comes round to the topic of 'motivation', however the word is defined. For this
reason, and coupled with the fact that many exercise and sport researchers have devoted a
great deal of time and energy to the topic, an understanding of motivation would appear critical if progress is to be made in the study and promotion of physical activity as a health
behaviour. This chapter, and those that follow in Part II, will cover key issues in exercise and
physical activity motivation. This chapter will highlight definitions, delimitations and
historical trends as a precursor to the following two chapters, in particular, which deal with
central theoretical perspectives in more detail.

The need for a motivational perspective

Few topics can claim to be more central to human behaviour than motivation. For example, we acknowledge that many behaviours can contribute significantly to an individual's healthy lifestyle but, at the same time, considerable difficulties are often faced by many people when attempting to start, maintain or resume involvement in such activities. The study of motivation in this context, therefore, would appear to be more than just of academic interest. It is also central to the understanding of behavioural choice and decision-making.

As discussed in Chapter 1, the World Health Organization (1986) has published targets for the European regional strategy for 'Health for All' for the year 2000. Scrutiny of Target 15 on 'knowledge and motivation for healthy behaviour' and Target 16 on 'positive health behaviour' shows a strong emphasis on motivational processes. For example, WHO, in statements associated with Target 16, suggested that 'positive health behaviour constitutes a conscious effort by individuals to actively maintain their health' (World Health Organization 1986: 64). However, they also acknowledged that 'positive health behaviour is by far the most challenging field for a health promotion policy' (65). Clearly these targets and statements make implicit and explicit reference to motivation and the problems of changing health behaviours.

Definition and current trends in motivation

The study of human motivation has been central to psychology since its earliest days and has developed through many different perspectives (Weiner 1992). Maehr and Braskamp's (1986) components of motivation will be offered as an operational definition of motivation. This is followed by a brief historical overview of the development of human motivation theories so that contemporary perspectives and theories used in exercise psychology are contextualised.

Defining motivation

Although motivation is often viewed in terms of direction and intensity, Maehr and Braskamp offer a more detailed view when they state that: 'most motivational talk arises from observations about variation in five behavioral patterns, which we label direction, persistence, continuing motivation, intensity, and performance' (Maehr and Braskamp 1986: 3).

Direction

The first indicator of motivation, according to Maehr and Braskamp (1986), is that of direction. This implies a choice has been made and so decision-making is central to understanding motivation. In the context of exercise, for example, there is the basic choice of whether to exercise or not, as well as choices of alternative leisure-time activities. Two important issues arise here. First, to what extent is exercise (and certainly habitual physical activity) consciously chosen? Some may be forced into walking or cycling through a lack of personal resources to travel in any other way. Different psychological processes may be involved here. Given that exercise is mostly structured and likely to take place in particular locations, such as exercise facilities, and at certain times, choice is important. For more everyday physical activities, this may not be the case. Second, one needs to consider the issue of alternative behavioural choices. This has often been lacking in the exercise psychology literature. Someone may not be rejecting exercise in any conscious way, but merely choosing activities that are seen as higher priorities. Some physical activity choices are likely to be made in an effort to reinforce personal perceptions of competence, or behaviours that are coherent with one's sense of self.

It is also noteworthy, however, that we are faced with physical activity choices throughout a normal day, and often quite unrelated to self-perceptions of competence. Will I climb the stairs or take the lift? Will I walk or drive? Some choices may be made relatively subconsciously and this in itself provides a challenge to health and exercise professionals.

Persistence

Maehr and Braskamp's (1986) second motivation factor, persistence, refers to the degree of sustained concentration on one task. Persistence, and hence motivation, might be inferred about someone who walks to work alongside a bus route. Lack of persistence is inferred when the walker gives up after five minutes and takes the first available bus. Of course, persistence is also a reflection of choice and decision-making and is likely to be correlated with how important something is to the individual. In addition, such persistence at a task may be high in order to enhance positive self-presentational aspects: 'I want to be seen walking to work as this confirms my identity (to me and others) that I am an active person'. Interestingly, Leary, Tchividjian and Kraxberger (1994) have argued that some such behaviours may not always be healthy. For example, for some (usually male) adolescents the desire for a muscular physique can be very strong. This, in turn, can lead to the use of potentially harmful drugs, such as anabolic-androgenic steriods, all in the cause of seeking a positive social impression.

Continuing motivation

This is when people regularly return to a task after a break. Indeed, Maehr and Braskamp suggest that 'it is almost as if a certain tension exists when a task is left incomplete; the person simply cannot leave it alone' (Maehr and Braskamp 1986: 4). There is some evidence that a few individuals feel highly committed in this way to structured exercise (Szabo 2000; Veale 1987), the so-called phenomenon of exercise dependence (see Chapter 9). At a more moderate level, many people report 'feeling good' from exercise and less good when they have missed exercise for several days.

One aspect of exercise motivation currently poorly understood involves continuing motivation. Although we have accumulated information on exercise maintenance, we know much less about the processes involved in resuming exercise after a break – the 'relapse' or 'stop-start' syndrome we discuss more fully in Chapter 6 (Sallis and Hovell 1990). Seeing that few people adopt exercise without periods of 'relapse', this would appear to be an important area for future study.

Intensity

Behavioural intensity is another indicator of motivation. This is important in relation to the debate about 'how much exercise is enough for health gains?', since more moderate forms of exercise require less intense levels of motivation. Certainly we have argued many times before that promoting exercise on the basis of 'vigorous' activity, regardless of any physiological rationale, is often doomed to failure due to the perceived, or actual, motivational effort (intensity) required, namely, it's too much like hard work!

One could argue that motivational intensity is more likely to be associated with competitive sports participants than recreational exercisers, but it is also associated with how much the person has invested their identity and self in an activity. This may be congruent with Csikzentmihalyi's (1975) investigations of highly motivated behaviour where people invest far more time than external rewards offered for the activity would suggest is warranted. Similarly, running over thirty miles per week is more than is necessary for 'health' and appears to be more than a simple recreative 'time filler'. Such behavioural and motivational intensity must relate to wider issues of the self and other perceived outcomes.

Performance

Finally, Maehr and Braskamp (1986) refer to performance as an indicator of motivation, although this is more problematic than the other indicators. The inference of motivation, they suggest, is made when performance cannot be explained simply in terms of competence, skill or physiological factors. This may be a less relevant component of motivation in the context of health-related physical activity and exercise.

Weiner (1992) suggests that the fundamental motivational question concerns the 'why?' of human action rather than the 'how?' Certainly this is a central theme reflected in this book: why is physical activity adopted, maintained, shunned or resumed?

Putting motivation in an historical context

As with much psychological research and theorising, the dominant themes, perspectives or paradigms in the study of human motivation have shifted a great deal over time. Initial perspectives emphasised people's motivation more in terms of mechanistic processes or 'drives', or what Weiner (1992) has described in terms of 'the machine' metaphor. Many behaviours, using this perspective, were seen to be largely involuntary and predetermined, fixed and routine, and described in terms of energy transmission. Should the 'machine' be out of balance, movement takes place to restore the balance. Such theoretical perspectives include psychoanalytic, ethological, sociobiological, drive and gestalt theories of motivation, and these were particularly popular until the mid-1950s and, with some exceptions, had a rather 'meteoric rise and fall' (Weiner 1992: 149). In concluding his review of these theories Weiner states that 'it is argued that a mechanistic theory can parsimoniously account for some of the vast variety of data that it generated, although other aspects of human behavior must be examined with other metaphors' (Weiner 1992: 151). It is probably fair to say that most exercise and health psychologists would prefer to adopt, and have adopted, more contemporary approaches to the study of motivation.

As drive-based theories waned in popularity, motivational psychologists adopted a more expectancy-value orientation, or what Weiner (1992) has described as the 'God-like metaphor'. Humans are seen to be 'all-knowing', fully informed about possible behavioural options, have complete rationality, and are able to calculate 'their most hedonic course of action' (Weiner 1992: 159). Such theories include achievement motivation, such as the approach advocated by the famous psychologist John Atkinson and his colleagues, locus of control, and attribution theories, although the latter overlap with the social-cognitive approach.

This paradigmatic shift is clear to see in exercise and sport psychology. In a content analysis of all motivation articles published in the *Journal of Sport and Exercise Psychology* and the *International Journal of Sport Psychology* between 1979 and 1991, attributions, self-confidence and achievement motivation were the three most popular topics. Both self-confidence (largely self-efficacy approaches) and achievement motivation (through an increased interest in achievement goal orientations) increased in popularity over the time period studied (Biddle 1994a). A similar emphasis can be found in the contemporary social psychological study of health (Ogden 1996; Stroebe and Stroebe 1995).

Even more recent perspectives in motivation research recognise that humans are not quite so 'all-knowing' as suggested in the theories above. Indeed, Weiner (1992) says that humans are not perfectly rational decision-makers and that their information processing capacities are more limited than sometimes acknowledged. He therefore extended the God-like metaphor to 'person as judge', a label he used to describe more recent work often labelled the 'social cognitive' perspective, although the distinction between some expectancy-value and social cognitive approaches is not always clear. Nevertheless, this new approach relies more on emotionality and on evaluation of outcomes rather than simple expectations of what will happen if we act in a certain way. Bandura says that in the social cognitive view, people are 'neither driven by internal forces nor automatically shaped and controlled by external stimuli' (Bandura 1986: 18). In other words, we operate cognitive evaluations of behaviours, cognitions and environmental events in a reciprocal way ('reciprocal determinism') and anticipate future consequences. In this approach Bandura discusses the importance of self-regulatory and self-reflective aspects of behaviour:

> Another distinctive feature of social cognitive theory is the central role it assigns to self-regulatory functions. People do not behave just to suit the preferences of others. Much of their behavior is motivated and regulated by internal standards and self-evaluative reactions to their own actions'.
>
> (Bandura 1986: 20)

By this process, people evaluate their actions, often against some expectation or desire, and then modify their actions accordingly. For example, some people may be motivated to exercise for weight control if they perceive a discrepancy between what they are currently like and what they want to be. The self-reflective elements of Bandura's social cognitive approach are central to human action. This operation of 'meta-cognition' (thinking about our own thoughts) is recognised through Bandura's seminal work on self-efficacy, and this will be discussed in more detail in Chapter 4.

In summary, contemporary social cognitive approaches to motivation emphasise self- and other-person perceptions, emotional feelings, and decision-making often based on the evaluation of outcomes. Reverting to Weiner's (1992) metaphors, approaches labelled 'person as judge' are, in fact, closely overlapping and conceptually similar to those described as 'all-knowing', and recent theorising in health, exercise and sport psychology has emphasised both, including approaches covered in this book, such as self-efficacy theory, intrinsic motivation and perceived autonomy, competence motivation and goal perspectives theory (Biddle 1999b).

Components of a general theory of motivation: does exercise psychology match up?

Many of the early researchers in exercise psychology recognised that their work was largely atheoretical in its approach (Rejeski 1992; Sonstroem 1988). Since the mid-1980s research has become more theoretically focused, usually by exercise psychologists borrowing well-known theories from educational, motivational and social psychology. This in itself could be criticised as being parasitic on the parent discipline, yet it also seems a sensible approach, at least in the initial stages as the atheoretical work is superseded. As we start to discuss the different approaches used in the study of physical activity and exercise motivation, it might be useful to consider Weiner's (1992) principles for the construction of a general theory of motivation to see how exercise psychology matches up in its approach.

Weiner considers eight issues:

1   *A theory of motivation must be built upon reliable (replicable) empirical relations.* Can the theories we discuss be demonstrated to 'work' with some certainty? This may seem rather ambitious given the complexities of human social behaviour but Weiner believes it is important if we are to have a general theory. As far as exercise and physical activity research is concerned, some of the theories discussed here are based on replicable results, albeit quite small in number in some cases. For example, the links between achievement goals, beliefs about success and intrinsic motivation in young people are fairly robust. Similarly, Godin (1993) has reviewed the exercise research on attitude-behaviour theories and found the associations between the attitude component of the Theories of Planned Behaviour and Reasoned Action and intentions to be quite consistent. However, initial efforts at building an exercise theory through the 'psychobiological theory' (Dishman and Gettman 1980), incorporating the construct of self-motivation, have not been so reliable, although self-motivation is usually a predictor of supervised exercise adherence (Dishman and Sallis 1994).

2   *A theory of motivation must be based on general laws rather than individual differences.* Weiner argues that while individual differences exist, he considers it much more important to search for general laws first rather than person x situation interactions. Certainly exercise psychologists have generally not been overly involved with the identification of individual differences and have concentrated instead on attitudes, beliefs and perceptions more specific to the situation at hand. However, some individual difference measures have been used, such as self-motivation (Dishman, Ickes and Morgan 1980), achievement goals (Duda 1993), and physical self-perceptions (Fox 1997a). These are appropriate if adding to the refinement of a theory of human motivation.

3   *A theory of motivation must include the self.* Weiner says that the concept of the self has been neglected in motivation research, this being a point made elsewhere in the context of physical activity and health (Biddle 1997a). 'the self lies at the very core of human experience and must be part of any theoretical formulation in the field of human motivation' (Weiner 1992: 361). Exercise psychology is increasingly recognising such an approach as it enthusiastically embraces self-perception and social-cognitive approaches to motivation, such as self-efficacy theory, self-esteem, competence theories etc.

4   *A theory of motivation must include the full range of cognitive processes.* Regrettably, exercise psychology has been restricted in its approach to cognition. While expectancies and self-perceptions have dominated, few studies have addressed information search or retrieval, memory or some aspects of decision-making in exercise.

5   *A theory of motivation must include the full range of emotions.* Motivational theories are increasingly incorporating emotions, and a wider range of emotions than previously. Emotion should be at the core of any motivational theory of exercise given the potential for strong reactions to exercise. Although emotion – mainly mood, anxiety and depression – has been studied a great deal as an outcome of exercise and physical

activity, it has rarely been incorporated into a motivational approach. The reinforcement of exercise through positive affect is likely to be an increasingly important topic for exercise psychology in the future. At present, however, we don't match up too well to this criterion of an adequate theory of human motivation.

6   *A theory of motivation must include sequential (historical) causal relations.* The typical cross-sectional correlational or ANOVA studies in motivation have led to an ahistorical approach where causal relations are not able to be specified. Contemporary approaches to data analysis, such as structural equation modelling, may help in this regard, although true longitudinal and prospective studies are still required. Exercise psychologists interested in motivation might also consider the identification of both distal and proximal variables. At present we have not done this very well.

7   *A theory of motivation must be able to account for achievement strivings and affiliative goals.* Given the dominance of achievement and social interaction, Weiner argues that a general motivation theory must account for these two domains of human action. Both are also central to exercise, although habitual physical activity, such as recreational walking, may not be explained by either. Nevertheless, achievement (competence, self-enhancement etc.), and affiliation do feature in many theories adopted in exercise, although we may need to broaden our approach. For example, a great deal of research has focused on the two achievement goals of task and ego orientations (see Duda 1993), yet have largely excluded the possibility of important motivational outcomes being associated with social goals (Urdan and Maehr 1995). Vallerand (1997), however, has accounted for competence, autonomy and relatedness (social) needs in his proposed hierarchical model of intrinsic and extrinsic motivation.

8   *A theory of motivation must consider some additional commonsense concepts.* Weiner believes that we need to further our understanding of commonsense terms associated with motivation, such as value, importance and interest. Exercise researchers have dealt with these and have, in a limited way, recognised them as central to furthering our understanding of volitional exercise behaviour. For example, in describing his hierarchical and multidimensional approach to the assessment of self-perceptions, Fox (1997a) proposes that perceptions of, say, sport competence are unlikely to affect physical self-worth or global self-esteem unless the domain of sport and related competence perceptions are themselves deemed important. However, we have not really studied the 'interest' or 'value' attached to exercise by different people. Even if someone says that they 'like' exercise, it may still be far enough down their own value hierarchy that it fails to be part of their lifestyle. This is probably reflected in the most reported barrier to exercise: 'lack of time'. The Theories of Reasoned Action and Planned Behaviour do deal with this issue by requiring individuals to rate both beliefs and values associated with outcomes.

Weiner's (1992) analysis of a general theory of motivation should not be used to judge research in our field too rigidly. Rather our purpose was to highlight some interesting and important issues in the development of good physical activity motivation theory and to give some context for the discussion that follows.

Descriptive approaches to the study of physical activity motivation

A common approach to the study of motivation in physical activity settings has been to look at participation motives. This is a descriptive approach using self-reported perceived reasons for starting, maintaining or ceasing involvement in some form of physical activity. It could be argued that this atheoretical approach is limited in scope, but it does provide a useful starting point for understanding people's 'surface' motivation. It does not, of course, help explain exercise behaviour in more theoretical terms.

A great deal of the literature on motives has dealt with children, usually in volunteer sport situations (Gould 1987). A more limited literature exists on adults, although this includes more on exercise and health-related physical activity (Biddle 1995c). Given the differences in both activities and perceptions that exist between children and adults, these two groups will be reviewed separately.

Descriptive research on adults

Typically, researchers in this field have asked questions concerning motives for participation and also about reasons for dropping out of activity. Questionnaire and structured interview have been used.

Motives for participation

A study we conducted is fairly typical of this research (Ashford, Biddle and Goudas 1993) and will be used as an illustration. We studied participants in fourteen activities in six English public sports centres. Recreational participants in age categories from 16–19 years up to 65 years and over were studied. Fifteen motives for participation were derived from prior research and rated on a simple interview-administered questionnaire. The motives included fitness, health, skill development, social interaction, relaxation etc. A factor analysis produced four clear factors, two being related to performance ('assertive achievement' and 'sports mastery and performance'), with two related to fitness and health ('physical well-being' and 'socio-psychological well-being'). Males were higher than females on ratings of the two performance factors. Younger subjects tended to be less interested than others in the factor of socio-psychological well-being.

The 'check-off' approach we adopted is convenient but may not provide a replicable instrument for future studies. Most participation motives studies have used this approach and while there is a great deal of commonality of findings, not all studies are directly comparable. For this reason, Markland and Hardy (1993) have developed an instrument to assess motivation for exercise. The 'Exercise Motivations Inventory' (EMI) consists of twelve subscales labelled stress management, weight management, re-creation, social recognition, enjoyment, appearance, personal development, affiliation, ill-health avoidance, competition, fitness and health pressures. An initial study revealed that 18–25 year old men reported that they exercised more for competition and social recognition and less for weight management than women of the same age. The most strongly endorsed factors for women were re-creation, fitness, enjoyment and weight management, whereas for men they were re-creation, competition, fitness and personal development. Although this approach does not yield extra information to the descriptive approaches already discussed, the standardised instrument should allow for better comparison across studies in the future.

POPULATION SURVEYS

Several population surveys in recent years have addressed issues associated with motivation. With some exceptions, such as the Campbell's Survey of Well-Being (Wankel and

Mummery 1993), the breadth of data collection attempted has precluded much theoretical work taking place. Consequently, most such surveys provide descriptive data on beliefs, attitude statements and motives. Nevertheless, given the large samples often included in these works, these can provide valuable descriptive data.

In 1992, the results of the Allied Dunbar National Fitness Survey (ADNFS) (The Sports Council and Health Education Authority 1992) were published. This was an ambitious project involving over 4,000 16–74 year olds from thirty regions of England. Home interviews took place on 1,840 men and 2,109 women for up to an hour and a half, with subsequent physical measures taken in the home and in mobile laboratories.

The home interview involved questions on involvement in physical activities as well as health, lifestyle and health-related behaviours, barriers and motivation for exercise, social background, personal attributes and general attitudes. The most important motivational factors for physical activity were 'to feel in good shape physically', 'to improve or maintain health', and 'to feel a sense of achievement'. Motives associated with weight control and physical appearance were also important for women. Motives of 'fun' were more likely to be reported by younger people whereas older respondents reported the factor of 'independence' higher than others.

Participants in the ADNFS also rated highly the importance of exercise for health. A small trend showed that the level of importance declined across the age groups of 16–34 years, 35–54 and 55–74. Surprisingly, however, relatively little is known about changes in motives across the adult life cycle, although Mihalik, O'Leary, McGuire and Dottavio (1989) did study 6,720 adults from the cross-sectional Nationwide Recreation Survey in the USA. They studied the extent to which participation 'expanded' or 'contracted' across the life cycle. They found that there was an 'addition' of activities between 18–28 years, but a decline in participation in 29–36 year olds. This was attributed to changes in job and family circumstances. An increased rate of 'deleting' activities occurred through the middle years, a trend reversed from about 50 years of age, probably due to children leaving home and greater financial independence. However, changes in activity patterns across the life cycle have yet to be systematically investigated alongside motivational factors and yet this is an important area of study. Greater collaboration with other social science researchers is required.

FURTHER ISSUES ON MOTIVES

British research has shown interesting differences in motivation for those within the same type of activity. Schlackmans (1986), a research company, studied nearly 2,000 women in ten English towns. Exercise and fitness classes were studied, and these included 'traditional' keep-fit, jazz-dance and aerobics. Through qualitative analyses, six main types of participants were identified. These were 'sporty socialisers', 'weight conscious', 'keen exercisers', 'modern mothers', 'social contact' and 'get out of the house'. These are outlined in Table 2.1 and show that motivation for exercise is diverse and not just related to factors associated with the exercise itself. A number of associated social and environment factors are also important and should be recognised by those wishing to promote exercise participation. For example, some individuals may use exercise as the most convenient way of meeting people or 'getting out of the house'. Exercise serves a purpose unrelated to fitness, health or other such factors.

One salient dimension that is likely to affect motives for participation is that of the intensity of the exercise. For example, the anxiety-reducing effects of exercise, so keenly

Table 2.1 Clusters of participant groups for women's exercise classes

Group (% of exercise market)	Description
Sporty socialisers (25%)	• interested in social aspects of participation • physically quite fit • good at other sports • interested in their own exercise progress.
Weight conscious (18%)	• exercise as a means to weight loss • self-perception of being overweight • less likely to take part in other sports.
Keen exercisers (17%)	• interested in physical fitness benefits • not interested in social aspects of participation • good at sport • perceive themselves to be quite fit.
Modern mothers (16%)	• keen on sport • perceive themselves to be quite fit • interested in their exercise progress.
Social contact (15%)	• older than 'modern mothers' group • women who live alone or had children who have left home • exercise seen mainly as a means for social contact.
Get out of the house (8%)	• youngest group • little interest in social or physical benefits • class used as a means of getting away from the house.

Source: Data from Schlackmans 1986.

promoted in the popular and research literature (see Chapter 8) have been shown to be less likely to occur at higher levels of exercise intensity (Steptoe and Bolton 1988; Steptoe and Cox 1988). This suggests that motives other than, or in addition to, psychological well-being, might be found in studies of vigorous exercise.

Motives for participation can offer a useful 'surface' analysis of motivation as long as it is recognised that this is all you get. However, a more problematic issue is that most surveys and studies capture people's motives either while they are active or ask people to recall 'what would' be a motive. What we need are more data on people at the time they start an exercise programme and to see how motives change over time. It is quite likely that initial motives reflecting, say, health, may change to motives of fun and relaxation. That is to say that motives to start exercising will focus on health outcomes, but motives for exercise maintenance will focus more on immediate outcomes. This has been proposed before but is not well documented (Dishman, Sallis and Orenstein 1985).

Reasons for ceasing participation

'Dropping out' of exercise should not be seen as an 'all or none' phenomenon (Sonstroem 1988) but as an on-going process of change. For example, Sallis and Hovell (1990) have proposed a process model of exercise in which at least two different routes could be taken by adults who cease participation. One route is to become sedentary while the other is to cease participation temporarily but return at a later date. Motivational factors affecting these routes may be different. Indeed, why some adults resume participation after a period of inactivity is poorly understood and is a priority for future research efforts.

One of the problems with research in this area is that once again only 'surface' reasons are offered, although one could argue that such responses are important to document. The ADNFS reported the reasons given for stopping regular participation in moderate to vigorous sport, exercise and active recreation. The three most frequently cited reasons were associated with work, loss of interest and the need for time for other things. The factors of marriage/change in partnership and having or looking after children were also important factors, but more so for women.

Perceived lack of time is frequently cited as the major reason for non-participation. Owen and Bauman (1992) reported on just over 5,000 sedentary Australians and found that the reason 'no time to exercise' was much more likely to be reported by those in the 25–54 age group compared with those over 55 years. This confirms the results from the ADNFS. Similarly, the barrier of time in the Australian study was not reported as often by those with higher education levels. Those who had children, however, did report a perceived lack of time more than others. Again, these data show the need to study motives and barriers in a wider social context.

THE STUDY AND MEASUREMENT OF EXERCISE/PHYSICAL ACTIVITY BARRIERS

In discussing motives for participation, we have suggested differentiating motives for adoption from those of maintenance. Similarly, when discussing reasons for ceasing participation one could identify barriers that prevent people from being more active as well as the reasons why those who were previously active are no longer so.

In the ADNFS, reported barriers to preventing adults from taking more exercise were classified into five main types: physical, emotional, motivational, time and availability. This is a useful way of analysing barriers for large population surveys as it gives a wider picture of barriers and some information for possible interventions. Figure 2.1 shows the main gender differences for the main barriers in each the categories, except 'availability'. Figure 2.2 shows age differences for women, and Figure 2.3 for men. Each barrier category is explained in more detail in Table 2.2.

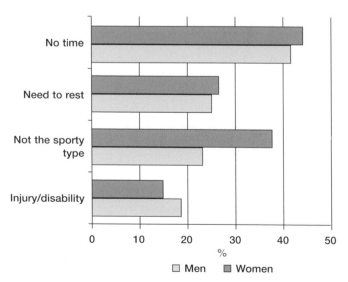

Figure 2.1 Percentage of English men and women reporting selected physical activity barriers from the ADNFS

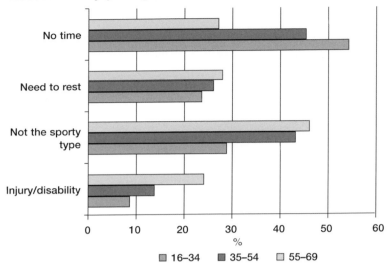

Figure 2.2 Percentage of three different age groups of English women reporting selected physical activity barriers from the ADNFS

Time barriers appeared to be the most important for both men and women, although women were likely to report emotional barriers to exercise (for example, 'I'm not the sporty type') more than men. This is likely to be related to perceptions of competence and will be discussed in more detail in Chapter 4. On a more anecdotal note, it is sad to think that participation in something as simple as cycling or jogging might be avoided on the basis of

Table 2.2 Factors given as barriers by people aged 16–69 years in the Allied Dunbar National Fitness Survey for England

Barrier label	Barriers
Physical	• I have an injury or disability that stops me • I'm too fat • My health is not good enough • I'm too old.
Emotional	• I'm not the sporty type • I'm too shy or embarrassed • I might get injured or damage my health.
Motivational	• I need to rest and relax in my spare time • I haven't got the energy • I'd never keep it up • I don't enjoy physical activity.
Time	• I haven't got the time • I don't have time because of my work • I've got young children to look after.
Availability	• There is no one to do it with • I can't afford it • There are no suitable facilities nearby • I haven't got the right clothes or equipment.

Source: Sports Council and Health Education Authority 1992.

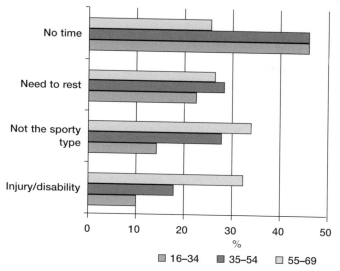

Figure 2.3 Percentage of three different age groups of English men reporting selected physical activity barriers from the ADNFS

self-presentational concerns. It makes one wonder how people developed such self-presentations and whether early experiences of 'exercise' in school were not as appropriate as perhaps they should have been. Certainly one can understand the self-presentational concerns in sport where competence levels are so clearly displayed.

Predictably, in the ADNFS, the physical and emotional barriers increased across the age groups, while time barriers decreased, at least for those over 55 years of age. This again shows the importance of a lifespan approach.

Useful though the approach used in the ADNFS is, again it does not provide a replicable instrument that has been psychometrically validated. In attempting to address this inconsistency in measurement, both Sechrist, Walker and Pender (1987) and Steinhardt and Dishman (1989) developed scales for the assessment of exercise barriers, as well as perceived benefits. Initial psychometric work by Steinhardt and Dishman revealed the barriers of time, effort, obstacles and 'limiting health'. Sechrist *et al.* (1987) identified barriers labelled exercise milieu, time expenditure, physical exertion and family encouragement. Although the development of such scales is welcomed, little research has been done to further validate the scales. Similarly, one might question the need for two scales and encourage, instead, an integration of the two. The scales do appear to reflect though the reported barriers from population surveys.

Descriptive research on children and youth

Much of the research on children's participation motivation tends to focus on competitive sport rather than more diverse aspects of exercise and physical activity. However, this is not surprising as children are less likely to participate in fitness pursuits currently favoured by adults, at least not until mid- to late adolescence. Nevertheless, it is important that we understand more fully the reasons children give for participation or non-participation in recreational play or the taking of non-motorised forms of transport.

Motives for participation

Research in Wales on youth and young adults 16–24 years of age (Heartbeat Wales 1987) found that non-participants would find the following to be incentives to become active in sport: fitness/weight loss, having more free time and as an aid to maintaining good health. Incentives declined with age, although the relative strength of the main incentives remained fairly constant within each age group. Similarly, a study in Finland (Telama and Silvennoinen 1979) of over 3,000 11–19 year olds, showed clear changes in motivation for physical activity as a function of age and gender. Boys and younger adolescents were more interested in achieving success in competition but by late adolescence very few showed interest in this factor. This trend was reversed for motives associated with relaxation and recreation. Fitness motivation was strongest among those who often thought about sport and took part in sports club activities. This fitness motive was unimportant for 18–19 year olds, or for those uninterested or inactive in sport. This has important implications for the way we promote fitness in youth and illustrates the need to distinguish between sport and exercise.

In a large study in Italy with over 2,500 participants in youth sports, responses to open-ended questions showed that enjoyment was reported as a reason for participation by 49.2 per cent of the sample. This was followed by physical (health/fitness) motives (32 per cent), social reasons (8.9 per cent), competition (4.2 per cent), skill motives (2.9 per cent), and social visibility or status (2.8 per cent) (Buonamano, Cei and Missino 1995). A factor analysis of a structured questionnaire revealed factors of success/status, fitness/skill, extrinsic rewards, team factors, friendship/fun, and energy release. A further analysis provided five typologies of motives for sport. These are shown in Table 2.3 and demonstrate the potential importance of taking into account social and demographic factors in understanding likely determinants of physical activity participation.

German research (Brettschneider 1992) has shown that the participation of adolescents in sport has actually increased in recent years. Activities now featuring more often in

Table 2.3 Five typologies of youth sport motives reported by Buonamano *et al.* (1995)

Cluster/type	Description
Enthusiasts	• belief that sport leads to success and fame • most motives endorsed positively • from large families • medium-to-low educational level • live in south of Italy.
Looking for socialisation	• most play team sports • mainly from north-central Italy • medium-to-high educational level • represented by athletes dropping out of swimming.
Competitors	• competitiveness and winning seen as a means to self-realisation • social status not a main motive • independent from other variables.
Individualists	• not interested in socialising • motivated for sport to improve body shape, gain skill and release energy.
Non-competitors	• negative responses to many motives • need to receive extrinsic reinforcement • more likely to live in north Italy • medium-to-high educational level.

comparison to those in the 1950s are 'new individual sports such as bodybuilding, jogging and surfing as well as the Eastern movement forms and the different forms of aerobic dancing' (Brettschneider 1992: 541). Brettschneider, similar to Buonamano *et al.* (1995), reports on research with 2,000 adolescents and young adults in which distinctive profiles of adolescent lifestyle could be seen. For example, 5 per cent of the group were categorised as a 'no sports group' since they preferred other leisure-time pursuits. Another 4 per cent were motivated by body image and general image promotion, whereas 13 per cent were characterised by individuality and self-expression and 'are disposed to health-related hedonism' (Brettschneider 1992: 548). Such typologies were confirmed through both quantitative and qualitative data.

Data from over 3,000 children in Northern Ireland (Van Wersch 1997; Van Wersch, Trew and Turner 1992) have shown that 'interest in physical education' remains relatively constant for 11–19 year old boys, whereas during the same period interest declines sharply for girls. 'Interest' was assessed by questionnaire items pertaining to attitude, behaviour, motivation and perceptions of fun in the PE setting.

Data from the English Sports Council's survey of young people and sport (Mason 1995) shows that from a sample of over 4,000 6–16 year olds, motives are diverse, ranging from general enjoyment to fitness and friendships. Similar results have been reported in North American research such as the Canada Fitness Survey (1983a) which sampled over 4,500 young people aged 10–19 years of age.

In an international study (King and Coles 1992), children aged 11, 13 and 15 years rated the degree to which they thought certain reasons were important for liking sport or physical activity. Comparable data were only obtained between Canada and Poland, but some strong differences emerged, suggesting the need for more cross-national studies. For example, Canadian 11 year olds were much more likely to rate 'have fun' as very important than their Polish counterparts, whereas the trend was reversed for the item 'to win' (see Figure 2.4).

North American research, however, (Gould and Petlichkoff 1988; Canada Fitness Survey 1983a; Wankel and Kreisel 1985) generally confirms reports from Europe that children are motivated for a variety of reasons. Reviews have concluded that children are motivated for diverse reasons, including fun and enjoyment, learning and improving skills, being with friends, success and winning, and physical fitness and health (Biddle 1999a). The latter factor might also include weight control and body appearance for older youth. However, more research is needed to understand the differences in motives across activities, levels of participation, and developmental stages, although so far the research shows some similarity in motives across settings and groups.

Reasons for ceasing participation

Various surveys are available on the reasons children and youth give for non-participation or ceasing involvement in sport and exercise (Heartbeat Wales 1987; Mason 1995; Canada Fitness Survey 1983a). Gould and Petlichkoff (1988) make the important distinction between sport-specific dropout (ceasing participation in one sport) and domain-general dropout (ceasing sport participation altogether). This may need to be incorporated into future studies.

As with motives for participation, there appear to be numerous reasons why children and youth cease their involvement. For example, Coakley and White (1992) conducted sixty in-depth interviews with 13–23 year olds, half of whom had decided to participate in one of five different sports initiatives in their local town. The others had either ceased involvement or

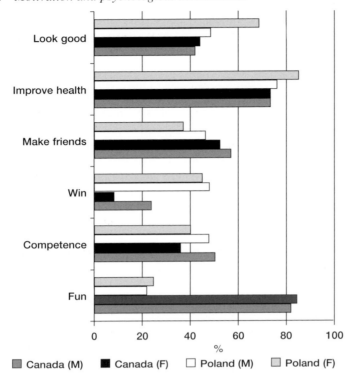

Figure 2.4 Reasons reported as 'very important' for liking sport or physical activity by 11-year-
old male (M) and female (F) Canadian and Polish children (data from King and Coles
1992)

had decided not to participate at all. The decision to participate or not appeared to be influenced by perceptions of competence, by external constraints, such as money and opposite sex
friends, degree of support from significant others, and past experiences, including school PE.
Negative memories of school PE included feelings of boredom and incompetence, lack of
choice, and negative evaluation from peers. Mason's (1995) analysis of data on over 4,000
youth in England provides support for this. She found that some children reported feelings of
embarrassment in sport settings, mainly due to perceived incompetence or concerns over
self-presentation associated with their physique during puberty.

Gould (1987) summarised the reasons for children's non-participation as conflicts of
interest, lack of playing time, lack of fun, limited improvement in skills or no success,
boredom and injury. Competitive stress and dislike of the coach have also been cited in sport
settings. Children, therefore, appear to have multiple motives for involvement and non-
involvement in sport, although less research is available on more diverse physical activity
settings.

Early exercise motivation research

The next two chapters address theoretical approaches to the study of exercise motivation. In
the following section early research is discussed that did not rely on known theoretical
approaches of the time. This is not necessarily to single out such studies as weak but merely
to differentiate them from those based on theories developed in other settings and branches

of psychology. In fact, some of these studies could be labelled as 'pioneering' in what has now become known as 'exercise/physical activity determinants'. Most of the variables under investigation, however, are more likely to be correlates than true determinants of action.

Comparisons of adherers and dropouts

A number of studies attempted to differentiate exercise adherers from non-adherers on the basis of psychological and other variables (Dishman 1987; Dishman and Buckworth 1997). For example, data from the Ontario Exercise Heart Collaborative Study showed that adherence to a post-coronary exercise programme was related to the convenience of the exercise facility, perceptions of the exercise programme and family/lifestyle factors (Andrew *et al.* 1981; Andrew and Parker 1979). In particular, spouse support was a significant predictor of adherence. However, what is interesting to note now, some twenty years later, is that the issue of social support remains an underdeveloped area of determinants research (Dishman 1994a; Taylor, Baranowski and Sallis 1994).

One of the earliest attempts to characterise the exercise 'dropout' was reported by Massie and Shephard (1971). They found that both physiological and psychological factors at entry to a fitness programme differed between adherers and dropouts such that dropouts tended to be overweight, but stronger, were more likely to smoke (a finding supported by Andrew *et al.* 1981), and were more extraverted. Other studies have also reported physiological differences between adherers and dropouts at entry to a programme, and factors such as muscle fibre type (Inger and Dahl 1979), functional capacity (Blumenthal *et al.* 1982), and

---

Box 2.1 Adherence, compliance, motivation ... what's in a word?

When discussing the topic of involvement in exercise, one can often get into a definitional minefield. Early on it was quite common to refer to exercise 'compliance', a term borrowed from medical settings where people were under some compulsion to follow a medical programme of rehabilitation or other treatment. However, is exercise the same thing? Should we talk about 'compliance' to exercise? It creates images of compulsion that we want to avoid in exercise promotion.

Other researchers have used the word 'adherence'. For example, whereas exercise psychologists use the word adherence to mean staying with (or dropping out of) an exercise programme others have broadened the construct to refer to the study of participation in exercise from a multidisciplinary approach. Using it in this way means that it goes beyond the construct of 'motivation'. For example, adhering to an exercise programme has physiological effects that can then legitimately be studied under the title 'adherence'. Motivation, as we discuss here, is more focused on choice, persistence etc. and reflects a psychological approach to involvement.

Finally, we have mentioned compliance, adherence and motivation here mainly in the context of structured exercise. What about habitual physical activity, such as walking to the shops or cycling to work? This now opens up a difficult issue. How volitional is the behaviour? You may cycle to work because there is no other alternative. The increasing study of habitual physical activity, to compliment that of exercise programmes, needs to address this issue more closely. Certainly, the use of the word 'compliance' seems inappropriate here also, but 'adherence' and 'motivation' . . .?

body composition (Dishman 1981) have been significant. In all cases the most likely explanation is that biological factors which make exercise a more difficult or less reinforcing experience will predict dropout. For example, exercisers with greater amounts of body fat will experience more discomfort in exercise, and may also experience some embarrassment.

A psychobiological model

Perhaps the most widely cited study of the discriminating power of physiological and psychological variables in predicting adherence to exercise is that of Dishman and Gettman (1980). In this study the researchers investigated the predictive utility of both psychological and biological variables in a prospective design. A twenty-week exercise programme was used whereby all participants were assessed at entry on a variety of psychological measures, including self-motivation, physical activity attitudes, health locus of control, perceived competence and attraction to physical activity. Biological variables assessed were metabolic capacity (predicted oxygen consumption), body weight and percentage body fat.

The results reported by Dishman and Gettman (1980) showed that both psychological and biological factors predicted adherence after twenty weeks. This led the authors to propose a 'psychobiological model' of adherence. Specifically, adherers and dropouts could be significantly discriminated from each other on the basis of body fat, self-motivation and body weight. Further analysis showed that just under 80 per cent overall (and slightly less for dropouts) could be classified correctly as adherers or dropouts based on their scores on these three variables.

A partial replication of the Dishman and Gettman (1980) study was carried out by Ward and Morgan (1984) who studied 100 men and women in a prospective investigation over thirty-two weeks of an exercise programme. Complete data were provided by seventy-six participants on seven biological variables in addition to the assessment of self-motivation and mood. Ward and Morgan analysed the adherence patterns at three time periods: 10, 20 and 32 weeks. After 32 weeks the accuracy of predicting adherence was estimated by using the regression equation developed by Dishman and Gettman (1980). The overall prediction accuracy was satisfactory for adherers (71 per cent) but poor for dropouts (25 per cent). Self-motivation scores were not significant discriminators between adherers and dropouts at any of the three time periods however.

Although a psychobiological model retains some intuitive appeal, it has not been possible to support it fully since the Dishman and Gettman (1980) research. While psychological and physiological variables may interact to predict participation, which variables become important may differ across exercise settings. For example, adherence to a high intensity aerobic endurance programme is likely to require high self-motivation and favourable physiological factors such as a high percentage of Type I ('slow twitch') muscle fibres and low body fat. However, this may not be true for other exercise regimes or habitual physical activity of an unstructured nature. Similarly, the psychobiological model was only developed on sixty-six people and is therefore in need of validation with larger and more diverse samples. We said this in 1991 and see no reason to change our opinion.

Personality and individual difference factors

One approach to the study of exercise adherence has been to attempt to identify stable characteristics of the exerciser, although this approach has waned somewhat since we reviewed such factors in 1991 (Biddle and Mutrie 1991). Some studies, however, have found that certain personality variables distinguish between adherers and non-adherers, but there remains a lack of consistency across studies. However, the notion that a persistent, committed or self-motivated individual will more likely persevere with exercise, particularly more intense forms, holds intuitive appeal, as discussed in the context of a psychobiological approach.

SELF-MOTIVATION

Given the role that self-motivation played in the early exercise determinants research, we will briefly review the main issues, although it should be noted that self-motivation is usually only studied in a more multivariate research design in contemporary work.

Dishman and his co-workers have reported research which suggests that 'self-motivation' is an important factor in adherence (Dishman *et al.* 1980; Dishman and Gettman 1980; Dishman and Ickes 1981). Initial psychometric research led to the development of the 'Self-Motivation Inventory' (SMI), a forty-item questionnaire measuring 'a generalised, nonspecific tendency to persist in habitual behaviour regardless of extrinsic reinforcement and is thus largely independent of situational influence' (Dishman 1982: 242).

Although the SMI was found to correlate with social desirability and ego-strength, a study investigating adherence to a rowing training programme demonstrated that it was the SMI score that was the most important in terms of predicting adherence, and did so independently of social desirability and ego-strength. Similarly, Dishman and Gettman (1980), as already reported, found that self-motivation was a clear discriminator between exercise adherers and dropouts.

Wankel, Yardley and Graham (1985) tested the utility of the SMI and motivational interventions in predicting short-term adherence to exercise. In their first study results showed no effect for self-motivation. In a follow-up study they assessed women enrolled on an aerobic dance programme. After administration of the SMI three groups were created: high, medium and low self-motivation groups. The motivational treatment in this study was 'structured social support material'. Results revealed a trend for social support but not for SMI.

Wankel *et al.*'s (1985) data, therefore, suggest that short-term adherence rates appear to be unaffected by self-motivation. This conclusion is not surprising nor a necessary criticism of the self-motivation construct. It is quite likely that if self-motivation does exist, particularly as a relatively permanent trait, then it will be influential in predicting long-term adherence rather than attendance over a few sessions. Indeed, the initial validation of the SMI used a thirty-two-week period.

Self-motivation, and the use of the SMI, remains an intuitively appealing area of adherence. However, although the results may appear to be equivocal as to the importance of self-motivation in exercise, it is likely that environmental factors also need to be considered. Despite the original definition suggesting that self-motivation was 'largely independent of situational influence', the effects for self-motivation are likely to be seen when the situation is relatively unfavourable from a motivational perspective and few extrinsic motivators are in evidence. This requires testing in a longitudinal design extending the methodology of Ward and Morgan (1984) who studied adherence at different time intervals.

We have modified the SMI for use with children and youth (SMI-C) (Biddle *et al.* 1996) and, using confirmatory factor analysis, confirmed a one factor structure for a twenty-item version. SMI-C scores were correlated with fitness test scores, but not physical activity assessed through continuous heart rate monitoring.

Knapp, in her cogent review of behavioural management techniques in exercise, suggests that the exact nature of the behavioural tendency to persevere is not clearly defined but:

> it may be useful to hypothesise that self-motivation is a learned set of skills and habitual responses that function to assist individuals to adhere to activities that are not adequately cued and reinforced by the environment or that may even be punished.
>
> (Knapp 1988: 220)

EXERCISE COMMITMENT

A related construct to self-motivation is that of 'commitment'. Although the construct of 'commitment' may seem to reflect commonsense, little is known about it in physical activity contexts. Also, in line with Weiner (1992), we need to know more about common sense notions of motivation, and commitment seems to be an appropriate construct here. Indeed, in introducing their work on sport commitment, Scanlan *et al.* (1993) say that commitment has intuitive appeal and face validity.

Carmack and Martens (1979) provided preliminary data on the psychometric properties of a 'commitment to running scale' and showed that runners reporting higher levels of commitment tended also to report greater running distances, higher perceived addiction to running, and greater discomfort if a run was missed. An extension of the concept of commitment to running was provided by Corbin *et al.* (1987) who developed a modification of the commitment to running scale so that it became applicable to a wide range of physical activities. This led to the 'commitment to physical activity (CPA) scale'. A significant difference in CPA scores between groups differing in activity levels was observed.

A recent exploration of the construct of commitment has been through the development of a 'sport commitment model' by Scanlan and associates (Carpenter *et al.* 1993; Scanlan *et al.* 1993) and also through the study of commitment to a career in physical education teaching (Moreira, Sparkes and Fox 1995). However, neither approach may be wholly appropriate for the study of exercise commitment, although they provide useful frameworks for development.

Scanlan's group attempted to define sport commitment and operationalise it through psychometric scale development. They drew on well-established social psychology literature where investment in, and commitment to, interpersonal relationships has been studied (Rusbult and Farrel 1983). The sport commitment model proposed by Scanlan and co-workers identifies the following antecedents of commitment: sport enjoyment, involvement alternatives, personal investments, involvement opportunities and social constraints (Scanlan and Simons 1992). Involvement alternatives reflect the extent to which people have viable alternative behaviours. In sport and exercise it may appear that we are free to chose our involvement (the 'want/don't want to' perspective of commitment). On the other hand, some aspects of life, such as a job, may involve the 'have to' approach to commitment. Although some people may feel trapped by their involvement and see few involvement alternatives (see Moreira *et al.* 1995), when talking about health-related exercise and physical activity, it is likely to be the 'want/don't want' perspective that is most appropriate (see discussion on self-determination theory in Chapter 3). In the sport commitment model, it was proposed that involvement alternatives would be negatively related to commitment. However, in a test of the model in a youth sport context using structural equation modelling, it was found that social constraints also negatively, though weakly, related to commitment. Social constraints refer to social norms and feelings of obligation to stay involved in the sport, a kind of social pressure. Its relationship is probably best explained in terms of pressure and compliance and hence the tendency to force a more extrinsic motivational orientation. It is not surprising, therefore, that this was inversely related to commitment.

The commonsense notion of commitment requires further consideration. Study of the antecedents of exercise commitment would appear to be necessary if we are to progress in this field. Early attempts at investigating commitment tended to be atheoretical and therefore it is recommended to consider the sport commitment model and its social psychological foundations, as a point of departure for the study of exercise commitment.

Chapter summary and conclusions

Central to our understanding of exercise behaviours is motivation. Clearly such an all-embracing construct cannot explain all that we do, but it remains at the core of the psychology of exercise determinants. In this chapter, therefore, we have:

- Defined motivation.
- Put motivation in an historical context so that contemporary approaches currently favoured in exercise psychology are contextualised.
- Discussed possible components of a general theory of motivation to see how exercise research compares.
- Reviewed the literature on descriptive approaches to exercise motives and reasons for dropout for both adults and young people.
- Described some early exercise determinants research, including studies of comparisons of adherers and dropouts, a psychobiological model, and the self-motivation construct.
- Discussed the construct of commitment to exercise.

The chapter has been necessarily broad to allow for a more focused discussion in the subsequent chapters on motivation. In summary, therefore, we conclude:

- Despite well-known benefits, only a minority of people in industrialised countries are sufficiently physically active to have a beneficial effect on their health. This necessitates a greater understanding of the determinants of involvement in exercise and physical activity, including motivation.
- Motivation involves different behaviours, including choice, persistence, continuing motivation and intensity.
- Motivation research has changed over the years from mechanistic approaches to contemporary perspectives emphasising cognitive and social-cognitive theories and exercise psychology has followed suit.
- A general theory of motivation is not really available, but judging the criteria offered by Weiner (1992), some facets are being addressed in exercise psychology, while others are not.
- Descriptive research on participation motives has tended to reflect motives for children's involvement in sport and adult's involvement in exercise and recreational physical activity. For children and youth common motives are fun, skill development, affiliation, fitness, success and challenge, whereas for adults motives change across stages of the life cycle. Younger adults are motivated more by challenge, skill development and fitness, whereas older adults are more interested in participation for reasons of health, relaxation and enjoyment.

- Reasons for ceasing participation are numerous and have included for children conflicts of interest, lack of fun or playing time, lack of success, injury and competitive stress. For adults, physical, emotional, motivational, time and availability barriers seem to be prominent, with time nearly always cited as a factor preventing participation.
- Early research on exercise determinants involved static comparisons of profiles of exercisers and non-exercisers, but did identify some potentially important variables, such as self-motivation. Such studies usually lacked a theoretical focus.
- A psychobiological model was proposed but results have been equivocal. However, the concept of both psychological and biological variables explaining exercise participation is still valid.
- Single motivational constructs, such as self-motivation and commitment, have been proposed and could still prove useful as variables within larger studies. However, more recent approaches have advocated the testing of social-cognitive theories rather than variables in isolation.

3　Motivation through feelings of control

In my letters to my children, I regularly urged them to exercise.

Nelson Mandela
(*Long walk to freedom*, 1994)

Chapter objectives

The purpose of this chapter is to extend the motivational analysis of exercise started in the previous chapter and to focus on theoretical perspectives that have contributed, in some way, to the literature on exercise and physical activity behaviours. In particular, we consider the notion of feelings of 'control' through reviewing theories of locus of control, intrinsic motivation and attribution. Specifically, we have the following objectives for the chapter:

- To appreciate the potential of perceptions of control, expectancies and value as determinants of exercise behaviour.
- To understand the principles of the construct of locus of control, including its structure and measurement in health and exercise settings.
- To critique the construct of locus of control as it has been applied in health and exercise.
- To develop an understanding of intrinsic motivational processes, specifically in terms of cognitive evaluation theory and perceptions of autonomy (self-determination theory).
- To consider the role of rewards and reinforcement in affecting intrinsic motivation and behaviour.
- To consider the basic principles of attribution theory and perceptions of control and their application to health and exercise motivation.
- To understand the role of beliefs concerning athletic ability in exercise motivation.

Introduction

In our short historical analysis of human motivation research in the previous chapter, in which we drew on Weiner's (1992) use of metaphors, it was mentioned that after the relative demise of many of the 'man as machine' theories, researchers adopted more expectancy-value theories. These are reflected in the metaphor of 'humans as all-knowing decision makers' (Weiner 1992: 159), or the God-like metaphor. The main approaches adopted here, which have also been used in exercise research, include Rotter's 'Locus of Control' theory and attribution theory (a 'person as scientist' approach). Both perspectives emphasise the important role of perception of control and expectations. Similarly, research investigating intrinsic motivation processes has used the notion of perceived control to help explain variations in motivation and behaviour. In addition, new perspectives currently being adopted in exercise and sport emphasis the role of autonomy in motivation. For these reasons we have joined in one chapter the expectancy-value and 'control' theories of locus of control, intrinsic motivation and attributions. They are linked, conceptually, through feelings of control.

Expectancy-value theories make the assumption that people's behaviour is guided logically by the anticipated consequences of their behaviour (expectancies) and the value or importance they attach to such outcomes. Whether we actually make such logical decisions is, of course, debatable, but such theories have demonstrated explanatory power. However, as Weiner (1992) proposes, perhaps they expect humans to be too logical and rational. Developments from these perspectives, therefore, have also been proposed and the chapter that follows will deal with theories of motivation that draw on competency-based (social-cognitive) and autonomy-based approaches.

Recognition of the importance of perceptions of control in exercise and health

The research and popular literature contains numerous references to the fact that changes in exercise and health behaviours are thought to be associated with the need to 'take control' or 'take charge' of personal lifestyles. The information that many of the modern diseases linked with premature mortality are 'lifestyle-related' (Powell 1988) has the implicit message that we, as individuals, are at least partly responsible for our health and well-being, thus implying the need for personal control and change. For example, in describing their 'wellness' approach to exercise and fitness, Patton *et al.* state that 'wellness-oriented health/fitness programs have a philosophical base similar to that of humanistic psychology and humanistic education, which recognise self-responsibility as being integral to genuine self-growth' (Patton *et al.* 1986: 26). Similarly, Weiner says that in spite of evidence linking obesity with biological and genetic factors 'fatness tends to be perceived as controllable, and people are considered responsible for being overweight' (Weiner 1995: 75). Such notions may have motivational implications, as we discuss later.

It should also be recognised, however, that there are potential problems with health messages that consistently encourage personal control as the only way of changing behaviour. This approach is often associated with the 'health fascist' label adopted in the 1980s. Some have argued that a greater emphasis should be placed on social determinants of health, and some accuse those who over-emphasise the need for personal control of adopting the 'victim blaming approach'. Feelings of guilt can develop when problems arise that are out of one's control (for example, disease related to environmental pollution), whereas others might blame the victim for a lack of motivation. Similarly, a great deal of good can be achieved by giving control to others, such as doctors, in some circumstances.

A framework for the study of 'control'

Psychological constructs centred on 'control' are numerous, such as self-efficacy, intrinsic motivation, locus of control and attributions (Biddle 1999b). In attempting to integrate some of these constructs and make sense of apparently disparate constructs, we draw on Skinner's

Box 3.1 The politics of personal control and victim blaming

A governmental discussion paper ('Green Paper') was published in 1991 concerning a strategy for health for England (other countries in the UK also had on-going, but separate, health strategies). This was the launch of the 'Health of the Nation' (HON) initiative that led to a published strategy and targets. Specifically, five key areas were identified: coronary heart disease and stroke, cancers, mental illness, HIV/AIDS and sexual health, and accidents. Numerous targets were set and many 'Task Forces' were established to consider contributions to these areas, including a 'Physical Activity Task Force'.

All governments face the dilemma of taking responsibility for certain actions, or stating that the responsibility lies with 'the people'. The former approach could lead to popularity if resources and energy follow, but the government also faces the potential of large costs and possibly the accusation of 'central control' and 'nannying'. 'Giving' responsibility to the people may free some resources but it also leaves the government open to criticism on the grounds of cutting costs or shirking responsibility. Who'd be a politician?

Of course, healthcare falls perfectly into this dilemma and illustrates the problem of responsibility, or what we have discussed in psychology as the issue of personal control. Broadly speaking, right wing policies support the supremacy of personal choice. Left wing policies would include more central control as a counter to the view that disadvantaged groups in society have no 'real' choice.

The HON document (Department of Health 1993) was a policy statement of a Conservative (right wing) government of the time and makes many references to personal choice and responsibilities, and some have accused it of being 'victim blaming'. For example, Marks (1994) outlines what he perceives to be 'fatal flaws' in the Health of the Nation document. These include:

- It assumes that behaviour is determined without reference to economic and social influences.
- Victims of preventable diseases are seen as irresponsible and unworthy of care.

This is similar to Weiner's (1995) analysis of responsibility and blame. The study of perceived control in psychology, therefore, clearly is not divorced from personal philosophy and politics.

(1995; 1996) theorising. In particular we will outline her agent–means–ends analysis and her 'competence system' model.

Agent–means–ends and different belief systems   Skinner (1995; 1996) makes the point that one way to conceptualise the vast array of control constructs is to analyse them in relation to their place within the tripartite model of agent, means and ends. This is illustrated in Figure 3.1.

Agent–means and capacity beliefs   Agent-means connections involve expectations that the agent (self) has the means to produce a response (but not necessarily an outcome). This

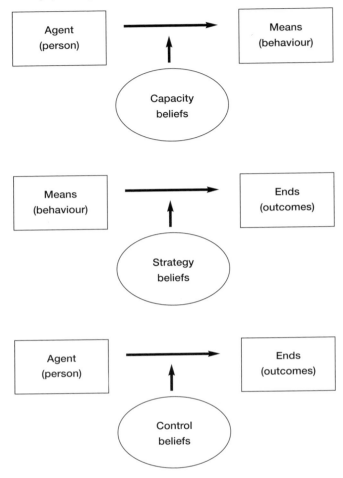

Figure 3.1 An agent–means–ends analysis and different types of beliefs mediating such links (adapted from Skinner 1995; 1996)

involves capacity beliefs, beliefs concerning whether the agent has the ability to produce the appropriate cause. For example, if effort is deemed important to produce success in road running, then positive capacity beliefs must involve the belief that 'I can try hard in road running'. Self-efficacy research has adopted this approach and has become a major force in motivational research in exercise and sport psychology. This will be discussed in the next chapter. Similarly, perceived competence approaches adopt the agent–means approach.

Means–ends and strategy beliefs   Means–ends connections involve beliefs about the link between potential causes and outcomes. This involves strategy beliefs, beliefs concerning the necessary availability of means to produce the desired outcomes. For example, if trying hard is necessary in successful road running, a strategy belief is 'I need to try hard to be successful at road running', thus contrasting with the capacity belief 'I can try hard'. Typically, means–ends relations involve attributional approaches, outcome expectancies and locus of control, constructs familiar in exercise and sport psychology.

Agent–ends and control beliefs   As Skinner put it, 'connections between people and outcomes prescribe the prototypical definitions of control' (Skinner 1995: 554), hence this connection involves control beliefs. These involve the belief by the agent that a desirable outcome is within their capability: 'I can be successful at road running if I want to'. This has to involve both capacity *and* strategy beliefs.

Agent–ends connections are less easy to recognise in exercise and sport psychology. Outcome expectancies can involve agent–ends as well as means–ends. Behavioural regulations, as depicted in self-determination theory (Deci and Ryan 1985) may also suit an agent–ends analysis.

Plotting beliefs on a competence system   Skinner (1995) proposes that humans have a need to seek competence. If this is the case, we can analyse control-related beliefs within a system of competence seeking or what Skinner (1995) refers to as the 'competence system'. This suggests that action is regulated by initial control beliefs. Action, in turn, produces some form of outcome that is evaluated and interpreted in respect of other beliefs (self, causes); these can lead to further control beliefs. The place of beliefs within this system are important in analysing the contributions of control-related constructs in exercise. For example, locus of control beliefs precede performance and are proximal to behaviour; attributions are beliefs interpreting past behaviour and are likely to be less proximal or even quite distal to future actions.

Locus of control

The locus of control (LOC) construct stems from a social learning theory approach to personality (Rotter 1954) where general beliefs are thought to develop from expectations based on prior reinforcements and the value attached to such reinforcements, and hence is an expectancy-value approach to motivation. Locus of control of reinforcements refers to the extent that people perceive that reinforcements are within their own control, are controlled by others or are due to chance. In Rotter's seminal monograph on LOC he says 'it seems likely that, depending on the individual's history of reinforcement, individuals would differ in the degree to which they attributed reinforcements to their own actions' (Rotter 1966: 2). This led Rotter to formalise the construct of LOC and suggest that a generalised belief existed for internal versus external control of reinforcement. Rotter (1966) defined 'internals' and 'externals' as follows:

> If the person perceives that the event (the reinforcement) is contingent upon his/her own behaviour or his/her own relatively permanent characteristics, we have termed this a belief in internal control.
>
> (Rotter 1966: 1)

> When a reinforcement is perceived . . . as following some action of his/her own but not being entirely contingent upon his/her action, then . . . it is typically perceived as the result of luck, chance, fate, as under the control of powerful others, or as unpredictable. . . . When the event is interpreted in this way . . . we have labelled this a belief in external control.
>
> (Rotter 1966: 1)

In the same monograph Rotter presented psychometric evidence for the measurement of

LOC with his internal–external (I–E) scale. This was a measure of 'individual differences in a generalised belief for internal or external control of reinforcement' (Rotter 1966: 1–2). The twenty-nine-item scale yields one score of LOC (high score indicating high externality) thus suggesting that LOC is a unidimensional construct. This has been challenged by a number of researchers. It should be noted, however, that Rotter stated that his I–E scale was a measure of *generalised* expectancy and therefore was likely to have a relatively low behavioural prediction but across a wide variety of situations. It was also likely to have greater predictive powers in novel or ambiguous situations since in specific well-known contexts more specific expectancies will be used (see discussion on self-efficacy Chapter 4).

Two developments in LOC research that have a bearing on physical activity are the multidimensional nature of LOC and the behavioural specificity of measuring instruments.

Multidimensional LOC

In terms of multidimensionality, a number of researchers have suggested that the unidimensional I–E split is insufficient (Palenzuela 1988), although not all agree on the exact nature of the multidimensionality. Nevertheless, there is some agreement that at least the external pole of LOC should be divided into 'chance' and 'powerful others' since those believing that their life is 'unordered' (chance 'control') would be different from those believing in events being controlled by powerful others.

Specificity of measurement

Since Rotter's I–E scale was developed as a generalised measure, it was inevitable that researchers would predict that more situation-specific measures of LOC would allow for better prediction of specific behaviours (see Figure 3.2). One of the most widely used of such measures is the Multidimensional Health Locus of Control Scale (MHLC) (Wallston, Wallston and DeVellis 1978) which yields scores on internal, chance and powerful others sub-scales. The MHLC, however, has had mixed success in predicting health behaviours, largely because of the wide range of possible behaviours it encompasses. It is also orientated towards illness and therefore may have little relationship with more overt health-enhancing behaviours such as exercise, although Dishman and Steinhardt (1990) did find the internal subscale of the MHLC scale to be predictive of habitual 'free-living' physical activity, but not of exercise. Despite the equivocal nature of findings, early reviews of the literature (Strickland 1978; Wallston and Wallston 1978) concluded that there was evidence for a link between health LOC and specific health behaviours.

Exercise research and LOC

Research investigating the link between perceived control, as measured by LOC scales, and participation in exercise has taken three routes. First, some researchers have tried to identify links between generalised LOC and exercise, some have used health LOC, and others have used exercise- and fitness-specific measures.

General and health LOC measures

One of the first studies investigating LOC and exercise was conducted by Sonstroem and Walker (1973). Specifically, they studied the relationship between LOC and both physical

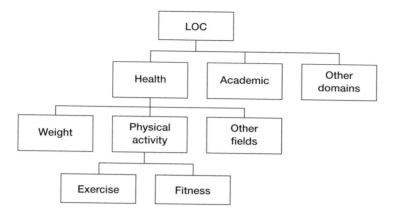

Figure 3.2 Specificity of the locus of control construct

fitness and activity levels. They administered the Rotter I–E scale, a general measure of activity attitudes, and a questionnaire assessing the extent of voluntary participation in physical activity to a sample of final year American university students. In addition, a 600 yard run was administered as an index of cardiovascular fitness (although now this test is considered a poor indicator of this component of fitness). The same test had been administered to these students in their first year at the university.

Internals with a positive attitude ran significantly faster, and had generally higher activity levels than others, although some of these trends were quite small. Nevertheless, these results are suggestive that LOC may have a small influence on activity and fitness scores. However, the fitness results are questionable on grounds of test validity.

A more popular approach in exercise LOC studies has been to administer the MHLC scale and then try to discriminate between groups of exercisers and non-exercisers. O'Connell and Price (1982) compared those who adhered to a ten-week exercise programme delivered on-site to employees of an American insurance company with those who dropped out and a control group of non-participants. The results showed small, but significant, differences such that the adherers were more internal than the dropouts who, in turn, were more internal than controls. No differences were found for the chance or powerful others sub-scales.

Dishman and Gettman (1980) used a unidimensional health LOC measure as part of a battery of measures in attempting to predict exercise adherence and dropout in a twenty week prospective study of adult men (see Chapter 2). Health LOC did not significantly add to the discrimination between adherers and dropouts even though adherers had higher internal scores than dropouts. Nevertheless, it was found that subjects with an external health LOC and low health/fitness value score were less likely to adhere to the programme than those with an internal health LOC and high health/fitness attitude score.

Dishman and Gettman's (1980) data provide, at best, moderate support for the concept of health LOC in predicting participation in a supervised exercise programme. Given their use of multivariate statistics in researching variables that discriminate between adherers and dropouts, it is possible to conclude that LOC is a relatively weak influence when placed in the context of other factors.

These results collectively provide weak support for LOC in predicting fitness and exercise behaviours, although the extent that this could be a reflection of the inadequacies of the fitness or LOC measures remains to be seen. At best these studies suggest that some group differences may exist between exercisers and non-exercisers at a cross-sectional level on LOC. However, one cannot ascertain whether such differences developed as a result of involvement or whether they were influential in initial decisions to become active. The conclusion from these studies, therefore, appears to be that health LOC does not strongly predict, or relate to, exercise behaviour although some association has been found in some studies.

Such an equivocal conclusion has prompted researchers to ask why such is the case. Three main possibilities exist. First, the theory could be wrong or not applicable to exercise; second, the measuring tools are not sensitive or appropriate enough to demonstrate a relationship between LOC and exercise participation, and third, fitness/exercise 'externals' are rare people thus making it difficult from a research perspective to demonstrate relationships or discriminate between groups. Given the theoretical predictions of LOC research, and the extensive testing of the theoretical constructs involved, one could still propose that a relationship should exist. Most of the studies where no relationship has been found suggest that the LOC measures have not been specific enough to exercise and fitness behaviours, and this includes health LOC. Not all people will perceive exercise as a health promoting behaviour anyway. Calls for greater specificity in measurement have been met with several studies that have addressed this issue in exercise and physical fitness.

Measurement of exercise and fitness LOC

Several researchers have attempted to develop exercise or fitness LOC scales (see Table 3.1). In a study of female participants in a university health education evening class programme, Noland and Feldman (1984) tested parts of their proposed exercise behaviour model (EBM). They assessed physical activity and physical activity attitudes and values. LOC was assessed with their own 'exercise locus of control' scale (EXLOC). This scale was purported to measure internal, chance, powerful others and environment sub-scales of LOC. The researchers, in terms of the internal scale, said 'it deals with the belief that the individual controls his/her own exercise behaviour' (Noland and Feldman 1984: 34). This is conceptually different, of course, from locus of control beliefs of reinforcement as postulated by Rotter (1966). Small but significant relationships between attitude and exercise, and the environment subscale of the EXLOC and exercise were found, suggesting that exercise is related to positive attitude and inversely related to beliefs that the environment (for example, weather, exercise equipment) has some control over exercise participation.

In a follow-up study, also of women, Noland and Feldman (1985) assessed the variables of exercise, attitude, values and EXLOC once again. In addition, they assessed the extent to which the women perceived fifteen barriers to exercise, including costs and lack of time. For those aged 25–45 years, no relationship was found between any of the EXLOC scales and exercise. For the older group (aged 46–65 years), it was found that greater amounts of exercise were related to higher scores of internal control and lower scores on the chance and powerful others scales. The Noland and Feldman (1984; 1985) studies were the first to report an exercise-specific LOC scale. However, scant psychometric validation procedures for EXLOC are reported.

McCready and Long (1985) also reported the use of an exercise-specific LOC scale. They studied women participating in an aerobic exercise programme who had exercised regularly (two to three times week) during the past year. The study investigated the influence of LOC

Table 3.1 A summary of research studies investigating exercise/fitness locus of control, exercise and physical fitness

Study	Sample[1]	LOC measure	Purposes	Results	Conclusion[2]
Noland and Feldman (1984)	Adult women (N = 64)	Exercise LOC (EXLOC) scale	Relationship between aspects of the 'exercise behaviour model' (EBM), including EXLOC and exercise participation.	External (environmental) subscale of EXLOC inversely related to exercise participation.	+
Noland and Feldman (1985)	Adult women (N = 215)	EXLOC	Same as for Noland and Feldman (1984) above.	No relationship between EXLOC and participation in exercise.	−
McCready and Long (1985)	Adult Canadian women in fitness programme (N = 61)	Exercise Objectives LOC scale (EOLOC)	Relationship between exercise adherence, physical activity value and EOLOC scores.	EOLOC unrelated to adherence.	−
Long and Haney (1986)	Sedentary adult Canadian women (N = 68)	EOLOC	• To assess the impact of counselling on initiating an active lifestyle. • To assess EOLOC and other variables in the context of the above purpose.	Weak relationship between increased physical activity and the combined effects of EOLOC and exercise value.	+(?)
Whitehead and Corbin (1988)	Three groups of undergraduate students (N = 377)	Physical Fitness LOC (FITLOC) scale	Psychometric construction and testing of FITLOC scale.	Some evidence of reliability and validity of FITLOC. Weak evidence of association with physical activity.	+(?)
Dishman and Steinhardt (1990)	Undergraduate students (N = 84)	MHLOC and EOLOC	Prospective study for the prediction of: • supervised exercise • free-living physical activity both from internal subscales of MHLOC and EOLOC.	• Internal HLOC predicted free-living physical activity, but not exercise. • Internal EOLOC did not predict either exercise or physical activity.	+ (HLOC) − (Exercise LOC)
(Doganis, Theodorakis, and Bagiatis 1991)	Greek women in fitness programmes (N = 96)	EOLOC	• To assess the psychometric properties of Greek version of EOLOC. • To assess the relationship between EOLOC and self-esteem.	• Support for psychometric properties of the scale. • Small significant correlations between internal (positive), chance (negative), and powerful others (negative) subscales and global self-esteem.	+(?)

Notes
1 Study participants are American unless stated otherwise.
2 + = evidence for positive role of exercise/fitness LOC in exercise behaviours.
+(?) weak or inconsistent evidence for positive role of exercise/fitness LOC in exercise behaviours.
− = no evidence for role of exercise/fitness LOC in exercise behaviours.

and attitudes on adherence to the programme. Measures were taken using Levenson's LOC scale, a revised version of the children's attitude toward physical activity (CATPA) scale, a social desirability scale and the 'exercise objectives locus of control' scale (EOLOC). Preliminary evidence for validity and reliability of the EOLOC was also presented.

EOLOC assesses internal, chance and powerful others scales through an eighteen-item inventory. The factor structure is still in need of clarification since McCready and Long reported two factor analyses producing five factors, and with only internal and chance looking fairly pure.

Analyses revealed that those classified into low, moderate and high attendance groups did not differ from each other on the EOLOC or CATPA scales. In predicting attendance, results showed that three attitude scores and the two external scales of Levenson's inventory were weak predictors, and EOLOC did not predict attendance at all. This led McCready and Long to conclude that 'individuals with higher percent attendance tended at the beginning of the fitness programme to have less positive attitudes toward physical activity as a means of continuing social relations and achieving health and fitness, and more positive attitudes toward physical activity for release of tension. They also held weaker beliefs that their reinforcements are controlled by powerful others and a stronger belief that chance elements affect their lives' (McCready and Long 1985: 352).

These results might seriously question the EOLOC as a measure of exercise-specific LOC, particularly when the general scale of Levenson's was more predictive. However, the results reported by McCready and Long showed that most of their participants had very high scores on the internal scale, thus weakening any statistical analyses relating adherence to internal EOLOC. This supports the comment made earlier about the likelihood of not finding many exercise/fitness externals.

Long and Haney (1986) also used the EOLOC scale in a study of sedentary women. They investigated the effects of counselling on the initiation of a physical activity programme. Three groups were studied: counselling plus information (about programmes and services in the community), counselling with no information, and a wait-list control group. All were followed-up after one month.

The two counselling groups increased their activity levels significantly over the one month period compared with the control group. However, in attempting to predict the increase in exercise from a combination of EOLOC and attitude scores only weak support was found for these variables. In the control group it was found that those who scored less on EOLOC powerful others and who did not view exercise as a means of risk taking and hard training were more likely to increase their activity levels. However, no such trend emerged for the counselling groups. Regardless of group, however, internal EOLOC, combined with positive attitudes towards activity as means of improving body shape, and enhancing health and reducing tension, were related to an increase in activity. This relationship, however, was statistically weak.

Dishman and Steinhardt (1990) provide a useful test of locus of control hypotheses by employing measures of both health and exercise LOC and relating them to both 'free-living' (habitual) physical activity and structured supervised exercise in a prospective design. However, they studied only a small (N = 84) sample of college students. Interestingly, they found that habitual physical activity was predicted by health LOC, but not by exercise LOC (using the EOLOC scale), while for exercise neither health nor exercise LOC measures were significant predictors. These results were obtained after controlling for the effects of initial fitness levels as well as expectancy value for health outcomes and perceived barriers to physical activity.

In predicting habitual physical activity, internal health LOC was a stronger factor in Week 5 than in Week 2. In addition, internal health LOC significantly added to the discrimination found between high and low active subjects. In sum, Dishman and Steinhardt provide support for the role of internal health LOC in predicting habitual, but not supervised, activity, but found no support for the validity of the EOLOC scale. In a footnote to their paper, Dishman and Steinhardt say that 'our results question the construct validity of exercise locus of control assessed by EOLOC scales' (Dishman and Steinhardt 1990: 394). They remind us that the original work by Long and colleagues (Long and Haney 1986; McCready and Long 1985) was based on small samples of adult women, hence 'the robustness of the scale's measurement properties in other groups may be limited. . . . Further work on the construct validity of exercise locus of control seems warranted because other existing measures of locus of control that are specific to exercise . . . also have weak evidence of construct validity when judged against conventional psychometric standards' (Dishman and Steinhardt 1990: 394).

The consensus has to be that EOLOC has failed to provide evidence that a LOC measure that is specific to exercise is a better predictor than other LOC measures. Indeed, one could safely argue that it does not predict exercise behaviours at all well. Again, no substantive additional work has been published since we made this conclusion in 1991.

One of the problems with the exercise-specific measures of LOC so far reported is that the psychometric properties of the scales (that is, EXLOC and EOLOC) are still unclear. A more rigorous attempt to develop a LOC scale for physical fitness behaviours has been reported by Whitehead and Corbin (1988). They present preliminary evidence for the validity and reliability of FITLOC – multidimensional scales for the measurement of locus of control of reinforcement for physical fitness behaviours – with American college students. Items were written to reflect the three dimensions of internal, chance and powerful others, and 'physical fitness behaviours' were defined as 'any behaviours which would be likely to result in a change in a subject's organic physical fitness status' (Whitehead and Corbin 1988: 110). But again, concurrent validity was demonstrated rather weakly with correlations between the FITLOC scales and a measure of physical activity recall. The correlation coefficients, while in the expected directions, were unconvincing in their strength. Whitehead and Corbin suggested that future research needs to include measures of value if concurrent validity is to be adequately demonstrated. Their own analysis had to assume that value scores were equal across participants. This scale, too, has remained untested in subsequent research.

A critique of locus of control

The research on LOC so far reported has originated from the construct as outlined by Rotter (1966). Subsequent developments have included the use of multidimensional and situation-specific instruments. However, the overall conclusion one can reach about the relationship of LOC (however measured) and participation in exercise or fitness activities is largely weak or inconclusive and appears to have changed little in the past few years, a time when rapid development has occurred in other areas of exercise psychology. A more critical look at the LOC construct itself, or at least the way it has sometimes been used in research, may shed some light on the problem.

Rotter (1975) has outlined three main problems and misconceptions about the I–E LOC construct:

1   Avoidance of measuring reinforcement value. It would be an over-simplification to suggest that internals will act in a certain way simply because of their control beliefs.

Differences in their interests and values associated with the behaviour could easily override any internal or external orientation. In terms of exercise behaviour this could account for some of the equivocal results reported, although some of the studies have attempted measures of value (or often simply affective 'attitude'). For example, the current interest in some forms of exercise (for example, mass jogging, aerobics, mountain biking) might suggest that one important factor operating here is social compliance to a 'fashion' or social pressure. Research suggests that externals may be more compliant than internals. If some externals valued health and physical fitness and wanted to comply with the current fashion of mass jogging, one would predict higher levels of involvement for externals rather than internals.

2   Specificity-generality. Rotter suggests that the ambiguity of the situation may also be important in determining whether LOC has an effect on behaviour. In novel and ambiguous situations people have little or no information to draw on, hence they are more likely to be influenced by generalised beliefs in LOC. However, for more familiar situations, LOC beliefs are likely to be less important since beliefs specifically related to the behaviours in question may acquire greater salience. Again, this may account for the weak relationships between LOC and participation reported in the sport and exercise literature. It could be hypothesised that people already possess beliefs about their physical abilities, competence and so on. They are more likely, therefore, to draw on these specific beliefs than more generalised LOC beliefs. The success of the self-efficacy construct in predicting participation (see Chapter 4) bears this out. Indeed, as Rejeski (1992) states 'one would not expect generalised locus of control to predict exercise behavior. It is inconsistent with the definition of the construct, except for subjects who have never had experience with exercise – in which case it may predict initial involvement' (Rejeski 1992: 143).

3   'Good guy – bad guy' dichotomy. By this Rotter meant that researchers had often erroneously assumed that it was 'good' to be internal and 'bad' to be external. Although it may be an advantage to hold internal LOC beliefs at times, it could also be argued that such beliefs can be maladaptive. Palenzuela (1988) has argued this in his cogent analysis of the LOC construct. He suggests that an interactionist perspective is required such that the 'advantage' of internal or external beliefs will depend on the situation one is in. Guilt and frustration may be created in a child who has always been led to believe that their propensity for being overfat was 'their fault' (high internality) whereas it may be more a function of their parents' influence on the child's lifestyle, a case of genuine lack of control. Weiner's (1995) analysis of attributions and responsibility beliefs concerning obesity and other social 'stigmas' bears this out.

Several authors have questioned the concepts of locus of control of reinforcement and locus of causality of behaviour (Ajzen 1988; Palenzuela 1988). For example, Ajzen's 'theory of planned behaviour' (outlined in Chapter 5), includes the variable 'perceived behavioural control' rather than generalised beliefs in LOC of reinforcement. Ajzen (1988) has argued that such generalised beliefs are likely to be unrelated to specific behavioural tendencies when target, action and context factors are considered. He therefore concludes that generalised LOC beliefs cannot 'be expected to permit accurate prediction' (Ajzen 1988: 104). He goes on to say that 'in terms of conceptualising control beliefs that are compatible with a particular behaviour of interest, one need not stop at the level of perceived achievement responsibility or health locus of control. Instead, one can consider perceived control over a given behaviour or behavioural goal.'

Ajzen (1988) suggests that Bandura's theory of self-efficacy (see Chapter 4) is an appropriate framework here. However, self-efficacy and LOC are conceptually different. Self-efficacy refers to the beliefs that one is capable of a particular action whereas LOC beliefs are those associated with the generalised belief in control over reinforcements. Indeed, Bandura's distinction between efficacy and outcome expectations is important since outcome expectancies are more closely related to LOC beliefs than efficacy expectancies.

Skinner's (1995; 1996) analysis also sheds light on the nature of LOC. Plotting LOC onto Skinner's competence system, we can conceptualise LOC as a set of regulative beliefs *preceding* action and outcome, thus we would expect LOC to have a strong impact on behaviour. However, we have suggested many reasons why this is not the case. LOC is a construct that fits the 'means–ends' part of the figure in Figure 3.1. This suggests if LOC is primarily involving means–ends relations, and hence strategy beliefs, it is concerned with thoughts about what is *required* for success (contingency) rather than beliefs about whether one actually possesses such requirements (competence). This may weaken the predictive power of LOC on behaviour (Biddle 1999b).

In conclusion, the often-stated belief that one needs 'control' over behaviour in order to lead active or healthy lives has not been supported by the LOC literature. This is probably due to a combination of weak methodology, inadequate instrumentation, the role it plays in contingency rather than competence beliefs, and the likelihood that LOC is only a small part of the explanation of exercise and physical activity behaviours anyway. Future work needs to consider its place in a wider research model and, by implication, its relationship with related constructs.

Intrinsic motivation, perceptions of control and autonomy, and exercise

So far, we have discussed the notion of feeling 'in control'. However, we have not linked this overtly to processes of motivation, yet it seems clear from everyday experiences that we prefer, or are more motivated by, situations where some choice, control and 'self-determination' exists. Conversely, we usually prefer not to be controlled and pressured too much. These constructs underpin the link between perceptions of control and motivated behaviour and are central to intrinsic motivation.

Intrinsic and extrinsic motivation are well known constructs in psychology and, although often under different names, in everyday situations too. Certainly those involved in promoting exercise believe that intrinsic motivation is key to sustaining involvement. Intrinsic motivation is motivation to do something for its own sake in the absence of external (extrinsic) rewards. Often this involves fun, enjoyment and satisfaction, such as recreational activities and hobbies. The enjoyment is in the activity itself rather than any extrinsic reward such as money, prizes or prestige from others, and participation is free of constraints and pressure. Such intrinsically pursued activities are referred to as 'autotelic' (self directing) by Csikszentmihalyi (1975). Such a notion is useful for the present discussion since it suggests that intrinsically motivated behaviour is linked to feelings of self-control or self-determination, or what we shall call 'autonomy' (Deci and Ryan 1985).

Extrinsic motivation, on the other hand, refers to motivation directed by rewards, money, pressure or other external factors. This suggests that if these rewards or external pressures were removed, motivation would decline in the absence of any intrinsic interest. Later, we shall introduce motivational constructs that shed extra light on a continuum of motivation, including motivational processes 'between' pure intrinsic and extrinsic motivation.

The development of intrinsic motivation theories

Deci and Ryan (1985; 1991) suggest that four approaches to the study of intrinsic motivation can be identified in the literature. These are free choice, interest, challenge and 'needs'. Studying intrinsic motivation through the assessment of free choice allows some behavioural measure to be estimated. In the absence of extrinsic rewards, those intrinsically motivated will be those who choose to participate in their own time. Intrinsically motivated behaviour is also performed out of interest and curiosity, as well as challenge. Finally, Deci and Ryan outline the important role of psychological needs identified over time through constructs such as 'effectance', 'personal causation', and 'competence' and 'self-determination'.

It is generally acknowledged that the initiation of the shift towards the study of a cognitive perspective on motivational needs was White's (1959) paper on 'effectance motivation'. White suggested that humans have a basic need to interact effectively with their environment. He reviewed a wide range of studies and argued convincingly that operant theories could not account for behaviours such as mastery attempts, curiosity, exploration and play. For all these, and other similar activities, there seems to be no apparent external reward except for the activity itself, and such activities have been termed intrinsically motivating. White argued that successfully mastering such tasks led to feelings of efficacy which, in turn, intrinsically motivated future behaviour.

An alternative approach was taken by deCharms (1968). He argued that self-determination is a basic human need and consequently individuals will be optimally and intrinsically motivated when they perceive themselves to be the 'origin', or in control of, their own behaviour. DeCharms (1968) used Heider's concept of perceived locus of causality (PLOC) to describe individuals' sense of autonomy or self-determination. PLOC refers to the perception people have about the reasons they engage in a particular behaviour. People with an internal PLOC feel as initiators or 'origins' of their behaviour. On the other hand, people feeling that their actions are initiated by some external force are said to have an external PLOC. External and internal PLOC are not mutually exclusive and they represent opposite ends of a continuum, as we have discussed already in terms of generalised LOC. According to deCharms, people are more likely to be optimally and intrinsically motivated when they have an internal PLOC.

Deci and Ryan (1985) propose that three key psychological needs are related to intrinsically motivated behaviour. These are the needs for competence, autonomy and relatedness. Competence refers to strivings to control outcomes and to experience mastery and effectance. Humans seek to understand how to produce desired outcomes. Autonomy is related to self-determination. It is similar to deCharms' notion of being the 'origin' rather than the 'pawn', and to have feelings of perceived control and to feel actions emanate from the self. Finally, relatedness refers to strivings to relate to, and care for, others; to feel that others can relate to oneself: 'to feel a satisfying and coherent involvement with the social world more generally' (Deci and Ryan 1991: 245).

Deci and Ryan state that 'these three psychological needs . . . help to explain a substantial amount of variance in human behavior and experience' (Deci and Ryan 1991: 245). People seek to satisfy these needs, but of more importance from the point of view of enhancing intrinsic motivation is that they predict the circumstances in which intrinsically motivated behaviour can be promoted. We will return to this later. First, let us consider a perspective on intrinsic and extrinsic motivation that has captured some attention in sport and exercise research.

Cognitive evaluation theory

The relationship between intrinsic and extrinsic motivation was, at one time, thought to be quite simple: 'more' motivation would result from adding extrinsic to existing intrinsic motivation! This appeared logical given the evidence demonstrating that reinforcements (that is, extrinsic rewards) will increase the probability of the rewarded behaviour reoccuring. However, a number of studies and observations, mainly with children, started to question whether intrinsic motivation was actually undermined by the use of extrinsic rewards. This was done through 'cognitive evaluation theory' (CET).

CET (Deci 1975; Deci and Ryan 1985) reconciled the two conceptions of White and deCharms by postulating that variations in individuals' feelings of competence and perceptions of autonomy will produce variations in intrinsic motivation. Providing individuals with rewards for their participation in an already interesting activity often led to a decrease in intrinsic motivation. Deci (1975) theorised that this was due to a shift in PLOC. Thus, individuals who had an internal PLOC for performing an activity shifted their locus of causality to a more external orientation when they received a reward, and consequently their intrinsic motivation decreased. Intrinsic motivation can also be affected by changes in perceptions of competence.

Lepper, Greene and Nisbett (1973) tested the relationship between intrinsic motivation and extrinsic rewards with pre-school children. Baseline data on intrinsic interest were collected. Intrinsic motivation was operationally defined as the amount of time spent playing with brightly coloured 'magic marker' highlighting pens during a break in the school day. The children were then assigned randomly to one of three groups:

1   'Expected reward condition': the children agreed to play with the pens and expected a reward for doing so (a certificate with seal and ribbon).
2   'Unexpected reward condition': the children agreed to play with the pens but were not told anything about receiving a reward, although they did receive one afterwards.
3   'No reward condition': these children neither expected nor received a reward for playing with the pens.

The children then participated in the experimental manipulation and were tested individually in a separate room in one of the three conditions. They were later observed, on another occasion, unobtrusively by the use of a one-way mirror. The pens were available in a classroom alongside a variety of other play equipment. The amount of time, expressed as a percentage of free-choice time, spent playing with the pens for each of the three groups showed that the expected reward group played for a significantly smaller amount of time than the other two groups.

A similar experiment was conducted by Lepper and Greene (1975) with children of the same age as in the previous study. This time they used two reward conditions: expected reward and unexpected reward. In addition, the researchers had three surveillance conditions. Some children were told that while they were playing their performance would be monitored by a video camera most of the time (high surveillance), occasionally (low surveillance) or not at all (no surveillance). Up to three weeks after the experimental manipulation, the children were unobtrusively observed playing. The results showed that intrinsic motivation was lower under surveillance and expected reward conditions.

These two studies supported earlier work by Deci (see Deci and Ryan 1985) who found that people paid to work on intrinsically motivating tasks spent less time on the tasks when given an opportunity in free time. Collectively, the results of these studies suggest what has been termed an 'over-justification effect'. By rewarding people for participating in an intrinsically interesting task, subsequent involvement in the task when the reward in no longer available is reduced.

The over-justification effect is based on the premise that the behaviour would have occurred anyway, without the need for extrinsic rewards. However, with the use of expected rewards a shift in perceptions occurs from intrinsic to extrinsic. The task is pursued for reasons of obtaining the reward rather than for intrinsic value. Therefore, the reward 'over-justifies' the behaviour and, in the event of the reward no longer being offered, the individual shows reduced intrinsic motivation.

The studies by Lepper and his co-workers, however, demonstrated that it was not the rewards *per se* that were the problem, but whether the rewards were expected or not. This suggests, therefore, that rewards need not be detrimental to intrinsic motivation in all situations. This led to the formulation of cognitive evaluation theory which states that rewards are likely to serve two main functions:

1   Information function. If the reward provides information about the individuals' competence then it is quite likely that intrinsic motivation can be enhanced with appropriate rewards.
2   Controlling function. If the rewards are seen to be controlling behaviour (that is, the goal is to obtain the reward rather than participate for intrinsic reasons), then withdrawal of the reward is likely to lead to subsequent deterioration in intrinsic motivation.

Attribution theory provides the framework for this analysis since the controlling function of rewards suggests that attributions for participation will be externally focused. This will likely reduce positive emotions under conditions of success and lead to perceptions of lack of control in situations of failure (Biddle 1993; Weiner 1986). While the informational function of rewards can be positive due to the recognition of competence, this will, of course, only be true for those who experience success. Regular use of rewards for successful outcomes to individuals in groups (for example, at school) could equally de-motivate unsuccessful people as they have their incompetence reinforced. This is referred to by Deci and Ryan (1985) as the 'amotivating' function of rewards and is conceptually related to the concept of helplessness. Figure 3.3 summarises these possibilities.

It is important to note that informational events are those events that are perceived to convey feedback about one's competence within the context of autonomy. Events where positive feedback occurs under pressure may be less powerful in influencing intrinsic motivation.

In summarising CET, Deci and Ryan present three propositions:

> Proposition 1. External events relevant to the initiation and regulation of behaviour will affect a person's intrinsic motivation to the extent that they influence the perceived locus of causality for that behaviour. Events that promote a more external locus of causality will undermine intrinsic motivation, whereas those that promote a more internal perceived locus of causality will enhance intrinsic motivation.
>
> (Deci and Ryan 1985: 62)

Deci and Ryan say that events that lead to an external locus of causality undermine

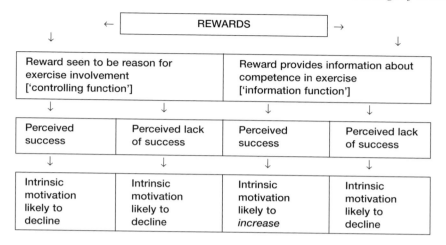

Figure 3.3 Possible links between rewards structures and intrinsic motivation in exercise settings

intrinsic motivation because they deny people 'self-determination', that is they control peoples' behaviour. On the other hand, internal locus of causality may enhance intrinsic motivation by facilitating feelings of self-determination, thus creating greater autonomy.

> Proposition 2. External events will affect a person's intrinsic motivation for an opti- mally challenging activity to the extent that they influence the person's perceived competence, within the context of some self-determination. Events that promote greater perceived competence will enhance intrinsic motivation, whereas those that diminish perceived competence will decrease intrinsic motivation.
>
> (Deci and Ryan 1985: 63)

As Proposition 2 suggests, intrinsic motivation is not just about feelings of control but also about perceived competence. The two right-hand routes in Figure 3.3 relate to compe- tence perceptions.

> Proposition 3. Events relevant to the initiation and regulation of behaviour have three potential aspects, each with a functional significance. The informational aspect facili- tates an internal perceived locus of causality and perceived competence, thus enhancing intrinsic motivation. The controlling aspect facilitates an external perceived locus of causality, thus undermining intrinsic motivation and promoting extrinsic compliance or defiance. The amotivating aspect facilitates perceived incompetence, thus undermining intrinsic motivation and promoting amotivation. The relative salience of these three aspects to a person determines the functional significance of the event.
>
> (Deci and Ryan 1985: 64)

Deci and Ryan (1985) conclude that, generally speaking, choice and positive feedback are perceived as informational, while rewards, deadlines and surveillance tend to be con- trolling. Negative feedback is seen to undermine motivation and is therefore referred to as 'amotivating'.

COGNITIVE EVALUATION THEORY IN EXERCISE AND PHYSICAL ACTIVITY

Since exercise and some forms of physical activity often require persistence, effort, time management, self-regulatory skills and many other things related to motivation, it is relevant to consider the role of intrinsic motivation and self-determination in exercise psychology. Research has mainly focused on competitive sport in the physical domain, although some studies are related to general intrinsic motivation processes, physical fitness or exercise (Chatzisarantis and Biddle 1998; Chatzisarantis, Biddle and Meek 1997; Goudas, Biddle and Fox 1994b; Markland 1999; Mullan and Markland 1997; Mullan, Markland and Ingledew 1997; Vallerand and Fortier 1998; Vallerand and Losier 1999).

Whitehead and Corbin (1991) tested Proposition 2 from CET in the context of fitness testing with children. Studying 12–13 year olds on an agility run test, they sought to test whether changes in perceived competence would vary with changes in intrinsic motivation. They used the Intrinsic Motivation Inventory (IMI) to assess four dimensions of intrinsic motivation: interest/enjoyment, competence, effort/importance, and pressure/tension.

After completing the agility run course, two groups of children were given bogus feedback, stating that they were either in the top or bottom 20 per cent for their age. A third group was given no feedback. Clear support for CET was found with the low feedback group (low competence) showing less intrinsic motivation than those receiving the more positive feedback. Intrinsic motivation scores were shown to be influenced by perceptions of competence.

An early study of exercise motivation (Thompson and Wankel 1980) provided some evidence for the role of perceived choice and control in exercise. This study investigated the influence of activity choice on adherence and future exercise intentions. Adult women who enrolled at a health club were asked to list their activity preferences. They were then matched on the basis of these preferences and then randomly assigned to either a 'choice' or 'no choice' group. The choice group were told that their exercise programme was based solely on the choices they had made, whereas the no-choice group were told that their programme was based on a standard format for exercise rather than their own preferences. In reality both groups received activities they had initially selected. The experimental manipulation was in terms of *perceived* choice only. The results showed that the choice group had a significantly better attendance record after six weeks, suggesting that perceived choice is an important factor in exercise motivation. This is consistent with an intrinsic motivation perspective.

COGNITIVE EVALUATION THEORY: A REAPPRAISAL WITH META-ANALYSIS

Although CET has met with general approval in the domain of physical activity, some researchers have attempted clarification of the relationships between rewards and intrinsic motivation. The first of five meta-analyses addressing these issues was reported by Rummel and Feinberg (1988). They included studies that tested the relationship between extrinsic rewards and intrinsic motivation and where the reward was conveyed in such as a way as to make it 'controlling'. A very large range was found, although only 5 of the 88 effect sizes contradicted CET. The overall mean effect size was –0.329 (see Table 3.2). It was concluded that rewards do have a moderate detrimental effect on intrinsic motivation and CET was supported.

A small meta-analysis was conducted by Wiersma (1992) on studies in industrial and organisational settings. Only twenty studies were analysed, with those on children and

Box 3.2 The DOs and DON'Ts of intrinsic motivation for promoting physical activity and exercise

Exercise motivation expert Dr Jim Whitehead, from the University of North Dakota, has provided some useful practical guidelines for translating the theory of intrinsic motivation into practical exercise promotion (Whitehead 1993).

He suggests some DOs and DON'Ts.

DO:
- Emphasise individual mastery.
- Promote perceptions of choice.
- Promote the intrinsic fun and excitement of exercise.
- Promote a sense of purpose by teaching the value of physical activity to health, optimal function, and quality of life.

DON'T:
- Over-emphasise peer comparisons of performance.
- Undermine an intrinsic focus by misusing extrinsic rewards.
- Turn exercise into a chore or a bore.
- Create amotivation by spreading fitness misinformation.

We fully support these proposals. Indeed on one occasion when Stuart was leading a course on the teaching of health-related exercise for physical education teachers, he suggested that lessons should be made more motivating. One proposal was to use music, either as a beat to follow or just a pleasant and motivating background creating a good climate. However, one teacher said that his headteacher did not allow music in lessons because the lessons might become too much fun! There ended the lesson on intrinsic motivation!

verbal rewards excluded. Analyses were performed separately for free time involvement in a task and for actual performance. The results are shown in Table 3.2 and show that when free time measures of intrinsic motivation are used, rewards have a detrimental effect, but when performance is assessed, rewards have a positive effect. Wiersma concluded that the results show the importance of how intrinsic motivation is operationalised and that performance measures may be combining both intrinsic and extrinsic motivation. For free time measures, at least, CET was supported.

Cameron and Pierce (1994) conducted a meta-analysis of studies investigating the relationships between rewards, reinforcements and intrinsic motivation across various domains of behaviour, including physical activity. Four main measures of intrinsic motivation were analysed: free time on a task, attitude (for example, self-reported task interest, enjoyment etc.), willingness to volunteer for a task in the future, and performance. They found that intrinsic motivation did not follow the expected trend predicted by CET for any of the measures of intrinsic motivation (see Table 3.2). However, when they looked at the type of reward being offered, they found that those rewarded with verbal praise or positive feedback had higher intrinsic motivation in comparison with those not rewarded. This trend was reversed

Table 3.2 Results from five meta-analyses on rewards and intrinsic motivation

Study	Measure of intrinsic motivation	Effect size
Rummel and Feinberg (1988)	Various	− 0.329[1]
Wiersma (1992)	a free time	a − 0.50
	b performance	b 0.34
Cameron and Pierce (1994)	a free time overall	a − 0.04
	b free time: verbal praise	b 0.38
	c free time: tangible reward	c − 0.22
	d attitude overall	d 0.14
	e attitude: verbal praise	e 0.30
	f attitude: tangible reward	f 0.05
	g performance	g − 0.0004
	h willingness to volunteer.	h 0.05
Tang and Hall (1995)	a task-contingent rewards	a − 0.51
	b performance-contingent rewards	b − 0.35
	c unexpected rewards.	c 0.34
Deci et al. (1999)	a engagement-contingent rewards	a − 0.40
	b completion-contingent rewards	b − 0.36
	c performance-contingent rewards.	c − 0.28

Note:
1 Sign is reversed from Rummel and Feinberg's 1988 paper to enable comparison with other studies.

for tangible rewards when time on task was the measure of intrinsic motivation, but the effect was small. This meta-analysis has been criticised by Deci, Koestner and Ryan (1999) for mixing interesting and boring tasks, using inappropriate control groups and misclassifying several studies.

Tang and Hall's (1995) meta-analysis looked at the over-justification effect. Their results supported the proposition from CET that expected tangible rewards undermine intrinsic motivation (see Table 3.2).

Deci *et al.* (1999) considered that further study was necessary to resolve some of the inconsistencies and controversies in the prior meta-analyses. Consequently, they conducted a comprehensive meta-analysis of 128 experimental studies. Their results are summarised in Table 3.2 and show clear support for CET.

From these meta-analyses, therefore, CET is largely supported. The literature in sport and exercise also appears to be supportive although clearly there are issues still to be developed. One way forward might be to progress beyond the distinction of intrinsic and extrinsic and, instead, look at a continuum of self-directed behaviour ranging between intrinsic and extrinsic roles and the extent to which people feel self-directed or controlled.

Moving towards self-determination

CET involves the processing of information concerning reward structures. Extending this perspective and including the psychological needs of competence, autonomy and related-ness, Deci and Ryan (1985; 1991) have proposed their 'self-determination theory' (SDT) approach to intrinsic motivation. The nature of motivated behaviour, according to Deci and Ryan, is based on striving to satisfy these three basic needs. This, they say, leads to a process of 'internalisation': internalising behaviours not initially intrinsically motivating.

Deci and Ryan (1985) have linked the internalisation concept to that of extrinsic and intrinsic motivation. In contrast to their earlier formulations in which they regarded these two motivational types as mutually exclusive, they proposed that they form a continuum where different types of extrinsically regulated behaviour can be located. Although not all theorists depict the continuum in the same way (Fortier *et al.* 1995; Pelletier *et al.* 1995), Deci and Ryan (1991) suggest that the continuum concerns extrinsic motivation rather than one end point being intrinsic motivation. They refer to the contiuum as one representing 'the degree to which the regulation of a nonintrinsically motivated behavior has been internalized' (Deci and Ryan 1991: 254). Although we have represented intrinsic motivation at one end of the continuum in Figure 3.4, it is the differentiation between external and integrated regulation – the four forms of extrinsic motivation – that are important in understanding the shift from earlier conceptions of a dichotomous variable to one of a continuum.

Types of extrinsic and intrinsic motivation

The four main types of extrinsic motivation are external, introjected, identified and integrated regulation, as shown in Figure 3.4. External regulation might be illustrated by the feeling 'OK, I'll exercise if I really must'. This is an example of where behaviour is controlled by rewards and threats. This may be relevant in the case of, say, coercion of patients by medical personnel where physical activity is prescribed for the reduction of health risk factors.

Introjected regulation might be when one says 'I feel guilty if I don't exercise'. This is more internal in the sense that the individual internalises the reasons for acting, but is not truly self-determined. The individual is acting out of avoidance of negative feelings, such as guilt, or to seek approval from others for their performance or behaviour. The term introjection has been used a great deal in different areas of psychology over the years and refers to someone 'taking in' a value but, at the same time, not really identifying with it; it is not accepted as one's own. As Ryan, Connell and Grolnick (1992: 174) suggest, 'in introjected regulation the external regulation has been 'taken in' in the form of intrapsychic, self-approval based contingencies'. Gestalt theorists have referred to introjects as being 'swallowed but not digested'. It is an 'internally controlling' form of behavioural regulation illustrated by thoughts such as 'I have to' or 'I ought to'. Vallerand (1997: 13–14) describes introjected regulation as saying it is 'as if individuals replace the external source of control by an internal one and start imposing pressure on themselves to ensure that the behavior will be emitted'. This is likely to be quite common in exercise; people often state they feel guilty when missing exercise sessions.

Identified regulation might be illustrated by the phrase 'I want to exercise to get fit/lose weight'. This is further towards the self-determined end of the motivation continuum where action is motivated by an appreciation of valued outcomes of participation, such as disease prevention or fitness improvement. This is positively correlated with future intentions and in physical activity can be the most strongly endorsed reason for exercising (Chatzisarantis and Biddle 1998). Whitehead (1993) has called this stage the 'threshold of autonomy'. It is behaviour acted out of choice where the behaviour is highly valued and important to the individual. It is illustrated by feelings of 'I want to' rather than the 'ought' feelings of introjection. The values associated with the behaviour are now 'swallowed and digested'.

Integrated regulation is illustrated by Whitehead (1993) through the phrase 'I exercise because it is important to me and it symbolises who and what I am'. Integrated regulation is the most self-determined form of behavioural regulation and the behaviour is volitional 'because of its utility or importance for one's personal goals' (Deci *et al.* 1994: 121). However, it is important to note that even though the behaviour may be fully integrated, it

Extrinsic motivation

AMOTIVATION	External regulation	Introjected regulation	Identified regulation	Integrated regulation	Intrinsic motivation
• capacity–ability beliefs • strategy beliefs • capacity–effort beliefs • helplessness beliefs					• to know • to accomplish • to experience stimulation

Self-determination

− ←   ↑   +

Figure 3.4 A continuum of self-determination in terms of different types of motivation

can still be extrinsically motivated. This is because it may be an instrumental action, done to achieve personal goals rather than for the pure joy of the activity itself. This is why the self-determination continuum can be construed as forms of extrinsic motivation without intrinsic motivation. In addition, some behaviours may never be performed for intrinsic reasons, although leisure-time physical activities can be.

In contrast to these forms of extrinsic motivation, intrinsic motivation is shown through feelings of enjoyment: 'I exercise because I enjoy it'. The individual participates for fun and for the activity itself. Clearly moving towards intrinsically, or integrated, motivated forms of behavioural regulation are advised for higher levels of intention and sustained involvement in exercise since they are likely to involve stronger feelings of personal investment, autonomy and self-identity. Some have also proposed three types of intrinsic motivation: intrinsic motivation 'to know', 'to accomplish' and 'to experience stimulation' (Vallerand 1997).

Ryan and Connell propose:

> that the constructs described in internalisation theories can be related to several distinct classes of *reasons* for acting that in turn have a lawful internal ordering. That is, these classes of reasons can be meaningfully placed along a continuum of autonomy, or of self-causality.
>
> (Ryan and Connell 1989: 750)

They suggest that the continuum should be able to be demonstrated through a simplex-like or ordered correlation structure where variables are ordered 'such that those deemed more similar correlate more highly than those that are hypothetically more discrepant' (Ryan and Connell 1989: 750). We have shown this in the context of children's motivational orientations towards school physical education lessons (see Table 3.3) (Goudas *et al.* 1994b). Similarly, by weighting each subscale, an overall 'Relative Autonomy Index' (RAI) can be computed, with higher scores indicating higher internality.

In addition, it has been suggested that the state of 'amotivation' exists where the individual has little or no motivation to attempt the behaviour. Whitehead (1993) describes the move from amotivation to external regulation as crossing the 'threshold of motivation'. Amotivation refers to the relative absence of motivation where a lack of contingency between actions and outcomes is perceived and reasons for continuing involvement cannot be found (Vallerand and Fortier 1998). Vallerand (1997) has likened amotivation to a feeling of learned helplessness although, as shown in Figure 3.4, there may be several types of amotivation involving not just beliefs of helplessness, but also feelings that one has inadequate ability,

Table 3.3 Correlations between self-determination theory variables, demonstrating the simplex-like pattern predicted by Ryan and Connell (1989)

Motivational orientation	External		Introjected		Identification		Intrinsic	
	F and N	Gym	F and N	Gym	F and N	Gym	F and N	Gym
Amotivation	0.55	0.53	− 0.14	− 0.15	− 0.62	− 0.70	− 0.72	− 0.75
External			0.23	0.10	− 0.25	− 0.50	− 0.38	− 0.50
Introjection					0.42	0.35	0.33	0.25
Identification							0.87	0.78

Source: data from Goudas *et al.* 1994b.

Note: F and N = football and netball; Gym = gymnastics.

effort and strategies. Amotivation is a construct in need of further study in exercise. Many adults report feelings of physical inadequacy that prevents participation in physical activity. They display amotivation. There is concern that too few youth are active enough for health gains and further work is required in identifying correlates of physical activity and motivation. Vallerand and Fortier (1998) suggest that the study of amotivation 'may prove helpful in predicting lack of persistence in sport and physical activity' (Vallerand and Fortier 1998: 85).

Surprisingly, the use of SDT for studying intrinsic motivation has not been extensive in physical activity. We have used the autonomy continuum, and the RAI, in analyses of adult physical activity and children's motivation within physical education. So far we have found that perceptions of autonomy, assessed with the RAI, are predictive of intrinsic interest in physical activity (Goudas, Biddle and Fox 1994a).

We have also investigated the role of perceived autonomy in exercise motivation using Ajzen's (1988) theory of planned behaviour framework (Chatzisarantis and Biddle 1998; see also Chapter 5). First, we found for adults that those with an internal PLOC, or high feelings of autonomy towards exercise, reported stronger intentions to be physically active and higher levels of actual physical activity than those with a more external orientation. Consistent with this, those high in autonomy reported more positive beliefs about exercise than those low in autonomy. Finally, we found that the interaction between autonomy and attitude added significantly to the prediction of self-reported levels of exercise beyond that accounted for by intention.

These results suggest that the construct of autonomy is an important one in the prediction of exercise behaviour. Indeed, and despite the proposals of Deci and Ryan (1985), it is possible to argue that perceptions of autonomy are the forgotton elements of intrinsic motivation, since most researchers seem to rely more on explanations associated with perceptions of competence. As we argue in the next chapter, perceptions of competence are important, but there are many behaviours in health and elsewhere where feelings associated with autonomy may be equally or more important. Individuals who have successfully lost weight often report greater feelings of 'control' over themselves and their lives. Similarly, exercisers may feel 'good' about themselves through the mechanisms of autonomy rather than competence. There are many joggers out there (including us!) who have minimal levels of jogging competence but feel good about the efforts we make to stay active.

This analysis must also recognise the 'double-edged sword' of autonomy. The SDT continuum from external to internal motivational influences means that some behaviours will be motivated, at least in the short term, by guilt and frustration, not recommended forms of long-term motivation. Pressures vary along this continuum and health behaviours, such as weight control, are often motivated by external influences. The key must be to find ways of moving towards the self-determined end of the continuum.

Skinner (1996: 557) has stated 'constructs related to autonomy are outside the proper domain of control'. This reflects Deci and Ryan's (1985) distinction between a need for competence *and* a need for autonomy. In addition, Deci and Ryan have stated that autonomy concerns freedom in initiating behaviours whereas control is concerned with perceiving a contingency between action and outcome. In this regard, autonomy is agent–means (competence) and control is agent–ends (competence and contingency). But where does this leave self-determination in terms of perceived control? Although the continuum uses language similar to that of control – intrinsic, external – it is essentially about *reasons for acting* or, what has been termed behavioural regulations. These vary by degrees of self-determination (autonomy), but not necessarily control or competence. Deci says that in his own work with Richard Ryan he has 'proposed that intentional (i.e., motivated, personally caused) behaviours differ in the extent to which they are self-determined versus controlled' (Deci 1992: 168). He goes on to say that 'there is a great advantage to specifying different regulatory processes (or motivational orientations); namely, it provides a motivational means of explaining different qualitative aspects of human functioning'.

As Deci and Ryan state:

> the need for self-determination is an important motivator that is involved with intrinsic motivation and is closely intertwined with the need for competence. . . . It is important to emphasize that it is not the need for competence alone that underlies intrinsic motivation; it is the need for self-determined competence.
>
> (Deci and Ryan 1985: 31–2)

In other words, intrinsically motivated states must involve competence and autonomy. To use the well-known example of slaves, they have perfect competence in rowing the ship but no autonomy; they are likely to have no intrinsic motivation. Given freedom of choice, in all likelihood they would not choose to row the boat. The study by Chatzisarantis *et al.* (1997) demonstrated this point by showing that the correlation between intentions and physical activity was high only when intentions were seen as autonomous.

Competence and autonomy, therefore, are part of the wider picture of control, but we should be aware of the differences between the major constructs involved. If intrinsically motivated behaviour, or behaviour regulated by integrated means, is what we strive for in our exercisers, children etc., we need both competence and autonomy. Each is 'necessary but not sufficient' since controlling competence or autonomous incompetence will not lead to self-determination. But with integrated regulation of behaviour almost certainly comes heightened feelings of competence and control. Internalised reasons for acting become experienced as self-regulated.

These analyses demonstrate the potential importance of self-perceptions of autonomy in motivated behaviour. It seems to make sense that perceptions associated with self-determined effort will enhance motivation, and is wholly consistent with other approaches, such as attributions (Biddle 1993; Weiner 1992) and self-theories (Dweck 1999), to which we move shortly.

A hierarchical model of intrinsic and extrinsic motivation

Vallerand (1997) organises the constructs of intrinsic and extrinsic motivation into a hierarchical model, as shown in Figure 3.5. Essentially, Vallerand (1997) proposes that intrinsic and extrinsic motivation, as well as amotivation, feature at global, contextual and situational levels. At each of these levels, there are antecedents (such as either global, contextual or situational factors, and needs for autonomy, competence and relatedness), as well as affective, cognitive and behavioural consequences. The global level refers to a general motivational orientation to which people typically subscribe. The contextual level of the model refers to domains of life, such as education, work, leisure, interpersonal etc. Finally, the situational level is concerned with situation-specific motivation.

This model is useful for conceptualising the different processes in intrinsic and extrinsic motivation and should help understanding of these constructs in physical activity. For example, patients entering a GP-referral exercise scheme will bring with them their global motivational orientation, yet the activity counsellor or exercise leader is in a position to influence situational cues to alter situation-specific motivation. Indeed, Deci and Ryan

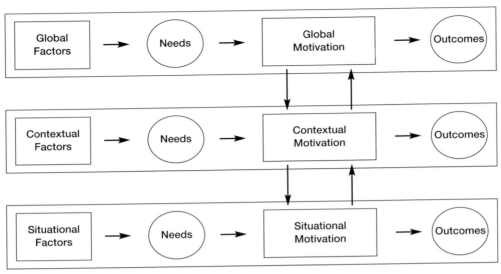

Figure 3.5 A hierarchical model of intrinsic and extrinsic motivation proposed by Vallerand (1997)

(1991) suggest that moving individuals from external to integrated regulation is more likely by altering situational or contextual factors. These include providing a meaningful rationale for the behaviour, acknowledging the behaver's perspective, and conveying choice rather than control. In exercise, therefore, the exercise leader might explain why certain exercises are 'good' and others 'bad' and what effect they might have. Empathy with how exercises feel concerning incompetence, inadequacy, exertion etc. will also help. Finally, the leader will allow some choice of activities, pace, difficulty etc.

Further implications for exercise participation

It is generally accepted that intrinsic motivation is a desirable quality for continued involvement in physical activities. However, the complex inter-relationship between intrinsic motivation, perceptions of control and autonomy, and extrinsic rewards remains to be fully tested in exercise settings. Summary evidence on adherence (Dishman *et al.* 1985) suggests that adults will adopt exercise for reasons of health yet are more likely to continue participation because of the more intrinsic feelings of well-being and enjoyment. Large population surveys also show that intrinsic reasons, such as 'feeling better', are important to both active and inactive people, although to varying degrees (Canada Fitness Survey 1983b). This suggests that adults may have an intrinsic orientation to exercise, whether they exercise or not. No doubt the more extrinsic influences of wanting to look 'good' in front of others, or participating to please others, will also be important factors for some people.

Exercise leaders and health promoters should be aware, given our previous discussion, of the inter-relationship between rewards and intrinsic motivation. For example, the use of reward systems ('token economies') in health clubs has been a common strategy (Franklin 1988), though no systematic evaluation of their effectiveness has been reported. While the short-term influence on adherence may be positive, the research reported in this chapter suggests that those wishing to promote greater exercise participation must be cautious in their use of extrinsic rewards, particularly for those already high in intrinsic motivation.

Rewarding competence may be appropriate, and it may also be better to reward and reinforce exercise behaviours rather than performance. In other words, encourage the process of activity by reinforcing frequency and participation, rather than solely reinforcing the product of exercise through rewarding high fitness scores or the use of comparative reward structures. The rewarding of participation is more likely to lead to feelings of autonomy.

Box 3.3 Reconciling theory and practice: the youth fitness incentive schemes conundrum

If you talk with coaches and teachers they nearly always will tell you that badges and other extrinsic reward systems 'work' for children. But haven't you read about cognitive evaluation theory I ask them?! This area oftens creates in us a potential clash between the theory and what the practitioners say. Who's right?

The issue of motivating children to become and remain physically active has attracted the attention of physical and health educators, yet there is still relatively little evidence on the motivation of children and youth in the exercise settings beyond the arena of volunteer competitive sport. Despite this it is commonplace in schools and within some national agencies to operate extrinsic reward systems for the promotion of children's sporting and fitness behaviours. British examples include the 'five-star' award scheme for (track and field) athletics, an award scheme for gymnastics, and a plethora of badges available through various swimming and life-saving activities. Similar schemes exist elsewhere and in the USA there has been much debate about the type of award scheme to implement for physical fitness (Corbin, Whitehead and Lovejoy 1988; Whitehead, Pemberton and Corbin 1990). Ironically, the award scheme implemented by the President's Council for Physical Fitness and Sports (PCPFS) requires participants to achieve very high goals before they are rewarded (reaching the 85th percentile on five test items), yet they state that one of their goals is to 'motivate boys and girls to develop and maintain a high level of physical fitness' (AAHPER 1965, cited in Corbin *et al.* 1988). Such standards seem more likely to demotivate than anything else given that so few are likely to achieve them.

The American Alliance for Health, Physical Education, Recreation and Dance (1988) has developed the 'Physical Best' fitness award scheme. This scheme promotes three types of awards ('recognition system') as shown in Table Box 3.3.

Table Box 3.3 The 'Physical Best' 'Recognition System'.

Award	Behaviour
Fitness Activity Award	Recognition of the student's participation in physical activities outside of school physical education. Student keeps an 'activity log/diary' and sets personal goals and activities in consultation with the teacher.
Fitness Goals Award	Recognition for obtaining individual fitness and exercise goals, set in consultation with the teacher. Goals can be set in cognitive, psychomotor and affective learning domains.
Health Fitness Award	Recognises the attainment of fitness levels associated with minimal risk or risks of health problems. Students have to attain the standards for all six items (distance run, skinfold measures, body mass index, sit and reach flexibility test, sit-up, and pull-up).

Source: adapted from AAHPERD 1988; McSwegin *et al.* 1989.

In explaining their three awards, McSwegin, Pemberton and Petray (1989: 25) state that 'extrinsic rewards . . . may not always motivate children and youth to strive to develop activity habits beneficial to lifelong fitness. How a student views an award influences that student's behaviour, prompting that student to be more involved or less involved in the activity'. Ah! McSwegin *et al.* have read about cognitive evaluation theory! They are aware of the potential problems of extrinsic rewards and the over-justification hypothesis. This makes a pleasant contrast to the often stated belief in physical education that awards are motivational, regardless of the circumstances.

Some physical educators have suggested that children should be rewarded for participation in exercise (what Corbin *et al.* (1988) call 'process awards'), rather than superior performance against others. Not only could the latter approach produce spurious results in terms of implications for health ('I'm fitter than X therefore I don't need to exercise'), but it is also likely to lead to a more external perceived locus of causality. Of course, rewarding exercise behaviour is also open to the negative aspects of rewards as many 'performance awards' are, but, as with all reward schemes, the key must lie in their use as information on competence by providing positive feedback. As Corbin *et al.* conclude, 'in the absence of research to document various award schemes designed to motivate fitness and regular exercise among youth, we would be wise to apply the best theoretical evidence available' (Corbin *et al.* 1988: 213).

The conundrum continues!

Attributions and exercise

The role attributions may play in perceived control of exercise behaviours is potentially important (Knapp 1988) although, as yet, research focussing specifically on exercise (as opposed to competitive sport) is sparse (Biddle 1993; Biddle, Hanrahan and Sellars, in press). Nevertheless, any discussion on control and expectancy-value theories of motivation relevant to exercise would be incomplete without some consideration of attributional processes. Similarly, attributions are considered important mediators of some other health behaviours (Adler and Matthews 1994; Stroebe and Stroebe 1995).

Attributions are the perceived causes and reasons people give for an outcome or behaviour and, because the focus is often on the perceived causality of behaviour, the term 'causal attributions' is sometimes used. Although the study of attributions has been applied to many settings, it is in achievement contexts that a great deal of research has been accumulated, particularly concerning academic achievement (see Weiner 1986; 1992), but also in sport (Biddle 1993; Biddle *et al.*, in press). Although little has been written about the role of attributions in health-related exercise contexts, this has increased somewhat since we last reviewed the area (Biddle and Mutrie 1991).

Attributions and perceptions of control

One of the most widely known approaches to attributions is that proposed by Weiner (1986; 1992; 1995). Although originally working in the field of educational achievement, Weiner's theory of achievement motivation and emotion has application to a broader range of issues.

The main attribution elements used in Weiner's research were ability, effort, task difficulty and luck. Table 3.4 summarises some of the cues used in making such attributions and gives examples from exercise. The classification model used for categorising such elements into the dimensions of locus of control (later renamed locus of causality) and stability is well known. The locus of causality dimension classifies attributions as they relate to the individual (internal) or reside outside of the individual (external). The stability dimension refers to the classification of attributions in relation to their temporal stability, with some attributions being transient (unstable) and others relatively permanent (stable) over time.

Weiner (1979) modified his earlier locus x stability model to include a 'dimension of controllability'. The locus of control dimension then became locus of causality to better reflect the distinction between this and the 'new' dimension. The controllability dimension classifies attributions in terms of whether they are controllable or uncontrollable. For example, effort is often seen to be internal yet unstable whereas ability (at least in the 'natural ability' sense) is internal but stable. One could argue, therefore, that effort is controllable whereas ability is not. This kind of argument led to the creation of the extra dimension.

Weiner has argued that the attribution dimensions are related to the consequences that attributions may have for motivation, cognition and emotion. For example, making attributions to stable factors is likely to lead to expectations that similar results will occur again in the future, whereas unstable attributions provide less clear-cut information about expectations. Similarly, attributions to internal factors are thought to heighten emotional feelings whereas external attributions may be related to a lessening of emotion. This has subsequently been refined such that locus of causality is thought to be related to feelings of self-esteem and pride whereas the controllability dimension is thought to be related to social emotions, such as guilt and pity. For example, attributing the completion of a half-marathon to well-planned training (internal) could increase the feeling of pride associated with the run. If, however, the run was not completed due to a lack of personal effort (controllable), guilt may ensue or, in the case of someone trying hard but failing due to a perceived lack of ability (uncontrollable), others may feel pity for the individual (Weiner 1995).

Table 3.4 Antecedents of the main attribution elements applied to exercise and physical activity

Attribution element	*Antecedents*	*Examples from exercise and physical activity*
Ability	Percentage, number and pattern of successes; level of difficulty of the task; ego-involved goals.	Regular success at completing exercise regimens; successfully negotiating known difficult tasks, such as marathons; regular involvement in distance walking found to be quite easy.
Effort	Relationship between performance and value of the task/goal; perceived physical effort; mastery goals; persistence.	Completion of effortful tasks; conscious decision-making for persistence and self-improvement.
Task difficulty	Social norms and comparison; characteristics of the task.	Completion of task known by others to be difficult. Comparison of exercise tasks in relation to what others can do.
Luck	Unique outcome; independence, randomness of outcome.	Work place relocates to twenty minutes walk from home, with no motorised transport available.

One area of attribution research and perceptions of control that may be important in the study of exercise is that of learned helplessness. Again, the relationship with exercise is speculative due to a lack of research, although evidence in educational and clinical psychology does exist (Abramson, Seligman and Teasdale 1978; Peterson and Seligman 1984). Apart from a position paper by Dweck (1980) surprisingly little research has been generated in sport or motor performance contexts (Biddle 1993).

Abramson *et al.* (1978) suggested that uncontrollable failure, when attributed to personal inadequacy (internal, stable attributions), and generalised to other situations ('global' attribution), would generate feelings of helplessness. As a result of such proposals, attribution 'retraining' methods were suggested in an effort to change maladaptive attributions for failure (Forsterling 1988).

Learned helplessness hypotheses retain a great deal of intuitive appeal although there is much disagreement as to the exact mechanisms underpinning such phenomena. Research based on this might be a fruitful avenue for investigating those who dropout from, or do not initiate, an exercise programme and could be investigated alongside similar constructs such as amotivation. Studies could look at the cognitions of adults quitting, or failing to initiate activity programmes, and compare them with their more active counterparts. Developments should also include investigations of attributions at the point of drop out, or over time for those who never participate. Longitudinal studies are required which investigate the development of cognitions in childhood and their relationships, if any, with participation patterns in adulthood.

Attribution research in health

The general notion of perceived control in health has a long history, although it is more recent to see formal attribution paradigms being applied. Several researchers have investigated the causal beliefs attached to chronic illness. Patients studied by Lowery and Jacobsen (1985) were interviewed and asked to respond to a question about how well they were doing with their illness. Patients who attributed their illness to external, unstable or uncontrollable factors tended to perceive themselves as having been unsuccessful in their illness outcome. However, only 66 per cent of the 'failure' patients offered an attribution at all. For the 'success' patients, attributions were offered by 79 per cent and tended to be internal and somewhat controllable (mainly effort-based). The sample studied by Lowery and Jacobsen (1985) was strongly optimistic and therefore did not expect failure in the long term. Overall, the results partially supported attribution predictions for chronically ill patients.

Bar-On and Cristal (1987) studied male post-myocardial infarction (MI) patients who were admitted to an intensive coronary care unit after their first MI. Two main questions were posed: 'why did the MI happen?' and 'what will help you cope with it?' Patients who attributed their MI and its outcomes after hospital treatment to luck/fate returned to work more slowly and were lower on a score of physical functioning compared with patients who attributed the MI to personal strengths and weaknesses. Similarly, Haisch, Rduch and Haisch (1985) investigated the effects of attribution retraining in weight loss and found positive effects. Those who were taught to reattribute weight problems to internal and unstable (controllable) factors were more successful in weight control after a twenty-three-week intervention programme than those not participating in attribution retraining. This was also shown to be successful after a ten-month follow-up. Similarly, attributions have been found to have important roles in the understanding of health behaviour change (Schoeneman and Curry 1990), dietary and smoking behaviours (Eiser and van der Pligt

1988; Hospers, Kok and Strecher 1990; Schoeneman *et al.* 1988a; Schoeneman *et al.* 1988b), and persuasion to attend screening (Rothman *et al.* 1993).

Lewis and Daltroy (1990), in their short review of attributions and health behaviour, propose six possible applications of attributional principles to health education. These have some relevance to exercise promotion. The six applications are:

1   Development of therapeutic relationships: eliciting attributions can assist in the development of empathy between patient and carer, or between other relationships in health settings.
2   Creation of correct attributions: assistance in developing informed judgements about one's health status may be important for psychosocial adjustment, particularly where illness is concerned.
3   Alteration of incorrect attributions: attributional change may be functional, either through misattribution alteration or through changes made in the dimensional structure of the attributions formed.
4   Alteration of the focus of the attribution: sometimes the attributional focus may need to be shifted away from one area (for example, uncontrollable illness) to another. This may act as a coping mechanism or assist in personal adjustment.
5   Attribution of characteristics of the individual: health educators and other health professionals can use attributional statements in reference to the individual client or patient. These might motivate behaviours if the statements give certain cues to the individual, such as how good a person they are or how capable they are.
6   Maintenance of perceived personal effectiveness: making the right attributions will have an influence on perceived competence and efficacy for the maintenance of their health behaviours.

Clearly there is some potential in the application of attributions to health behaviours, particularly as they relate to perceptions of control and subsequent motivation.

Attribution research in exercise

Knapp (1988) suggests that attributional factors may be important in behavioural change strategies in exercise. Studies investigating attributions in health-related exercise are summarised in Table 3.5. In a cross-sectional retrospective survey of beliefs, including attributions, of exercisers and non-exercisers, we interviewed 433 adults in a street survey (Biddle and Ashford 1988). It was found that aerobic exercisers differed from non-exercisers such that exercisers had significantly higher perceptions of control over their cardiovascular health.

In a follow-up study of 468 adults in another city, we also assessed attributions made in relation to exercise behaviours rather than cardiac health (Biddle and Ashford 1988). Again, exercisers and non-exercisers were different in their attributions. Exercisers reported higher scores on internality (locus) and controllability over exercise, as well as higher scores on consensus and consistency attribution information. This suggests that exercisers were more likely to have been active in the past (consistency) and were more likely to have modified other health habits (consensus).

More recently, in a study of adherence to exercise in a commercial health/fitness club, we found clear differences in attributions for adherence between adherers and non-adherers (Smith and Biddle 1990). Adherers were more likely to attribute their attendance to personal

Table 3.5 Studies investigating the role of attributions in health-related exercise contexts

Study	Sample	Attribution measures	Purpose	Results	Conclusion
Biddle and Ashford (1988): Study I	Random sample of British adult men (n = 234) and women (n = 199).	Single items in larger interview/survey assessing locus, stability and controllability of personal cardiac health.	To differentiate self-reported aerobic exercisers from non-exercisers.	More control over cardiac health perceived by younger exercisers.	Health attributions differentiate exercisers from non-exercisers.
Biddle and Ashford (1988): Study II	Random sample of British adult men (n = 238) and women (n = 230).	Single items in larger interview/survey assessing locus, stability and controllability of exercise; consensus, consistency, distinctiveness attributions for exercise.	To differentiate self-reported aerobic exercisers from non-exercisers.	• More control over exercise perceived by exercisers. • Exercisers more likely to have exercised in the past (high consistency) and to have consensus attributions.	Exercise attributions differentiate exercisers from non-exercisers.
Smith and Biddle (1990)	New adult members (n = 96) of a fitness club in England.	Single item measures of ability, effort, task difficulty and luck for programme adherence.	To discriminate adherers from non-adherers on attribution elements.	Adherers attributed their behaviour to effort and task ease, where non-adherers used attributions to luck, task difficulty, low effort and low ability. 95.7% correct classification of subjects into adherence groups based on attributions.	Exercise adherence strongly associated with attributions for adherence.
McAuley et al. (1990)	Asymptomatic, sedentary, middle-aged American males (n = 28) and females (n = 36) who had previously dropped out of a structured exercise programme.	Causal Dimension Scale II (CDSII)	To ascertain attributions for exercise cessation, and relationships between attributions and emotional reactions associated with dropout.	• Lack of motivation and time management primary reasons for dropping out of exercise. • Attributions for dropout mainly internal, unstable and personally controllable. • Attribution dimensions associated with feelings of guilt (locus), shame (stability and personal control) and displeasure (personal control).	Exercise-related emotion is associated, in a small way, to attributions for dropping out of exercise.

Study	Participants	Measure	Purpose	Findings
McAuley (1991)	Middle-aged, sedentary American males (n = 37) and females (n = 43) halfway through a five-month structured exercise programme.	CDSII	To examine relationships between attribution, self-efficacy and exercise emotion for previously sedentary adults.	• Those who exercised more frequently were higher in self-efficacy and made more internal, stable and personally controllable attributions for their exercise progress. • Positive exercise emotion associated with self-efficacy, as well as internal, stable, and personally controllable attributions.	Positive feelings concerning exercise are associated with attributions for exercise progress.
Vlachopoulos et al. (1996)	British school children (n = 304) aged 11–15 years in school physical education lessons.	CDSII modified for children.	To investigate psychological determinants of childen's affective reaction to exercise testing.	• Attributions largely unrelated to exercise-induced feelings. • Feeling states strongly associated with a task goal orientation and perceived competence.	Attributions unrelated to exercise-related emotion in children.
Vlachopoulos and Biddle (1997)	British school children (n = 1070) aged 11–16 years.	CDSII modified for children.	To investigate psychological determinants of children's achievement-related affective reaction to past school physical activity/education experience.	• Personally controllable attributions augmented positive affect and minimized negative affect, regardless of levels of perceived ability. • Task goal orientation positively associated with controllable attributions.	Positive post-exercise feeling states are associated with personally controllable attributions.

effort while non-adherers were more likely to cite luck as a factor for their behaviour. These findings were supported by qualitative data from a follow-up study of office workers. One participant expressed the view that 'I am an active person because I made a decision to exercise and not because I have any physical ability', while another said 'I believe I have adopted a sedentary lifestyle basically because I am lazy' (Smith 1995).

McAuley and colleagues have studied attributions in exercise employing Weiner's (1986) theory of achievement attributions and emotions. McAuley, Poag, Gleason and Wraith (1990) studied a small group of middle-aged men and women who had previously dropped out of a structured exercise programme. Using the Causal Dimension Scale II (CDSII) (McAuley, Duncan and Russell 1992), study participants generally reported internal, unstable and personally controllable attributions for ceasing participation in the programme. Results also showed that attributions for dropping out were associated, in a small way, to feelings of shame, guilt, displeasure and frustration.

Similarly, McAuley (1991) investigated attributions, self-efficacy and emotion midway through a five-month exercise programme for previously sedentary middle-aged adults. Analyses showed that attributing their exercise progress to internal, stable and personally controllable factors was associated with feelings of positive emotion, as was exercise efficacy. However, Vlachopoulos, Biddle and Fox (1996) found that attributions had a negligible effect on exercise-induced feeling states for children involved in track running, while a task goal orientation and perceived competence had strong effects. However, while similar trends were found by Vlachopoulos and Biddle (1997) when studying children's overall feelings about physical education, they did find that personally controllable attributions augmented positive affect and minimised negative affect, regardless of levels of perceived ability.

Attributional thinking, placed within Skinner's (1995; 1996) competence system, as we know, primarily about interpretation of outcomes, the consequences of which may impact on future regulative beliefs and actions. They are, therefore, more distant from (future) actions and outcomes than most regulative beliefs such as LOC. This may explain the difficulty researchers have had in demonstrating strong relationships between attributions and behaviour in physical activity. Only prospective studies can test this, and these are sparse. It also assumes that little will change between making the attributions and subsequent behaviour, yet we have not tested the longevity or consistency of attributions over time. To make matters worse, we have nearly always assessed attributions immediately after performance. Attributional processing reflects means–ends connections (Skinner 1995) and these involve strategy, not capacity, beliefs. Accordingly, attributional thinking looks to identify causes of outcomes (for example, ability, effort and luck) rather than appraising whether the individual has access to these causes (for example, effort). In reality, one could argue that true attributional thinking, while primarily being about identification of causes, is also a response to questions such as 'why did *I* fail at this task?' thus necessitating control beliefs (namely, strategy *and* capacity beliefs). If so, attributions are more central to control beliefs and will also involve agent–ends connections. True perceptions of control, through control beliefs, require a combination of competence and contingency. Attributions, but not LOC, include both. Attributional processing is likely to involve both means–ends (contingency) and agent–ends (competence).

Further study is required to tease out the relative importance of these beliefs. Given that effort and ability are central constructs both to the beliefs in Skinner's tripartite model and within attribution theories, continued linkage in research seems prudent. Certainly the evidence points to the utility of addressing attributions people make in health and exercise settings. Attributions remain an important component of motivational theories using the perspective of perceived control.

Perceptions of the incremental nature of ability

An interesting development in the study of control, goals and attributions has been Dweck's theorising concerning the perceived stability of ability (Dweck 1999; Dweck, Chiu and Hong 1995; Dweck and Leggett 1988). Initially in the domain of intelligence, and more recently extended to include views of morality and stereotyping, Dweck and colleagues have proposed that two clusters of beliefs underpin people's judgements and actions (Dweck 1992; Dweck 1996; Dweck *et al.* 1995; Dweck and Leggett 1988; Levy, Stroessner and Dweck 1998; Mueller and Dweck 1998). These beliefs centre on the way people view the malleability of attributes, such as intelligence. Those subscribing to the view that a particular attribute is fixed and relatively stable hold an 'entity' view or 'entity theory'. Conversely, those seeing the attribute as changeable and open to development hold an 'incremental' view or theory.

Research has shown that those holding an entity view are more likely to have negative reactions, such as helplessness, when faced with achievement setbacks (Dweck and Leggett 1988). Entity theorists are more likely to endorse performance (ego) goals whereas incremental theorists have been shown to endorse learning (task) goals more.

There has been little attention given to implicit beliefs in the physical activity domain. This is despite similar notions in prior research, such as ability and effort beliefs in attribution research (Biddle 1993), or beliefs concerning the causes of success in goal orientations research (Duda 1993). In replicating the study by Dweck and Leggett (1988), Sarrazin *et al.* (1996) found some support for the relationship between implicit beliefs concerning the nature of athletic ability and the adoption of different goals in physical activity (specifically sport) for children aged 11–12 years. Those choosing a 'learning' (task) goal were more likely to endorse incremental beliefs about sport ability than those adopting performance (ego) goals. Biddle, Soos and Chatzisarantis (1999) tested a model predicting intentions from perceived competence, achievement goals and implicit beliefs. They found that data from Hungarian youth fitted the model well when sub-domains of entity beliefs (beliefs that sport ability is general and a gift) were modelled to predict an ego goal orientation, and incremental beliefs (learning and incremental/changeable sub-domains) were modelled to predict a task orientation. However, the path coefficients were generally small.

In a small-scale experiment, Kasimatis, Miller and Macussen (1996) told some students that athletic co-ordination was mostly learned, to create an incremental condition, and told others that co-ordination was genetically determined (entity condition). After initial success, participants were subjected to a difficult exercise task through video. Results showed that in the face of such difficulty, more positive responses were found for those in the incremental condition. Specifically, such participants reported higher motivation and self-efficacy and less negative affect. However, the implicit beliefs held by the students were not assessed. The nature and extent of entity and incremental beliefs in this sample, therefore, as well as the longevity of such effects, are not known.

The physical activity research reviewed so far suggests that relationships do exist, albeit small at times, between implicit beliefs and goal orientations, as well as other motivational indicators. This could prove to be a useful development in the study of attributional thinking in exercise. If sedentary individuals feel that exercising 'ability' is fixed and cannot be developed, they are less likely to try. This is supported by the ADNFS data reported in the previous chapter where over 40 per cent of women with feelings that they were 'not the sporty type' presented a significant barrier to physical activity.

Chapter summary and conclusion

As stated at the beginning of this chapter, the popular health/fitness literature constantly makes reference to the concept of 'control' over lifestyle, fitness and health. The evidence presented here has been accumulated from three main sources derived from expectancy-value and control theories of motivation: locus of control, intrinsic motivation and attribution-related theories. In the chapter, we have:

- Reviewed the evidence concerning locus of control in health and exercise.
- Reviewed the evidence in physical activity and other settings concerning the role of rewards and reinforcements in intrinsic motivation.
- Reviewed recent developments in intrinsic motivation theory, concerning the role of a continuum of autonomy and self-determination.
- Reviewed the principles of attribution theory, and beliefs concerning ability, and provided evidence in the health and exercise domains.

   Having reviewed the evidence, we conclude:

- That current research findings are not supportive of locus of control being a strong determinant of exercise. However, this could be due to numerous problems with the way that much of this research has been carried out. In particular, most studies violate the original assumptions of locus of control theory and measuring instruments have not been fully tested or have been inappropriately applied.
- That cognitive evaluation theory remains a viable theory for the study of motivational processes in exercise.
- That self-determination theory is a viable perspective for the study of exercise motivation and is likely to increase our understanding of exercise motivation in the future, and in particular the different types of extrinsic motivation that might exist in physical activity.
- That despite limited evidence in the exercise domain, the tenets of attribution theory are applicable to health and exercise and could provide an important perspective for understanding cognitive, affective and behavioural aspects of most health domains.
- Beliefs concerning the stability of exercise competence may be important motivational factors.

4 I can! Motivation through feelings of competence and confidence

> I did manage to influence some of my more sedentary colleagues. Exercise was unusual for African men of my age and generation. After a while even Walter [Sisulu] began to take a few turns around the courtyard in the morning. I know that some of my younger comrades looked at me and said to themselves 'If that old man can do it, why can't I?' They, too, began to exercise.
>
> Nelson Mandela
> (*Long walk to freedom*, 1994)

Chapter objectives

This chapter continues the saga of exercise motivation through reviewing a number of interrelated theories and perspectives. The unifying theme of the chapter is the study of self-perceptions of competence and confidence. Specifically, in this chapter we aim to:

- Move from general to specific self-perception theories relevant to the study of exercise.
- Review how people perceive competence in the physical domain, including general notions of competence, how we assess competence and different definitions of competence.
- Outline achievement goal perspectives and related theories as viable ways to study motivation in exercise.
- Briefly discuss the role of self-schemata in exercise.
- Review self-efficacy theory (SET) and present a comprehensive overview of research findings, methods and issues.
- Present some alternative views on confidence relevant to the study of physical activity.

So far, we have discussed a number of issues associated with motivation for physical activity. In Chapter 2 we provided an overview of the area, including a review of descriptive approaches to exercise motivation. This was then followed, in Chapter 3, by a discussion of theories that have been used in exercise research that have drawn on perceptions of control. However, it is actually quite difficult arriving at a clear demarcation of theories as far as labels are concerned. For example, attribution theory is discussed by Weiner (1992) as an expectancy-value approach, but is labelled as 'social cognitive' by Fiske and Taylor (1991). Yet Roberts' book on motivation in sport and exercise largely ignores attribution theories and claims that the book 'is firmly placed within the present zeitgeist of social cognitive per-spectives on motivation' (Roberts 1992: vii). However, it should be noted that Roberts (1992) does acknowledge the central role attribution theory has had in the development of the social cognitive approaches he presents.

In drawing together self-perception, competence and social-cognitive theories in this chapter, we fully recognise that such demarcations are difficult and often somewhat tenuous. Indeed, discussion on control theories in the previous chapter could easily have prefaced the forthcoming discussion on competence perceptions, and the work on attitude theories (see Chapter 5) could be accommodated within a social cognitive theme. One has to draw the line somewhere! But to help orientate yourself, our rationale is as follows.

The approach in Chapter 3 shows humans to act rationally, yet contemporary thinking suggests that this may be exaggerated and these theories 'present too positive a picture of the capacities and capabilities of humans' (Weiner 1992: 298). The 'social cognitive' approach is based more on emotion and choice than rational decision-making. This is not dissimilar to Weinstein's (1988) 'messy desk analogy' used in discussing the 'precaution adoption process' in health psychology. Essentially, he proposes that we do not act in life as if we have an ordered set of priorities on our desk, each one carried out in logical order regardless of competing pressures or priorities. Instead, circumstances, limitations of resources and other factors, prevent such logical behaviour. Some items even get lost under a pile of other things! Consequently, we are more likely to act through various pressures, such as social prompting ('have you seen those papers I left on your desk?'), or just personal preference (emotion).

Bandura delimits his social cognitive theory as follows: 'the social portion of the terminology acknowledges the social origins of much of human thought and action; the cognitive portion recognizes the influential causal contribution of thought processes to human motivation, affect and action' (Bandura 1986: xii). As such, we shall address issues of exercise and physical activity motivation that draw on cognitive processes of the self. By this we mean the thinking that goes on that may determine whether we exercise or not, and the role of self-perceptions of competence and confidence in maintaining such involvement.

Maddux describes a general social cognitive theory as 'an approach to understanding human cognition, action, motivation, and emotion that assumes that people are capable of self-reflection and self-regulation and are active shapers of their environments rather than simply passive reactors to their environments' (Maddux 1993: 119). Drawing on Bandura's (1986) work, Maddux goes on to outline five central points of this approach:

- People can symbolise events and have the capacity to anticipate consequences through forethought.
- This forethought guides behaviour through goals.
- People are self-reflective: 'these metacognitive, self-reflective activities set the stage for self-control of thought and behavior' (Maddux 1993: 119).
- People can self-regulate through the selection and alteration of environmental conditions.
- 'Environmental events, inner personal factors (cognition, emotion and biological events) and behavior are mutually interacting influences' (Maddux 1993: 119).

Dominant theories of motivation where self-perception has been a central feature in the contemporary sport and exercise literature are theories based on the constructs of self-efficacy, self-perceptions of worth and competence motivation, and, more recently, perceptions of success and definitions of achievement goals. Some time ago, we recognised the importance of such theories in determining approach and avoidance tendencies in exercise (Biddle and Fox 1989). As discussed above, there are other social cognitive or similar approaches that, we believe, best fit in other chapters, so will not be discussed here.

These include attitude-behaviour theories such as the theory of planned behaviour. In Chapter 6 we bring together these theories in a discussion on theoretical and conceptual convergence.

From general to specific self-perceptions

Contemporary self-esteem theory proposes that our global view of ourselves ('global self-esteem') is underpinned by perceptions of specific domains of our lives, such as social, academic and physical domains (Shavelson, Hubner and Stanton 1976). Based on this approach, Ken Fox has developed an operational measure of physical self-perceptions whereby psychometrically sound scales assess the higher order construct of 'physical self-worth' (PSW) and its self-perception subdomains of sport competence, perceived strength, physical condition and attractive body (Fox 1997a; Fox and Corbin 1989). This hierarchy is shown in Figure 4.1.

It is proposed that everyday events are likely to affect more specific perceptions of self, such as the belief that one can run one mile which, if reinforced over time, may eventually contribute to enhanced self-perceptions of physical condition or even PSW. As such, self-perceptions can be viewed in terms of being more 'domain general'; that is they operate at the level of general self-perceptions of competence and worth, such as PSW. These are 'carried around' with us at a general level of abstraction and are unlikely to be modified by short-term or trivial experiences. Nevertheless, they could be important psychological constructs guiding general motivated behaviour. Self-perceptions can also be viewed in more specific terms, such as specific competency perceptions: 'can I finish this run?'; 'I have just walked two miles for the first time'.

In line with this analysis, we can identify common theoretical threads running through the exercise psychology literature. At the domain-general level are theories of competence and self-perceptions that, while not exactly trait-like, are generalisable across specific situations within the physical domain. These approaches include competence motivation, exercise self-schemata and goal orientations. At the level of situation-specific perceptions, the dominant approach has been Bandura's 'self-efficacy theory' (Bandura 1977; 1986; 1997). For consistency and completeness, we also address other approaches to physical activity/exercise confidence, even though they may not fit perfectly with our representation of the domain-general/situation-specific hierarchy.

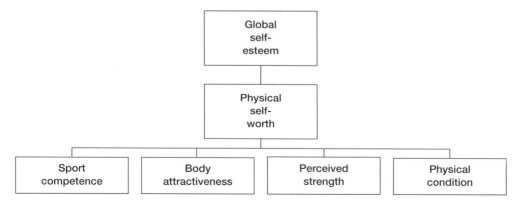

Figure 4.1 Physical self-perception hierarchy proposed by Fox (1990)

Domain-general approaches to physical activity motivation

In this section we discuss competence motivation theory, exercise self-schemata and recent perspectives on achievement goals and definitions of competence that are higher-order social-cognitive constructs of motivation and self-perception.

Self-perceptions and competence motivation theory

Attempts at explaining human behaviour through an individual's desire to seek situations where they can display competence are not new in psychology. As we discussed in Chapter 3, White's (1959) seminal paper on 'effectance' (competence) motivation argued against the mechanistic explanations of the time in favour of a more cognitive approach. A comprehensive, and more contemporary, interpretation of competence motivation has been made by American developmental psychologist, Susan Harter (Harter 1978; Harter and Connell 1984). She developed White's theory in several ways. First, she conceptualised competence as multidimensional by specifying domains of competence perceptions, such as scholastic and athletic competence. These domains are likely to become more differentiated with age, as shown in Table 4.1. Second, she related self-perceptions of competence to motivational orientations and perceptions of control. Finally, she developed measuring instruments for the assessment of domains of competence and self-perceptions of adequacy.

Many sport psychologists have followed the lead of Harter and tested her theory, or parts of the theory, in physical activity settings (Ommundsen and Vaglum 1991; Van Wersch 1997; Weiss 1986; Weiss, Bredemeier and Shewchuk 1986). However, it has largely been ignored in exercise psychology.

Harter's theory suggests that individuals are motivated in achievement domains where their competence can be demonstrated, particularly if they also feel intrinsically oriented in

Table 4.1 Competence perception/adequacy subdomains as represented in measures by Harter and colleagues

Children <8[1]	Children[2]	Students[3]	Adults[4]
Cognitive competence	Scholastic competence	Creativity	Sociability
Physical competence	Social acceptance	Intellectual ability	Job competence
Peer acceptance	Athletic competence	Scholastic competence	Nurturance
Maternal acceptance	Physical appearance	Job competence	Athletic abilities
	Behavioural conduct	Athletic competence	Physical appearance
		Appearance	Adequate provider
		Romantic relationships	Morality
		Social acceptance	Household management
		Close friendships	Intimate relationships
		Parent relationships	Intelligence
		Humour	Sense of humour
		Morality	

Sources
1 Harter and Pike (1983).
2 Harter (1985).
3 Neeman and Harter (1986).
4 Messer and Harter (1986).

that area and see themselves as having an internal perceived locus of control. Successful mastery attempts under such conditions are associated with positive emotion and low anxiety. Harter's theory predicts that those high in perceived physical competence would be more likely to participate in physical activity. Such a relationship has been found, although it is not strong, probably due to the influence of other variables and, if Harter is correct, these might include perceptions of control and motivational orientations. Few physical activity studies have tested the full model. Also, an over-reliance on perceptions of competence through achievement settings may make this approach less relevant to the recreational/health-related context we are mainly concerned with in this book.

Nevertheless, the strength and attraction of Harter's theory centres on the development of psychometrically sound and developmentally-based instruments for the testing of her model. But, as stated, only parts of the model, such as motivational orientation, or domain-specific perceptions of competence, have been tested against behaviour and related variables.

The hierarchical model of physical self-worth proposed by Fox (1997a) presents another view of competence perceptions and motivation. The so-called 'self-enhancement' model of self-esteem is applicable here (see Chapter 8). This is where positive self-perceptions play a motivational role in behaviour. For example, if I feel competent in the exercise domain it is more likely that I will want to demonstrate that competence, and hence be motivated to exercise. Indeed, the reverse (lack of motivation through perceptions of incompetence) is likely to be a major determinant of current sedentary habits of adults in industrialised countries. In addition, with exercise being a health behaviour, other motivations will be relevant. Not all exercisers participate to show competence; indeed some probably have relatively low perceptions of competence but are driven by motives of appearance, health, psychological well-being etc. The picture is a complex one. Nevertheless, it is widely accepted that people have a need to maintain or enhance their self-esteem, thus they seek out situations where this is possible.

ASSESSING PERCEPTIONS OF COMPETENCE

Harter's scales for the assessment of perceived competence have been used extensively in studies on physical activity, either in the original (Ulrich 1987) or modified form (Weiss, Bredemeier and Shewchuk 1985). Recently, scales have been developed assessing more specific physical self-perceptions. These have included the Physical Self-Perception Profile (PSPP) for adults (Fox and Corbin 1989) and children (Whitehead 1995), and the Physical Self-Description Questionnaire (PSDQ) (Marsh *et al.* 1994). However, few authors have challenged the way that competence perceptions have been assessed. Is 'competence' referred to in social comparative terms (for example, 'are you better than kids your age?'). Contemporary literature on goal orientations supports the view that people can construe ability, competence and success in different ways, as we discuss later.

An analysis of the physical adequacy/competence items in the Harter scales from Table 4.1 shows that the term 'good at . . .' is used a great deal in Harter's scales. This could be interpreted as either social comparative or mastery, so may not be a problem. Of the six items for pre-school/kindergarten children, five use the term 'good at'. The other item ('can tie shoes') is criterion referenced and mastery oriented. All six items for Years (Grades) 1–2 use the term 'good at'.

Harter's scale for children (see Table 4.2) contains six items in the 'athletic competence' subscale. This instrument uses the alternative choice format where children are asked to read two contrasting statements, choose the one which reflects them, and then to rate whether it is 'sort of true for me' or 'really true for me'. From the six items, one (item 4) reflects a clear comparative emphasis (using the reference 'better than'), and two could be construed as more comparative, with reference to 'do very well' (1) and 'good enough' (2). Only one item, in our opinion, is clearly mastery-oriented by making reference to participation and task involvement (item 5). A similar conclusion can be drawn from scrutiny of the student and adult scales in Table 4.1.

Harter's contribution to the understanding and measurement of perceived competence should not be underestimated. However, it is our belief that the scales that have so readily been accepted in sport and exercise psychology require further scrutiny, at least as far as the definition of perceived competence is concerned.

In reference to his PSPP, Fox (1990) states quite clearly that he uses three orientations in assessing perceived competence. For the sport competence subscale, he assesses perceptions of sport/athletic *ability* (for example, '[some people] feel that they are really good at just about every sport'), ability to *learn* sport skills (for example, '[some people] always seem to be among the quickest when it comes to learning new sports skills'), and *confidence* in the sports environment (for example, '[some people] are among the most confident when it comes to taking part in sports activities'). Even here, though, comparative elements inevitably creep in, such as with reference to 'among the most confident', even though the subject of the statement is mastery (participation)-oriented. It would appear, therefore, from this analysis of the assessment of perceived competence, that more account needs to be taken of recent advances in achievement goal orientations and the different ways people have of defining competence and success.

Differential definitions of competence and success: goal perspectives theory

Early research in sport and exercise psychology followed the theoretical perspectives associated with 'need for achievement' and expectancy-value theories of Murray, Atkinson and McClelland (see Weiner 1992). However, a major change of direction in the study of achievement motivation and perceptions of ability and competence can be traced to the work of Maehr and Nicholls (1980). They influenced the thinking of many people interested in achievement-related constructs and behaviour, and in particular in education. Such an approach was readily adopted by those in sport psychology, although has not been included much in the study of exercise. However, where it is relevant to the present discussion is in the research utilising a goals perspectives approach in children's physical activity, and in

Table 4.2 Athletic competence items from the Self-Perception Profile for Children. Only the positively worded of the two statements is shown (emphases added)

Item (actual number)	Statement
1 (3)	[some kids] *do very well* at all kinds of sports.
2 (9)	[some kids] feel they are *good enough* at sports.
3 (15)	[some kids] think that they could *do well* at just about any new sports activity they haven't tried before.
4 (21)	[some kids] feel that they are *better than* others their age at sports.
5 (27)	[some kids] usually *play* (games and sports) rather than watch.
6 (33)	[some kids] are *good at* new games right away

Source: Harter 1985.

physical education in particular. This is because the determinants of children's physical activity are poorly understood (Sallis *et al.* 1992b) and that most children can be studied through physical education programmes rather than those self-selecting themselves into voluntary programmes. Sallis *et al.* (1992b) identify secondary school-based interventions as a research priority.

FOUNDATIONS OF GOALS PERSPECTIVES THEORY

In rejecting many of the assumptions of Atkinsonian achievement motivation theory, Maehr and Nicholls argued that:

> success and failure are not concrete events. They are psychological states consequent on perception of reaching or not reaching goals. . . . It follows that, if there is cultural variation in the personal qualities that are seen to be desirable, success and failure will be viewed differently in different cultures.
>
> (Maehr and Nicholls 1980: 228)

Maehr and Nicholls (1980) defined three types of achievement motivation: ability-orientated motivation, task-orientated motivation and social approval-orientated motivation. Ability-orientated motivation is when 'the goal of the behavior is to maximize the subjective probability of attributing high ability to oneself' (Maehr and Nicholls 1980: 237). This has been modified in sport psychology to refer to 'ego' goal orientations where success is defined as the demonstration of superiority over others (Duda 1993).

In task-orientated motivation, according to Maehr and Nicholls (1980), 'the primary goal is to produce an adequate product or to solve a problem for its own sake rather than to demonstrate ability' (Maehr and Nicholls 1980: 239). This is the 'task' goal orientation (Duda 1993).

The third goal – social approval-orientated motivation – has been investigated less than the other two goals (Urdan and Maehr 1995). This dimension of achievement motivation was defined by Maehr and Nicholls in terms of demonstration of 'conformity to norms or virtuous intent rather than superior talent' (Maehr and Nicholls 1980: 241–2).

Nicholls (1989) has argued that the two main orientations here – task and ego – are based on how people construe competence. In a task perspective, ability and effort are less clearly differentiated and hence is referred to as the 'less differentiated conception of ability'. Cues used to assess competence are effort and task completion and hence are self-referenced. The 'more differentiated conception of ability' (ego orientation) is where competence is judged relative to others, and ability and effort are differentiated as causes of outcomes. This means that an externally-referenced view is adopted. Nicholls (1989) also argues that these conceptions of ability give rise to corresponding goals in achievement settings, and these are the task and ego goals referred to. Further, it has been suggested that individuals will be predisposed to task or ego orientations, although we shall clarify this shortly.

GOAL ORIENTATIONS AND LINKS WITH MOTIVATION

Two interrelated areas of goals and competence perceptions have now been studied in the context of physical activity and shed light on important motivational processes in the physical domain. These are:

- The relationships between individual differences in goal orientations and motivational constructs such as intrinsic motivation and perceptions of ability.
- Underlying belief structures and goals. The related area of the links between situational achievement cues, such as group climate and motivational responses will be discussed in Chapter 7.

There is now consistent evidence that the adoption of a task goal in physical activity settings can be motivationally adaptive (see Duda 1993). However, ratings of task and ego goal orientations are usually found to be uncorrelated. Hence, we have argued elsewhere (Fox *et al.* 1994) that goal 'profiles' should be studied whereby combinations of task and ego are accounted for. In other words, some people will be 'low' in both task and ego, some 'high' in task but 'low' in ego, or any other combination. We have found that children low in both task and ego goal orientations have lower perceived sport ability than other groups. Similarly, this group is often over-represented by girls, whereas for the high task/high ego group boys strongly outnumber girls. One reason for this gender bias could be associated with socialisation and personal identity. It could be argued that it is more important for boys in our society to demonstrate 'competence', however construed, in physical activity settings.

Whereas Fox *et al.* (1994) found that the high task/high ego and high task/low ego groups were similar in their motivational responses when asked about sport in general, in a study of motivational responses following a specific physical fitness task, we found that children in the high task/low ego group had the most motivationally adaptive profile (Goudas *et al.* 1994a). In addition, a similar study showed that the high/high and high task/low ego groups showed the best motivational profile, depending on the variables assessed (Vlachopoulos and Biddle 1996). It appears, therefore, that a high task orientation is positive, either singly or in combination with a high ego orientation.

An important issue is to investigate how and why different goal orientations or profiles are developed. Dweck and Leggett (1988), for example, suggest that academic goals are related to underlying beliefs about the nature of intelligence. Those believing that intelligence is relatively fixed are more likely to adopt a 'performance' (ego) goal whereas others who believe that intelligence is more changeable will be predisposed to a 'learning' (task) goal (see Chapter 3).

We first replicated Dweck and Leggett's (1988) method, with some modifications, by studying the relationship between goal choice and notions of the incremental nature of sport ability (Sarrazin *et al.* 1996). A small difference was noted between children choosing a learning (task) goal and those preferring a performance (ego) goal such that the former were more likely to believe that sport ability was incremental or changeable. However, the results were less clear than those shown by Dweck and Leggett (1988) for classroom settings. In a follow up study with French school students, we extended the notion of conceptions of sport ability to include several 'scientific' and 'lay' conceptions of ability, such as believing that sport ability was the product of learning, was a 'natural gift', was stable etc. Results were clearer than in the earlier study with a relationship demonstrated between a task orientation and beliefs that sport ability was incremental and the product of learning. An ego goal orientation was associated with beliefs that sport ability is general and is perceived more as a 'natural gift' (see Figures 4.2 and 4.3).

In addition to the motivational consequences of task and ego goals, we have studied emotional responses to exercise in relation to goals (Vlachopoulos *et al.* 1996). Children reported their emotions following an 800m race/time trial in school physical education

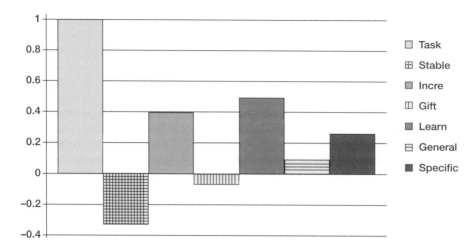

Figure 4.2 Conceptions of the nature of sport ability and their relationship with a task goal orientation shown through canonical correlation coefficients (Sarrazin *et al.* 1996)

using the Exercise-Induced Feeling Inventory (EFI). This instrument yields scores of 'positive engagement', 'revitalisation', 'tranquility' and 'physical exhaustion'. Results showed clear associations between task orientation and feelings of enhanced positive post-exercise feelings and reduced perceptions of physical exhaustion, whereas ego orientation was unrelated to post-exercise affect. Also, in a meta-analysis of the relationship between task and ego goals and affective responses to various types of physical activities, we have found a clear positive relationship between a task goal and positive affect (Ntoumanis and Biddle 1999b).

Typically, the issues addressed here have not been dealt with in the exercise psychology literature on adults. Our earlier work (Biddle and Mutrie 1991) gave little space to goal

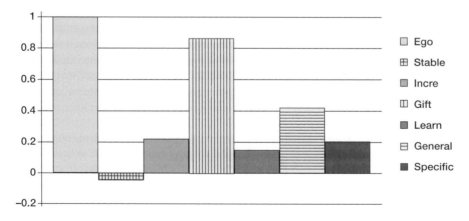

Figure 4.3 Conceptions of the nature of sport ability and their relationship with an ego goal orientation shown through canonical correlation coefficients (Sarrazin *et al.* 1996)

orientations, but since that time there has built a consistent body of knowledge that sheds light on motivational issues that contribute to the identification of physical activity determinants, at least for children and young people.

Exercise self-schemata

The current section of this chapter on 'domain-general' approaches to physical activity motivation has emphasised the role of generalised beliefs and perceptions in exercise and health behaviour and actions, such as goals and beliefs in competence. One approach currently favoured in contemporary social psychology is that of information processing guided by self-schemata. Fiske and Taylor (1991: 98) define a schema as 'a cognitive structure that represents knowledge about a concept or type of stimulus, including its attributes and the relations among those attributes'. Such knowledge is gained through experience and schemata are thought to guide the way we retrieve, select and interpret information.

Kendzierski (1988; 1990b; 1994) has applied this construct to exercise through work on 'exercise self-schemata'. Such generalised views of oneself may be important determinants of exercise behaviour. Specifically, Kendzierski (1994) has defined three main types of individuals:

- Exerciser schematics: these are people who describe themselves in terms of being an exerciser, being physically active and 'in shape', and rate these constructs as important to their own self-image.
- Non-exerciser schematics: these people view exercise/physical activity descriptors as clearly not applying to them, but rate these descriptors as important to their self-image.
- Aschematics: do not rate exercise/physical activity descriptors as particularly descriptive of them, nor do they view them as important to their self-image.

Initial validation of a measure of these three types has proved successful, such as finding that exercise schematics were more likely than the other two groups to report starting an exercise programme (Kendzierski 1990b), and that they reported doing more exercise (Kendzierski 1988). However, although some of these data are prospective, it still appears slightly tautological. Where, for instance, could we intervene? Do we attempt to develop positive associations with exercise and self-image such that the development of an exercise self-schemata promotes the likelihood of greater exercise, or is it only through positive exercise experience, and presumably greater importance attached to this aspect of the self, that the self-schemata develops? Perhaps the answer is both, similar to self-esteem theory. Kendzierski (1994) argues that experience is a necessary but not sufficient condition for schemata development and that an exercise self-schemata is not merely a reflection of exercise experience.

The notion of exercise self-schemata is an interesting one. For instance, current clothes fashion includes a great deal more sports/leisure wear than in the past. Whether this will encourage the development of exercise self-schemata remains to be seen. It would appear more likely than if such clothes were very unfashionable. However, more work is required in this area to clarify key issues. One way forward may be to integrate this approach with the hierarchical self-esteem model of physical self-perceptions (Fox 1997a), particularly in respect of the perceived importance of subdomains of physical self-worth. Kendzierski suggests that exercise self-schemata research:

could provide a basis for future work involving (a) the identification of individuals most likely to benefit from interventions aimed at promoting exercise behavior and (b) the identification of individuals who may require extra encouragement and/or closer supervision to achieve their exercise goals.

(Kendrzierski 1990b: 80)

The discussion so far has centred mainly on 'domain-general' theories of motivation, that is to say the theories that operate at a higher and more abstract level of generality. In addition, contemporary research has reflected a desire to study more state-specific conceptions of cognition and motivation. Such constructs are liable to be more open to influence, at least in the short term, and hence may have more practical appeal to practitioners attempting to change physical activity and health behaviours.

State-specific theories of exercise motivation

The social-cognitive perspectives currently favoured in the exercise psychology literature have drawn extensively on self-efficacy theory and this approach has had a large impact in both exercise (McAuley 1992; McAuley and Courneya 1993) and health (Stroebe and Stroebe 1995).

Motivation and confidence: self-efficacy theory

Confidence has been identified at the anecdotal and empirical level as an important construct in exercise motivation. Statements associated with self-perceptions of confidence are commonplace in studies on exercise and sport. For example, in the Allied Dunbar National Fitness Survey for England (The Sports Council and Health Education Authority 1992), emotional, motivational and time barriers were identified as factors preventing people being more physically active (see Chapter 2). All are likely to be associated, in one way or another, with feelings of confidence to initiate or maintain activity.

Physical self-efficacy is seen as a central construct in Sonstroem and Morgan's (1989) exercise and self-esteem model (Figure 4.4). Using the notion of a hierarchy, Sonstroem and Morgan place efficacy as a lower-order 'specific' construct in the model that represents the 'lowest generality level of the competence dimension. Self-conceptions at this level should be the most accurate and the most readily influenced by environmental interactions' (Sonstroem and Morgan 1989: 333). This concurs with Bandura's notions of self-efficacy. Sonstroem and Morgan's model proposes that physical self-efficacy is the first cognitive link between higher order psychological constructs and actual behaviours. The assumption is that behavioural outcomes influence self-efficacy and onwards to self-esteem. This reflects a 'psychological consequences' approach to self-efficacy. However, self-efficacy theory also supports the reciprocal nature of the relationship between efficacy perceptions and behaviour by stating that the behaviour will not be indulged in unless efficacy perceptions are sufficient. This is dealing with the motivational role of self-efficacy and will be the approach adopted here.

BASIC TENETS OF SELF-EFFICACY THEORY IN PHYSICAL ACTIVITY AND EXERCISE

The need for studying the theories and mechanisms of confidence should be self-evident. However, there are a number of issues that need addressing. It is not known whether there are different types of confidence in exercise, such as the confidence to initiate exercise in the

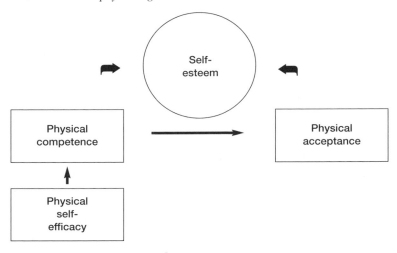

Figure 4.4 Sonstroem and Morgan's (1989) exercise and self-esteem model

first place or the confidence that exercise will bring about desired results, such as weight loss or gains in fitness. The role of state versus trait factors is not known, although contemporary approaches to the study of self-confidence suggest that situational cues will dominate over and above any trait confidence factors. Also, the permanence of confidence in particular situations, or across different groups (for example, age, gender, class, ethnicity) is rarely studied. This all suggests that self-confidence, despite recent interest in this area of psychological research, and the intuitive logic and appeal of the topic, requires further study before application can be made in some fields.

The shift from reliance on stable personality traits as predictors of behaviour to a more social-cognitive approach has led to the development of a number of theoretical perspectives on self-confidence. These approaches range from efficacy expectations (Bandura 1997) to performance expectations (Corbin 1984), perceptions of competence (Harter 1978), and cognition-emotion relationships with likely behavioural consequences (for example, learned helplessness; Abramson, *et al.* 1978).

This diversity of approaches has been mirrored in the physical activity literature with studies on self-efficacy theory, performance expectancies, trait and state sport confidence, and movement confidence (Feltz 1988; 1992; McAuley 1992; Vealey 1986).

Self-efficacy theory (SET) originated in clinical settings but it has subsequently been tested in a variety of physical activity and health contexts, such as sport (Feltz 1992), weight loss (Weinberg *et al.* 1984), exercise (Ewart 1997; McAuley 1992), and with other health-related behaviours (Schwarzer 1992; Strecher *et al.* 1986). Schwarzer, for example, states that 'self-efficacy has proven to be a very powerful behavioural determinant in many studies, and its inclusion in theories of health behaviour, therefore, is warranted' (Schwarzer 1992: 223).

Bandura (1986) defines perceived self-efficacy as:

> people's judgements of their capabilities to organise and execute courses of action required to attain designated types of performances. It is concerned not with the skills one has but with judgements of what one can do with whatever skills one possesses.
>
> (Bandura 1986: 391)

The key phrase here is 'capabilities to organise and execute courses of action' since Bandura has always differentiated between efficacy expectations and outcome expectations. By this it is meant that beliefs related to the ability to carry-out a particular behaviour are *efficacy* expectations whereas beliefs as to whether the behaviour will produce a particular result are *outcome* expectations. For example, efficacy expectations might be the belief that one can successfully adhere to a programme of brisk walking five times each week for thirty minutes each. However, outcome expectations might refer to whether one believes that such activity will produce the weight loss that was desired at the beginning.

Although Bandura's SET refers to the two expectancies as being different, they are both part of the self-confidence concept in physical activity and exercise. People are likely to be concerned about both types of expectancy and both require study in exercise psychology research (Desharnais, Bouillon and Godin 1986). For example, it is important to know whether efficacy expectations are influential in the adoption of exercise programmes, yet it is also likely that outcome expectations will affect the maintenance of such programmes and the reinforcement necessary for continued involvement. Studies apparently testing SET, however, do not always make it clear whether they are investigating efficacy or outcome judgements.

SOURCES OF EFFICACY INFORMATION

Four main sources of information for self-efficacy beliefs have been identified by Bandura (1986; 1997). These are:

- prior success and performance attainment
- imitation and modelling
- verbal and social persuasion
- judgements of physiological states.

Performance attainment   This is thought to be the most powerful of efficacy sources since it is based on personal experience of success and failure. However, the appraisal of such events (namely, attributions) is likely to influence expectations of future success. Bandura states that 'successes raise efficacy appraisals; repeated failures lower them, especially if the failures occur early in the course of events and do not reflect a lack of effort or adverse external circumstances' (Bandura 1986: 399). Attribution theory (Weiner 1986) predicts that internal and stable causes of failure, such as lack of ability, are more likely to lead to debilitating and demotivating cognitions and negative emotions than factors which appear more changeable, such as lack of effort or poor strategy.

The study of attributional variables in relation to perceptions of self-efficacy in exercise contexts has been sparse. McAuley (1991) integrates the two theories by studying previously sedentary middle-aged adults midway through a five-month exercise programme. As predicted by theory, efficacious exercisers reported more personally controllable attributions for their exercise progress. In addition, self-efficacy, as well as attributions, predicted exercise emotion.

Attributional factors may also be important in determining the extent that efficacy expectations gained in one context generalise to other contexts. Although this has not been tested in exercise research, Bandura (1986) suggests that some generalisation is likely and is predicted to be strongest in similar events to the original source of efficacy judgements. For example, research into learned helplessness has suggested that the nature of the attributions given in response to failure may influence the extent to which negative perceptions generalise beyond the event itself. 'Global' attributions for failure are those which generalise beyond the situation in which failure occured. If an individual believes that their inability to play a competent game of tennis is due to their lack of co-ordination, this will probably generalise to other sports situations. However, a 'specific' attribution for failure will not generalise and is regarded as a more positive way to think about such situations as it is more likely to protect self-esteem (Abramson *et al.* 1978).

Bandura (1990) has argued that outcome expectancies and attributions are different motivational processes, although both operate through the anticipation of future behaviour and performance. Expectancies operate through the process of forethought while attributions constitute retrospective reasoning. Both, however, are important sources of information for the development of efficacy perceptions.

Imitation and modelling   Self-efficacy may also be developed through imitation and modelling processes. Observing others succeed or fail could affect subsequent efficacy beliefs, particularly if the individual has little or no prior experience to draw on. Interestingly, Bandura (1986) suggests that social comparison information is important in self-efficacy beliefs. However, whether this is true about health-related exercise in comparison to, say, competitive sport, is difficult to say. Although confidence may be associated with certain self-presentational processes, such as social physique anxiety (Leary 1992; Leary *et al.* 1994), it could be argued that health-related exercise is less likely to evoke social comparison than some other situations. Nevertheless, public exercise behaviours, such a street jogging, public swimming or exercise classes are likely to evoke strong self-presentation influences and could be a major source of motivational variation.

Bandura suggests that the social comparison element of vicarious experience is important because in some situations it is not always possible to gauge your success without some kind of reference point, such as another person's score: 'Because most performances are evaluated in terms of social criteria, social comparative information figures prominently in self-efficacy appraisals' (Bandura 1986: 400).

Another point on vicarious processes in self-efficacy concerns the use of certain types of individuals in promoting exercise to non-exercisers or certain groups, such as the obese. It is common in the mass media to use elite sport models, or models displaying high levels of fitness or physique/figure development. Bandura contends that vicarious influences such as modelling are more likely to have an influence when the individual has some empathy with the model. On the other hand, anecdotal evidence suggests that elite models are 'interesting' and 'motivational'. This needs resolving to make effective use of models in exercise promotion. Indeed, in our own research, we found that older patients referred into an exercise programme by their family doctor were more confident when exercising with similar individuals. They also reported feeling uncomfortable when around young vigorous exercisers (Biddle, Fox and Edmunds 1994a; Fox *et al.* 1997).

Verbal and social persuasion   Depending on the source of such efficacy information, persuasion from others is likely to influence perceptions of self-efficacy. However, it is thought to be a relatively weak source in comparison to the two already mentioned and has not been studied in any systematic way in exercise research. The success of persuasion is also dependent on the realistic nature of the information. Given the potential for regular contact between exerciser and instructor in supervised programmes, verbal persuasion is likely to be a source of self-efficacy worthy of note in some situations.

New approaches to health and exercise promotion through social marketing might be applicable, such as through market research, ongoing evaluation of campaigns and strategies, and the use of consumer behaviour and communication models (Donovan and Owen 1994; Wankel and Hills 1994; Wankel and Mummery 1993).

Judgements of physiological states   The original theorising on SET was based on experiences in clinical settings, and in particular the modification of reactions to aversive events, such as phobias (Bandura 1977). In such situations it was found that self-efficacy was related to how one appraised internal physiological states such as heart rate. Bandura (1986) says that 'treatments that eliminate emotional arousal to subjective threats heighten perceived self-efficacy with corresponding improvements in performance' (Bandura 1986: 401). The use of such somatic feedback can be a positive influence on self-efficacy, however the evidence in sport has been inconsistent (Feltz 1992) and hardly studied at all, to our knowledge, in exercise, although teaching people how to monitor physiological signs may provide for the possibility of enhancing efficacy perceptions. It seems that studies need to address the links between the concepts of self-efficacy, effort perceptions and the capabilities people have for self-monitoring physical exertion during exercise. This is particularly important for people apprehensive about exertion, such as in rehabilitation contexts.

Self-efficacy, therefore, is believed to develop from four main sources. Ewart summarised the application of these in the context of promoting exercise in a rehabilitation situation by saying that:

> the most effective way to encourage patients to adopt exercise activities for which they lack self-efficacy is to expose them to the recommended activity in gradually increasing doses [performance], arrange for them to see others similar to themselves performing the activity [modeling]; have respected healthcare providers offer encouragement by providing reassurance and emphasizing the patient's accomplishments [persuasion], and arrange the setting of the activity so as to induce a relaxed but 'upbeat' mood [arousal; physiological state].

(Ewart 1989: 684; words in brackets added)

Box 4.1 Applying self-efficacy theory to exercise promotion

Self-efficacy theory gives clear intervention possibilities through each of its four sources of efficacy information. For promoting health-related activity, the following guidelines are proposed.

Performance attainment   In recreational activity it is likely to be less important to participants whether they succeed in an objective way (namely, win the game). However, efficacy expectations for the adoption of exercise are likely to be enhanced by prior experience in similar situations. Regrettably many people's experience of physical activity stem from a narrow range of competitive games at school. Coakley and White (1992), for example, provided evidence from an English study that showed that negative perceptions of school physical education (PE) could be related to post-school participation. In their study of young people in south-east England they attempted to identify the factors which young people based their decisions about participation in leisure time sport and recreation. They found that involvement in sport reflected factors beyond those associated with competitive sport itself. One factor deemed important by these people was the experience they had had in school PE and sport. Lack of participation was related to negative memories of PE, with boredom, lack of choice, negative evaluation from peers, and feelings of stupidity and incompetence being the most commonly cited factors. Girls were more likely to associate physical education experiences with discomfort and embarrassment and this seemed to affect their orientation to leisure time. Such experiences, according to SET, are likely to alter efficacy expectations in those activities experienced in school PE. These may then generalise, to differing degrees depending on the activities, to other exercise modes.

A similar analysis is possible for school leavers who have experienced courses in health and fitness activities. Their self-efficacy for initiating their own activity programme is likely to be influenced by their experience at school. The traditional images of 'drill' and 'exercise as punishment' have almost certainly been negative influences on activity patterns in leisure time. Interventions, therefore, must come in the form of enjoyable and reinforcing physical activity where individual perceptions of mastery and intrinsic motivation are enhanced.

Vicarious experience   It could be argued that early experience in exercise, and the success of those around you, will influence self-efficacy expectations and, hence, exercise patterns. Seeing people of similar build and physical ability 'succeed' in exercise is likely to have positive effects. However, such effects have a greater probability of occurrence when 'success' is perceived in individualistic mastery-oriented terms (that is, a self-improvement 'task orientation'). Constant comparison with others (an ego-orientation) is more likely to lead to disappointment and potential dropout.

Social and verbal persuasion   Although this usually refers to persuasion from others, self-talk has sometimes been found to be an effective strategy for enhancing self-efficacy, although the results have been mixed. In terms of exercise, it is likely that self-talk and personal perceptions of the costs and benefits of exercise will play a role in exercise adoption or maintenance.

Judgements of physiological states   This is probably more important in avoidance behaviours although a relaxed approach to exercise may enhance the mental health benefits. A greater awareness of physiological symptoms of effort and pain could also be beneficial in maintaining an exercise programme at an appropriate level. High levels of anxiety, such as social physique anxiety, may hinder exercise participation.

MEASUREMENT OF SELF-EFFICACY

Self-efficacy will vary along the dimensions of magnitude, strength and generality (Bandura 1986):

- Magnitude of self-efficacy refers to the ordering of tasks by difficulty, such as feeling that one is capable of sustaining a walking programme but not one for running half marathons.

- Strength refers to the assessment of one's capabilities for performing a particular task. For example, people are able to subjectively rate their likelihood of maintaining a walking programme of three miles every other day.
- Generality of self-efficacy refers to the extent to which efficacy expectations from one situation generalise to other situations, such as efficacy gained through a walking programme generalising to the lifting of weights in a body conditioning programme (Ewart *et al.* 1983). Each of these measures of efficacy perceptions should, if conforming to Bandura's theory, be taken. Rarely is this actually the case. While all studies measure strength of self-efficacy, fewer measure magnitude and generality. The operational measures of self-efficacy, therefore, in exercise settings appear to be limited.

Self-efficacy in exercise: research findings

When we reviewed this field in 1991 (Biddle and Mutrie 1991) we located only nine studies that had investigated self-efficacy and health-related exercise. This has now changed and self-efficacy has become a popular topic of study within the exercise domain. In addition to the number of studies increasing, there has also been a trend to study non-patient populations in an effort to counterbalance the early bias towards patient groups.

RESEARCH WITH PATIENTS

Ewart and co-workers conducted a number of the early studies on self-efficacy and exercise and they shed light on some important issues (see Ewart 1989). Ewart *et al.* (1983) studied self-efficacy in the context of treadmill running with post-myocardial infarction (MI) patients. Before and after treadmill exercise, assessment of self-efficacy to take part in walking, running, stair climbing, sexual intercourse, lifting and general exertion (but not all at once!) was made. The improvements in self-efficacy are illustrated in Figure 4.5.

These results show that positive changes in self-efficacy took place following treadmill exercise, and that this was greatest for running, suggesting that efficacy effects do generalise but appear to have stronger effects on similar exercise modes. When counselling also took

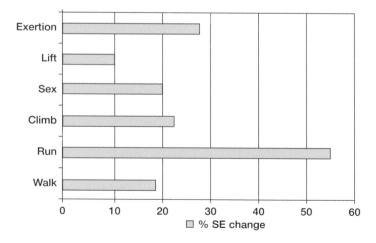

Figure 4.5 Increases in self-efficacy after treadmill running for post-MI men (data from Ewart *et al.* 1983)

place it was found that efficacy perceptions for sexual intercourse, lifting and general exertion significantly increased above the level attained after treadmill running. This was not true for the other activities indicating that generalisability of self-efficacy is enhanced for dissimilar activities when additional intervention is given.

Ewart *et al.* (1986) investigated the specificity of self-efficacy perceptions of men with coronary heart disease (CHD). Circuit weight training was used and self-efficacy ratings taken prior to a variety of physical fitness tests were shown to correlate more strongly with test results for activities specific to the self-efficacy judgements. For example, efficacy ratings for the performance of lifting activities were significantly correlated with the arm strength test but not with the aerobic endurance treadmill test. Conversely, self-efficacy ratings of jogging were significantly correlated with the aerobic endurance test but not with tests of arm, grip or leg strength.

Kaplan, Atkins and Reinsch (1984) studied patients with chronic obstructive pulmonary disease (COPD) and tested whether generalised expectancies (that is, health locus of control; see Chapter 3) would differ from specific expectancies (self-efficacy) in exercise behaviour change. The results showed superior effects for self-efficacy as a mediator of changes in walking behaviour and this generalised to similar activities such as stair climbing.

The studies discussed so far have focused on those with known medical symptoms, such as documented CHD. The extent that such studies can be generalised to other people remains problematic. Given that SE is a social-cognitive variable open to environmental and perceptual intervention, it might be unwise to generalise from these studies. For example, Ewart (1989) suggests that post-coronary patients are often limited more by fear of exertion than their actual medical condition. This is quite different from individuals free of disease symptoms. Studies on medical patients in exercise rehabilitation suggest that:

- Self-efficacy judgements can generalise but will be strongest for activities similar to the activity experienced.
- Self-efficacy in 'dissimilar' activities can be enhanced through counselling.
- Self-efficacy better predicts changes in exercise behaviour than generalised expectancies of LOC.

RESEARCH WITH NON-PATIENT GROUPS

A number of researchers have now investigated non-patient groups in exercise and physical activity. Self-efficacy has been shown to predict walking in a large adult sample contacted by mail (Hofstetter *et al.* 1991), it has predicted exercise change over time in a large community sample (Sallis *et al.* 1992a), has discriminated adherers from dropouts in an exercise weight loss programme (Rodgers and Brawley 1993), has predicted positive affect after exercise (Bozoian, Rejeski and McAuley 1994), and has negatively correlated with psychobiological markers of negative affect (Rudolph and McAuley 1995).

Sallis *et al.* (1986) studied potential predictors of changes in community activity levels. Three measures of physical activity were examined over one year with over 1,400 Californian adults. Results showed that self-efficacy was predictive of the adoption of vigorous activity for both sexes, was predictive of the maintenance of vigorous activity and the adoption and maintenance of moderate exercise for women only. We also found clear gender differences when studying the role of efficacy in predicting self-reported physical activity levels in a university workforce sample (Biddle, Goudas and Page 1994b). In our study, in which we assessed self-efficacy alongside variables from the theory of planned

behaviour (TPB) (Ajzen 1988) (see Chapter 5), self-efficacy was a factor adding significantly to attitudinal variables from the TPB in the prediction of intention to exercise for
women, but not men. This is consistent with research on self-confidence and gender where
it has been argued that women need higher self-confidence to overcome social and psychological barriers to exercise in comparison to men (Corbin 1984; Lirgg 1991). For men in our
study, attitudes were the best predictors of intention whereas intention and self-efficacy
predicted actual activity for women, but only attitude and intention did so for men.

Poag-DuCharme and Brawley (1993) extended the analysis of self-efficacy in exercise
in their study of two samples of adults. They compared the role of self-efficacy for those
starting exercise and those already involved. They also investigated different exercise
contexts, such as structured classes and unstructured exercise sessions, and they sought to
measure self-efficacy in diverse ways. For their sample of exercise beginners, they
assessed 'scheduling' (for example, planning and scheduling strategies) and 'barrier' (for
example, injury or transport problems) efficacy, whereas for the group of current exercisers involved in structured classes they assessed efficacy perceptions for completing in-
class components of the programme, in addition to the scheduling and barrier efficacy
ratings.

In the study concerning those beginning an exercise programme, Poag-DuCharme and
Brawley (1993) found that barrier and scheduling efficacy predicted exercise intentions in
equal amounts at the beginning of the programme. However, for those remaining in the
programme, scheduling efficacy became a more important predictor of intention, although
barrier efficacy was still a significant predictor. For actual exercise behaviour it was found
that participation during weeks 9–16 was best predicted by scheduling efficacy, with barrier
efficacy and intention not adding to the prediction.

For the experienced exercisers only in-class efficacy predicted intentions at the outset of
the programme, but after 6–7 weeks both barrier and scheduling efficacy made small, but
significant, predictions of intentions. In predicting programme adherence between weeks
7–12, it was found that scheduling efficacy and intentions were the strongest predictors.

The studies reported by Poag-DuCharme and Brawley (1993) bring out some important
points. Specifically, they found that:

- Self-efficacy was predictive of both intentions to exercise and actual participation in
  exercise.
- Self-efficacy was predictive within two exercise contexts: unsupervised and structured
  classes.
- Different types of self-efficacy were predictive of intentions and participation at
  different stages of the exercise process.

Although Poag-DuCharme and Brawley's (1993) research is small-scale, and some of the
efficacy measures predict only small amounts of variance, they raise some new issues and
illustrate some important concepts for exercise psychology researchers to note. The issue of
exercise stages will be addressed in Chapters 6 and 11.

McAuley's work on exercise self-efficacy has been influential (McAuley 1992;
McAuley and Courneya 1993; McAuley and Mihalko 1998). In particular, McAuley and
colleagues have studied self-efficacy responses of older adults, a population previously
under-represented in the exercise psychology literature. Several studies by McAuley and
co-workers focus on a group of previously sedentary 45–64 year olds. These studies have
shown that for older adults exercise self-efficacy:

- Can be increased through intervention.
- Will predict participation, particularly in the early stages of an exercise programme.
- Declines after a period of inactivity.
- Is associated with positive exercise emotion.

Dzewaltowski (1989) compared Bandura's (1986) social cognitive theory (SCT), the central part being self-efficacy, with Fishbein and Ajzen's (1975) theory of reasoned action (TRA; see Chapter 5). The results showed that SCT predicted exercise better than the TRA, and that self-efficacy was a stronger predictor than other SCT variables. However, while this might suggest that SCT should be used instead of the TRA, the measure of behavioural intention, central to the TRA in linking attitudes and social norms to behaviour, was very high in nearly all participants, and hence had a very restricted range. This reduced the possibility of intention predicting behaviour. Similarly, the study suffers from a crude measure of exercise. Only the number of days on which exercise took place was assessed, and this was elicited via unvalidated self-report rather than known measures of activity recall. However, perhaps of greater concern is the fact that all participants were recruited from required physical education classes. The extent of their activity is almost certain to be affected by being in such a situation. Had the classes had some element of voluntary attendance about them, such as in commercial fitness clubs, then the theories would have been tested in a more useful context.

Despite these criticisms, Dzewaltowski (1989) has provided an important step in comparing two well-known psychological perspectives in predicting exercise (see McAuley and Courneya 1993). A more realistic situation is required for future research of this kind before different models can be adequately compared. However, Dzewaltowski (1994) is critical of the approach of simply adding self-efficacy to other theories. In explaining why he believes this 'strategy is misdirected' (Dzewaltowski 1994: 1396), he says that self-efficacy should be evaluated within Bandura's social cognitive theory. This seems overly restrictive to us and, given the conceptual similarity and overlap between many of the variables used in social cognitive approaches (see Chapter 6), it would appear to be a good strategy to assess the relative strengths and weaknesses of key variables from several, not one, perspective.

In summary, the studies investigating self-efficacy in non-patient exercise groups show a consistent relationship between efficacy and exercise participation, as well as relationships with other important factors, such as post-exercise emotion.

Methodological issues in self-efficacy research

The methodological issues associated with self-efficacy have never been easy. First, it has always been argued by Bandura (1977) and others (for example, McAuley 1992), that self-efficacy needs to be assessed in relation to specific behaviours if increased magnitude of behavioural prediction is required. Generalised perceptions of confidence are not the same as perceptions of efficacy. Nevertheless, we need more studies on the generalisability of self-efficacy across exercise settings. Similar to the attitude-behaviour correspondence issue in social psychology, the utility of self-efficacy is likely to be greater when measures correspond closely to the behaviour in question, such as cycling three times per week, rather than using a general reference such as 'exercise'. For this reason, one must question the assumptions underpinning Ryckman *et al.*'s (1982) Physical Self-Efficacy Scale. Their rationale for developing such a scale was based on the need for measuring self-efficacy for exercise in preference to more global measures of self-concept. However, they too have only assessed generalised perceptions of physical ability and 'self-presentation confidence', and not self-efficacy as defined by Bandura.

Sherer *et al.* (1982) also report the development of what they call 'The Self-Efficacy Scale'. However, inspection of the test items and rationale for test construction suggests that their inventory is more akin to a general self-motivation scale and does not approximate Bandura's conceptualisation of self-efficacy. Similarly, Sallis *et al.* (1988) have developed scales for the assessment of self-efficacy for diet and exercise behaviours. For exercise they derived factors labelled 'resisting relapse' and 'making time for exercise'. Data showed that the two subscales correlated only 0.32–0.40 with self-reported vigorous physical activity.

The second methodological issue to be considered concerns the behaviours associated with efficacy perceptions. Assessing self-efficacy in any meaningful way requires the behaviour to be associated with effort, potential barriers and behavioural self-regulation. In other words, habitual behaviours, such as tooth brushing, are likely to be unrelated to feelings of efficacy whereas physical exercise may be highly associated with efficacy beliefs because exercise requires planning, effort and often considerable barriers. This is probably why self-efficacy emerges as one of the most consistent predictors of physical activity behaviours, particularly when physical activity includes elements of vigorous exercise.

Other approaches to the study of confidence and physical activity

Although SET has dominated the literature linking confidence perceptions and exercise, other perspectives and approaches have been adopted and shed some interesting light on related issues.

PERFORMANCE ESTIMATION

Bandura's SET and SCT clearly differentiate between efficacy and outcome expectations. However, earlier on it was stated that both types of expectancy are likely to be important in physical activity settings. Using a similar construct to outcome expectations, Corbin and his co-workers have investigated the issue of self-confidence in exercise from the view point of performance estimations (see Corbin 1984). This research programme was based on theorising by Lenney (1977) in the area of women and achievement behaviour. She suggested that while evidence pointed to under-achievement by females in some achievement contexts, this was not invariably so. Lenney pointed out that female self-confidence was dependent on 'situational vulnerability' which was determined by three main factors:

- The sex-typed nature of the task: confidence is likely to be low in situations where the task is perceived as 'inappropriate'. That is to say a role conflict may be apparent such as in performing tasks sex-typed as 'masculine'. An example would be women in the context of a weight training class where some might lack self-confidence.
- Social evaluation: Lenney (1977) has suggested that females will underestimate their ability when they are being evaluated or compared, such as in competition.
- Feedback: it has been proposed that females achieve better levels of performance when given objective and accurate feedback.

These factors point to important variables in the exercise environment and, while originating from the study of women in achievement contexts, could also apply to men in some situations, such as activities sex-typed 'female' or 'feminine' (for example, dance and aerobics). However, given the predominantly masculine stereotyping of many physical activities, particularly sports, the emphasis has been placed on research into female self-confidence (Corbin 1984). Unfortunately, little progress has been made in the exercise domain using this perspective since our last review (Biddle and Mutrie 1991).

SPORT CONFIDENCE

Vealey (1986) developed a sport-specific, interactional model of self-confidence in which she constructed scales for the measurement of state and trait sport self-confidence. A scale measuring perceptions of competitive orientation was also developed. This is analogous to Nicholls' (1989) ego-oriented and task-oriented goals in achievement motivation. Vealey's (1986) rationale for using such a conceptual framework was that it allowed for individual differences in defining the meaning of success in sport.

Vealey defined 'sport-confidence' as 'the belief or degree of certainty individuals possess about their ability to be successful in sport' (Vealey 1986: 222). However, the focus of this book is more aligned to recreational involvement in physical activity from the point of view of health rather than sports performance. Moreover, little research has used this approach in recent years.

MOVEMENT CONFIDENCE

Griffin, Keogh and co-workers have proposed a model of movement confidence that they claim is different from other conceptualisations of self-confidence (Griffin and Keogh 1982). Griffin and Keogh (1982: 213) state that 'we are viewing movement confidence as an individual feeling of adequacy in a movement situation'. However, although they recognise the similarities between their model and other conceptualisations of competence and motivation, they say that they are 'proposing an important additional consideration for movement situations in terms of the sensory experiences which are directly related to moving' (215). Hence, their 'movement involvement cycle' depicts movement confidence being a product of an interaction between movement competence (that is, perceptions of personal skill within the confines of a particular task), and movement sense ('personal expectations of sensory experiences related to moving'; 214). Movement confidence itself then mediates participation (choice, persistence and performance) which, in turn, influence the interaction between competence and movement sense.

The uniqueness of the components of the model have been questioned by Feltz (1988) who says that the movement confidence model can be explained in terms of self-efficacy theory. The 'unique' addition of movement sense to the model is, according to Feltz, already part of SET since one source of efficacy information is autonomic perception. While the search for the nature and make-up of confidence appears appropriate, the research programme based around the movement confidence model has failed to support initial propositions that confidence is more than just competence. Nevertheless, the utility of this approach may be most evident in settings involving young children and, as such, requires further testing.

Self-presentational processes in exercise confidence

The following constructs are just some of those listed in the contents page of Leary's (1995) book on 'Self-Presentation': physical appearance, gestures and movement, public self-consciousness, weight, appearance and physique anxiety, and modesty. Clearly, there is great potential for using such constructs in furthering our understanding of physical activity and perceptions of confidence.

Self-presentational concerns may affect physical activity choice, such as when one perceives the activity to be incompatible with one's image (for example, aerobic dance, lifting weights etc.), or where anxiety is felt in displaying low levels of physical competence. As Leary (1992: 342) says 'people are unlikely to devote themselves to activities that convey impressions that are inconsistent with their roles, others' values, or social norms'.

Hart, Leary and Rejeski, for example, have studied the construct of 'social physique anxiety'. Specifically, they propose that people high in such anxiety, in comparison to those not anxious:

> are likely to avoid situations in which their physique is under scrutiny of others (for example, swimming in public) ... avoid activities that accentuate their physiques (including aerobic activities that might be beneficial to them) ... and attempt to improve their physiques through a variety of means, some of which may be harmful (for example, fasting).
>
> (Hart *et al.* 1989: 96)

Further testing of the social physique anxiety construct in health contexts, alongside other self-presentational factors, is warranted (Leary *et al.* 1994). For example, the ADNFS data showed that concerns about lack of sports competence were major barriers to participation in physical activity. How generalisable such feelings are remains to be seen. For some individuals, feelings of 'not being the sporty type' may generalise across many different physical activities, whereas for others they may only affect one of two specific activities. Indeed, most physical activities such as sports occur in such public settings that self-presentational issues are hard to ignore. Coupled with this is the widespread social acceptance and admiration of physical expertise. This means that social anxiety in physical activity contexts is likely to be common. People are more likely to experience social anxiety when they are motivated to make desirable impressions on others but have low feelings of self-efficacy in being able to so (Leary 1995).

Chapter summary and conclusions

In this chapter, we have attempted to review and synthesise some of the major theoretical approaches in exercise motivation that have focused on self-perceptions of efficacy and competence. Specifically, we have:

* Moved from 'domain-general' approaches, including physical self-perceptions, competence motivation, exercise self-schemata and goal orientations, to more state-specific conceptions of competence, such as through self-efficacy theory.
* Reviewed how people perceive competence in the physical domain, including general notions of competence, how we have assessed competence, and the different definitions of competence.
* Outlined how task and ego achievement goals are viable ways to study motivation in exercise.
* Briefly discussed the role of self-schemata in exercise.
* Reviewed self-efficacy theory and presented a comprehensive overview of research findings, methods and issues.

- Presented some alternative views on confidence relevant to the study of physical activity, including self-presentational concerns.

From our review of the literature, we conclude:

- That exercise participation is associated with perceptions of competence, in whatever form competence is operationalised. However, more specific perceptions of competence/efficacy are likely to be better predictors of specific behaviours than generalised beliefs in competence.
- Defining 'competence' is not easy and there may be a bias towards social comparative definitions of competence.
- Goal perspectives theory proposes that people can define competence and success in different ways, the main ones being ego and task orientations. Research is consistent in showing the motivational benefits of a task orientation, either singly or in combination with an ego orientation.
- Relatively new perspectives, such as exercise self-schemata, have potential to contribute to the understanding of exercise motivation, although the current research base is inadequate.
- Research using self-efficacy with patient groups demonstrates that exercise self-efficacy can be developed in 'diseased' populations; self-efficacy judgements can generalise but will be strongest for activities similar to the activity experienced; self-efficacy in 'dissimilar' activities can be enhanced through counselling; self-efficacy better predicts changes in exercise behaviour than generalised expectancies.
- Research with non-patient groups has shown that exercise self-efficacy can be increased through intervention, will predict participation, particularly in the early stages of an exercise programme, will decline after a period of inactivity, and is associated with positive exercise emotion.
- Self-presentational processes offer additional understanding to exercise confidence and anxiety. However, little research exists and so represents an area for development for the future.

5 Linking attitudes with physical activity

> We all feel we know what it is to have an attitude towards something or somebody.
>
> J. R. Eiser
> (*Attitudes, chaos and the connectionist mind*, 1994)

Chapter objectives

The purpose of this chapter is to review key attitude theories used in contemporary exercise and health research. Specifically, in this chapter we aim to:

- Define and delimit the attitude construct.
- Briefly overview the early descriptive approach to the study of physical activity attitudes.
- Review the theoretical foundations and contemporary exercise research of the theories of reasoned action (TRA) and planned behaviour (TPB).
- Summarise the health belief model (HBM) and research findings from exercise.
- Briefly discuss protection motivation theory (PMT) and Triandis' theory of social behaviour (TSB) in the light of health and exercise research.
- Consider the implications of exercise research using subjected expected utility (SEU) and action control (AC) theories.
- Reach a consensus on the role of attitudes in exercise behaviour.

Health education or promotion campaigns are often aimed at changing beliefs or knowledge on the assumption that such changes are necessary to bring about a change in behaviour. Unfortunately, changes in awareness, attitudes, beliefs and knowledge far from guarantee changes in behaviour, although they may be an important first step in such a process (see Chapter 6). Although any inference of a causal link between beliefs and behaviour cannot usually be sustained, it does seem reasonable that beliefs and attitudes will have some influence on our actions. Indeed, such an assumption has occupied social psychologists for many years in health research (Conner and Norman 1996; Stroebe and Stroebe 1995).

A number of theoretical models have been proposed that attempt to explain the role of attitudes in human behaviour. The purpose of this chapter, therefore, is to outline the major integrating theories in health-related attitudes, and to report research findings that have a bearing on exercise and physical activity behaviours.

Defining attitudes

It is often seen to be a statement of the obvious that attitudes are about feelings and behaviour. However, the study of attitudes in social psychology has a long, yet controversial history, particularly when attempting to predict behaviours from stated attitudes. Even so, Olson and Zanna (1993: 118) report that 'attitude and attitude change remain among the most extensively researched topics by social psychologists'. Unfortunately, the extensive usage of the word attitude in everyday speech has rendered it prone to misinterpretation, or to be used in a way that is ill-defined or too general. For example, the Allied Dunbar National Fitness Survey (ADNFS) (The Sports Council and Health Education Authority 1992) uses the sub-heading 'Attitudes to exercise and fitness' to cover a range of psychological factors associated with exercise participation. In one sense they do cover 'attitudes', but they do not refer to well-known social psychological theories of attitude prominent in the health and exercise literature.

No universally agreed definition of attitude exists, although the structure of attitudes can be delimited to a certain extent (Olson and Zanna 1993). A three-component model of attitude (Hovland and Rosenberg 1960) suggests that in addition to attitudes having a belief (cognitive) component, they also have affective (emotional) and behavioural components (see Figure 5.1).

Attitude, like personality, motivation and some other psychological constructs, is hypothetical and not open to direct observation. The responses often used to infer attitudes can be either verbal or non-verbal in each of the cognitive, affective and behavioural categories of the three-component model. These are illustrated in Table 5.1, with examples from physical activity. In addition, Olson and Zanna (1993) propose that most attitude theorists agree that attitudes are represented in memory.

Attitudes toward physical activity: descriptive approaches

The study of attitudes has interested sport and exercise scientists for a long time, although the initial research efforts were primarily descriptive. For example, Kenyon (1968), in his widely cited research, developed the 'attitude toward physical activity' (ATPA) inventory in which he identified six sub-domains. These reflected Kenyon's belief that physical

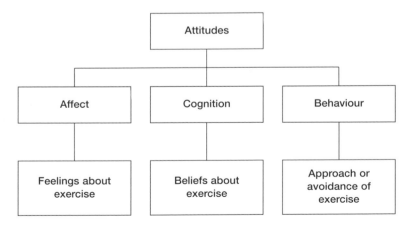

Figure 5.1 The three-component view of attitudes applied to physical activity

Table 5.1 Inferring physical activity attitudes from different responses

Response mode	Cognitive	Response category Affective	Behavioural
Verbal	Expressions of *beliefs* concerning physical activity.	Expressions of *feelings* (likes, dislikes etc.) concerning physical activity.	Expressions of intention to be physically active or inactive.
Non-verbal	Perceptual reactions to physical activity.	Physiological reactions (independent of effort) to physical activity.	Approach or avoidance of physical activity and related contexts.

Source: adapted from Ajzen 1988.

activity could be reduced to more specific components based on their 'perceived instrumentality'. Kenyon's model, therefore, suggested that physical activity could be perceived in terms of:

- a social experience
- health and fitness
- the pursuit of vertigo (thrill and adventure seeking activities)
- an aesthetic experience
- catharsis
- an ascetic experience.

Numerous studies have used the ATPA scale, as well as a modified version for children (Schutz *et al.* 1985). However, while the description of attitudes about physical activity may have some use in research and be of some heuristic value, such expressions of attitudes have been found to be poor predictors of actual behaviour. For example, Sidney, Niinimaa and Shephard (1983) found differential attitude profiles on the ATPA among over-60 year olds in an endurance exercise programme, but these attitudes were unrelated to reported participation patterns, daily records of activity and measures of physical fitness.

Kenyon (1968) states that the area of social attitudes has been plagued by problems of definition and measurement. However, Kenyon defines attitude as: 'a latent or nonobservable, complex, but relatively stable behavioural disposition reflecting both direction and intensity' of feeling *toward a particular object*' (Kenyon 1968: 567; our emphasis). This definition, therefore, means that the ATPA scale will assess a generalised attitude toward physical activity rather than attitude toward a specific behaviour, such as jogging or walking. It is not surprising, therefore, that specific behaviours are not strongly predicted from such a measure.

Nevertheless, there are occasions when global attitudes can provide useful information. For example, the first step in understanding a problem is description. To this end, describing attitudes in this way can help formulate more substantial research questions. Just knowing the sub-components of physical activity attitudes may be useful, even if they may not predict specific behaviours too well. Similarly, it is not possible, in large epidemiological surveys, to assess highly specific attitudes, yet population data are vital for furthering our understanding of physical activity behaviours. Generalised attitude measures then become important and useful.

To this end, we developed a generalised measure of attitudes toward physical activity for older adults (Terry *et al.* 1997) as this age group had been neglected in previous research as far as appropriate measurement instruments was concerned. Working from first principles in psychometric test construction, a four-factor scale was developed with 471 Canadian adults aged over 50 years. The four subscales confirmed were tension release, health promotion, vigorous exercise and social benefits.

Often, this approach is the only one available within the constraints of large population surveys, although some have managed to include enough items to assess the basic principles of attitude theories (Wankel and Mummery 1993). Where possible, more direct tests of attitude-behaviour links are desired in preference to descriptive approaches of generalised physical activity/exercise attitudes.

Models and theories linking attitudes and behaviour in physical activity research

The descriptive approach to attitude measurement inevitably led researchers to question whether attitudes actually did predict behaviours at all: the 'attitude–behaviour discrepancy'. Indeed, Eiser states that this discrepancy is 'essentially an artefact of the haphazard selection of *specific* behavioural indices which researchers have tried to relate to *general* verbal measures of attitudes' (emphasis added), but goes on to say that 'if we are as selective in our choice of behavioural indices as we are at present in our choice of verbal indices, the 'attitude–behaviour discrepancy' may disappear as a substantive problem' (Eiser 1986: 60).

Such a critique is consistent with a more contemporary view of the role of attitudes in predicting behaviour. In social psychology in general, as well as exercise psychology research in particular, the 'theory of reasoned action' (TRA) and 'theory of planned behaviour' (TPB) models have been used extensively in the belief that specific measures of attitude, in conjunction with social influences, will predict behavioural intention and subsequent behaviour.

The theory of reasoned action

Proposed by Ajzen and Fishbein (Ajzen and Fishbein 1980; Fishbein and Ajzen 1975), the TRA is concerned with 'the causal antecedents of volitional behaviour' (Ajzen 1988: 117). It is based on the assumption that intention is an immediate determinant of behaviour, and that intention, in turn, is predicted from attitude and subjective (social) normative factors. The TRA is illustrated in Figure 5.2 and has been used extensively in exercise research, as we discuss later.

Ajzen and Fishbein suggest that the attitude component of the model is a function of the beliefs held about the specific behaviour, as well as the evaluation, or value, of the likely outcomes, thus their approach is an expectancy-value interaction. The measurement of such variables, they suggest, should be highly specific to the behaviour in question in order to achieve correspondence, or compatibility, between assessed attitude/subjective norm questions and the behaviour being predicted. It is recommended that questionnaire item content for testing the TRA be derived from interview material gathered from the population to be studied. Four factors should be considered in terms of achieving correspondence:

- Action: attitude and behaviour need to be assessed in relation to a specific action, such as taking part in an aerobic exercise class, rather than a general attitude object such as physical activity.

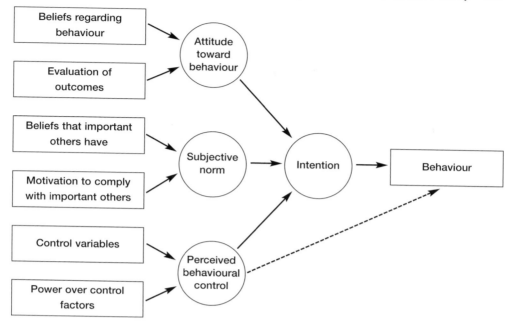

Figure 5.2 Theories of reasoned action (excluding perceived behavioural control) and planned behaviour (including perceived behavioural control)

- Target: reference should be made to specific target groups, such as aerobic exercisers, or specified significant others.
- Context: reference should be made to the context in which the behaviour takes place (for example, 'at this health club').
- Time: time should be clearly specified (for example, 'attending this exercise class three times/week over the next two months').

Ajzen (1988) proposes that these four factors should be assessed at the same level of generality/specificity. Of course, very high correspondence, such as predicting attendance at the fitness club on Tuesdays from items that refer only to exercising at the club on Tuesdays, will have limited generalisability. While vague attitude measures about 'exercise' may be less than precise and be weak predictors, we also want to have the ability to generalise, thus some compromise between the two may sometimes be necessary, depending on what it is we wish to predict. The descriptive measures discussed above, such as Kenyon's ATPA, assess only the target (physical activity) and not the action, context or time. Perhaps this has led to some researchers being confused about the role of attitudes in exercise. For example, Dishman and Sallis (1994) conclude, in their review of studies both pre- and post-1988 in supervised and unsupervised settings, that attitudes are largely unrelated to physical activity. This is a surprising conclusion given the clear evidence presented by Godin (1993), and updated here, that shows that both intentions and attitudes are related to physical activity when appropriate theoretical models, such as the TRA, are used. Similarly, King *et al.* (1992) say that intentions do not predict actual behaviour in adult studies of exercise. This also is not correct and, indeed, intentions are even better predictors of physical activity than attitudes. Correlations between intention and physical activity are consistently positive and statistically significant. Indeed, Sallis and Owen (1999), in reference to meta-analytic evidence from Hausenblas, Carron and Mack (1997), describe the correlations between intentions and exercise as 'substantial' (118).

The subjective norm component of the TRA ('normative component') is comprised of the beliefs of significant others and the extent that one wishes or is motivated to comply with such beliefs or people. The relative importance of the attitudinal and normative components will depend on the situation under investigation. For example, one might hypothesise that adolescent health behaviours, in some contexts, will be more strongly influenced by the normative component than the attitudinal component, but that this trend may be reversed with adults.

The TRA has generally received support in recent years. For example, Sheppard, Hartwick and Warshaw (1988) conducted a meta-analysis of eighty-seven studies with over 11,000 people using the TRA in a variety of settings and found a weighted average correlation between intention and behaviour of 0.53. Similarly, the correlation between attitude and subjective norm with intention was 0.66. Both results give clear support to the TRA.

The theory of reasoned action and exercise research

The TRA has received a great deal of attention in social psychology generally (Ajzen 1988; Sheppard *et al.* 1988) and in health contexts (Conner and Armitage 1998; Conner and Sparks 1996; Stroebe and Stroebe 1995). Although not without its critics, particularly in respect of the causal structure of the model (Liska 1984), it has also been recommended and used in exercise research (Doganis and Theodorakis 1995; Godin 1993).

In one of the first tests of the theory, Riddle (1980) used the TRA in predicting jogging behaviour in adult women and men. Specifically, she found that the intention to jog was significantly predicted from both the attitudinal and normative components of the model, although the attitudinal component was stronger. The beliefs held about the consequences of jogging were the factors most clearly distinguishing joggers from non-exercisers with, as expected, joggers having the more positive beliefs.

The work of Gaston Godin and co-workers in Canada has provided the most extensive test of the TRA in exercise settings. Godin (1993) reports that about 30 per cent of the variance in intention is explained by the attitudinal and normative components of the TRA, although the attitudinal component is nearly always the stronger of the two predictors. Indeed, the normative component is inconsistently associated with physical activity participation.

Hausenblas *et al.* (1997) analysed thirty-one exercise studies using meta-analysis. It yielded 162 effect sizes (ES) with over 10,000 participants, and they found that intention had a large effect on exercise behaviour, and attitude had a large effect on intention. The effect of attitude was twice that of subjective norm.

Godin and Shephard (1986a) tested the predictive utility of Kenyon's model against the TRA. In terms of predicting intention to be physically active and actual past exercise behaviour, the TRA attitude component was superior to the sub-domains of Kenyon's model, thus supporting our earlier statements about the need to measure specific attitudinal factors to achieve a stronger prediction of behaviour. In a further test of the theory, Godin and Shephard (1986b) studied 698 Canadian children aged 12 to 14 years of age. They found that boys were more active than girls and that boys had a greater intention to exercise, and higher scores on the attitudinal and normative components of the TRA, although these declined in both boys and girls across the three cohorts studied. Overall, the TRA was only partially supported in its ability to predict exercise intentions. The attitude component was found to be a better predictor of intention than the normative component and is illustrative, in this respect, of many other exercise TRA studies.

Box 5.1 Subjective norms assessed through questionnaire and interview

It is interesting to note that the statistical information on the role of subjective norms in the TRA and TPB discussed in the main text suggests that subjective norm, or social support, does not really matter much in physical activity. But is this really the case? Our own personal experiences suggest a different story. This confusion could be the result of the way we are measuring subjective norms in questionnaires. Dr Andy Smith, a leading physical activity specialist in the UK, conducted some interviews with participants of an exercise class he had supervised for initially inactive adults. For example, an older member of the class close to retirement said that 'I used to walk a lot, but my friends have scattered and I am less active now'. Another remarked on the support from her spouse: 'I enjoyed myself [on the programme] and having my husband with me helped my motivation'. The following comments from programme members also suggest that social norms/support are important:

- 'good to be with like-minded people'
- 'the course is socially important'
- 'enjoyed the course and social occasion'
- 'enjoyed the social opportunity'.

Who said social aspects are not important? We need to look into this further.

The theory of reasoned action: conclusion and critique

The TRA has received support in exercise contexts, and Godin suggests that 'when attitude is measured within a proper theoretical framework, it seems an important determinant of exercise behavior' (Godin 1994: 122). The TRA qualifies as one such 'proper theoretical framework'. Based on the evidence presented, the TRA attitudinal component appears to be influential in predicting intentions to exercise and intentions predict behaviour to a certain extent. From a practical standpoint this suggests that interventions that attempt to alter beliefs and affective perceptions of the outcomes of exercise may be useful. We need to know more about the physical sensations and senses of satisfaction and enjoyment attached to beginning exercise routines before definitive statements can be made here. However, it appears that the physically demanding routines associated with rigorous training regimes would be quite unsuitable for the majority of people wishing to start and maintain a health-related exercise programme. Educational interventions in terms of both the cognitive and affective components of exercise attitudes appears warranted.

Although the normative component of the TRA has not been a strong predictor of exercise intentions, it has sometimes contributed in a small way. Interventions that are possible include public health campaigns that persuade the public that exercise is 'normal' and not just for the young, fit and 'sporty'. (The concept of persuading people through 'fear appeals' will be dealt with later in the chapter.) Unfortunately, the evidence from the Allied Dunbar National Fitness Survey that we have discussed earlier in this book shows that personal beliefs that they are 'not the sporty type' are strong barriers to physical activity, particularly for women. However, subjective norms, such as through the role of the exercise leader, may play an important motivational role for those already possessing positive attitudes (Smith and Biddle 1999).

The TRA has not been without its critics. For example, the following points highlight issues for consideration:

- The TRA is a unidirectional model and fails to offer the possibility that variables in the model can act in a reciprocal manner.
- The model relies solely on cognitions and omits other potentially important determinants of action, such as environmental influences.
- The TRA predicts behaviour from measures of behavioural intention taken at one point in time. Similar attitudinal models of behaviour (Bentler and Speckart 1981; Triandis 1977) take into account prior behaviour or 'habit'. In the exercise context, habitual physical activity is often the goal of public health initiatives and therefore research may usefully investigate the role of habit in addition to other TRA variables. As it stands, the TRA may only predict new behaviours rather than habitual ones. The distinction between exercise adoption and maintenance is important. However, the role of past behaviour is a difficult one to judge at times. It can appear rather obvious, and even unhelpful if we wish to identify behavioural determinants, to state that past behaviour is the best predictor of current or intended behaviour.
- The distinction between intentions and expectations may be important (Olson and Zanna 1993). We could decide (intend) to exercise but realise that it rather too difficult (expectation). This is similar to Kendzierski's (1990a) distinction between exercise decision-making and exercise implementation, and is something future exercise attitude studies might need to consider.
- The TRA was developed to account for behaviours that are under volitional control (Ajzen 1988). Consequently, the theory may not predict behaviours where other factors may be influential. In the case of exercise, there may be a number of behavioural barriers preventing the behaviour being totally volitional (for example, responsibilities to others, job etc.). A revised TRA – the 'theory of planned behaviour' (TPB; see later in this chapter) – is an attempt to account for behaviour under 'incomplete' volitional control.
- Insufficient attention has been paid to the measurement of behaviour within the TRA. Without an accurate measure of the behaviour under investigation, the principle of correspondence cannot be applied. This casts some doubt on several of the studies cited here, such as when assessment relies on unvalidated self-reports. Of course, the assessment of physical activity through self-report can be very difficult, but these are issues that need addressing in the future. The definition of the behaviour and its measurement presents particular problems for the study of exercise adherence within the TRA.
- The TRA allows the investigation of the inter-relationships between attitudes, subjective norms, intentions and a single behaviour. It does not account for alternative behaviours (Smith and Biddle 1999). For example, although many people intend to be more physically active, few see this through to action. This could be due to exercise being of lower priority than other behaviours, and so just does not get to the top of 'things to do'. Attitude studies should also look at competing behaviours and choices

(Sheppard *et al.* 1988), similar to the formulations of subjective expected utility (SEU) theory (Edwards 1954), as discussed later in this chapter.

- Intention should predict behaviour quite well when both intention and behaviour are measured in close proximity or, in the case of measurement taking place some time apart, the prediction will be affected by how intentions change during this time interval (Ajzen and Fishbein 1980). This is the issue of 'intentional stability' and is one that has largely been ignored in exercise research (Chatzisarantis and Biddle 1998).
- Finally, there appears to be a potential discrepancy between the inconsistent role of subjective norms in exercise research using the TRA and the belief that social support is a determinant of exercise (Dishman and Sallis 1994). Although social support may not be exactly the same as social influence/subjective norm (Taylor *et al.* 1994), the similarities are such that we should expect the social normative component of the TRA to be more closely linked to exercise behaviour than has typically been the case. Although this discrepancy still needs to be resolved, two explanations are possible. First, we may not be assessing subjective norms appropriately in TRA studies and this may be forcing respondents to misinterpret the meaning behind the statements. A second possibility is that some people may be reluctant to admit that they require motivation from others and certainly do not want to admit that they wish 'to comply' with these people (for example, adolescents with parents). These points require testing.

In summary, the TRA has been at the forefront of re-establishing attitude research as a powerful force in social psychology and both health psychology and exercise psychology have been quick to utilise such an approach. The TRA has proved to be a viable unifying theoretical framework that has been successful in furthering our understanding of exercise intentions and behaviours. It has also been instrumental in moving exercise determinants research from being largely atheoretical to theoretical in the past ten years or so.

The theory of planned behaviour

The TRA has provided a model that has been successful in predicting behaviour and intentions for actions that are primarily volitional and controllable. However, in the case of physical exercise, and other health-related behaviours such as smoking and weight control, volitional control is likely to be 'incomplete' (Ajzen 1988), although Godin (1993) suggests that different types of physical activity may differ from each other in this respect. As already discussed (see Chapter 4), the role of perceptions of control is a potentially important one in many health-related behaviours.

Ajzen's theorising and research (Ajzen 1985; 1988; 1996; Ajzen and Madden 1986; Schifter and Ajzen 1985) suggests that the TRA is insufficient for behaviours where volitional control is incomplete. Consequently, Ajzen has proposed an extension of the TRA for such behaviours and has called this the theory of planned behaviour (TPB). The TPB is the same as the TRA but with the additional variable of 'perceived behavioural control', as illustrated in Figure 5.2. Perceived behavioural control is defined by Ajzen as 'the perceived ease or difficulty of performing the behaviour' (Ajzen 1988: 132) and is assumed 'to reflect past experience as well as anticipated impediments and obstacles'. Figure 5.2 links perceived control with both intentions and behaviour. This suggests that the variable has a motivational effect on intentions, such that individuals wishing to exercise, but with little or no chance of doing so (because of largely insurmountable behavioural barriers at the time), are unlikely to exercise regardless of their attitudes towards exercise or the social factors operating. This overcomes one of the problems of the TRA alluded to earlier when a distinction was made between intentions and expectations.

Ajzen (1988) argues that perceived behavioural control will accurately predict behaviour only under circumstances when perceived control closely approximates actual control (hence the use of broken line in Figure 5.2). For example, whereas some people may have a strong perception of control over their bodyweight, the reality might be different since there are biological factors likely to affect weight gain and loss that are beyond personal control. In such situations one would not expect perceived control to be a strong predictor of weight change, although it is possible for it to predict to a lesser degree. Similarly, one would expect better predictions of exercise *behaviour* (for example, frequency of exercise) from perceived control compared with exercise *performance* (for example, a fitness test score) since the latter is less controllable due to factors such as heredity, practice and the test environment.

Evidence from the theory of planned behaviour

The TPB is appropriate for use in the study of exercise, particularly as exercise is a behaviour that has many barriers, thus it is only partly under volitional control. The testing of the TPB in exercise is expanding. Godin (1993) located eight published papers and we have found additional papers from the English language literature.

Most studies in this area are relatively small, yet Wankel and Mummery (1993) managed to integrate TPB items into the large population survey 'The Campbell Survey of Well-Being'. This involved over 4,000 Canadians who had previously participated in the 1981 Canada Fitness Survey. Although the survey allowed for a test of the TPB, space limitations in the survey, which was assessing far more than physical activity attitudes, did not allow for a strict operationalisation of the TPB variables. However, despite this, the study provides the first population-based assessment of attitudes using the framework of the TPB. Wankel and Mummery used the measures that are outlined in Table 5.2.

The data set was large enough to allow for analyses to include four age groups for both males and females, and retain suitable cell sizes. In predicting physical activity intention, Wankel and Mummery (1993) found that across the different age and gender groups, variance in intentions accounted for by attitudes, social norm/support and perceived behavioural control ranged from 25 to 35 per cent. For the total sample, 31 per cent of the variance in intentions was explained by the three TPB variables. This is a reasonable approximation of estimates from other studies. Godin (1993) claimed that about 30 per cent of the variance in intention is explained by the attitude and subjective norm components and that anything between 4 and 20 per cent extra variance is accounted for by perceived behavioural control. Wankel and Mummery's data, therefore, are broadly compatible with this which, given the large population sample used, coupled with the problems of operationalising the variables precisely in line with the TPB, is encouraging for the TPB itself.

In a meta-analysis of our own (Chatzisarantis and Biddle 1999), we found that perceived behavioural control was strongly correlated, after correcting for sampling and measurement error, with sport and exercise behaviour (0.50) and intention (0.60). In addition, PBC correlated with intentions even when attitudes and subjective norm were statistically controlled. These results suggest that the TPB may be superior to the TRA for the study of physical activity behaviours, a conclusion consistent with the research of Kimiecik (1992). The meta-analysis conducted by Hausenblas *et al.* (1997), involving only exercise studies, found a strong effect for PBC on intention and behaviour.

Table 5.2 TPB and other variables used in Wankel and Mummery's (1993) population survey of Canadians

Variable	Assessment
Behavioural intention	Intention to participate in vigorous physical activity over the coming twelve months. Six-point scale collapsed to three-point scale: 1 = less than once/week; 2 = 1 or 2 times/week; 3 = 3 or more times/week.
Attitudes toward the behaviour	Six evaluative semantic differential five-point scales to assess feelings about participation in vigorous physical activity.
Subjective (social) norms	Not assessed directly. Instead, a measure of social support was used. Degree of social support for vigorous physical activity received from significant others assessed on five-point scales.
Perceived behavioural control	Two questions, using five-point scales, concerning perceived control over participation in vigorous physical activity.
Indirect measures of beliefs	Fourteen indirect belief items were included, although not directly derived from the TPB. The stem was 'How much does (or would) participation in vigorous physical activity help you?' (for example, feel better mentally; have fun; get together with other people).
Indirect measures of barriers/control	Fourteen indirect barrier/control items were included following the stem 'How important are the following in keeping you from being more physically active?' (for example, lack of partner; lack of athletic ability; fear of injury).

The theory of planned behaviour: conclusion and critique

Many of the criticisms of the TRA already discussed can be applied to the TPB, with the exception of the point concerning volition since the inclusion of perceived behavioural control accounts for this. However, as Godin (1993) has suggested, it is unclear which physical activities are perceived to be volitionally controlled and which are not. It seems reasonable to suggest that walking will be seen by most people to be quite controllable, yet activities requiring facilities and high costs are likely to be seen to be much less controllable. This needs to be taken into account in future studies as we seek to predict participation in both structured and unstructured physical activities. However, Ajzen (1988) warns that:

> at first glance, the problem of behavioral control may appear to apply to a limited range of actions only. Closer scrutiny reveals, however, that even very mundane activities, which can usually be executed (or not executed) at will, are sometimes subject to the influence of factors beyond one's control.
>
> (Ajzen 1988: 127)

One problem with the TPB is the lack of consistency in defining and assessing perceived behavioural control. For example, originally Ajzen (1988: 106) said that perceived behavioural control was 'closely related to self-efficacy beliefs' and that it 'refers to the perceived ease or difficulty of performing the behavior and it is assumed to reflect past experience as well as anticipated impediments and obstacles' (132). The similarity with self-efficacy has also been noted by Olson and Zanna (1993), and Stroebe and Stroebe (1995). However, more recently, Ajzen (1991) defines perceived behavioural control in terms of both perceived resources and opportunities as well as perceived power to overcome obstacles, thus the construct represents both control beliefs and perceived power.

Studies incorporating self-efficacy and PBC often find that they make independent contributions to the prediction of intentions or behaviour. For example, Terry and O'Leary (1995) found items reflecting self-efficacy and PBC to be factorially distinct. Moreover, they found that self-efficacy predicted intentions to be physically active, but not activity itself, whereas PBC predicted physical activity but not intention. The two constructs require further testing in this regard. PBC seems to include beliefs built on past experience as well as external barriers whereas self-efficacy refers to beliefs concerning agent-means connections (Skinner 1995; 1996) without necessarily distinguishing types of constraints.

Alternative attitude models for the study of physical activity

In addition to the widely cited theories of reasoned action and planned behaviour, other models of attitude have been proposed. The models we review are: Triandis' theory of social behaviour, the health belief model, and Rogers' protection motivation theory. Finally, a brief comment will be made concerning studies in physical activity utilising the two decision-making theories of subjective expected utility theory and action control theory. Although these models have either very few research studies to support them in the physical activity domain, or their applicability to physical activity could be questioned, they are included in the current discussion for the sake of completeness. In addition, some aspects of the models may be particularly useful for the study of exercise as a health behaviour and so further our understanding of exercise determinants, even though the model in full may be largely untested in exercise/physical activity or found to be limited.

Triandis' theory of social behaviour

Triandis (1977) proposed an attitude model that has some similarities with the TRA and TPB although stresses less conscious decision-making at some points in the model (Godin 1994; Valois, Desharnais and Godin 1988; Wallston and Wallston 1985). The model specifies that the likelihood of acting out a particularly behaviour will be dependent upon:

- prior behaviour ('habit')
- behavioural intention
- facilitating conditions.

In contrast to the TRA, the Triandis model suggests that as the strength of habit increases, so the level of volition decreases, hence Triandis proposes that in addition to intention researchers must also assess habit and facilitating conditions.

Valois *et al.* (1988) compared the Triandis model with that of the TRA in predicting both exercise behaviour and intention. With 166 adults aged 22 to 65 years of age, Valois *et al.* found that the two models were equally effective in predicting actual exercise behaviour, but they also found that whereas the Triandis model accounted for 25 per cent of the variance in exercise intentions, the TRA accounted for only 9 per cent. This suggests a difference between intentions, in the form of 'decision-making' and actual behaviour or 'decision implementation', as we discuss later (Kendzierski 1990a).

In a similar study by Godin *et al.* (1987) measures were taken of past exercise behaviour (habit), attitude, subjective norm, and both proximal (after three weeks) and distal (after two months) exercise participation. The results showed that intention was directly influenced by both attitude and habit, proximal behaviour was the result of habit only, and distal behaviour was influenced by a combination of intention and proximal behaviour. These researchers concluded that their results had two clear practical implications:

- If the target group is sedentary adults, intervention should take place through the attitude component as it is this that influences intention and not subjective norms.
- For children the intervention should be in the form of developing the exercise habit and positive attitudes since this group are unlikely to have developed these adequately at this age.

Triandis' model has really only been tested by Godin and colleagues and so the quantity of information we have in physical activity is limited. Nevertheless, the model allows for other variables to be considered and some have been shown to be important. The extent to which 'habit' is necessary for exercise, however, is debatable. Although some health behaviours, such as tooth brushing or the taking of some medications, may be relatively automatic, it is unlikely that an infrequent and high effort activity like exercise can be seen in the same way. Whether more moderate physical activity, such as walking, is the same remains to be seen. Certainly for vigorous exercise too much planning and effort is involved, although it could be claimed that people do develop 'routines' that might predispose them to degrees of sedentary or active behaviour. This is close to the idea that people are at different 'stages of contemplation' for exercise, and this is discussed more fully in the next chapter.

The health belief model

The question of why people do, or do not, seek healthcare has been an important one for health psychologists and other social scientists over the past few decades. Indeed, the field was initially typified by diverse findings and an apparently irreconcilable set of behavioural predictors. However, in the 1950s, a group of American social psychologists attempted to integrate the work on health behaviours by developing an attitude-based model of health decision-making: the health belief model (HBM) (Becker *et al.* 1977; Conner and Norman 1994; Janz and Becker 1984; Sheeran and Abraham 1996).

The HBM developed from Kurt Lewin's 'field theory' and an expectancy-value approach to motivation and behaviour (see Chapter 3). Lewin's phenomenological perspective advocated that behaviour is influenced by the individual's characteristics and the environment.

Lewin's field theory stated that we exist in a 'life space' of regions of both positive and negative value, and forces attract and repel us from these. Illness is a region of negative value and hence we are motivated to avoid it most of the time and this formed a central tenet of the HBM.

The HBM was devised in an attempt to predict health behaviours, primarily in response to low rates of adoption and adherence of preventive healthcare behaviours. Becker *et al.* (1977) stated that the HBM was adopted as an organising framework for four main reasons:

- The model has potentially modifiable variables.
- The model is derived from sound psychological theory.
- Although the HBM was first developed to account for preventive health behaviours, it

has also been employed successfully to account for 'sick-role' and 'illness' behaviours. 'Sick-role' behaviours are primarily associated with seeking treatment or a remedy for illness, whereas 'illness' behaviours are primarily associated with seeking advice or help on the nature and/or extent of the illness.

- The HBM is consistent with other health behaviour models.

The HBM has been applied to a wide variety of health behaviours, including exercise. Indeed, Rosenstock says that 'for more than three decades, the model has been one of the most influential and widely used psychosocial approaches to explaining health-related behavior' (Rosenstock 1990: 39). The model hypothesises that people will not seek (preventive) health behaviours unless:

- They possess minimal levels of health motivation and knowledge.
- View themselves as potentially vulnerable.
- View the condition as threatening.
- Are convinced of the efficacy of the 'treatment'.
- See few difficulties in undertaking the action.

These factors can be modified by socio-economic and demographic factors, as well as 'cues to action', such as media campaigns or the illness of a close friend or relative. The HBM is illustrated in Figure 5.3.

The majority of the HBM research has involved illness, sick-role or preventive behaviours. Rosenstock stated that 'it should be noted explicitly that the Model has a clear-cut avoidance orientation' (Rosenstock 1974: 333) and, initially at least, concerning one-shot behaviours such as clinic attendance. To what extent this can be applied to exercise or physical activity without modifications, therefore, remains to be seen and will be discussed later.

In 1984, after a decade of systematic research using the HBM, a state-of-the-art review

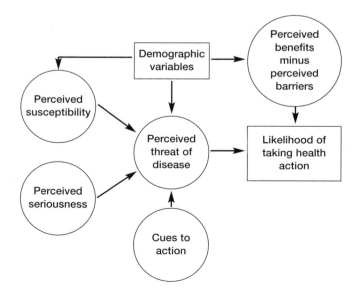

Figure 5.3 A simplified version of the health belief model

was published (Janz and Becker 1984). It was reported that 'the HBM has continued to be a major organising framework for explaining and predicting acceptance of health and medical care recommendations' (Janz and Becker 1984: 1). They concluded that:

- There was substantial support for the model across more than forty studies.
- The HBM is the most extensively researched model of health-related behaviours.
- 'Perceived barriers', when studied, was the most consistently powerful predictor.
- Beliefs associated with susceptibility appeared to be more important in preventive health behaviours.
- Beliefs in the perceived benefits of action seemed more important in sick-role and illness behaviours.
- Despite the variability of measuring instruments, the HBM has remained robust across a wide variety of settings and with a wide variety of research techniques.

Despite this optimistic view, Harrison, Mullen and Green (1992) went further and tested the HBM with adults using meta-analysis but with much stricter criteria for inclusion of studies than Janz and Becker (1984). From 147 research studies, Harrison *et al.* excluded all but sixteen on various criteria, including lack of a behavioural dependent variable, did not measure susceptibility, severity, benefits and costs in the same study, and lack of information about scale reliability. Overall, small but significant effect sizes were found for all four dimensions of the model but effect sizes varied greatly across the dimensions. In addition, they reported that prospective studies had significantly smaller effect sizes than retrospective ones, thus further weakening the case in favour of the HBM.

THE HEALTH BELIEF MODEL AND EXERCISE RESEARCH

Despite its illness avoidance orientation, the HBM has been used as a framework for investigating exercise behaviours. Lindsay-Reid and Osborn (1980) studied 124 sedentary male fire fighters in Canada. A prospective design was used whereby health beliefs were measured at the beginning of an exercise programme and also six months later. The number of exercisers reporting low perceptions of risk of heart disease and illness probability was significantly more than non-exercisers. It was concluded that those who adhered to the exercise programme tended to have beliefs associated with reduced susceptibility of CHD and general illness, contrary to the HBM. Feelings associated with illness susceptibility, therefore, were not motivating for this sample in terms of adopting and maintaining physical activity.

The results of this prospective study were supported in a cross-sectional retrospective survey we conducted (Biddle and Ashford 1988). In our first study of 433 adults, those classified as non-exercisers reported greater perceptions of vulnerability to general and cardiac ill-health when compared to exercisers. In a second study of 468 adults, we found similar results. Specifically, exercisers were higher in exercise intention, importance and benefits, and also had stronger beliefs in exercise control, were more likely to have been active in the past, and were more likely to have modified other health habits. Non-exercisers had higher perceptions of general health vulnerability.

These two sets of results suggest that perceptions of vulnerability to ill-health are related to *inactivity* rather than positive health behaviours as predicted by the HBM. This may be the result of thinking that exercise is something to be done 'when well' and that some forms of exercise may be hazardous, particularly for certain groups.

A comprehensive social psychological study of exercise adherence conducted by Olson and Zanna (1982) included the measurement of health beliefs. Specifically, sixty new members of four fitness clubs in Toronto, Canada were studied for three months. The HBM was used as the basis for measuring health beliefs. Susceptibility, seriousness and the efficacy of exercise in prevention were assessed for each of four health 'problems': heart, lungs, blood pressure and obesity. Consistent with Lindsay-Reid and Osborn (1980) and Biddle and Ashford (1988), but inconsistent with the HBM, Olson and Zanna found that exercisers ('regular attenders') considered heart, blood pressure and respiratory problems to be less serious (at the time of joining the club) than other subjects. However, male adherers reported greater susceptibility to problems associated with heart, lungs and obesity than male non-adherers, whereas female adherers reported less susceptibility to these health problems than female non-adherers.

THE HEALTH BELIEF MODEL: CONCLUSIONS AND CRITIQUE

From the evidence presented here on exercise and the HBM, it is clear that the optimistic conclusions of Janz and Becker (1984) and, to a certain extent the low but significant effect sizes reported in Harrison *et al.*'s (1992) meta-analysis, do not necessarily hold true for exercise behaviours. Although isolated variables, such as barriers, may relate to some exercise behaviours, the model as a whole has been relatively unsuccessful in predicting the adoption and/or maintenance of physical activity and exercise. Indeed, it could be argued that there is greater support for beliefs from the HBM predicting non-participation in exercise.

There is little doubt about the general heuristic appeal of the HBM. However, a number of points can be made in criticism of the model and associated research, and in particular in relation to its use in exercise settings (Godin 1994; Sonstroem 1988; Stroebe and Stroebe 1995; Wallston and Wallston 1985).

First, one must question the holistic nature of the model. Is it one model or merely a collection of individual variables? Indeed some have argued that because the list of potential variables is so large, the model is untestable (Wallston and Wallston 1985). Similarly, what relationships exist between the variables and how should the model variables be tested? Some research studies test the variables in linear combination while others test interactions. In addition, Harrison *et al.*'s (1992) meta-analysis tested the effect of individual variables only.

Second, there has been a lack of consistency in the operationalising of variables and the measuring tools used. Although Janz and Becker (1984) point out that the results obtained from a diversity of measuring instruments adds to the validity of the model, it does not make for easy comparison across studies. Indeed, Harrison *et al.* (1992) rejected a large number of studies from their meta-analysis because of measurement problems or lack of information provided in studies. However, recent psychometric developments have been made in the measurement of exercise benefits, outcomes and barriers (Sechrist *et al.* 1987; Steinhardt and Dishman 1989) but these instruments were not developed as tools for the direct assessment of the HBM.

Another criticism is that many of the studies measure health beliefs retrospectively, although some prospective studies do exist in health (King 1982) and exercise (Lindsay-Reid and Osborn 1980). Inevitably the retrospective studies fail to resolve the temporal patterning of beliefs and behaviour. Harrison *et al.* (1992) found weak effects for prospective health studies in their meta-analysis.

In terms of exercise research, one of the major problems associated with the HBM is that it was developed to predict isolated illness-avoidance behaviours, such as attendance at a clinic. Many such behaviours are one-shot behaviours, often supported by health professionals. Exercise, on the other hand, is a complex behaviour and, at least where adherence is concerned, is an on-going process rather than a single behaviour. For example, exercise is likely to involve stages of adoption, maintenance, relapse and re-adoption in many cases. Similarly, motives for adopting and maintaining exercise can be diverse, and may not include health enhancement or illness avoidance motives. The evidence presented here suggests that the illness-avoidance orientation of the model is not appropriate for the explanation or prediction of exercise behaviours. However, the increasing recognition of exercise and physical activity as a health behaviour, manifesting itself in promotion schemes such as family doctor-initiated 'exercise on prescription' schemes (Fox *et al.* 1997; Taylor 1999) may mean that the HBM is an appropriate framework for some exercise and physical activity contexts.

Parts of the HBM, or at least beliefs themselves, may remain within a wider model of exercise behaviour. Although the HBM may not be wholly appropriate for the prediction of exercise, its historical significance should not be underestimated. However, there appears to be a strong case for modifying the existing HBM for the prediction of exercise behaviours. For example, in predicting health behaviours that involve long-term behaviour change and maintenance, the inclusion of self-efficacy beliefs may be necessary and this point has been recognised by HBM researchers (Rosenstock 1990).

Some researchers have proposed a modified model for the study of exercise. However, Noland and Feldman's (1984; 1985) 'exercise behaviour model ' (EBM) has failed to be verified and exercise researchers are probably better seeking modifications to the HBM if they are interested in the role of health beliefs in exercise decision-making.

Protection motivation theory

A model that has some similarities with the HBM, as well as with the TRA/TPB, is that of Rogers' 'protection motivation theory' (PMT) (Rogers 1983). This too is a cognitive model based on expectancy-value principles and was originally developed as an explanation for the effects of 'fear appeals' in health behaviour change. Some have argued that 'health threats' might be a better term as the model is really one of health decision-making (Wurtele and Maddux 1987). Health behaviour intentions ('protection motivation') are predicted from the cognitive appraisal mechanisms shown in Figure 5.4 (Boer and Seydel 1996).

Support has been found for the model (Rippetoe and Rogers 1987). Similarly, Prentice-Dunn and Rogers (1986) contrast the PMT with the HBM and suggest that the PMT has some distinct advantages. They say that the PMT has more of an organisational framework and is not open to the criticism of merely being a catalogue of variables. Second, the division of cognitive appraisals into threat and coping categories helps to clarify how people think about health decision-making. Third, PMT includes self-efficacy, a variable found to be a powerful mediator of behaviour change in other studies (see Chapter 4).

To our knowledge, only three studies have directly tested PMT in an exercise context, although other studies provide evidence indirectly (see Godin 1994). Stanley and Maddux (1986) tested PMT alongside self-efficacy theory in the prediction of exercise behaviour of American undergraduate students. Using an experimental design, they found that manipulations of perceived response efficacy (outcome expectancy) and self-efficacy through written persuasive communications successfully predicted intentions to exercise.

Wurtele and Maddux (1987) asked 160 sedentary undergraduate women to read

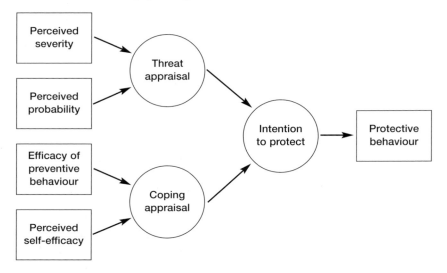

Figure 5.4 A simplified version of protection motivation theory

persuasive appeals for increasing their exercise. The appeals were varied along the four dimensions of severity, vulnerability, response efficacy and self-efficacy. Consistent with Bandura's (1977) theory of self-efficacy, PMT includes two types of efficacy. 'Response efficacy' refers to the belief that a response will produce the desired outcome whereas 'self-efficacy' refers to the belief in one's ability to initiate and maintain the desired behaviour (see Prentice-Dunn and Rogers 1986).

Wurtele and Maddux (1987) found that only vulnerability and self-efficacy predicted intentions to exercise, which in turn were predictive of self-reported exercise. Those with high self-efficacy also had strong intentions to exercise even though they were not exposed to the vulnerability-enhancing or response efficacy – enhancing conditions in the study. This confirms the important role of self-efficacy in behaviour change. It was also found that the threat appeals were ineffective in changing exercise intentions, although this could be a function of the young age of the participants. Typically, motivation for exercise involves increasing health-related beliefs as one ages (see Chapter 2).

Fruin, Pratt and Owen (1991) studied Australian adolescents and their beliefs about cardiovascular disease risk and the role of exercise. Response efficacy, response costs and self-efficacy were manipulated in an experimental design such that students received short essays with either 'high' (positive) or 'low' (negative) information on the variable in question (for example, response costs). Results revealed that students in the high self-efficacy condition reported stronger intentions to exercise, and those in the low response efficacy condition reported greater feelings of hopelessness and fatalism. Again, efficacy beliefs have been shown to be important in exercise contexts.

Godin concluded that:

> in general, messages conveying a persuasive threat seem effective in enhancing participants' intention to change their behaviors, but they are less effective in inducing and sustaining changes in behavior. . . . The PMT thus has limited usefulness for the study of exercise behavior.

(Godin 1994: 117)

Given the results of the three studies just reported, this conclusion may be premature. Although one may not be comfortable with physical activity motivation based on fear or health threats, and also noting that the results of PMT research are more favourable towards the role of self-efficacy than health threats *per se*, research so far suggests PMT sheds light on some important constructs and processes in physical activity decision-making that warrant further study.

Other decision-making theories

Kendzierski has studied the role of attitudes and exercise from the perspective of decision-making theories (Kendzierski 1990a; Kendzierski and LaMastro 1988). In particular, Edwards' (1954) 'subjective expected utility' (SEU) theory and Kuhl's (1985) 'action control' perspective are highlighted.

SEU theory suggests that decisions about exercise are made on the basis of the individual's belief in the worth or value of exercise, or more specifically of the outcome from exercise, and the probability that this outcome will occur should participation take place. Whether exercise takes place, or the type of exercise participated in, will be determined by the behavioural alternative with the most 'favourable' value and probability. Interestingly, SEU theory considers alternative courses of action, and thus when used in exercise research will shed light on the individual's beliefs about not exercising as well as about participation itself (Smith and Biddle 1999). This approach has rarely been used in exercise research but may be important in physical activity contexts. For example, some people with favourable attitudes and intentions towards physical activity may still have this behaviour low enough down their personal list of priorities that it never gets to the point of being acted upon. In short, we need to know where exercise is in peoples' overall value structure. This might be close to a notion of 'stages of contemplation' whereby we can identify the readiness of someone to act out their intentions. This may reflect the salience or value of exercise in relation to competing alternatives.

Kendzierski and LaMastro (1988), however, found that SEU theory predicted interest in exercise (weight training) but not actual adherence. They concluded that SEU theory may be more useful in situations involving simple choices, whereas they argue that exercise adherence is a complex behavioural process.

Kendzierski (1990a) conducted further research along these lines. Specifically, she investigated SEU theory and Kuhl's (1985) action control theory in predicting intentions, adoption and adherence to aerobic exercise. Kuhl states that 'action control . . . will be used here . . . to denote those processes which protect a current intention from being replaced should one of the competing tendencies increase in strength before the intended action is completed' (Kuhl 1985: 102).

Kendzierski (1990a) assessed people on Kuhl's 'action control scale' which categorises people into action-oriented or state-oriented individuals. Action-oriented are those who tend to focus on and plan for future actions, whereas state-oriented individuals are those who do not plan for the future and focus on the present or past. Kendzierski found that SEU theory predicted exercise intentions but not adherence, leading her to suggest that it was important to make the distinction between decision making and decision implementation. The correlation between intention and behaviour was slightly stronger for action-oriented individuals, giving some support to Kuhl's theory. However, Kuhl suggests that state-oriented individuals may have cognitions related to a 'catastatic' mode of control (that is, change preventing) or a 'metastatic' mode of control (that is, change inducing). 'As long as an individual is in a catastatic mode of control, the enactment of action-oriented intentions seems to be more difficult than when the individual is in a metastatic mode of control' (Kuhl 1985: 102).

Kendzierski (1994) later suggested other directions in addition to these decision-making approaches, such as the study of self-schemata, for advancing the understanding of exercise decision-making processes. This was discussed more fully in Chapter 4. However, action control theory may be a theoretical perspective useful for investigating perceptions of control and the use of planning strategies in exercise since self-regulatory planning skills may be important in the exercise adherence process.

Chapter summary and conclusions

Most people would agree that an important area for understanding of exercise and physical activity is attitudes. However, as with motivation (see Chapters 2–4), such an all-embracing construct cannot explain all that we do, but it remains central to the psychology of physical activity determinants. The conceptual overlap between the approaches reviewed is clear to see but this will be discussed more fully in the next chapter.

In this chapter, therefore, we have:

• Defined attitude and components of the attitude construct.
• Reviewed the early approach to physical activity attitudes.
• Summarised the approach adopted through the theories of reasoned action and planned behaviour, the two most commonly used theories in exercise attitude research.
• Described other approaches to the study of attitudes, including Triandis' theory of social behaviour, the health belief model, and protection motivation theory, as well as briefly mentioning two other decision-making approaches.

In summary, therefore, we conclude that:

• The early physical activity attitude research was mainly descriptive and focused on Kenyon's ATPA scale or similar generalised measures. ATPA assesses only the target of physical activity and not the action, context or time elements of attitude thought to be critical in linking attitude with behaviour. This approach, therefore, has limited utility in predicting participation in physical activity although may be of use in eliciting descriptive information in population surveys.
• The TRA has consistently predicted exercise intentions and behaviour across diverse settings and samples; attitude accounts for about 37 per cent of the variance in intentions, but subjective norm is only weakly associated with intentions.
• The TPB appears to add to the predictive utility of the TRA in physical activity; perceived behavioural control has been shown to account for 36 per cent of the variance in intentions.
• Both TRA and TPB models are limited by their focus on conscious decision-making through cognitive processes, they are essentially static and uni-dimensional approaches, and the prediction of physical activity from intentions may depend on the proximity of measurement of these two variables.
• The TRA and TPB have, however, been the most successful approaches in exercise psychology linking attitudes and related variables to intentions and participation; intentions share about 30 per cent of the variance in physical activity assessment.
• The health belief model has been shown to be a reasonably effective integrating social

psychological framework for understanding health decision-making, although meta-analytic results suggest small amounts of variance in health behaviours are accounted for by the major dimensions of the HBM. Its utility in physical activity settings has not been demonstrated, probably due to the inappropriate emphasis of the HBM on illness-avoidance and 'one-shot' behaviours.

- Protection motivation theory may be useful in predicting exercise intentions, but current data are more supportive of the role of efficacy beliefs rather than health threats themselves.

- Other decision-making approaches, such as subjective expected utility theory and action control theory hold some promise for furthering understanding of exercise and physical activity determinants, but few data exist. SEU theory suggests that researchers need to look at alternative or competing behaviours that may prevent physical activity being carried out.

- Attitudes are important determinants of physical activity, although subjective norms less so. Intentions and behaviour can be predicted from attitudes if appropriate social psychological theories and procedures are applied. To this end, and until data suggest otherwise, the TRA or TPB are recommended for this purpose.

6 Physical activity theories and models

Stages, phases and overlap

Welcome or not, change is unavoidable.

J. O. Prochaska, J. C. Norcross and C. C. DiClemente
(*Changing for good,* 1994)

Chapter objectives

The purpose of this chapter is to discuss the differences and similarities, or what might called 'conceptual convergence', between the different theoretical approaches so far discussed on physical activity determinants. In addition, models describing a more dynamic 'process' approach to exercise will be considered. Specifically, in this chapter we aim to:

- Discuss the conceptual overlap or convergence between constructs used in the key social-cognitive and expectancy-value approaches in contemporary exercise psychology.
- Judge the degree of convergence and the issue of whether theories should be tested in competition or whether studies should integrate similar constructs.
- Highlight the need for better measurement of variables in these models.
- Outline the popular 'stages of change' approach to exercise decision-making, including contemporary research findings and processes of change.
- Discuss the 'natural history' model of exercise proposed by Sallis and Hovell (1990) and suggest which determinants might be important at the different phases of the model.
- Describe the lifespan interaction model and show how it provides a good global framework for the study of the complex factors associated with participation in exercise and physical activity.

A great deal has been said in recent years on the likely determinants of exercise and physical activity. Much of this has been centred on psychological and social psychological issues. In this book alone we have considered the following approaches, amongst others: Rotter's social learning theory/locus of control approach, intrinsic motivation (with cognitive evaluation and self-determination theories), attribution theory, goal perspectives theory, competence motivation theory, exercise self-schemata, self-efficacy theory, theories of reasoned action and planned behaviour, theory of social behaviour, protection motivation theory and the health belief model. Can this fractionation be justified or can we bring together some of the approaches that are similar to each other? In this chapter we consider the important issue of conceptual convergence between the major approaches used in the study of exercise and physical activity behaviours. Clearly, we cannot analyse all of the theories listed above, but we shall consider the main ones and, in particular, where convergence is more obvious. This should help us become more focused on the important constructs for investigation in future exercise and physical activity research. Similar efforts have been made before in exercise (Brawley 1993; Maddux 1993) and health psychology (Mullen, Hersey and Iverson 1987; Weinstein 1993), and readers are recommended to consult these references. However, some researchers also sound a note of caution about this process, as we shall discuss later.

We shall also consider 'process' models of exercise which describe stages or phases of exercise behaviour, rather than provide the static picture usually found in cross-sectional research that adopts a perspective based only one theoretical perspective or one period in time. The process approaches to be discussed are the 'transtheoretical model' of behaviour change, or 'stages of change' approach, Sallis and Hovell's (1990) model of a 'natural history' of exercise and Dishman's (1990) 'lifespan interaction model'. All were developed for different reasons yet provide useful insights into the complex process of different phases of exercise decision-making and behaviour.

Conceptual convergence of key approaches to physical activity determinants

The first point to make is that all of the major theoretical approaches considered so far have some merits. They have not been included in this book to satisfy any sense of theoretical completeness, but rather to shed light, however small and doubtful at times, on physical activity behaviours. Perhaps the most important issue to remember is that theory, or at least good theory, provides an integrating framework to allow a clearer picture to emerge from what is likely to be complex process. Participation in structured exercise or active living through habitual physical activity is a complex behavioural phenomenon and certainly needs good theoretical research for us to make sense of it. As we have already stated, much of the early research in exercise psychology was atheoretical and was guided more by common-sense and intuition. This was a good start, but obviously progress could only be made by borrowing or developing theoretical approaches. The former approach has been more common.

Some of the approaches already discussed have either involved few or single constructs, such as self-efficacy, focus on specific outcomes, such as intrinsic motivation, or have only just emerged in exercise research, thus making it premature to evaluate fully, such as exercise self-schemata. Appraisals of theories in exercise have been made by numerous researchers in recent years, and a selection of these is summarised in Table 6.1. However, not all of the reviews listed in the table make explicit reference to conceptual convergence between theories. This is best done by Brawley (1993), Maddux (1993) and Weinstein (1993), although readers are also recommended to consult Rejeski's (1992) thought-provoking analysis of exercise behaviour research.

Testing within or between theories?

Despite a strong emphasis towards some reconciliation between theoretical approaches, some researchers have expressed reservations about this. Dzewaltowski (1994) defends the position of Bandura's social cognitive theory and suggests that research be carried out within one theoretical framework. While recognising that one strategy is to look for

Table 6.1 Selected reviews of social psychological theories of exercise/health

Author	TRA	TPB	HBM	PMT	SET	TSB	LOC	Others
Sonstroem (1988)	√		√		√		√	Sonstroem's psychological model; psychobiological model; self-esteem; perceived competence.
Biddle and Fox (1989)	√		√		√	√		
Rejeski (1992)	√	(√)	√		√	√	√	
Brawley (1993)	√	√			√			
Rodgers and Brawley (1993)	√	√			√			Behavioural management; mass change strategies; social persuasion.
Dishman (1993)	√	√	√		√	√	√	Expectancy-value decision theories; personal investment theory; self-regulatory theory; opponent-process theory; relapse prevention model.
Maddux (1993)	√	√	√	√	√			Habit.
Weinstein[1] (1993)	√		√	√				SEU.
Godin (1994)	√	√	√	√	√	√		
Biddle (1994b)	√	√	√		√		√	Competence and self-presentation.
Biddle (1995c)					√			Competence motivation; attributions and achievement goals; decision-making theories.
Biddle (1997a)					√			Competence motivation; goal perspectives theory; exercise self-schemata; self-determination and intrinsic motivation.

Key
√ Construct existing within theoretical framework.
(√) Construct exists in similar form.

Note:
1 Referred to 'health' rather than exercise, but is an important paper in drawing attention to commonalities between the theories discussed.
  Abbreviations
  TRA: theory of reasoned action   TPB: theory of planned behaviour
  HBM: health belief model   PMT: protection motivation theory
  SET: self-efficacy theory   TSB: theory of social behaviour
  LOC: locus of control and Rotter's social learning theory

convergent and discriminant validity between constructs of the different theories, Dzewaltowski says that:

> another strategy, and I believe a more effective strategy, is to evaluate constructs on their ability to contribute to understanding physical activity *within* a constructed theoretical framework. In other words, I believe researchers should develop one effective language to account for the processes determining physical activity rather than compare languages.
>
> (Dzewaltowski 1994: 1396)

One has to question whether we are able to be so certain about the theoretical framework in the first place. For example, although Dzewaltowski is correct in saying we need to establish one language, we are not yet in a position to know what that language is. Even his own research has proposed testing one theory *against* another (Dzewaltowski, Noble and Shaw 1990), which suggests that one theory is better than another. One may well be better, but at this stage there is so much conceptual overlap that we need to test a variety of constructs and models together, not in competition, in order to better understand physical activity determinants.

Dzewaltowski (1994) is critical of efforts that have attempted to integrate self-efficacy into the TPB, yet, as we have already discussed in Chapter 5, it is not even clear how close self-efficacy is to the construct of perceived behavioural control, as conceived by Ajzen in the development of the TPB. For this reason, we need to look at self-efficacy, and measures of perceived behavioural control, if indeed they are different, in order to sort out the conceptual confusion currently existing. To 'ring fence' theories and their constructs is not a wise strategy in our opinion.

Perhaps Dishman (1994b) is closer to the mark when he suggests that we need to resolve the measurement redundancy in these models before testing 'competing' theories. It is true that further measurement refinement in necessary if progress is to be made. Part of this process can be achieved by testing constructs (assuming that they are properly constituted and operationalised) simultaneously. As Dishman says:

> the proliferation of measures of psychological determinants requires some degree of standardisation. Better discriminant and convergent evidence for the validity of measures and their underlying constructs is needed to permit clear contrasts of several social-cognitive variables related to outcome-expectancy values and perceptions of the self.
>
> (Dishman 1994: 1384)

Judging the similarities between theories

For the sake of clarity, only the following theoretical frameworks will be considered in attempting to formulate some convergence: theory of reasoned action, theory of planned behaviour, health belief model, protection motivation theory, Triandis' 'theory' (model) of social behaviour, and self-efficacy theory. An attempted mapping of construct overlap appears in Table 6.2.

All of the approaches listed in Table 6.2 are expectancy-value/social cognitive approaches. As such they stress the role of thoughts about actions and the consequences of those actions, as well as the value or importance of likely outcomes. In addition, the social cognitive emphasis stresses the role of thoughts about what other people may be thinking and about their beliefs concerning one's own behaviour. In his analysis of the similarities of some social cognitive theories of health and exercise, Maddux says the 'assumptions made by social cognitive theory . . . underscore the theme that these theories are compatible rather than competing' (Maddux 1998: 119). Similarly, Brawley's (1993) analysis of three of these theories – TRA, TPB and self-efficacy theory – suggests that nineteen determinants of exercise identified in previous reviews (Dishman 1990; Sallis and Hovell 1990) can be linked to variables from these three theories.

Returning to the broader range of theories shown in Table 6.2, these most explicitly deal with the role of intention, outcome expectancies, outcome value, social factors/norms and efficacy or perceived control. Fewer deal directly with situational cues or perceived vulnerability/severity. Interestingly, self-efficacy theory does not contain reference to outcome value that, as Rejeski (1992) says, is a strange omission. Why should someone want to pursue exercise, even with high self-efficacy, if they did not value the outcomes? However, according to Maddux (1993), attempts to include outcome value alongside self-efficacy have yielded mixed results. Similarly, the role of outcome value has not been addressed in the

Table 6.2 A mapping of construct convergence across six theories applied to exercise behaviour and determinants

Theory	Intention	Outcome expectancy	Outcome value	Social norm	Self-efficacy	PBC	Habit/past behaviour	Situational cues	Perceived vulnerability/severity
TRA	√	√	√	√					
TPB	√	√	√	√		√			
HBM		√		(√)	(√)			√	√
PMT	√	√	?	(√)	(√)	(√)	√	(√)	√
TSB	√	(√)		(√)	√		√	(√)	
SET		(√)	(√)	(√)	√	(√)	(√)	(√)	

Key
√ Construct existing within theoretical framework.
(√) Construct exists in similar form.
? Possible inclusion but not clear from operational definitions.

Abbreviations
TRA: theory of reasoned action
TPB: theory of planned behaviour
HBM: health belief model
PMT: protection motivation theory
TSB: theory of social behaviour
SET: self-efficacy theory

Notes:
1 The labels used to describe the constructs may not correspond exactly to the labels used in the original theory. More generic labels have been used to allow comparison across theories.
2 Self-efficacy theory is problematic to include in this table for two reasons. First, nearly all studies in exercise have simply addressed the construct of self-efficacy rather than tested other components of Bandura's (1986) social cognitive theory. Second, much of the overlap suggested here is only partial and is achieved by estimating the true meaning of factors associated with self-efficacy beliefs. However, it remains in the table as most people recognise self-efficacy as a core social-cognitive variable in determinants research in exercise and physical activity.

HBM, where only outcome expectancy, via perceptions of threat, is considered. In PMT, it is possible to identify outcome value through the role of intrinsic rewards, although this is rather an indirect reference to value.

Towards an integrated model?

The discussion so far suggests that there is indeed a great deal of overlap between the various social psychological approaches used in contemporary physical activity and exercise research and perhaps more effort should be devoted to rationalising the key variables for future research. Maddux (1993) proposes an integrating framework, based on the TPB, for including these key variables.

Maddux's model proposes that exercise behaviour will be determined directly by intentions, self-efficacy and cues to action. Intentions will be a function of attitude toward the new and current behaviour, social norms and self-efficacy. This model now includes perceived benefits and costs and is therefore close to the notions used in subjective expected utility theory when behavioural choices are made after consideration of both action and inaction.

Similarly, Dishman (1994b) proposes a model for the testing of the inter-relationships between components of decision-making theories. This model proposes relationships based on the TPB, self-efficacy theory, social cognitive theory and expectancy theory.

From construct convergence to 'stage' models

Having identified points of convergence in key social psychological models that have been applied to exercise and physical activity, a logical step is to review dynamic 'stage' approaches. The discussion so far on conceptual convergence and the integrated models, points towards the use of more process-oriented approaches. For example, in Maddux's (1993) model, it is suggested that several time phases are operating. Likewise, Dishman's (1994a; 1994b) path model, as with many of the other social psychological approaches, suggests that behaviour is predicted by intentions which, in turn, are preceded by various time-phased cognitions or cues, varying on a proximal/distal dimension.

Several researchers have proposed a stage approach to advance understanding of how people move into or out of participation in exercise or physical activity. In addition to Dishman's (1990) heuristic model of exercise (the lifespan interaction model), we shall review two main dynamic stage approaches to exercise. First, the transtheoretical model, or 'stages of change' approach, will be discussed, and this will be followed by Sallis and Hovell's (1990) 'natural history of exercise' and an analysis of possible determinants at different stages of exercise involvement. Dishman's (1990) interaction model will be used to summarise key points.

Stages of change and exercise

Research into the nature of behaviour change in smokers and those presenting themselves for psychotherapy has suggested that recovery from problem behaviours, or successful behaviour change, involves movement through a series of stages (Prochaska and Velicer 1997; Prochaska, DiClemente and Norcross 1992; Prochaska *et al.* 1994a; Prochaska *et al.* 1994b). This notion has now been successfully applied to exercise behaviours (Buxton, Wyse and Mercer 1996; Ingledew, Markland, and Medley 1998; Marcus *et al.* 1994; Marcus *et al.* 1992b; Marcus *et al.* 1992c). Even those attempting self-change, as well as those in therapy, seem to move through 'stages of change' (SOC). The SOC approach is currently popular in psychotherapy and now other areas of health and exercise. The term 'trans-theoretical model', a term used to describe the wider framework encompassing SOC, refers to Prochaska's early work in which he identified common change stages and processes across diverse theoretical systems of psychotherapy. We review the evidence on SOC and physical activity in this chapter and then make application to interventions in Chapter 11.

The following stages have been identified, although not all have necessarily been used in all exercise studies (see p. 264 for European prevalence data):

- Precontemplation: includes people who are not currently exercising and have no intention of doing so in the near future. Prevalence information from a large sample (n = 1063) of worksite employees in the USA (Marcus *et al.* 1992b) showed that only 8 per cent were at this stage. If the definition is changed to those who are not at a criterion level of physical activity (for example, five periods per week of thirty minutes of moderate activity) and have no intention of reaching criterion within a specified time period (say six months), then the prevalence is likely to rise steeply. Using a question referring simply to 'exercise', with no further delimiting references, for a large (n = 4404) representative sample of Australian adults 12.7 per cent were found to be precontemplators (Booth *et al.* 1993).
- Contemplation: this stage includes current non-exercisers but who have an intention to start exercising in the near future. Marcus *et al.* (1992b) identified 21.1 per cent of their sample in this category while Booth *et al.* (1993) reported 9.6 per cent, with a further 23.3 per cent classified as 'occasional exercisers and thinking of doing more'.
- Preparation: these are individuals who are 'currently exercising some, but not regularly' (Marcus and Owen 1992: 6), or, as Prochaska and Marcus (1994) suggest, these people are intending to take action in the next month or so. This stage has not always been used in exercise research and could be quite unstable as sporadic involvement occurs.
- Action: this stage represents people who are currently exercising, but have only recently started. As such, Prochaska and Marcus (1994) suggest that it is an unstable stage during which individuals are at high risk of relapse. Marcus *et al.* identified 36.9 per cent of their sample at this stage.
- Maintenance: this stage includes those who are currently exercising and have been doing so for some time – at least six months – and included 34 per cent of the sample studied by Marcus *et al.* (1992b). In Booth *et al.*'s (1993) Australian sample, action and maintenance stages were combined to reveal 38.2 per cent of the population.
- Termination: this has not been used in exercise research but does feature in other SOC research, such as on smoking and alcohol abuse in which about 15–17 per cent of those in the maintenance group were classified. Prochaska and Marcus define this stage as the point at which people have 'no temptation to engage in the old behaviour and 100 per cent self-efficacy in all previously tempting situations' (Prochaska and Marcus 1994: 163).
- Relapse: this has not been tested much in exercise but is consistent with Sallis and Hovell's (1990) model. While data are available from smoking and alcohol research on the risk of relapse from the maintenance phase, little data are available in exercise. However, Marcus and Simkin (1994) suggest that maybe 15 per cent fall into the category of being 'relapsers' (that is, regressive movement back to either contemplation or precontemplation).

A meta-analysis of sixty-eight studies, involving 68,580 participants, estimated that 14 per cent were in precontemplation, 16 per cent in contemplation, 23 per cent in preparation, 11 per cent in action, and 36 per cent in maintenance (Marshall and Biddle 2000).

The stages outlined suggest a steady linear progression from one stage to the next. However, certainly in addictive behaviours, where most of the SOC approach has been investigated, a linear pattern has given way to the belief that change is cyclical (see Figure 6.1). In the context of exercise, Marcus and Simkin (1994) suggest that several attempts at change are likely before maintenance is reached. Indeed, Prochaska *et al.* (1992) say that for many the process of cycling may help strengthen behaviour change in the long run as people learn from their mistakes and relapses. However, as they succinctly put it, 'much more research is needed to better distinguish those who benefit from recycling from those who end up spinning their wheels' (Prochaska *et al.* 1992: 1105).

More recently, stage models of health behaviour have received more critical appraisal. For example, Weinstein, Rothman and Sutton (1998) present what they see as defining features of stage theories. These are a classification system for defining stages, an ordering of stages, common barriers to change facing people in the same stage, and different barriers to change facing people in different stages. They suggest that cross-sectional comparisons across stages have limited value in testing whether a stage process is followed in health behaviour change.

The research on SOC and exercise is still in its infancy. Nevertheless, there is some consistency in the evidence, much with sizeable samples for this type of social psychological research, to suggest that SOC is an important construct worthy of serious consideration in both exercise research and practice. Marcus and her colleagues, who have undoubtedly led

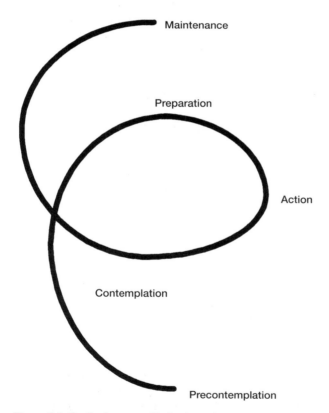

Figure 6.1 Cyclical stages of behaviour change

the way in applying SOC to exercise, have provided evidence showing that increasing self-efficacy is associated with greater exercise readiness, and that perceived benefits increase and costs decrease through the stages in a predictable way (Marcus and Owen 1992). The 'pros' and 'cons' of exercise and decision balance is also consistent with SOC (Marcus, Rakowski and Rossi 1992). In addition, progress has been made on the measurement of stages and processes of change (Marcus *et al.* 1992b; Wyse, *et al.* 1995), and it has been shown that interventions can move people between stages (Cardinal and Sachs 1995; Marcus *et al.* 1992a).

Processes of change and interventions

The stages of change discussed so far refer to the temporal patterning of behaviour change. By also identifying *processes* of change we are able to understand why and how this temporal shift might take place. Processes of change, therefore, are important for interventions designed to move people between stages. This is discussed in Chapter 11.

Conclusions and critique of stages of change

There is no doubt that a dynamic approach to understanding exercise and physical activity that includes different stages of 'readiness' is an appropriate way forward. The success of the SOC model in other health settings also lends confidence to its application to physical activity. Similarly, Marcus and co-workers, as well as other researchers, have shown the utility of SOC in exercise across three countries and in adults of differing ages, and processes of change have been proposed, thus increasing the likelihood of SOC being applied successfully in intervention trials.

Peer-reviewed published SOC research in physical activity, however, is still relatively small, although growing. It is often descriptive and has merely identified different, and at times predictable, variables associated with each stage. Limited information is available on processes of stage or on how best to move people from one stage to another. The following limitations have been identified (see Marcus and Simkin 1994):

- Studies have mainly relied on self-report of physical activity.
- Consistency of defining and assessing stages is required.
- Studying SOC across both structured exercise and habitual physical activity settings is required.
- Studies are largely cross-sectional; longitudinal research is required to study behaviour change more effectively.
- More intervention studies are required for testing the effectiveness of matching processes and stages, including testing whether mismatching processes and stages produce no behaviour change (see Weinstein *et al.* 1998).
- Greater use of representative and diverse samples is desired.

In the measurement of stages some misclassification may occur as a result of the way the stages are operationally defined. For example, classically, stages are assessed by defining precontemplation as not being at the level of the behavioural criterion (for example, moderate physical activity for thirty minutes for five days of the week) and not intending to be at the criterion within six months. However, most exercise studies define precontemplation as 'non-exercisers' with no intention of exercising. This is a more severe definition and probably accounts for why exercise studies show such low numbers in the precontemplation stage; numbers much lower than epidemiological studies of physical activity levels seem to suggest.

A natural history model of exercise

Throughout our discussions we have said that exercise behaviour and determinants are complex and can only really be studied effectively through multivariate models and theories. Also, early studies that investigated differences between 'adherers' and 'dropouts' (see Chapter 2) gave the mistaken impression that exercise was an 'all or none' phenomenon (Sonstroem 1988) rather than a process open to considerable change over time. As suggested by the SOC approach, people move between stages of contemplation, decision-making, and behavioural involvement, and even then not in any linear fashion, but often taking steps backwards as well as forwards.

In reviewing the determinants of exercise, Sallis and Hovell (1990) produced a 'natural history' model that has considerable utility in understanding the process of exercise. Their model is shown in Figure 6.2 and depicts the three important transition phases:

- sedentary behaviour to exercise adoption
- exercise adoption to maintenance or dropout
- dropout to resumption of exercise.

We know little about the exercise adoption process, and hardly anything about exercise resumption. Most research on determinants has investigated maintenance and dropout. However, even this model oversimplifies things, as Sallis and Hovell (1990) recognised. The following additional factors should be taken into account when considering the natural history model:

- There are degrees of 'exercising'. When is someone 'sedentary' for example? For the sake of clarity, the model assumes that exercise is a dichotomous rather than a continuous variable. The notion of sporadic activity, and its determinants, is a challenge for future research.

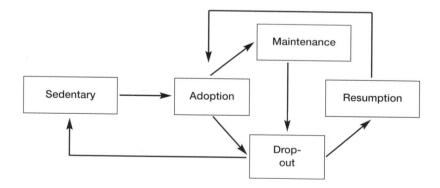

Figure 6.2 Sallis and Hovell's (1990) natural history model of exercise. Reproduced, with permission of Lippincott, Williams and Wilkins, from J. F. Sallis and M. Hovell (1990) 'Determinants of exercise behavior', *Exercise and Sport Sciences Reviews* 18: 307–30.

- The model is simply a useful device for focusing on the dynamic process of exercise. There are many other factors to be considered for a full picture of determinants across the lifespan. For example, we need to consider developmental/lifespan stages, socio-demographic characteristics, and actual activity differences. All are likely to operate slightly differently across the phases described here. In fact, when we attempted an analysis of the natural history model before (Biddle 1992), it was suggested, not altogether seriously, that at least 210 permutations of determinants exist on the basis of categorising determinants into seven major categories (for example, social and environment, attitude etc.), six developmental periods, and at least five stages of the natural history model!
- The model is unlikely to be applicable to children as it refers primarily to structured exercise. Children are more likely to involve themselves in sporadic physical activity, through play and personal transportation, as well as structured activities (for example, sport). In addition, strong influences will be social norms and parents rather than independent decision-making on the part of the child. The model will become increasingly relevant as young people progress through adolescence.

Determinants may differ across exercise phases

Although the data are not yet complete enough for us to be sure about the different determinants of exercise for each of the phases in Sallis and Hovell's model, we are in a position to speculate. As Sallis and Hovell say, 'those who study determinants of exercise behavior must carefully define which transition they are studying, because the determinants are likely to be different at each transition point' (Sallis and Hovell 1990: 310). Given the extensive discussion on possible determinants that has already taken place in the preceding chapters, this section will consider the factors that could be most influential at each of the phases, or transitions, in the natural history model. For the sake of clarity, we shall describe the model in terms of phases as follows and as shown in Figure 6.2:

- Phase 1: moving from being sedentary to adopting exercise.
- Phase 2: maintaining involvement in exercise.
- Phases 3 and 4: ceasing involvement in exercise.
- Phase 5: resuming exercise after previously ceasing participation.

STARTING EXERCISE

Sallis and Hovell (1990) are pessimistic about this phase of their model. They conclude that 'we understand almost nothing about why some people start exercising' (Sallis and Hovell 1990: 313). They are, of course, correct as most studies, even if they claim to study the adoption process, usually have self-selected or narrow samples, such as CHD patients. Sallis' own work (Sallis *et al.* 1986) is one of the few population-based studies of exercise adoption, but by his own admission the study of determinants lacked a theoretical focus. Their work did show, however, that self-efficacy, knowledge and attitudes were generally associated with the adoption of vigorous and moderate exercise. Logic also dictates that much of the material reviewed in the previous chapter on attitudes, as well as that on self-efficacy (Chapter 4), appears to be appropriate for understanding the adoption process. Similarly, the SOC research in exercise has shown that self-efficacy levels of contemplators are usually lower than for those in the action or maintenance stages, and that those not yet exercising have more negative beliefs about exercise.

These issues do not need re-examining as they have been discussed in some detail already, but suffice to say at this point that these approaches address likely predisposing factors for the adoption of change in lifestyle. In addition, for some people, variables associated with health vulnerability and severity may be important, as depicted in the health belief model and protection motivation theory. These may be particularly important for patients being recommended exercise for medical reasons. Interventions aimed at changes in belief structures and perceived barriers, therefore, may have some success.

The natural history model deals with exercise and it is not known how appropriate such a model is for habitual physical activity, such as walking or stair climbing. However, it is these habitual activities that may hold the key to moving people from being sedentary to active. The behavioural barriers associated with structured exercise may be much greater than those of habitual physical activity, yet at this point we are not able to demonstrate whether encouraging habitual physical activity will be any more successful than providing structured exercise programmes. This is another direction for the future.

Box 6.1 Does becoming more habitually active predispose people to taking up structured exercise?

Recently, I (SB) was working as a consultant with Dr Andy Smith. Andy and I had been asked by the leisure department of a local district council to conduct field research on why three of their leisure/sport centres were struggling to attract customers. After our research and written report we felt that a good way to move forward would be to have a one-day informal meeting/discussion with the three centre heads, the director of leisure for the district council and the two researchers/consultants.

Half way through the day, Andy raised the issue of centre staff expecting people to come to the centre. He suggested 'why not go out into the community and take your product to them'? This could be done, for example, by initiating work site schemes, or community physical activity plans, like 'cycling to work' days. This, we suggested, might then encourage people to be more physically active which, in turn, might help them take the step into structured exercise at the leisure centres.

To be honest, we don't have any data to guide us on this. We were advising this strategy on the basis of wanting to encourage greater physical activity, but whether it would create more clients in the sports centres was not possible to say. Some have argued that it would take clients away if they could exercise elsewhere. One of the reasons why people take structured exercise these days is that everyday situations no longer give us enough activity.

This is a conundrum that we are not yet able to solve. Would promoting greater habitual physical activity also increase the number of people using sport/exercise facilities?

As stated, the data on adoption of exercise are sparse and much of these comments reflect speculation and educated guess work. Nevertheless, it seems reasonable to propose that enabling factors of beliefs, attitudes, self-efficacy, social support, and the perception of few barriers will be a step in the right direction for exercise adoption. Certainly these are consistent with strategies proposed for moving precontemplators to contemplation and preparation (Prochaska *et al.* 1994a).

MAINTAINING EXERCISE

We are on much firmer ground when proposing determinants of the maintenance phase of exercise and we have already discussed many of these issues at length in this book. In addition to the factors identified for adoption, two important issues need to be considered as far as psychological determinants are concerned. First is the issue of psychological reinforcement from exercise, and second is the issue of self-regulation.

The reinforcement associated with exercise has also been raised by Sallis and Hovell (1990). They proposed a closer look at learning theories and the role of reinforcement and punishment in exercise. Population studies have shown that many people do not find the effort of physical activity at all pleasant (The Sports Council and Health Education Authority 1992; Canada Fitness Survey 1983b) whereas some individuals have reported high levels of enjoyment, with a few even reporting some measure of dependence or 'addiction' to exercise (Polivy 1994).

What appears to be emerging, therefore, is the important role of psychological outcomes from exercise. Typically, the so-called 'mental health' benefits of exercise have been studied from the point of view of outcomes only (this is reviewed in more detail in Chapters 8–10). From the view of determinants of exercise maintenance, however, we should also consider the mental health outcomes as *reinforcers* of subsequent exercise. Although Sallis and Hovell suggest that 'the punishment of vigorous exercise remains immediate and salient, while the reinforcers of improved health or weight loss are greatly delayed and silent' (Sallis and Hovell 1990: 320), it is possible to suggest that the mood enhancing and 'feel better' effects of exercise can also be perceived in the short term. The key is to structure exercise experiences such that the probability of perceiving exercise as rewarding is increased. We suggest the 'physiological' message of 'vigorous' and prolonged exercise, which for so long has been standard, has not served us well.

Early reviews on exercise and physical activity determinants support the point we are making. Dishman, Sallis and Orenstein (1985: 166) said that 'feelings related to well-being and enjoyment seem more important to maintaining activity than concerns about health'. Similarly, most reviews on children and physical activity stress the importance of enjoyment and development of perceptions of competence as a means of encouraging physical activity (De Bourdeauhuij 1998).

In addition to exercise being reinforcing through positive psychological outcomes, maintenance of exercise is likely to be enhanced, at least for some people, through the operation of self-regulatory strategies and skills. Evidence from the stages of change approach suggests that those in the action and maintenance phases are more likely to have arrived at a positive 'balance' of exercise 'pros' (benefits) and 'cons' (costs) (Prochaska 1994), and this process of decision-balance is itself a conscious exercise in self-regulation. Similarly, some adherence studies show the importance of 'self-motivation' in distinguishing adherers and dropouts (Dishman and Gettman 1980). Self-motivation includes elements of self-regulation such as goal-setting and self-monitoring. Goal-setting itself has often been found to be effective as a short-term behaviour change strategy (Atkins *et al.* 1984), as has self-monitoring (Juneau *et al.* 1987). Further discussion on individual behaviour change interventions for exercise can be found in Chapter 11.

CEASING EXERCISE

The study of exercise 'dropout' has been controversial, mainly because early studies were not able to identify if those ceasing participation in a structured programme had quit altogether or had merely gone elsewhere to exercise. The word 'dropout', therefore, was difficult to define. Gould and Petlichkoff (1988), in a review of youth sport participation, differentiated between those children dropping out altogether from those merely switching allegiance to another sport. This is something that exercise studies need to do.

The cessation of exercise may also be dependent on a variety of lifecycle influences. For example, Mihalik *et al.* (1989) found that in a study of adults aged from 18 to over 50 years, it was those in the 29–36 year old range who most 'contracted' their physical activity and sport involvement. This is suggestive of key life events, such as marriage, having children, and job changes, being influential in physical activity levels.

The message that 'healthy' exercise has to be 'vigorous' has already been criticised from a behavioural point of view. In addition, the promotion of vigorous exercise in structured classes, while enjoyable and appropriate for some, has been implicated in dropout. The issue of exercise intensity is addressed more fully in the next chapter.

Box 6.2 Establishing guidelines for the promotion of physical activity: scientific 'proof' or common sense?

In 1993, I (SB) took part in the 'Moving On' conference in England set up to establish guidelines for physical activity promotion in England as part of the Government's 'Health of the Nation' strategy. After several days of scientific evidence and discussion, one key message agreed was that adults should be encouraged to reach the 'target' of 30 minutes of moderate activity on most days of the week. Discussion ensued as to whether the 30 minutes could be achieved in two blocks rather than all at once. The 'scientific' evidence seemed to point to 30 minutes being optimal, and not enough evidence appeared in defence of the 2x15 minutes message. But I refused to accept this! I spoke up and said to Steven Blair, the Chair, that I couldn't really accept that under the 30 minute principle, I would be classified as not having reached the target. At the time I walked to work everyday (I cycle now) and it was 22 minutes there (it's uphill!), and only 20 minutes back! Steve agreed to write to the Prime Minister and ask for special dispensation for me! More importantly, we agreed that it would be nonsense to 'not count' such activity. Consequently, the current message is 30 minutes, in bouts of at least 15 minutes. A victory for common sense over 'science' in my opinion!

RESUMING EXERCISE

In discussing the determinants of resumption of exercise after dropout Sallis and Hovell are quite clear:

> this phase of the natural history of exercise has been completely neglected by both theoreticians and empirical investigators. The extent to which drop-outs resume exercise later has never been studied, to our knowledge. Thus, there are no studies

on the determinants of resumption of exercise. Research on these issues is desperately needed with both participants in specialised programs and with the general population.

(Sallis and Hovell 1990: 315)

Sallis and Hovell's comment has sparked interest in the resumption process but still no coherent data have emerged, although Mihalik *et al.*'s (1989) cross-sectional study of physical activity 'expansion' and 'contraction' across the adult lifecycle provides interesting data of some relevance to this problem. However, we are once again left to speculate about possibilities, one of which is the process of relapse studied in other health fields.

Marlatt (1985) has proposed a 'relapse prevention' model for the explanation of poor adherence to abstaining from various addictions and negative health behaviours, such as excessive alcohol and nicotine consumption. Marlatt defines relapse as 'a breakdown or set back in a person's attempt to change or modify any target behavior' (Marlatt 1985: 3).

Although this definition, as well as the relapse prevention model, provides a starting point for the analysis of exercise resumption, it may not be wholly suitable. Knapp (1988), for example, notes that the behaviours addressed in addiction relapse are high frequency, undesired behaviours yet exercise is low frequency and desired. Nevertheless, until we have something better, it provides us with a workable model in which to identify possible determinants of exercise resumption. Marlatt's model, modified for possible application to exercise, is illustrated in Figure 6.3.

The starting point is identified in Figure 6.3 as the high risk situation of ceasing exercise. This risk situation is the threat to self-control that could produce 'relapse' back to a sedentary lifestyle. For those with addiction problems, Marlatt (1985) has identified interpersonal conflict, negative emotional states and social pressure as the three primary high-risk situations. Certainly the latter two have been identified as predictors of (in)activity. Whether these situations lead to relapse will be dependent on the adequacy of the individual's coping

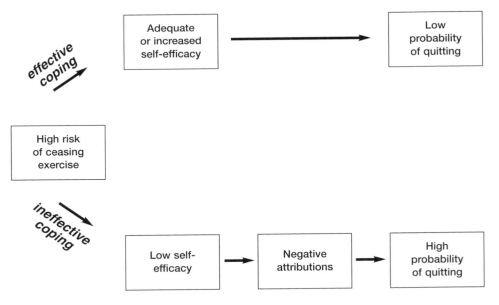

Figure 6.3 Relapse prevention model applied to exercise

skills and responses. A high risk situation for lack of exercise might be extra work pressures, thus producing a perception of reduced time for exercise. The probability of relapse from this is associated with the adequacy of coping response, such as time management skills, as well as self-efficacy towards exercise. A lack of coping response may lead to decreased efficacy and an expectation of less exercise taking place. In the case of drug use, this has been identified as a time when the pleasurable effects of the drug are highlighted. In the case of exercise, this is when rest from physical exertion might be seen as pleasurable. The 'abstinence violation effect' could lead on from this and is where the individual displays feelings of guilt and self-blame, depending on the attributions made for the relapse. For example, attributions reflecting negative personal characteristics and feelings of helplessness and lack of control will increase the probability of a sustained relapse.

Although the model presented is speculative as far as exercise is concerned, relapse prevention has been successfully applied in exercise research. King and Frederiksen (1984) demonstrated its success, alongside social support, for a small group of previously sedentary college women attempting increases and maintenance in jogging frequency. In addition, the relapse model is consistent with other exercise determinants research in having a central role for self-efficacy. Also, attributions for relapse or dropout may be important factors in determining the strength of the motivational deficit associated with relapse. These two psychological constructs should be pursued further in research on exercise resumption. However, we wish to stress the likely differences between exercise and addictive behaviours, the latter of which has been addressed more substantially in relapse research.

Can we prioritise determinants across phases of the natural history of exercise?

Having made the general point concerning the role of different determinants across the phases of exercise, is it possible to put them into any priority or pattern? We have attempted this before (see Biddle 1992) but admitted that it was for heuristic value and was in need of verification. It is not really possible to be any more optimistic today, but we still believe that an effort to identify, however crudely, the key determinants for adoption, maintenance, dropout and resumption should be attempted. Our effort is shown in Table 6.3 and is a modification of that produced in Biddle (1992) but also includes the more global categories of determinants proposed by Sallis and Hovell (1990).

A lifespan interaction model

So far we have considered two 'process' models of exercise. The SOC approach tackles exercise from the point of view of stages in individual decision-making, thus it is a dynamic model operating primarily from an ideographic approach. Sallis and Hovell's (1990) natural history model is way of viewing the dynamic process of exercise participation that could be applied to the study of determinants at a nomothetic level. In our final model, we discuss a global overview of exercise behaviours through the 'lifespan interaction model' proposed by Dishman and Dunn (1988) and refined by Dishman (1990). The model is shown in Figure 6.4.

Rather than explaining the process of exercise and physical activity involvement, it provides a useful global framework for understanding the multifactorial nature of physical activity and the factors that require investigation if understanding is to be advanced. The left segment of the model highlights three broad categories of determinants: psychological, biobehavioural and social environmental. The middle segment concerns the characteristics

Table 6.3 Possible determinants of exercise across different stages and phases of exercise and physical activity

Stages[1] →	Pre	Con	Prep action maintenance	Relapse
Phases[2] → Factors/determinants (adapted from Biddle 1992)	Adoption		Maintenance	Dropout	Resumption

	Adoption	Maintenance	Dropout	Resumption
Attitudes	**	*	*	**
Social norms	**	**	*	**
Self-efficacy/control/ competence	***	***	***	***
Personality/self-motivation	*	**	**	*
Environmental	**	**	*	**
Biological	*	**	***	*
Mental health outcomes	*	***	***	**
Self-regulatory skills	**	***	***	***
Attributions	*	*	**	***
Determinants categories (from Sallis and Hovell 1990)				
Environmental	**	**	*	**
Social	**	**	*	**
Cognitive	**	**	***	**
Physiological	*	**	***	*

Key
* some influence possible   ** expected influence   *** likely strong influence

Notes:
1 Stages: according to the transtheoretical 'stages of change' model; pre = precontemplation; con = contemplation; prep = preparation.
2 Phases: according to Sallis and Hovell's (1990) 'natural history' model.

of physical activity, such as phases of involvement, type or frequency, settings etc. The right segment highlights different population groups that may have characteristics or specific issues that interact with the other factors in the model.

The three categories of determinants are very broad and this book has really addressed primarily psychological determinants. However, the model is right to highlight other factors. Sallis and Hovell (1990) use the categories of environmental, social, cognitive, physiological and 'other personal' factors. Whatever the classification system used, it is important to recognise that determinants are multifactorial. However, the extent to which we are able to test such complex models is debatable. Taking the categories proposed by Sallis and Hovell, and their distinction between 'distal' and 'proximal' determinants, and then superimposing this onto a model including adoption, maintenance, dropout and resumption, we have a very complex system indeed! Nevertheless, this is what Dishman (1990) is really trying to highlight: the complexity of the exercise/physical activity process and thereby warning against over-simplified conclusions about why people do or

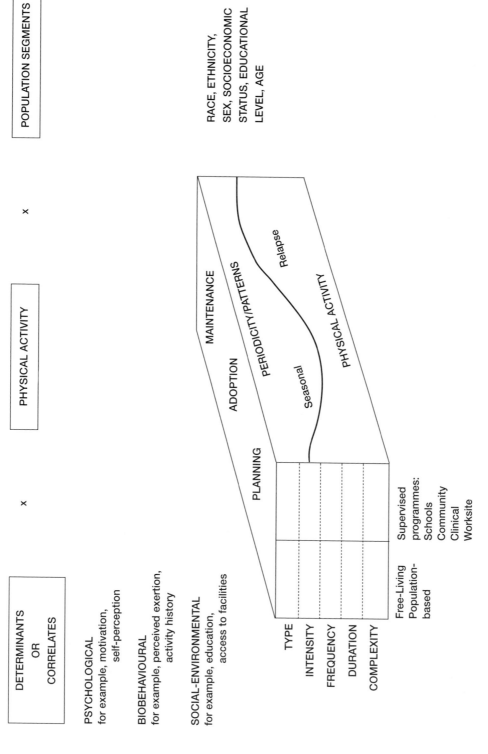

DETERMINANTS
OR
CORRELATES

PSYCHOLOGICAL
for example, motivation,
self-perception

BIOBEHAVIOURAL
for example, perceived exertion,
activity history

SOCIAL-ENVIRONMENTAL
for example, education,
access to facilities

×

PHYSICAL ACTIVITY

×

POPULATION SEGMENTS

RACE, ETHNICITY,
SEX, SOCIOECONOMIC
STATUS, EDUCATIONAL
LEVEL, AGE

PLANNING ADOPTION MAINTENANCE

PERIODICITY/PATTERNS

Relapse

Seasonal

PHYSICAL ACTIVITY

TYPE
INTENSITY
FREQUENCY
DURATION
COMPLEXITY

Free-Living
Population-
based

Supervised
programmes:
Schools
Community
Clinical
Worksite

Figure 6.4 Dishman's lifespan interaction model

do not exercise. For this reason, the lifespan interaction model, untestable though it may be, serves a useful unifying function.

Chapter summary and conclusions

The research and theorising on the psychological determinants of exercise and physical activity is becoming increasingly complex. Theories have been borrowed, adapted and developed from other branches of the psychological and behavioural sciences and, as such, there is a need to not only review the contribution of these theories to the understanding of exercise, as we have done elsewhere in this book, but also to consider the conceptual overlap, or convergence, between the theories. In addition, we need to consider more dynamic, process-oriented, approaches to exercise behaviour.

In this chapter, we have:

- Discussed the conceptual convergence between key theoretical frameworks commonly used in contemporary exercise psychology for predicting exercise and physical activity participation.
- Considered the integration of aspects of these models into a composite model that might be more predictive than any one of the current models alone.
- Reviewed and critiqued the dynamic change processes or stages that people may go through when involved in decision-making about physical activity.
- Outlined a 'natural history' model of exercise and discussed determinants appropriate for different phases of the model.
- Described a lifespan interaction model of exercise and physical activity as a useful guiding framework for understanding the complexities of exercise and physical activity determinants.

In summary, therefore, we conclude:

- There is considerable conceptual convergence between the major theoretical approaches adopted in contemporary exercise psychology, particularly those using a social-cognitive or expectancy-value approach.
- Greater convergence should be attempted in preference to 'ring fencing' theories, as some have advocated.
- Measurement problems require resolution before convergence can progress satisfactorily.
- The stages of change approach to decision-making provides an important advance on static models of exercise and physical activity determinants.
- Measures of stages and processes of change are now available and require validation across more diverse samples.
- SOC research needs to advance beyond description of predictable cross-sectional differences between stages.
- Applicability of the processes of change to exercise and physical activity is required.
- A natural history model of exercise is a useful framework for identifying key stages in exercise behaviour.
- More needs to be known about which determinants are more or less important at each of the phases of the model.
- The lifespan interaction model provides a valuable overarching model for the identification of the complex interactions determining exercise and physical activity involvement.

7 What I feel and where I am

Exercise perceptions and social environments

Thoughts have no meaning in isolation.

J. R. Eiser
(*Attitudes, chaos and the connectionist mind*, 1994)

Chapter objectives

The purpose of this chapter is to discuss concepts associated with how people view the stimulus of exercise and physical activity and how they view group exercise environments. Specifically, in this chapter we aim to:

- Discuss the role of biobehavioural issues in exercise psychology.
- Consider perceptions of, and reactions to, the stimulus of exercise.
- Highlight the importance of perceptual processing in exercise and the adoption of a social-psychobiological approach to exercise perceptions.
- Cover important issues associated with social environments in exercise.
- Discuss exercise leadership issues and models.
- Discuss the importance of group climate in the development of exercise motivation.
- Consider the role of social and family support in the encouragement of physical activity.
- Look at present and possible future research dealing with exercise group settings, and specifically group cohesion and collective efficacy.

It would be doing a disservice to the issues addressed here to refer to this chapter as a 'pot pourri' of topics, but there a number of important issues in motivation and exercise determinants research that require consideration but are either inadequately researched or require relatively brief comment. As such, we have tackled two themes under which various concepts can be dealt with. The themes concern exercise perceptions, and in particular exercise as reinforcement or punishment, and associated issues of exercise intensity and effort. Some refer to these issues as 'biobehavioural' (Dishman 1990). The second theme concerns the exercise environment and the group settings that constitute an important location for many current and potential exercisers.

Biobehavioural issues in exercise perceptions

Although earlier in this text (see Chapter 2) we cast doubt on the validity of the exact specifications of the 'psychobiological model' of exercise adherence proposed in the early 1980s, the concept of an interaction between psychological and biological factors in affecting exercise behaviours seems appropriate. Indeed, our discussion of Sallis and Hovell's (1990) natural history model of exercise in Chapter 6 included reference to the likely reinforcing and punishing aspects of exercise as determinants, and Sallis and Hovell themselves advocate strongly such a learning theory approach. Reviews of exercise determinants have also shown that aspects of physical activity, such as exercise intensity, may be associated with adherence (Dishman and Sallis 1994). We can even support a biobehavioural approach with reference to school physical education. Why else is exercise sometimes used as punishment – against our advice (see Box 7.1) – if teachers don't know that physical activity can have aversive as well as rewarding outcomes?

Box 7.1 Exercise as punishment: Last one in – ten press-ups!

Those of you who have taught exercise classes, and certainly those who have taught children, will likely have used exercise as punishment, or, if you prefer, for motivation! Go on, admit it – we have in the past but don't now! Rather than feel guilty about it, let's analyse the situation.

   For years, in places like the military and schools, exercise has been used as an aversive experience and yet, at the same time, we hear all about the good qualities of exercise and the need to encourage it! What a contradiction! It is likely that if members of the public were asked what they thought of 'cross-country running' or 'press-ups' they would give quite negative replies. It seems to make perfect sense to us, as psychologists and exercise promoters, that if we wish to encourage exercise we need to make the exercise experience as positive and reinforcing as possible. This means never allowing the association between exercise and pain/punishment to be established.

   If you need to punish someone, but believe in the benefits of exercise, try something other than exercise. It makes good psychological sense.

Hackfort (1994: 178), in a critical review of the literature on exercise and mental health, says 'that not only the objective person–task–environment constellation has to be taken into account from a psychology perspective but also the subjective representation (perception, evaluation), which also is a determinant for intentional behavior'. In short, it is clear that biological factors, and certainly perceptions of biological factors, can affect exercise participation. The most obvious physical parameter of exercise that is likely to affect perceptions of the exercise experience is that of exercise intensity.

Perceptions and preferences of effort and intensity

The rating of 'effort sense' (ratings of perceived exertion or 'RPE') has received considerable attention as a result of the work of Gunnar Borg and the use of his RPE scales. Effort ratings have been used in field and laboratory settings with exercising participants for the verbal reporting of a number read from a scale representing the continuum of effort from minimal to maximal. However, while the use of effort ratings has been reported as a reliable index of the metabolic cost of exercise (Borg 1998), about 30 per cent of the variance between RPE and physiological parameters remains unexplained (Dishman and Landy 1988; Williams and Eston 1989). This suggests that further investigation is warranted into the psychological mechanisms of effort perceptions. This is supported by Rejeski and Thompson (1993: 18) who mentioned exceptions to the 'exclusive physiological orientation' of the RPE construct, such as research that has shown that psychological factors can affect RPE (Noble and Robertson 1996; Robertson and Noble 1997).

Rejeski himself (Rejeski 1981; 1985) developed a broader psychological view of RPE. His 1981 review was written to 'underscore the fact that exertional responses are *not* analogous to muscle reflexes or amenable to a strict psychophysical paradigm. Rather, psychological dispositions and social-cognitive variables constitute potent mediating mechanisms in the perceived sense of effort' (Rejeski and Thompson 1993: 18). Similarly, Dishman and Landy (1988: 314) speculate that 'although day-to-day fluctuation in exercise tolerance might be explained as physiological or biochemical variation, it is reasonable to suppose that cognitive and affective variables also play a major psychobiological role in such changes'.

The area of cognitive mediation in exercise perceptions, therefore, is important. Personality research suggests that pain tolerance differs between introverts and extraverts, with the latter demonstrating higher tolerance. However, no differences have been found in pain tolerance between different sport or activity groups, and there are no studies on the relationship between pain and exercise adoption, maintenance or resumption (O'Connor and Cook 1999).

Self-presentational issues may also affect exercise behaviour. For example, it has been suggested that individuals high in public self-consciousness may report lower RPEs in an effort to present a more favourable social image. Hardy, Hall and Prestholdt (1986) did find that RPEs were lower when exercising with another person present. This was also found to be true when the coacting exerciser exhibited non-verbal signs that the exercise intensity was low.

Individual differences in RPE have also been reported when those differing in sex-role perception have been studied and this presents a most intriguing line of investigation. Social psychologists have often used psychometric scales to measure the extent individuals endorse predominantly masculine characteristics in describing themselves, predominantly feminine characteristics, or a mixture of both (Bem 1974). When both characteristics are equally strongly endorsed, people are described as being androgynous and are thought to have a propensity for flexible sex-role behaviour in the light of gender-related cues and thus be less prone to sex-role stereotypic behaviour.

Rejeski and his co-workers have studied this issue in relation to exercise intensity. Based on his social psychophysiological model of effort perception, Rejeski (1981) has proposed that exercise tolerance may partly be related to past experience with fatigue and the social context of the behaviour. This suggests that those with limited experience of exercise fatigue or those who are inhibited by the social situation of physical exercise (for example, believe that the exercise is sex-role 'inappropriate') will inflate effort ratings. This was supported by Hochstetler, Rejeski and Best (1985). They had women run on the treadmill for thirty minutes at 70 per cent of $VO_{2\ max}$ and they recorded RPEs at five-minute intervals, plus a number of related physiological variables. Three groups were created as a result of psychometric assessment of sex-role orientation: masculine-typed, feminine-typed and androgynous. Results showed that greater RPEs were reported by feminine-typed women compared with the other two groups. Also, the feminine-typed group reported greater unease and less self-assurance prior to the run than the other groups. Despite some methodological problems these data provide interesting directions for future work on social psychology and exercise intensity.

Rejeski and Sanford (1984) studied RPE during cycle ergometry for feminine-typed females. However, in addition to having women pedal for twenty minutes at 80 per cent $VO_{2\,max}$, they were shown a video of a model participating in the task. The model was either showing signs of exercise tolerance or intolerance. The results showed that higher RPEs were reported by those who were shown the intolerant model, again suggesting the importance of social cues in exercise intensity perceptions. To what extent this reaction is unique to feminine females is not possible to ascertain.

These studies point to a wider perspective on exercise prescription and adherence. Instead of rigid compliance to physiological guidelines, it may be appropriate to consider affective and cognitive factors too, such as exertion preferences in addition to exertion perceptions. It may be important, as Hardy and Rejeski (1989) suggest, not just to look at *what* one feels during exercise but *how* one feels. In other words, similar RPEs may have different meaning for different individuals.

Hardy and Rejeski (1989) report the use of a 'Feeling Scale' (FS) to assess affective reactions during exercise. RPE and FS were moderately correlated but overall the results showed that feelings about exercise intensity are not identical to perceptions of effort loading, although the two constructs become more similar with increasing workloads. Similarly, Parfitt, Markland and Holmes (1994) found that physically active participants reported more positive feelings, using the FS, after a bout of exercise at 90 per cent workload than inactive participants, but such a difference was not evident at a 60 per cent workload.

Physiologically-driven guidelines for optimal fitness development have dominated the field of exercise prescription yet these may need to be reviewed from a behavioural point of view. Dishman suggests that 'the optimal volume of exercise for promoting adherence and health outcomes remains to be identified. Not only may rigid prescriptions be too behaviorally challenging for some, they may not be biologically necessary' (Dishman 1988a: 53). The move to accepting more moderate levels of exercise as health promoting may alleviate this problem.

Until recently little was known about the reactions of exercisers to different intensities of exercise. Steptoe and co-workers have studied this and, although similar work will be discussed later when we consider the psychological outcomes of exercise in more detail, Steptoe's results also shed light on the issue on the biobehavioural issues of adherence (Steptoe and Bolton 1988; Steptoe and Cox 1988).

Steptoe and Cox (1988) studied the effect of acute aerobic exercise on mood using female medical students aged 18 to 23 years. Four eight-minute trials of exercise were carried out by each participant with two at a 'high' intensity (2kg/100W) and two at a 'low' intensity (0.5kg/25W). Participants were also classified as 'fit' or 'unfit' based on their heart rate response to exercise. Mood was assessed before and after each trial. The results showed that exercise intensity related to post-exercise mood. Specifically, the high intensity condition produced elevated levels of tension-anxiety, while the low intensity condition produced elevated levels of vigour and exhilaration. These mood changes were largely unaffected by physical fitness levels.

This study was partially replicated by Steptoe and Bolton (1988). Female students were studied in both high (100W) and low (25W) exercise intensity conditions. Mood states were assessed before and after fifteen minute exercise bouts on a cycle ergometer. Results showed that anxiety reduced significantly from pre-exercise levels when assessed at six and twelve minutes into the exercise period, but only for those in the low intensity condition. Increases in tension-anxiety scores from the Profile of Mood States (POMS) for the high intensity group were also found, thus supporting Steptoe and Cox (1988).

These results show that positive mood changes are evident only with lower exercise intensities. This is an important finding for exercise adherence and strongly supports the notion of carefully graded exercise experiences for novices. Steptoe and Bolton conclude by saying that 'it may be that particular schedules can be devised that lead to immediate positive mood responses, and that these will in turn promote greater uptake and adherence to exercise programmes' (Steptoe and Bolton 1988: 104–5). One note of caution, however, is that while more positive affect was noted for lower exercise intensities, it is possible that moderate and higher intensity exercise groups reported positive feelings after further recovery.

Is there a dose-response relationship in exercise for psychological responses?

In concluding our discussion of biobehavioural issues associated with exercise adherence and determinants, we wish to consider the dose-response relationship from a psychological point of view. Although this has already been done ably by Rejeski (1994) and Ekkekakis and Petruzzello (1999), it is necessary to revisit some issues.

The objective of the chapter so far has been to alert readers to the important role of perceptions in physical activity and exercise, rather than just accept a biological or reductionist approach to exercise. Consequently, various social psychological issues have been raised. However, given that much of the biological data in exercise research support a dose-response relationship is this also the case for psychological factors? Rejeski concludes 'it is premature to reach any definitive conclusions regarding the effects of varying doses of acute and chronic exercise on psychological outcomes' (Rejeski 1994: 1052). This would appear to be consistent with the issues discussed, such as sex-role perceptions, self-presentation and effort perceptions. All show marked individual differences suggestive of strong psychological and social psychological interactions with the biological markers of activity, hence the need to study exercise from a biopsychosocial interaction perspective. As Rejeski says:

> when people exercise they are doing far more than simply moving physically. As numerous studies suggest, the social environment provided with exercise training (e.g., enjoyment, peer support, or interactions with exercise leaders) may be as important to psychosocial outcomes as the activity itself.
>
> (Rejeski 1994: 1053)

So it appears too simple to attempt to reduce psychological responses to exercise to a simple dose-response gradient but, instead, continue the search for important social psychological influences on exercise behaviours and determinants. As such, our discussion will now address some important social environmental issues of adherence and determinants.

Social environments and exercise

A great deal of structured exercise takes place in a social context, such as an exercise class or public facility. Consequently, the role of social environmental factors may be important in furthering our understanding of exercise determinants. Indeed, as already discussed, self-presentational factors have been shown to influence individual perceptions of the exercise stimulus. Also, common sense notions in fitness classes will support the important role of the exercise environment, including the class leader.

Exercise leadership

Surprisingly little has been written about the role of the exercise leader, at least from the point of view of research findings, yet for this type of exercise setting, the leader could be the single most influential factor for adherence. The growth of 'personal trainers' is support for the motivational role of an exercise leader.

Weber and Wertheim (1989) investigated the influence of staff attention on the adherence patterns of new recruits to a community gymnasium in Australia. The fifty-five women, on arrival at the exercise facility, were randomly allocated to one of three groups: control, self-monitoring of gym attendance and self-monitoring plus extra staff attention. Over a twelve-week period it was found that attendance was highest for the self-monitoring group and lowest for the control group. However, the attendance of the self-monitoring plus staff attention group, although slightly better than the control, was not significantly superior. The intervention based on the exercise leader, therefore, was not successful over and above that of self-monitoring. It may be that trying to identify one set of successful leadership behaviours in health-related exercise will prove as unfruitful as in other contexts, including sport, due to the complex interaction between personal and environmental factors. Nevertheless, exercise leaders will almost certainly be important individuals in helping exercisers maintain participation.

In contrast to the paucity of information concerning exercise leaders, a great deal has been said on the role of leadership in sport settings (Chelladurai 1993). After initial, and somewhat unsuccessful, attempts to identify leadership 'types' through personality profiling, leadership research in sport has supported two main approaches. First, there is the 'situational' approach advocated by Ronald Smith and Frank Smoll whereby they propose a set of 'universal' behaviours associated with good coaching (Carron and Hausenblas 1998; Smith and Smoll 1996; Smith, Smoll and Curtis 1979). These characteristics can be modified with training and are observable through the 'coaching behavior assessment system' (CBAS). The CBAS involves observers noting the 'reactive' and 'spontaneous' behaviours of coaches, usually in youth sport settings.

The second approach to sport leadership has been an interactional and multidimensional one proposed by Chelladurai (1993). His model is based on the premise that there are antecedents to leader behaviour, such as situational, leader and group member characteristics, different dimensions of leader behaviour, such as required, actual and preferred behaviours, and finally, there are consequences of these interactions for behaviour and satisfaction. The model is shown in Figure 7.1.

The important point about Chelladurai's model is that it allows for different aspects of leadership to be considered. Not only is the actual behaviour of the leader included, but so is the behaviour required of the situation, and the behaviour preferred by the group members. Chelladurai developed a psychometric scale for the assessment of preferred leadership behaviours through the 'Leadership Scale for Sports' (LSS) (Chelladurai and Saleh 1980). Although this scale has not been applied to exercise, the point has already been made that the perceptions and preferences of individuals in the exercise context may be crucial for adherence. The application of the LSS to exercise, at least in principle, is clear to see. For example, one of the dimensions of the LSS is 'training and instruction'. This refers to the extent to which people prefer coaching behaviour aimed at strenuous and hard training with

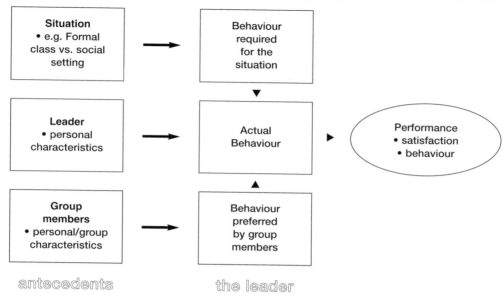

Figure 7.1 Modified version of Chelladurai's multidimensional model of leadership

the intent of improving performance. While this might be wholly appropriate and desired by some individuals in exercise, others will find that form of exercise leadership aversive. Another subscale from the LSS refers to 'social support'. This is the extent to which individuals prefer their coaches to be concerned about the welfare of the group members and to create good interpersonal relations within the group. This is likely to be a very important factor for some exercise classes.

The application of leadership theory from sport to exercise is long overdue. Chelladurai's model may be a suitable start although the applicability of all of the LSS subscales to exercise will require scrutiny. However, the importance of exercise leadership is clear to see and will feature in future exercise psychology studies (Carron, Hausenblas and Estabrooks 1999).

Group climate and exercise motivation

Closely related to the issue of leadership is that of the climate, or atmosphere, created within the exercise group. In Chapter 4 we discussed the role of individual perceptions of success – 'goal orientations' – and showed how they were related to motivation. A similar line of research has evolved concerning individual perceptions of the group climate. This work started in classroom environments (Ames and Archer 1988) and has now been extended to include sport and physical education settings (Biddle *et al.* 1995; Duda and Whitehead 1998; Ntoumanis and Biddle 1999a; Papaioannou 1995; Papaioannou and Goudas 1999), but little has been said about health-related exercise contexts for adults. This would appear to be an important direction for the future.

Individual achievement goals have referred to mastery/task and ego/comparative elements. Perceptions of the 'motivational climate' can be categorised as 'mastery' or 'performance'. A mastery climate is one in which the group members perceive that the dominant ethos is one of self-improvement, where mistakes are viewed as part of learning, and praise may be given for high effort regardless of the actual outcome. A 'performance' climate, however, is one where students are often compared to each other, where praise will usually only be given for normatively superior performance, and where anxiety is often felt about making mistakes.

Biddle *et al.* (1995) and Papaioannou (1994) have worked on the development of psychometric scales for the measurement of class climate in physical education. Papaioannou (1994) was the first to assess PE class goals by developing the 'learning and performance orientations in PE classes questionnaire' (LAPOPECQ) from data on over 1,700 Greek school students. The questionnaire comprised the two higher-order constructs of learning (mastery) and performance, and were underpinned by subscales assessing:

- Learning: 'teacher-initiated learning orientation'; 'students' learning orientation'.
- Performance: 'students' competitive orientation'; 'students' worries about mistakes'; 'outcome orientation without effort'.

We modified this slightly to construct a questionnaire comprising four mastery and two performance subscales (Biddle *et al.* 1995; Goudas and Biddle 1994). The mastery subscales were: 'class mastery orientation', 'teachers' promotion of mastery orientation', 'student perception of choice', and 'teacher support'. The performance subscales were 'class performance orientation' and 'worries about mistakes'. Similarly, translation and further scale development in French also resulted in two higher-order constructs of learning and performance/comparison (Biddle *et al.* 1995).

Ames and Archer (1988), in a classroom study, found that students' perceptions of class mastery goals were positively related to attitudes towards their class, a preference for challenging tasks, and to the use of effective learning strategies. Conversely, perceptions of a performance climate were associated with maladaptive motivational patterns, such as attributing failure to lack of ability. Similarly, Seifriz, Duda and Chi's (1992) study of motivational climate in basketball teams found that team mastery goals were associated with higher intrinsic motivation and beliefs that sport success was the result of trying hard. Intrinsic motivation was also correlated with mastery climate perceptions in a study of British (Goudas and Biddle 1994) and Greek (Papaioannou 1994) physical education classes. Similarly, analysis of two PE activities for the same group of children showed that perceptions of a mastery class climate were good predictors, either directly or indirectly through individual task goals and perceptions of autonomy, of intrinsic interest and future intentions to participate (Biddle *et al.* 1995).

In an intervention study, we manipulated the teaching style offered to a class of girls being taught track and field athletics (Goudas *et al.* 1995). It was found that motivation was consistently higher in the classes taught with a style that included more student choice, itself a dimension of a mastery climate. Interventions to change the climate of groups and classes, therefore, should be possible and a future avenue for exercise research.

A recent meta-analysis of climate studies across all physical activity settings quantified the links between climates and positive psychological outcomes (such as satisfaction, intrinsic motivation and positive emotion) and negative psychological outcomes (such as anxiety and boredom) (Ntoumanis and Biddle 1999a). The overall effects from fourteen studies (n = 4,484) showed a large effect for mastery climate on positive outcomes, a moderate effect for performance climate on negative outcomes, and small-to-medium effects for performance climate on positive outcomes and mastery climate on negative outcomes. The effect sizes are shown in Figure 7.2.

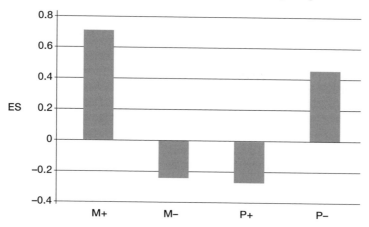

Figure 7.2 Effect sizes from a meta-analysis of motivational climate in physical activity showing relationships between mastery and performance climates and positive and negative psychological outcomes (Ntoumanis and Biddle 1999a)

Note: correlations have been corrected for measurement and sampling error.
Key: M: mastery climate; P: performance climate; +: positive psychological outcomes (for example, enjoyment); –: negative psychological outcomes (for example, anxiety).

In summary, the lead given by researchers investigating group climates in educational and sport settings provides a good platform for exercise researchers. The anecdotal recognition of the importance of exercise class climate now requires verification through research. Although group exercise settings are not necessarily the best ways of promoting mass participation in exercise across the community, they provide an important setting for exercise for many people. In discussing the possibilities for studying exercise motivational climate, Ntoumanis and Biddle say:

> When using or developing scales for this area of research, elements unique to the exercise context should be included, such as items relating to the perception of social norms associated with fitness or body appearance. For example, it would be relevant to know whether instructors in exercises classes stress individual improvement in fitness or whether they promote interpersonal comparison.
>
> (Ntoumanis and Biddle 1999a: 662)

Social and family support of physical activity

In addition to the role of group environments, where interpersonal relationships may be weak or transient, an important area for consideration for the social psychology of exercise is that of close social support. Again, this has not been studied extensively in exercise and remains an area for development.

In health psychology, social support has been studied and found to be beneficial for health and well-being, such as stress control (Stroebe and Stroebe 1995). However, from the point of view of exercise determinants, we are defining social support in motivational terms in respect of the social influence of people on the physical activity patterns of others. Sheridan and Radmacher (1992: 156), for example, define social support as 'the resources

---

Box 7.2 Creating the right environment for GP referral exercise patients

In the UK over the past decade there has been a tremendous increase in the number of 'GP-referral' exercise schemes (GP: 'general practitioner' – family doctor). During the latter part of 1993 and the first few months of 1994, one of us (SB), along with colleagues Ken Fox and Laurel Edmunds (Fox *et al.* 1997), conducted a review of GP-referral exercise schemes throughout England. In addition to telephone and mailed survey data, we conducted eleven case study visits throughout the country.

One of the factors that clearly had been addressed in some community sports/leisure centres was the need to create the 'right' environment for a group of people not used to using such facilities. One centre manager was very aware of this and had changed the lighting and the music in the fitness room to accommodate this new client group. They even enlarged the cycle seats to accommodate a new type of physique!

This case study was illustrative of facility managers becoming aware of the need to create a motivational climate that was suitable for a specific group. Further interviews with the patients themselves confirmed the importance of this and of the need to change the 'young/sporty' image of the facilities if older patient groups were to be accommodated properly.

---

provided to us through our interactions with other people'. As discussed in Chapter 5 on attitude theories, the concept of 'subjective norms' in the Theories of Reasoned Action and Planned Behaviour approximates social support, although the two constructs are not identical.

Modelling and adult encouragement

Social support is usually seen in terms of emotional, informational and material support (Stroebe and Stroebe 1995; Taylor *et al.* 1994), and Table 7.1 shows the possible role of each in exercise. However, although some data exist on the family aggregation of physical activity, suggestive of a social influence effect, there is little data to guide us on social support mechanisms in adult exercise settings. Taylor *et al.* conclude:

> studies with children of different ages, with families of different ethnic backgrounds, and with different methods of assessing physical activity consistently found significant familial resemblance in activity habits. The studies with the most reliable and valid methods . . . demonstrated significant familial associations, with most correlations in the range of .3 to .5.
>
> (Taylor *et al.* 1994: 320)

The exact reasons for such a relationship are still unclear and could be explained through several competing hypotheses.

Social support, however, is not always positive from the point of view of physical activity. Many parents are concerned about the safety of their children and, as such, actively prevent them from taking some forms of physical activity. The two most obvious are cycling on busy

Table 7.1 Types of social support and examples from exercise and physical activity

Type of social support	Example
Emotional support	Empathy from others in your attempt to be physically active. You feel that they 'are on your side'.
Informational support	Information and advice is given by others concerning exercise, such as details of a local running event.
Material (instrumental) support	Direct help, such as driving children to a sports centre or buying them a bicycle for transportation to school.

roads and walking or playing in areas where they perceive a risk of physical attack. In both cases, motorised transport is likely to be used instead of physical activity, such as for getting to school. For understandable reasons, therefore, the social influence of parents could be detrimental to children's physical activity.

Box 7.3 The influence of fashion over safety in cycling

A good illustration of the role of social influence in exercise is the recent conversion of many people, in the UK at least, to the wearing of safety helmets while cycling. Only a few years ago, children considered them 'silly' and were embarrassed to wear them. However, they gradually became fashionable, along with other colourful and trendy cycle-wear. It is our belief, therefore, that the increase in cycle helmets is more to do with fashion and social influence of peers than concern over safety, although the latter may well have helped.

The literature on modelling effects in physical activity largely deals with observational learning of motor skills. Although modelling has been identified as an important construct in Bandura's social cognitive theory, and specifically as a source of self-efficacy (Bandura 1997; see this text, Chapter 4), little is known about the role of modelling in the development of active lifestyles for children or adults. Indeed, the limited data available are not clear. This probably reflects the low levels of physical activity of adults anyway and hence their influence on children's physical activity, in terms of modelling, is likely to be limited. It would appear to make more sense to look at various adult models, including teachers, since most children and youth will have considerable exposure to these as models. For this reason, we tested the relationships between adult encouragement of physical activity, other social cognitive variables, and self-reported strenuous physical activity among boys and girls aged 13–14 years (Biddle and Goudas 1996). In this cross-sectional survey we found physical activity correlated with 'adult encouragement' ($r = 0.37$) more than other variables. In a path analysis, we found that adult encouragement directly predicted intentions to be active in the future, as well as current strenuous physical activity. It also predicted strenuous activity indirectly through perceived sport competence.

Sallis (1998) has reviewed the evidence for the effectiveness of family interventions in increasing the physical activity of youth. Studies with healthy youth using educational methods have been unsuccessful in changing physical activity levels. However, more success has been reported with behaviour modification techniques used with obese young people (Epstein, Koeske and Wing 1984).

Further work is required, however, to tease out the differential influence of adults at different stages in childhood. For example, when do teachers influence children more than parents, if at all? What, if any, are the gender effects between children and adult modelling? The literature has portrayed a confused picture on this issue. When do parents have less influence than peers? Future studies should investigate these social influence issues, particularly given the paucity of data on children's physical activity determinants. Until we have a clearer picture, it may be best to support a commonsense approach, such as that of the Centres for Disease Control and Prevention (1997) who recommend that parents and guardians are included in activity instruction and programmes and are encouraged to support their children's participation.

Group cohesion and collective efficacy in exercise

Having discussed leadership and perceptions of group climate, as well as likely social influence variables in exercise, it is also important to consider factors associated with exercise group cohesion and collective efficacy. Indeed, Franklin (1988) has proposed that a lack of group spirit is likely to predispose people to drop out of group exercise programmes. Carron *et al.* state their case in stronger terms: 'the need for interpersonal attachment is a fundamental human motive – a fact that has important implications or promoting adherence in exercise and physical activity' (Carron *et al.* 1999: 4). It appears that strategies designed to increase adherence should include the encouragement of group participation.

Exercise group cohesion

The study of group dynamics, cohesion and individual adherence to group activities, such as exercise, is an important line of research if we are interested in structured exercise contexts. Although group cohesion is a very old topic of research and discussion in psychology, it has not been studied in exercise until quite recently.

Cohesion is defined as the forces attracting members to remain in the group as well as forces preventing group disruption (Carron and Hausenblas 1998). Two areas of investigation have dominated the research on group cohesion in sport: the measurement of group cohesion and the relationship between cohesion and performance. Group cohesion is nearly always considered important in sport yet whether it is important for exercise, where group performance is rarely a desired outcome, remains to be seen. However, it is likely that some aspects of cohesion, such as group attraction, could influence adherence patterns.

Carron, Widmeyer and Brawley (1988) continued their research programme on group cohesion in sport (Carron and Hausenblas 1998; Carron *et al.* 1999; Widmeyer, Brawley and Carron 1985; Widmeyer, Carron and Brawley 1993) by investigating cohesion and adherence in fitness and recreation contexts. Carron *et al.* (1988) looked at fitness class adherers and non-adherers as well as elite sport adherers and non-adherers. These four groups were assessed using the Group Environment Questionnaire (GEQ) (Widmeyer *et al.* 1985). The GEQ is a self-report instrument yielding scores on four subscales: individual attraction to the group – task (ATG–T), individual attraction to the group – social (ATG–S), group integration – task (GI–T), and group integration – social (GI–S). Slight modification was made to the GEQ to allow it to be administered to the fitness groups since the original scale was written for sport groups. Analysis of the fitness group scores showed that two of the GEQ variables significantly discriminated adherers from non-adherers. Specifically, adherers had higher scores on both ATG subscales thus showing that dropouts were less personally attracted to the group's task and to the group as a social unit.

In a meta-analysis by Carron, Hausenblas and Mack (1996), small-to-moderate effects were found between social influence variables and exercise behaviours. Key findings from the meta-analysis are:

- Moderate effects were found for exercise adherence for the variables of task cohesion, the exercise class leader, and social support from important others and family.
- Intention to exercise and exercise affect were positively associated with family and important others.
- Support from family members was stronger when involving exercise prescription from a health professional in comparison to other exercise programmes.

Considerably more work is required, however, in understanding the nature and extent of social psychological variables of the group and exercise adherence. The following issues require attention:

- The type of exercise may be crucial. Studies on diverse activities such as distance running, weight training and aerobic exercise-to-music may reveal different results.
- The type of participant and exercise leader are important ingredients in this type of research. Although it is usual to encourage sedentary people to take part in exercise with a partner or in groups, much more needs to be known before specific advice about the nature of such group factors and exercise adherence can be made. For example, it is now common for exercise-to-music classes to consist of more than fifty people. We know little about the motivational effects of being in such a large group, the concomitant lack of individualised instruction and attention, or whether these are unimportant given enjoyable exercises and motivating music. Alternatively, the anonymity of exercising in a large group may be perceived as a positive feature for some people from the point of view of reducing self-presentational pressures, yet the degree of social loafing in large groups is likely to be quite high. Group size, therefore, requires further investigation.
- Although a group environment may be perceived positively in the short term, longer term adherence to exercise may suffer if individual behavioural skills are not taught or learned, particularly if the exercise group ceases after a period of time. Typically, exercise prescriptions in supervised settings work on 10–12 week schedules.
- The GEQ was developed from a conceptual model of sport group cohesion. Half of the GEQ is concerned with group task aspects. The extent to which exercise groups perceive themselves to have a 'task' is debatable. Further work is required on group cohesion measurement in exercise.

Carron *et al.* (1999) propose some principles for promoting group adherence in exercise, such as:

- Distinctiveness: feelings of group distinctiveness, such as wearing group T-shirts or logos, can increase feelings of cohesion.
- Group norms: cohesion can increase by having group members share common expectations.
- Interaction and communication: cohesion and interaction between members of the group are positively correlated.

Exercise group efficacy

The literature on the determinants of individual participation in exercise and physical activity is quite clear in identifying self-efficacy as a consistent and important determinant (see Chapter 4). However, recently the concept of group, or collective, efficacy has been proposed for the study of group motivation. For example, Bandura says 'people do not live their lives in social isolation. Many of the challenges and difficulties they face reflect group problems requiring sustained collective effort to produce any significant change' (Bandura 1986: 449). Bandura suggests that collective efficacy will influence group motivation by affecting what people do, how much effort is exerted, and their motivation in adverse circumstances, such as group failure. Interestingly, Bandura (1986: 449) does not see self-efficacy as divorced from collective efficacy, but rather collective efficacy is rooted in self-efficacy: 'inveterate self-doubters are not easily forged into a collective efficacious force'.

As with group cohesion, one can see the relevance of collective efficacy for sport groups (George and Feltz 1995). However, whether some exercise groups require collective efficacy is likely to be variable. Nevertheless, it is another area that needs to be considered, and we have identified the following two areas of investigation associated with exercise motivation:

- What is the relationship, within exercise groups and classes, between collective efficacy and group and personal goal-setting? The favourable influence of goal-setting has been recognised by many researchers and the group effect may be important for some individuals.
- What effect might collective efficacy have in exercise classes on the attributions made for success and failure? For example, would classes high in collective efficacy be more likely to attribute group 'failure' to unstable controllable factors, thus making them more amenable to change?

These issues, and others, suggest that the study of collective efficacy might be an important direction for the future. Certainly it is currently understudied yet has potential.

Chapter summary and conclusions

This chapter has considered a range of issues associated with perceptions of exercise, from both biobehavioural and social psychological points of view. Specifically, in this chapter we have:

- Discussed the importance of individual perceptions of the exercise stimulus.
- Shown how leadership and group climate need to be considered in exercise motivation theory and practice.
- Considered the issue of social influence in physical activity and discussed directions for future research.
- Discussed the potential of studying group cohesion and efficacy in furthering our understanding of exercise groups.

In summary, therefore, we conclude:

- That the psychological and perceptual responses of individuals to the stimulus of exercise is not uniform.

- A number of factors influence how people perceive the intensity of exercise, possibly including personality, sex-role orientation and self-presentational influences.
- Feelings about exercise intensity are not identical to perceptions of effort loading.
- Mood state reactions to the exercise stimulus appear to be more favourable for moderate, rather than high, intensity exercise, at least in the short term.
- A dose-response relationship between exercise and psychological responses does not seem appropriate given clear individual differences in perceptions of exercise.
- Insufficient evidence is available to conclude about the most appropriate way of studying exercise leadership, but research in sport settings suggests that Chelladurai's multidimensional model of leadership has many characteristics that might be appropriate for future research in exercise.
- Extrapolating from studies in sport and physical education, mainly with children, the development of a mastery motivational climate in exercise classes and groups appears to be desirable for motivational and other positive psychological outcomes.
- Evidence exists of familial aggregation of physical activity, but the role of parental and other adult encouragement is less clear.
- Research on group cohesion has shown that exercise group dropouts have lower perceptions of cohesion than those who stay. However, the direct applicability of a conceptual model of group cohesion developed for sport requires further testing in exercise.
- There is a positive relationship between exercise behaviour and some social influence variables, such as family support.
- The notion of collective efficacy in exercise groups is presently untested, although remains a viable area of study for the future.

Part III

Psychological outcomes of physical activity

8 The feel-good factor

Physical activity and psychological well-being

Exercise dissipates tension, and tension is the enemy of serenity.

Nelson Mandela
(*Long walk to freedom*, 1994)

Chapter objectives

The purpose of this chapter is to review the evidence on the relationship between participation in physical activity and exercise and psychological well-being (PWB). Specifically, we review the areas of mood and affect, including enjoyment; self-esteem; anxiety and stress reactivity; non-clinical depression; cognitive functioning; personality and adjustment; and sleep. Specifically, in this chapter we aim to:

- Highlight the concept of health-related quality of life and how it is typically measured.
- Review the evidence linking physical activity and exercise with measures of mood and affect.
- Highlight the definitional problems associated with the construct of enjoyment in exercise and present four approaches to the study of enjoyment in physical activity.
- Comment on the psychological effects of depriving people of exercise.
- Provide evidence on factors moderating the relationship between exercise and mood/affect.
- Summarise the evidence linking physical activity with the development and enhancement of self-esteem and physical self-perceptions.
- Review the findings from investigations of exercise and anxiety responses, including physiological reactivity to psychosocial stressors for people differing in fitness.
- Summarise the evidence linking exercise with non-clinical states of depression.
- Comment on studies investigating the links between exercise and cognitive functioning, and exercise and personality/psychological adjustment.
- Briefly highlight results from meta-analyses on the effect of exercise on sleep.

A case was made in Chapter 1 for the diverse health benefits of a physically active lifestyle. However, although there is plenty of anecdotal support for the view that physical activity has positive effects on psychological well-being, the emphasis is often placed more firmly on the physical outcomes. Nevertheless, the publication of health-related documents in England by the British Government in the 1990s (Department of

Health 1993b) marked a significant change in approach in healthcare and promotion in England and placed greater emphasis on aspects of well-being. The overall aims of *The Health of the Nation: A strategy for health for England* (HON) (Department of Health 1993b) were:

- 'Adding years to life': reduce premature mortality and improve life expectancy.
- 'Adding life to years': improve the quality of life.

This is also reflected in the national 'Active for Life' campaign in England promoted by the Health Education Authority. Similarly, the influential Surgeon General's report on physical activity and health in the United States (Department of Health and Human Services 1996) recognises the importance of physical activity for well-being as well as disease prevention.

The promotion of health through physical activity and exercise, therefore, now incorporates the recognition of the importance of psychological well-being. This chapter reviews the evidence on the links between physical activity and psychological well-being.

Evidence has been drawn from an extensive literature. Narrative and meta-analytic reviews, epidemiological surveys, and controlled trials are reviewed in an effort to reach conclusions from varied approaches. In addition, we will discuss a range of topics associated with psychological well-being, including:

- health-related quality of life
- emotion and mood
- enjoyment
- exercise deprivation
- self-esteem
- anxiety and reactivity to stress
- non-clinical depression
- personality and psychological adjustment
- exercise and sleep.

Health-related quality of life

Rejeski, Brawley and Shumaker (1996) suggest that it is typical for health-related quality of life (HRQL) to be defined in terms of participants' perceptions of function. They outline six types of HRQL measures:

- Global indices of HRQL: these might include general life satisfaction, or self-esteem.
- Physical function: perceptions of function; physical self-perceptions; health-related perceptions.
- Physical symptoms: fatigue; energy; sleep.
- Emotional function: depression, anxiety, mood, affect, emotion.
- Social function: social dependency; family/work roles.
- Cognitive function: memory; attention; problem-solving.

Rejeski *et al.* (1996) state that the National Institutes of Health in the USA now mandate researchers to include measures of HRQL in most clinical trials. However, HRQL measures are usually viewed simply in terms of physical function and this is a narrow view. There are many HRQL instruments and these include affective measures. Some (Muldoon *et al.* 1998) suggest a simple division of HRQL into functional measures and those assessing quality of life.

Key HRQL measures include the SF-36, the Nottingham Health Profile (Hunt, McEwan and McKenna 1986) and the EuroQol (Buxton, O'Hanlon and Rushby 1990; Buxton *et al.* 1992). The SF-36 is the best known measure and is a thirty-six-item questionnaire designed to assess eight health dimensions covering functional status, well-being, and overall evaluation of health (Dixon *et al.* 1994). Dixon *et al.* (1994) conclude that the SF-36 is not designed for specific patient groups, is not directly based on lay views and has little evidence that it detects change. An over-reliance on the use of the SF-36 in HRQL studies is unadvisable and, where possible, more specific measures should be sought.

Rejeski *et al.* (1996) provide a comprehensive review of HRQL and physical activity (PA) and offer the following conclusions:

- HRQL test batteries should include general and condition- or population-specific measures.
- The degree of change observed in HRQL through physical activity will depend on baseline levels.
- The degree of impact of physical activity on HRQL will depend on both the physiological stimulus as well as social and behavioural characteristics of the treatment or intervention.
- People vary in the extent to which they value certain health-related outcomes from physical activity, hence this will affect HRQL perceptions of those in intervention studies.

HRQL, therefore, includes an affective dimension that requires further consideration, such as through measures of mood, self-esteem, anxiety, and depression.

Emotion and mood

The mood states and emotions associated with exercise have a potentially important role in physical activity and health promotion. If we believe that physical activity is a positive health behaviour to be encouraged and promoted, how people feel during and after activity may be critical in determining whether they maintain their involvement. This means that the extensive discussion in earlier chapters concerning motivation and adherence cannot be divorced from aspects of psychological well-being. Emotion and mood may have motivational properties for an important health-related behaviour. In addition, positive mood and affect are important health outcomes in their own right.

What are emotions and moods and how do we measure them?

Although moods and emotions are closely related and often synonymous concepts, mood can be seen as a global set of affective states we experience on a day-to-day basis and may last hours, days, weeks, or even months (Oatley and Jenkins 1996). Mood can be conceptualised in terms of distinct mood states, such as vigour and depression, and it is then that it becomes similar, or the same as, emotion. Emotion is normally defined in terms of specific feeling states generated in reaction to certain events or appraisals. They are likely to last for minutes or hours, but not longer (Oatley and Jenkins 1996). The distinction between mood and emotion in physical activity research studies is often not clear. Readers are referred to Oatley and Jenkins (1996) and Vallerand and Blanchard (2000) for further discussion on definitional issues.

In psychology, there is a debate concerning the nature of emotion (Cacioppo, Gardner and Berntson 1999; Diener 1999; Green, Salovey and Truax 1999; Russell and Barrett 1999; Watson *et al.* 1999). Some prefer to define emotion in terms of discrete emotional reactions, such as pleasure and fear (Clore, Ortony and Foss 1987; Lazarus 1991; Weiner 1995). Others suggest that emotions are best defined in terms of their common properties, or dimensions, such as positive and negative affect (Watson, Clark and Tellegen 1988). Lazarus (1991), however, argues that the distinct qualities of emotional reactions are lost, or blurred, when reduced to a few dimensions. He argues that each emotion is unique because it is created by a different appraisal of the perceived significance of an event. However, it is also logical to see emotions clustered according to common categories. Watson *et al.* (1988) have derived two major factors from an analysis of emotions: positive affect and negative affect. The former refers to feelings such as alert and active, whereas negative affect refers to unpleasant affective states such as anger and fear.

Russell has also advocated a dimensional approach to the study of emotions (Russell 1980). In his 'circumplex' model, he suggests that emotion can best be defined in terms of the two dimensions of valence (that is, pleasant–unpleasant) and arousal (that is, high–low). This gives rise to emotions being classified into four quadrants:

- high arousal/low pleasure (for example, tense)
- high arousal/high pleasure (for example, excited)
- low arousal/high pleasure (for example, relaxed)
- low arousal/low pleasure (for example, depressed).

Measures of mood have typically involved the Profile of Mood States (POMS) (McNair, Lorr and Droppleman 1971), although McDonald and Hodgdon (1991) also located exercise studies using the Multiple Affect Adjective Check List (MAACL) (Zuckerman and Lubin 1965) which assesses only anxiety, depression and hostility. The POMS assesses five negative mood scales and only one positive scale (vigour) although the bi-polar form of the POMS (Lorr and McNair 1984; Lorr, Shi and Youniss 1989) allows the assessment of both a positive and negative pole. The sub-scales in the bi-polar version are energetic–tired, elation–depression, confident–unsure, composed–anxious, agreeable–hostile and clearheaded–confused. However, a large sample size is required to produce sufficient statistical power to detect changes and it is a matter of judgement as to the practical significance of small changes. For this reason, the bi-polar version of POMS may not be the most suitable or sensitive instrument for exercise or physical activity studies. The POMS can also be varied, however, according to the instructions, such as how participants feel 'right now' or 'over the past few weeks'.

Abele and Brehm (1993) report a number of studies they have conducted in Germany using the *Befindlichkeitsskalen* (BFS). This scale places mood states along the continua of

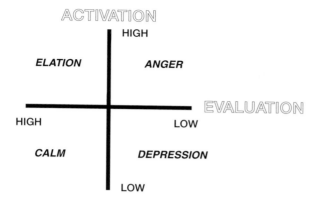

Figure 8.1 Diagrammatic representation, with example moods, of the BFS (*Befind-lichkeitsskalen*) developed by Abele and Brehm (1993)

high/low activation and positive/negative mood and is similar to Russell's (1980) circumplex model (see Figure 8.1).

Measures of mood and affect in exercise research

In addition to more generic measures of mood and affect, some researchers have developed scales for the assessment of exercise-related feeling states. Both types of measures used in physical activity research are summarised in Table 8.1.

In reaction to their dissatisfaction with global measures, such as the PANAS, Gauvin and Rejeski (1993) developed the Exercise-induced Feeling Inventory (EFI) in an effort to capture four distinct feeling states in exercise: revitalisation, tranquillity, positive engagement and physical exhaustion. Psychometric support has been reported for adults (Gauvin and Rejeski 1993) and children (Vlachopoulos *et al.* 1996), although the conceptual underpinnings of such 'exercise-specific' measures have been criticised (Ekkekakis and Petruzzello 2000; in press-a).

With adults, Gauvin and Rejeski (1993) found that positive engagement, revitalisation and tranquillity scores all correlated highly with PANAS positive affect scores, thus demonstrating concurrent validity. In addition, these researchers were able to show that the EFI sub-scales were sensitive to environmental cues. For example, positive engagement scores were higher after exercise in a 'real-world' setting than after exercise in a laboratory.

In a similar vein, McAuley and Courneya (1994) developed the Subjective Exercise Experiences Scale (SEES) comprising three factors of positive well-being, psychological distress and fatigue, and this, too, now has support with children (Markland, Emberton and Tallon 1997) although, again, has been criticised in relation to its conceptual underpinnings (Ekkekakis and Petruzzello, in press-b). Both the SEES and EFI are scales that can easily be used in field assessments of exercise affect.

Emotion, mood and physical activity

There are a very large number of studies investigating the relationship between exercise and affective states. Conclusions are drawn mainly from three types of studies: narrative and meta-analytic reviews, large-scale population surveys and experimental trials.

Table 8.1 Summary of mood and affect measures commonly used in exercise research

Instrument	Reference	Measures	Comments
POMS (profile of mood states)	McNair et al. (1971)	Sixty-five-item scale assessing: • tension • depression • anger • vigour • fatigue • confusion.	• Only one positive sub-scale. • Used extensively in PA research. • Short and bipolar forms available. • Time instructions can be varied. • Can be a state or trait scale. • General scale not specific to physical activity.
PANAS (positive and negative affect schedule)	Watson et al. (1988)	Two ten-item affect scales assessing: • Positive affect: for example, excited, enthusiastic, inspired. • Negative affect: for example, distressed, hostile, irritable.	• Good psychometric properties. • Assesses only two general dimensions. • Time instructions can be varied. • Can be a state or trait scale. • General scale not specific to physical activity.
BFS (Befindlichkeitsskalen)	Abele and Brehm (1993)	Forty-item scale devised in Germany to assess two dimensional model of mood: activation (high/low) and evaluation (positive/negative). eight sub-scales: • activation (high/positive) • elation (high/positive) • calmness (low/positive) • contemplativeness (low/positive) • excitation (high/negative) • anger (high/negative) • fatigue (low/negative) • depression (low/negative).	• Extensive German research supporting validity of scale in sport and exercise settings. • State scale.
MAACL (multiple affect adjective check list)	Zuckerman and Lubin (1965)	• Scale comprises 132 adjectives. • Assesses anxiety, depression and hostility.	• Time instructions can be varied. • Can be a state or trait scale. • General scale not specific to physical activity. • Some doubts expressed about psychometric properties (see McDonald and Hodgdon 1991).

Scale	Reference	Description	Characteristics
FS (feeling scale)	Hardy and Rejeski (1989)	• Single-item scale assessing hedonic tone (pleasure–displeasure).	• Developed for exercise research. • State scale. • Eleven-point scale ranging from −5 to +5.

EFI (exercise feeling inventory)	Gauvin and Rejeski (1993)	• Twelve-item adjective scale assessing four dimensions:
		  • positive engagement
		  • tranquillity
		  • revitalisation
		  • physical exhaustion.
			• Developed for exercise research.
			• Sound psychometric properties.
			• State scale.

SEES (subjective exercise experiences scale)	McAuley and Courneya (1994)	• Twelve-item adjective scale assessing three dimensions:
		  • positive well-being
		  • psychological distress
		  • fatigue.
			• Developed for exercise research.
			• Sound psychometric properties.
			• State scale.

Narrative and meta-analytic reviews

From the numerous narrative reviews available, there is cautious support for the proposition that exercise is associated with enhanced affect and mood (Biddle 2000). The caution comes from the relatively weak research designs utilised. For example, the comprehensive review by Leith (1994) showed that experimental evidence was less convincing than for pre- or quasi-experimental studies. Leith demonstrated that the percentage of studies finding positive mood effects drops from pre-experimental studies (100 per cent) to quasi-experimental (79.2 per cent) to true experimental studies (62.5 per cent). Such cautiously positive conclusions are enhanced, however, by the fact that the reviews span several countries and populations, such as those in the workplace, women and people with disabilities. Also, diverse methods and measuring instruments are used yet yield similar findings. In addition, hardly any studies report negative mood effects.

McDonald and Hodgdon (1991) report a meta-analysis on exercise and mood. They delimited their review to aerobic fitness training studies and found that researchers used mainly the uni-polar POMS or MAACL. Results for mood suggest a clear relationship between exercise and vigour and a lack of negative mood and this corresponds to the typical 'iceberg profile' (see Figure 8.2). McDonald and Hodgdon concluded that 'aerobic fitness training produces some positive change in mood ... at least on a short-term basis' (McDonald and Hodgdon 1991: 98).

Interestingly, Schlicht (1994b) reported a brief meta-analysis of exercise and mental health in which the proposed relationship between physical activity and PWB was not supported. The analyses involved thirty-nine studies and over 8,000 research participants. However, the studies selected were not listed in his paper and additional information is required on study selection criteria before more can be concluded. It is not clear how many of the studies included are in German or English, the latter being more likely to be included in the North American meta-analyses that have supported a link between physical activity and other indices of mental health (Petruzzello *et al.* 1991). Nevertheless, Schlicht (1994b) reported an overall ES of only 0.15, but with a large range, and the overall ES was not significantly different from zero.

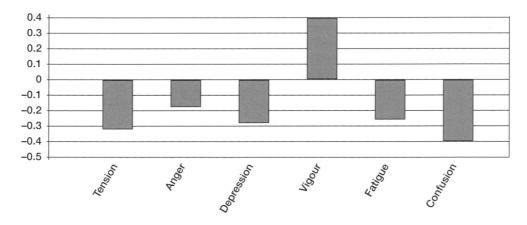

Figure 8.2 Effect sizes from McDonald and Hodgdon's (1991) meta-analysis of aerobic fitness training and mood states

Population surveys

Although often suffering from methodological shortcomings, population (epidemiological) surveys have the advantage over some other studies in so far as they usually have large samples, are representative of the population and hence allow good generalisability of findings. Five such studies from Britain are summarised in Table 8.2 and show clear positive relationships between physical activity and psychological well-being. Confidence in these results is enhanced by noting that the surveys cover both adolescents and adults, use clinical, non-clinical, quantitative and qualitative assessments, and cover a total sample of over 23,000. However, as noted by Thirlaway and Benton (1996), not all groups seem to benefit from PA. In addition, one cannot conclude that these are exercise-induced effects. Although the Allied Dunbar National Fitness Survey (ADNFS) (The Sports Council and Health Education Authority 1992) demonstrated that the same trend was evident for those in poor as well as good health, large-scale surveys offer few clues on the cause of PWB.

Nevertheless, the British studies are comparable to Stephens' (1988) secondary analysis of four North American surveys. Across several measures, and with over 55,000 adults, there was a clear association between PA and psychological well-being. For example, positive affect was associated with PA for both men and women in the two age groups under and over 40 years. Stephens provided the following clear conclusion:

> the inescapable conclusion of this study is that the level of physical activity is positively associated with good mental health in the household populations of the United States and Canada, when mental health is defined as positive mood, general well-being, and relatively infrequent symptoms of anxiety and depression. This relationship is independent of the effects of education and physical health status, and is stronger for women and those age 40 years and over than for men and those age under 40. The robustness of this conclusion derives from the varied sources of evidence: four population samples in two countries over a 10-year period, four different methods of operationalizing physical activity and six different mental health scales.
>
> (Stephens 1988: 41–2)

Evidence from population surveys, therefore, supports a relationship between physical activity and mood/affect. The nature of such surveys means that we can only conclude that participation in exercise, or the quantity of PA taken, is associated with PWB over time. Acute effects of exercise cannot be studied in this way. Similarly, whether this relationship can be said to be causal remains to be seen. In this regard, evidence from experimental trials is required.

Experimental trials

Few studies have investigated the effects of exercise on affect and mood through controlled experimental trials. Five British studies are summarised in Table 8.3. These show that the intensity of exercise is important in determining the effects of exercise on mood, something not suggested in other types of studies such as large-scale surveys. Three of the studies by Steptoe and his colleagues (Moses, *et al.* 1989; Steptoe and Bolton 1988; Steptoe and Cox 1988) show that moderate, but not high intensity exercise, has mood enhancing effects. Figure 8.3 illustrates results from Steptoe and Bolton's study. Similarly, Parfitt, Markland and Holmes (1994) show that feeling states in exercise are significantly worse at a higher

Table 8.2 Summary of findings from British population surveys investigating the relationship between physical activity and psychological well-being

Study	Survey design and scope	Results and conclusions
Hendry, Shucksmith and Cross (1989)	Postal and supervised survey of 5,862 14–20 year olds in Scotland. Assessment with General Health Questionnaire and sports participation.	• GHQ (mental health) scores improved as participation in sport increased for both boys and girls. • Competitive sports 'types' had better mental health than non-competitive 'types'.
Sports Council and Health Education Authority (1992)	Allied Dunbar National Fitness Survey (ADNFS) for England of 16–74 year olds (N = 4,316). One section of interview assessed perceived well-being.	• Small but consistent trend showing relationship between PA and well-being. Same trend evident for those in poorest health, reducing the chance that only those who are 'well' choose to exercise. • Association between PA and well-being stronger for those 55 years and over. • Trends evident for all age groups and both sexes.
Thirlaway and Benton (1996)	National Health and Lifestyle Survey data. Representative British sample (N = 6,200). Assessed on PA and General Health Questionnaire. (Unpublished survey data reported in book chapter.)	• Higher PA associated with better mental health in women over 30 years and men over 50 years. • No relationship for those under 30 years of age.
Steptoe and Butler (1996)	Investigation of the association between emotional well-being and regular sport/vigorous PA in 16 year olds (N = 5,061). Data from 1986 follow-up to 1970 British Cohort Study.	• Greater sport/vigorous PA was positively associated with emotional well-being independent of gender, SES or health status. • Participation in non-vigorous activity was associated with high psychological and somatic symptoms on Malaise Inventory.
Gordon and Grant (1997)	1,634 teenagers from Scotland (aged 13.5–14.5 years). Qualitative method used with open-ended questionnaire responses to 'how do you feel today?'	• About one quarter reported that sport made them feel happy and good about themselves. • Large gender differences.

intensity for less active individuals, and Boutcher, McAuley and Courneya (1997) found that greater positive affect was reported after aerobic treadmill exercise for trained runners in comparison to matched untrained participants. This suggests that training status may account for post-exercise affective responses. Hardy and Rejeski (1989) reported more negative moods after higher intensity exercise than after less intense activity. Such findings led Leith to recommend that 'moderate-intensity exercise appears to have the best potential to impact on participant mood states' (Leith 1999: 146).

Raglin (1997) has suggested that high-intensity activity may delay rather than eliminate post-exercise anxiety reductions. The increases in negative mood after high intensity exercise reported in Steptoe's research may be due to the higher exertion required, but studies have shown that positive mood is still enhanced some time later. The temporal nature of changes in mood after different intensities of exercise requires further investigation. However, even if the post-exercise negative mood effect is transitory, it may be enough to affect adherence and reduce physical activity participation. Given that Steptoe's research involved primarily untrained participants, it may not be surprising, and is consistent with Boutcher *et al.* (1997), that only moderate intensity exercise produces positive affective responses.

Finally, in a controlled trial of healthy American adults, King *et al.* (1989) found that participants assigned to a six-month physical activity intervention, in comparison to controls, showed significant improvements in body appearance satisfaction, perceived physical fitness and satisfaction with weight. No differences, however, were found for depressed mood, tension/anxiety, or confidence/well-being. These results suggest that psychological changes are more likely if they are closely linked to the physical changes associated with an exercise programme.

Enjoyment and physical activity

If physical activity is associated with psychological well-being, it seems obvious that an element of enjoyment of physical activity must also be present. Enjoyment is an important element of motivation, particularly when physical effort might be required, like in fitness/exercise classes. Despite all of this, enjoyment has remained an elusive concept for

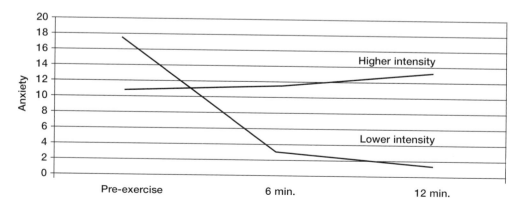

Figure 8.3 Interaction effects between the intensity of exercise and anxious mood pre- and post-exercise (data from Steptoe and Bolton 1988)

Table 8.3 Controlled experimental trials from Britain investigating physical activity, exercise and psychological well-being

Study	Participants	Design and treatment	Results and conclusions
Steptoe and Cox (1988)	Sample: female students (N = 32)	• Single session experiment testing the effects of exercise intensity and music on mood. • All participants exercised for four periods: at both low and moderate intensity with music and metronome.	• Moderate intensity exercise produced more negative mood states (increased tension-anxiety, reduced vigour and exhilaration). • Low intensity exercise produced favourable mood state changes. • Ratings of Perceived Exertion were slightly lower when exercising with music rather than a metronome. • No mood effects for music.
Steptoe and Bolton (1988)	Female students (N = 40)	• Replication and extension of Steptoe and Cox (1988): exercised for fifteen minutes at either moderate or low intensity.	• Immediately after higher intensity exercise, participants reported higher tension-anxiety and mental fatigue than those in the low intensity condition. • Both groups showed a decline in these states during the exercise recovery period.
Moses *et al.* (1989)	Sedentary adults (N = 109)	• An experimental study of the effects of exercise training on mental well-being: participants assigned to either high intensity aerobic exercise, moderate intensity aerobic exercise, attention-placebo, or waitlist control. • Ten-week training period undertaken.	• Only the moderate intensity exercise group showed reductions on the tension-anxiety and confusion mood scales, and a measure of coping deficits.
Steptoe *et al.* (1993)	Sedentary adults (N = 33) within borderline or 'definite' range for anxiety	• Experimental study of the effects of exercise on psychological stress and mood responses (only mood effects reported here). • Participants assigned to either moderate exercise or attention-placebo control conditions.	• Exercise group showed significant reduction in confusion and improvement in perceived stress coping. • These trends not shown in attention-placebo group.
Parfitt *et al.* (1994)	Students (N = 80)	• Experimental test on affective reactions to exercise as a function of exercise intensity and exercise history. • High and low active participants reported psychological affect in the last 30 seconds and 5 minutes after exercising at 60% and 90% of VO_{2max}.	• High-active participants reported greater positive affect in the high intensity condition in comparison to the low-active group. • No differences at the lower intensity.

many years. It is only recently that psychologists have better understood the construct, although even now there is disagreement about how enjoyment should be conceptualised (Kimiecik and Harris 1996; Wankel 1997). Kimiecik and Harris (1996) adopted Csikzentmihalyi's approach and defined enjoyment in terms of 'flow' (see next section). They suggest that enjoyment is not positive affect but an optimal psychological state. In other words, 'enjoyment is a psychological state that leads to . . . positive feelings states' (Kimiecik and Harris 1996: 256). They also suggest that enjoyment is 'not an affective product of the experience, but a psychological process that is the experience' (257).

At least four approaches to enjoyment can be identified that have relevance to physical activity, although not all are consistent with Kimiecik and Harris' (1996) definition:

- Csikzentmihalyi's 'flow' model
- intrinsic motivational processes
- Scanlan's study of sport enjoyment in children
- exercise-induced feeling states.

Enjoyment and flow

Csikzentmihalyi (1975) studied why people invested huge amounts of time and energy in tasks appearing to yield limited external rewards. One of his conclusions was that motivation seemed highest when the difficulty of the task was matched by the personal abilities and skills of the individual. This matching led to a state of 'flow', or supreme enjoyment and engagement in the task. A mismatch can lead to either boredom (low challenge/high skills) or anxiety (high challenge/low skills).

Kimiecik and Stein (1992) draw on Csikzentmihalyi's work to propose six dimensions of flow in sport. Application to wider exercise settings is needed. The six dimensions are:

- Matching of action and awareness: this occurs when the matching of skills with the challenge produces feelings that the action itself is spontaneous and automatic, and awareness of oneself does not differ from awareness of the activity.
- Clear goals and unambiguous feedback.
- Concentration on the task at hand.
- The paradox of control: flow is associated with feelings of control and, at the same time, feelings that reflect a lack of worry concerning the loss of control.
- The loss of self-consciousness: less conscious awareness of one's actions.
- Transformation of time: flow is often associated with loss of awareness of time; time is 'distorted by the experience' (Kimiecik and Stein 1992: 148).

Enjoyment and intrinsic motivation

The development of intrinsic motivation is a key consideration for many promoting physical activity and has already been discussed in Chapter 3. High intrinsic motivation includes high effort, feelings of enjoyment, competence, and autonomy (self-determination), and low levels of pressure and anxiety (Deci and Ryan 1985).

Intrinsic motivation, enjoyment and flow are clearly interrelated, although Kimiecik and Harris (1996) suggest that they are similar but not the same. They argue that enjoyment allows for the development of intrinsic motivation. Csikzentmihalyi (1975) spoke of 'autotelic' (self-directed) activities being the ones where flow was most likely, and Deci and

Ryan (1985) speak about the 'self-determination' of behaviour through intrinsic motivation. How interrelated these constructs are in exercise and physical activity remains an unanswered research question.

Scanlan's sport enjoyment model

Scanlan first proposed a preliminary model of sport enjoyment for children (Scanlan and Lewthwaite 1986) after studying 9–14 year old American boys. Sport enjoyment was defined as 'an individual's positive affective response to his or her competitive sport experience which reflects feelings and/or perceptions such as pleasure, liking, and experiencing fun' (Scanland and Lewthwaite 1986: 32). They proposed a preliminary model of sport enjoyment centred on the two continua of intrinsic–extrinsic and achievement–non-achievement. Predictors of enjoyment in the intrinsic–achievement quadrant refer to personal perceptions of mastery and competence; intrinsic–non-achievement to physical movement sensations and excitement. Predictors of enjoyment in the extrinsic–achievement quadrant are perceptions of competence derived from others (for example, social approval); extrinsic–non-achievement factors are non-performance related, such as affiliation.

Exercise-induced feeling states

Earlier, we suggested that Abele and Brehm's (1993) *Befindlichkeitsskalen* in Germany better represents both the activation and evaluation dimensions of mood (see Figure 8.1). Positive feelings, accompanied by high activation, could be associated with enjoyment during physical activity. Similarly, the positive engagement sub-scale of the EFI is closely associated with enjoyment. However, while enjoyment is a key to motivation, its nature and measurement is still in need of development and refinement. The only specific scale purporting to assess physical activity enjoyment is Kendzierski and DeCarlo's (1991) eighteen-item Physical Activity Enjoyment Scale (PACES).

Exercise, menstruation and mood

Exercise as a treatment for menstrual cycle symptomatology is not a new idea. It has been advocated in the lay literature for some time now (Cowart 1989) but such recommendations have lacked theoretical rationale and empirical support. Only two intervention studies have been carried out, one to assess the effects of exercise on dysmenorrhea (Israel, Sutton and O'Brien 1985) and the other to assess the effects on premenstrual syndrome (Prior and Vigna 1987). The results of both studies are suggestive of positive effects of exercise in alleviating premenstrual syndrome or dysmenorrhea, although neither study measured psychological states.

Data from cross-sectional studies indicate strong associations between physical exercise and positive psychological states during the menstrual cycle. Choi and Salmon (1995) prospectively monitored women who exercised at different levels for a whole month. The women, who had regular menstrual cycles, completed a specially devised mood adjective checklist on a daily basis. There were three groups: thirty-three high exercisers (those who regularly exercised more than three times a week), thirty-six low exercisers (those who exercised less than three times a week) and thirty-nine sedentary women. The results showed that not only were positive mood and negative mood related to cycle phase in all groups, high exercisers experienced the most positive mood and the least negative mood throughout the cycle. In addition, a significant interaction showed that not only did the high exercisers feel better emotionally than the other two groups over the whole cycle, they did not experience a decline in positive mood from mid-cycle to the premenstrual phase. A similar trend was seen in negative mood although this only approached statistical significance. Similar results did not emerge for the menstrual phase of the cycle. This may reflect different mechanisms that lower mood premenstrually and menstrually. For example, acute pain that is often present while menstruating, but not premenstrually, suggests one obvious way in which the sources of distress and discomfort may be different. Furthermore, it is not clear how self-perceptions influence either the reporting of menstrual discomfort or the role of exercise in alleviating discomfort. Cultural influences passed from mother to daughter may lead to the view for some women that menstruation is a time of incapacity; participation in exercise runs counter to this view and may therefore operate to influence feelings of strength rather than incapacity. This viewpoint is reflected in the current advertising trend for sanitary products to be associated with women who lead physically active lives.

Choi and Salmon (1995) suggest that their findings indicate possible protection from premenstrual deterioration in women who routinely take high levels of exercise. This is, of course, a tentative suggestion because of the cross-sectional design of the study. The association may be the result of more severe premenstrual symptoms, or a perception of incapacity during menstruation, leading to some women being sedentary. Equally those women with fewer symptoms premenstrually may be more inclined to be active. There is a clear need for further experimental research to follow up the promising results from the cross-sectional data. However, the possibility of a mood-enhancing effect from exercise may have important implications for women who do suffer negative moods at certain points of the menstrual cycle.

Exercise deprivation

The literature on exercise deprivation also lends some support to the notion that physical activity is associated with psychological well-being. Exercise deprivation occurs when regular exercisers are forced (often for experimental purposes) to give up their usual pattern of exercise. Studying the psychological consequences of such deprivation provides an interesting way of looking at the benefits of exercise and an insight into why some people continue in regular activities. It may also assist in our understanding of the mechanisms of psychological benefits from exercise.

Researchers have asked regular exercisers to stop exercise for a period of days, weeks (Morris, Steinberg, Sykes and Salmon 1990) or months (Baekeland 1970) and have found that deprivation caused a 'feel worse' effect which disappeared once exercise was reinstated. However, despite the appeal of this paradigm, the difficulty of recruiting those who are willing to give up their exercise routines for research purposes has prevented there being a substantial literature in this area. A recent review by Szabo (1995) suggests that findings from survey, cross-sectional and experimental studies, show that interruption to the normal exercise pattern of an habitual exerciser will have a negative impact on psychological well-being. This negative impact is most frequently expressed as a series of 'withdrawal' symptoms such as guilt, irritability, tension and depression.

This literature provides us with two possible ways of understanding psychological outcomes and physical activity. Firstly, it is suggested that some regular exercisers experience withdrawal on deprivation of their usual exercise because this deprives them of regular enjoyable experiences, such as mood enhancement, social interaction and the joy of movement (Pierce 1994). Alternatively, and perhaps even simultaneously, some exercisers need the increase in arousal level that exercise brings in order to avoid negative feelings from low sympathetic arousal such as lethargy and sluggishness (Pierce 1994). Thus, the benefit of exercise can be seen as a way maintain good feelings and avoid bad feelings associated with inactivity.

Factors moderating the relationship between mood/affect and exercise

The evidence that exists for a link between physical activity and psychological well-being is sometimes weak or inconsistent, suggesting that factors may be operating as moderators of this relationship. For example, it could be that exercise studies attract people who are already psychologically healthy and thus have little room for improvement in any of the standard measures. In the population attracted to Kelly and Mutrie's (1997) study, all baseline scores on POMS were within one half of a standard deviation of the standardised mean. And yet, exercisers subjectively report feeling better for exercise. Perhaps regular exercisers use their exercise to help them cope with the daily and weekly fluctuations in mood which we all experience, thus the net result from regular activity is one of positive mood states.

In terms of our understanding of psychological outcomes from regular exercise this suggests that we should not expect to see huge benefits to mood from exercise for psychologically healthy people. Instead it might be suggested that regular exercise is a way of helping maintain the feel good factor rather than enhance it; logically people cannot continue to feel better and better from exercise as this would result in manic behaviour. This is consistent with the experimental literature that has suggested that if people have normal mood profiles to begin with exercise appears to make little impact, while larger improvements will be noticed if people do not have normal mood profiles to begin with (Steptoe *et al.* 1989).

There is some evidence in population surveys (Stephens 1988) that more positive affect results from physical activity for women and those over 40 years of age. However, when specific aspects of affect are studied, such as depression, the picture is not clear. Also, positive mood effects have been reported in studies involving people of both genders and all ages. It is not known whether specific forms of exercise, such as aerobic exercise, are more beneficial than others when affect is considered. However, data already reported suggest that training status may be important in determining whether positive affect is experienced after exercise (Boutcher *et al.* 1997).

One popular area of research in sport psychology may shed some light on contextual factors influencing exercise affect (see Chapters 4 and 7). The goals people have in approaching physical activity, and the environment perceived by the participants (climate) may be important. Two main achievement goals have received considerable research attention in physical activity in recent years (Duda and Whitehead 1998). A task goal orientation is held when success is defined primarily in terms of self-improvement and task mastery. It is highly correlated with the belief that effort will bring success. An ego goal orientation is held when success is defined in terms of winning and demonstrating superiority over others. This correlates highly with the belief that ability is necessary for success.

We conducted a meta-analysis of thirty-seven studies, with a total of forty-one independent samples (N = 7950), investigating the relationship between task and ego goals and positive (PA) and negative affect (NA) (Ntoumanis and Biddle 1999b). After correcting for measurement and sampling error, the correlation (effect size (ES)) between task orientation and positive affect was moderate-to-high while correlations were generally small for relationships between task and NA, ego and PA, and ego with NA. These results, shown in Figure 8.4, suggest that adopting a task goal orientation in sport and physical activity will lead to more positive affective reactions.

In another review, we calculated effect sizes for the relationship between task and ego climates in physical activity and positive and negative affect (Ntoumanis and Biddle 1999a). Climates refer to the perception of contextual cues in a situation (for example, an exercise class) that may emphasise more of a task climate or an ego climate (see Chapter 7). In the former, group members perceive they have greater involvement in decision-making, success is defined and evaluated in terms of individual effort and improvement, and new learning strategies are encouraged. An ego climate, on the other hand, emphasises interpersonal comparison, and evaluation is based on normative standards. Calculations from fourteen studies with over 4,400 people revealed that a task climate was associated quite strongly with positive affective and motivational outcomes (see Figure 7.2).

The nature of the exercise experience could also moderate the relationship activity and PWB. For example, studies of the acute effects of exercise have generally been successful in demonstrating that physical activity makes you 'feel good'. However, longer-term studies investigating the effects of chronic exercise have been less successful, at least in experimental settings.

Mood and affect: summary

Based on the evidence reviewed, the following summary statements can be made:

- Participation in exercise and physical activity is consistently associated with positive affect and mood.
- Where quantified trends have been identified, aerobic exercise has a small-to-moderate effect on vigour (+), fatigue (−) and confusion (−), and a small effect on anger (−).
- The relationship between physical activity and psychological well-being has been confirmed in several large population surveys, in the UK and elsewhere, using different measures of activity and well-being.
- Experimental trials support an effect for moderate intensity exercise on psychological well-being, particularly for acute exercise.

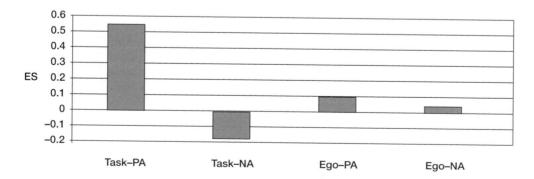

Figure 8.4 Effect sizes calculated for the relationship between achievement goals (task and ego) and positive (PA) and negative (NA) affect. ESs are correlations corrected for sampling and measurement error (Ntoumanis and Biddle 1999b)

- The effect for high intensity exercise on affect and mood is less clear, although may occur after a period of post-exercise recovery.
- Quantified trends support the contention that a task oriented (self-referenced) goal in physical activity is associated with positive affect.
- Quantified trends support the contention that a mastery (task) motivational climate in physical activity settings is associated with positive motivational and affective reactions.

Exercise and self-esteem

Self-esteem is often seen to be the single most important measure of psychological well-being. Indeed, enhanced self-esteem resulting from physical activity is often claimed by those promoting exercise and sport participation, and is a common rationale for the teaching of physical education for children. Sonstroem, in a review of the effects of exercise on self-esteem, concluded that:

> the consistently positive results . . . suggest a basis for the belief in the salutary effects of physical training programs. It is concluded that exercise programs are associated with significant increases in the self-esteem scores of participants. These score increases are particularly pronounced in subjects initially low in self-esteem. . . . These conclusions refer to exercise programs rather than fitness increases, and to increases in self-esteem scores rather than in self-esteem *per se*.
>
> (Sonstroem 1984: 138)

Self-esteem refers to the value placed on aspects of the self, such as academic and social domains. It is an extension of the construct of self-concept, which merely describes aspects of the self. Self-esteem, therefore, attaches a value to such descriptors. Until recently, the measurement of self-esteem was a factor preventing substantial progress being made in understanding the potential links between exercise and self-esteem. Often researchers have employed a global measure of self-esteem rather than a multidimensional one. It has been shown that self-esteem is a global construct underpinned by a multidimensional and hierarchical structure. Global self-esteem is composed of differentiated perceptions of the self, such as physical, social and academic self-perceptions. These, in turn, are underpinned by increasingly transient perceptions of worth and competence, such as sport ability or physical appearance for the physical sub-domain of global self-esteem (Fox 1997b; 1998; Fox and Corbin 1989). Figure 4.1 in Chapter 4 shows Fox's physical self-perception model based on this approach.

Two approaches to self-esteem and exercise can be identified. First, there is the 'motivational approach' or 'personal development hypothesis' (Sonstroem 1997a; 1997b) whereby self-esteem (SE) acts as a motivational determinant of physical activity (see Figure 8.5a). Here individuals high in self-esteem, or more specifically in physical self-worth (PSW) and related physical self-perceptions, are more likely to approach physical activity contexts since this is an area where competence and self-worth can be maintained or enhanced.

In addition, there is the 'skill (personal) development' hypothesis (Sonstroem 1997a, 1997b). This proposes that self-esteem can be changed through experience, either positive or negative, through development in skills, task mastery, success and so on (see Figure 8.5b). This refers to self-esteem more as an outcome of involvement in, say, physical activity, in contrast to the motivational emphasis of the self-enhancement hypothesis. The skill development hypothesis underpins many physical education programmes for children. Of course,

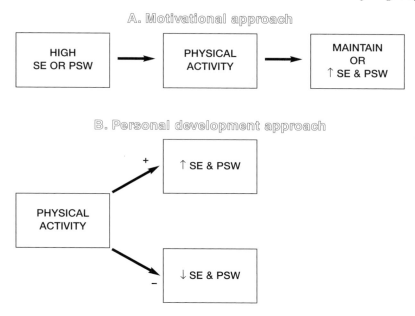

Figure 8.5 'Motivational' and 'self-enhancement' approaches to self-esteem

in reality, the two approaches are not mutually exclusive as initial involvement in physical activity, which may be externally motivated, may lead to enhanced self-perceptions of esteem and worth which, in turn, become motivators of subsequent activity (Biddle 1997a).

Measurement of self-esteem in the physical domain

Such theoretical advances are now being met with concurrent advances in psychometric assessment. Fox and Corbin (1989) developed the Physical Self-Perception Profile (PSPP) (Fox 1998). This is a measure of physical self-worth and four sub-domains of this construct: sport competence, body attractiveness, perceived strength and physical condition. These factors were derived initially from research on an American student population.

What the PSPP and other similar instruments, such as Marsh's 'Physical Self-Description Questionnaire' (PSDQ) (Marsh *et al.* 1994), should allow is for the investigation of how exercise might affect differential aspects of self-perceptions, and how these might impact on self-esteem. For example, participation in exercise may increase positive feelings about physical condition that may, in turn, affect physical self-worth and self-esteem. These relationships are thought to be more likely if the domain in question is seen to be important to the individual (Fox 1998). However, surprisingly few studies have assessed this. In a comprehensive analysis of this issue, Marsh and Sonstroem (1995) studied over 200 adult aerobic dance participants in the USA. Measures were taken of general self-esteem and the four sub-domains of the PSPP (body attractiveness, perceived sport competence, physical condition and perceived strength), as well as the physical self-worth scale from the PSPP. In addition, Fox's (1990) Perceived Importance Profile (PIP) was administered. This inventory provides eight items, two each for the sub-domains of the PSPP, each item assessing the perceived importance of that sub-domain. Finally, the sample was assessed on self-reported physical activity.

A number of different models and methods were tested, but essentially the results provided little support for the notion that physical exercise participation is better predicted by domain-specific physical self-perceptions in combination with importance ratings than by self-perceptions alone. However, Marsh and Sonstroem (1995) raise the issue of the function and specificity of importance ratings. For example, someone who perceives themselves to have low body attractiveness, but attaches high importance to that domain, may act in a similar way to another individual who has strong positive self-perceptions of their attractiveness and also high importance for the domain. The first person could be motivated for improvement (for example, weight loss) whereas the second seems to demonstrate the effect of competence on behaviour: they are motivated because they are competent or look good in the aerobics context. In other words, 'although self-concept researchers have often asked subjects to rate the importance of different self-concept domains, they may need to ask why a particular domain is important or in what situations it is important' (Marsh and Sonstroem 1995: 101).

Narrative and meta-analytic reviews

McDonald and Hodgdon (1991) reported an overall ES of 0.56 (n = 41) for studies investigating the link between aerobic fitness training and 'self-concept', and this term included most standard measures of self-perceptions, including self-esteem. Thirteen different inventories were used, none conforming to contemporary self-esteem theory where measures would include domain-specific perceptions of physical self-worth. The ESs varied across the different scales, but at times very small numbers of studies were located. For example, the highest ES (1.45) involved only two studies using a fairly obscure inventory, while the lowest ES (0.23) was a mean of four studies using the Secord and Jourard (1953) Body Cathexis Scale.

McDonald and Hodgdon (1991) included self-related measures from personality tests to form their 'self-esteem cluster'. This involved all measures from the 'self-concept' studies above, plus the self-sufficiency (scale Q2) and insecurity (scale O) sub-scales from the 16PF. The ES was 0.35 for the cluster: a moderate effect.

In a meta-analysis of play and physical education programmes for children, Gruber (1986) calculated an overall ES of 0.41 for self-esteem from twenty-seven studies. 61 per cent of the studies produced positive effects on self-esteem. These results support a positive effect for physical activity on the self-esteem of youngsters. However, an average ES of only 0.12 was reported from three randomised controlled trials (RCT) for youth reviewed by Calfas and Taylor (1994).

Doan and Scherman (1987) analysed the relationship between various personality measures, including self-esteem/concept and exercise. Of eleven pre-experimental studies, seven showed a positive effect and four no effect; for quasi-experimental studies, five were positive and three showed no change, while of the ten experimental studies, five were positive and five showed no change. No study reported a negative effect for exercise on self-esteem.

A systematic review by Fox (2000) identified thirty-six RCTs in the literature since 1970, with nine being unpublished postgraduate theses. Positive changes in physical self-perceptions or general self-esteem were found in 76 per cent of all RCTs. Fox concluded that exercise can be used to promote positive physical self-perceptions, but the mechanisms underpinning such changes are not clear.

An emerging area of importance concerns physical self-perceptions during pregnancy. In comparison to the literature available on the physiological issues of exercise during pregnancy (Lokey *et al.* 1991) there is very little literature on the psychological issues. The transition to parenthood can be seen as a developmental crisis and there are emotional as well as social changes during pregnancy. The pregnant woman may feel that she is perceived of only as a 'pregnancy' and that her own identity becomes submerged (Alder 1994). In addition a woman's perception of her pregnancy will be influenced by both peer and cultural pressures. Strang and Sullivan (1985) reported that pregnancy resulted in negative changes in body image for many women. Wallace *et al.* (1986) conducted a cross-sectional study of pregnant women who were participants in aerobic exercise compared to pregnant women who were sedentary and found that the exercising women had higher self-esteem scores and lower discomfort scores than the sedentary women. Hall and Kaufmann (1987) reported that pregnant women who had exercised during pregnancy retrospectively had improved self-image, reduced tension and decreased discomfort during the time of participation. In a prospective study, Slavin *et al.* (1988) found that exercise allowed women to feel more in control of their bodies and helped them maintain a positive self-image during pregnancy. These authors suggest that one of the most consistent benefits of exercise during pregnancy is psychological, because it allows women to feel control over their bodies at a time when many bodily changes that occur are biologically driven. In addition, post-natal depression may respond to exercise programmes, since the effects of exercise on mild and moderate depression are well established (see later in this chapter). To date, however, no specific studies on the effects of exercise on post-natal depression have been carried out.

Self-esteem: summary

Exercise is related to positive changes in self-esteem, although more information will be obtained about the nature of such changes through domain-specific measures of self-perceptions. Sonstroem has updated his 1984 review (Sonstroem 1997a) and many of his earlier conclusions have been repeated. However, several key questions were posed by Sonstoem (1997a) and these are summarised in Table 8.4. On balance, evidence does support a positive link between exercise and self-esteem and a similar conclusion was reached by Fox (2000) in his review of RCTs.

Table 8.4 Responses to four key questions posed by Sonstroem (1997a) on the relationship between exercise and self-esteem

Key question	Summary of Sonstroem's response
1 Are increases in self-esteem directly related to increases in physical fitness?	No. It is the perception of improvement in fitness or other factors rather than actual fitness change that is associated with more positive self-perceptions.
2 Are increases in self-esteem limited to those subjects with initially lower self-esteem?	Yes, but. . . . Positive changes in self-esteem are more likely for those initially low in self-esteem and those initially low in fitness or ability but want to change this factor, and it is important to them.
3 Are increases in self-esteem independent of confounding factors such as the placebo effect, response distortion and social desirability?	Yes. Although many studies have not controlled for such factors, evidence exists for independent effects of exercise on self-esteem.
4 Do increases in self-esteem disappear after several months?	No. Where follow-up data are available, self-esteem scores persist over time.

Exercise and anxiety

The study of the proposed anxiety-reducing effects of exercise has a long history in sport and exercise psychology and has remained an area of considerable interest to researchers. Anxiety is defined in terms of both state (transitory) and trait (enduring) characteristics, and sometimes with reference to both cognitive (worry) and somatic (bodily tension) elements. In addition, exercise researchers have been interested in the psychophysiological stress reactions of participants differing in fitness levels.

Although many mood and affect studies include measures of tension and anxiety (such as those using the POMS), it is clearer conceptually to deal with anxiety as a separate construct, partly because of the volume of such research. Most studies of exercise and anxiety have assessed state anxiety using either the state scale of the State–Trait Anxiety Inventory (STAI) (Spielberger, Gorsuch and Lushene 1970), POMS tension sub-scale (McNair *et al.* 1971) or the MAACL anxiety sub-scale (Zuckerman and Lubin 1965). When trait anxiety has been assessed, studies have used almost exclusively the trait scale of the STAI.

Meta-analytic findings

The results from four meta-analyses (Long and van Stavel 1995; McDonald and Hodgdon 1991; Petruzzello *et al.* 1991; Schlicht 1994a) help in reviewing the effects of exercise on anxiety. Schlicht (1994a) located twenty-two samples between 1980 and 1990 and found a small and non-significant effect size of –0.15, thus concluding that exercise had little effect on anxiety. However, Petruzzello (1995) criticised this paper strongly by pointing out that Schlicht had under-represented the field by not locating all of the studies (Schlicht 1995). Although Schlicht (1994a) analysed twenty-two samples from twenty studies, Petruzzello *et al.*'s (1991) meta-analysis used fifty for Schlicht's time period, and 104 overall. Consequently, Schlicht was unable to conduct moderator analyses and his meta-analysis lacked statistical power (see Schlicht 1995). Table 8.5 summarises results from three meta-analyses.

Petruzzello *et al.* (1991) have conducted the most comprehensive meta-analysis of the field to date. We review their findings alongside the more focused meta-analyses of

Table 8.5 Summary results from three meta-analyses on exercise and anxiety

Study	Outcome variables	Activity/fitness measure	No. of effect sizes	Mean effect size[1]
McDonald and Hodgdon (1991)	State anxiety	Aerobic fitness training	13	0.28
	Trait anxiety	Aerobic fitness training	20	0.25
Petruzzello *et al.* (1991)	State anxiety	Exercise	207	0.24
	Trait anxiety	Exercise	62	0.34
	Psycho-physiological indicators	Exercise	138	0.56
Long and van Stavel (1995)	Within-group pre-post studies	Exercise training	26	0.45
	Contrast group studies	Exercise training	50	0.36

Note:
1 All effect sizes are significantly different from zero.

McDonald and Hodgdon (1991) and Long and van Stavel (1995). Petruzzello *et al.* (1991) analysed data from 124 studies that examined the effect of exercise on anxiety. They included studies published between 1960 and 1989 that investigated state anxiety, trait anxiety and psychophysiological indicators of anxiety. Published and unpublished studies were included, as well as studies varying in methodological design. By coding such variables, the effect for methodological adequacy could be tested.

McDonald and Hodgdon (1991) restricted their meta-analysis to studies investigating the effects of aerobic fitness training on psychological outcomes, one of which was anxiety. This yielded thirty-six effect sizes from twenty-two studies. No date limitation was reported in their search procedures. However, they did not consider unpublished studies, abstracts and dissertations and included only studies using standardised anxiety measures, as well as fitness measures, and pre- and post-test measures. Finally, Long and van Stavel (1995) restricted their meta-analysis to adults involved in quasi-experimental or experimental training studies using standardised anxiety measures. Clinical studies (psychiatric and Type A) were omitted leaving forty studies and seventy-six effect sizes.

The main findings from these meta-analyses are summarised in Table 8.5 and show that exercise has a significant small-to-moderate effect on anxiety. Petruzzello *et al.* (1991) found that for state anxiety studies using no-treatment control groups and motivational control groups both showed a significant ES, but the ES was larger for studies utilising a pre-post within-subjects design. McDonald and Hodgdon (1991) found that survey studies produced a lower ES than experimental studies. These findings suggest that the internal validity of the study may not necessarily influence effect sizes but anxiety change can occur when motivational factors are controlled. In addition, Petruzzello *et al.* (1991) found that exercise was as effective as other anxiety-reducing treatments. This finding may be particularly important given the low cost of exercise.

Aerobic exercise showed greater effects than non-aerobic exercise, but caution must be expressed concerning this result since only thirteen effect sizes were used to calculate the effects of non-aerobic exercise by Petruzzello *et al.* (1991). They found no differences between types of aerobic exercise, a finding supported by McDonald and Hodgdon (1991).

Interestingly, the length of the exercise session might be related to anxiety. Petruzzello *et al.* (1991) showed superior effects for exercise lasting 21–30 minutes in comparison to sessions less than this. However, when the effect sizes in the 0–20 minute category that were calculated from comparisons with other anxiety-reducing treatments were eliminated, the ES increased from 0.04 to 0.22, and was not significantly different from the 0.41 for 21–30 minute duration.

When reviewing exercise and affect, we suggested that higher intensity exercise may not produce such positive effects as more moderate exercise. However, for state anxiety, Petruzzello *et al.* (1991) found that effect sizes for the intensity of exercise were homogeneous. For psychophysiological indices of anxiety, though, the meta-analysis showed the highest effect size for 40–59 per cent of HR_{max} or VO_{2max} (ES = 1.06; n =13) and this was significantly different from 70–79 per cent intensity (ES = .41; n = 24). All four intensity categories, though, including 80 per cent and above, showed effect sizes significantly different from zero. These results suggest that moderate intensity exercise may be particularly beneficial for anxiety reduction, but other higher intensities can also be beneficial.

Population surveys

The extensive secondary data analysis of physical activity and mental health reported by Stephens (1988) includes evidence on anxiety. Data on over 10,000 adults in Canada showed that reporting symptoms of anxiety was less likely in more active individuals. This held for men of all ages, and for women over 40 years, but not for younger women. Other large-scale epidemiological data sets (see Sports Council and Health Education Authority 1992; Thirlaway and Benton 1996) provide only general well-being measures, thus it is not possible to detect changes in anxiety. This is also the case for Steptoe and Butler's (1996) data with 5,061 adolescents. However, they do report that 'greater participation in vigorous sports and activities was associated with lower risk of emotional distress, independently of sex, social class, illness during the previous year, and use of hospital services' (Steptoe and Butler 1996: 1791).

Experimental trials

In a review of exercise and anxiety, Leith (1994) identified twenty experimental studies. Of these, fourteen (70 per cent) showed reduced anxiety from exercise, with the rest showing no change. None showed increased anxiety from exercise. A series of experimental trials in the UK by Steptoe and his colleagues provides a useful framework for drawing conclusions concerning experimental work on exercise and anxiety (see Table 8.3).

Steptoe and Cox (1988) studied the psychological responses of thirty-two female medical students to both high (cycle ergometry exercise of 50rpm against 2kg/100W) and low (0.5kg/25W) intensities. For the anxiety–tension sub-scale scores from the POMS, they found a significant level x time interaction. This showed a significant increase in anxiety from pre- to post-test for the high intensity condition and a non-significant decrease for low intensity exercise.

Moses *et al.* (1989), testing sedentary adults across high intensity, moderate intensity, attention-placebo and waiting list conditions, also found evidence for anxiety reduction in the moderate but not high intensity group. In fact, those exercising at a higher intensity reported increases in anxiety from pre- to post-test. Moderate intensity exercise undertaken by low-active anxious adults in the study by Steptoe *et al.* (1993) was also associated with anxiety reduction whereas an attention-placebo condition showed no change.

These studies illustrate that exercise is associated with anxiety reduction under experimental conditions. However, Steptoe's data are particularly striking as they suggest that it is moderate rather high intensity exercise than produces anxiety reduction during exercise, although anxiety has also been shown to reduce in the post-exercise recovery period. This was discussed in the section on mood and affect earlier in this chapter.

Exercise and stress reactivity

Studies have investigated physiological reactivity to psychosocial stressors. A typical experimental design is for participants to be assigned to 'low' and 'high' aerobic fitness groups on the basis of laboratory tests of aerobic fitness and then to be assessed on their physiological reactivity (for example, blood pressure) to a stressor such as cold water immersion. Crews and Landers (1987) conducted a meta-analysis of thirty-four such studies and reported a mean ES of 0.48, showing a moderate effect for fitness on stress reactivity with fitter individuals showing less reactivity. Stronger effects were shown after acute exercise rather than chronic involvement in exercise. The majority of studies used blood pressure and heart rate as dependent measures, but these may be confounded with the independent variable of fitness measurement.

A national review and research consensus process in England on physical activity and psychological well-being (Biddle *et al.* 2000) also considered reactivity to stress. After considering the evidence, Taylor (2000) concluded that 'single sessions of moderate exercise can reduce short-term physiological reactivity to and enhance recovery from brief psychosocial stressors'.

While the reviews by Crews and Landers (1987) and Taylor (2000) provide useful data on exercise and stress reactivity, this field has a number of methodological concerns. For example, there are only a few experimental studies and many studies are correlational. The influence of fitness, independent of physical activity history, has yet to be determined, and all studies employ short-term stressors. In addition, Taylor suggested that we need to know more about the effects of exercise on naturally occurring stressors.

If exercise does affect stress reactivity, further knowledge is needed on the underlying mechanisms of such effects. Crews and Landers (1987) suggest that changes in sympathetic nervous system activity as a result of exercise, or changes in endogenous opiode release, may be factors.

Factors moderating the relationship between exercise and anxiety

Moderators of the relationship between exercise and anxiety have been alluded to in the results of the meta-analyses and other studies. In summary, exercise-induced anxiety reduction is evident across all ages and both genders. Where differences have been identified, these have not been consistently observed across studies. Data are lacking on differences between groups varying by ethnicity, SES and education.

Anxiety: summary

Based on the evidence reviewed, the following summary statements can be made concerning exercise and anxiety:

- Meta-analytic findings suggest that exercise is associated with a significant small-to-moderate reduction in anxiety.
- This holds for acute and chronic exercise, state and trait anxiety, psychophysiological indices of anxiety and groups differing by gender and age.
- Evidence concerning the different effects for aerobic and non-aerobic exercise is unclear.
- Experimental studies support an anxiety-reducing effect for exercise, mainly for moderate exercise during activity, but for both moderate and high intensity exercise post-activity.
- Large-scale epidemiological surveys support an anxiety-reducing effect for exercise
- Physiological reactivity to psychosocial stressors appears to be reduced for those high in aerobic fitness.

Exercise and non-clinical depression

The relationship between exercise and depression for those with clinical levels of depression is reviewed in Chapter 9. Here we investigate such a relationship for non-clinical populations, that is, those with mild-to-moderate depression and not classified as having clinical levels of depression.

McDonald and Hodgdon (1991) identified five measures of depression in their meta-analysis of aerobic training studies. These were the BDI, the Centre for Epidemiological

Studies Depression Scale (CES-D) (Radloff 1977), Lubin's (1965) Depression Adjective Check List (DACL), the Symptom Check List 90 (SCL-90) (Derogatis, Lipman and Covi 1973), and Zung's (1965) Self-Rating Depression Scale (SDS). In addition, the POMS depression sub-scale has been used (see Leith 1994) although McDonald and Hodgdon used this as part of their analysis of mood rather than depression *per se*.

Meta-analytic findings

Two meta-analyses have been conducted on exercise and depression. McDonald and Hodgdon ('1991), already reported in the sections on mood and anxiety in this chapter, have also meta-analysed depression as an outcome variable for their study of aerobic fitness training. In addition, North, McCullagh and Tran (1990) reported a meta-analysis of eighty studies yielding 290 effect sizes on exercise and depression. The main results from these two meta-analyses are summarised in Table 8.6.

The optimistic conclusions from these meta-analyses are not shared by all (Dishman 1995; Dunn and Dishman 1991). North *et al.* (1990), for example, conclude that both acute and chronic exercise are associated with depression reduction and that this is also the case in follow-up and the effect sizes are mainly moderate in strength. Similarly, McDonald and Hodgdon's (1991) more focused review showed that aerobic fitness training studies also provided evidence for a moderate effect of exercise on depression. In addition, when logical clusters of effect sizes were calculated, the depression cluster was found to have a higher ES than for anxiety, self-esteem and psychological adjustment (McDonald and Hodgdon 1991).

Although these meta-analyses probably constitute the best evidence in this area to date, there are a number of issues that should caution over-confidence. Many of these are argued well by Dunn and Dishman (1991) and Dishman (1995). For example, some studies in the meta-analyses may have included individuals suffering from depression with a primary anxiety component. Dunn and Dishman argue this point on the basis of evidence showing a large number of people meeting DSM–II–R criteria for agoraphobia and panic attacks also suffer from depression or have a history of depression. In these cases, exercise may reduce state anxiety and elevate mood that could then produce changes in depression. North *et al.*'s meta-analysis is also questioned on the basis of non-uniformity in defining depression, as well as the discrepancy between the results of the meta-analysis and other studies. Dunn and Dishman suggest that the meta-analytic finding that acute bouts of exercise are associated with depression reduction is not consistent with effects observed for tricyclic antidepressant drugs: 'it is difficult to explain this discrepancy in terms of pharmacological and neurobiological pathways' (Dunn and Dishman 1991: 49).

Population surveys

The large-scale survey analysis reported by Stephens (1988) and discussed earlier, provides evidence concerning physical activity and depression assessed with the CES-D. Results from over 3,000 North American adults from the first National Health and Nutrition Examination Survey (NHANES–I) showed that depression was highest for those reporting 'little/no exercise' in comparison to those classified in the 'moderate' and 'much' exercise categories (see Figure 8.6). Interestingly, this difference suggests that moderate exercise may be sufficient for anti-depressant effects and that additional activity yields no additional benefit. Further support was provided in follow-up data in NHANES–II (Farmer *et al.* 1988).

Table 8.6 Summary results from two meta-analyses on exercise and depression

Study	Outcome variables	Activity/Fitness measure	No. of effect sizes	Mean effect size[1]
North et al. (1990)	Depression	Exercise	290	0.53
	Depression	Exercise programmes	226	0.59
	Depression	Follow-up	38	0.50
	Depression	Single exercise sessions	26	0.31
	Depression	Exercise for initially non-depressed	143	0.59
	Depression	Exercise for initially depressed	120	0.53
	Depression	Weight training	7	1.78
	Depression	Various aerobic	54	0.67
	Depression	Walk and/or jog	89	0.55
	Depression	Aerobic class	13	0.56
	Depression	Jogging	66	0.48
McDonald and Hodgdon (1991)	Depression	Aerobic fitness training	17	0.97
	Depression 'cluster'[2]	Aerobic fitness training	Mean of seven combined effect sizes	0.55
	SDS	Aerobic fitness training	7	0.66[3]
	BDI[4]	Aerobic fitness training	5	1.22[3]
	DACL[4]	Aerobic fitness training	3	1.54[3]
	CES–D	Aerobic fitness training	2	0.73[3]
	SCL–90	Aerobic fitness training	1	1.02

Notes:
1 All effect sizes are significantly different from zero unless stated (or with ES n = 1); signs disregarded (all ES scores reflect a decrease in depression with exercise).
2 Cluster comprised: depression scores from the MAACL, POMS, MMPI and other 'mixed tests'; POMS confusion scale; POMS vigour scale (reversed); POMS fatigue scale.
3 No significance levels reported.
4 Both BDI and DACL were used in one study together.

Many individuals included in these surveys are not depressed in the first place and measurement may be capturing simply transient mood or general well-being. Measures of physical activity are weak, often using single item self-report measures assessed in a cross-sectional rather than prospective design.

Experimental trials

Leith (1994) reports forty-two studies investigating exercise and depression and 81 per cent show anti-depressant effects. Nine of the thirteen experimental studies reported by Leith show changes in depression. The work of Martinsen and colleagues in Norway has been

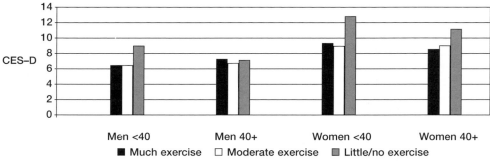

Figure 8.6 Depression scores (from the CES–D scale) for over 3,000 American men and women below and above 40 years of age differing in amount of leisure time physical activity (data from Stephens 1988)

particularly influential in demonstrating experimentally the anti-depressant effects of exercise. However, these are with clinical patients and will be discussed in Chapter 9.

Factors moderating the relationship between exercise and non-clinical depression

The results reported so far suggest that exercise is associated with reduced depression. However, the evidence is not strong in indicating clear differences between groups, such as men and women or across different ages. Evidence could not be located in groups differing by SES or ethnicity, although some studies have controlled for these factors and still located anti-depressant effects for exercise (for example, Farmer *et al.* (1988) for SES). Common sense dictates, however, that the greatest effects are likely for those with higher initial levels of depression. Non-depressed individuals cannot become 'more non-depressed' as a result of exercise!

In attempting to locate moderators for exercise and depression, it is important to recognise a number of factors identified by O'Connor, Aenchbacher and Dishman (1993) in their review of exercise and depression in the elderly. For example, they highlight that age is confounded by health status. Factors likely to lead to depression, such as poor health status, will be disproportionately represented in elderly groups. This means that any correlations between physical activity and depression in the elderly could be explained by many factors often not controlled for.

O'Connor *et al.* (1993) suggest that depression is more difficult to assess in the elderly and that age may by confounded by inactivity. The latter point concerns cohort effects for activity, such as evidence showing that the social acceptability of exercise is less in older adults than in their younger counterparts. Therefore, age *per se* may not be the factor accounting for age differences in physical activity in the elderly. Finally, the assessment of physical activity is particularly problematic in the elderly. Combining the four issues identified by O'Connor *et al.* (1993) highlights the potentially problematic area of locating moderators of the relationship between exercise and depression, at least in this age group.

In looking for moderators in this field what we are attempting is to identify how confident we are in concluding that exercise or physical activity *cause* a reduction in depression. To this end, some researchers have suggested that we adopt criteria used in epidemiological research for this purpose (see Dishman 1995; Mutrie 2000). This is used to judge the results of clinical studies in Chapter 9.

Non-clinical depression: summary

Based on the evidence reviewed, the following summary statements can be made concerning exercise and non-clinical depression:

* Meta-analytic findings suggest that exercise is associated with a significant moderate reduction in depression.
* This holds for acute and chronic exercise, different exercise modalities and groups differing by gender and age.
* Experimental studies support an anti-depressant effect for exercise.
* Large-scale epidemiological surveys support the claim that a physically active lifestyle is associated with lower levels of depression.

Exercise and cognitive functioning

> I found that I worked better and thought more clearly when I was in good physical condition.
>
> (Nelson Mandela, *Long walk to freedom*, 1994)

Subjective reports from runners (Mutrie and Knill-Jones 1986) suggest that over half of those questioned perceived that after running they can think more clearly. This would suggest that running and maybe other forms of activity can have a positive effect on some form of cognitive functioning. The term cognitive functioning embraces a wide variety of tasks ranging from simple reaction time to complex information processing.

Kirkendall (1986) concluded that a modest positive relationship existed between motor performance and intellectual performance in children and that this relationship was strongest in the early stages of development. Intervention techniques for learning-disabled children have also been investigated but a meta-analysis of 180 studies (Kavale and Mattson 1983) showed no positive effect on academic, cognitive or perceptual motor performance from perceptual-motor training on children whose average IQ was 88 at the age of 8 years. In an experimental study, MacMahon and Gross (1987) found no effect on academic performance for a group of boys with learning disabilities who were given a twenty-week vigorous aerobic exercise programme. A more recent narrative review of the use of exercise with learning-disabled children (Bluechardt, Wiener and Shephard 1995) also concluded that exercise programmes had not been successful in improving motor performance. Claims that exercise for children helps them perform better academically have been used in support of daily physical education programmes (Dwyer *et al.* 1983; Pollatschek and O'Hagan 1989), although a review by Shephard led him to conclude that 'daily programs of physical education should not be introduced with the expectation that they will lead to major gains in academic performance' (Shephard 1997: 123).

The literature on physical activity and cognitive development in children shows the strongest links in the early, pre-school years. Research in perceptual-motor development has suggested that the early development of psychomotor function and neuromuscular control could assist academic learning in young children. Increases in cerebral blood flow have been documented after physical activity, and this could assist in cognitive functioning. Similarly, activity will increase blood flow in the prefrontal somatosensory and primary motor cortices of the brain (Williams 1986). However, despite these plausible mechanisms, the studies of cognitive change in children exposed to physical activity interventions have been poorly controlled and open to severe methodological criticism.

Tomporowski and Ellis (1986) reviewed literature on the effects of exercise on cognitive processing and concluded that there was conflicting evidence. The explanation for this seems to lie in the experimental designs used. There is a need for studies to rule out the effects of different fitness levels (rather than just the effects of exercise) by having participants work at relative rather than absolute work loads, and it may be that differing intensities and duration of exercise will have differing effects. In addition, at least two questions can be addressed; firstly, the effect on cognition during exercise and, secondly, the post-exercise effect. Finally, the tests used to measure cognitive functioning must be free from influences of prior experience and learning.

Boutcher (2000) reviewed fourteen experimental studies on physical activity and cognitive functioning in older adults and found that only five showed positive effects after aerobic training. Etnier *et al.* (1997) conducted a meta-analysis of 134 studies and reported a mean overall ES of 0.25: a relatively small, though significant, effect. The effect was small for acute (ES = 0.16) and chronic (ES = 0.33) designs, but larger for cross-sectional (ES = 0.53) and mixed designs (ES = 0.54). In addition, more threats to the internal validity of both acute and chronic exercise studies yielded larger effect sizes. More well-controlled trials are needed.

Exercise, personality and adjustment

The question every sport and exercise psychologist has confronted is 'does physical activity affect personality?' Indeed, it is still commonly accepted that playing sport, at least for children and youth, is inherently 'good' and associated with 'character development'. Similarly, companies are willing to pay for their staff to attend outdoor activity centres in the belief that such activities assist in the development of leadership skills, positive group dynamics, etc. However, while this topic has occupied the minds of psychologists for many years, it has also been one of the most controversial and there are many factors likely to mediate any effects of physical activity on personality.

The European Federation of Sport Psychology ('Fédération Europeene de Psychologie des Sports et des Activités Corporelles': FEPSAC) has published a position statement summarising the positive and problem outcomes of involvement in sport for children (FEPSAC 1996). Some of the possible positive effects include the opportunities for challenge, social interactions, skill enhancement and physical development. Alternatively, some problem outcomes may arise, such as anxiety if the environment or adult leadership is inappropriate.

Given that this area is replete with anecdotal evidence and potentially biased claims, it is important to seek some kind of scientific consensus. Three reviews of the field provide guidance. First, McDonald and Hodgdon (1991) report a meta-analysis of aerobic fitness training and trait personality measures; second, Doan and Scherman (1987) review studies of exercise and personality; finally, Leith and Taylor (1990) provide a review of exercise and psychological well-being, including personality and self-perceptions.

McDonald and Hodgdon (1991) found nine different personality inventories used in studies of aerobic fitness training, but only three had a sufficient number of studies to analyse quantitatively. These were the 16PF (Cattell, Eber and Tatsuoka 1970), the Eysenck Personality Inventory (EPI) (Eysenck and Eysenck 1963) and the Minnesota Multiphasic Personality Inventory (MMPI) (Hathaway and McKinley 1943). No significant effects were found for aerobic fitness training on extraversion or neuroticism subscales of the EPI, but increased scores on the 16PF were found for intelligence (ES = 0.38) and self-sufficiency (ES = 0.30), and reduced scores for insecurity (ES = –0.18) and tension (ES = –0.38). Such

Box 8.1 Physical activity as 'nation building'

Much discussion in sport and other physical activity settings centres on the proposed links between involvement in physical activity and individual 'character development', as we have discussed. However, an extra dimension to this issue has recently re-entered the sport and exercise psychology arena: the role of physical activity (sport) in nation building. We say re-entered since the link between sport success and the promotion of 'good' in the nation is not new. It was fundamental to the role of sport in the past few decades in the former socialist countries of central and eastern European, and indeed continues in this way for similar political regimes, such as China and Cuba.

But a recent example has put a more humanistic face on this issue. In 1995, South Africa hosted, and won, the 3rd Rugby Union World Cup tournament. After the dismantling of apartheid and years of international sporting isolation, South Africa at last had an opportunity to be 'centre stage' in world sport. The team adopted the slogan 'one team, one nation', and it was widely reported that the event (greatly helped by the host nation – 'The Springboks' – winning!) substantially helped in the creation of a 'feel good' and united effect in a country where racial discrimination had created such division. Afterwards, President Nelson Mandela said 'The Springboks now identify with the aspirations of all the South African people – one team, one nation' (Kidane 1995: 27).

In presenting evidence on exercise and mental well-being at an international conference recently, one of us was asked by a South African delegate about the evidence on physical activity as 'nation building'. There is little or no 'scientific' evidence, although simple observation of recent events tell us a great deal. Clearly, physical activity (in this case vicarious involvement in sport as a spectator) has the potential to 'nation build' in a positive way. Whether all of the practices associated with this process are good remains to be seen.

results are consistent with other areas reviewed in this book, such as cognitive functioning (intelligence), anxiety (tension), and mood and psychological well-being (insecurity and self-sufficiency).

Studies using the MMPI mainly involved clinical groups so generalising to other populations is not possible. However, six of the ten clinical scales in the MMPI showed favourable changes. In addition, McDonald and Hodgdon's 'adjustment cluster' of hypochondriasis (–), social introversion (–), intelligence (+), schizophrenia (–), and hysteria (–) yielded an overall ES of 0.33, suggesting a small positive effect for aerobic fitness training on personality and adjustment.

Doan and Scherman (1987) listed sixteen 'personality' studies in their review and found that six of eight pre-experimental studies showed positive effects, but only three of six quasi-experimental studies and one of two experimental studies showed positive effects. None showed negative effects. This area, however, is plagued with measurement and definitional problems and caution is advised in interpreting these data.

Finally, Leith and Taylor (1990) used the same approach as Doan and Scherman (1987) and analysed results of studies according to whether they were pre-experimental, quasi-experimental, or experimental. Of three pre-experimental studies investigating personality, all showed 'positive' effects for exercise, with two also demonstrating improvements in fitness. All of these studies used the 16PF to assess personality. Of the forty-six quasi-experimental studies, only one was considered to assess personality. This showed a positive effect for exercise and fitness was also improved. Of the twenty-six experimental studies Leith and Taylor reviewed, only one referred to 'psychological adjustment' and none were classified as studying personality. The study of psychological adjustment showed no change in fitness and no change in psychosocial adjustment. In conclusion, positive associations between exercise and personality and adjustment have been found.

Exercise and sleep

There is anecdotal evidence and a common-sense belief that exercise can improve quality of sleep. In addition, a number of reviews suggest that sleep can be positively affected by exercise (Horne 1981; O'Connor and Youngstedt 1995). In addition, two meta-analyses have been conducted. Kubitz *et al.* (1996) found that acute exercise yielded significant effect sizes for a number of sleep variables. The ESs showed that individuals who exercised fell asleep faster, and slept longer and deeper than those not exercising. The meta-analysis by Youngstedt, O'Connor and Dishman (1997) confirmed these findings, with the exception of sleep onset latency. For chronic exercise, Kubitz *et al.* (1996) found that fitter individuals fell asleep faster, and slept deeper and longer than less fit individuals. ESs were small to moderate for both acute and chronic exercise.

Exercise and the menopause

The psychosocial challenges of the transitional years during which women gradually lose their reproductive function (medically termed the climacteric, but more commonly known as the menopause) are many. These include coming to terms with the end of reproductive years, changing roles in the family as children mature and leave home, potential increase in health problems of parents, self and partner, and opportunities for dedicating more time to career and self-development. Many women report that the climacteric is a positive time of change and an opportunity to experience more independence (Musgrave and Menell 1980). However, some women may experience a certain amount of physical and psychological distress during the climacteric. Vasomotor symptoms such as nocturnal sweating and hot flushes are the most commonly reported physical symptoms and are related to hormonal changes (Hunter, Battersby and Whitehead 1986). There is also evidence of non-clinical psychological symptoms with loss of self-confidence, depression and anxiety being the most frequently reported (Barlow *et al.* 1989; Hunter and Whitehead 1989). There are equivocal findings regarding sexual function. It has been suggested that loss of self-esteem is the most general climacteric symptom and several factors combine to reduce a woman's sense of self-esteem during the climacteric. These factors are low socioeconomic status, negative attitude towards the menopause and its consequences, limited social network, poor marital relationships and stressful life events.

Gannon (1988) has noted that there is potential for the use of exercise to alleviate some of the symptoms commonly reported by women during the climacteric. However, there is very little research to support this suggestion. Bachman *et al.* (1985) randomly assigned post menopausal women to either an exercise group (n = 12) or a control group (n = 10) and noted improvements in fitness and psychological well-being, with no change in sexual vitality, after thirteen weeks of exercise. Crammer, Neiman and Lee (1991) found similar results from a ten-week exercise programme for premenopausal women. In this study the women were randomly assigned to either a walking programme or to a sedentary control group. The exercise group showed improvements in cardiovascular function and psychological well-being but no change in percentage body fat after the ten-week programme.

No other experimental studies on women during the climacteric years could be found in searching the literature. However, Harris, Rohaly and Dailey (1993) provided qualitative data on why middle-aged, menopausal women exercise. They identified five primary motives for exercise from their analysis of interview data:

1   Personal power/control: 'I really like being in shape . . . there's a certain element of personal power that's involved in it'; 'I feel fairly good about myself, and confident in the things that I can do'.
2   Reclaiming the body: 'When I look in the mirror, I want to see a fit body'; 'Exercise has probably enabled me to look better in my clothes and feel better about myself'.
3   Well-being: 'It relieves me of a lot of tension'; 'I think the main reward in exercising is just feeling good. I know how much better I feel when I exercise regularly'.
4   Enjoyment: 'I really love the walk'; 'I enjoy having fun'.
5   Adjusting to the years: 'This is the way I want to grow old – active and thin'; 'I guess I want to be independent. I want to feel stronger'; '[As I get older I want to] look the way I want to look and feel about myself the way I want to feel'.

Although the women in this study were not asked directly about their menopausal symptoms it is evident from the examples of responses that their high self-esteem, happiness and satisfaction with the process of ageing are being attributed to physical exercise. These qualitative data provide information not attainable by traditional experimental designs. We recommend that further qualitative studies are undertaken which help us understand why some women exercise throughout their lives and why others stop. For example, use of the life history approach suggested by Sparkes (1997) may prove fruitful.

Further evidence on the association between exercise and menopausal status is available from cross-sectional studies. In one such study of women attending a hospital clinic for menopausal symptoms, thirty-eight were interviewed as they waited for their appointment (Mutrie and Choi 1993). They also completed a questionnaire on exercise habits, the Climacteric Symptoms Scale (Greene 1991) and the Physical Self-Perception Profile (PSPP) (Fox and Corbin 1989). On the basis of their responses the group were divided into those who were exercising for health or leisure purposes for at least sixty minutes per week (n = 17) and those who were sedentary (n = 21). The exercisers reported a higher estimation of their physical self-worth and physical condition than the non-exercisers and a trend to have less anxiety than the non-exercisers. This suggests that either those women who exercise have positive psychological advantages over non-exercisers or that more positive psychological dispositions allow women to exercise. The next generation of research must disentangle the cause and effect relationship, but it does appear from previous research that exercise can cause positive changes. Since this was a clinical sample, and remembering that it has been suggested that a reduction in self-esteem is the most general symptom of the climacteric, then exercise could be used as an adjunctive and or alternative treatment for this population of women.

Together the studies suggest that exercise may be a useful self-help and clinical treatment for menopausal symptoms and may be particularly important in promoting positive changes in body image and physical self-perceptions. Future experimental research must establish the effectiveness of such a treatment.

Physical activity and psychological well-being: mechanisms

This chapter suggests that physical activity is associated with numerous dimensions of psychological well-being. However, this is not enough. We also need to know *why* and *how* such effects occur. This necessitates a brief discussion on the mechanisms of such links.

Mechanisms explaining the effects of exercise on PWB have not been clearly identified. Several proposed mechanisms are plausible, including biochemical, physiological and psychological (Biddle and Mutrie 1991; Boutcher 1993; Morgan 1997). Possible biochemical and physiological mechanisms include:

* Changes associated with an increase in core body temperature with exercise: the thermogenic hypothesis (Koltyn 1997).
* Increase in endorphin production following exercise: the endorphin hypothesis (Hoffmann 1997)
* Changes in central serotonergic systems from exercise: the serotonin hypothesis (Chaouloff 1997).
* The effects of exercise on neurotransmitters, such as the norepinephrine hypothesis (Dishman 1997).
* The 'feel better' effect from PA may result from changes in physical self-worth and self-esteem from mastering new tasks, having a greater sense of personal control, or from time away from negative or more stressful aspects of our lives (Fox 1997b; Fox, in press).

In an elegant analysis of possible mechanisms and their interaction with exercise experience, Boutcher (1993) proposes that for those just starting exercise (that is, in the 'adoption phase'), greater emphasis should be placed on psychological mechanisms since the exerciser had not adapted, physiologically, to the exercise stimulus. In the maintenance phase, Boutcher suggests that both psychological and physiological mechanisms are likely to be important, and in the final habituation phase, he suggests that emphasis should be placed on physiological mechanisms and the influence of behavioural conditioning. These ideas are appealing since they integrate the context and experience of exercise with possible mechanisms. However, they require further testing.

Researchers looking at the psychological outcomes of exercise are strongly advised to attempt to refine our understanding of mechanisms. Possible explanations for why physical activity might influence mental health are likely to work in a synergistic way in which people may feel better, perceive an increased sense of control, notice less tension in muscles, sleep better, use less effort in daily tasks and have higher levels of circulating neurotransmitters. Perhaps it is this *gestalt* which provides the effect rather than one mechanism explaining one outcome. The problems for researchers do not get easier!

Chapter summary and conclusions

The relationship between physical activity and psychological well-being is one of the oldest areas of study in philosophy and psychology. It is not surprising, therefore, that evidence is both voluminous and controversial. Much of the debate stems from weak research designs and low statistical power in many studies, thus creating doubt about the true effects of exercise on PWB. However, nearly all areas studied show positive effects for exercise across diverse methods of investigation, including meta-analyses, population surveys and experimental trials, and virtually none show negative effects.

In this chapter, we have:

- Reviewed the evidence on physical activity and various indices of psychological well-being, including mood and affect, self-esteem, enjoyment, anxiety, non-clinical depression, cognitive functioning, personality and sleep.
- Used meta-analyses, population surveys and experimental trials, where available, to reach a research consensus.
- Summarised the likely mechanisms linking physical activity with pschological well-being.

In summary, therefore, we conclude:

- That exercise and physical activity participation is consistently associated with positive mood and affect.
- Quantified trends show that aerobic exercise has small-to-moderate positive effects on vigour, and small-to-moderate negative effects for fatigue and confusion.
- Experimental trials support the effect of moderate exercise on psychological well-being (PWB), but the trends for vigorous exercise are less clear.
- Exercise is related to positive changes in self-esteem and related physical self-perceptions.
- State, trait and psychophysiological measures of anxiety are less following exercise bouts or programmes; the effects are small-to-moderate.
- Aerobically fit individuals appear to have a reduced physiological response to psychosocial stressors.
- Exercise is associated with a moderate reduction in non-clinical depression.
- The effects of exercise on cognitive functioning appear to be small, though significant.
- Exercise can have a positive effect on personality and psychological adjustment
- Small effects suggest that individuals who exercise fall asleep faster, and sleep longer and deeper than those not exercising.
- Exercise can have positive effects for women during the climacteric.

9   Depression and other mental illnesses

Running and worrying don't mix.

W. Glasser
(*Positive addiction*, 1976)

Chapter objectives

This chapter reviews the role of physical activity and exercise in the treatment and prevention of depression and mental illness. Specifically, the chapter will:

- Introduce the topic of mental illness.
- Provide context for identifying the prevalence of depression and mental illness.
- Discuss the lack of acknowledgement of the role of physical activity in prevention and treatment of mental illness.
- Provide and in-depth review of the literature on physical activity and exercise on depression.
- Provide reviews of the role of physical activity in other mental illness, such as anxiety disorders, schizophrenia and alcohol and drug dependence.
- Note the possibility of negative effects from exercise.
- Draw conclusions about what we know.
- Make recommendations for researchers and practitioners.

Introduction

Depression and mental illness are considered as clinical issues and the chapter will be restricted to studies that have clinically defined populations. There is more literature on the topic of physical activity and depression than other mental illnesses and so it has been singled out in the title and will be given more attention. Mental illness has various definitions and is commonly studied under the heading of abnormal psychology. Other terms include psychiatric disorders, psychological disorders and mental disorders.

Mental disorder had been defined by the American Psychiatric Association (1994) as:

a clinically significant behavioral or psychological syndrome or pattern that occurs in an individual and that is associated with present distress (e.g., a painful symptom) or disability (i.e., impairment in one or more important areas of functioning) or with a significantly increased risk of suffering death, pain, disability, or an important loss of freedom. In addition, this syndrome or pattern must not be merely an expectable and culturally sanctioned response to a particular event, for example, the death of a loved one.

(American Psychiatric Association 1994: xxi)

In the area of public health, mental illness is the most commonly used term and UK Government initiatives currently prioritise mental illness as an area of concern (Department of Health 1998). Classifying the various types of mental illness is commonly done with reference to either the Diagnostic and Statistical Manual of Mental Disorders (DSM), of which version IV is the most recent (American Psychiatric Association 1994), or the International Classification of Diseases – 10 (ICD–10) (World Health Organization 1993) which classifies (and gives a numerical code) all diseases including mental and behavioural disorders. These classification systems allow both clinicians and researchers to have a common language concerning the various disorders and a known method of diagnosis, although experience and expert training in psychiatry or psychology is required to undertake any diagnosis. DSM–IV has five axes on which the classification of mental illness is made. The first two list all possible disorders and the remaining three allow the diagnosis to characterise physical health, the extent of stressful life circumstances and the overall degree of functioning. Table 9.1 shows the five axes. The ICD–10 (1993) chapter on mental and behavioural disorders contains classifications as specified by codes F00–F99 which are shown in Table 9.2.

Table 9.1 Five axes from DSM–IV for classifying mental illness

Axis	Description
1 Clinical disorders	In this axis each major disorder is described and criteria listed. The headings include depressed mood, anxiety, unexplained physical symptoms, cognitive disturbance, problematic substance abuse, sleep disturbance, sexual dysfunction, abnormal eating, psychotic symptoms, psychosocial problems and other mental disorders such as manic symptoms.
2 Personality disorders	In this axis dysfunctional personality traits are described and disorders usually first diagnosed in infancy, childhood or adolescence such as academic skills disorders or impaired social interaction.
3 General medical conditions	This axis is often the starting point of diagnosis since symptoms may be related to a recognised disorder. For example depressed mood may be related to hypothyroidism and that is a different diagnosis than depressed mood with no related medical condition.
4 Psychosocial and environmental problems	In this axis family, educational, housing, economic and legal problems are assessed.
5 Global assessment of functioning	The global assessment of functioning has a 100-point scale (GAF) which allows assessment of psychological, social and occupational functioning. The GAF scale ranges from 'persistant danger of severely hurting self or others' which would get a score of 1–10, to 'serious symptoms or any serious impairment in social, occupational, or school functioning' which would score 41–50 and to 'superior functioning in a wide range of activity' which would score 91–100.

Table 9.2 ICD–10 codes for mental and behavioural disorders

Numerical code	Description
F00–F09	Organic, including symptomatic, mental disorders (for example, dementia).
F10–F19	Mental and behavioural disorders due to psychoactive substance use (for example, dependence syndrome).
F20–F29	Schizophrenia, schizotypal and delusion disorders (for example, paranoid schizophrenia).
F30–F39	Mood (affective) disorders (for example, depression).
F40–F48	Neurotic, stress-related and somatoform disorders (for example, phobias).
F50–F59	Behavioural syndromes associated with physiological disturbances and physical factors (for example, eating disorders).
F60–F69	Disorders of adult personality and behaviour (for example, kleptomania).
F70–F79	Mental retardation (for example, mild mental retardation).
F80–F89	Disorders of psychological development (for example, developmental disorders of speech and language).
F90–F98	Behavioural and emotional disorders with onset usually occurring in childhood and adolescence (for example, hyperkinetic disorders).
F99	Unspecified mental disorder.

Treatment

Settings for treatment of psychological disorders include general practice, hospitals, specialist clinics (or resource centres), private therapy and informal settings. Many treatments include drug therapy thus requiring a GP or psychiatrist to be involved. In extreme cases more invasive procedures such as electroconvulsive therapy or psychosurgery (such as prefrontal lobotomy) are performed. More common therapies include focusing on the way the person is thinking or feeling and acknowledging their social circumstances. The range of trained professionals who might undertake this therapy include psychiatrists, clinical psychologists, counselling psychologists and social workers. Within this area there are many approaches ranging from psychoanalysis (which perhaps is the lay person's impression of therapy involving a couch and a person taking notes), to client-centred and cognitive-behavioural approaches. Sometimes the whole family may be involved in the therapeutic process. Of interest to us is the role of physical activity in the prevention and treatment of psychological disorders. Physical activity could be seen as part of a treatment programme that might assist with enhancing moods and self-esteem, encouraging socialising and improving physical health. In thinking about how physical activity might prevent psychological disorders, it is possible that it provides a means by which one's sense of self develops (Fox 1997b), allows competencies to develop, provides opportunities for socialisation and promotes physical health and fitness.

Prevalence

The prevalence of mental illness is clearly a concern for public health. In the UK, the Office for Population Census and Surveys (OPCS) published a survey on the prevalence of psychiatric morbidity in 1995 (Meltzer *et al.* 1995). This survey used the Clinical Interview Schedule (CIS) to classify neurotic disorders, functional psychosis, and alcohol and drug dependence. The survey was representative of adults aged 16–64 years in Great Britain and involved over 10,000 interviews. It was concluded that 160 per 1,000 adults had suffered a neurotic disorder in the week prior to interview, with the most common disorder being mixed anxiety and depression. Neurotic disorders were more common amongst women than men. There was a much smaller incidence of functional psychosis such as schizophrenia with a prevalence rate of 4 per 1,000 noted. Alcohol and drug dependence had prevalence rates of 44 and 22 per 1,000 respectively, but young adults aged between 16–24 years had much higher incidences for both alcohol dependency (176 per 1,000) and drug dependency (111 per 1,000), making alcohol dependence a problem for one in six young adults. Overall about 14 per cent of the population scored twelve or above on the CIS, thus indicating mental illness. Table 9.3 shows the prevalence of common cardiovascular conditions in Scotland as reported in the 1995 Scottish Health Survey (Dong and Erins 1997). It can be seen from this table that none of the common cardiovascular conditions are as prevalent as mental illness. Thus mental illness is not a trivial issue affecting small proportions of the population, rather, it is as common as high blood pressure and much more common than heart attacks and strokes. In addition, the survey statistics just described only relate to adults aged 16–64 years. The prevalence of mental health problems among children in the UK is estimated at up to 20 per cent with 7–10 per cent having moderate to severe problems which prevent normal functioning (Kurtz 1992).

In terms of physical activity, the OCPS survey (Meltzer *et al.* 1995) asked two very simple questions about walking and sports participation. However, these data do not appear in the analysis of issues which relate to the prevalence of mental illness. This analysis must be undertaken in future surveys, but more appropriate measures of physical activity are required. In the Scottish Health Survey 1995 (Dong and Erins 1997), physical activity was assessed by self-report and covered activity at home, at work, and sports and exercise. The responses were then classified into six levels from 0–5 and are similar to the criteria adopted in the English National Fitness Survey (The Sports Council and Health Education Authority 1992). Table 9.4 shows the classifications.

The Scottish survey did report a relationship between levels of physical activity and psychological well-being, as measured by the General Health Questionnaire (GHQ) (Goldberg *et al.* 1970). For both men and women the percentage with a GHQ score over four (indicating mental health problems) was lowest in activity level 5 and highest in activity level 0.

Given the universal consensus on the role of physical activity for health, there is now a need for a global agreement on how to measure physical activity in surveys relating to all aspects of health. In both England and Scotland physical activity task forces have been recommended or already set up and one target for these groups must be to make recommendations about how to measure physical activity in surveys to allow meaningful comparisons to be made over time. What is also required are prospective studies that track populations over time and can therefore provide good evidence for the relationship between activity levels and the onset of mental illness. Steptoe and Butler (1996) suggested that this could be done with British data from

Table 9.3 Prevalence of common cardiovascular conditions in Scotland

Condition	Percentage of men reporting condition	Percentage of women reporting condition
Angina	3.1	2.5
Heart attack	2.4	1.1
Stroke	1.0	0.5
Hypertension	13.3	13.9
Diabetes	1.5	1.5
Heart murmur	2.1	3.2

Source: Dong and Erins 1997.

Table 9.4 Classifications of six levels of activity used in the Scottish Health Survey

Level	Criterion
5	Three or more occasions of vigorous activity per week.
4	Three or more occasions of a mixture of vigorous and moderate activity per week.
3	Three or more occasions of moderate activity per week.
2	More than one, less than three occasions of moderate or vigorous activity per week
1	One occasion of moderate or vigorous activity per week or less
0	No occasions of moderate or vigorous activity per week

Source: Dong and Erins 1997.

a cohort study initiated in 1970, which they have already used to show a positive association between sport participation and emotional well-being for the cohort during adolescence.

Lack of acknowledgement from mental health professionals of the role of physical activity and exercise

Over the past twenty years the literature in the area of physical activity/exercise and mental health has been growing (see Chapters 8 and 10). However, as Dishman (1995) points out, the evidence has not persuaded mental health agencies, such as the American Psychiatric Association, to endorse the role of exercise in treating mental illness such as depression. In the UK, a recent overview of depression and its treatment did not mention the value of exercise at all (Hale 1997). This is in contrast to coronary artery disease in which inactivity is now recognised as a primary risk factor (Pate *et al.* 1995). Perhaps the evidence for the role of exercise in treating and preventing mental illness is not convincing. Maybe the mental health literature is suffering from a dualist tendency to treat the mind (mental health) and body (physical health) as separate issues, thereby failing to recognise the mental outcomes of a physical treatment such as exercise (Beesley and Mutrie 1997). Rejeski and Thompson are more optimistic in suggesting that we are moving away from dualism: 'The mind–body distinction has slowly, but noticeably yielded to the concept of biopsychosocial interactions – the position that the body, the mind, and the social context of human existence are reciprocally interdependent on one another' (Rejeski and Thompson 1993: 7). If we are indeed moving away from dualism then perhaps we would expect those who treat mental health problems to promote exercise as part of treatment. However, McEntee and Halgin (1996) reported that while many psychotherapists believe in the therapeutic value of exercise, very few (around 10 per cent) recommend exercise to their clients. From their survey of 110 practising psychotherapists, McEntee and Halgin concluded that one of the major reasons for this reluctance to discuss exercise was that it was perceived as inappropriate in so far that exercise was perceived as being very directive and perhaps dealt with better by physicians or physical recreation specialists. 'Many therapists simply do not see their work as pertaining to the body, and they believe that most clients come to therapy to discuss psychological ailments, not physical or exercise-related ones' (McEntee and Halgin 1996: 55). It would therefore seem that there is much work to be done to convince those who deliver mental health services to focus on the links between mind and body and to look more positively on the role of exercise in mental health issues.

Another aspect of the treatment of mental illness that suggests that it is worthwhile to pursue the possibility of the use of exercise is that of patient choice. In the UK, drugs continue to be the most frequently used treatment for depression although psychotherapy and ECT are also used (Hale 1997). Patients often report that they do not want drugs (Scott 1996). Consequently, exercise is a reasonable option with few negative side effects and could be cost-effective in comparison to other non-drug options such as psychotherapy. Studies on the cost-effectiveness and cost-benefit of exercise versus drugs or other therapies must be undertaken so that the potential economic advantages of exercise can be measured. Perhaps the economic arguments will be the most powerful in persuading mental health professionals to include exercise as a treatment option. On a more positive note, recent leaflets from the Royal College of Psychiatrists and from the Health Education Authority suggest that taking exercise is a good self-help strategy for depression.

Depression

Depression is one of the most common psychiatric problems. An estimated 20 per cent of patients in primary care have some degree of depressive symptomology (Paykel and Priest 1992). In addition, by analysing American employee health insurance data, depression is the most common complaint in the workplace with a higher prevalence in women than men (Anspaugh, Hunter and Dignan 1996). It has been estimated that clinically defined depression affects 5–10 per cent of the population of most developed countries (Weismann and Klerman 1992). Taken together this evidence suggests a large and expensive burden in healthcare resources in the treatment of depression.

Definitions of depression range from episodes of unhappiness that affect most people from time to time, to persistent low mood and inability to find enjoyment. In addition, depression may be secondary to other medical conditions, such as alcohol addiction. Most cases of depression are treated in general practice but more severe cases are referred to psychiatric services.

Defining clinical depression

One issue that has plagued our understanding of the relationship between physical activity and depression is the lack of agreement amongst researchers concerning the criteria defining depression. Many previous reviews have included cases of 'depression' that would not reach clinically defined criteria and may be better defined as transitory negative affect. In this chapter only clinically defined depression will be included. Discussion on depressive mood is included in Chapter 8. For clinically defined depression, patients will have sought help for their symptoms and a diagnosis made using standard instruments or interviews. The DSM–IV criteria for a major depressive disorder are summarised in Table 9.5.

The most common questionnaire used for assessment, especially in exercise studies, is the Beck Depression Inventory (BDI) (Beck *et al.* 1961). Moderate depression on the BDI is defined as a score of sixteen or above. However, many exercise studies have included people with scores lower than sixteen at baseline. This is considered as a transitory or normal score and such studies are not included in this chapter. In respect of clinical interview, diagnosis of depression is made using criteria listed in the DSM–IV (American Psychiatric Association 1994), or the ICD–10 (World Health Organization 1993). In research studies, the Research Diagnostic Criteria are often used (Spitzer, Endicott and Robins 1978). Depression can also occur with other chronic diseases and mental disorders and such cases will be included in this section of the chapter, but all will have met the criteria for clinical depression.

Consensus statements

In Chapter 8, consensus statements were reported showing that there is considerable agreement that exercise is associated with good mental health. This chapter aims to deal with

Table 9.5 Summary of DSM–IV criteria for major depressive episode

Category	Criteria
A	At least five of the following symptoms have been present during the same two-week period, nearly every day, and represent a change from previous functioning. At least one of the symptoms must be either 1 depressed mood or 2 loss of interest or pleasure.
A(1)	Depressed mood (or alternatively can be irritable mood in children and adolescents).
A(2)	Markedly diminished interest or pleasure in all, or almost all, activities.
A(3)	Significant weight loss or weight gain when not dieting.
A(4)	Insomnia or hypersomnia.
A(5)	Psychomotor agitation or retardation.
A(6)	Fatigue or loss of energy.
A(7)	Feelings of worthlessness or excessive or inappropriate guilt.
A(8)	Diminished ability to think or concentrate.
A(9)	Recurrent thoughts of death, recurrent suicidal ideation without a specific plan, or a suicidal attempt or a specific plan for committing suicide.
B	Symptoms are not better accounted for by a Mood Disorder Due to a General Medical Condition, a Substance-Induced Mood Disorder, or Bereavement (normal reaction to death of a loved one).
C	Symptoms are not better accounted for by a Psychotic Disorder (for example, Schizo-affective Disorder).

depression and mental illness, and only three of the National Institute of Mental Health consensus statements (Morgan and Goldston 1987b) relate to this topic. These are:

- Anxiety and depression are common symptoms of failure to cope with mental stress, and exercise has been associated with a decreased level of mild to moderate depression and anxiety.
- Severe depression usually requires professional treatment which may include medication, electroconvulsive therapy and/or psychotherapy with exercise as an adjunct.
- Physically healthy people who require psychotropic medication may safely exercise when exercise and medication are titrated under close medical supervision.

Studied in this way the consensus statements about exercise having a therapeutic effect on clinical cases of mental illness is not that convincing since there is only an agreement of an association, rather than a causal link, for exercise and mild-to-moderate depression; exercise is only mentioned as an adjunct to the treatment of more severe depression with no specific mention of the benefits this might provide; and the final point that it is safe to exercise whilst using psychotropic medication is a guide to practice rather than a consensus on the use of exercise in such situations. Keeping in mind that only clinical cases (that is, people who have sought help from health professionals for their condition or those who have been diagnosed by clinicians) are being discussed in this chapter a more detailed look at the evidence will now be made.

Epidemiological evidence for the role of exercise in the prevention of depression

We owe a great debt to the work of William Morgan who pioneered much of the initial research investigating the role of exercise and mental health (Morgan 1968; 1969; 1970a;

1985; 1994; 1997; Morgan and Goldston 1987a; Morgan and O'Connor 1988). It was per-haps his early findings that fitness levels, for both male (Morgan 1968; 1969) and female (Morgan 1970b) psychiatric patients, were lower than non-hospitalised controls which led to experimental work in using exercise as part of a treatment regime for such patients. Martinsen *et al.* 1989d) replicated these findings with Norwegian psychiatric patients near time of admission. Morgan (1970a) also showed that patients admitted to a psychiatric hospital, but discharged after a short period of time (on average sixty-one days), had higher levels of muscular endurance on admission than patients with similar initial levels of depression who remained in hospital for longer (at least one year). Such cross-sectional data raised intriguing questions about whether lack of exercise can cause depression or whether depression causes lack of exercise and whether increasing fitness levels could influence recovery. There were also questions about how much heredity and motivation play a part in the results of fitness tests obtained in these studies. However, some of these early questions have now been answered. In the next section, the review of epidemiological evidence suggests that depression is indeed associated with low activity/fitness and that those who maintain activity are less likely to develop depression.

The strongest epidemiological evidence comes from four prospective studies that have followed cohorts over time. In all of the studies depression was clinically defined and in one study depression was diagnosed by psychiatric interview (Weyerer 1992). Statistical adjust-ments for potential confounding variables, such as age and socio-economic background, were also made in each of the studies.

Farmer *et al.* (1988) reported a follow-up of 1,497 respondents to a large survey with par-ticular regard to activity and depression. They showed that, over a period of eight years, women who had engaged in little or no activity were twice as likely to develop depression as those who had engaged in 'much' or 'moderate' activity. The effects of age, employment, income, education and chronic medical conditions were all statistically accounted for. There was no significant association over the same time period for men, but for those men who were depressed at baseline, inactivity was a strong predictor of continued depression at the eight-year follow-up.

Camacho *et al.* (1991) also found an association between inactivity and incidence of depression in a large population from Almeda County in California. Baseline data were collected in 1965 and followed up in 1974 and 1983. Physical activity was categorised as low, medium or high. In the first wave of follow-up (1974), the relative risk (RR) of developing depression was significantly greater for both men and women who were low active in 1965 (RR 1.8 for men, 1.7 for women) compared to those who were high active. There is some evidence for a dose-response relationship with those who were moderately active in 1965 showing lower risk of developing depression than those who were low active (see Figure 9.1).

In the second follow-up in 1983, four categories of activity status were created. These categories are shown in Table 9.6 and are defined as follows:

1   Those who were low active in 1965 and remained low in 1974 (low/low).
2   Those who had been low active in 1965 but had increased activity level in 1974 (low/high).
3   Those who had been high active in 1965 and decreased activity by 1974 (high/low).
4   Those who had been high active at both time points (high/high).

Those who were inactive in 1965 but had increased activity in 1974 were at no greater

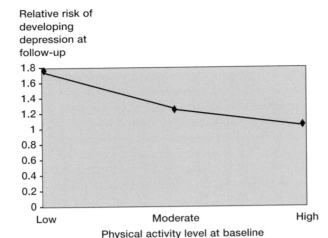

Relative risk of
developing
depression at
follow-up

Physical activity level at baseline

Figure 9.1 Relative risk of developing depression at follow-up from different levels of baseline
physical activity (Camacho *et al.* 1991)

risk of developing depression in 1983 than those who had been active at both times points
(the reference group for computing the odds ratio). This suggests that physical activity may
have a protective effect. None of the odds ratios computed for risk of depression in 1983
showed significant difference between the four activity categories. The largest odds ratio,
however, was for those who had relapsed from activity in 1965 to inactivity in 1974. They
were 1.6 times more likely to develop depression in 1983 than those who had maintained
activity, but it must be remembered that this odds ratio did not reach significance. The
authors note, however, that this odds ratio was relatively unaffected by adjustments for age,
sex, physical health, socio-economic status, social support, life events, anomie, smoking
status, relative weight, 1965 level of depression and alcohol consumption. This leads them
to believe it is a robust finding. Given that only 137 people were in this category, it is
perhaps not surprising that the odds ratio did not reach significance. However, the evidence
from the 1974 follow-up did provide statistically significant evidence that low activity
preceded the reported depression.

Similar findings have been reported by Paffenbarger, Lee and Leung (1994b) from the
Harvard Alumni studies which followed men for 23–27 years. In that study, men who
engaged in three or more hours of sport activity per week at baseline had a 27 per cent
reduction in the risk of developing depression at follow-up compared to those who played
for less than one hour per week. When the authors combined the various indices of physical
activity (sports play, walking, stair climbing) evidence for a dose-response relationship
emerged. Those who had expended 2,500 kcal or more/week were 28 per cent less at risk of
developing clinically recognised depression than men who expended less than 1,000
kcal/week, while those who expended between 1,000 and 2,499 kcal/week had a 17 per cent
reduction in risk compared to the least active group. This dose-response trend was
significant and is illustrated in Figure 9.2 in terms of relative risk.

All of these studies have been conducted on North American populations but Weyerer
(1992) showed that in a community sample from Bavaria (n = 1,536), the physically inactive were over three times more likely to have depression than those who were regularly
physically active. All people in this study were interviewed by a research psychiatrist and

Table 9.6 Changes in physical activity status and subsequent depression

Activity status 1965/1974	Odds ratio for developing depression in 1983	Confidence interval for odds ratio
1 low/low	1.22	0.62–2.38
2 low/high	1.11	0.52–2.21
3 high/low	1.61	0.80–3.22
4 high/high	1.00	reference group

Source: Camacho *et al.* 1991.

8.3 per cent were identified as depressed using a clinical scale There was some evidence for a dose-response relationship. Those reporting only occasional physical activity were 1.55 times more likely to have depression than those who were regularly physically active, although this was not statistically significant. These cross-sectional data are open to the criticism that the relationship is created because the depressed are inactive. The strongest counter to this argument, which we have seen in the three studies already reviewed, is follow-up data which show the least active are most at risk of developing depression at a later point in time. However, low physical activity was not a predictor of depression at a five-year follow-up to this study. The time scale of the Weyerer follow-up was shorter than any of the other studies and this may be the reason for this apparent difference in results.

All four of these studies show an association between activity and depression with the least active having the greatest incidence of depression. In three of the four studies follow-up data suggested that inactivity at baseline was predictive of developing depression at follow-up. This suggests that inactivity precedes depression. It is important to reiterate that other possible variables, such as physical health status, were accounted for since people may well be inactive because they are disabled or prevented from taking part in activity because of a medical condition. However, there are other reasons, such as lack of social skills or socio-economic status, which could also predict both inactivity and depression which may not have been fully accounted for. Hopefully, there will be more epidemiological data of this nature that will help us form a picture of the time course of the onset of depression in relation to inactivity and allow for further exploration of variables predicting inactivity and depression. In particular, longitudinal studies are required to elucidate the possible benefits and risks of involvement in physical activity for youth on adult psychological functioning. Steptoe and Butler (1996) suggested that this could be done with British data from a cohort

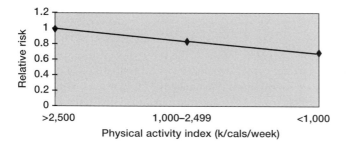

Figure 9.2 Relative risk of developing depression at follow-up from different levels of physical activity at baseline (adapted from Paffenbarger *et al.* 1994)

study initiated in 1970, which they have already used to show a positive association between sport participation and emotional well-being for the cohort during adolescence. Thus the epidemiological data are strongly suggestive of a protective effect from activity but yet more data are required. A final point to note is that there is no evidence to suggest that increasing physical activity or exercise increases the risk of depression.

Meta-analyses on exercise and depression

Two meta-analytic reviews of the use of exercise as a treatment for depression have provided further substantial evidence for positive effects from exercise, as reported in Chapter 8 (McDonald and Hodgdon 1991; North *et al.* 1990). Both report effect sizes of around one half of a standard deviation of change in depression scores which suggests that exercise does have an anti-depressant effect. Calfas and Taylor (1994) report a small meta-analysis of five RCT studies on healthy and psychologically 'at risk' adolescents. They reported an effect size of –0.38 for exercise on depression, although the small number of studies involved means that this must be a cautious conclusion.

The outcome of meta-analytic reviews are subject to the quality of the input. Dishman (1995) suggests that averaging together results from studies with different designs and different methods of measuring the variables of interest is not helpful and concludes that there are too few studies with similar features to warrant confidence in the results of meta-analyses in this area. The issue of whether depression has been clinically defined is particularly important for this chapter. In fact, very few studies included in North *et al.*'s (1990) or McDonald and Hodgdon's (1991) meta-analyses on depression had clinically diagnosed individuals.

Craft and Landers (1998) have addressed this issue and conducted a meta-analysis confined to those with clinically defined depression. This meta-analysis included thirty studies, many of which were unpublished dissertations. The average effect size was calculated at –0.72. Further analysis of the moderating variables showed that the effect sizes for mode of exercise (aerobic versus non-aerobic) did not differ, nor was there a difference between exercise treatment and psychotherapeutic or behavioural interventions. However, there was a greater effect size for those initially classified as moderate-to-severe in depression compared to those classified as mild-to-moderate. The results of this meta-analysis are therefore very encouraging. Nevertheless, even with a well-conducted meta-analysis, Dishman's (1995) criticisms remain valid since in some of the comparisons (for example, with different entry level of depression) there are still very few studies. It seems best, therefore, to also look at individual studies in detail rather than relying solely on conclusions from meta-analyses.

Key studies

Most narrative reviews (Biddle and Mutrie 1991; Byrne and Byrne 1993; Gleser and Mendelberg 1990; Martinsen 1989; Morgan 1994) of the topic of exercise and depression make cautious positive conclusions but note the methodological limitations of many studies and this criticism has been echoed many times (Dishman 1995). However, with the exception of Martinsen (1989; 1993; 1994), reviews to date have included non-clinical depression and Morgan (1994) noted that one of the most reliable findings in this area is that exercise will not decrease depression in those who are not depressed in the first place. It would seem appropriate, therefore, to examine all studies in which exercise has been used to treat those with clinical depression and to limit the discussion to studies having the best design features. All studies from 1970 that could be located by standard search methods, incorporating random assignment of participants to groups, and including a clinically defined measure of depression were reviewed. This process excluded some well-designed studies, such as McCann and Holmes (1984), because depression levels were below sixteen on the BDI and there was no clinical interview to confirm the diagnosis. The eleven key studies identified are summarised in Table 9.7.

Conclusions from key studies

The first and obvious conclusion from Table 9.7 is that more studies are required. Only four could be found that had been conducted in the 1990s. It could also be concluded that both internal and external validity are high, given that only those studies with good design features were included, and given that they have been conducted in North America and Europe, all with similar results. From the table it is concluded that exercise programmes (both aerobic and non-aerobic) can reduce clinically defined depression and that the reduction of depression is of the same order as that found for a variety of standard psychotherapeutic treatments. Furthermore, these anti-depressant effects are feasible in a short time frame (4–8 weeks) and persist from two months to one year. The findings apply to middle-aged and older adults. These findings are similar to those from meta-analyses and thus add confidence to the meta-analytic conclusion that exercise can have a substantial anti-depressant effect.

What we do not know is the comparative effects of exercise treatment with drug treatment. This seems surprising given that drugs are the most common treatment for depression in the UK, and it is also surprising that so few studies have been conducted in the UK. The studies in Table 9.7 have mean ages of participants between 29–71 years, suggesting that exercise effects for depression levels for youth have not been studied. Only one study on the use of exercise as an adjunctive treatment in clinically diagnosed mental illness in children was found (Brown *et al.* 1992), but it was excluded from the table of key studies since it did not reach the design criteria. In addition, we do not know much about adherence levels to exercise especially in the follow-up phases. Some studies do report this but in most cases the details are missing.

It is clearly difficult to conduct studies with good design features in this area. Even by selecting those studies with random assignment to treatment conditions methodological difficulties remain which limit the strength of the conclusions. These difficulties include:

- Achieving a large enough sample to ensure statistical power (could the findings of 'no difference' between some conditions be a Type 2 statistical error?).
- Equalising time in contact with professionals in the different treatment conditions.
- Avoiding resentful demoralisation in a no treatment group or a group given the 'routine' as opposed to the 'new' treatment.
- Controlling for the effects of the positive characteristics of an exercise leader.
- Conducting long term follow-up.
- Finding adequate measures of the variables of interest including fitness changes.

The next stage for research is to overcome these methodological difficulties.

Evaluating the evidence for the anti-depressant effect of exercise

It is still difficult to conclude that there is a causal link between exercise and reduction in depression because there are many peripheral issues (such as the effect of an exercise

Table 9.7 Randomised controlled studies of exercise treatment for clinically defined depression

Authors/location	Subjects and clinical assessment	Design	Treatment groups	Measures	Results (statistically significant at 0.05)
(Greist et al. 1979) USA	n = 28 (15 women), RDC criteria for depression.	Ten weeks of treatment one and three month follow-up.	1 10 sessions of time-limited psychotherapy. 2 Time-unlimited psychotherapy. 3 Running with a leader 3 x 30–45 mins/week.	SCL.	The running treatment was as effective as the two psychotherapy treatments.
(Klein et al. 1985) USA	n = 74 (53 women), mean age 30 years, recruited via media, RDC criteria for depression.	Twelve weeks of treatment and one, three and nine month follow-up.	1 Running with a leader, 2 x 45 mins/week. 2 Group meditation, 2 hours/week. 3 Group therapy, 2 hours/week.	SCL and psychiatric interview.	The running treatment was as effective as the other two treatments.
(Martinsen, Medhus and Sandvik 1985) Norway	n = 43, mean age 40 years, hospitalised depressives; clinical assessment by DSM–III.	9 weeks of treatment.	1 Exercise group, aerobic training, 50–70% $VO_{2\,max}$, 1 hour, 3/week. 2 Control group, occupational therapy, 1 hour, 3/week.	BDI; predicted $VO_{2\,max}$.	The exercise group decreased depression scores and increased fitness more than the control group.
(Doyne et al. 1987) USA	n = 40 (all women) recruited through mass media; mean age 29 years; clinical assessment by RDC.	Eight weeks of treatment; one, seven, twelve month follow-up.	1 Aerobic group (running); 4/week. 2 Non-aerobic group (weight-lifting); 4/week. 3 Waiting list control group.	BDI; HRSD; cardiovascular fitness. (METS) from sub-maximal test.	Both exercise conditions reduced depression more than waiting list control. Levels of depression remained lower than baseline to one year follow-up.
(Fremont and Craighead 1987) USA	n = 49, recruitment via advertisement, BDI scores of 16 and above.	10 weeks of treatment and 2 month follow-up.	1 Cognitive therapy 1 hour/week. 2 Running with a leader, 3 x 20mins/week. 3 Both cognitive therapy and running.	BDI.	All three groups improved. Improvements maintained at two month follow-up.

Study	Sample	Duration	Intervention	Measures	Results
(Mutrie 1988) UK	n = 24 (20 women), mean age 42 years, clinical assessment by GP diagnoses and BDI scores of 16 and above.	Eight weeks of treatment; assessment at four weeks, eight weeks and twenty week follow-up.	1 Aerobic exercise conducted at home (walk/jog) 3 x 20–30 mins./week 2 Non-aerobic strengthening and stretching exercise conducted at home, 3 x 20–30 mins./week 3 No treatment for four weeks, then combination of aerobic and non-aerobic exercise, 3 x 20–30 mins/week.	BDI, POMS, standard step-test for aerobic fitness, standard sit-up test for strength.	After four weeks only the aerobic group made significant reductions on BDI. After eight weeks all groups decreased BDI scores and these scores were maintained at twenty weeks with no group differences. There were no group differences in fitness test results with no change noted at four weeks and all groups improving by eight weeks.
(Martinsen et al. 1989a) Norway	n = 99 (63 women), mean age 41 years, hospitalised depressives, RDC classification.	Eight weeks of treatment.	1 Aerobic training, 3 x 1 hour/week. 2 Strength and flexibility training, 3 x 1 hour/week.	Montgomery-Asberg rating scale, predicted $VO_{2\,max}$.	Both groups decreased depression scores. Only the aerobic group made gains on $VO_{2\,max}$.
(Veale et al. 1992) trial 1 UK	n = 83 (53 women) mean age 36 years, clinical assessment by CIS.	Twelve weeks of treatment.	1 Standard treatment. 2 Aerobic exercise (3/week running) adjunctive to standard treatment.	CIS, BDI, predicted $VO_{2\,max}$.	Exercise group reduced depressive symptoms (CIS) and trait anxiety more than standard group despite incomplete adherence by some S's.
(Veale et al. 1992) trial 2 UK	n = 41; clinical assessment by CIS.	Twelve weeks of treatment.	Each group received standard treatment and either: 1 Aerobic exercise (3/week) or 2 Non-aerobic exercise (stretching, yoga) (3/week).	CIS, BDI, predicted $VO_{2\,max}$.	Both exercise groups showed similar changes to that seen in trial 1 above. No differences between groups on any measures.
(Bosscher 1993) Netherlands	n = 24 (12 women), mean age 34 years, hospitalised depressives, RDC classification, SDS >40.	Eight weeks of treatment.	1 Standard movement therapy of mixed games and exercises, 50 mins 3 x week. 2 Running 45 mins 3 x week.	SDS.	Only the running group showed significant decreases in depression although scores still above entry level criteria. No fitness measures taken.

Table 9.7 (continued)

(Singh, Clements and Fiatorone 1997) USA	n = 32 (20 women), mean age 71 years, clinical assessment by DSM–IV criteria.	Ten weeks of treatment.	1 Progressive resistance training (PRT) 3 x week. 2 Attention – control group meeting 2 x week.	BDI, HRSD, SF–36, strength (1 repetition max.).	All depression measures, strength, SF–36 subscales of bodily pain, vitality, social functioning and role emotional showed significantly greater improvements in PRT group than controls (95% compliance).

Abbreviations
RDC (Research Diagnostic Criteria) (Spitzer *et al.* 1978)
DSM–III or IV (Diagnostic and Statistical Manual of Mental Disorders) (American Psychiatric Association 1980; 1994)
SCL (Symptom Checklist) (Derogatis *et al.* 1973)
BDI (Beck Depression Inventory) (Beck *et al.* 1961)
HRSD (Hamilton Rating Scale) (Hamilton 1960)
POMS (Profile of Mood States) (McNair *et al.* 1971)
CIS (Clinical Interview Schedule) (Goldberg *et al.* 1970)
SDS (Zung Depression Scale) (Zung, Richards and Short 1965)
SF–36 (Medical Outcomes Survey Short Form) (Ware, Snows, Kosinski and Gandek 1993)

leader, or a class effect) associated with most of the successful programmes. Also there are relatively few experimental studies. Nevertheless, given the recent addition of epidemiological data to the discussion it may be appropriate to use Hill's (1965) classic criteria for deciding whether there is an association or a causal link between observed illness (in this case depression) and some environmental condition (in this case exercise status). Hill suggested eight criteria which can be used to help scientists and practitioners decide if a causal interpretation of evidence can be made. These eight criteria will be used to draw conclusions concerning any anti-depressant effect of exercise. The eight criteria are:

1   strength of association
2   consistency of evidence
3   specificity of effect
4   temporal sequencing
5   dose-response relationship
6   biological plausibility
7   coherence
8   experimental evidence.

STRENGTH OF ASSOCIATION

The first of Hill's criteria is strength of the association. Meta-analytic studies show an effect size between 0.53 and 0.72 for exercise on depression. Epidemiological studies suggest a relative risk of around 1.7 for the inactive reporting depression at a later date. This evidence is not quite as strong as that for exercise and coronary heart disease, where a range of relative risk of between 1.5 to 2.5 for the inactive have been reported (Pate *et al.* 1995). Nevertheless, the strength of association between exercise and depression can be seen and is described as moderate-to-large.

CONSISTENCY

Hill's second criterion is consistency: the question of whether or not the association between exercise and depression has been shown in different places, with different people, at different times and in different circumstances. If we look at Table 9.7 we can see that experimental evidence has been found in the USA, UK and elsewhere in Europe. The same is true of the epidemiological evidence. Men and women have been studied, the data span three decades of work, and the circumstances include community, hospitals and primary care settings. So it does seem that the findings are consistent.

SPECIFICITY

Specificity, the third of Hill's criteria, refers to whether or not other associations exist between the conditions and disease. Hill argues that if specificity can be claimed (that is, limiting the conditions to the disease, such as smoking and lung cancer) this strengthens the argument for causation. In exercise studies specificity does not exist. Depression is not the only condition linked to inactivity (Blair *et al.* 1989), and depression itself has multiple causes (Kaplan *et al.* 1987). However, Hill also argued that if specificity is not present other criteria may supply extra evidence.

TEMPORAL SEQUENCE

The fourth of Hill's criteria is temporal sequence. In order to conclude that there is a causal link between inactivity and depression we must demonstrate that inactivity precedes the onset of depression. Early cross-sectional studies could not provide an answer to this question because it was equally likely that depression preceded inactivity. However, at least three prospective populations studies have shown that the inactive are more likely to develop depression. Thus there is some evidence for the temporal sequence which strengthens the causation argument.

DOSE-RESPONSE RELATIONSHIP

Hill's fifth criterion is evidence for a dose-response curve or biological gradient. Two prospective epidemiological studies have shown a dose-response gradient with the least active at baseline being most at risk of developing depression at follow-up, while the most active had the lowest risk. In terms of experimental studies, there is insufficient evidence at present to suggest that different doses of exercise produce different psychological outcomes. Although both aerobic and non-aerobic exercise have produced an anti-depressant effect, almost all the aerobic exercise has been based on moderate intensity (60–75 per cent) levels with a typical prescription of three times per week for 20–60 minutes. However, it has also been noted that negative effects in terms of mood occur in athletes who far exceed the typical prescription (Morgan 1994). Thus the evidence for a dose-response curve is modest.

PLAUSIBILITY

The sixth criterion is biological plausibility. Here we are looking for the explanation of the observed association. There is agreement that the underlying mechanisms of the effects of exercise on mental illness are not yet known (Biddle and Mutrie 1991; Morgan 1997; Morgan and Goldston 1987a; Plante 1993). Several possible mechanisms, including biochemical changes such as increased levels of endorphins and psychological changes such as an increased sense of mastery, have been proposed (La Forge 1995; Petruzzello *et al.* 1991). The studies showing an anti-depressant effect for non-aerobic exercise suggest that improvement in aerobic fitness is not a key issue. However, objective measures of all possible fitness parameters (aerobic, strength, flexibility and body composition) should be included in studies to provide evidence that the exercise programme has had the desired fitness effect and to shed light on potential mechanisms.

The fact that we do not know which mechanism operates should not prevent us saying they remain 'plausible'. Dishman (1995), in his excellent review of this topic, concludes that our lack of knowledge about the biological plausibility of the association between exercise and mental health is a major shortcoming. This may contribute to the lack of acceptance of the role of exercise by psychiatrists (Hale 1997). However, Hill reminds us that we should not demand too much of this criterion because 'what is biologically plausible depends upon the biological knowledge of the day' (Hill 1965: 298). Determining the mechanisms for the psychological effects of exercise in general and for depression in particular is perhaps the greatest challenge to exercise scientists trying to illuminate the relationship between exercise and mental health. Until we have more appropriate technology to study in humans during exercise, it would appear that much of the knowledge has to be developed using animal models. Brain imaging, though, is one possible technology that may advance our understanding of the mechanisms. It is clear that the answer to this complex question will not be found in exercise laboratories alone. We must collaborate with colleagues in neuroscience and psychological medicine to expand our knowledge.

COHERENCE

The possible mechanisms should not conflict with what is understood to be the natural history and biology of mental illness. This is Hill's criterion of coherence. While, as with many other aspects of these criteria, the evidence is far from complete, one example might show coherence. More women than men report depression and women report less activity than men. Development of animal models to study inactivity and depression and the use of exercise to combat depression will provide further evidence for coherence.

EXPERIMENTAL EVIDENCE

Perhaps the best evidence comes under Hill's criterion of experimental evidence. This has already been discussed in the conclusions from the key studies represented in Table 9.7. The experimental evidence supports a causal link with exercise programmes and depression reduction.

In reviewing the evidence using Hill's (1965) criteria it can be seen that only the criterion not satisfied is that of specificity. Other criteria, such as temporal sequence, dose-response, plausibility and coherence, have only modest evidence, but it does seem reasonable to conclude that there is supportive evidence for a causal link between inactivity and depression. There are those who might say that the evidence is still insufficient and therefore we should not recommend the use of exercise in the treatment of depression or consider inactivity to be a factor in the onset of depression. However, as Hill reminded us,

> All scientific work is incomplete – whether it be observational or experimental. All scientific work is liable to be upset or modified by advancing knowledge. That does not confer upon us a freedom to ignore the knowledge we already have, or postpone the action that it appears to demand at a given time.
>
> (Hill 1965: 12)

The potential benefit of advocating the use of exercise as part of treatment for depression far outweighs the potential risk that no effect will occur. There are very few possible negative side effects (for example, injury, exercise dependence) and there have been no negative outcomes reported in the literature. In addition, there are potential physical health benefits such as an increase in fitness, weight reduction and decreased coronary artery disease risks. Therefore, physical activity and exercise should be advocated as part of the treatment for clinically defined depression.

Anxiety disorders

There is strong evidence of the anxiety reducing effects of exercise from several meta-analytic reviews, and these have been reviewed in Chapter 8 (Long and van Stavel 1995; McDonald and Hodgdon 1991; Petruzzello *et al.* 1991). However, almost none of the studies included in these reviews involved clinically diagnosed anxiety disorders. Taylor (2000), in a recent review of the anxiety reducing effects of exercise, notes that for studies of acute exercise the majority of study participants were college students and that for chronic exercise only three studies (out of twenty-seven reviewed) focused on groups with an anxiety disorder. Presenting symptoms for a person with a clinical level of anxiety might include fear, worry and inappropriate thoughts or actions. Diagnosis might include phobias (such as agoraphobia), panic attacks, obsessive-compulsive disorder, stress disorders (such as post-traumatic stress) and generalised anxiety. The ICD–10 (WHO 1993) section on neurotic, stress-related and somatoform disorders (codes F40–F48) covers phobias, anxiety disorders, obsessive–compulsive disorders, reactions to severe stress, dissociative disorders (namely, lack of integration of past and present) and somatoform dysfunctions such as unexplained pain. Anxiety itself is therefore an inadequate heading but one which is commonly used in the literature. DSM–IV provides criteria for all of these conditions. An example of the diagnostic criteria for Generalised Anxiety Disorder is:

- Excessive anxiety and worry, for more days than not, that are out of proportion to the likelihood or impact of feared events.
- The worry is pervasive and difficult to control.
- The worry is associated with symptoms of motor tension (for example, trembling, muscle tension), autonomic hypersensitivity (for example, dry mouth, palpitations), or hyperarousal (for example, exaggerated startle response, insomnia).
- The anxiety, worry, or physical symptoms cause clinically significant distress or impairment in social, occupational, or other important areas of functioning.
- The condition has lasted for at least six months.

Only four studies could be found in which participants had clinically diagnosed anxiety disorders. The first is a study by Orwin (1981), in which eight patients diagnosed as agoraphobic were treated with a running programme. Patients were asked to run to situations that they found fearful, such as supermarkets. Such places normally create feelings of anxiety for those with agoraphobia, but these patients were taught to attribute increased respiration and heart rate to the running and not to their phobic response. Orwin (1981) reported that all eight patients recovered from such repeated exposure after running and had similar success with situational phobias. Here the running seemed to be operating as a method of desensitising patients to the onset of anxiety symptoms by attributing bodily changes to the demands of the exercise. However, no other studies in which phobic patients have been treated this way, have been reported. Of course, Orwin's studies were pre-experimental with no control group, thus providing little evidence that exercise could be used as a treatment for phobias.

A series of Norwegian studies have tried to unravel some of the issues in the use of exercise for treating anxiety disorders. Martinsen, Sandvik and Kolbjornsud (1989c) included patients with agoraphobia in an exploratory study of the value of exercise for ninety-two non-psychotic patients who had various different psychiatric diagnoses. Exercise involved an eight-week programme which was an adjunct to other treatment. There was no control group. Results showed short-term gains for those diagnosed with agoraphobia with panic disorder but these were not maintained at the one year follow-up. At the end of the programme fitness improvement and symptom reductions were significant. However, without a control group it is not clear if the symptom reductions were part of the normal course of recovery or accelerated by the exercise.

Martinsen, Hoffart and Solberg (1989b) undertook a further study of exercise in the treatment of anxiety disorders. The anxiety disorder was diagnosed by clinical interview (using DSM–III criteria) and patients (n = 79) in a Norwegian psychiatric hospital were participants. The patients were randomly assigned to aerobic exercise (jogging or walking) or non-aerobic exercise (strength and flexibility training). Both training programmes lasted about sixty minutes for three times each week for eight weeks. Both groups decreased anxiety as rated by therapists blind to treatment conditions, but only the aerobic exercise group increased maximum oxygen consumption. These results are identical to those reported for the depressed patients by the same authors (Martinsen, Hoffart and Solberg 1989a). The results suggest a beneficial effect of both aerobic and non-aerobic exercise on anxiety disorder. The fact that aerobic fitness improvement was not required to produce the beneficial effects suggests that the explanatory mechanisms are more likely to be psychological than physiological. However, one major drawback of this design is the lack of a control group. The exercise was alongside other treatment but did involve work with specialist instructors. The psychological effect of gaining extra attention and support from these instructors was therefore not controlled.

Another Norwegian study examined the effects of different intensities of aerobic exercise on anxiety disorders (Sexton, Maere and Dahl 1989). Participants were in-patients (n = 52) in a 3–4 week programme in a psychiatric hospital and were diagnosed by DSM–III criteria as having non-psychotic anxiety disorders. Patients were randomly assigned to moderate (walking) or vigorous activity (jogging) and had supervised exercise (thirty minutes 4–5 each week) for the duration of their programme. They were expected to continue the activity unsupervised for a total of eight weeks and were also followed up at six months. Both intensities of exercise showed reductions in anxiety symptoms at eight weeks and six months. Fitness gains were greater for the jogging group at eight weeks but the difference between groups had disappeared by six months. Aerobic gain did not correlate with reduction in anxiety. More joggers than walkers dropped out of the programme leading the authors to recommend the moderate rather than vigorous activity for other therapy programmes. Despite several good design features this study did not have a non-exercising control group required to show that the exercise had an effect over and above the normal treatment effect of the psychiatric programme.

From these studies we can conclude that there is a suggestion that exercise, both aerobic and non-aerobic, can help reduce clinical anxiety symptoms. Moderate intensity exercise seems best for adherence and higher levels of intensity do not necessarily improve the outcome. However, since none of the studies included a non-exercising control group it is difficult to conclude that there is a causal link.

There has also been a suggestion that exercise is contra-indicated for those suffering from anxiety neurosis. Pitts and McLure (1967) suggested that exercise could lead to the onset of anxiety symptoms in such patients, due to increases in lactate levels in the bloodstream. This hypothesis was refuted by Morgan (1979), but the evidence for the refutation came from studies on non-clinical participants. For some reason, perhaps an ethical one, the Pitts–McLure hypothesis has not been properly tested in a well-designed study involving patients with clinical anxiety.

Clinical anxiety: conclusions

Very little is known about how exercise effects clinical anxiety disorders in comparison to what is known about depression. This may partly be due to the number of diagnoses at the clinical level which could include symptoms of anxiety. A further difficulty in the area of anxiety disorders is separating anxiety from depression. Sometimes the symptoms of these two conditions present together and are diagnosed as mixed anxiety and depression. In their exploratory study, Martinsen *et al.* (1989c) found that patients with a single rather than a mixed diagnosis has better outcomes from exercise. From the studies reported, it is only possible to conclude that there is a potential association between exercise and reduction in symptoms. Further studies, which incorporate control groups, are needed to expand the knowledge in this important area of mental health.

Schizophrenia

Schizophrenia is a psychotic illness affecting a small proportion of the population, but is the most common serious mental illness and, as such, places a disproportionately heavy burden on resources in psychiatric care (Faulkner and Biddle 1999). It is characterised by thought disturbance such as delusions, speech disturbance, difficulties in interpersonal functioning, inappropriate behaviours and emotional responses, and is most commonly treated with antipsychotic medication. A brief description of the DSM–IV criteria for schizophrenia is as follows:

- A disturbance that lasts for at least six months and includes at least one month of active-phase symptoms (for example, delusions, hallucinations, disorganised speech, grossly disorganised or catatonic behaviour, negative symptoms.
- There must be significant impairment in one or more major areas of functioning (for example, work, interpersonal relationships) for most of the time since the onset of the disturbance, and the functioning must be significantly lower than that prior to the onset of the disorder.

There is a potential role for exercise in the treatment of schizophrenia. Chamove (1986) noted that physical activity and fitness levels are known to be low in schizophrenic patients especially those in psychiatric hospitals. Early studies of the effect of increasing activity for such patients had positive outcomes but these studies tended to be pre-experimental. Some of the positive effects for increased activity noted in a study of forty schizophrenic patients were:

- less psychotic features
- less movement disorder
- improved mood
- more social interest and competence (Chamove 1986).

Patients seemed to understand these benefits themselves. For example, Falloon and Talbot (1981) reported that as many as 78 per cent have used exercise as a way of reducing hallucinations. Pelham and Campagna (1991) reported three single-subject case studies which incorporated quantitative information from standard fitness tests, Beck Depression Inventory and Mental Health Inventory scores with qualitative information from interviews. The results showed physiological and psychological benefits and information was also gathered on long-term exercise adherence. The article concluded with a useful set of guidelines on exercise programmes for schizophrenic patients.

The same researchers (Pelham *et al.* 1993) also reported an experimental design which showed that psychiatric patients (diagnosed with schizophrenia or major affective disorder) who undertook a twelve-week aerobic exercise programme decreased depression scores and increased aerobic fitness. The control group undertaking non-aerobic exercise did not show these improvements. This does not support Martinsen's findings that both aerobic and non-aerobic exercise decreased depression scores for a group of hospitalised depressed patients (Martinsen 1990a; 1990b). However, only five individuals were assigned to each group in the Pelham *et al.* (1993) study and the statistical conclusions may therefore not be valid. In addition, it may be that schizophrenic patients respond differently than other psychiatric patients to exercise or it may be that initially low fitness levels influenced the results. Furthermore, Pelham *et al.* (1993) seemed to focus on depression as the major dependent variable which is only one aspect of schizophrenia.

In reviewing the very limited evidence for the use of exercise in the treatment of psychoses such as schizophrenia, Plante concluded that 'the current research results suggest that exercise may assist these patients with mood and self-esteem factors much more than with thought disturbances associated with psychotic symptomatology' (Plante 1993: 367). Similarly, Faulkner and Biddle concluded from a review of eight pre-experimental, three quasi-experimental and one experimental study that:

> the existing research does not allow firm conclusions . . . as to the psychological benefits of exercise for individuals with schizophrenia. It does, however, support the potential efficacy of exercise in alleviating negative symptoms of schizophrenia and as a coping strategy for the positive symptoms.
>
> (Faulkner and Biddle 1999: 453)

In the UK, Faulkner and Sparkes (1999) have reported a qualitative study of exercise as therapy for schizophrenia. Three patients who began a ten-week exercise programme implemented in their hostel setting, were studied through an ethnographic approach. Two of the three patients perceived the exercise programme to be very beneficial, while the third patient ceased participation after seven weeks. One main theme which emerged from the analysis was the role of exercise in encouraging patients out of their 'internal world' and into the 'social world', such as a swimming pool or a walking route. Another theme was that exercise helped the secondary symptoms of depression and low self-esteem, helped control auditory hallucinations and promoted better sleep patterns and general behaviour. The authors recommended that care plans for schizophrenic patients should include exercise, but comment on how difficult that is to achieve. In the hostel where the exercise programme was carried out the staff were very enthusiastic about the way in which exercise had helped patients and noted deterioration when the programme stopped. Despite this there were no plans to ensure that the exercise programme would become a routine element of treatment. The lack of standard randomised controlled trial data on the physical and mental benefits of exercise for schizophrenic patients may be one reason for the reluctance to spend money on exercise as parts of treatment packages. However, in this area it will be very difficult to find sufficient partcipants to conduct such as study and the environment of a hostel or hospital setting is not conducive to random assignment to groups without contamination or resentment. Thus, a qualitative approach is appropriate and the evidence from such studies indicates that there are many potential benefits for exercise programmes to be put in place. Future study in this area must continue to evaluate exercise programmes in a variety of ways (for example, physical and mental health benefits, cost-effectiveness, patient and staff perception of benefit). In addition, they need to include the issue of how to negotiate with administrators, psychiatrists and those in charge of care, in hospitals, hostels or in the community, about the inclusion of exercise in the management and treatment of schizophrenic patients.

Alcohol dependence

The topic of dependence on alcohol and drugs falls into all of the commonly used classifications of mental illness. Using ICD–10 (World Health Organization 1993), a diagnosis of dependence is made through noting various dependence syndromes. These features are noted in Table 9.8. If three or more of these features are present then a diagnosis of dependence is made.

Alcohol dependence is a common problem affecting one in six adults aged 16–24 years. Other surveys have shown that 24 per cent of men and 7 per cent of women drink at levels above the recommendations for safe limits (HMSO 1992), indicating a large percentage of the population who are at risk of becoming dependent.

The topic of appropriate treatment for alcohol abuse has received much discussion with no one method showing distinct advantages (Heather, Roberston and Davies 1985). Rehabilitation from an addictive behaviour involves establishing self-control strategies and finding coping strategies for the emotions involved with withdrawal and continued abstinence (Marlatt and Gordon 1985). Self-esteem is often very low as the problem drinker faces the need for treatment and realises the physical and mental damage that alcohol may have caused (Beck, Weissman and Kovacs 1976). It is intriguing to note that one of the earliest documented pieces of research in exercise psychology was in the area of alcohol rehabilitation (Cowles 1898) although several decades passed before the research was replicated. Cowles' conclusion provides a challenge to current researchers to provide experimental evidence of the declared benefits of exercise:

> The benefits accruing to the patients from the well-directed use of exercise and baths is indicated by the following observed symptoms: increase in weight, greater firmness of muscles, better colour of skin, larger lung capacity, more regular and stronger action of the heart, clearer action of the mind, brighter and more expressive eye, improved carriage, quicker responses of nerves, and through them of muscle and limb to stimuli. All this has become so evident to them that only a very few are unwilling to attend the classes and many speak freely of the great benefits derived.
>
> (Cowles 1898: 108)

Problem drinkers often have low levels of cardiorespiratory fitness and muscle strength

Table 9.8 ICD–10 classification of dependence syndrome

Classification	Dependence syndrome
Compulsion	Desire/compulsion to take the substance.
Impaired control	Difficulty in controlling behaviour in regard to onset, termination and level of substance taking.
Withdrawal	Physiological withdrawal states occurs when substance withdrawn.
Relief use	Substance used to avoid or relieve withdrawal symptoms.
Tolerance	Increased amount of substance required to achieve effect similar to lower dose.
Salience	Increased amounts of time spent in obtaining or taking substance or recovering from its effects. Persistence despite awareness of harmful response.

Source: World Health Organization 1993.

and appropriate programmes of exercise have been shown to be effective in improving these physical parameters (Donaghy, Ralston and Mutrie 1991; Tsukue and Shohoji 1981). Since regular exercise has been associated with improved mental health, decreased levels of depression and anxiety, and increased self-esteem, and these are commonly reported problems in alcohol rehabilitation, the use of exercise as part of the treatment for alcohol rehabilitation has been piloted in several locations (Donaghy *et al.* 1991; Frankel and Murphy 1974; Gary and Guthrie 1972; Murphy, Pagano and Marlatt 1986; Palmer, Vacc and Epstein 1988; Sinyor *et al.* 1982). In these studies the exercise programmes can be considered to be lifestyle interventions providing the problem drinker with the skills to undertake a positive health promoting behaviour (exercise), simultaneously providing self-control strategies, coping strategies and an alternative to drinking (Marlatt and Gordon 1985; Murphy *et al.* 1986).

Donaghy and Mutrie (1998) reported a randomised controlled trial in which 117 problem drinkers were assigned to either a three-week supervised exercise programme (followed by a twelve-week home-based programme), or a placebo group. The latter received a stretching programme for three weeks and advice to continue exercising for the next twelve weeks. The exercise group improved scores on physical self-worth and perceptions of strength and physical condition at one and two months after entry to the programme. The between-groups difference in physical self-perceptions was not evident at five months, but this may be due to drop off in exercise adherence (Donaghy and Mutrie 1997). Evidence exists, therefore, that a structured exercise programme added to a three-week treatment programme can help problem drinkers improve their perception of physical self-worth. Adherence to exercise was a problem with 26 per cent having left the treatment programme (not just the exercise) at the end of three weeks and by the second month follow-up a further 30 per cent had dropped out. Activity levels were sustained for the exercise groups for 8–12 weeks following the three-week programme but had dropped to the level of the control group by five months.

Special challenges for this population include low starting levels of fitness and muscle weakness, relapse to drinking with consequent effects on exercise behaviour, social isolation and lack of support. There is clearly a need for help, such as telephone contact or regular meetings, to sustain activity levels initiated in treatment programmes for this patient group. There is also a need to integrate the exercise into other treatments such as discussion groups, self-help groups or forms of cognitive behavioural therapy. Reinforcing the value of exercise and encouraging adherence could be topics for group leaders and therapists in these other forms of treatment.

Drug rehabilitation

Evidence for the use of exercise in drug rehabilitation programmes is very hard to find. Indeed the only evidence appears to come from unpublished dissertations (Adamson 1991; Hyman 1987; Murdoch 1988). There is anecdotal support for the use of sport and exercise in drug rehabilitation from a group in Glasgow called Carlton Athletic. The group is run by former drug users and involves sport participation as the primary vehicle used to support rehabilitation. Unfortunately, no evaluation has yet been carried out on this self-help process. The problems faced in drug rehabilitation are similar to those in alcohol rehabilitation; high levels of anxiety and depression are often reported as well as low self-esteem (Banks and Waller 1988) and thus it might be assumed that exercise could have the same potentially therapeutic effect. One unique problem for drug rehabilitation is the variety of drugs and their effects both during addiction and withdrawal. In addition, drug misuse often involves the use of many drugs by the same person (Arif and Westermeyer 1988). It may be that this variety of responses makes the standard 'clinical' trial experiment untenable, because there is likely to be a large variation in the dependent variables but only small numbers of participants available because of the nature of the treatment programmes. In addition, these are often residential. Qualitative methodology may therefore be the best way to gather information in this area.

Exercise programmes for those attempting to withdraw from drugs have a particular challenge in overcoming adverse withdrawal effects from drugs. Such patients are liable to forget appointments for exercise, and the withdrawal effects may prevent exercise completely on some days or an inability to leave the house to go to an exercise facility. Keeping in regular contact with these patients is very helpful to them. Perhaps home-based exercise, such as through an exercise videotape, could provide some support through difficult phases, but regular phone calls and visits may also be required.

Exercise dependence

In the previous chapters there has been more evidence of psychologically beneficial effects of physical activity or exercise than detrimental effects. Anyone who has had negative experiences of being ridiculed for lack of skill by schoolmates may tell a different story. Novice exercisers who judge themselves failures because they give up their exercise plan may also have trouble accepting that exercise is good for mental health. There is an acknowledged 'dark side' to physical activity in which self-esteem may be damaged or physique anxiety created as a result of poor experiences (Brewer 1993), but much less literature exists on that topic than the beneficial effects. Also such negative experiences, while damaging at the time, are unlikely to lead to mental illness which is the topic of this chapter. However, recent evidence has suggested that some people can approach exercise in a way that many would see as mentally unhealthy. Some can become dependent on, or addicted to, exercise and will exhibit very high levels of activity on a daily or twice-daily basis. There is often informal discussion amongst various professionals about the risk of creating people who are dependent on exercise when using exercise as part of treatment. This is particularly true in working with other dependencies such as alcohol or drug use in which it is easy to suggest that the clients are swapping one dependency for another. The term exercise dependence was first used by Veale (1987) to describe a state in which exercise has become a compulsive behaviour. Previous literature describing this phenomenon was hampered by lack of an agreed definition. For example, the term obligatory exercise has been used and a questionnaire exists to measure this trait (Thompson and Pasman 1991). Davis, Brewer and Ratusny (1993) note that lack of agreement on terminology and measurement has plagued this area of research. Veale (1987) provided a set of diagnostic criteria to help researchers and clinicians describe this kind of exercise behaviour in a consistent manner. These are shown in Table 9.9. In addition, he distinguished between primary exercise dependence and exercise dependence that is secondary to eating disorders.

Exercise dependence is characterised by:

- A frequency of at least one exercise session per day.
- A stereotypical daily or weekly pattern of exercise.
- Recognition of exercise being compulsive and of withdrawal symptoms if there is an interruption to the normal routine.
- Reinstatement of the normal pattern within one or two days of a stoppage.

Table 9.9 Diagnostic criteria for exercise dependence

Criteria	
A	Narrowing of repertoire leading to a stereotyped pattern of exercise with a regular schedule once or more daily.
B	Salience with the individual giving increasing priority over other activities to maintain the pattern of exercise.
C	Increased tolerance to the amount of exercise performed over the years.
D	Withdrawal symptoms related to a disorder of mood following the cessation of the exercise schedule.
E	Relief or avoidance of withdrawal symptoms by further exercise.
F	Subjective awareness of the compulsion to exercise.
G	Rapid re-instatement of the previous pattern of exercise and withdrawal symptoms after a period of abstinence.
Associated features	
H	Either the individual continues to exercise despite a serious physical disorder known to be caused, aggravated or prolonged by exercise and is advised as such by a health professional, or the individual has arguments or difficulties with his/her partner, family, friends, or occupation.
I	Self-inflicted loss of weight by dieting as a means towards improving performance.

Source: Veale 1987.

The problems that exercise dependence can create range from tiredness and chronic injury to relationship problems and eating disorders (Veale and Le Fevre 1988). However, there is no known prevalence for this problem and no universal agreement on these criteria. Szabo (2000) suggests that it is very rare.

There is also a need for a validated questionnaire to measure exercise dependence. Davis *et al.* (1993) have provided some evidence for the validity of the Commitment to Exercise Scale which is related to, but not based on, Veale's concept of exercise dependence. Szabo (2000) has conducted a review of research into this field, but of the seventeen studies he cites not one of them is actually measuring exercise dependence. Measures used included questionnaires on commitment to running, self-perceived addiction to running, negative addiction, obligatory running, and in-depth qualitative interviews and case studies. Thus it is difficult to draw conclusions about the extent of the problem.

Exercise dependence may well present at a mental health clinic, sports injury clinic, or be associated with eating disorders. Given that only 20–30 per cent of the population exercise three times per week (The Sports Council and Health Education Authority 1992), it is likely that only a very small percentage of the overall population could be diagnosed as exercise dependent and so it is not a public health problem. Nevertheless, the media seem interested in this more 'sensational' aspect of exercise and give it greater coverage than sometimes it deserves.

Furthermore, it is difficult to say how harmful exercise dependence really is to an individual. If the person continues to exercise against medical advice then the risk of chronic injury is clear. It may also be economically harmful to neglect work responsibilities in favour of exercise. Damage to personal and social relationships may be psychologically harmful. It is clear in these cases that the exercise dependent individual needs to regain a balance in terms of their need to exercise and other important life issues. If exercise professionals notice someone who appears to be dependent then some information on seeking appropriate advice or following some self-help strategies should be made available. As with other behaviour change, raising awareness of the issue is a first step. Box 9.1 offers a format for use in creating a poster in gyms and sports injuries clinics to raise awareness and offer avenues of advice.

Box 9.1 An example of a poster format for raising awareness and offering self-help strategies for potential exercise dependents

1   Do you think exercise is compulsive for you?
2   Is exercise the most important priority in your life?
3   Is your exercise pattern very routine and rigid? Could people 'set their watches' by your exercise patterns?
4   Are you doing more exercise this year than you did last year to gain that feel good effect?
5   Do you exercise against medical advice or when injured?
6   Do you get irritable and intolerable when you miss exercise and quickly get back to your exercise routine if you are forced to change it?
7   Have you ever considered that you were risking your job, your personal life or your health by overdoing your exercise?
8   Have you ever tried to lose weight just to make your exercise performance better?

If you answered YES to most of these questions, or if you are worried about becoming dependent on exercise please speak to a member of staff or follow these self-help strategies:

• Use cross-training to avoid over-use injuries; remember aerobic fitness, strength and flexibility are all important aspects of fitness.
• Schedule a reasonable rest period between two bouts of exercise to prevent mental and physical fatigue.
• Schedule one complete rest day each week and notice how energetic you feel the next day.
• Exercise your mind by getting involved in mental and social activities that can lower anxiety and lift self-esteem.
• Try to learn a stress management technique such as relaxation, yoga, tai chi or meditation.

Source: Veale 1987; Zaitz 1989.

Someone who is exercise dependent (that is, fulfils criteria A – G in Table 9.9) may manage to prevent physical, personal or financial harm, but may still acknowledge a compulsion to exercise. Is this harmful, or is it what Glasser (1976) describes as 'positive addiction'? Veale (1995), the author of the suggested diagnostic criteria, admits that he has, in his professional capacity as a psychiatrist, interviewed very few people who could be diagnosed as having primary exercise dependence. Many people who may have the characteristics of dependence are probably functioning quite well and have no need to seek help. Iannos and Tiggemann (1997) found no evidence of personality dysfunction in a cross-sectional study examining various personality characteristics of high level exercisers (more than eleven hours of exercise per week) compared to moderate and low level exercisers. They concluded that these high levels of activity may be psychologically beneficial to these exercisers since it could help maintain feelings of self-esteem and personal control.

Veale (1995) also pointed out that cases of secondary exercise dependence are more frequently encountered, that is, a person who uses excessive exercise as part of another disorder, such as an eating disorder. He recommended studies that attempt to determine whether or not primary exercise dependence exists independently of eating disorders. Davis *et al.* (1998) suggested that around 80 per cent of patients with anorexia nervosa have exercised extensively, thus indicating the extent of secondary exercise dependence. There is also a suggestion that high levels of exercise may trigger eating disorders, although there is considerable controversy in the literature. For example, Brehm and Steffan (1998) showed in a cross-sectional study that adolescents who were categorised as obligatory exercisers were more likely to have a drive for thinness (a major element in defining eating disorders) than adolescents who did exercise but were not classified as obligatory exercisers. The authors concluded that obligatory exercise could trigger eating disorders. Iannos and Tiggemann (1997) showed that for women who exercised more than eleven hours per week there was a high level of eating disordered behaviour. This association was not evident for the men in the study who exercised at equally high levels, which suggests that there may be different motivations for men and women who are exercise dependent. On the other hand, Szabo (2000) reviewed sixteen studies which have explored the association between eating disorders and exercise and noted that the conclusions are equivocal and that some of the discrepancies in findings related to the definitions of exercise used. This again outlines the need for standardised ways of measuring exercise dependence.

Exercise dependence secondary to eating disorders may not always be negative. Some treatment programmes may require cessation of exercise, but given that there may be some psychological gain from exercise in such conditions, it could be that modified exercise could be used as part of the treatment. For example, the caloric expenditure of an exercise session could be modified. Non-aerobic activities, such as strength training or flexibility training, will typically use fewer calories than aerobic activities undertaken for the same period of time and may help prevent the loss of lean tissue. Thus the psychological benefit may be retained for less caloric expenditure if strength and flexibility training was substituted for some aerobic activity. Alternatively, lower intensity activity, such as walking rather than running, for the same amount of time could save calories, but provide a positive aspect to treatment. Exercise itself could be used as a reward (a pleasurable experience) in a programme in which eating patterns are being modified. However, there is one example of a randomised trial in which exercise was used as a positive aspect of treating eating disorders. Levine, Marcus and Moulton (1996) successfully used a walking programme to help control binge eating in obese women.

One particularly difficult area in the definition of exercise dependence is whether or not competitive athletes in training would be defined as dependent. At first glance many athletes would fulfil the criteria in Table 9.9, but their 'dependence' is almost a requirement of the pursuit of their primary goal which is the enhancement of performance.

Perhaps the major concerns for athletes are the associated features H and I in Table 9.9 that can clearly lead to physical and mental harm over time. Weight loss that may appear similar to an eating disorder is a secondary condition in both exercise dependence and in sports in which 'leaness' is an advantage (for example, distance running), or in which weight control for competition categories is required (for example, judo, weightlifting). Coaches, exercise leaders and athletes must be aware of possible risks to long term eating patterns which could be created by pressure to be a certain weight (Dummer *et al.* 1987), although the prevalence of eating disorders in these sports is not well described (1992). In addition, Morgan (1994) reminded us that over-training can have detrimental mental health effects such as mood disturbances and depression. Coaches and sports scientists should therefore be aware of the harmful effects of exercise dependence and over-training and be ready to counsel and assist athletes who appear to be displaying such features, or mood disturbances over prolonged periods of time.

It is not clear why exercise dependence occurs. It has been shown that such extreme exercise behaviour in men is associated with an obsessive-compulsive personality trait (Davis *et al.* 1993) or that exercise dependent people are literally 'running away' from other, perhaps undiagnosed, problems. Szabo (2000) suggests that the literature points to self-esteem being negatively related and anxiety positively related to exercise dependence. It has also been proposed that a person who is exercise dependent has become addicted to the feelings associated with increased endorphin or adrenaline production as a result of exercise (Pierce 1994) but these speculations remain difficult to demonstrate empirically. Another physiologically-based explanation has been termed the 'sympathetic arousal hypothesis' (Thompson and Blanton 1987). Regular exercise may cause decreased sympathetic arousal at rest that feels like lethargy to the individual. Dependence may occur because such an individual seeks out further bouts of activity to help achieve a preferred state of arousal. Beh, Mathers and Holden (1996) offered some support for this notion. They measured EEG in dependent and non-dependent exercisers and found that those classified as dependent had higher alpha frequencies than those non-dependent. The authors interpreted this as suggesting that dependent exercisers have higher levels of tonic arousal. This runs counter to the idea that sympathetic arousal is depressed as a result of exercise but is consistent with the notion of a preferred arousal level.

Other suggestions about why exercise dependence occurs include the possibility that exercise is an analogue for anorexia nervosa, although this has been heavily criticised and no supportive evidence has been produced (Biddle and Mutrie 1991). However, Davis *et al.* (1993) did show an association between excessive exercising and weight pre-occupation in both men and women and while this finding may not show an analogue to more serious eating disorders, it certainly suggests a link. Furthermore, we know that exercise dependence is very often present with eating disorders, but what we do not know is whether primary exercise dependence occurs for the same reasons that eating disorders occur. Davis *et al.* (1998) have suggested, from quasi-experimental studies on anorectic patients, that those with higher levels of obsessive-compulsive symptomatology also have higher levels of excessive exercising. This finding led these authors to conclude that excessive exercising may exacerbate obsessive symptomatology when an eating disorder has developed. This particular connection provides some clinical evidence for an animal model of anorexia nervosa which shows that when experimental animals are deprived of food and have free access to a running wheel, they will reduce food intake and increase physical activity (Epling and Pierce 1988). This appears counter to self-preservation (as does excessive exercise and self-imposed starvation in humans), but can perhaps be explained by the similar effect which exercise and starvation have on increased 5-HT (serotonin) synthesis and turnover. The hypothesis for the biological link between the need to reduce food intake and increase exercise, as explained by Davis *et al.*, is that 'activity-induced 5-HT stimulation or turnover leads to reduced food intake and body weight which in turn provides a further stimulus for physical activity' (Davis *et al.* 1998: 193).

Further investigation of this intriguing biological mechanism may help explain exercise dependence and provide a new theory as to why it is seen so often in those with eating disorders. Techniques involved in these studies may also shed light on the positive psychological outcomes noted from physical activity such as a mood enhancing effect or an antidepressant effect.

Exercise dependence: conclusions

All health professionals should be aware of the characteristics of exercise dependence. Although the public health risk is negligible, an individual who is exercise dependent may be at risk of mental or physical ill health. All professionals who are likely to come in contact with such individuals should raise awareness of the issue and offer avenues for seeking help. Those treating eating disorders will be aware of the use of exercise in these conditions but might also consider how exercise could play a positive role in the treatment of eating disorders. Coaches must be aware that there is a risk of triggering eating disorders by demanding a particular body weight or shape. Such issues need to be carefully handled to avoid long term harm. Finally, further research is required to understand the prevalence and characteristics of those who are exercise dependent. In particular a measurement scale, which could be validated against the diagnostic criteria, is required.

Mechanisms: what explanations can be offered for the psychological benefits of physical activity and exercise in depression and mental illness?

There is considerable agreement that the underlying mechanisms related to the positive effects from exercise on mental health are not yet known (Biddle and Mutrie 1991; Morgan 1997; Morgan and Goldston 1987a; Plante 1993). Several possible mechanisms, including biochemical changes (for example, increased levels of endorphins) and psychological changes (for example, increased sense of mastery), have been proposed (Petruzzello *et al.* 1991). What we appear to be searching for is a parallel to understanding psychosomatic processes since the body's activity affecting how we feel can easily be classed as 'somatopsychic' (Harris 1973). This body–mind relationship is challenging to a number of disciplines such as philosophy, psychology and neuroscience. What is intriguing to scholars who place importance on physical activity is that the relationship is usually studied from mind to body and, in Western thought at least, the mind is given the lead role in most discussions: hence mind–body and psychosomatic. However, evolution has ensured that we have skilful bodies engineered for movement and we believe that our search for the somatopsychic processes, which will provide an answer to why physical activity might help people feel better, must at least equate the importance of body and mind. In this respect La Forge (1995) has suggested a possible model.

La Forge (1995) has provided one of the best reviews of the possible mechanisms because he started from a standpoint of integrating the possible mechanisms rather than describing them as separate processes. This integration occurs via neural connections and to accept La Forge's model one has to accept the philosophical position that all emotions have a neurological explanation. Table 9.10 shows the mechanisms La Forge has integrated. This table provides a brief summary and commentary on these hypotheses. He also points out that all of the mechanisms in Table 9.10 overlap in terms of structure and function and in terms of neuro-anatomic pathways. The integrated model he proposes accepts this overlap and suggests that it is the integration that must be studied rather than the isolated mechanisms.

However, and paradoxically, this seems only to be achievable by researchers focusing on each part, and then bringing their research together. This leads to the call for inter-disciplinary research and the need to employ the latest imaging technologies to enhance understanding of what happens in the exerciser's brain.

What is particularly appealing in this integrated model is that, in terms of mental illness, exercise can be seen to play the same role as some antidepressant drugs but at the same time it could have more widespread, and potentially beneficial, effects. However, some of these effects are not yet accounted for in this model. One notable exception is that of how exercise can provide a sense of mastery and control. For example, one theory of depression suggests that depression is a result of feeling that there is no action that can be taken to alleviate a problem. This feeling of helplessness is learned over a period of time and from a variety of situations, and results in the person having an external locus of control (Abramson *et al.* 1978; Peterson, Maier and Seligman 1993; Seligman 1975). It has been suggested that exercise can play a role in helping the person who is suffering in this way to gain control in one area of life, namely the physical self. In addition, if the exercise is programmed correctly, the sense of achievement and progression from week to week builds on this sense of control and may even provide a sense of mastery (Greist *et al.* 1981). Self-esteem enhancement has therefore featured as a potential explanation for how exercise can alleviate depression and anxiety (Ossip-Klein *et al.* 1989). La Forge's integrated model, as it stands, does not account for the neurobiology of achievement or self-esteem enhancement, but it could. New technologies will soon be able to show which areas of the brain are activated when we sense achievement and such pathways will undoubtedly link to those already identified by La Forge. A way forward in this area might be to use the hierarchical model of physical self-worth (Fox 1997a; 1997b; Fox and Corbin 1989) to explore how exercise may alter this for those suffering from mental illness and then finally to map the areas of the brain responsible for the perceptions of these changes.

The final comment on this model is that it also has to account for the apparent pleasure in inactivity which the vast majority of the population experience. Can we have learned that homeostasis (staying still and inactive) is more pleasurable than all the built-in connections which seem to reward activity? In evolutionary terms it is easy to see that activity needed to be rewarded, but perhaps the rewards are only available once we get past a certain level of conditioning (readiness to be active for survival) and prior to that our responses to activity are suggestive of pain and punishment (safer to be still) rather than reward and pleasure. For deconditioned people it is more pleasurable to maintain inactivity. For health professionals keen to get more of the population active the slow and gradual approach is essential if we are to gain the feelings of pleasure which are potentially available for activity and not evoke pain. There is still much to learn but the integrated model is a starting point on which both theories of motivation to exercise and explanations of psychological effects from exercise can be built. La Forge provided this sensible guide to future practice:

> The mechanism is likely an extraordinary synergy of biological transactions, including genetic, environmental, and acute and adaptive neurobiological processes. Inevitably, the final answers will emerge from a similar synergy of researchers and theoreticians from exercise science, cognitive science and neurobiology.
>
> (La Forge 1995: 28)

This synergy of researchers is not always easy to achieve in the current academic climate

Table 9.10 Mechanisms for exercise-associated mood changes reviewed by La Forge (1995)

Name of hypothesis	Indicative reference	Major principles	Comments
Opponent-process theory	(Solomon 1980)	Processes which oppose the heightened state of arousal brought about by exercise seek to return the body's systems to homeostasis. These opponent processes get stronger through training and thus may cause relaxation and anxiety reduction post exercise in trained individuals.	Very difficult to obtain empirical evidence as many processes could potentially oppose. Thus hypothetically linked to all the other processes mentioned.
Opioids	(Schwarz and Kindermann 1992)	Opioids (for example, endorphins, enkephalins, dynorphins) are associated with increased mood and decreased pain sensations. Exercise increases plasma levels of opioids and thus opioids could therefore be responsible for post-exercise mood enhancement. This system is linked to the cardiovascular, respiratory, reproductive and immune systems.	It is not clear if the plasma levels reflect the central nervous system levels of opioids and research investigating the exercise and mood link has been equivocal.
Monoamines	(Chaouloff 1989)	Monoamines (dopamine, norepinephrine, epinephrine, serotonin) are involved in depression and anxiety. Much anti-depressant medication is aimed at increasing the amounts of these amines. Exercise may also stimulate production.	Most of the exercise research is animal-based but since medications have extensive human research it is a very plausible hypothesis.
Neocortical activation	(Kubitz and Landers 1993)	Incoming signals from muscles etc. during movement stimulate areas of the cortex responsible for mood. In addition exercise may cause a shift to right hemisphere processing. Links to the concept of exercising to find 'optimal' levels of arousal.	Methods have been inconsistent and often no mood or anxiety measure taken. Associating mood states with activity in specific brain regions is not an exact science at present.
Thermogenic changes	(Petruzzello et al. 1991)	Increased core temperature decreases muscle tension and has been hypothesised to reduce anxiety. Certain types of exercise will increase core temperature.	Very little support for this hypothesis has emerged from the literature. Given the body's ability to maintain core temperature against hostile environments this does seem an unlikely explanation but the process of maintaining temperature may link to the opiods or to cortical activity.
Hypothalamic-pituitary-adrenal (HPA) axis changes	(Peronnet and Szabo 1993)	The HPA axis is the framework for mind–body communication; it plays a role in depression, eating disorders and stress response. Stress hormones are released by this axis in response to physical (exercise) and mental stress. High levels of stress hormones are associated with negative moods. Training decreases the amount of stress hormone release, but overtraining increases it.	The mechanisms which elicit responses by the HPA axis to exercise stress and to psychosocial stress are probably different and need to be better understood before this hypothesis can be advanced.

in which resources follow demarcated research groups, but it is an ideal worth pursuing for those with a passion to find out exactly why exercise may help us feel better.

Guidelines for practice

We offer the following practical guidelines in respect of physical activity and mental health problems and illness:

- Practitioners (GPs, psychologists, psychiatrists, care workers, therapists, community mental health workers) should attempt to incorporate regular activity into the lives of all patients.
- Physical activity/exercise should be advocated as part of the treatment for institution-alised patients especially where activity and fitness levels are low.
- It would appear that most drugs used in the treatment of mental illness are not contraindicated with exercise, but practitioners must be aware of potential interactions (such as the effect of beta blockade on heart rate or the effect of serotonin re-uptake inhibitors on exercise tolerance).
- Health promoters must include the prevention of mental illness in the rationale for the need to increase the percentage of the population engaged in regular physical activity.
- Exercise leaders, sports centres and sports injury clinics should raise awareness of the characteristics of exercise dependence.

Future directions for research

We offer the following points in respect of future research directions:

- Surveys of health and mental health must include good measures of physical activity.
- Further epidemiological evidence is required to show the relationship between exercise and mental illness.
- Cost effectiveness and cost benefit studies of exercise are required in the area of depression and other mental illnesses.
- Randomised controlled trials of exercise versus drug treatment for depression are required in primary care and in psychiatric care.
- Randomised controlled trials are required in the area of anxiety disorders and exercise.
- There is a need for qualitative studies with patients groups (such as schizophrenia or those in drug rehabilitation) in which RCTs are unlikely to be feasible.
- The prevalence of exercise dependence needs to be established and a validated scale to measure exercise dependence is required.
- Exercise scientists must form collaborative teams with researchers in physiology, neuroscience, cognitive science and psychological medicine in order to expand the knowledge about the mechanisms by which exercise can provide positive psychological benefits in mental illness.
- The potential for exercise to assist in the treatment of other mental illnesses, which have not yet been explored in the exercise literature, should be examined in studies in which exercise becomes adjunctive to standard treatment for that problem. This research model has limitations in that it is difficult to equate time in treatment for the two groups (standard treatment versus standard treatment plus exercise) or to prevent resentful demoralisation in the group not receiving exercise, but it is easy to put in place and has

few ethical concerns. Examples of disorders which might benefit include cognitive disturbance, sleep disturbance, psychosocial problems and childhood problems such as attention deficits or social interaction problems.

Conclusions

In this chapter, we have:

- Introduced the topic of mental illness and provided a context for identifying the prevalence of depression and mental illness.
- Reviewed the literature on physical activity and exercise on depression.
- Reviewed the role of physical activity in other mental illness, such as anxiety disorders, schizophrenia and alcohol and drug dependence.
- Considered the possible negative effects from exercise.
- Discussed likely mechanisms explaining the positive role of physical activity in preventing or alleviating mental health problems.
- Provided guidelines for practice and future research directions.

Having reviewed this field, we conclude:

- Exercise (both aerobic and non-aerobic) can reduce clinically defined levels of depression and evidence from epidemiological studies, meta-analysis and experimental studies suggests that this is a causal link.
- There is very limited knowledge of the effects of exercise on anxiety disorders and at best an association between exercise and reduced symptoms has been shown.
- No negative effects of exercise in mentally ill patient groups have been noted although there is an hypothesised contra-indication for certain anxiety disorders.
- Exercise has the potential to improve certain symptoms in schizophrenia.
- Exercise does not decrease drinking behaviour in problem drinkers, but does influence fitness, physical self-perception and activity levels.
- Exercise can play a positive role in assisting those who are being treated for drug dependence.
- A very small percentage of exercisers can become dependent on exercise.
- The mechanisms of the psychologically beneficial effects of physical activity and exercise are not clear at this time but there are many plausible mechanisms.

10 The psychology of exercise for clinical populations

Exercise was invented and used to clean the body when it was too full of harmful things.

Christobal Mendez 1500–1561

(Berryman 2000)

Chapter objectives

This chapter aims to review the role of physical activity and exercise in the treatment of a variety of clinical populations. Mental illness has been excluded from this chapter and is comprehensively reviewed in Chapter 9. We use the American College of Sports Medicine's (ACSM) classification of disease and disability as a framework and examples of psychological issues for specific conditions from each category have been given. Specifically, this chapter will:

- Highlight the psychological issues associated with exercise for clinical populations.
- Discuss the role of exercise psychology in a clinical team.
- Use the American College of Sports Medicine's framework for classifying disease and disability.
- Provide examples of psychological issues for each category in the ACSM framework, with the exception of mental health issues (see Chapter 9), including:
  1 cardiovascular and pulmonary diseases
  2 metabolic diseases
  3 immunological and haematological disorders
  4 orthopaedic diseases and disabilities
  5 neuromuscular disorders
  6 cognitive, emotional and sensory disorders.
- Summarise what we know in this area of exercise psychology.
- Offer a guide to good practice.
- Provide recommendations for conducting research in exercise psychology with clinical populations.

Clinical populations can be defined as those people who have sought help for a particular medical condition, who are under medical observation, or who have been diagnosed by a relevant clinical specialist. Structured or supervised exercise has been promoted for a host of medical conditions for some time. Bouchard, Shephard and Stephens (1994) listed twenty-four medical conditions for which exercise has a potential therapeutic role. Research on the efficacy of exercise for these clinical groups grew out of the knowledge that had been accumulated on the prevention and treatment of cardiovascular disease through exercise and activity (Pate *et al.* 1995). Initial interest in the role of exercise for clinical populations came from physicians and exercise physiologists who used exercise tests as part of a medical diagnosis or who sought physical improvements and decreased morbidity and mortality for their patients. More recently it has been recognised that longevity is perhaps not the key issue for exercise with these patients groups, and that quality of life and the ability to function in everyday activities are more salient issues. The American College of Sports Medicine (ACSM) has produced a comprehensive text on managing exercise programmes for clinical populations to assist the increasing number of exercise specialists in this area (ACSM 1997a). Moore, in the introductory chapter of this text, summarised the short history of the rationale for exercise programmes with clinical populations as follows:

> in the 1980s, research and clinical applications for exercise expanded to populations with a variety of chronic diseases and disabilities, for whom exercise is perhaps more fundamentally related to quality of life rather than quantity of life. Perhaps the greatest potential benefit of exercise is its ability to preserve functional capacity, freedom and independence.
>
> (Moore 1997: 3)

There are two issues to be considered in discussing the psychological aspects of exercise for clinical populations. First, exercise clearly has a contribution to make to enhancing quality of life for clinical populations. Quality of life could be considered as a broad heading under which various psychological outcomes from exercise programmes could be placed. Exercise psychologists are able to assess the relationship between exercise and quality of life by various psychometric techniques and by qualitative research.

Second, if exercise is to be beneficial to patients we must be able to keep them involved in activity over the longest time possible and thus psychologists clearly have a role to play. The process of keeping people involved in beneficial activity has been under-researched in comparison to the medical outcomes from such activities. In order to promote exercise adherence for patients who have a defined medical condition, an understanding of the psychological factors which affect adherence, along with an understanding of the particular challenges to exercise which the various medical conditions create, is required. The prescribed exercise treatment may present problems because patients are not confident of their physical abilities or the medical conditions themselves may present difficulties for the intending exerciser.

The focus of this chapter will be the assessment of quality of life and the psychology of starting and maintaining exercise for these patients groups. Guidelines for good practice and for researching psychological outcomes and adherence are also provided.

Working with clinical populations

It is likely that exercise specialists working with clinical populations will be part of a team of clinicians and paramedical staff such as physiotherapists. Exercise is one part of a multi-treatment package designed to help the patient. It is clear that such exercise specialists need an understanding of the physiological demands of exercise and the adaptations and limitations that various conditions will impose. Such specialists may be in charge of exercise testing for diagnostic or exercise prescription purposes. Thus a solid background in exercise physiology is required. However, it is clear that knowledge of exercise psychology is also very important. Exercise psychology will provide an understanding of the psycho-social issues that will affect test results (for example, anxiety will affect tests involving voluntary termination) and the ability to undertake the prescription of exercise (for example, the patient may not believe exercise will help and is thus unlikely to adhere to the programme). In addition there are beneficial psychological outcomes from exercise participation which may play an important motivational role (Fox 1997b). Some hospitals now employ exercise therapists who work alongside physiotherapists providing appropriate exercise prescriptions. Some specialists groups, such as the British Association of Cardiac Rehabilitation (BACR) provide training courses for exercise specialists working in cardiac rehabilitation and this training includes exercise psychology. The British Association of Sport and Exercise Sciences (BASES) provides an accreditation system to ensure quality control. There have also been efforts to create a specialist field of exercise therapy for working with such clinical populations. It would seem that this is an expanding field of application.

It is likely that the prevailing ethos in clinical settings is one that adheres to a medical model that focuses more on diagnosis and prescription of treatment than on the person. This model would normally lead to the same exercise prescription being offered for all patients, such as group classes in cardiac rehabilitation. However, with regard to exercise adherence, a person-centred approach should be considered. This implies that the same exercise prescription is not suitable for all people. Instead the exercise prescription must be tailored to each person's circumstances and provide them with control over their exercise rather than maintaining control within the hospital setting. The long-term goal must be independent exercisers and not exercisers who are dependent on hospital supervision. This idea fits very well with the current 'Active Living' recommendations for increasing activity; this suggests that sedentary people should aim to accumulate around thirty minutes of moderate intensity activity, such as walking, most days of the week (Pate *et al.* 1995).

Loughlan and Mutrie (1995) have advocated a counselling approach which uses a variety of cognitive-behavioural techniques, to maximise adherence to recommendations (see Chapter 11). It is likely that patients are not active and therefore a counselling approach may be more appealing to them. This approach includes:

- Understanding the person's exercise and activity history.
- Allowing them to say what they feel are the benefits and drawbacks of increasing activity levels.
- Helping them see ways to overcome stated barriers to activity.
- Looking for ways to assist motivation like finding an exercise 'buddy'.
- Getting support from family and friends.
- Helping them set realistic short and long term goals concerning their activity levels.

Categories of clinical populations

The framework suggested by ACSM (1997a), which is shown in Table 10.1, classifies forty separate medical conditions into six categories of disease or disability. This framework has been adapted for use in this chapter. The topic of mental illness has already been covered in Chapter 9. Within each category examples will be given of the known physical and psychological benefits of exercise, special challenges for adherence will be outlined and what is known about motivations, barriers and adherence rates will be discussed. The inclusion of certain conditions within each category was based on current literature searches using adherence (and associated words) or psychological benefits as key terms, and this may have resulted in omissions of work which do have information on adherence or psychological outcomes but did not list any of the associated key words.

Cardiovascular and pulmonary diseases

Chronic obstructive pulmonary disorders (COPD)

COPD includes asthma, chronic bronchitis and emphysema (Higgins 1989). As much as 10 per cent of the world's population suffer from asthma and the incidence of asthma is increasing, particularly for children. In the UK, asthma is the most frequent medical reason for children being absent from school and for repeated visits to their GP (Holgate 1993). There is often a spiral of inactivity from COPD sufferers since one main symptom is dyspnea (the sensation of breathlessness). When dyspnea is experienced activity levels are likely to drop and this leads to further 'deconditioning', meaning that activity may feel more difficult and non-adherence is therefore more likely. Pulmonary rehabilitation programmes based on exercise have a short but reasonably successful history (Lacasse *et al.* 1996). Adherence to exercise programmes for people with COPD has been studied (Atkins *et al.* 1984) and the results have enhanced knowledge on the effectiveness of various adherence strategies. These studies show that cognitive behaviour modification strategies will work with this patient group, with simple techniques such as goal-setting increasing the number of minutes walked in an eleven-week programme almost four times as much as the control group. These results are shown in Figure 10.1.

Exercise programmes also confer psychological benefits in terms of increased quality of life and decreased depression and anxiety (Singh *et al.* 1997). It would appear that part of the explanation of such benefits lies in the social interaction which exercise classes provide and the reassurance that other people of a similar age and with the same illness can cope and improve their exercise capacity. It has also been noted that such rehabilitation programmes can benefit the patient's family by providing them with reassurance that other families cope with breathlessness and that exercise is to be encouraged (Petty 1993). Special challenges for COPD patients and exercise include the issue that for some asthmatics exercise is a double-edged sword. On the one hand it can improve overall functional capacity and reduce breathlessness but, on the other hand, it can also induce an asthmatic attack (Belman 1989). Exercise programmes must be tailored to avoid breathlessness and there may be the need to overcome a belief from such patients and their families that they should not exercise. Special advice on how and when to use medication in conjunction with exercise is usually required (Gordon 1993b).

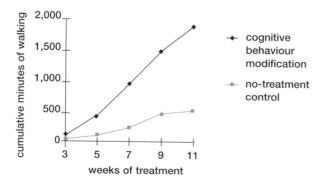

Figure 10.1 The effect of cognitive behaviour modification strategies on walking for COPD patients (data from Atkins *et al.* 1984)

Table 10.1 The American College of Sports Medicine's classification of diseases and disabilities

Major category of disease/disability	Sub-categories
1 Cardiovascular and pulmonary diseases	Myocardial infarction Coronary artery bypass grafting angioplasty Angina and silect ischemia Pacemakers and implantable cardioverter defibrillators Valvular heart diseases Congestive heart failure Cardiac transplant Hypertension Peripheral arterial disease Aneurysms and marfan syndrome Pulmonary disease Cystic fibrosis
2 Metabolic diseases	Renal failure Diabetes Hyperlipidemia Obesity Frailty
3 Immunological/Hematological disorders	Cancer Anemia Bleeding disorders Acquired immune deficiency syndrome Organ transplant Chronic fatigue syndrome
4 Orthopaedic diseases and disabilities	Arthritis Low back pain syndrome Osteoporosis
5 Neuromuscular disorders	Stroke and head injury Spinal cord injury Muscular dystrophy Epilepsy Multiple sclerosis Polio and post-polio syndrome Amyotrophic lateral sclerosis Cerebral palsy Parkinson's disease
6 Cognitive, emotional and sensory disorders	Mental retardation Alzheimer's disease Mental illness Deaf and hard of hearing Visual impairment

Source: American College of Sports Medicine 1997a.

Cardiac rehabilitation

Exercise-based cardiac rehabilitation programmes are in widespread use in the USA (Naughton 1985) but their introduction has been relatively slow in the UK (Gloag 1985), despite the greater percentage of the UK population who will suffer a myocardial infarction (MI) (Tunstall-Pedoe and Smith 1986). The reasons for such caution in the UK are unclear. Perhaps the reason is as simple as finding the extra cost of mounting these programmes within an already stretched National Health Service budget. Perhaps the reason is the more complex point that medical consultants review success in medical treatment of MI in terms of decreased mortality and the early evidence for that via exercise was equivocal (Naughton 1985). However, Oldridge *et al.* (1988) conducted a meta-analysis of RCTs and concluded that MI patients who had a cardiac rehabilitation programme that included exercise had a 25 per cent reduction in mortality compared to controls.

Given the need to heal infarcted heart tissue and improve the efficiency of the cardiovascular system, it is not surprising to note that most research on the effect of exercise during cardiac rehabilitation has focused on physiological and cardiovascular parameters (Dugmore 1992). Oldridge *et al.* (1988) suggested that improvements in psychological well-being and quality of life may be more beneficial than changes in exercise tolerance.

Anxiety and depression are perhaps the most frequently measured psychological outcomes. Milani, Lavie and Cassidy (1996) estimated that 20 per cent of cardiac patients exhibit symptoms of depression 4–6 weeks after a cardiac event. There has been more work on psychological outcomes for this group of patients than any other clinical group. Kugler, Seelbach and Kruskemper (1994) completed a meta-analysis of fifteen studies that had investigated anxiety and/or depression as outcomes of exercise-based cardiac rehabilitation programmes. These authors found low to moderate effect sizes (ES) for anxiety (ES = 0.31) and depression (ES = 0.46) as a result of exercise-based cardiac rehabilitation. These effects are perhaps under-estimates of the true effects of exercise on anxiety and depression because not all the participants in the studies reported will have symptoms of anxiety or depression. Thus there appear to be both physiological and psychological benefits associated with exercise in cardiac rehabilitation.

The field of exercise adherence has benefited from the research conducted in cardiac rehabilitation settings and the findings suggest that we need to learn about how to maintain long term adherence. Oldridge, Donner and Buck (1983) report that 40–50 per cent of Canadian patients drop-out of cardiac rehabilitation programmes six to twelve months after referral. In the UK, Pell *et al.* (1996) reported a 58 per cent completion rate for Glasgow hospital-based rehabilitation programmes. Quaglietti and Froelicher (1994) noted that adherence declines over time with only 30–55 per cent of patients continuing to exercise four years after the initial cardiac event. Finally, and most pessimistically, Prosser, Carson and Phillips (1985) established that only 12 per cent of patients were doing regular exercise six to nine years after a short hospital-based programme.

An example of a study that highlights the issue of long-term adherence was completed by Rovario, Holmes and Holmsten (1984). They randomly assigned cardiac patients to either a three times per week supervised exercise programme (n = 27) or a routine care programme which included exercise advice but no supervised sessions (n = 19). After three months of supervised training and at a follow-up four months later, patients in exercise-based rehabilitation had improved more than those in routine care on measures of cardiovascular functioning, self-perceptions and psychosocial functioning, including reduced employment related stress, more frequent sexual activity and increased house-hold activities. However, when these patients were followed up six years later (Holmes 1993), the advantages for the original exercise-based groups had disappeared. The authors suggested that the explanation lay in the increased level of activity in the routine care group and the decreased level in the group who initially had supervised exercise. This issue raises the question of how the exercise classes within a hospital setting might achieve the long term goal of creating independent exercisers who can find ways of continuing exercise after the initial supervision.

There is a concern, therefore, that many patients do not get the benefits from exercise programmes because they do not complete it. There have been some excellent studies of the factors associated with such drop-out (Oldridge *et al.* 1983) and there is a general conclusion that individual factors and factors related to the programme itself provide reasons for drop-out (see Chapter 2). Given the concern over adherence levels in cardiac rehabilitation it is surprising that very few studies have sought patient viewpoints on the content of the programme. In the UK, Campbell *et al.* (1994) interviewed twenty-nine patients who had recently suffered a myocardial infarction. The most frequently suggested element for the cardiac rehabilitation programme was exercise, but it was also clearly noted that the hospital was not the best location. Programmes in more local centres with supervision were requested. It was also noted by a majority of patients that bad weather was off-putting for walking programmes and other imaginative alternatives must be considered such as walking round large DIY stores or shopping centres.

A variety of exercise programmes have been tried including hospital-based and home-based, aerobic and strength-based programmes and differing exercise intensities. Home-based programmes that encourage walking seem to have the best chance of long term adherence. Moving from Phase III (hospital-based) to Phase IV (community-based) is a particularly challenging time for exercise adherence. Gillies *et al.* (2000) showed that providing patients with an exercise counselling session at the end of Phase III was more effective than providing exercise information alone in increasing physical activity levels in the short term. For managers of cardiac rehabilitation programmes, Quaglietti and Froelicher offer the following suggestions:

> reduce the waiting time, provide expert supervision, tailor the exercise to avoid physical discomfort and frustration, use variable activities including games, incorporate social events, recall absent patients, involve the patient's family or spouse in the program, and involve the patient in monitoring his or her progress.
>
> (Quaglietti and Froelicher 1994: 599)

Special challenges for this patient group include fear of another MI, and the possible interaction of exercise with commonly prescribed drugs such as beta-blockers. Beta-blockers will attenuate heart-rate response and thus exercise intensity is best introduced to the patient via ratings of perceived exertion. Perhaps because of the fear of further MI there is a concern that patients become dependent on the hospital environment and it is a challenge to assist patients to become independent exercisers and to sustain this. The British Association of Cardiac Rehabilitation is addressing the problem directly by providing training for exercise leaders and physiotherapists in what is described as Phase IV (community-based) cardiac rehabilitation. The issues of exercise psychology and long term adherence are addressed in this training.

Metabolic diseases

Perhaps the most prevalent of metabolic disorders is obesity (see Chapter 1). Recent reviews suggest that physical activity is a critical behaviour in reducing the risks of obesity (Blair and Brodny 1999; Prentice and Jebb 1995). However, obesity itself is not often viewed as a disease and will not be reviewed here. Readers are referred to the report of a consensus conference held on the topic of obesity and exercise for excellent reviews of this issue (*Medicine and Science in Sports and Exercise* 1999: supplement to 31(11)). In this section diabetes has been chosen as the most frequent metabolic disease.

Diabetes

Both Type 1 (insulin dependent, IDDM) and Type 2 (non-insulin dependent, NIDDM) diabetics are usually advised to exercise as part of their treatment along with medication, modification of diet and monitoring of glucose levels (Wing *et al.* 1986) (see Chapter 1). A joint position statement by ACSM and the American Diabetes Association (1997b), provides anyone involved with either Type 1 or 2 diabetic patients with a comprehensive set of guidelines concerning exercise. In this position statement benefits to cardiovascular, peripheral arterial and metabolic systems from exercise are described, and preparing the diabetic patient for exercise is discussed. Interestingly, from the point of view of exercise adherence, no reference is made to maintenance of exercise or psychological outcomes. The psychological effects of facing a lifetime of dealing with diabetes, and the consequent emotional and social adjustments are very well documented by health psychologists, as is the need for patient education about treatment (Dunn 1993). Given the wealth of literature on these psychological issues in diabetes, and the standard recommendation that exercise should be part of treatment, it is surprising that neither the psychological benefits of exercise for diabetics, nor patient education in appropriate exercise have received much attention from researchers. Literature searches suggest that no experimental work has been carried out on the psychological effects of exercise on IDDM or NIDDM. Two articles based on anecdotal evidence suggest that there are psychological effects of exercise for diabetics such as sense of control and a reduction in stress (Norstrom 1988; Vasterling, Sementilli and Burish 1988). A two-year observational study showed positive associations between physical activity and psychological well being in Type 2 diabetics (Stewart *et al.* 1994).

It is possible that central to these reported benefits is a changing view of the physical self from one which is compromised by the need to monitor food intake and blood sugar levels to one coping with exercise and feeling improvements in physical condition. Berg suggested that:

> The psychological effects of exercise may be just as important as the more readily measured physical and physiological effects. The realisation that participation in physical activity, including vigorous sport, can be engaged in safely and even beneficially may do much to create a positive feeling about life. Physically active diabetics may even be encouraged to maintain a higher degree of control of their condition so that they can maintain a vigorous lifestyle.

(Berg 1986: 428)

Some recent work (Swift *et al.* 1995) has shown that among NIDDM patients who regularly participated in exercise, over half selected diabetes control as the main reason for starting and continuing with exercise. Barriers to exercise included physical discomfort from exercise, fear of reactions from low blood sugar, being too overweight to exercise and lack of family support. A large-scale survey (n = 1,030) of IDDM patients' motivations and barriers to exercise (Marsden 1996) suggested that fear of a hypoglycaemic event was not seen as a major barrier. Instead, and similar to non-diabetic populations, time constraints were listed as the major barrier. Motivations to exercise were to avoid future diabetic complications and to improve physical health.

Marsden's (1996) work also revealed that less than a third of IDDM patients took regular exercise, but that at least another third are contemplating starting or are doing some exercise on an irregular basis. This work highlights the need for exercise education to be part of diabetic patient care. There is also a clear need for further professional training for the medical team because the majority of patients in Marsden's survey had not received advice about exercise from their hospital clinic. Ary *et al.* (1986) showed that only 20 per cent of Type 2 patients received any specific advice about how to exercise despite the fact that the majority of patients were told that they ought to exercise. A recent study of knowledge and attitude towards exercise amongst children with IDDM also underlines the need for education for patients and professionals. Rickabaugh and Saltarelli (1999) found some serious gaps in knowledge about IDDM and exercise amongst children and their parents and physical education (PE) teachers. They recommended that PE teachers in particular needed pre-service training on the management of exercise for IDDM.

The need to take into account individual motivations and barriers and the lack of advice regarding exercise for this patient group, suggests that both IDDM and NDDM patients need similar exercise counselling (Loughlan and Mutrie 1995) to that recommended for non-clinical populations (see Chapter 11). Two pilot studies have confirmed that, for both Type 1 and Type 2 patients, an exercise consultation increased physical activity more than exercise information from the British Diabetic Association's exercise leaflet. Hasler *et al.* (1997) showed that the exercise consultation was effective for Type 1 patients in increasing activity over a three-week period. A similar design, used with Type 2 diabetics attending a routine appointment, showed that the exercise consultation increased physical activity levels more than the standard leaflet over a five-week period (Kirk *et al.* 2000). Marsden (1999) has provided an excellent practical guide for undertaking exercise consultations and constructing exercise programmes for diabetic patients.

The special challenge to Type 1 diabetics is to balance insulin control, glucose and exercise bouts. Patients need adequate knowledge of how to do this including the knowledge that exercise should not be undertaken with high levels (>250 mg/dl) of blood glucose. Blood glucose monitoring should therefore be encouraged before and after exercise. Type 2 patients may have different challenges that include being overweight and perhaps less motivated to deal with their condition. The special challenge in working with overweight individuals is to find activities which do not increase the stress on joints and which avoid potential embarrassment. Swimming might seem like an obvious non-weight bearing activity, but swimsuits and public swimming pools may be too threatening for many obese people. Cycle and rowing ergometers may therefore be more realistic exercise modes.

Immunological and haematological disorders

Cancer

It has long been recognised that coping with the diagnosis and treatment of cancer may require assistance in the form of psychological interventions (Anderson 1992). It is also recognised that exercise as part of treatment has the potential to improve both physical (for example, fatigue, nausea, weight change) and psychological functioning, although exercise is unlikely to have positive effects on the cancer itself (see Chapter 1). Simon (1990) concludes his discussion of an excellent review of exercise immunity, cancer and infection by Calabrese by stating:

> There is little systematic information dealing with the role of exercise in the functional or psychological rehabilitation of cancer patients. There is little reason to expect that exercise training will help induce remissions in these patients, but there is good reason to expect that exercise may improve their quality of life.
>
> (Simon 1990: 586)

Friedenreich and Courneya (1996) reviewed the use of exercise with cancer patients and found only nine studies on this topic and all of them related to breast cancer. The results, though, are encouraging since the overall conclusion was that exercise resulted in both physical and psychological improvements. Friedenreich and Courneya report that the issues of recruitment and adherence to exercise have been poorly studied (or reported) in the existing literature and that all of the exercise interventions were supervised.

Clear objectives for future research with exercise and cancer patients are to investigate different types of exercise, including home-based and non-supervised programmes, to understand motivations and barriers, and to estimate adherence rates at various stages of the disease including treatment and long term follow-up.

Special challenges for exercise prescription with cancer patients include exercising whilst recovering from intensive treatment such as chemotherapy, muscle weakness and perhaps embarrassment in public facilities because of hair loss due to treatment or fear of what people might think of a mastectomy scar.

HIV/AIDS

There is increasing interest in the use of exercise as part of a treatment schedule for people who have contracted Human Immunodeficiency Virus (HIV) (Lawless, Jackson and Greenleave 1995; Rigsby *et al.* 1992). These initial studies focused on the immune system response to exercise and they found that there were no adverse effects (Birk 1996). Indeed, LaPerriere *et al.* (1991) suggested that physical training can increase CD4 cell counts (the helper cells which are important in immune response) by around fifty cells per cubic millimetre, which is comparable to the effect of certain AIDS drugs, but with none of the side effects.

Other studies show the potential for exercise to have positive psychological effects for the HIV population, including increased ability to cope with HIV+ status (LaPerriere *et al.* 1990), increased perception of well-being (Lox, McAuley and Tucker 1995) and improved quality of life (Stringer *et al.* 1998). However, this important outcome from exercise may be ignored by researchers. Stringer (1999), in reviewing the available evidence of the effects of aerobic exercise for this population, summarised six studies with good design features, but only two of them measured quality of life.

Clearly, there are some special concerns for adherence to exercise for this population since 75 per cent dropped out of one twenty-four-week study of the effects of exercise on HIV (McArthur, Levine and Berk 1993). However, a recent study, which compared the effects of high and moderate intensity aerobic training with a control group, had more optimistic adherence results. Stringer *et al.* (1998) reported a study in which thirty-four individuals with HIV+ were enrolled and 77 per cent completed the six-week programme. In addition, the authors reported 91 per cent adherence to the two exercise regimes that included three session of cycle ergometry per week for six weeks. There was no discussion from the authors of these excellent adherence results about how the programme compared to previous exercise programmes with this population. This was unfortunate since future researchers have no guidance about how to structure an exercise programme to maximise adherence. Clearly a six-week programme is much less of an adherence challenge than the twenty-four-week programme of McArthur *et al.* (1993). Nevertheless, to get good adherence at twenty-four weeks, there must be good adherence earlier and we clearly need to know more about the time course, modalities and intensities of activity which provide the best adherence.

HIV+ patients may have limitations to their exercise such as reduced aerobic capacity, but Stringer (1999) noted that the majority of these patients are deconditioned and that aerobic capacity can be returned to normal with appropriate exercise programmes. Almost all studies in this area have focused on aerobic training, but there may be advantages in including strength training, especially if muscle wasting has occurred. Siafakis (1999) has reported preliminary data suggesting that strength training not only increases strength but can enhance mood and physical self-perceptions in this population. Special challenges in working with such individuals include obtaining ethical approval for studies which involve laboratory testing, protection of confidentiality, public prejudice against this group if exercise is conducted in public facilities, poor muscle mass and muscle weakness.

Orthopaedic diseases and disabilities

Arthritis

Sharratt and Sharratt (1994) present an excellent summary of the role of exercise in both rheumatoid arthritis (inflammation of membrane surrounding the joint) and osteoarthritis (degeneration of cartilage within the joint). It would seem that in this particular disease there is a consensus that exercise can enhance the quality of life by maintaining range of movement and functional capacities connected with daily living (Stenstrom 1994). Despite this consensus there is still a paucity of research that can contribute to our understanding of how to promote exercise to this patient group to maximise long term adherence.

In one of the few studies addressing motivations and barriers for this patient group, Neuberger *et al.* (1994) surveyed 100 patients with either rheumatoid or osteoarthritis to determine perceptions about exercise. They established that perceiving benefits from exercise was a significant predictor of exercise participation; those with less formal education and a longer duration of arthritis perceived fewer benefits from exercise. In addition, those who exercised in their youth reported more benefits of exercise.

The major challenge for arthritis sufferers who are exercising is the issue of joint pain and the type of activity that should be undertaken. Exercise should take place at the time of day at which inflammation is at its lowest and non-weight bearing activities such as swimming and cycling are particularly recommended. If inflammation or increased pain occurs as a result of exercise, then the exercise may have to be adjusted so that the affected joint is not so stressed. Gordon (1993a) has written a very good guide to exercise for those suffering from arthritis which deals directly with the issue of pain and is essential reading for anyone constructing exercise opportunities for this patient group.

Osteoporosis

Osteoporosis is the condition in which there is a decrease in absolute amount of bone, rendering the skeleton susceptible to breakage and fractures (see Chapter 1). Osteoporosis can affect both males and females because there is a gradual decline in bone density with age. However, the loss of bone mass accelerates for women when ovarian function decreases during and after menopause. Thus postmenopausal women are more susceptible to osteoporosis than any other segment of the population (Kanis *et al.* 1990). In addition, osteoporosis sufferers often have to contend with pain, disability, depression and decreased confidence in their physical abilities (Rickli and McManus 1990; Vaughn 1976).

A variety of treatments have been tested but none are without controversy. Hormone replacement therapy slows down the process of bone loss (Gannon 1988) but if treatment ceases, this effect will be sustained for up to three years only (Lindsay *et al.* 1976). The role of calcium and vitamin D supplementation is not yet clear (Smith 1982). Several reviews have suggested that physical activity can enhance bone density and therefore should be considered as part of the treatment for osteoporosis (Gannon 1988; Marcus *et al.* 1992d). Clinical trials suggest that appropriate weight bearing activity can enhance bone density by around 4 per cent, which is similar to improvements noted from drug therapies (Chow, Harrison and Notarius 1987; Simkin, Ayalon and Leichter 1987; Smith *et al.* 1990).

Kriska *et al.* (1986) have noted that adherence to exercise programmes has been the major problem in most studies evaluating the effect of exercise on bone, but very few studies have attempted to study adherence issues. Mitchell, Grant and Aitchison (1998) reported very high adherence to a twelve-week class-based programme of exercise for osteoporotic women. On average, the sixteen exercisers in this study attended 87 per cent of the target of twenty-four classes. However, very little is known about exercise behaviour over a longer period of time for this patient group. This includes motivations and barriers, how patients view activity and the benefits it may provide, or what strategies the medical professions might adopt to increase or maintain adherence for a period of time which would allow bone measurements to alter as a result of exercise (namely, 9–12 months). One study on this issue used a postal questionnaire to a local branch of the National Osteoporosis Society to establish current activity patterns and attitudes towards activity (Paton 1993). A response rate of 55 per cent was achieved (seventy-four out of 140) but no follow up of non-respondents was possible because the society required that responses be anonymous. Thus the results may not be representative of the larger group of osteoporotic patients. All of the respondents had been diagnosed as osteoporotic for at least five years. Twenty-six percent of this group were sedentary and of the 74 per cent who reported that they were physically active more than half were participating in three exercise bouts each week. The most popular activity was walking. The three most commonly noted motivations for exercise were 'to feel better physically', 'to prevent further osteoporosis' and 'to feel better mentally'. The three most commonly perceived barriers to exercise were 'no facilities nearby', 'no knowledge of how to exercise' and 'not fit enough'. It is interesting to note that only 24 per cent of these respondents reported that they had been advised to begin exercise on diagnosis of the condition. Clearly, further studies on this population are required to enhance the understanding of motivation to exercise, but based on these results it would seem that exercise is perceived to have benefits and that barriers could be overcome through education on how to undertake exercise.

Special challenges for this population exist, including:

- Finding enjoyable weight bearing activity that will influence bone density.
- The need for both aerobic and strength-enhancing components in the exercise programme.
- Overcoming fear of falling or worsening the condition by undertaking exercise.
- Decreased mobility and low fitness levels.
- The need to modify programmes depending on limitations imposed by the disease.

Chronic low back pain

Managing chronic low back pain (that is, pain that is almost always present in the lower spine) is a serious problem for health services (see Chapter 1). In the UK, low back pain as a reason for being absent from work has increased by 104 per cent in the last decade (Klaber Moffet *et al.* 1995) and is the most common reason for attendance at out-patient physiotherapy clinics (Jette *et al.* 1994). There appears to be no consensus as to the most effective treatment (Waddell 1992) although both general and isokinetic exercise (Timm 1991) have been suggested as being effective. Frost *et al.* (1995) showed that a four-week supervised fitness programme was more effective than a home-based programme in reducing perceived disability and pain and in increasing self-efficacy for daily living tasks. The difference in perceived disability between the two groups was maintained at a six-month follow up. These authors suggested that the changes in self-efficacy may be due to endorphins released during exercise decreasing pain perception or increasing feelings of well-being, although the two groups did not differ in psychological change as measured by the General Health Questionnaire. Klaber Moffat *et al.* (1999) showed that back pain classes, which teach patients how to move safely and exercise, were more effective than traditional general practitioner management in reducing perceived disability and pain for up to twelve months. In addition, the patients who received the back pain classes had fewer days off work and used fewer healthcare resources thus making the back pain classes cost effective. What is becoming evident in this area of research is that the patient's psychological state (including pain perception, depression and self-efficacy) may be very important in determining recovery. In this sense the psychological outcomes of exercise programmes designed to manage low back pain may be just as important as the physiological responses such as increased strength, flexibility or aerobic performance.

Frost *et al.* (1995) described a teaching style used by the physiotherapist conducting the fitness programme. This incorporated psychological principles such as increasing self-efficacy for exercise, and reinforced positive physical self perceptions (for example, 'I am a regular exerciser') rather than negative perceptions (for example, 'I am a disabled patient'). This suggestion emphasises the important role of exercise psychology in exercise programmes designed to manage low back pain. It is important to note that this teaching approach produced very high (87 per cent) adherence levels over four weeks. However, it is presumably easier to attend for a short duration, and the authors do not report adherence to exercise in the six-month follow-up results. No other adherence statistics for exercise as part of back pain management could be found.

Special challenges for this group include overcoming the fear that movement will cause further injury. Perhaps what is required in the early stages is not an exercise programme but a movement education programme. Once patients realise that movement does not necessarily involve pain then gentle exercise can begin. There is also the challenge of finding enjoyable and interesting low impact activities.

Neuromuscular disorders

Two examples of the psychological aspects of exercise in the treatment of neuromuscular disorders have been chosen. The first is stroke and brain injury. The pathophysiology of stroke and brain injuries is often similar and so they have been linked together in this brief review. However, there are certain dissimilarities as well, not least of which is the variety of causes of brain injury (for example, car accidents) and therefore brain damage. In assessing the risks associated with exercise for those with brain injury, physical, psychological (such as aggressiveness) and behavioural (such as disruptive behaviour) issues all have to be considered (Vitale *et al.* 1995). In a review of the benefits of aerobic exercise after stroke, Potempa *et al.* (1996) concluded that enhanced motor unit recruitment, improved functional capacity, reduced cardiovascular risk and increased confidence in physical activity were all potential benefits for this patient group. Exercise has become a recommended aspect of treatment after brain injury for a variety of reasons including increasing cognitive function, increasing blood perfusion to certain areas of the brain, influencing neurotransmission and decreasing fatigue. However, most of the information about the effects of exercise come from quasi-experimental designs because of the low numbers of patients at any one time, but these studies show that 12–16 weeks of training are required to show effects (Jankowski and Sullivan 1990; Wollman *et al.* 1994). Grealy, Johnson and Rushton (1999) showed that a single session of exercise, which also involved engagement in a virtual reality environment, significantly improved movement and reaction times. These authors reported that over four weeks the exercise and virtual reality training improved verbal and visual learning in comparison to scores on these tests for participants in a control group with similar injuries. Enriching the environment in this way may have added advantages for other clinical populations and is worthy of investigation.

Special challenges for these patients include the mode of exercise. Very often the exercise will have to be conducted on a piece of stationary equipment, such as a cycle ergometer, because of other movement limitations. Even then special precautions may have to be taken to ensure patient safety and comfort such as a chest brace or handlebar adjustments. Poor concentration may also be a problem and exercise may have to be accumulated in short bouts.

The second example of a neuromuscular disorder is Parkinson's disease. The main features of this disease are tremor and rigidity in muscles, poor gait and posture, and hypokinesia. For most patients, physical activity reduces during the course of this disease but increasing physical activity and exercise has the potential of improving motor function and impacting on how these patients feel about themselves. Specific stretching and strengthening exercise can have an impact on the physical features of this disease but exercise may also have an effect on the neurotransmission problems that are the root cause of the disease. In Chapter 9, possible mechanisms for the psychological benefits of exercise were explored and it was noted that dopamine release occurs during exercise and that this may be one way in which psychological benefits occur. In Parkinson's disease, there is a loss of dopamine production and so there is added potential for exercise to be beneficial. One study has shown decreased mortality for Parkinsonian patients who were regularly exercising over a four-year period (Kuroda *et al.* 1992).

A handful of studies have attempted to show the effects of intervening with a form of exercise on motor ability but none have measured how patients perceive this treatment. Interventions have ranged from passive mobilisation conducted by physiotherapists, to sports training such as karate (Palmer *et al.* 1986). The results have been equivocal and the study designs, because of the preliminary nature of this work, have not been strong. Banks (1989) showed that home-based physiotherapy could improve activities of daily living but there was no control group for comparison. On the other hand, Gibberd *et al.* (1981) concluded that physiotherapy for these patients did not improve functional capacity, but the programme of exercise was not standardised. One randomised controlled trial (RCT) has been reported on the effects of an intensive physical rehabilitation programme (Comella *et al.* 1994). This study showed positive effects for the intensive programme on daily activities and motor function, but these effects had been lost after six months. Adherence to intensive programmes without supervision is clearly a problem. Reuter *et al.* (1999) provided training in motor co-ordination and muscle function in gymnasia and swimming pools, which they describe as 'sports training', to sixteen Parkinsonian patients. They found that there were significant improvements in motor abilities, subjective well-being and cognitive function at the end of the fourteen-week training period. These improvements had not been lost six weeks after the training had finished. However, this was a one group pre-post design and it is therefore not clear if the subjective improvements are related to group membership and extra time from therapists. The value to the patients was clear since they refused to be without the sports training for more than six weeks. There is clearly a need for more RCTs in this area.

Special considerations include knowledge of how to construct an exercise programme that will focus on the particular motor problems faced by these patients, and altered heart rate and blood pressure responses.

Cognitive, emotional and sensory disorders

Mental illness is listed in this final section of the ACSM's categorisation of disease and disability. There has been a great deal of research into the benefits of exercise in mental illness and this had been covered separately in Chapter 9. Cognition is also an area that has attracted considerable research interest from exercise scientists, but the application of this interest to individuals with clinical problems has been restricted to those with stroke or brain injury, as reported above. Etnier *et al.* (1997) conducted a meta-analysis of all the available studies (n = 134) that had examined the influence of fitness and exercise on cognitive function and found an overall effect size of 0.25. This suggests that exercise improves cognitive function by a small, but significant, amount. They noted that this effect was smaller with increasing experimental rigour and larger when longer term programmes were examined. They investigated a wide range of moderator variables including normal or impaired mental fitness that could be considered as a clinical condition. However, mental fitness did not have a significant impact on the effect size noted above, which suggests no added advantage to this potential clinical group. Impaired mental fitness may not equate to a clinical condition and so it is probably better to conclude that there are potential cognitive gains for 'clinical' individuals, such as those with brain injury, as discussed above.

Also in this final category are hearing and visual impairments and in both these conditions potential benefits to the patient's self-image, confidence and social skills are noted along with more physical benefits such as balance and fitness (American College of Sports Medicine 1997a). However, there is almost nothing in the published research literature that can help us with creating and sustaining adherence to exercise for these patients. Similarly, although Alzheimer's disease and mental retardation are listed in this category, again there is very little research to guide us about the potential benefits of exercise for these populations or any special considerations in relation to exercise adherence. There is an obvious need for further research here.

Guidelines for practice

- Medical teams in clinical settings should encourage regular activity for most patient groups. There are few contraindications.
- Medical teams should undertake training in the basic principles of exercise psychology.
- Use continuing professional development (such as the British Association of Cardiac Rehabilitation courses) to keep staff up-to-date in specialist areas.
- Where physical activity/exercise is advocated as part of treatment (for example, cardiac rehabilitation or diabetes), the goal should be to create independent exercisers. Supervised exercise should be restricted to initial phases.
- Where physical activity /exercise has been recommended, records of activity levels should be recorded at all clinic appointments.
- Use Quaglietti and Froelicher's (1994) suggestions for improving adherence in cardiac rehabilitation as a guide for all clinical settings in which exercise is recommended:

> reduce the waiting time, provide expert supervision, tailor the exercise to avoid physical discomfort and frustration, use variable activities including games, incorporate social event, recall absent patients, involve the patient's family or spouse in the program, and involve the patient in monitoring his or her progress.
>
> (Quaglietti and Froelicher 1994: 599)

Recommendations for research with clinical populations

- There is plenty of scope for research in the areas of adherence to exercise and psychological outcomes from exercise for most clinical populations.
- Researchers should try to form links with medical teams dealing with specific conditions.
- Qualitative research may often provide a starting point for such research because many of the situations do not lend themselves to standard clinical trials.
- Explore a variety of programmes such as home-, community- and hospital-based, or combinations of these. While close supervision may be required in the early stages, the long-term goal is independent exercise for these populations.
- Both researchers and practitioners should operate with a model of adherence to guide them (see Chapters 2–6). At the very least stage of exercise behaviour change should be recorded for the six months prior to exercise commencing and the processes of change recorded after exercise has commenced (see Chapters 6 and 11). Other suitable models include the theory of reasoned action or the health belief model both of which may help to explain why some people do adhere to the recommended exercise and others do not (see Chapter 5).
- Activity must be recorded before and after any exercise programme or intervention. The seven-day recall (Lowther *et al.* 1999a) is a suggested tool but other measurements might include monitoring movement via a motion sensing device such as Caltrac.
- Report the uptake for any exercise programme from the potential client population.
- Investigate motivations and barriers to exercise in each patient group as a whole and also for those who have taken up the offer or completed an exercise programme.
- Record and report (via a register or via contact) adherence at regular intervals (for example, weekly class register or monthly phone calls for home-based programmes). Report adherence to exercise prescription as a percentage of target in as many ways as

possible, for example, minutes of activity per week, number of sessions completed, full weeks of exercise. If this is self-report data provide corroboration via class registers, friends and relatives, pedometers etc. Once this is done various outcomes, including motivations and barriers, can be described for high and low adherers.

- Report drop-out rate. This will involve reporting those who dropped out before commencing and those who did not complete different stages. A definition of non-completion is required and completion of less than a half of the required programme is suggested as a working definition. Provide a between-groups analysis of drop-out rate so that potential causes can be investigated. Make every effort to contact drop-outs to establish reasons for not continuing.
- Ideally include qualitative and quantitative analysis on motivations and barriers for high, low or no adherence.
- Describe the exercise programme and the amount of supervision and encouragement given.
- Aim to provide adherence information at six months but a longer follow-up is even better.
- Include relevant psychological outcomes in all intervention studies.
- Include the issue of the potential mechanisms of psychological benefit.
- Use standardised questionnaires that have known validity and reliability.
- If possible provide qualitative information from health professionals and medical staff of their view of the role of exercise for any given patient group.

Chapter summary and conclusions

This chapter has:

- Considered the role of physical activity and exercise in the treatment of a variety of clinical populations.
- Used the American College of Sports Medicine's classification of disease and disability.
- Provided examples of psychological issues for specific conditions from each category.

We conclude:

- Patients in almost all categories of disease and disability could benefit from exercise. There are few contraindications.
- Knowledge about adherence and psychological outcomes is incomplete. The area of cardiac rehabilitation offers the most information on adherence.
- Good short-term adherence (4–12 weeks) can be achieved from supervised programmes of exercise. However, for some populations, such as those in drug rehabilitation or those with HIV + status, even short-term adherence may need special support systems.
- Long term adherence (1–4 years) is poor and not well documented. The best information comes from follow up of those in cardiac rehabilitation which suggest that 30–55 per cent are still exercising after four years. This is the area that requires most research. The cardiac rehabilitation statistics can serve as a benchmark for other clinical populations. Home-based walking programmes seem to offer the best hope for long term adherence but other modalities must be explored.
- Very little is known about the level of exercise in clinical populations. For example,

only one third of Type 1 diabetics are regular exercisers despite the fact that exercise is well recognised as part of diabetic treatment.

- Drop-out from exercise programmes is associated with factors to do with the programme and factors to do with the person and his/her circumstances.
- Motivations for exercise are clearly to do with improved health.
- Barriers to exercise are similar to non-clinical populations (for example, lack of time) but also include issues to do with the particular disease state (for example, fear of another MI or fear or worsening osteoporosis) which could be overcome through appropriate patient education.
- Cognitive behavioural strategies can be effective and the use of a counselling approach which encourages decision balance, overcoming perceived barriers and setting individualised goals should be encouraged in all clinical settings.
- Psychological outcomes are often mentioned anecdotally but are rarely measured in exercise programmes or interventions. The potential psychological benefits range from increasing a person's sense of confidence, control and self-esteem, improving mood, increasing social opportunities, improving cognitive function and improving quality of life.
- There is a need for raising awareness in some medical teams concerning the role of exercise, the potential psychological benefits and the need to assist patients with adherence to exercise.

Note

1 This chapter is based on one by Nanette Mutrie published in S. Bull (ed.) (1999) *Adherence issues in sport and exercise*. Copyright John Wiley and Sons Limited. Reproduced with permission.

Part IV

Interventions, applications and future directions

11 Making a difference I

Intervention strategies for the individual

The drama of behaviour change and resistance to it plays itself out across the full spectrum of daily life.

S. Rollnick, P. Mason and C. Butler
(*Health behaviour change: A guide for practioners*, 1999)

Chapter objectives

The purpose of this chapter is to twofold: to present current messages concerning physical activity that are aimed at the general public and to give examples of interventions designed to increase physical activity.

Specifically, in this chapter we will:

- Provide a framework for discussing interventions aimed at increasing physical activity levels.
- Discuss the current messages being used by agencies to promote physical activity.
- Outline the transtheoretical model of behaviour change.
- Give examples of the use of the transtheoretical model in physical activity interventions.
- Describe the process of exercise consultation and show results of studies using this approach.
- Show how the primary care setting can be used to increase physical activity.
- Draw conclusions about current research knowledge in this field.
- Make recommendations for researchers and practitioners.

A framework for discussion

King (1991; 1994) has provided an excellent framework for discussing interventions which aim to increase physical activity in the general population. There are four levels presented within this framework. The first level, which is the focus of this chapter, refers to interventions aimed at individuals. The second level is more concerned with how leaders, teachers and programmes providers can create the most appropriate intra- and interpersonal climates, including various choices, to encourage groups of people to increase or maintain activity (see section on motivational climate in Chapter 7). The third level of the framework is focused on how communities and organisations, such as workplaces, can promote activity. The fourth level is about how policies and environmental infrastructure, such as the mandatory provision of bicycle paths, can influence activity levels (the third and fourth levels are discussed in Chapter 12).

Several reviews have been conducted in this area and provide us with guidance for practice. Hillsdon and Thorogood (1996) conducted a systematic review of intervention strategies for the promotion of physical activity and found that, at least in 1996, there was not one single UK trial which fitted their review criteria. Their conclusions suggest that individual interventions that do not require attendance at a facility, such as walking, are likely to be most successful and that regular follow-up improves adherence. Dishman and Buckworth (1996) conducted a meta-analysis of the research examining the promotion of physical activity. Overall they found a moderately large effect size ($r = 0.34$) for a variety of interventions. There were no differences, in terms of effect size, between males and females, white or non-white participants or between age groups. However, effect sizes were larger for studies that used behaviour modification approaches and for programmes that promoted unsupervised compared to supervised activity. These findings support those of Hillsdon and Thorogood (1996) and suggest that programmes using behaviour modification strategies, such as goal-setting and reinforcement management, and which do not limit exercise to supervised classes are likely to be the most successful.

Dunn (1996) conducted a systematic review of physical activity adoption strategies and concluded that there was very little research at community and policy level to guide practice and that most research had been concerned with individual behaviour change. Dunn's review suggested four trends in the published literature on ways of helping individuals become more physically active. These were:

- The use of theories to guide the development of interventions.
- The use of statistical techniques to predict factors which are important in physical activity adoption.
- Targeting those who are ready to change behaviour.
- Exploring various modes of delivering the messages such as written materials, phone and electronic contact.

However, the major conclusion from Dunn's (1996) review was that we simply do not know enough about how to help people adopt and maintain physical activity to have clear guidance about what will, and what will not, work. Before we provide examples of these interventions, the recent changes in the content of the messages that are being transmitted to the general public, about physical activity, will be explained.

Current recommendations about physical activity

The American College of Sports Medicine (ACSM) established position statements (1978; 1990; 1998b) giving recommendations on the quantity and quality of exercise required for the development and maintenance of cardiorespiratory and muscular fitness. The recommendations stated that aerobic exercise should be undertaken 3–5 times per week, at an intensity of 60–90 per cent of maximum heart rate (or 50–85 per cent of $VO_{2\ max.}$ or Heart Rate Reserve) and should be of a continuous nature, lasting 20–60 minutes. A minimum threshold for the acquisition of cardiovascular fitness was, therefore, cited as being a weekly minimum of three sessions of at least twenty minutes of continuous, vigorous intensity aerobic exercise. This recommendation was developed from evidence from a variety of clinical and randomised controlled trials (RCT) which established that individuals who participated in this amount of physical activity could achieve measurable changes in fitness outcomes, such as increased $VO_{2\ max.}$ and decreased body fat. Despite this message being widely publicised by health promotion agencies, medical personnel and fitness profession-als, the vast majority of the population has failed to achieve the minimum thresholds described above. Evidence from the Allied Dunbar National Fitness Survey in England (The Sports Council and Health Education Authority 1992), indicated that over 70 per cent of men and 80 per cent of women failed to achieve 3 x 20 minutes of vigorous and/or moderate activity in the four weeks prior to the survey.

A more recent review of literature completed by the ACSM and American Centers for Disease Control (CDC) has led to new recommendations which are based, not on the acquisition of physical fitness but, on potential health benefits from physical activity participation. The new recommendation is that:

- Every adult should aim to accumulate thirty minutes or more of moderate intensity physical activity over the course of most days of the week.

This new recommendation has taken into account increasing epidemiological evidence that has indicated that even moderate intensity activity can lead to potential *health gain* amongst sedentary individuals. The key differences between the two messages relate to the change of emphasis from *vigorous* to *moderate* intensity from *continuous* to *accumulated* activity and from *distinctive periods of exercise* to *daily physical activity*. Moderate intensity activities are those with an energy expenditure of 4–7 METS (work metabolic rate/resting metabolic rate). This includes activities such as walking (3–4 miles per hour pace), gardening and stair climbing. The need for *regular* activity is emphasised by suggesting that thirty minutes should be accumulated on most days of the week. While there is limited evidence to support the case that accumulated, small bouts of activity may influence fitness, this new message suggests that for sedentary individuals any increase in physical activity is likely to be of benefit to their health. It also takes into account the many psychological barriers faced by sedentary individuals in achieving the fitness recommendations. The barriers cited frequently relate to lack of time, not perceiving one-self as 'sporty', and difficulties in accessing facilities (see Chapter 2). The emphasis in the new recommendations, therefore, is on *active living*. The active living message is that individuals should become *more active, more often* taking every opportunity to make active choices when they arise. The new message is clearly targeted at the sedentary majority of the population and is meant to be complementary to the previous message, rather than a replacement of it.

The complementary nature of active living and fitness messages has been further emphasised by the most recent position stance published by ACSM (1998b). In this state-ment, programmes of physical activity and exercise are recommended with the goal of encouraging a lifetime of physical activity. While it is aimed at developing and maintaining cardiorespiratory fitness, muscular fitness and flexibility, the idea that lower activity levels may still produce health (but not necessarily fitness) benefits is incorporated. The following quotations from the 1998 statement clarify the complementary nature of active living and fitness-oriented programmes:

> The ACSM now views exercise and physical activity for health and fitness in the con-text of an exercise dose continuum. . . . Many significant health benefits are achieved by going from a sedentary state to a minimal level of physical activity. . . . Although the fitness paradigm that is recommended in this ACSM position stand is adaptable to a

broad cross-section of the healthy adult population, it is clearly designed for the mid-dle-to-higher end of the exercise/physical activity continuum.

(ACSM 1998b: 976)

The current message for the promotion of physical activity should therefore take a two-step approach, as shown in Table 11.1. Messages aimed at young people are discussed in Chapter 12.

For older adults, a similar position statement has been made by ACSM (1998a). There is universal recognition that the proportion of older adults in developed countries is increasing rapidly. In parallel, there is growing recognition of the role that activity and exercise can play in promoting healthy ageing and in reducing functional decline that accompanies ageing. The position stand confirms the need for regular moderate activity for older adults. However, there is recognition that with increasing age aerobic exercise becomes more diffi-cult for a variety of limiting conditions such as arthritis and poor gait. The clear message is that strength training (at least two sessions per week) should be included for all exercise programmes for this age group and for the frail elderly strength and balance training become a pre-requisite for aerobic exercise.

In the UK, national campaigns with television advertising have been launched to support the two-step approach. For example, the Health Education Board for Scotland (HEBS) eval-uated an advert which promoted the idea that walking is a sufficient activity for health. Wimbush, Macgregor and Fraser (1997) reported that the evaluation had two components. The first was a population survey conducted pre and post the appearance of the TV advert. The second component of the evaluation was a survey, conducted at baseline with a ten-week and one year follow-up, of those people who chose to call the helpline ('Fitline') number given at the end of the advert. The population survey showed that during the first four weeks of the advert being screened 70 per cent of the Scottish population were aware of the advert. This is a very high level of coverage and companies buying advertising space on TV would consider this a huge success. However, only 16 per cent at best were aware of

Table 11.1 Current messages for the promotion of physical activity

Recommendation	Advice	Target group
Step one: Active living Aim to accumulate thirty minutes of moderate intensity physical activity on most days of the week.	Add physical activity into your daily routine so that being active becomes a way of life. • take the stairs • walk some of your journeys • think of yourself as active.	Inactive or irregularly active adults.
Step two: Regular exercise Aim to include three periods of vigorous intensity activity, which lasts for at least twenty minutes, in your routine each week.	Improve your fitness by gradually increasing the length of some of your bouts of activity • be more active more often • make your activities a little more energetic	Those achieving step one, who are already active at a moderate level, and would like to do more. Those wishing to achieve measurable changes to their fitness levels.

the Fitline telephone service and of that group only 5 per cent had actually used the service. Both forms of evaluation showed an increase in knowledge about walking as a form of exercise. There was no notable change in either intention to walk more or actual walking behaviour. In the Fitline survey, around half of the respondents claimed to be more active than they had been at the baseline survey and most of that group said their walking had increased. The authors concluded that, although there was no impact on walking behaviour at a population level, the advert did have an impact in terms of raising awareness and influencing knowledge and thus had an important role to play in terms of health education. In addition, the Health Education Authority in England is conducting an evaluation of the 'active for life' campaign.

The Scottish Office has recently set targets for increasing the percentage of the Scottish population which will meet the minimum guidelines for 'active living' by the year 2005 (The Scottish Office 1999). These targets are:

- The proportion of 11–15 year olds taking vigorous exercise 4/week should increase from 32 per cent in 1994 to 40 per cent in 2005.
- The proportion of men/women aged 16–64 taking thirty minutes of moderate activity 5/week should increase from 32 per cent/22 per cent in 1994 to 50 per cent/40 per cent in 2005.

Having discussed the context of contemporary promotional strategies and messages, we now consider specific approaches to physical activity behaviour change for individuals.

The transtheoretical model of behaviour change

Once the message about how much activity is required to achieve health and fitness benefits is clear, the task of encouraging individual change for the majority of the sedentary population still exists. A variety of behaviour change models have been suggested to underpin the practical work of stopping negative and harmful behaviour such as smoking or drug dependence. One practical approach has been to adapt the 'stage of change' or transtheoretical model (TTM), which has substantial support in the area of smoking cessation, for use with exercise and physical activity. The principles of this approach were discussed in Chapter 6. Here we focus on interventions using the TTM.

The TTM has four key elements (Reed 1999):

- A set of distinct categories that describe the stages of behaviour change that people go through.
- A set of ten processes which people use as they change behaviour.
- Self-efficacy underpins different stages.
- The recognition that the weighing up of pros and cons of changing behaviour will influence progress.

These four key elements will now be described as they relate to exercise and physical activity. By way of reminder, here are the five main stages:

- Precontemplation: no intention to become more active in the next six months.
- Contemplation: thinking about becoming more active in the next six months.

- Preparation: having a plan of action (for example, taking out a membership) or having attempted some exercise but not enough to meet the minimum criteria for active living.
- Action: people have become regular exercisers but only in the previous six months.
- Maintenance: achieved regular exercise for longer than six months.

People may fall back from their current stage for a variety of reasons and this is described as relapse and is sometimes listed as a separate stage. Regular exercise may be interrupted for a variety of reasons like injury, illness, moving house, or changing job. People who relapse can fall back to any stage and may begin the cycle of change again from any of the prior stages.

The stage of change process is dynamic; people move round the cycle, sometimes several times, in their efforts to change behaviour. On the other hand, some people may stay at a stage for a long period of time without movement. For example, a person may be contemplating beginning an activity programme for several years before they get round to doing something about that. Figure 11.1 shows the cycle of change.

Using a stage of exercise behaviour change approach suggests different kinds of intervention strategies will be useful at each stage. Table 11.2 outlines the five stages of behaviour change with suggested approaches and appropriate agencies for each. The needs of each group have been documented from evaluation studies (Health Education Authority 1995b).

The stages of exercise behaviour change can also be used to describe the population and provide information on the percentage of the population who might respond to any particular intervention. A recent European survey (Kearney, de Graaf, Damkjaer and Engstrom 1999) has provided excellent information in this regard. Figure 11.2 shows that in Europe a third of the population is in action and maintenance and that a third of the over 55 group are in pre-contemplation. This kind of information can also show change over time as a result of interventions that might be put in place.

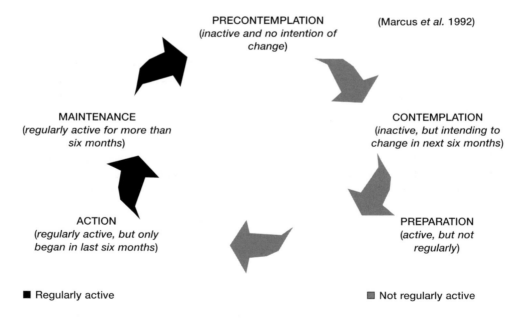

PRECONTEMPLATION
(*inactive and no intention of change*)

(Marcus *et al.* 1992)

CONTEMPLATION
(*inactive, but intending to change in next six months*)

PREPARATION
(*active, but not regularly*)

ACTION
(*regularly active, but only began in last six months*)

MAINTENANCE
(*regularly active for more than six months*)

■ Regularly active

■ Not regularly active

Figure 11.1 The stages of exercise behaviour change

Table 11.2 Matching promotional approaches to stage of exercise behaviour change

Stage of behaviour change	Characteristics	Needs	Appropriate initiatives	Appropriate agencies
Stage 1: Pre-contemplation	Little awareness of their inactivity and the consequences of inactivity to their own health.	Information about the problem; opportunities to personalise the situation.	National/local media, leaflets, posters.	National and local health promotion agencies.
Stage 2: Contemplation	Balances the potential benefits of taking activity against the costs (time, money, effect on others).	Opportunities for discussion; knowledge of facilities or opportunities; cues to action.	Taster sessions; promotional events and campaigns; advice from GP's; phoneline.	Local authority leisure services; local health education.
Stage 3: Preparation	Prepares to take action and then increases physical activity; is active on an irregular basis.	Opportunities for participation; feedback on progress.	Discussions with exercise or health professional; exercise consultation.	Local authority leisure services, local health education, workplace opportunities.
Stage 4: Action	Recently become physically active on a regular basis.	Feedback on progress.	Provision of a variety of opportunities and events.	Local authority leisure services, voluntary sector, workplace.
Stage 5: Maintenance	Has been regularly physically active for at least six months.	Support to maintain.	Clubs, support groups, co-participants.	Local authority leisure services, voluntary sector, workplace.

Processes of change

Along with stage of readiness to change behaviour is the notion that people make use of certain processes as they change from one stage to another. Processes of change are defined by Marcus *et al.* as 'the cognitive, affective, and behavioral strategies and techniques people use as they progress through the different stages of change over time' (Marcus *et al.* 1992a: 425). Table 11.3 describes ten processes of change and how they might be used in exercise and physical activity interventions. Five of these processes are described as experiential and the other five as behavioural. However, the relevance of these processes for exercise has not been fully established. However, as Table 11.4 shows, movement from one stage to another is associated with one or a set of processes of change. This is likely to be particularly important for interventions. Assessment of the current stage for an individual should, therefore, allow for interventions to be tailored to specific processes of change. It is this heuristic appeal that has led to the SOC approach being popular in health and exercise promotion, such as through family doctor (GP) referral exercise schemes.

Self-efficacy

The third element of the TTM is the concept of self-efficacy (see Chapter 4). For exercise and physical activity this has referred to various issues such as a person's confidence that

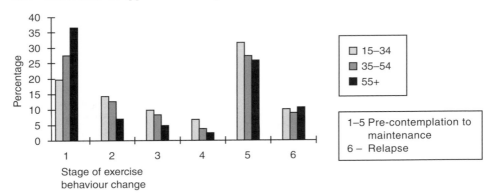

Figure 11.2 Percentage of each age group of the European population at each stage of exercise behaviour. Data from Kearney *et al.* (1999).

Table 11.3 Processes of change and physical activity intervention possibilities

Process	Description	Physical activity intervention possibilities
EXPERIMENTAL: Increasing knowledge (consciousness raising).	Increasing information about oneself and physical activity.	Talking with others about PA; observing others in PA and exercise; learning about the benefits of exercise.
Warning of risks (dramatic relief).	Experiencing and expressing feelings about (non) exercising.	Discussion; role-play; graphic materials.
Caring about consequences (self-re-evaluation).	Assessing how one feels about oneself and exercise/PA.	Clarification of values and attitudes associated with exercise and other competing behaviours; imagery of exercise.
Increasing health alternatives (social liberation).	Increasing alternatives for PA through society.	Physically active transport to work.
Environmental re-evaluation.	Assessing how (non) exercising is related to the physical environment.	Learning about physical activity opportunities in the community.
BEHAVIOURAL: Helping relationships.	Being open and trusting to someone about your exercise/physical activity.	Eliciting social support for your involvement.
Substituting alternatives (counter-conditioning).	Substituting alternatives for sedentary behaviour.	Increasing habitual activity.
Understanding benefits (self-liberation).	Commitment to exercise/PA and belief that one can exercise.	Resolutions to exercise; contracting to exercise.
Creating active opportunities (stimulus control).	Countering stimuli that increase the probability of sedentary behaviour.	Removing some labour-saving devices; making exercise clothes or equipment prominent.
Rewarding yourself (reinforcement (contingency) management).	Giving oneself a reward or receiving a reward from others.	Rewarding PA/exercise.

Table 11.4 Moving between stages and proposed dominant processes of change

Movement towards stage of: Contemplation	Preparation	Action	Maintenance
Increasing knowledge (consciousness raising)	Caring about consequences (self-re-evaluation)	Understanding benefits (self-liberation)	Rewarding yourself (reinforcement (contingency) management)
Warning of risks (dramatic relief) Environmental re-evaluation			Helping relationships
			Substituting alternatives (counterconditioning) Creating active opportunities (stimulus control)

they can overcome typical barriers to exercise, or confidence to undertake related behaviours such as going into a sports centre. Examples of items in a self-efficacy questionnaire are shown in Table 11.5.

Researchers have established a consistent relationship between self-efficacy and stage of behaviour change. Those in the action and maintenance stages report higher levels of self-efficacy that those in the earlier stages. This suggests that influencing self-efficacy may assist behaviour change, but also that changing behaviour may change self-efficacy.

Decisional balance

The final element of the TTM is the concept of decisional balance. The original research subdivided this into gains and losses to self and others and approval or disapproval by self or others. Subsequent analysis showed that the important elements were more simply expressed as the 'pros' and 'cons' of changing behaviour. Examples of items in a decisional balance questionnaire are shown in Table 11.6. Research has shown that at the early stages of behaviour change cons outweigh pros, that those in preparation may have more equality around the pros and cons, and that those who are in maintenance will perceive more pros than cons. This suggests that influencing perceptions of pros and cons may assist in behaviour change.

The Health Education Authority (1995a; 1995b) recommended this model as a way of approaching health behaviour change. Its strong points are the way in which populations can

Table 11.5 Example items from a scale to assess self-efficacy for exercise. A seven point Likert scale is used to score responses (not at all confident = 1 to very confident = 7).

	Stem: I am confident I can participate in regular exercise when:
1	I am tired
2	I am in a bad mood
3	I feel I don't have the time
4	I am on vacation
5	It is raining or snowing

Source: Marcus *et al.* 1992c.

Table 11.6 Example items assessing decisional balance ('pros' and 'cons'). A five-point Likert scale is used to score responses (not at all important = 1 to extremely important = 5).

---

1   I would be healthier if I exercised regularly

2   I would feel better about myself if I exercised regularly

3   Other people would respect me more if I exercised regularly

4   My family and friends would get to spend less time with me if I exercised regularly

5   I would feel that I was wasting my time if I exercised regularly

6   I would probably be sore and uncomfortable if I exercised regularly

---

Source: Marcus and Owen 1992.

be described and targeted for health promotion campaigns and the potential to explain the processes that people go through in making changes. However, it has also been criticised and some of these issues are addressed in Chapter 6. The next section will give examples of the use of this model for exercise and physical activity promotion.

Interventions based on the transtheoretical model of behaviour change

Project active

In the USA, Project Active (Dunn *et al.* 1997; 1998; 1999) aimed to establish if an active living approach to promoting physical activity could be as effective as a traditional fitness-oriented approach. The project used the TTM as a basis for the interventions aimed to change sedentary behaviour. The project recruited 116 men and 119 women (mean age 46 years) by press and other media in Dallas, Texas. The participants were randomly assigned to one of two groups. One group was labelled 'Structured Exercise' and followed ACSM guidelines for cardiorespiratory fitness via a traditional gym-based approach at the Cooper Aerobics Centre. Participants in this group were supervised for six months and then paid a fee to remain a 'member' of the aerobics centre. The second group was labelled 'Lifestyle Counselling' and followed the 'Active Living' guidelines. When they met they did not exercise but had group discussions designed to assist adoption and maintenance of active living. At first the meetings were weekly (first four months); these then tapered to bi-weekly from 4–6 months, monthly from 6–12 months, bi-monthly from 12–18 months, and finally tri-monthly from 18–24 months.

At six months, 85 per cent of the Structured group and 78 per cent of the Lifestyle group were achieving the minimum Active Living criteria. Both groups had improved cardio-respiratory fitness (although the Structured group improved more than the Lifestyle group). In addition, both groups reduced total cholesterol, total cholesterol/HDL–C ratio, diastolic BP and percentage body fat. There was a 15 per cent reduction in CHD risk overall (17 per cent Structured, 12 per cent Lifestyle).

By twenty-four months both groups increased total energy expenditure (TEE) and cardiorespiratory fitness from baseline and had similar decreases from six months. These results are illustrated in Figures 11.3 and 11.4. Twenty percent of the participants were still on or above the active living recommendations. There was a dose-response relationship with those doing the most consistent activity (maintaining minimum guidelines for 70 per cent of the twenty-four weeks) showing the best fitness and TEE responses. In addition, both groups decreased BP and percentage body fat while body weight remained unchanged. The authors drew the conclusion that the lifestyle approach was as effective as a traditional fitness

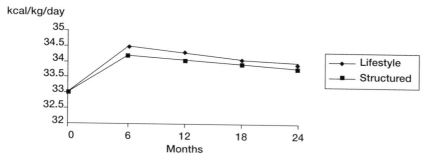

Figure 11.3 Changes in total energy expenditure in both lifestyle and structured groups in Project Active. Data from Dunn *et al.* (1999).

approach in improving activity, fitness, BP and body composition and declare this to be good news for those who could not tolerate or maintain the 'fitness' approach. However, there are aspects of this project limiting both the internal and external validity of the results.

It could be said that this is not a true randomised controlled trial since there is no control group. The lack of a control group raises the issue of whether or not anyone motivated to sign up for such a project would have made similar changes over twenty-four months even if they had not received either of the interventions? Given the wealth of evidence suggesting that long-term exercise is difficult to achieve, this is possible but unlikely. The changes which were recorded were modest (for example less than 2 per cent body fat loss and less than 2 ml/kg/min. improvement in aerobic fitness) and only 20 per cent of participants were still achieving the active living recommendations at twenty-four months. On the one hand it could be argued that if this kind of change could be achieved across the population substantial health gains could also be achieved. On the other hand it could be argued that this was an expensive method of achieving minimal changes in activity levels, which also may be difficult to generalise to other locations. It is hard to imagine any local health promotion agency being able to sustain the regularity of meetings required for the lifestyle counselling group (twenty hours in the first six months) with a population who do not have the motivation for being involved in a research project. In addition, Project Active recruited a population of participants who were well educated and likely to be interested in healthy lifestyles. Is it possible that the same techniques could be successful with a more representative population?

Overall, the findings support the concept of the Active Living approach and this is the

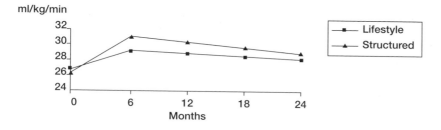

Figure 11.4 Changes in maximum oxygen uptake in both lifestyle and structured groups in Project Active. Data from Dunn *et al.* (1999).

first piece of research demonstrating long-term outcomes. This means that health promoters can be more confident in suggesting that the Active Living approach can produce fitness and health benefits. However, we need further research that tests cheaper and more readily applicable means of changing physical activity behaviour if we are to achieve changes across all socio-economic groups.

Promoting physical activity through active commuting

Increasing physical activity levels by active commuting, that is walking or cycling to and from locations, has become an increasingly political issue because of the need to reduce traffic congestion and fuel consumption, and thus enhance the environment, in many cities. Vuori, Oja and Paronen (1994) established that walking or cycling to work could increase fitness and that this form of active commuting was a feasible health and exercise promotion strategy. Oja *et al.* (1991) have implemented a workplace physical activity programme in Tampere, Finland, through the promotion of active commuting to work. Initial research suggested that during the summer 38 per cent were physically active in commuting to work on a regular basis, 15 per cent irregularly, 17 per cent used motorised transport but did consider physically active commuting a possibility, while 30 per cent perceived little other option than using motorised transport.

A programme was initiated in a paper manufacturing company over a six-month period. This involved three work sites and 1,200 employees. 'The programme was targeted to increase the awareness and knowledge of possibilities to use walking and cycling as forms of transportation to and from work and to stimulate the participation in safe walking and cycling during work commuting' (Oja *et al.* 1991: 237). The company management was supportive of the initiative and the administration was handled by the health personnel of the company.

The promotion campaign was found to have a positive effect in terms of greater awareness, increased participation in walking and cycling as a means of commuting to work, particularly among older workers, and an increase in physical activity in leisure time. However, problems associated with pedestrian and road safety were noted and highlight the importance of environmental changes in the promotion of physical activity.

In conclusion, Oja *et al.* said that their findings suggest

> that walking and cycling during work commuting are feasible forms of regular physical activity for a sizeable section of the working-age population. . . . Work-commuting exercise appears to be a plausible alternative with which to promote exercise among the general, often inactive, working population.
>
> (Oja *et al.* 1991: 238)

Oja, Vuori and Paronen (1998) concluded the following with respect to cycling or walking to work:

- Poor and unsafe conditions for walking or cycling are major impediments for active commuting to work.
- Walking and cycling to work on a regular basis produce measurable positive changes in several health and fitness parameters.
- Increasing walking or cycling to work is possible through a targeted programme; co-operation with local traffic and safety groups may be beneficial.

Similar initiatives are underway in the UK (Davis 1999). For example, in Glasgow, a group charged with creating an inter-agency policy for increasing physical activity levels in the city, conducted a randomised controlled trial. The aim was to establish if a cognitive behavioural intervention, delivered via written interactive materials, could increase active commuting behaviour in workplace settings (Mutrie *et al.* 1999). The intervention was based on the transtheoretical model of behaviour change and the target population was those who were thinking about active commuting (contemplators) and those who were doing some irregular active commuting (preparers).

Participants identified through screening (n = 333) were sent a baseline questionnaire. This measured demographic variables, stage of change and self-efficacy for active commuting, using an adapted version of a scale by Marcus *et al.* (1994), seven-day recall of physical activity (Lowther *et al.* 1999a) and physical and mental functioning by the SF–36 (Ware *et al.* 1993). Participants were matched for average distance travelled to work and randomly assigned to a control group or an intervention group who received the intervention materials. Follow-up questionnaires were sent at six months to both groups.

Completed baseline questionnaires were received from 295 participants (intervention group n = 145, control group n = 150). The mean age was 38 years (range of 19 to 69 years), 64 per cent were female and 36 per cent were male. The response rate at six months was 67 per cent (n = 198). Over six months, a significantly larger percentage of the intervention group (49 per cent) progressed to a higher stage of active commuting behaviour change compared to the control group (31 per cent). The average difference between the two groups was 18 per cent. Analysis of the physical activity using the seven-day recall revealed a significantly greater average time spent walking to work for those in the intervention group compared to controls for those who had not walked to work at the start of the study. There was also a significant increase in the average time spent walking to work, in favour of the intervention group, among those who already walked to work. The average relative increase in the time spent walking to work at six months, for someone given the intervention, was 1.93 times any increase in walking time for a corresponding control individual who walked the same amount at baseline.

More of those who progressed, compared to those who regressed in stage of active commuting behaviour, rated certain motivations as important. These motivations for active commuting were getting some fresh air, sense of enjoyment/independence and no necessity for parking. There were no significant differences on the rating of importance in any of the barriers between those who progressed and those who regressed on stage of active commuting.

The intervention, however, was not successful in increasing cycling. Only eighteen participants reported cycling to work at six months and there was no difference in the reported average weekly minutes of cycling between cyclists in the intervention group (n = 9) and control group (n = 9). Follow-up focus group research identified barriers faced by cyclists which were difficult to overcome, such as perception of traffic danger and lack of safe cycle parking. This is important to note since many transport campaigns have focused on cycling as an alternative. This research tells us that in a city with a reasonable network of cycle lanes there is still a perception of danger and difficulty associated with cycling. Campaigns which seek to promote cycling must work on a long-term strategy of changing public perception by continual support for safe cycling, driver education about cyclists on the road and helping local authorities create safe routes and cycle parking facilities. Wardman, Hatfield and Page (1997) have calculated that significant increases in cycling are unlikely to be achieved by provision of cycle routes alone. Recent research suggests that a significant shift to cycling will only happen if co-ordinated action is taken in three areas: promotion of individual and social behaviour change, promotion of organisational change and implementation of situation and environmental measures (Davies *et al.* 1997).

An interesting finding was related to participants' responses to the SF–36 – a measure of perceptions of physical and mental health functioning. At six months the experimental group had significantly higher scores than the control group on general health, vitality and mental health. This suggests that active commuting could increase quality of life perceptions and this may be related both to increasing activity and diminishing dependence on other forms of transport and even decreasing the stress of other forms of transport. One participant in the project, who had sold her car as a result of her involvement, reported the following experience:

> I dislike driving especially in rush hour traffic and have found it no hardship to give up my car – in fact I no longer have my own vehicle. The cost of my monthly rail pass is less than I was paying out in petrol. I look at the faces of the motorists and I think – I am glad that is not me! I enjoy the feeling of getting exercise and arrive at work with plenty of energy and quite relaxed.
>
> (*University of Glasgow Newsletter*, 3 March 1999: 20)

In terms of the TTM model, the intervention group did not differ from the control group in the most frequently used processes of change. For both groups the most frequently used processes of change were self-liberation, counter-conditioning and self-re-evaluation. Perhaps the processes questionnaire, which had been adapted from processes used in smoking cessation, needs to be made more specific for physical activity or even active commuting before changes will be seen as a result of interventions.

Twenty five percent of the initial intervention group were still actively commuting to work one year after they received the intervention, comparing well to interventions aimed at changing other health behaviours. For example, only 2 per cent of smokers successfully quit and did not relapse after one year after personal advice on how to stop (Law and Tang 1995). There was no evidence to suggest a seasonal impact on the efficacy of the intervention, nor were there gender, age or distance-to-work effects noted.

This intervention is a cheap and effective way of assisting the achievement of targets for physical activity (The Scottish Office 1999) and the environment (Department of the Environment, Transport and the Regions 1998). It was successful in increasing walking but not cycling. Nevertheless, the intervention pack could help those who want to walk more and the Health Education Board for Scotland plan to distribute it to all local authority health boards to compliment existing activity promoting strategies and to assist in the search for alternative modes of transport. The pack can be tailored for different locations by inserting local information as appropriate. The study design from this project is shown in Figure 11.5 and the main results in Figure 11.6.

Promoting physical activity in university students

Woods, Mutrie and Scott (1999) used a postal intervention based on the stage of change model, to encourage sedentary undergraduate students to become more physically active. The design of this study involved almost 3,000 first year students at a large city university. Baseline information was collected from these students while they waited in line to register at the university. The baseline information included current stage of change for physical

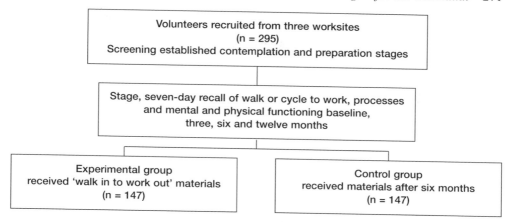

Figure 11.5 Study design for the Active Commuting Project (Mutrie *et al.* 1999)

activity and exercise, participation pattern for physical education in the last two years of schooling, and intentions towards activity in the next six months. Those who were categorised as precontemplators or contemplators (n = 459) were randomly assigned to an experimental or control group. The experimental group was sent, by post, stage-matched materials that were designed to encourage participation in Active Living or in the university's structured exercise programmes. Follow-ups were conducted at seven and nineteen months on all students. This design of this study is shown in Figure 11.7.

The baseline results showed that 46 per cent of the student population was not achieving the current minimum physical activity targets. Thirty five percent had not taken part in PE during their final two years at school. There was a significant positive association between taking part in PE at school and current activity. Those who had participated in PE were more likely to be in the regularly active stages of change and to intend to exercise in the future. This association is shown in Figure 11.8. This shows the potentially important part that schools can play in promoting attendance at PE that clearly relates to continued involvement in activity beyond the years of schooling.

At seven months, more of the experimental group (80 per cent) than control group (68 per cent) had increased stage of change and, at nineteen months, more of experimental group (42 per cent) than control group (27 per cent) were in action and maintenance stages of

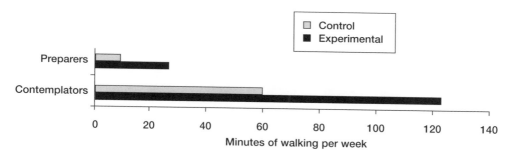

Figure 11.6 Increases in minutes of walking per week for participants in the Active Commuting Project (Mutrie *et al.* 1999)

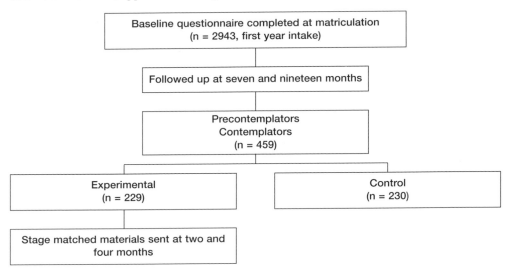

Figure 11.7 Study design for a postal intervention targeted at precontemplating and contemplating students (Woods *et al.* 1999)

exercise behaviour. The most frequently used processes of behaviour change, for those who improved their stage of change over time, were self-reevaluation, self-liberation and reward management. These results suggest that using postal, self-instruction material, is a cheap way of encouraging the least active students into an active lifestyle as they arrive at university and that the effect can last into their second year at university.

Some of the most interesting material from this research came from qualitative data. Nine focus groups were carried out to explore the perceptions of these students about physical activity during their initial years at university. Several important findings emerged from both a content analysis and a group dynamics analysis. The results revealed how young adults talk about their past and current experiences of physical activity, how

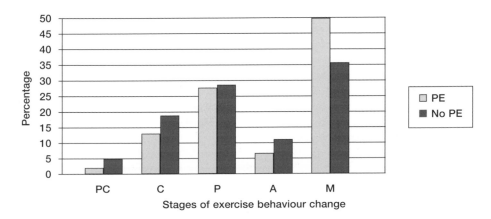

Figure 11.8 Percentage of students at each stage of exercise behaviour change who had participated in physical education (PE) during the final two years of schooling (Woods *et al.* 1999)

these experiences influenced current levels of participation, and what might help them to be active in the future. Themes to emerge from the data included the importance of social determinants (for example, the role of significant others) and self-empowerment (for example, belief in your ability to be part of an exercise culture) in physical activity adoption and maintenance. The following excerpt from the transcription of the focus group discussions shows the importance of social support in overcoming feelings of incompetence in certain activities:

> I suppose it was recently we started exercising again because I thought people will laugh at me and I didn't do anything till this year again because it was just I thought will people laugh at me I'm not any good at this, why should I bother I've not been good at it before. The only thing that I enjoyed was swimming. I'm still a bit overweight. I recently lost a lot of weight and I wouldn't have gone in a pool in a swimming costume or anything. It's friends that encouraged me to go back and I'm so glad I did because I really enjoy it now but not beforehand.

The data also supported the staging of individuals though the stage of change questionnaire, as individuals could be categorised into different levels of activity and inactivity due to their comments in the interviews. These corresponded favourably to their self-selected stage of change in a questionnaire. Focus group participants viewed the intervention materials as quite useful, but they concluded that the materials should be more realistic to young adults. For example, they felt that the statistics on levels of inactivity should refer only to young adults and preferably to those at the university. Future research into the production of intervention materials in physical activity should examine the effect of stage matching, but also make the intervention age- or population-specific.

Using an exercise consultation approach for increasing physical activity

Many local authority and private leisure centres offer fitness testing/assessment for members as a way of encouraging attendance. However, there has been surprisingly little evidence to support the notion that fitness assessment could be motivating for long-term exercise. Computerised fitness assessments are now commercially available, and this has become a popular service to members of facilities. In contrast, a more person-centred approach was also becoming popular, such as being based on the concept of motivational interviewing, pioneered by Miller and Rollnick (1991). Loughlan and Mutrie (1995) offered guidelines about using a person-centred exercise consultation approach to increasing activity levels. These guidelines were based on the available knowledge of what assists people in making exercise behaviour change. The person doing the consultation must have excellent communication and reflective listening skills, and empathy for the people who are seeking help. Exercise consultants must also have good knowledge about physical activity for general and clinical populations, including the current activity recommendations and any contraindications for particular groups. Finally, exercise consultants must understand the various theories of behaviour change and the various factors that will influence whether or not a person will succeed in becoming more active.

A similar model of physical activity counselling has been described by Laitakari and Asikainen (1998). They advocate a more detailed assessment procedure that includes quality of life, health status, health practice and living environment. Such details may be helpful but they may also take more time. A trade-off between details and time may be required. Laitakari and Asikainen have not yet reported on the efficacy of their counselling approach but results will be helpful in determining if a longer consultation is effective. The consultation approach described by Loughlan and Mutrie (1995) has now been tested in several settings.

Loughlan and Mutrie (1997) randomly assigned 179 National Health Service employees to receive a fitness assessment, an exercise consultation or an information booklet. The participants were all in the contemplation or preparation stage of exercise behaviour change. Using a seven-day recall of physical activity questionnaire (Loughlan and Mutrie 1995) all three groups were found to increase activity levels at four weeks, three months and six months post intervention. There was evidence that on-going support was needed to maintain initial increases in physical activity. It was suggested that exercise consultation showed trends to sustain activity more than the fitness assessment or information. It would seem that when people are ready to change even simple and cheap interventions such as information could provide a short-term stimulus to change.

A further study on the same theme was undertaken over twelve months to assess the longer-term effectiveness of the consultation process. Lowther, Mutrie and Scott (1999b) compared the effectiveness of fitness assessment and exercise consultation in increasing activity levels in a community setting. Almost 400 people responded to a local mailshot offering them the chance to participate in a physical activity project. Respondents chose whether they wanted a fitness assessment or an exercise consultation and then were randomly assigned to experimental or control groups. The control groups received information about physical activity and the experimental groups received either an exercise consultation or a fitness assessment with a three-month follow-up. The study design is summarised in Figure 11.9. The measures included stage and processes of change and a seven-day recall of physical activity.

The results showed that, for those who were not regularly active at baseline, by three months all groups had significantly increased physical activity. This supports our earlier findings that information alone can assist people in making a short-term change in activity levels (Loughlan and Mutrie 1997). At six months, both experimental groups had maintained the initial increases in physical activity but both control groups relapsed back to their baseline levels. This finding suggests that support is required to maintain activity since both

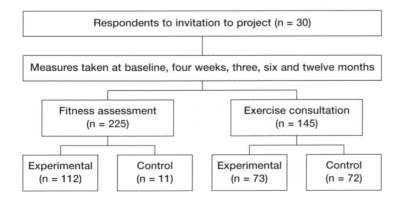

Figure 11.9 Design for community trial of exercise consultation versus fitness assessment (Lowther *et al.* 1999b)

experimental groups received a second assessment or consultation after three months. At twelve months only the exercise consultation experimental group reported significantly more physical activity than at baseline. This supports the view that the cognitive behavioural skills, which are the focus of the consultation process, may have the best long term effects in increasing physical activity for individuals.

This study also provided excellent information on the kind of person who might chose an exercise consultation. Figure 11.10 shows that significantly more of the people who chose an exercise consultation were classified in pre-contemplation, contemplation or preparation stages than in action and maintenance stages. This was not true for fitness assessment, which attracted equal numbers of active versus inactive people. In addition, older rather than younger adults were more likely to chose exercise consultation in preference to fitness assessment (Lowther *et al.* 1999b). Thus, offering an exercise consultation service from a leisure centre may attract different segments of the population in comparison to the standard opportunity to have a fitness assessment. For example, Bailey and Biddle (1988) found that only 17.3 per cent of men and 14.4 per cent of women who volunteered for a fitness test at the Health Fair of the 1986 National Garden Festival in England were found to be below average on age-related fitness norms. In addition, of the 3,000 individuals analysed in this study (from a total of 13,373 who completed a fitness test), only 21 per cent of women and 18 per cent of men were over 45 years of age. These data reflect the bias towards the young and fit individual being attracted to such an activity and lend further support to the potential efficacy of exercise consultation in attracting a wider population.

Primary healthcare interventions

The promotion of physical activity and exercise in primary healthcare (PHC) has increased greatly in the USA and UK in recent years (Fox *et al.* 1997; Pender *et al.* 1994). There are several good reasons why PHC should address physical activity promotion more than it has done in the past. These include:

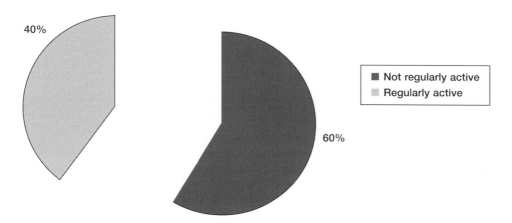

Figure 11.10 Percentage of the participants who opted for exercise consultation by physical activity status (Lowther *et al.* 1999b)

- PHC has become increasingly oriented towards prevention, therefore physical activity can more easily be promoted alongside other health behaviours, such as smoking cessation and dietary modification.
- the PHC team has regular contact with large numbers of people who could benefit from increases in physical activity. It is estimated in England that 90 per cent of a PHC practice population visit their surgery within a three-year period, and about 70 per cent annually.
- GPs (family physician; 'General Practitioner') are thought to be particularly influential in changing attitudes and behaviours since they are often viewed as credible sources of information.

Little systematic evaluation has taken place across the many PHC interventions in physical activity. However, some researchers have suggested that the GP is well placed to provide advice about physical activity although some may lack knowledge about physical activity and how to promote it (Gould *et al.* 1995). A survey of 161 GPs in Finland showed that they rated further training for themselves in exercise counselling less important than ten other health behaviours (Miilunpalo 1991).

Reed, Jensen and Gorenflo (1991) attempted to identify factors associated with GPs in the USA who encouraged more than 50 per cent of their patients to exercise. The higher rates of patient encouragement were given by more experienced GPs (more than ten years in practice), by GPs who estimated that greater than 10 per cent of their patients had a personal exercise programme, participated in an exercise programme of their own and had a method of patient follow-up. The extent that PHC personnel are active themselves may be an important precursor to getting an interventions started (Fox *et al.* 1997), although evidence on whether these individuals are good role models is not particularly encouraging (Pender *et al.* 1994).

Trends in PHC physical activity interventions

Physical activity promotion in PHC has generally not been well documented. In England, the Health Education Authority (HEA) funded a national research project on PHC promotion of physical activity to find out the nature of extent of this type of intervention (see Fox *et al.* 1997). An initial search revealed 121 schemes, of which 40.5 per cent were labelled 'practice-based'. These involved the management of the patient residing primarily in the PHC setting, such as with the Practice Nurse or an exercise counsellor/leader. Most schemes were 'leisure centre-based' schemes (59.5 per cent), most of which were in the pilot stage. These schemes involved the GP or other member of the PHC team handing over the management of the patient to a local leisure/sports centre. In addition, fifty-two schemes were planned, suggesting that a large expansion in schemes was likely to follow. This has indeed been the case and the proportion of schemes adopting the leisure-centre model has increased further. In-depth analysis of eleven schemes identified several issues that appeared to be important for this form of intervention.

MANAGEMENT OF THE PATIENT

The majority of physical activity promotion schemes in PHC in England involve an alliance between the PHC team and leisure centres. The other schemes are essentially PHC practice-based, varying in complexity. Some of the practice-managed schemes centred on one GP who is particularly enthusiastic about promoting physical activity. He or she might have organised other elements in the practice, such as local classes or an in-house clinic, or they may simply increase their consultation periods to emphasise a physically active lifestyle.

Other practice-managed schemes involved GPs referring patients to a practice-based clinic held at fixed times in the week. The clinics were sometimes staffed by a practice nurse or someone employed on a part-time basis as an physical activity leader/counsellor. Patients received assessment, advice and support, often with the opportunity of attending an in-practice class or one held in the community. Alternatively, patients were advised on self-directed behaviour change. A more comprehensive alternative was where patients can be referred, often after in-house assessment and counselling, to community-based facilities and activities. However, the management and monitoring of the patient remained within the practice.

For the leisure-centre managed schemes, GPs referred directly to a local leisure/sports centre where staff supervised all aspects of the intervention, including assessment, programme design and exercise supervision. While such centres have personnel trained in exercise, as well as attractive surroundings and sophisticated exercise equipment, it was also noted that they can be intimidating environments for the inexperienced exerciser. Nevertheless, the research project identified many successful schemes where leisure centre staff changed the environment to suit the patients.

Both leisure centre and practice-based schemes have their own advantages and disadvantages, and these are summarised in Table 11.7. However, the best system is likely to be a comprehensive community-linked scheme with the GP referring directly to a physical activity clinic.

Regardless of how the patient was managed, the schemes given the most positive feedback by patients reflected a common programme philosophy of 'wellness' promotion. Here indicators of programme success emphasised gradual and comfortable changes in lifestyle, the 'process' of involvement in physical activity and exercise rather than the 'product' of physical outcomes, and the social and mental benefits accruing from physical activity.

TRAINING OF PHC PERSONNEL

The PHC resource in England, 'Better Living, Better Life' (Department of Health 1993a), in reference to physical activity promotion in PHC, states that 'a general lack of experience of this aspect of health promotion in primary care means that further training will often be advisable'. Similarly, Pender *et al.* (1994) identified further training for doctors and nurses in physical activity expertise and counselling.

The delivery of effective physical activity interventions in PHC is potentially complex since any one scheme might involve a GP, practice nurse, health visitor, a physical activity counsellor and an exercise leader. Each will bring different expertise to bear and, at the same time, require different expertise to be developed for specific roles within the intervention. For example, the GP may need to be well versed on methods of eliciting physical activity levels of patients through interview methods, but will probably not require 'hands on' expertise of fitness testing procedures. The reverse could be true for other members of the PHC team. The areas of expertise associated with members of the PHC team are identified in Table 11.8.

The Physician-Based Assessment and Counselling for Exercise (PACE) project in the USA was developed to assist GPs and other PHC professionals, to better counsel patients for physical activity (see Pender *et al.* 1994). The system involves the GP assessing initial activity levels as well as physical and psychological readiness for exercise, the latter being

Table 11.7 Advantages and disadvantages of different PHC schemes for promoting physical activity

Type of PHC Scheme	Advantages and disadvantages
1 Practice-managed schemes	Advantages • counselling can be made available on site • available to larger percentage patients • physical activity can be delivered within a 'healthy lifestyle' message • greater flexibility for patients who can be directed to a choice of several outlets in the community • better opportunities for record-keeping. Disadvantages • facilities not often available on site • finding trained personnel may be difficult • may not provide sufficient motivational boost to get patients started • difficult to provide support with patients left too much on their own • difficult to create social atmosphere unless exercise class takes place on site • the scheme may be perceived as medical rather than intrinsically worthwhile and enjoyable.
2 Leisure centre managed	Advantages • eases the burden of the GP • no costs for PHC • facilities readily available on site • trained personnel are usually available • motivation and support for the patient can be high • social benefits for the patient can be high. Disadvantages • sporty image has to be overcome in order to attract patients • physical activity is restricted to discrete exercise sessions rather than lifestyle change • facilities are often only available during slack day-time hours • scheme often has an end-point with limited follow-up • doctors may not be willing to refer patients • currently schemes attract a very small percentage of patients • some schemes could not cope with large numbers of patients.

based on the stages of change model already discussed (see Chapter 6 and earlier in the present chapter). Based on the interaction between these assessments, patients are given one of three protocols:

- Protocol 1: 'getting out of your chair'; designed for those at a low level of readiness and addresses benefits and barriers of moderate level physical activity.
- Protocol 2: 'planning the first step'; designed for those contemplating and 'ready' for exercise and involves both behavioural and exercise guidance for the adoption of physical activity.
- Protocol 3: 'keeping the PACE'; designed for those already active, this intervention involves reinforcement as well as maintenance and relapse prevention strategies and advice.

EFFECTIVENESS OF PROGRAMMES

Reliable data on the effectiveness of PHC interventions to change physical activity behaviours and health outcomes are sparse. Tai, Gould and Iliffe (1997) suggested that, although the benefits of increasing activity have been well documented, the feasibility of providing interventions based in primary care has not been well tested. Their paper focused primarily on older people and provided a helpful analysis of how to design and evaluate interventions aimed at increasing physical activity. They recommended that a series of feasibility studies are needed to refine recruitment strategies and that continuing professional development is required for GPs about the health benefits of exercise before full scale testing of exercise promotion within primary care is undertaken.

Swinburn, Walter *et al.* (1998) showed that giving patients written advice about increasing activity was more effective than verbal advice. The same authors (1997) conducted qualitative research with the GPs involved in their study and established that GPs were positive about the notion of prescribing exercise and that training and resource materials, including patient follow-up, were considered important aspects of a successful programme.

There have only been a handful of studies that have attempted to determine the effectiveness of primary care based schemes in increasing physical activity or providing health benefits. In the UK, two randomised controlled trials of methods of promoting activity in primary care have produced different conclusions. A controlled trial was undertaken in a well-publicised scheme in the south of England by Taylor, Doust and Webborn (1998a). They targeted GP patients with at least one coronary heart disease risk factor. One hundred and forty two patients were randomly assigned to attend a ten-week exercise programme at

Table 11.8 Areas of expertise required in GP-referral exercise schemes

Knowledge and skills	Personnel		
	General practitioner	Activity counsellor	Exercise leader
KNOWLEDGE			
Health benefits of physical activity	***	***	***
How much physical activity is enough	***	***	***
National participation patterns	**	*	*
Contra-indications of physical activity	***	***	***
Behavioural determinants of physical activity involvement	***	***	***
Barriers to physical activity	***	***	***
Behaviour change strategies	***	***	***
Monitoring progress	***	***	**
Measurement of programme effectiveness	***	**	*
SKILLS			
Assessment of physical activity	***	***	*
Screening for contra-indications	***	***	***
Activity counselling	**	***	*
Implementing behaviour change strategies	**	***	***
Exercise teaching: individuals	*	***	
Exercise teaching: groups	*	***	
Monitoring programme effectiveness	***	**	**

Key: * useful   ** desirable   *** essential

a local leisure centre or to be in a control group. At eight weeks and at sixteen weeks the intervention group reported more vigorous activity than the control group but by the final thirty-seven-week follow-up activity levels had returned to baseline. However, the control group had no significant changes over the course of the study. In addition, more of the intervention group (61 per cent) than the control group (23 per cent) reported that they were in the action or maintenance stages of exercise behaviour change at the final follow up. Thus there is evidence from this study that short-term changes in activity are possible from leisure centre-based GP referral schemes but that long-term change is difficult to achieve.

The second study was conducted in Newcastle (England) and produced different, but questionnable, conclusions. Harland *et al.* (1999) ran an ambitious and well-designed study aimed at determining if different motivational strategies produced different adherence to exercise over twelve months. Participants were patients attending their GP's clinic who were randomly assigned to one of four groups:

- A control group (who received a fitness assessment, activity information and advice).
- A brief motivational interview group.
- A group who received financial incentives as well as a motivational interview.
- A group who received more intensive interviewing.

However, despite the good research design (good numbers of participants all randomly assigned to groups with twelve-month follow-up) there were methodological flaws which resulted in negative conclusions being drawn by the authors despite what appears to be positive data. The authors wanted to know whether there was a difference between the various interventions and controls in changes in physical activity score from twelve weeks to one year. At one year there were no statistical differences between the four groups in terms of the percentage of participants who were physically active. The *British Medical Journal* (BMJ) issue in which the article was published put the headline in the 'Today in the BMJ' section of the journal: 'exercise prescription is a waste of scarce resources'. This, of course, is a very serious accusation and may have influenced budget controllers to think again about existing or potential exercise referral schemes. However, we think that Harland *et al.* (1999) asked the wrong question of the data. Instead of looking at differences between groups, a better question would have been to ask whether any group had increased their activity at one year compared to baseline. According to the data the authors present in Table 2 of their paper, the percentage of participants who had increased physical activity scores at one year compared to baseline, ranged from 23 per cent in the control group to 31 per cent in Intervention Group 3. If these are significant changes from baseline then the conclusion might have been that even the control condition can have a substantial impact in increasing physical activity over one year. Further economic analysis might then determine that the control group (which seemed to include the basis of many intervention techniques such as assessment, feedback and the provision of information) was the most cost-effective intervention. The authors' conclusion that brief interventions are of questionable effectiveness is wrong since none of their interventions or even the control condition could be described as brief. The previous section of this chapter shows that much briefer interventions and even information alone can positively influence physical activity levels. We also think that the outcome measures asked the wrong questions since they were based on an outdated questionnaire. This focused on fitness rather than active living. A better option would have been to determine if participants had achieved the current targets for sedentary individuals of accumulating thirty minutes of moderate activity on most days of the week.

The authors also claimed that the research was based on the stage of change model. However, they did not report how interventions were tailored to stages, any details of pre or post intervention stages, effectiveness of interventions by stage, or of the other crucial elements of this model described earlier in this chapter and in Chapter 6, such as the processes of change and self-efficacy measures.

These flaws mean that the key messages from this paper are very misleading and that the conclusions drawn are not based on the evidence. Such misinterpretation could severely limit future research and service developments. Clearly, there is a need for further trials of methods of promoting physical activity in the primary care setting in the UK.

There are also lessons to be learned from studies in primary care which have focused on improving healthy behaviour in general and not just physical activity. For example, Steptoe *et al.* (1999) reported on a large scale (over 800 participants) trial of the use of behaviourally oriented counselling for primary care patients at increased risk of coronary heart disease. The intervention group received counselling from the practice nurse who had been trained in an approach based on the stage of change model. At both four and twelve months the intervention group, in comparison to the control group, had a favourable reduction in cigarette smoking, reduction in fat intake and increased physical activity. Biomedical outcomes, such as body mass index, diastolic blood pressure and total serum cholesterol concentrations, were not influenced by the intervention. This study demonstrated that physical activity, and other health behaviours, can be influenced by a counselling approach in the primary care setting. On the other hand, it also demonstrated the difficulty of translating such behaviour into biologically significant change.

There may, of course, be other outcomes of equal importance not measured by such studies. Butler *et al.* (1999) costed training in motivational consulting, similar to the counselling approach used by Steptoe *et al* (1999), for smoking cessation to be around £70 for each GP and the extra time needed around £14 for each patient. For example, participants who have made successful change in health behaviours may feel an increase in self-esteem or quality of life, which, in the longer term, may influence adherence to healthy living and make a difference to biological markers.

In the USA there have been two large-scale trials of promoting activity in primary care. Both of these have been informed by small-scale trials of training physicians to counsel patients to increase physical activity, for example Marcus *et al.* (1997), and many of the same authors are involved in the two larger scale trials. The first was Project PACE (Physician-based Assessment and Counselling for Exercise) which used the transtheoretical model to design short interventions that were delivered by family physicians (Patrick *et al.* 1994). The project intervention consists of providing brief (3–5 minute) counselling with each patient. The counselling focuses on benefits and barriers to increasing activity, self-efficacy and gaining social support for increasing activity. The strategies differ depending on the stage of exercise behaviour of each patient and in this sense the intervention is described as stage-matched. Physicians themselves find the PACE tools acceptable (Long *et al.* 1996) and a randomised controlled trial showed that the PACE interventions did increase physical activity, particularly walking (Calfas *et al.* 1996). In addition, Calfas *et al.* (1997) have shown that the intervention does influence the processes of change. This suggests that there is a good theoretical structure to the intervention tools although further refinements would enhance validity.

The second USA trial (activity counselling trial (ACT)) has not yet reported the final results but the design is worth describing. ACT is a large scale (over 800 participants) and long term (twenty-four month) trial of two different models of primary care activity counselling versus standard care (King *et al.* 1998). Again, the elements of the trans-theoretical model were used in the design of this project along with additional cognitive behavioural techniques known to assist behaviour change. The standard care model involves physician advice with limited written materials, and the two other models both utilise that same basic start point but add to it. The first model is described as staff assistance and added to the standard care by providing an educational video and a short counselling session that results in short term activity goals. Follow-up supportive materials are provided via twenty-four newsletters. The second model is described as staff-counselling and used all the materials and interventions of the staff assistance model but adds to that more personal contact in the form of telephone support, one-to-one counselling and behaviour change classes.

Two major reviews of interventions aimed at PHC or related settings are now available. Riddoch, Puig-Ribera and Cooper (1998) located twenty-five papers from the UK satisfying their inclusion criteria. They concluded that 'the majority of studies report some form of improvement in either physical activity or related measures. However, the size of the effect is generally small, and there is no real consistency across studies' (Riddoch, Puig-Ribera and Cooper 1998: 25). Similar conclusions were drawn from an analysis of non-UK studies.

Although not restricted to PHC, Simons-Morton *et al.* (1998), in their review of interventions in healthcare settings, concluded:

> interventions in healthcare settings can increase physical activity for both primary and secondary prevention. Long-term effects are more likely with continuing intervention and multiple intervention components such as supervised exercise, provision of equipment, and behavioral approaches.
>
> (Simons-Morton *et al.* 1998: 413)

RECOMMENDATIONS FOR PHYSICAL ACTIVITY PROMOTION IN PHC

There is in need for high quality personnel well-versed in a wide variety of physical activity knowledge and skills. This is particularly important given the apparent increase in the number of such schemes across developed countries. A key recommendation for the development of physical activity promotion in PHC, therefore, concerns training. Collaboration between medical and exercise/physical activity professionals is essential.

A second recommendation, and one that stems directly from our experience with the English national project, concerns communication between PHC team members. Two keys lines of communication can be identified:

* GP to physical activity counsellor: GP needs to inform the counsellor of the medical needs of the patient; the counsellor needs to communicate with the GP about suitability of some exercises, possible contraindications, and feedback progress being made.
* physical activity counsellor to exercise leader: there needs to be a suitable 'fit' between the advice given by the counsellor, such as on behaviour change, and that given by the exercise leader.

The PHC setting will become increasingly important as more GPs and health professionals embrace physical activity. To this end, the Surgeon General's report (Department of Health and Human Services 1996) encourages healthcare providers to talk routinely with patients about physical activity and how it can be accommodated in their lifestyles.

Summary and conclusions

In this chapter we have:

- Provided a framework for discussing interventions aimed at increasing physical activity levels.
- Considered the current messages being used by agencies to promote physical activity.
- Outlined the transtheoretical model of behaviour change and interventions based on this approach.
- Described the process and effectiveness of exercise consultation.
- Outlined the key issues and results concerning the primary care setting and the promotion of physical activity.

From our analysis, we conclude that:

- It is possible to increase the physical activity levels of sedentary individuals.
- Short-term (3–12 weeks) increases in PA are relatively easy to achieve.
- Long-term change (6–24 months) is hard to achieve.
- Cognitive behavioural techniques either one-to-one or written offer the best possibility of long term change.

In addition, we make the following recommendations for researchers:

- There is a clear need for research in the area of support for long-term exercise behaviour change.
- More specific relapse prevention strategies for exercise and physical activity must be explored and tested.
- There is a need to explore different and new media for delivering the messages such as information technology, video conferencing and telephone contact.
- Project Active is a good demonstration of how to promote physical activity and it must be repeated in other cultures and with more minimal intervention strategies.
- The effect of exercise counselling with a variety of follow-up options (such as another consultation, telephone support, postal reminders) needs to be tested over the long term.
- More work is required in primary care settings to establish how the primary care team can influence physical activity levels.

We offer the following recommendations for practice:

- Promoting physical activity in the community should involve unsupervised activity opportunities as well as supervised classes.
- The message for the sedentary population is that every adult should aim to accumulate thirty minutes or more of moderate intensity physical activity over the course of most days of the week.
- Walking offers the simplest and most accessible mode of physical activity for the majority of the sedentary population.
- All promotion should include cognitive behavioural principles of behaviour change.
- Primary care teams should consider training of staff in physical activity promotion.

12 Making a difference II

Interventions in organisations and communities

> Physical activity promotion can happen just about anywhere, and in fact for it to be success-
> ful, it needs to happen just about *everywhere*.
>
> Department of Health and Human Services
> (*Promoting physical activity: A guide for community action*, 1999)

Chapter objectives

The purpose of this chapter is to consider interventions to increase physical activity in organisations, including the school, workplace and primary healthcare, and in communities, as well as to consider interventions at governmental level. Specifically, in this chapter we aim to:

- Consider physical activity promotion and interventions in schools.
- Discuss the role of physical education in exercise promotion and to evaluate the evidence on specific interventions to change physical activity levels.
- Evaluate whether physical activity in childhood predicts participation in adulthood.
- Consider physical activity promotion and interventions in the workplace.
- Present a rationale for physical activity promotion in the workplace and associated evidence on its effectiveness.
- Consider physical activity promotion and interventions in the community.
- Discuss contemporary social psychological approaches to persuasion and attitude change.
- Highlight a social marketing approach to physical activity promotion.
- Discuss recent initiatives from national governments to promote physical activity within broader health policy.
- Show how an integration is possible between different levels of interventions in physical activity.

In the previous chapter we discussed interventions enabling the individual to become more physically active. However, there is also a need to intervene at a macro level. Clearly, macro and micro (individual) interventions are often complimentary since many strategies planned at, say, the community level, also need to be translated into individual action at the micro level. In addition to personal and interpersonal approaches to physical activity intervention, King (1991) has identified two levels of macro intervention: organisational/environmental and institutional/legislative. At the organisational/environmental level, King lists schools, worksites, neighbourhoods, coummunity facilities (for example, cycle paths) and organisations, and sites for 'daily living' activity which might include stairways, shopping centres and car parks. For the level of institutional/legislative interventions, King suggests that the main channel for change is through policies, laws and regulations. In addressing the problem of sedentary behaviour in developed nations, King said that an approach was required that:

> emphasizes all levels of interventions, including personal and interpersonal strategies that target individuals or small groups, and organizational, environmental, and societal strategies that influence the broader milieu. . . . Although gains in knowledge have been made, it is clear that to achieve a significant impact on the whole population, strategies that target the environmental and social forces influencing exercise behavior will require far greater attention.
>
> (King 1994: 183)

We shall consider both of the broad categories of intervention outlets identified by King (1991). Specifically, we shall discuss physical activity promotion in schools, the workplace, primary healthcare settings, as well as wider community initiatives. Finally, we consider broader political initiatives on health and physical activity.

Organisations

The importance of promoting physical activity through organisations is now recognised. The advantages of such 'captive audiences' make this an appealing area for intervention. Although there are many organisational settings where physical activity can, and sometimes is, promoted, such as prisons and churches, the three settings in which systematic work can be located in the exercise literature are schools, the workplace and, more recently, primary healthcare (Department of Health and Human Services 1999).

Schools have at least three obvious benefits for the targeting of physical activity. First, this captures a critical age range at which changes appear most likely to be possible; second, school-wide strategies should enable virtually all members of an age cohort to be targeted; third, a delivery structure, through physical and health education, is already in place.

The workplace, while targeted extensively in North America, has shown inconsistent involvement in physical activity promotion in other countries. Nevertheless, it has been estimated that most adults spend about one quarter of their time at their place of work during their working lives (Department of Health 1993b). Similarly, the workplace has the advantage of targeting large numbers of adults and, at least for larger companies, may have an infrastructure to support health promotion initiatives, such as medical support and sport/exercise facilities.

Physical activity promotion in primary healthcare settings has expanded hugely in some countries, such as the UK (Fox *et al.* 1997). The advantages centre on the availability of contacting exercise precontemplators, 'at risk' older adults, and the persuasive influence of medical and other health professional staff in such a setting.

Interventions in schools

In commenting on the promotion of physical activity in the American population, Iverson *et al.* said 'one community organization – the schools – underpins the whole effort to achieve the goal of national fitness' (Iverson *et al.* 1985: 219). Similarly, interest in the potential of schools to promote physical activity has been stated in policy documents in many countries. For example, the American College of Sports Medicine (ACSM) opinion statement on 'Physical Fitness in Children and Youth' stated the following recommendation:

> School physical education programs are an important part of the overall education process and should give increased emphasis to the development and maintenance of lifelong exercise habits and provide instruction about how to attain and maintain appropriate physical fitness.
>
> (American College of Sports Medicine 1988: 422)

This statement mirrors a concern in Britain and elsewhere in the Western world about the apparent lack of regular physical activity in some groups of children. For example, the review of the National Curriculum in England and Wales, undertaken by Dearing, proposed that 'we must encourage our young people to develop a fit and healthy lifestyle' (Dearing 1994: 45).

Judging by these statements, there would appear to be a need to look closely at the promotion of physical activity and exercise in schools. This has important implications from the point of view of socialising children into healthy lifestyles. The central part of a school that is identified with the promotion of exercise is that of physical education (PE), although the more generic health promotion activities can, and should, combine across curriculum areas.

Physical education and exercise promotion

The discussion paper produced by Her Majesty's Inspectors for schools in Britain on physical education across the years of compulsory schooling (HMI 1989) lists eleven aims of physical education, and these are shown in Table 12.1. From the standpoint of promoting health-related physical activity and exercise, Aims 2 and 3 are directly related to

Table 12.1 Aims of physical education for ages 5 to 16 years in England and Wales

1 To develop a range of psycho-motor skills.
2 To maintain and increase physical mobility and flexibility.
3 To develop stamina and strength.
4 To develop understanding and appreciation of the purposes, forms and conventions of a selection of physical activities.
5 To develop the capacity to express ideas in dance forms.
6 To develop the appreciation of the concepts of fair play, honest competition and good sportsmanship.
7 To develop the ability to appreciate the aesthetic qualities of movement.
8 To develop the capacity to maintain interest and to persevere to achieve success.
9 To foster self-esteem through the acquisition of physical competence and poise.
10 To develop self-confidence through understanding the capabilities and limitations of oneself and others.
11 To develop an understanding of the importance of exercise in maintaining a healthy life.

Source: HMI 1989.

Note: These aims are numbered for ease of identification in the text and are not in order of priority or importance.

physiological changes, while Aim 11 perhaps makes the assumption that changes in knowledge or value will change behaviour. Aims 9 and 10 clearly focus on psychological outcomes.

Physical education has taken a much more prominent role in health promotion in recent years and has changed from a narrow medical rationale to one based on a more holistic approach stressing lifetime participation, enjoyment and motivation. However, there is also an ideology centred on the disease-prevention medical model, and politicians have also applied pressure to bolster the 'games/sports' lobby, sometimes at the expense of health/fitness activities. It appears, however, that success at international sport has no relationship with physical activity levels of the population (Powell *et al.* 1991). Indeed, the 'Healthy People 2000' project in the USA states that one of its objectives is to increase the proportion of PE lessons in which children are active, 'preferably engaged in lifetime physical activities' (Department of Health and Human Services 1991: 102). These activities are defined as those 'that may be readily carried into adulthood because they generally need only one or two people. . . . Competitive group sports and activities typically played only by young children such as group games are excluded'.

Behavioural issues in health/fitness promotion with children

In Chapter 2, we introduced data describing motives for children's participation in physical activities. It was noted that much of the data were on structured sports settings. We know relatively little about behavioural issues of children's physical activity in recreational play or exercise. In discussing psychological factors associated with schools and physical activity, we shall consider the effects of PE programmes and special interventions, and whether patterns of behaviour in childhood 'track' through to adulthood.

INTERVENTIONS IN PHYSICAL EDUCATION PROGRAMMES

Interventions have mainly been conducted in Primary (elementary) schools, although secondary school interventions do exist. Studies vary from extensive increases in time, such as through daily PE interventions, to relatively minor changes in emphasis in existing curriculum time (Almond and Harris 1998; Harris and Cale 1997).

Two large-scale interventions in the USA have been reported: the Sports, Play, and Active Recreation for Kids (SPARK) project and the Child and Adolescent Trial for Cardiovascular Health (CATCH) project by McKenzie, Sallis and co-workers (McKenzie *et al.* 1996; 1997; Sallis *et al.* 1997). For example, Sallis *et al.* suggest:

> For public health benefit, physical education should promote generalization of physical activity outside of school, because physical activity recommendations cannot be met through physical education alone . . . specific programs to promote generalization must be developed and rigorously evaluated.
>
> (Sallis *et al.* 1997: 1328)

The SPARK and catch project inverventions   The SPARK intervention involved a number of American Primary schools in which PE classes were designed to promote and teach high levels of physical activity and movement skills that are enjoyable. Typically lessons were thirty minutes duration divided equally between health-related and skill (sport)-related activities. A classroom-based 'self-management' programme was also taught for thirty minutes each week in which students learned self-monitoring, goal-setting, reinforcement, and related skills. Homework and newsletters were designed to stimulate parent–child interaction.

Three groups of lessons were created. Some children were taught the SPARK intervention only by physical education specialists, others by classroom teachers who did not specialise in PE. In addition, there was a control condition in which 'normal' PE was continued. Overall, 955 students from seven schools provided complete data over a two-year period. Results showed that the amount of PE time was greater in the two experimental conditions compared with the control condition, and that within lessons children were more active in the PE specialist-led classes than those led by classroom teachers, with the control group children even less active. These results are shown in Figure 12.1. However, similar differences out of school were not observed although favourable changes in fitness measures were obtained, thus showing similar findings to those in Belgium by Pieron *et al.* (1996). Clearly, further work is required to see why out-of-school differences were not evident. Sallis *et al.* (1997) suggest several possibilities, including restrictions created by parents on safety grounds, and the lack of independent decision-making available to children of this age.

Further analysis of the SPARK project is reported by McKenzie *et al.* (1997). When a follow-up was conducted eighteen months after termination of the intervention, energy expenditure declined during lessons for those originally taught by PE specialists (see Figure 12.2). This suggests that the type of teacher is important in promoting health-related activity in lessons because the SPARK project has shown that the PE specialists create more time for this activity but this declines when other teachers replace them.

The CATCH intervention is described by McKenzie *et al.* (1996). It involved ninety-six primary/elementary schools studied for two years. After baseline assessment of various parameters, schools were randomly assigned to either a 'measurement only' or 'intervention' condition. For the intervention condition, schools were further randomly allocated into either 'school-based intervention' or 'school-based plus family intervention'. The intervention was multi-factorial and, in addition to PE interventions, included interventions on tobacco, food, classroom learning on cardiovascular health, school policy and a home/family component. As far as the PE goals were concerned, interventions were designed to improve existing PE programmes to promote 'children's enjoyment of and participation in moderate-to-vigorous physical activity during PE classes and to provide skills to be used out of school and

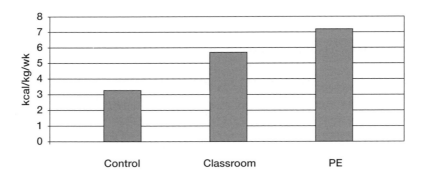

Figure 12.1 Energy expenditure of children taught in two experimental SPARK conditions and a control group condition (data from Sallis *et al.* 1997)

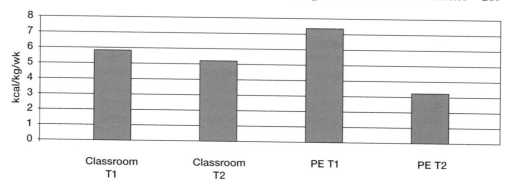

Figure 12.2 Energy expenditure of children taught either by classroom or PE teachers during the SPARK project. T1: data during the intervention; T2: data eighteen months after the end of the intervention (data from McKenzie *et al.* 1997).

throughout life' (McKenzie *et al.* 1996: 424). In addition, the PE intervention included curriculum content and materials, teacher training and on-site consultation to teachers.

The results showed that schools in which teachers were trained to deliver the intervention increased the amount of moderate-to-vigorous activity more than control schools. This activity increased by 39 per cent in intervention schools with such schools recording over 50 per cent of lessons in this type of activity. Similarly, intervention children had higher energy expenditure, higher energy expenditure per lesson and greater overall physical activity levels than those in the control schools.

McKenzie *et al.* (1996) point out that half of the lessons in the intervention conditions were taught by classroom teachers, not by PE specialists, thus showing that the programme can be effective for both types of teachers. In summarising the results, McKenzie *et al.* highlight that the effectiveness of the CATCH programme was 'accomplished through the implementation of a developmentally appropriate activity-based program and improved instruction and class management' (430). It is noteworthy that such results come from a large multi-site randomised controlled intervention.

Almond and Harris (1998) reviewed nineteen intervention studies for primary schools and five at the secondary age-level. They concluded for primary school interventions that:

- Fifteen of seventeen studies documented positive changes in physiological or clinical outcomes.
- All eight studies showed positive changes in physical activity, either in school or out of school.
- Five studies investigated cognitive change and two showed increases in health-related knowledge; one showed academic performance to increase significantly one non-significantly, and another showed no loss of academic performance despite extra time being allocated to PE.
- Three of four studies showed positive changes in attitude.

Similar conclusions were reached concerning children in secondary school, although only one out of the three studies found increases in physical activity out of school. A systematic review by Stone *et al.* reported that 'the strongest evidence base is with students in the upper elementary grades and school environmental changes' (Stone *et al.* 1998: 308). They also recommended more research on increasing out-of-school activity levels.

Childhood and adolescent physical activity and its transfer into adulthood

One objective for school PE programmes is nearly always the development of 'healthy' habits for adulthood. Although the assumption that behaviours learned in childhood and adolescence will transfer ('track') into adulthood seems reasonable, evidence to substantiate it is mixed. Many factors in the transition from school to adult life are likely to affect the levels and patterns of physical activity and changes in the adult life cycle itself will affect the extent that adults are active.

Evidence from the Allied Dunbar National Fitness Survey (ADNFS) in England (The Sports Council and Health Education Authority 1992) does support the view, at least indirectly, that early participation is associated with a greater likelihood of involvement later in life. Through interview, participants in the survey were requested to recall the moderate-to-vigorous physical activity they took part in at the ages of 16, 24 and 34 years. The results showed:

- That those currently over 55 years of age were much less active at age 34 than those currently younger than 55 years. This suggests that younger adults today are more active than their older counterparts.
- 'Adult participation in sport and recreation in later years was strongly associated with behaviour at an earlier age' (The Sports Council and Health Education Authority 1992: 64). This was supported by 25 per cent of those stating that they were very active between the ages of 14 and 19 years were active currently, whereas only 2 per cent currently active were inactive in the past during those teenage years. In addition, about 30 per cent of the adults in the survey remained in the same activity category across the three time periods studied.

Data from Sweden also supports the view that activity in childhood is a predictor of activity in adulthood. Engstrom (1991) followed 2,000 Swedish youths from 15 to 30 years of age. Using the fairly liberal definition of 'activity' as weekly involvement in activity of the intensity of jogging, he found a steep decline in activity between the ages of 15 and 20 years, with some levelling after that. To test for tracking effects from childhood to adulthood, Engstrom used three conditions an indicators of early (aged 15 years) activity involvement. These were:

- At least four hours per week of sports or physical activities at age 15 years.
- Being a member of a sports club at 15 years of age.
- Having a high grade in physical education in the eighth grade (in Sweden).

An index of 'psychological readiness' at the age of 30 was then calculated from 'attitude towards keep-fit activities and self-esteem concerning the body and sports capabilities' (Engstrom 1991: 478). Unfortunately, no further details on these measures were given. The results of Engstrom's analysis are shown in Figure 12.3. This shows a clear relationship between the number of conditions fulfilled for activity involvement at 15 years of age and high psychological readiness at aged 30. For example, for women fulfilling all three of the

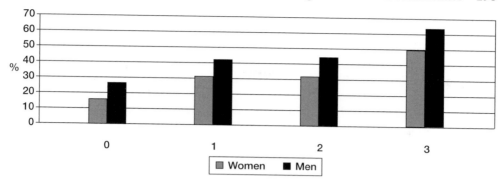

Figure 12.3 Percentage of individuals with high psychological readiness for physical activity at the age of 30 years according to indicators of sport experience at 15 years (data from Engstrom 1991)
Note: the number of conditions on the horizontal axis refer to the practice of sport at least four hours/week at the age of 15 years, member of a sports club at 15, and a high grade in PE at school.

criteria at 15 years, 52 per cent had a high psychological readiness at 30 years, whereas for those not fulfilling any of the criteria, only 17 per cent had a readiness.

These data are supported by a clear relationship between psychological readiness at age 30 years and actual involvement in physical activity for both men and women. Engstrom (1991) also analysed environmental circumstances and involvement in physical activity. The following four conditions were used to assess environmental circumstances:

- physically active mate/spouse
- most friends are physically active
- no children
- academic education.

Again, there was a clear relationship between the number of environmental conditions fulfilled at the age of 30 years, and current activity involvement. For example, for men not fulfilling any of the criteria, only 16 per cent were currently active, whereas for men fulfilling all four criteria, 80 per cent were active. This begs the question whether it is the environmental support or the psychological readiness that predicts activity since both correlated highly with physical activity. To answer this, Engstrom (1991) created four groups:

- low readiness/negative environment
- high readiness/negative environment
- low readiness/positive environment
- high readiness/positive environment.

The high/positive group showed very high activity levels in comparison with the low/negative group, as expected. However, of more interest was the finding that those with a positive environment, but low readiness, were more active than those with high readiness but a negative environment, suggesting a dominant role for environmental circumstances.

Engstrom (1991) provides an interesting perspective on the issue of physical activity tracking. Although his short conference paper did not allow full analysis of his methods, his results do lend clear support to the view that 'early experience with physical activity during childhood and adolescence . . . is of importance for the practice of keep-fit activities in adulthood' (Engstrom 1991: 480–1). However, the criterion measure of activity was quite weak. As Riddoch (1998) points out, the correlations for tracking among youth are weak when self-report measures are used. For one study using heart rate measures, though, the correlations were quite high (r = 0.57–0.66) (Pate *et al.* 1996). Even so, this study investigated 3–4 year olds over a three-year period. This is a time when relatively little change in environmental, social and psychological factors is expected. Stability of behaviour, therefore, is likely.

Riddoch's (1998) review of nine tracking studies published between 1992–7 involving young people concluded that they showed weak levels of tracking. The Health Education Authority's 'policy framework' for young people concluded that while low levels of tracking are evidenced from youth to young adulthood, a slightly higher relationship exists for children's activity tracking into youth (Biddle, Sallis and Cavill 1998).

In conclusion, while the picture is far from clear, there is some evidence for positive experiences early in life being associated with higher levels of activity later in life. The effects are, however, weak. Whether this small effect is real or the result of other factors, one cannot be sure. For example, it is quite possible that a third variable, say motor competence or even early maturation, is the key influence with children experiencing early success less likely to quit later on. We await studies to resolve these important issues.

SUITABILITY OF PHYSICAL EDUCATION FOR PROMOTING LIFETIME PHYSICAL ACTIVITY

Many have questioned the relevance of current PE curricula for the development of active lifestyles in adulthood. For example, Coakley and White (1992), in a qualitative study using in-depth semi-structured interviews with British adolescents, found that participation in community sport programmes was influenced by past experiences in school physical education classes. In particular, such memories guided future expectations of sport and exercise. Negative memories centred on boredom and lack of choice, feeling stupid and incompetent, and receiving negative evaluation from peers. This parallels theoretical developments in sport and exercise psychology in intrinsic motivation, enjoyment, achievement goal orientations and motivational climate, as we discussed in Chapter 4. For example, the reactions reported by Coakley and White are consistent with the need to promote intrinsic motivation. This is likely to be achieved through promoting high perceptions of autonomy and competence by allowing participants to make choices and have some involvement in decision-making procedures, and allowing for individual interpretations of success for the maximisation of enjoyment (Biddle and Chatzisarantis 1999). In addition, the class climate may need reappraising so that all pupils are valued for their own efforts. This might help reduce negative peer evaluation and increase intrinsic motivation (Papaioannou and Goudas 1999).

CYCLING AND WALKING TO SCHOOL

Promoting walking or cycling to school has a number of advantages, including a large potential population (children and parents/guardians), reduction in car use and the creation of healthy habits at an early age. Estimates show that some 62 per cent of primary age pupils walk to school compared to 45 per cent for those at secondary school. However, there are very few studies providing guidance on the motivational influences of walking to school. Nevertheless, the 'Safe Routes to School' project in England does provide some information about the nature of walking to school.

An analysis by Cleary (1996) showed more pupils walk home from school than to school. The trends for car use are opposite. This is interesting as it suggests that many pupils are within walking distance of school but appear to be driven there in the morning, possibly due to parents delivering their children on the way to work. The increase in employment rates among women over the past few decades may also be a factor here. Finally, traffic volume has been reported as a major deterrent to walking to school (The Pedestrians' Association 1997).

Walking to school is likely to be strongly influenced by social-environmental, rather than just psychological factors, although the social psychology of the parent may be important. The key social-environmental factors appear to be:

- work patterns of the parents
- convenience of driving children to school prior to going on to work
- proximity of school to home
- degree of parental consent to allow children to travel independently to school.

On an encouraging note, 84 per cent of local authorities in Britain surveyed by the Pedestrians' Association (1998) reported 'encouraging' walking to school. Initiatives included cycle lanes and traffic calming.

Schools: summary

As far as young people are concerned, whether they are involved in physical education programmes or not, current consensus on physical activity guidelines is apparent. Sallis and Patrick (1994) convened an international consensus conference on physical activity for adolescents, and in England a similar process was undertaken by the Health Education Authority, this time for all young people aged 5–18 years (see Biddle *et al.* 1998). The recommendations are given in Table 12.2. Recommendations for both school and community programmes for physical activity for young people are given in Table 12.3.

In reality, physical education, while a very important context for the development of health-related behaviours, cannot be expected to change children's physical activity and fitness. The current political climate in many Western European and North American countries appears to be favouring 'core' academic skills in the curriculum. This often leads to PE being forced to take a cut of available curriculum time. With the multitude of objectives physical educators have set themselves, fitness and activity change cannot realistically be achieved in the short term. Nevertheless, work must continue to find the best way to promote long term changes through the infrastructure already in place in schools. Intervention studies, such as SPARK and CATCH, provide some hope in this regard.

Interventions in the workplace

An area that has seen considerable expansion in the field of health and fitness promotion is that of worksite fitness and physical activity programmes. Young (1997) reports that for companies with between fifty and ninety-nine employees in the USA, about 33 per cent have worksite programmes, a figure rising to over 80 per cent for companies employing over 750 people. King (1994) suggests that more needs to be done with smaller worksites.

Workplace initiatives are often more extensive than just exercise and fitness programmes and may include other health behaviours, such as non-smoking. This expansion over the past decade or so is particularly evident in North America and Japan, although European

Table 12.2 Physical activity guidelines for young people

Source	Age group	Guidelines
Sallis and Patrick (1994)	Adolescents	• All adolescents should be physically active daily, or nearly every day, as part of play, games, sports, work, transportation, recreation, physical education, or planned exercise, in the context of family, school and community activities.
		• Adolescents should engage in three of more sessions per week of activities that last twenty minutes or more at a time and that require moderate to vigorous levels of exertion.

Biddle *et al.* (1998)	5–18 year olds	• Primary recommendations:
		  ○ All young people should participate in physical activity of at last moderate intensity for one hour per day.
		  ○ Young people who currently do little activity should participate in physical activity of at least moderate intensity for at least half an hour per day.

		• Secondary recommendation: At least twice per week, some of these activities should help to enhance and maintain muscular strength and flexibility, and bone health.

Table 12.3 Recommendations for school and community promotion of physical activity for young people

Area	Recommendation
Policy	Establish policies that promote enjoyable, lifelong physical activity.
Environment	Provide physical and social environments that encourage and enable safe and enjoyable physical activity.
Physical education	Implement PE curricula and instruction that emphasises enjoyable participation in physical activity, and that help students adopt and maintain physically active lifestyles.
Health education	Implement health education curricula and instruction that help students adopt and maintain physically active lifestyles.
Extra-curricula activities	Provide extra-curricula physical activity programmes that meet the needs and interests of all students.
Parental involvement	Include parents and guardians in physical activity instruction and in extra-curricular and community physical activity programmes, and encourage them to support their children's participation in enjoyable physical activities.
Personnel training	Provide training for education, coaching, recreation, health-care, and other school and community personnel that imparts the knowledge and skills necessary to effectively promote enjoyable, lifelong physical activity.
Health services	Assess physical activity patterns among young people, counsel them about physical activity, refer them to appropriate programmes, and advocate for physical activity instruction and programmes.
Community programmes	Provide a range of developmentally appropriate community sports and recreation programmes that are attractive to all young people.
Evaluation	Regularly evaluate school and community physical activity instruction, programmes and facilities.

Source: Department of Health and Human Services 1997.

initiatives also exist. European workplace initiatives have tended to focus on safety rather then preventive medicine, as seen in the UK's 1974 Health and Safety at Work Act, although with the recognition of the workplace as an important setting for health promotion this is now changing.

We have argued elsewhere (Smith and Biddle 1995) that to understand the cultural difference between European and North American initiatives in workplace health promotion, one needs an understanding of the motivation of the corporation, factory or office involved in the project. Often it can be a case of simply economic self interest. This motivation has accounted for the rapid growth of fitness campaigns in American corporations. The huge financial cost of private health insurance for American companies provides a powerful motivator for such initiatives. In the UK, the system of National Insurance contributions and the National Health Service has removed the urgency to address such issues. However, concerning the economic criteria for assessment, much of the rationale for worksite interventions in physical activity reflects a cost benefit analysis (CBA) approach whereby an evaluation of the economic effectiveness of the programme is performed. Other approaches could also be used, such as a cost effectiveness analysis (CEA) or a cost utility analysis (CUA). CEA evaluates the effectiveness of the intervention in relation to investment in other resources. CUA considers the effect the programme has on length and quality of life. It is likely that companies interested in developing a wellness programme will go beyond a cost-benefit analysis and look towards a cost-effectiveness analysis whereby competing resources are considered. However, ultimately, a cost utility analysis may be used whereby the quality of life of the employees may be the prime consideration. This suggests that the motivation and rationale for interventions in the workplace can be quite varied and need not necessarily be economic.

Workplace exercise and health promotion programmes: rationale and outcomes

Some of the major benefits claimed for programmes are improved corporate image and recruitment, better productivity, lower absenteeism and worker turnover, and reduced medical costs and incidence of industrial injuries. Gettman said that 'considering the evidence presented through a wide variety of studies, it is concluded that physical activity is economically beneficial' (Gettman 1996: 4). Opatz, Chenoweth and Kaman (1991) (cited in Kaman and Patton 1994), in an evaluation of health promotion in the workplace, concluded that the potential economic impact in the short term was 'moderate' for healthcare costs, and 'moderate-to-strong' for absenteeism and productivity. Similarly, Warner *et al.* (1988), in a review of twenty-eight articles on exercise in the workplace, suggest that the current evidence is as follows:

- Epidemiology: prevalence and health impact: generally quite good information, suggestive of an impact but not definitive.
- Health effects of behaviour change: prevalence and health impact: generally quite good information, suggestive of an impact but not definitive.
- Cost information (types, measurements): very little research.
- Cost-benefit or cost-effectiveness: very little research. However, Shephard concludes that 'in the short term, work-site fitness and health programs appear to yield corporate benefits that more than match program costs, although this view would be strengthened by more controlled experiments' (Shephard 1992: 366).

It has been argued that the type of person attracted to a company offering a comprehensive wellness programme will be a high achiever, have a low absenteeism record and good productivity. This is difficult to quantify although the improved company image that may stem from such an intervention should enhance recruitment prospects. Such factors may, directly or indirectly, increase worker satisfaction.

Subjective reports have indicated favourable changes in productivity with the introduction of a company fitness or wellness programme. However, many of the studies have examined the impact on white collar workers where the measurement of productivity is difficult. In addition, it is problematic to measure productivity of blue collar or shop floor workers since they are unlikely to support a wellness programme with productivity improvements as a key outcome. Kaman and Patton conclude that:

> in the absence of standardised, objective measures of productivity, this outcome may remain one with many hopeful claims, but with little substantive data to support them. . . . Nevertheless, there continues to be a thread of continuity between improved fitness and desirable work behaviors.
>
> (Kaman and Patton 1994: 139–40).

However, in a review by Shephard (1992), twenty-three of twenty-six studies did actually show increases in productivity, measured in a variety of ways, after intervention.

Similarly, studies on absenteeism and corporate fitness programmes are favourable, and Shephard (1992) reports such a trend in thirty-six of thirty-nine studies. It is possible, however, that a self-selection process is at work here with only the conscientious workers choosing the health/fitness programmes. Also, anecdotal evidence suggests that some workers will volunteer to participate in fitness programmes, if conducted in work time, in order to avoid their work commitments. Indeed, Kaman and Patton (1994) report that absenteeism is actually quite low even in companies that do not offer health promotion programmes.

There is little systematic evidence on the effects of fitness programmes on staff turnover. However, if the previous suggestions concerning recruitment, company image and worker satisfaction are true, one could expect a reduced turnover of staff with such a programme. This, of course, is not always positive as all corporations will want some turnover to maintain a freshness of approach and to generate new ideas. For the health economist, however, there is the conundrum of extra pension costs accruing from prolonged life for the healthy, but now retired, members of the company!

Research in North America suggests that medical costs can be reduced substantially through appropriate health/fitness interventions in the workplace (Shephard 1989; 1992). Kaman and Patton say that 'substantial evidence suggests that exercise program components within work site health promotion programs lower participants' health risks and therefore lower related healthcare costs' (Kaman and Patton 1994: 135). Similarly, estimates from Britain suggest that over two million people consult their family doctor about back pain in any one year with the peak occurring in the 45 to 65 year old group: often the most valuable to industry. Back pain also accounts for nearly 10 per cent of the days lost through certified incapacity for work (Wells 1985). Health/fitness interventions could reduce this burden on industry and on the individual. Exercise may be an appropriate strategy for some back pain sufferers, although other interventions are also possible, such as posture and lifting education classes, stress management and ergonomic considerations in the workplace. For example, based on the review by Biering-Sorensen *et al.* (1994), the consensus statement from the 2nd International Consensus Symposium in Toronto stated that 'a reduction of the amount of weight lifted and other ergonomic modifications of the work site can reduce the risk of certain types of occupational low back pain' (Bouchard *et al.* 1994: 51). Also, positive results have been reported from a small number of studies investigating fitness programmes and industrial injuries (Shephard 1989; 1992).

Despite the benefits summarised so far, a recent meta-analytic review has suggested that worksite interventions have yet to demonstrate improvements in physical activity or fitness (Dishman *et al.* 1998). Forty-five effect sizes were obtained from twenty-six studies (total n over 8,500). The average effect for a worksite intervention was no more than one quarter of a standard deviation, or increasing success rates from 50 to 56 per cent after the intervention.

PHYSICALLY ACTIVE COMMUTING TO WORK

Physically active commuting to work has several advantages as an intervention strategy. First, many adults commute to work on most days of the week, thus providing a huge group of people to target for regular activity. Second, the time allocated to work travel is clearly identifiable in the routine of the typical day and week. Again, this allows for effective intervention. It has been estimated in the UK that only one in ten commuter journeys are on foot (Transport 2000, no date). Physical activity as a means of commuting to work has been discussed more fully in Chapter 11.

Further psychological issues in workplace physical activity programmes

One of the most important issues associated with corporate physical activity and exercise programmes, as well as more general health promotion initiatives, is that of adherence. The investment in staff, facilities and other aspects of the programme may affect only a small percentage of the workforce if there is a high dropout rate.

In a review of the effectiveness of fitness promotion programmes in modifying exercise behaviours, Godin and Shephard (1983) suggested that the workplace offers a convenient and cost effective environment in which to promote physical fitness. However, they also recognise that changes must occur in society at large before physical activity and fitness promotion in the workplace becomes more successful than the current adherence rates suggest. Shephard's (1985) comments on the establishment of a corporate fitness programme suggest that more emphasis is required on psychological issues if such programmes are to be effective. He concluded:

- Only 20 per cent of employees will take up the offer of a regular exercise programme; half will have dropped out within a few months.
- Physicians (GPs) should be contacted for support of the company programme.
- Blue collar workers and people at the 'low end' of the white collar organisations need to be targeted.
- The most frequently pursued activities (for example, jogging, walking, swimming) require little organisation, equipment and no partner.
- The main perceived barrier is lack of time.
- A fairly slow rate of progression in exercise programmes should be adopted in order to avoid injury, discomfort etc.
- Graded classes should be provided to accommodate varying ability/fitness levels.

- The reasons why employees will want to become active are: looking good, feeling good, making social contacts, and better health.

Interventions in primary healthcare

The Health of the Nation initiative in England (Department of Health 1993b) identified the health services as central to achieving health change in the population. In particular, local and regional health authorities were encouraged to 'shift the focus towards health promotion' (Department of Health 1993: 34). This change to a more prevention-oriented approach is partly responsible for the increasing interest being shown in physical activity promotion in medical settings. In particular, this has taken place through the family doctor/physician (GP; 'general practitioner') and associated healthcare professionals in primary healthcare (PHC) settings (Fox *et al.* 1997; Pender *et al.* 1994). We have discussed interventions in PHC in Chapter 11.

The community

So far in this chapter we have considered interventions in organisations or specific settings, such as PHC. Although these techniques may have a significant effect on the lifestyle and health of some groups, they are likely to be local and somewhat restricted. For physical activity to have a significant effect on public health, interventions aimed at communities and mass populations must also be used. Unfortunately, there would seem to be an inverse relationship between the size of the target population and the degree of behavioural change achieved.

Persuasion and the social marketing of physical activity

In Chapter 5 we discussed approaches to exercise promotion based on attitude theories. At the time we were primarily concerned with individual behaviour and determinants of exercise. However, attitude theory is also central to understanding the communication of messages to large numbers of people, such as in community health campaigns. Unfortunately, some campaigns have been based on a simplistic and atheoretical understanding of the nature of attitude and its relationship with behaviour. Many physical activity campaigns have simply listed the potential positive outcomes that may accrue from participation, such as weight loss, improved aerobic fitness and an improved figure/physique. As Fishbein and Ajzen (1975) have demonstrated, these outcome beliefs must be supported by positive behavioural evaluations (values).

Social psychological approaches to persuasion and attitude change

An area of attitude theory relevant to this discussion is that of persuasion. Olson and Zanna say that 'the single largest topic within attitudes literature is persuasion: attitude change resulting from exposure to information from others' (Olson and Zanna 1993: 135). For example, McGuire's (1969) sequence of cognitive responses, or 'chain of persuasion', suggests that for a message to influence behaviour, it must involve the following:

- Exposure: the recipient must be exposed to the message.

- Attention: the message must be attended to.
- Comprehension: the message must be understood. It is thought that when the message is not clearly understood, attitudes may be more influenced by the credibility of the source, whereas this is thought not to be so important when the message is understood (Olson and Zanna 1993).
- Yielding: the message must be persuasive; the recipient is persuaded by the content.
- Retention: the message must be retained, even in the face of competing messages and influences.
- Retrieval: the ability to retrieve the message from memory when needing to act.
- Decision: a decision to act in accord with the message, sometimes in the face of competing messages.
- Behaviour: acting in accordance with the message.

The approach to attitude change advocated by McGuire (1969) suggests that attitudes are formed and changed as a result of careful thought and consideration of the relevant issues. This is similar to the Ajzen/Fishbein approach already discussed through the Theories of Reasoned Action and Planned Behaviour (see Chapter 5). Other attitude change theories suggest that the processing of information is not so logical. For example, the 'heuristic-systematic' model, proposed by Chaiken (1980), says that such thoughtful processing of information only occurs when the person is motivated and able to so. Persuasion may occur, however, if the person is unmotivated but this will be temporary and may depend on other factors, such as environmental cues. When motivated, the strength of the argument is thought to determine the degree of persuasion and attitude change is likely to be more permanent.

Similar to the heuristic-systematic approach is the 'elaboration-likelihood' model, proposed by Petty and Cacioppo (1986). They proposed that the 'central' route to attitude change involves an elaboration of the message through conscious thought, as in the heuristic-systematic model. The 'peripheral' route to attitude change and persuasion includes other forms of attitude change that are not related to deliberation or much thought, such as being exposed to the message. The elaboration-likelihood approach advocates that people are motivated to hold 'correct' attitudes. 'Elaboration involves making relevant associations, scrutinising the arguments, inferring their value, and evaluating the overall message' (Fiske and Taylor 1991: 478). Important factors to consider in these approaches to attitude change include:

- The communicator of the message, such as attractiveness and expertise.
- The message itself, including difficulty, repetition and 'involvement' with the message or attitude object.
- Audience involvement: 'the respondent's amount and valence of cognitive response determines the type of effect that occurs. Because cognitive responses demand an actively thinking recipient, audience involvement has influenced each of the effects [communicator and message] discussed so far' (Fiske and Taylor 1991: 487; words in brackets added for clarity).

These approaches to persuasion and attitude change have not been studied in the context of exercise and physical activity, at least not directly through research. However, recently, a 'social marketing' approach to community physical activity promotion has been advocated and this is consistent with some of the notions just discussed.

Social marketing and physical activity

While psychologists, and other behavioural scientists, may be well placed to advise on aspects of communication, attitude change and behaviour, they are not necessarily expert on the 'selling' of the message to appropriate target groups. This is one reason why techniques of successful marketing have been applied to health, and other persuasion, campaigns (Maibach and Parrott 1995). In an excellent overview of social marketing applied to physical activity, Donovan and Owen define social marketing as 'the applications of the principles and methods of marketing to the achievement of socially desirable goals' (Donovan and Owen 1994: 250). Readers are referred to Donovan and Owen (1994) for a comprehensive overview of this expanding area.

Box 12.1 Understanding what the consumer wants

We make the point in the text, when discussing social marketing, that the psychologist may not necessarily be the most expert person for the 'selling' of the community-wide message. A recent story illustrates this.

A small survey was carried out by a local team of health/exercise specialists in a health authority 'district' in England. They wanted to find out the type of health interventions that might be appealing to residents on a fairly deprived housing estate on the edge of a town. The 'classic' replies were expected, such as interventions to stop smoking, start exercising, eat more healthily etc. Instead, rather more 'basic' answers were given. The priorities for a 'healthy lifestyle' identified by these residents included 'proper lighting in alleyways' and 'keeping dog shit off the pavements'!

The need to match the message to the clients is clear to see.

MASS MEDIA AND SOCIAL MARKETING

One important distinction that Donovan and Owen (1994) make is between the use of mass media and the use of social marketing. Although mass media may be used as part of social marketing, it is only a part. Drawing on McGuire's 'chain of persuasion', Donovan and Owen propose that mass media advertising may work best in the early stages of this chain – for example, exposure, attention, comprehension – rather than at the level of behaviour change. This may account for the belief that mass media campaigns are not that successful at behaviour change (Redman *et al.* 1990). Indeed, the effectiveness of such methods for changing community activity patterns has been questioned. However, Aaro (1991) reports on the favourable outcomes of a combined community and mass media physical activity campaign in Norway. He suggests that the reasons for such success are twofold. First, local action is stimulated by mass media coverage, and, second, mass media brings more attractive and appealing material than traditional 'medical' approaches to health promotion. Both these reasons are consistent with the view just expressed about McGuire's chain of persuasion. Indeed, Aaro suggests that the process of behaviour change needs to be viewed in several ways:

It is important to point out that behavioural outcomes are not the only criteria of success in mass media campaigns promoting fitness. The change of health-related behaviour can be regarded as a process in which changes in the actual behaviour itself is an end product of a number of less visible (perhaps invisible) intermediate changes. Sometimes . . . a series of campaigns with no effect on behaviour produces a substantial change in behaviour when the results are summed.

(Aaro 1991: 199)

One presumes he is referring to changes in the early stages of the persuasion 'chain'.

The most extensive review of the impact of mass media on physical activity was conducted by Marcus *et al.* (1998). They located twenty-eight studies satisfying certain criteria, including the use of an experimental or quasi-experimental design. In summary, they concluded:

- Recall of messages was high.
- Little impact was detected on physical activity itself.
- Interventions using print or telephone were effective in changing behaviour in the short term.
- Interventions tailored to a target audience were most effective.

MARKET SEGMENTATION

An aspect of social marketing that develops from the broader impact of a mass media approach is that of market segmentation. Promotional messages need to be appropriate for different segments of the market, or target populations. This may differ in regard to the 'four Ps' of what Donovan and Owen (1994) call the 'marketing mix':

- product: range, types etc.
- price
- promotion
- place: for example, availability.

Successful techniques for the promotion of physical activity begin with a clear statement of the behaviour to be promoted. Fishbein and Ajzen's (1975) concept of the relationship between attitudes, social norm and confidence clearly illustrates the need for a specifically stated 'target behaviour'. The first step in defining the target behaviour is to distinguish between physical activity, exercise and sport. Unfortunately, these terms are often used interchangeably when each calls for a different form of promotion and marketing. From a community perspective, the target behaviour is most likely to be physical activity, such as walking programmes and 'lifestyle' activity. This target behaviour is selected because it is the least behaviourally challenging and is a possible stepping stone for a sedentary population to move on to exercise and sport.

Eadie and Leathar (1988) suggested that social marketing of fitness in the community should observe four main guidelines:

- It should have a positive appeal. Fitness was seen as relatively unimportant to many in their study. Therefore, negative fear appeals are likely to be rejected. Marketing should emphasise the more immediate social and mental benefits.
- A greater emphasis on 'universal representation' is required to make fitness and exercise a socially acceptable activity for all and not just for those fit and good at sport.

- Campaigns must recognise individuality by suggesting a wide range of opportunities for people to choose from.
- Fitness marketing should highlight the informal nature of participation since many people appear to be put off highly structured and professionalised activities.

Killoran, Cavill, and Walker (1994) have presented promotional messages for physical activity in England based on a segmentation analysis. Four groups were identified:

- sedentary
- irregular moderate activity
- regular moderate activity
- regular vigorous activity.

These were based on proposed targets for physical activity for England and will be discussed in more detail later in the chapter. The exact definitions of each group are not necessary at this stage since it is the concept of market segmentation that we wish to demonstrate. For sedentary individuals the message proposed by Killoran *et al.* was:

> be a little more physically active; anything is better than nothing. Try walking more often, taking it gently to start with, and then gradually increase the amount that you do. Check with your doctor if you're worried about your health, or if you're having problems being more active.
>
> (Killoran *et al.* 1994: 151)

For those classified as doing 'irregular moderate activity', the proposed message was:

> work up to being active on 5 days of the week. Aim for a total of 30 minutes of physical activity on each of these days. Make this total from shorter bouts of 10 minutes, if that is easier for you, but build up to these gently. You can do it!

For the 'regular moderate' group:

> keep it up at that level. You may want to do some vigorous level activities instead of some of your moderate level ones, or try putting a little more effort into the activities that you do. Step up the pace – gradually.

Finally, for the 'regular vigorous' segment: 'keep it up!' (151). Killoran *et al.* identified the sedentary and irregularly active as priority groups for targeting and recognised them as having 'distinct characteristics and promotional needs'. For example, sedentary adults in England tend to be older, overweight and from lower socio-economic backgrounds, as well as having some negative views about physical activity. This approach to segmentation is broadly in agreement with that advocated by Donovan and Owen (1994).

Killoran *et al.* (1994) state that the competition for the promotion of physical activity is intense with commercial interests being strong. With the increasing recognition by health and exercise specialists that more moderate forms of physical activity can give significant health benefits, 'the promotion of moderate physical activity will need to establish a specific 'niche' to be effective' (Killoran *et al.* 1994: 167). To a certain extent, therefore, as this 'moderate' message is assimilated, we are in a position of communicating a message that may require some time to be understood. This is because the public had often previously been told that exercise must be 'vigorous' to be healthy. An analysis of 'message effects' in the elaboration-likelihood model of attitude change suggests that a 'difficult' message can cause attitude change if the message is thought about and involves something deemed important. Comprehending the message will encourage persuasion (Fiske and Taylor 1991) – a challenge for the promotion of the 'new' message of moderate physical activity. Indeed, there is some evidence (Killoran *et al.* 1994) that people do not like general messages at all and that they want a clearer 'prescription' for exercise. This may make it more difficult for the marketing of moderate rather than vigorous physical activity.

Another segmentation strategy is that based on the stages of change approach (SOC) discussed more fully in Chapters 6 and 11. In other words, the marketing is based on the stage of readiness of the individual to consider and take up physical activity or exercise. Strategies then draw on appropriate characteristics of people classified within the segments. For example, research has shown that 'contemplators' hold less positive views about exercise and lack confidence to start exercise. Marketing appropriate persuasive messages for this segment should address these issues.

A summary of community intervention projects

A number of community projects have been reported that have included the promotion of physical activity (see Table 12.4). However, all of these are multiple risk factor interventions where physical activity is but one, and sometimes a peripheral, health behaviour that is targeted.

The ParticipAction campaign in Canada focused specifically on physical activity and primarily used mass media. Considerable resources were invested and it was suggested that a very high proportion of the Canadian population became aware of the campaign. However, increases in physical activity resulting from the intervention are unclear. Later messages centring on the concept of 'active living' provided a stronger orientation toward more moderate activity. As discussed earlier in the context of market segmentation, this message has not always been understood, particularly as some have seen it as a change from previous messages. King (1994) suggests that the following lessons can be learned from the ParticipAction campaign:

- Awareness and knowledge can be increased with a well-planned campaign.
- Changes in physical activity resulting from such awareness changes are not easy to quantify.
- More powerful behaviour change may result from focused messages and specific targeting.

At a more general level of analysis, Owen and Dwyer (1988) propose the following guidelines for the promotion of exercise in the community:

- 'Emphasise the role of environmental settings and social supports' (343): adoption is likely to be greater with facilities in workplaces, such as showers and child care, exercise facilities, as well as environmental changes that encourage greater physical activity, such as cycle paths.

Table 12.4 Examples of community physical activity interventions studies

Project	Individual outcomes	Organisational outcomes	Target audiences	Behaviour targets	Strategies	Significant changes
North Karelia (Finland)	None specifically targeted.	Media events and community organisations involved.	General; community organisations; GPs.	Multi-risk factor.	Mass media; community organisations.	Decrease in CVD> controls.
Stanford 5 Cities Project (USA)	Knowledge, awareness, participation, energy expenditure, bodyweight, resting HR.	Media events; availability of exercise facilities.	General; women; Hispanics; work sites; schools.	Multi risk factor.	Mass media; community events; fitness assessment; school and work site contests; talks; health contests; talks; health professional training.	Participation in moderate and vigorous PA> controls; resting HR <control.
ParticipAction (Canada)	Knowledge and awareness.		General.	Physical activity; active living.	Mass media; community organisation.	Awareness and knowledge.
Australia National Heart Foundation Campaign	Knowledge, awareness, intentions, self reported adoption and maintenance.	Media events.	General.	Physical activity.	Mass media; professional talks; use of personalities; state contests and events.	Awareness increased, especially for women; increase in walking, especially in adults>60 years.

Source: adapted from King 1994.

- 'Use a judicious combination of media': a combination of approaches is advocated, including the co-ordination of 'community events, classes, media promotions, self-help materials and other methods within the framework of a systematic campaign'. This is consistent with the view expressed earlier that mass media campaigns alone may only affect knowledge and awareness, whereas additional promotions and facility access may better promote the behaviour itself.
- 'Operate simultaneously on a number of different levels, and identify clearly those aspects of the process of behaviour change which are of concern': this recognises the concept of market segmentation and the need to target specific groups with appropriate interventions, such as knowledge and confidence for those contemplating exercise and, for example, social support networks for those attempting maintenance.
- 'Provide a variety of specific exercise options': again, this emphasises the need to target specific groups and provide varied, but appropriate options for each group.
- 'Develop and promote exercise options which are intrinsically interesting and appealing': consistent with intrinsic motivation theory (see Chapter 3) and the knowledge that people have multiple motives for participation in physical activity (see Chapter 2), it is important to allow people choice and variety, and to emphasise the intrinsic pleasure of exercise rather than promote exercise purely for health. The 'disease prevention' approach will not motivate many people over the long term.
- 'Make soundly-based information and instruction readily available' (344): while the need for expert exercise instructors is clear, it is also recognised that many people do not find exercise classes attractive and thus seek help in different ways. This necessitates good self-help materials, or a system of advice, such as through primary health-care counselling, as discussed earlier. Indeed, an integration of the two 'systems' is possible since one way to personalise the physical activity message to the community is through health professionals becoming more expert at physical activity promotion. For example, in Somerset, a training module for primary healthcare nurses has been established. The objective of this has been to empower such people to promote physical activity with their client groups. The training course has focused on behaviour change strategies rather than teaching a repertoire of physical movement skills. The nurses and health visitors will go back into their communities and promote physical activity rather then simply teach exercise classes. By the nature of their role, health visitors will come into contact with a large number of sedentary people. They deal with young mothers, older adults, and single-parent families. These groups would not normally come into contact with an exercise leader but can be advised through their existing relationship with a health professional (Smith and Biddle 1995).

Community physical activity promotion: an example

The 'active living' message suggests that sedentary public should be encouraged to add activity into their daily routine at every opportunity. Chapter 11 explored some of the interventions used at an individual level. A recent study has explored the community application of the active living message with particular regard to encouraging stair climbing. Blamey, Mutrie, and Aitchison (1995) aimed to discover if Scottish commuters would respond to motivational signs encouraging them to 'Stay Healthy, Save Time, Use the Stairs'. The signs were placed in Glasgow city centre underground station where stairs (thirty steps) and escalators were adjacent.

The study spanned a sixteen-week period and a total of 22,275 observations were made on Mondays, Wednesdays and Fridays between 8.30 and 10 a.m. during eight of these weeks. The eight observation weeks were split into four stages: a one-week baseline, a three-week period when the sign was present, a two-week period immediately after the sign was removed, and two one-week follow ups (during the fourth and twelfth weeks after intervention). Observers recorded the number of adults using the escalators and stairs and categorised them by sex. Those carrying luggage or with pushchairs were excluded. A comparison was made between the baseline week stair use and each of the seven subsequent observation weeks. This process was repeated for the total sample as well as for males and females separately.

Stair use during the one week baseline period was around 8 per cent. This increased to the order of 15–17 per cent during the three weeks that the sign was present. Figure 12.4 shows the overall percentage improvement from baseline compared to each of the subsequent seven weeks. Stair use significantly increased after the signs were in place and continued to increase during the three intervention weeks. A sudden decrease in stair use occurred once the sign was removed. At the twelve week follow up stair use remained significantly higher that at baseline. There is, however, an obvious downward trend suggesting a possible eventual return to baseline levels. It was found that females were more likely to use escalators than males at all times.

The results show that a motivational sign positively influenced stair use. The improvement was slightly greater than that found in a similar study (Brownell, Stunkard and Albaum 1980).

Interviews were also conducted as part of the Blamey *et al.* (1995) study. These were conducted during the time taken to go up the escalator or walk up the stairs: about forty-five seconds. Stair users reported saving time and health as the main motivating factors while escalator users cited laziness and stair climbing taking too much time and effort as the main barriers to stair climbing. In general, males reported higher levels of physical activity and lower perception of the effort required to climb stairs than females. Adults over 50 years of age gave a higher rating of the perception of effort required to climb the stairs.

The information gained from this study suggests that future campaigns designed to increase stair walking should focus on how little effort stair climbing takes and how easy it would be to be active, at least on some journeys. In addition, different motivational posters could be designed for older people and women and men.

The original study resulted in the Health Education Board for Scotland (HEBS) producing a resource pack to encourage stair use in the workplace. HEBS was also convinced of the need to reinforce this behaviour and produced further signs suggesting to stair walkers that if

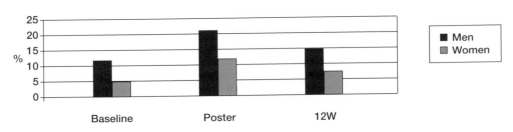

Figure 12.4 Stair-climbing before and after a promotional intervention (data from Blamey *et al.* 1995)

they walk up one set of stairs everyday for a year they will have climbed the equivalent of a 3,000 ft. mountain. Although this has not been tested as a method of reinforcing stair walking behaviour, it does appear intuitively appealing.

Concluding remarks on interventions in communities

Community-wide interventions pose a dilemma. They are potentially the most effective way of making a significant impact on public health yet they are the most difficult to manage in terms of appropriate targeting of messages to specific groups. An understanding of the social psychology of persuasion and attitude change, therefore, is important in making progress in this field. Recent developments, such as social marketing, may go someway to translating these concepts in actual behaviour change. However, at present, where evaluations of large-scale campaigns or interventions to increase community physical activity have taken place, the results have not been particularly encouraging for changing behaviour, although they are more optimistic for showing changes in awareness and knowledge. In a systematic review of interventions using a randomised controlled design, Hillsdon and Thorogood (1996) concluded:

- Physical activity can be increased.
- This increase can be maintained for up to two years.
- Sustainable increases are more likely for walking and exercise not requiring facilities.
- Follow-up contact enhances participation.

Dishman and Buckworth (1996) also supported the view that low-to-moderate intensity physical activity could be significantly increased through intervention. This was shown by an extensive meta-analytic review. In addition, they showed that interventions were effective using behaviour modification methods, for physical activity in leisure time and in general community settings. In conclusion, Dishman and Buckworth said:

> a conservative interpretation . . . is that interventions for increasing physical activity have a moderately large effect. . . . The analysis of effects weighted by sample size suggests that interventions based on the principles of behavior modification, delivered to healthy people in a community, are associated with large effects, particularly when the interventions are delivered to groups using mediated approaches or when the physical activity is unsupervised, emphasizing leisure physical activity of low intensity, regardless of the duration or frequency of participation.
>
> (Dishman and Buckworth 1996: 712)

Political initiatives and interventions for increasing physical activity

King (1991) identified several levels of physical activity interventions, from individual to legislative. Although physical activity is widely recognised as a key element in health promotion and disease prevention, it is only recently that we have seen political and governmental involvement. The initiatives in the USA, such as the 'Healthy People 2000' project (Department of Health and Human Services 1991), have been discussed by many physical activity researchers (Dishman 1994a). However, as King (1994) points out, physical activity is a free-choice behaviour and not a product that can be controlled like cigarettes or certain foods. Indeed, it could be claimed that governments have been rather 'lukewarm' about physical activity until very recently.

Legislative support for physical activity has now emerged in the UK. For example, The Health of the Nation initiative in the early 1990s had the aims of improving life expectancy and reducing premature mortality ('adding years to life'), and improving the quality of life ('adding life to years'). Physical activity has been identified as an important element to combat one of the five priority areas: coronary heart disease and stroke. This policy has continued with the Labour Government's initiative *Our Healthier Nation*. However, one shift of emphasis, reflecting the change in government in 1997, was to give much greater recognition to the inequalities in the health statistics. It is thought that by addressing social inequalities, health will improve, although the relationship between social class and physical activity is less clear than for some other health behaviours (Coggins, Swanston and Crombie 1999). A recent review of physical activity interventions in low-income groups and ethnic minorities showed most of the fourteen studies identified to use pre-post or quasi-experimental designs (Taylor, Baranowski and Young 1998b). Only two of the ten studies with ethnic minorities showed an increase in physical activity. In conclusion, Taylor *et al.*, said 'much work remains to develop effective interventions for these populations' (334).

In referring to the Allied Dunbar National Fitness Survey (ADNFS) (Sports Council and Health Education Authority 1992), the Department of Health said 'the Government will, in consultation with others, develop detailed strategies for physical activity in the light of the survey results' (Department of Health 1993b: 62). Consequently, a 'Physical Activity Task Force' (PATF) was established with the remit of recommending targets and strategies for physical activity for the English population. The following targets were recommended for the year 2005:

- To reduce by at least 10 per cent the proportion of men and women aged 16 to 74 taking no occasion of moderate intensity physical activity of at least thirty minutes each week. 1990 estimates gained from the data in the ADNFS meant the figures would drop from 29 to 19 per cent for men and from 28 to 18 per cent for women.
- To increase the proportion, by at least 15 per cent, of men and women aged 16 to 74 who take a minimum of thirty minutes of at least moderate intensity physical activity on five days of the week or more. This would achieve a change from 36 to 51 per cent for men and 24 to 39 per cent for women.
- To increase the proportion, by at least 10 per cent, of men and women age 16 to 64 taking on average three periods of vigorous physical activity of twenty minutes during a week. This would result in changes from 16 to 26 per cent for men and 5 to 15 per cent for women.

The recommendations were subsequently rejected by the Conservative Government who stated that official targets were no longer necessary. However, the implementation of strategies to increase physical activity in the community could still be based on the calculations presented. This reversal is not easily explainable although it is known that Government Ministers find physical activity a difficult health behaviour to deal with as they do not wish to 'nanny' people. While some sympathy with this view exists, it is not easy to see how physical activity differs from any other health behaviour in this respect. Indeed, increases in physical activity could improve public health much more than many other changes in health behaviours, thus necessitating a clear and strong line of intervention.

The American Healthy People 2000 project includes national objectives for physical activity levels, physical education provision, workplace physical activity promotion, avail-ability of community facilities and primary care interventions to increase physical activity. Clearly, national legislative initiatives can be important landmarks for legitimising physical activity promotion and interventions. Ultimately, of course, physical activity and health objectives can only be met with appropriate interventions, and these may come through organisations, such as schools and workplaces, or at the broader community level, and this requires co-ordination and integration.

Integration between levels of physical activity intervention

Before exercise psychology expertise can be used to promote physical activity within the community and across organisations and institutions, we have argued that it is important to have integration between areas of the health promotion system (Smith and Biddle 1995). In Britain, for example, this usually means that the exercise specialist must work alongside the health promotion team of a local health authority. An illustration of this is shown in Figure 12.5. Here we have represented a community-based strategy to increase physical activity as a 'planning pyramid'. This shows more specialised facilities and programmes, catering for fewer people, at the top of the pyramid, and mass community programmes at the base.

Pyramid I shows the overall physical activity strategy on face 'a'. The other faces of the

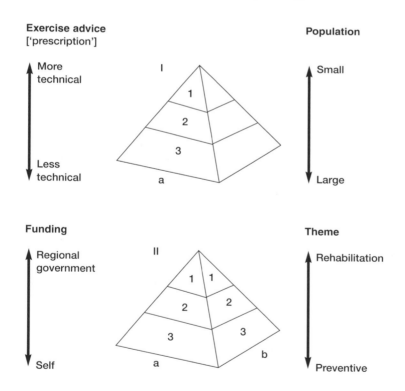

Figure 12.5 Integration of physical activity promotion through the use of 'planning pyramids'. (Reprinted, by permission, from S. J. H. Biddle (ed.) (1995) *European perspectives on exercise and sport psychology*, p. 94. Champaign, Ill.: Human Kinetics.)

pyramid could be modifications of 'a' for sub-populations or different geographical regions. Sector 1 of Pyramid I represents more technical medical rehabilitation taking place in hospitals and specialised clinics. Personnel are likely to include medical doctors, nurses, physiotherapists and, possibly, exercise scientists. The population here will be small and the exercise advice and 'prescription' precise and 'technical'. Moving down the pyramid, Sector 2 shows intervention at the level of recognised health clinics and centres staffed by physiotherapists and exercise scientists. At the lowest level, Sector 3, the largest population is targeted and the exercise advice least technical. This represents 'mass' physical activity promotion through, say, health-related exercise classes at leisure centres staffed by exercise leaders.

Pyramid II shows two more focused interventions based on the same principles of staffing and population size as just outlined. Face 'a' depicts interventions targeting coronary heart disease (CHD) while face 'b' is associated with the mental health outcomes of physical activity. For CHD, Sector 1 again represents medical and hospital CHD rehabilitation work. Sector 2 might include supervised exercise programmes at recognised centres for rehabilitation, as well as home-based programmes monitored by rehabilitation staff. Sector 3 includes community-based physical activity and exercise interventions for individuals with CHD risk factors, as well as general health-related exercise programmes.

Finally, interventions aimed at mental health are on face 'b' of Pyramid II. At the top of the pyramid might be exercise aimed at hospitalised clinical patients, while Sector 2 could involve community GPs prescribing exercise and physical activity for their patients suffering mild non-clinical disorders. Interventions in Sector 3 might involve community-based activity and exercise programmes that emphasise mental well-being and stress management.

Sallis and Owen (1996; 1999) propose the use of an ecological model approach to physical activity promotion and research. This recognises multiple levels of influence, such as intrapersonal, social-environmental and physical environmental. Policies governing incentives and resources for physical activity are part of the wider social-environmental factors of influence (Marks *et al.* 2000). Sallis and Owen (1996) specify some guiding principles of ecological approaches to health behaviour change (see Table 12.5). Successful interventions in physical activity will need to address this wider approach, difficult though this will be. Ecological approaches tend to be rather broad in orientation, making it difficult to identify key determinants or which aspects of an intervention were successful. Nevertheless, such an approach will capture the diversity of influences on physical activity (Sallis, Bauman and Pratt 1998).

Chapter summary and conclusions

This chapter has considered physical activity interventions at institutional, community and governmental levels. Specifically, we have:

- Considered physical activity promotion in schools, and in particular discussed the role of physical education and school-based interventions.
- Discussed physical activity promotion and interventions in the workplace and reviewed evidence on its effectiveness.
- Reviewed issues associated with physical activity promotion and interventions in the community, including attitude change, social marketing, and ecological approaches.
- Discussed recent initiatives from national governments to promote physical activity.

Table 12.5 Principles of ecological approaches to health behaviour change applied to physical activity

Principle	Description	Examples of application to physical activity
Multiple dimensions of influence on behaviour.	In addition to intra- and inter-personal influences, ecological models include social, cultural and physical environments as important influences on health behaviours.	• Social 'acceptance' of physical activity in different cultural groups. • Inhibitory physical environment for physical activity.
Interactions of influences across dimensions.	An ecological approach should say how the different types of determinants will interact to influence health behaviours.	A research study testing the interaction between intra-personal beliefs concerning walking and use of a pedestrianised city centre.
Multiple levels of environmental influences.	Ecological models specify levels of influence, such as different types of environment (for example, urban, climate).	The prevalence of physical activity in places differing in climate and inner-city cycle paths.
Environments directly influence behaviours.	Ecological models propose that environments directly influence health behaviours as well as indirectly through other factors such as individual beliefs.	Physical activity will be directly influenced by local traffic conditions regardless of intra- or inter-personal differences.

Source: based on Sallis and Owen 1996.

In summary, therefore, we conclude:

- That schools are well placed to promote healthy lifestyles, including physical activity, and that physical education has the potential to reach large numbers of children of all backgrounds and abilities.
- Interventions to increase physical activity in or through schools have met with mixed success or have not been properly evaluated. Two large controlled trials in the USA have shown some effectiveness.
- The objectives, content and delivery of health-related exercise in schools are often confused and sometimes PE has failed groups in the promotion of lifetime of physical activity.
- In some countries, the workplace has been identified as an important setting for physical activity and health promotion.
- There is evidence for the effectiveness of physical activity interventions in the workplace on absenteeism, productivity and reduced healthcare costs, but effectiveness in increasing physical activity has not be demonstrated.
- The greatest potential public health impact of physical activity promotion is likely to come through community interventions.
- Social psychological approaches to attitude change and persuasion hold considerable promise in the identification of appropriate strategies for community interventions.
- Principles of social marketing require further application to exercise and physical

activity, and, in particular, note should be taken of the importance of market segmentation and targeted groups.
- Governments of developed countries have only recently been involved in legislative initiatives in physical activity and this interest has helped to legitimise physical activity as an important health behaviour.
- Effective physical activity promotion requires co-ordination across all levels of interventions.

13 Conclusions and future directions

Better to hunt in fields, for health unbought,
Than fee the doctor for a nauseous draught.
The wise, for cure, on exercise depend.
                    John Dryden 1631–1700
            (*Oxford Dictionary of Quotations*, 1981)

Chapter objectives

The purpose of this concluding chapter is to summarise key points from the preceding twelve chapters and comment on future directions of each main theme. In addition, we shall suggest more general directions for future work in exercise psychology. We shall depart, at times, from what has been an evidence-based review of the field in so far as we offer personal observations and comments from our combined experience of some forty years professional involvement in physical activity. Specifically, in this chapter we shall:

- Summarise the key evidence on determinants, psychological well-being and interventions in exercise and physical activity.
- Provide future directions for research and practice.

When we wrote the first text specifically addressing exercise psychology in 1991, little did we know that the field was already expanding rapidly and would continue to expand. Indeed, the interest and activity in this area of research and practice continues to grow. Indictors of growth include:

- The marked increase in interest shown by policy makers and governments.
- The continued collaboration between agencies as diverse as transport, medicine and economics with health and physical activity agencies.
- The expansion of 'sport' science and 'sport' psychology to embrace health-related physical activity and exercise, often resulting in the word exercise being inserted in journal and society titles.
- An expansion in opportunities for employment and careers in physical activity promotion, through fields as diverse as mental health, cardiac rehabilitation, leisure services, primary healthcare, and higher education teaching and research.
- Continued media interest in exercise and health

These are important times for the study and promotion of physical activity.

Recognition of the importance of physical activity for health has grown and few can now dispute the central role that promoting active lifestyles has in health promotion and disease prevention. Yet, as we have stated many times in this book, exercise participation is low, health problems associated with inactive living have high prevalence, and various factors, such as the built environment, make it difficult to find easy solutions to the problem. When asked by journalists, for example, what we think about the prospects of increasing population physical activity levels, we often give both pessimistic and optimistic views. The optimistic perspective reflects the points just raised. There has never been as much interest or activity in exercise and active lifestyles. One could say the bandwagon is truly rolling. However, the pessimistic view might suggest that the bandwagon is in danger of being slowed or halted by a range of barriers associated with 'modern living': transport, environmental factors, changing work patterns, beliefs about sport and exercise, socio-economic and health inequalities, less time for physical education on school curricula and other factors. Are people really going to take a brisk walk for thirty minutes on most days of the week? Are young people really going to take one hour of activity on most days of the week? When stated in such bland terms, it is easy to adopt the pessimistic view. And herein lies the irony. At a time in human history when we *need* exercise, few people are doing it. Yet we know many would value the outcomes. A physically active life can help to address the 'mental malaise' sometimes referred to in society, the need we all have to 'feel good', the startling increase in obesity, and the hope that we live not just a long life but one free of disability with associated good quality of life.

So let's be optimistic! The experience of researchers and other physical activity specialists is that we have plenty of evidence and good practice that can make a difference. The evidence reviewed in this book points overwhelmingly to the importance of psychological factors in exercise and physical activity. We recognised early in this book that the psychological perspective is but one of many appropriate for understanding and promoting activity. Putting all of this together suggests we should be optimistic, even if it means we recognise that psychology alone cannot solve the problem. Indeed, it would be foolish to suggest anything close to that. We firmly believe that real progress will only come about when we integrate knowledge and practice across the diverse fields and agencies impacting on population physical activity levels.

Determinants of physical activity and exercise: summary of key findings

We have reviewed the main descriptive and theoretical approaches to exercise determinants, primarily using a motivational approach. We will summarise key conclusions from this review and make some additional comments.

Descriptive approaches

- For children and youth, common motives for involvement in sport and physical activity are fun, skill development, affiliation, fitness, success and challenge. For adults, motives change across stages of the lifecycle. Younger adults are motivated more by challenge, skill development and fitness, whereas older adults are more interested in participation for reasons of health, relaxation and enjoyment.
- Reasons for ceasing participation are numerous and have included for children conflicts of interest, lack of fun or playing time, lack of success, injury and competitive stress.

For adults, physical, emotional, motivational, time and availability barriers seem to be prominent, with time nearly always cited as a factor preventing participation.

Comment Descriptive approaches are easy to understand, have heuristic value, but lack detail and underlying theory explaining why people act in the way they do.

Theoretical approaches

- Single motivational constructs, such as self-motivation and commitment, have been proposed and could still prove useful as variables within larger studies. However, more recent approaches have advocated the testing of broader theories rather than variables in isolation.
- Research findings are not supportive of locus of control being a strong determinant of exercise. Most studies violate the original assumptions of locus of control theory and measuring instruments have not been fully tested or have been inappropriately applied. Greater precision in defining and assessing constructs related to perceptions of control is needed.
- Self-determination theory, including cognitive evaluation theory, is a viable perspective for the study of exercise motivation and is likely to increase our understanding of exercise motivation in the future, and in particular the different types of extrinsic motivation that might exist for physical activity.
- Exercise participation is associated with perceptions of competence, in whatever form competence is operationalised. However, more specific perceptions of competence/efficacy are likely to be better predictors of specific behaviours than generalised beliefs in competence.
- Goal perspectives theory proposes that people can define competence and success in different ways, the main ones being ego and task orientations. Research is consistent in showing the motivational benefits of a task orientation, either singly or in combination with an ego orientation.
- Research using self-efficacy with patient groups demonstrates that exercise self-efficacy can be developed in such populations; self-efficacy judgements can generalise but will be strongest for activities similar to the activity experienced; self-efficacy in 'dissimilar' activities can be enhanced through counselling; self-efficacy better predicts changes in exercise behaviour than generalised expectancies.
- Research with non-patient groups has shown that exercise self-efficacy can be increased through intervention, will predict participation, particularly in the early stages of an exercise programme, will decline after a period of inactivity, and is associated with positive exercise emotion.
- Early research on physical activity attitudes was mainly descriptive. Generalised attitude scales usually assess only the target of physical activity and not the action, context or time elements of attitude thought to be critical in linking attitude with behaviour. This approach, therefore, has limited utility in predicting participation in physical activity although may be of use in eliciting descriptive information in population surveys.
- The theory of reasoned action (TRA) has consistently predicted exercise intentions and behaviour across diverse settings and samples. The theory of planned behaviour (TPB) appears to add to the predictive utility of the TRA in physical activity.
- The health belief model has been shown to be a reasonably effective integrating social psychological framework for understanding health decision-making, although

meta-analytic results suggest small amounts of variance in health behaviours are accounted for by the major dimensions of the HBM. Its utility in physical activity settings has not been demonstrated.

Comments   The move from an atheoretical to a theoretical approach in exercise psychology is welcomed. However, greater precision in defining and choosing appropriate theoretical models, and better integration of models with other approaches, is now required. For example, it is widely accepted that perceptions of control are important motivational factors in exercise and other health behaviours. However, there is great diversity in how these perceptions are operationalised and this has led to some confusion.

The use of simply descriptive items in large-scale population surveys needs to be addressed. The collection of large-scale data using more complete theoretical approaches is needed. In addition, the experimental test of some theories is sparse and is now required.

- There is considerable conceptual convergence between the major theoretical approaches adopted in contemporary exercise psychology, particularly those using a social-cognitive or expectancy-value approach.
- Greater convergence should be attempted in preference to 'ring fencing' theories, as some have advocated.

Comments   While the practical reality of many research studies is that data are collected based on only one or two theoretical approaches, it is important that we do not lose sight of the 'bigger picture'. This is likely to require greater integration and discussion of findings drawing on wider theoretical approaches. There is overlap between commonly used theories and this overlap must be used to our advantage. This cannot occur if we:

- persist with theories that are redundant
- operationalise theories incorrectly
- measure constructs inadequately
- adhere too closely to one theoretical approach for all problems.

Integrative approaches

- The stages of change or transtheoretical approach to decision-making provides an important advance on static models of exercise and physical activity determinants but the application of all of the elements of the transtheoretical model (and not just the stages) is now required in physical activity.
- A natural history model of exercise is a useful framework for identifying key stages in exercise behaviour. However, more needs to be known about which determinants are more or less important at each of the phases of the model.
- The lifespan interaction model provides a valuable overarching model for the identification of the complex interactions determining exercise and physical activity involvement.

Comments   Understanding the process of exercise behaviour change is important. Such a complex behaviour can never be fully understood by examining people as either exercisers or non-exercisers, or as active or inactive. Improved understanding will emanate from approaches that recognise people move, often inconsistently, through phases and stages of involvement in physical activity and exercise. In addition, much greater attention needs to be paid to ecological approaches that account for intrapersonal, interpersonal, social and environmental factors.

Perceptual and social contextual approaches

- The psychological and perceptual responses of individuals to the stimulus of exercise are not uniform. A number of factors influence how people perceive the intensity of exercise.
- The development of a mastery motivational climate in exercise classes and groups appears to be desirable for motivational and other positive psychological outcomes.
- Evidence exists of familial aggregation of physical activity, but the role of parental and other adult encouragement is less clear.
- Research on group cohesion has shown that exercise group dropouts have lower perceptions of cohesion than those who stay. However, the direct applicability of a conceptual model of group cohesion developed for sport requires further testing in exercise.
- There is a positive relationship between exercise behaviour and some social influence variables, such as family support.

Comments These findings highlight the complexity of exercise behaviour. To fully understand exercise and physical activity determinants, social, social-environmental, and perceptual factors need to be accounted for.

Psychological outcomes of exercise: summary of key findings

We have reviewed the main approaches to the study of psychological outcomes from exercise. Again, we will summarise key conclusions from this review and make some additional comments.

Non-clinical populations

- Participation in exercise and physical activity is consistently associated with positive mood and affect. Experimental trials support the effect of moderate exercise on psychological well-being (PWB).
- Exercise is related to positive changes in self-esteem and related physical self-perceptions.
- State, trait and psychophysiological measures of anxiety are decreased following exercise bouts or programmes and aerobically fit individuals appear to have a reduced physiological response to psychosocial stressors.
- Exercise is associated with a moderate reduction in non-clinical depression.
- The effects of exercise on cognitive functioning appear to be small, though significant, and exercise can have a positive effect on personality and psychological adjustment.
- Small but positive effects are suggested for exercise on sleep.
- Exercise can have positive effects for women faced with reproductive events such as menstruation, pregnancy or the menopause.

Comments Anecdotal and research evidence consistently links exercise and physical activity with the 'feel good' effect. This conclusion is made more impressive by the range of psychological outcomes. This is, of course, not a new idea since the concept of a healthy mind in a healthy body has been around for many centuries. However, the research designs are often weak and we are some way from assessing the causality of this link with any certainty. Nevertheless, the evidence all points in the direction of positive psychological outcomes from physical activity and this may prove an effective and important issue in promoting more active lifestyles.

Clinical populations

- Exercise can reduce clinically defined levels of depression and evidence from varied sources suggests that this is a causal link.
- No negative effects of exercise in mentally ill patient groups have been noted although there is an hypothesised contra-indication for certain anxiety disorders.
- Exercise has the potential to improve certain symptoms in schizophrenia.
- Although exercise does not decrease drinking behaviour in problem drinkers, it can influence fitness, physical self-perception and activity levels. Exercise can play a positive role in assisting those who are being treated for drug dependence.
- A very small percentage of exercisers can become dependent on exercise.

Comments   The conclusion that exercise is causally linked to decreased clinical depression will be seen as controversial by some people. However, the diversity and strength of evidence favours such a conclusion. There is now a need for raising awareness of the role of exercise for mental health professionals.

- The mechanisms of the psychologically beneficial effects of physical activity and exercise are not clear at this time but there are many plausible mechanisms.

Comments   The lack of clarity about what causes exercise to have a positive psychological effect is a major weakness is the promotion of exercise in mental health. There is a clear need to identify what factors are at work in linking exercise with better psychological well-being. This will require multi- and inter-disciplinary research.

- Patients in almost all categories of disease and disability could benefit from exercise. There are few contraindications. However, very little is known about exercise participation levels in clinical populations and more work is required on understanding and improving long-term adherence in such groups.

Interventions to increase physical activity: summary of key findings

- It is possible to increase the physical activity levels of sedentary individuals and short-term increases are relatively easy to achieve. However long-term change is hard to achieve.
- Cognitive behavioural techniques, either one-to-one or written, offer the best possibility of long term change.

Comments   While short-term behaviour change is possible, the challenge is to maintain involvement in exercise over several years or indeed the whole lifespan. One area requiring attention is the testing of relapse prevention strategies. There is also a need to explore different and new media for delivering messages as well as testing interventions at various stages of involvement across different settings.

- Schools are well placed to promote healthy lifestyles, including physical activity, and physical education has the potential to reach large numbers of children of all backgrounds and abilities.

Comments   Much has been written about the importance of schools in all aspects of health promotion yet interventions in or through schools have met with mixed success or have not been properly evaluated. In relation to physical activity, schools too often have been associated with competitive sport to the exclusion of the promotion of active lifestyles for all children. Many sedentary adults report negative feelings about school physical education. Political rhetoric has not helped with unjustified claims that schools are no longer interested in competitive sport or that the priority should be put on winning Olympic medals. The middle ground in this argument – that sport is important but so are active lifestyles for those not interested in playing sport – seems unappealing to the media. Meanwhile, the physical education profession presents a confused and over-complicated mission statement to the policy makers and the public. Examinations in physical education seem to reinforce the notion that excellent performance is more important than understanding the health implications of active or inactive lifestyles. Meanwhile curricular time for physical education has decreased.

- There is evidence for the effectiveness of physical activity interventions in the workplace on absenteeism, productivity and reduced healthcare costs, but effectiveness in increasing physical activity has not been demonstrated.

Comments   While American or Japanese-style worksite exercise provision might not sit happily with British or other European cultures, the workplace has huge potential for promoting physical activity. In particular, active transport to work through walking and cycling could be a significant public health initiative. Changes will require major shifts in the 'culture' of car use and other forms of motorised transport. Multi-agency collaboration is vital, and in particular the links with transport and urban planning agencies.

- The expansion of exercise promotion into primary care is welcomed but further assessment of effectiveness is necessary. In addition, training of medical and paramedical staff and reimbursement to GPs for taking preventive action needs further consideration.
- The greatest potential public health impact of physical activity promotion is likely to come through community interventions. Social psychological approaches to attitude change and persuasion, as well specific social marketing methods, hold considerable promise in the identification of appropriate strategies for community interventions.
- Governments of developed countries have only recently been involved in legislative initiatives in physical activity and this interest has helped to legitimise physical activity as an important health behaviour. However, this is only one level of intervention and effective physical activity promotion requires co-ordination across all levels of interventions.

Comments   Although governments have shown increasing interest in physical activity, further lobbying is necessary. This will require evidence from large-scale well-controlled studies and the demonstration of cost-effectiveness of interventions. Recognition also needs to be given to competing interests of governments, such as taxation from tobacco, employment in the car industry and their fear of 'nannying' people on behaviour change.

Concluding remarks

It would easy in concluding a book of this nature to say we need more research. In some areas, such as testing the mechanisms of exercise and psychological well-being, this is true. In other areas we need to better understand the evidence we have, perhaps by meta-analysing findings or conducting qualitative follow-ups to existing studies. What appears necessary, though, is that the rapid increase in the *quantity* of exercise psychology studies needs to be associated more closely with better *quality* of research. We have too few large-scale randomised controlled trials and too many cross-sectional surveys, often small-scale themselves.

In addition to improved quality, perhaps we also need to look beyond our immediate confines of sport and exercise science and psychology and collaborate more with colleagues in other fields. In particular, research with other social scientists (for example, economists, sociologists), medical researchers and epidemiologists, and biomedical scientists (for example, in neurobiology, biochemistry, physiology), as well other professionals in urban planning, transport, and related fields can only move the field forward. Within such a framework, though, sound psychological theory and measurement must be central. Physical activities and exercise routines are *behaviours* and, as such, require a clear behavioural and psychological approach alongside other perspectives.

When we consider the vast sums of money that are spent by manufacturers on products which increase (perhaps inadvertently) sedentary behaviour such as cars, computer games, television and film viewing, it is clear that action must be taken to avoid an epidemic of inactivity. Researchers and practitioners cannot delay action until the knowledge base is perfect. As Hill reminded us:

> All scientific work is incomplete – whether it be observational or experimental. All scientific work is liable to be upset or modified by advancing knowledge. That does not confer upon us a freedom to ignore the knowledge we already have, or postpone the action that it appears to demand at a given time.
>
> (Hill 1965: 12)

We hope this book inspires many to encourage more people to be more active, more often.

Bibliography

Aaro, L. E. (1991) 'Fitness promotion programs in mass media: Norwegian experiences.' In P. Oja and R. Telama (eds), *Sport for all* (pp. 193–200). Amsterdam: Elsevier.

Abele, A. and Brehm, W. (1993) 'Mood effects of exercise versus sports games: Findings and implications for well-being and health.' In S. Maes, H. Leventhal and M. Johnston (eds), *International Review of Health Psychology* (vol. 2, pp. 53–80). Chichester: John Wiley.

Abramson, L. Y., Seligman, M. E. P. and Teasdale, J. D. (1978) 'Learned helplessness in humans: Critique and reformulation.' *Journal of Abnormal Psychology*, 87: 49–74.

Adamson, M. J. (1991) *The role of exercise as an adjunct to the treatment of substance abuse.* Unpublished M.Ed. thesis, University of Glasgow.

Adler, N. and Matthews, K. (1994) 'Health Psychology: Why do some people get sick and some stay well?' *Annual Review of Psychology*, 45: 229–59.

Ainsworth, B. E., Montoye, H. J. and Leon, A. S. (1994) 'Methods of assessing physical activity during leisure and work.' In C. Bouchard, R. J. Shephard and T. Stephens (eds), *Physical activity, fitness, and health* (pp. 145–59). Champaign, Ill.: Human Kinetics.

Ajzen, I. (1985) 'From intentions to actions: A theory of planned behavior.' In J. Kuhl and J. Beckmann (eds), *Action control: From cognition to behavior* (pp. 11–39). New York: Springer-Verlag.

—— (1988) *Attitudes, personality and behaviour*. Milton Keynes: Open University Press.

—— (1991) 'The theory of planned behavior: Organization behavior and human decision processes.' *Organizational Behavior And Human Processes*, 50: 179–211.

—— (1996) 'The directive influence of attitudes on behavior.' In P. M. Gollwitzer and J. A. Bargh (eds), *The psychology of action* (pp. 385–403). New York: Guilford Press.

Ajzen, I. and Fishbein, M. (1980) *Understanding attitudes and predicting social behaviour*. Englewood Cliffs, N.J.: Prentice-Hall.

Ajzen, I. and Madden, T. J. (1986) 'Prediction of goal-directed behaviour: Attitudes, intentions, and perceived behavioural control.' *Journal of Experimental Social Psychology*, 22: 453–74.

Alder, B. (1994) 'Postnatal sexuality.' In P. Y. L. Choi and P. Nicolson (eds), *Female sexuality: Psychology, biology and social context*. London: Harvester Wheatsheaf.

Almond, L. and Harris, J. (1998) 'Interventions to promote health-related physical education.' In S. J. H. Biddle, J. F. Sallis and N. Cavill (eds), *Young and Active? Young people and health-enhancing physical activity: Evidence and implications* (pp. 133–49). London: Health Education Authority.

American Alliance for Health, P. E., Recreation, and Dance (1988) *Physical best*. Reston, Va.: AAHPERD.

American College of Sports Medicine (1978) 'Position statement on the recommended quantity and quality of exercise for developing and maintaining fitness in healthy adults.' *Medicine and Science in Sports*, 10: vii–x.

—— (1988) 'Opinion statement on physical fitness in children and youth.' *Medicine and Science in Sports and Exercise*, 20: 422–3.

—— (1990) 'Position Stand: The recommended quantity and quality of exercise for developing and maintaining cardiorespiratory and muscular fitness in healthy adults.' *Medicine and Science in Sports and Exercise*, 22: 265–74.

—— (1997a) *ACSM's exercise management for persons with chronic diseases and disabilities.* Champaign, Ill.: Human Kinetics.

—— (1997b) 'American College of Sports Medicine and American Diabetes Association joint position statement: Diabetes mellitus and exercise.' *Medicine and Science in Sports and Exercise*, 29 (12): i–vi.

—— (1998a) 'Position Stand: Exercise and physical activity for older adults.' *Medicine and Science in Sports and Exercise*, 30: 992–1008.

—— (1998b) 'Position Stand: The recommended quantity and quality of exercise for developing and maintaining cardiorespiratory and muscular fitness, and flexibility in healthy adults.' *Medicine and Science in Sports and Exercise*, 30: 975–91.

American Psychiatric Association (1980) *Diagnostic and statistical manual* (3rd edn). Washington, D.C.: APA.

—— (1994) *Diagnostic and statistical manual of mental disorders–IV*. Washington, D.C.: APA.

Ames, C. and Archer, J. (1988) 'Achievement goals in the classroom: Students' learning strategies and motivation strategies.' *Journal of Educational Psychology*, 80: 260–7.

Anderson, B. L. (1992) 'Psychological interventions for cancer patients to enhance quality of life.' *Journal of Consulting and Clinical Psychology*, 60: 552–8.

Andrew, G. M., Oldridge, N. B., Parker, J. O., Cunningham, D. A., Rechnitzer, P. A., Jones, N. L., Buck, C., Kavanagh, T., Shephard, R. J. and Sutton, J. R. (1981) 'Reasons for dropout from exercise programs in post-coronary patients.' *Medicine and Science in Sports and Exercise*, 13: 164–8.

Andrew, G. M. and Parker, J. O. (1979) 'Factors related to dropout of post myocardial infarction patients from exercise programs.' *Medicine and Science in Sports*, 11: 376–8.

Anspaugh, D. J., Hunter, S. and Dignan, M. (1996) 'Risk factors for cardiovascular disease among exercising versus nonexercising women.' *American Journal of Health Promotion*, 10(3): 171–4.

Arif, A. and Westermeyer, J. (1988) *Manual of drug and alcohol abuse guidelines for teaching in medical and health institutions*. New York: Plenum.

Ary, D. V., Toobert, D., Wilson, W. and Glascow, R. E. (1986) 'Patient perspectives on factors contributing to nonadherence to diabetes regimen.' *Diabetes Care*, 9: 168–72.

Ashford, B., Biddle, S. and Goudas, M. (1993) 'Participation in community sports centres: Motives and predictors of enjoyment.' *Journal of Sports Sciences*, 11: 249–56.

Astrand, P.-O. (1994) 'Physical activity and fitness: Evolutionary perspective and trends for the future.' In C. Bouchard, R. J. Shephard and T. Stephens (eds), *Physical activity, fitness, and health* (pp. 98–105). Champaign, Ill.: Human Kinetics.

Atkins, C. J., Kaplan, R. M., Timms, R. M., Reinsch, S. and Lofback, K. (1984) 'Behavioral exercise programs in the management of chronic obstructive pulmonary disease.' *Journal of Consulting and Clinical Psychology*, 52: 591–603.

Atkinson, R. L. and Walberg-Rankin, J. (1994) 'Physical activity, fitness, and severe obesity.' In C. Bouchard, R. J. Shephard and T. Stephens (eds), *Physical activity, fitness, and health* (pp. 696–711). Champaign, Ill.: Human Kinetics.

Bachman, G., Leiblum, S., Sandler, B., Ainsley, W., Narcissioan, R., Sheldon, R. and Nakajima, H. (1985) 'Correlates of sexual desire in post menopausal women.' *Maruritas*, 7: 211–16.

Baekeland, F. (1970) 'Exercise deprivation: Sleep and psychological reactions.' *Archives of General Psychiatry*, 22: 365–9.

Bailey, C. and Biddle, S. (1988) 'Community health-related physical fitness testing and the National Garden Festival Health Fair at Stoke-on-Trent.' *Health Education Journal*, 47: 144–7.

Bandura, A. (1977) 'Self-efficacy: Toward a unifying theory of behavioral change.' *Psychological Review*, 84: 191–215.

—— (1986) *Social foundations of thought and action: A social cognitive theory*. Englewood Cliffs, N.J.: Prentice-Hall.

—— (1990) 'Perceived self-efficacy in the exercise of personal agency.' *Journal of Applied Sport Psychology*, 2: 128–63.

—— (1997) *Self-efficacy: The exercise of control*. New York: W. H. Freeman.

Banks, A. and Waller, T. A. N. (1988) *Drug misuse: A practical handbook for GP's*. London: Blackwell Scientific.

Banks, M. A. (1989) 'Physiotherapy benefits patients with Parkinson's disease.' *Clinical Rehabilitation*, 3: 11–16.

Barker, D. J. P. and Rose, G. (1990) *Epidemiology in medical practice*. Edinburgh: Churchill Livingstone.

Barlow, D. H., Grosset, K. H., Hart, H. and Hart, D. M. (1989) 'A study of the experience of Glasgow women in the climacteric years.' *British Journal of Obstetrics and Gynaecology*, 96: 1192–7.

Bar-On, D. and Cristal, N. (1987) 'Causal attributions of patients, their spouses and physicians, and the rehabilitation of the patients after their first myocardial infarction.' *Journal of Cardiopulmonary Rehabilitation*, 7: 285–98.

Beck, A. T., Ward, C. H., Mendelsohn, M., Mock, J. and Erbaugh, H. (1961) 'An inventory for measuring depression.' *Archives of General Psychiatry*, 4: 561–71.

Beck, A. T., Weissman, M. and Kovacs, M. (1976) 'Alcoholism, hopelessness and suicidal behavior.' *Journal of Studies on Alcohol*, 37: 66–77.

Becker, M. H., Haefner, D. P., Kasl, S. V., Kirscht, J. P., Maiman, L. A. and Rosenstock, I. M. (1977) 'Selected psychosocial models and correlates of individual health-related behaviours.' *Medical Care*, 15 (supplement): 27–46.

Beesley, S. and Mutrie, N. (1997) 'Exercise is beneficial adjunctive treatment in depression.' *British Medical Journal*, 315: 1542.

Beh, H. C., Mathers, S. and Holden, J. (1996) 'EEG correlates of exercise dependency.' *International Journal of Psychophysiology*, 23: 121–8.

Belman, M. J. (1989) 'Exercise in chronic pulmonary obstructive disease.' In B. A. Franklin, G. Seymour and G. C. Timmis (eds), *Exercise in modern medicine* (pp. 175–91). Baltimore: Williams and Wilkins.

Bem, S. L. (1974) 'The measurement of psychological androgyny.' *Journal of Consulting and Clinical Psychology*, 42: 155–62.

Bentler, P. and Speckart, G. (1981) 'Attitudes "cause" behaviours: A structural equation analysis.' *Journal of Personality and Social Psychology*, 40: 226–38.

Berg, K. (1986) 'Metabolic disease: Diabetes mellitus.' In V. Seefeldt (ed.), *Physical activity and well-being* (pp. 425–40). Reston, Va.: American Alliance for Health, Physical Education, Recreation, and Dance.

Berryman, J. W. (2000) 'Exercise science and sports medicine: A rich history.' *Sports Medicine Bulletin*, 35(1): 8–9.

Biddle, S. (1992) 'Adherence to physical activity and exercise.' In N. Norgan (ed.), *Physical activity and health* (pp. 170–89). Cambridge: Cambridge University Press.

—— (1993) 'Attribution research and sport psychology.' In R. N. Singer, M. Murphey and L. K. Tennant (eds), *Handbook of research on sport psychology* (pp. 437–64). New York: Macmillan.

—— (1994a) 'Motivation and participation in exercise and sport.' In S. Serpa, J. Alves and V. Pataco (eds), *International perspectives on sport and exercise psychology* (pp. 103–26). Morgantown, W. Va.: Fitness Information Technology.

—— (1994b) 'What helps and hinders people becoming more physically active?' In A. J. Killoran, P. Fentem and C. Caspersen (eds), *Moving on: International perspectives on promoting physical activity* (pp. 110–48). London: Health Education Authority.

—— (1995a) 'Exercise and psychosocial health.' *Research Quarterly for Exercise and Sport*, 66: 292–97.

—— (2000) 'Exercise, emotions, and mental health.' In Y. L. Hanin (ed.), *Emotions in sport* (pp. 267–91). Champaign, Ill.: Human Kinetics.

Biddle, S., Akande, D., Armstrong, N., Ashcroft, M., Brooke, R. and Goudas, M. (1996) 'The self-motivation inventory modified for children: Evidence on psychometric properties and its use in physical exercise.' *International Journal of Sport Psychology*, 27: 237–50.

Biddle, S., Cury, F., Goudas, M., Sarrazin, P., Famose, J. P. and Durand, M. (1995) 'Development of scales to measure perceived physical education class climate: A cross-national project.' *British Journal of Educational Psychology*, 65: 341–58.

Biddle, S., Fox, K. and Edmunds, L. (1994a) *Physical activity promotion in primary health care in England*. London: Health Education Authority.

Biddle, S. and Goudas, M. (1996) 'Analysis of children's physical activity and its association with adult encouragement and social cognitive variables.' *Journal of School Health*, 66(2): 75–8.

Biddle, S., Goudas, M. and Page, A. (1994b) 'Social psychological predictors of self-reported actual and intended physical activity in a university workforce sample.' *British Journal of Sports Medicine*, 28: 160–3.

Biddle, S., Soos, I. and Chatzisarantis, N. (1999) 'Predicting physical activity intentions using a goal perspectives approach: A study of Hungarian youth.' *Scandinavian Journal of Medicine and Science in Sports*, 9: 353–7.

Biddle, S. J. H. (ed.) (1995b) *European perspectives on exercise and sport psychology*. Champaign, Ill.: Human Kinetics.

—— (1995c) 'Exercise motivation across the lifespan.' In S. J. H. Biddle (ed.), *European perspectives on exercise and sport psychology* (pp. 5–25). Champaign, Ill.: Human Kinetics.

—— (1997a) 'Cognitive theories of motivation and the physical self.' In K. R. Fox (ed.), *The physical self: From motivation to well-being* (pp. 59–82). Champaign, Ill.: Human Kinetics.

—— (1997b) 'Current trends in sport and exercise psychology research.' *The Psychologist: Bulletin of the British Psychological Society*, 10(2): 63–9.

—— (1999a) 'Adherence to sport and physical activity in children and youth.' In S. J. Bull (ed.), *Adherence issues in exercise and sport* (pp. 111–44). Chichester: John Wiley.

—— (1999b) 'Motivation and perceptions of control: Tracing its development and plotting its future in exercise and sport psychology.' *Journal of Sport and Exercise Psychology*, 21: 1–23.

Biddle, S. J. H. and Ashford, B. (1988) 'Cognitions and perceptions of health and exercise.' *British Journal of Sports Medicine*, 22: 135–40.

Biddle, S. J. H. and Chatzisarantis, N. (1999) 'Motivation for a physically active lifestyle through physical education.' In Y. Vanden Auweele, F. Bakker, S. Biddle, M. Durand and R. Seiler (eds), *Psychology for physical educators* (pp. 5–26). Champaign, Ill.: Human Kinetics.

Biddle, S. J. H. and Fox, K. R. (1989) 'Exercise and health psychology: Emerging relationships.' *British Journal of Medical Psychology*, 62: 205–16.

Biddle, S. J. H., Fox, K. R. and Boutcher, S. H. (eds) (2000) *Physical activity and psychological well-being*. London: Routledge.

Biddle, S. J. H., Hanrahan, S. J. and Sellars, C. (in press) 'Attributions: Past, present, and future.' In R. N. Singer, H. Hausenblas and C. Janelle (eds), *Handbook of sport psychology*. New York: Wiley.

Biddle, S. J. H. and Mutrie, N. (1991) *Psychology of physical activity and exercise: A health-related perspective*. London: Springer-Verlag.

Biddle, S. J. H., Sallis, J. F. and Cavill, N. (eds) (1998) *Young and active? Young people and health-enhancing physical activity: Evidence and implications*. London: Health Education Authority.

Biering-Sorensen, F. S., Bendix, T., Jorgensen, K., Manniche, C. and Nielsen, H. (1994) 'Physical activity, fitness, and back pain.' In C. Bouchard, R. J. Shephard and T. Stephens (eds), *Physical activity, fitness, and health* (pp. 724–36). Champaign, Ill.: Human Kinetics.

Birk, T. J. (1996) 'HIV and exercise.' *Exercise Immunology Review*, 2: 84–95.

Blair, S. (1993) 'CH McCloy Research Lecture: Physical activity, physical fitness and health.' *Research Quarterly for Exercise and Sport*, 64: 365–76.

Blair, S. N. (1988) 'Exercise within a healthy lifestyle.' In R. K. Dishman (ed.), *Exercise adherence: Its impact on public health* (pp. 75–89). Champaign, Ill.: Human Kinetics.

—— (1994) 'Physical activity, fitness, and coronary heart disease.' In C. Bouchard, R. J. Shephard and T. Stephens (eds), *Physical activity, fitness and health* (pp. 579–90). Champaign, Ill.: Human Kinetics.

Blair, S. N. and Brodny, S. (1999) 'Effects of physical inactivity and obesity on morbidity and mortality: Current evidence and research issues.' *Medicine and Science in Sports and Exercise*, 31(11: supplement): S646–S662.

Blair, S. N., Kohl, H. W. and Goodyear, N. N. (1987) 'Rates and risks for running and exercise injuries: Studies in three populations.' *Research Quarterly for Exercise and Sport*, 58: 221–8.

Blair, S. N., Kohl, H. W., Gordon, N. F. and Paffenbarger, R. S. (1992) 'How much physical activity is good for health?' *Annual Review of Public Health*, 13: 99–126.

Blair, S. N., Kohl, H. W., Paffenbarger, R. S., Clark, D. G., Cooper, K. H. and Gibbons, L. W. (1989) 'Physical fitness and all-cause mortality: A prospective study of healthy men and women.' *Journal of the American Medicial Association*, 262 (17): 2395–401.

Blamey, A., Mutrie, N. and Aitchison, T. (1995) 'Health promotion by encouraged use of stairs.' *British Medical Journal*, 311: 289–90.

Bluechardt, M. H., Wiener, J. and Shephard, R. J. (1995) 'Exercise programmes in the treatment of children with learning disabilities.' *Sports Medicine*, 19: 55–72.

Blumenthal, J. A., Williams, R. S., Wallace, A. G., Williams, R. B. and Needles, T. L. (1982)

'Physiological and psychological variables predict compliance to prescribed exercise therapy in patients recovering from myocardial infarction.' *Psychosomatic Medicine*, 44: 519–27.

Boer, H. and Seydel, E. R. (1996) 'Protection motivation theory.' In M. Conner and P. Norman (eds), *Predicting health behaviour: Research and practice with social cognition models* (pp. 95–120). Buckingham: Open University Press.

Booth, M. L., Macaskill, P., Owen, N., Oldenburg, B., Marcus, B. H. and Bauman, A. (1993) 'Population prevalence and correlates of stages of change in physical activity.' *Health Education Quarterly*, 20: 431–40.

Borg, G. (1998) *Borg's perceived exertion and pain scales*. Champaign, Ill.: Human Kinetics.

Bosscher, R. J. (1993) 'Running and mixed physical exercise with depressed psychiatric patients.' *International Journal of Sport Psychology*, 24: 170–84.

Bouchard, C. and Despres, J. P. (1995) 'Physical activity and health: Atherosclerotic, metabolic, and hypertensive diseases.' *Research Quarterly for Exercise and Sport*, 66: 268–75.

Bouchard, C. and Shephard, R. J. (1994) 'Physical acivity, fitness, and health: The model and key concepts.' In C. Bouchard, R. J. Shephard and T. Stephens (eds), *Physical activity, fitness, and health* (pp. 77–88). Champaign, Ill.: Human Kinetics.

Bouchard, C., Shephard, R. J. and Stephens, T. (eds) (1994) *Physical activity, fitness and health: International proceedings and consensus statement*. Champaign, Ill.: Human Kinetics.

Bouchard, C., Shephard, R. J., Stephens, T., Sutton, J. R. and McPerson, B. D. (eds) (1990) *Exercise, fitness and health: A consensus of current knowledge*. Champaign Ill.: Human Kinetics.

Boutcher, S. (1993) 'Emotion and aerobic exercise.' In R. N. Singer, M. Murphey and L. K. Tennant (eds), *Handbook of research on sport psychology* (pp. 799–814). New York: Macmillan.

Boutcher, S. H. (2000) 'Cognitive performance, fitness, and ageing.' In S. J. H. Biddle, K. R. Fox and S. H. Boutcher (eds), *Physical activity and psychological well-being* (pp. 118–29). London: Routledge.

Boutcher, S. H., McAuley, E. and Courneya, K. S. (1997) 'Positive and negative affective response of trained and untrained subjects during and after aerobic exercise.' *Australian Journal of Psychology*, 49: 28–32.

Bozoian, S., Rejeski, W. J. and McAuley, E. (1994) 'Self-efficacy influences feeling states associated with acute exercise.' *Journal of Sport and Exercise Psychology*, 16: 326–33.

Brawley, L. R. (1993) 'The practicality of using social psychological theories for exercise and health reserach and intervention.' *Journal of Applied Sport Psychology*, 5: 99–115.

Brehm, B. J. and Steffen, J. J. (1998) 'Relation between obligatory exercise and eating disorders.' *American Journal of Health Behavior*, 22(2): 108–19.

Brettschneider, W. D. (1992) 'Adolescents, leisure, sport and lifestyle.' In T. Williams, L. Almond and A. Sparkes (eds), *Sport and physical activity: Moving towards excellence* (pp. 536–50). London: Spon.

Brewer, B. W. (1993) *The dark side of exercise and mental health*. Paper presented at the 8th World Congress of Sport Psychology, Lisbon.

British Nutrition Foundation (1999) *Obesity: The report of the British Nutrition Foundation Task Force*. Oxford: Blackwell Science.

Brown, S. W., Welsh, M. C., Labbe, E. E., Vitulli, W. F. and Kulkarni, P. (1992) 'Aerobic exercise in the psychological treatment of adolescents.' *Perceptual and Motor Skills*, 74: 555–60.

Brownell, K. D., Stunkard, A. J. and Albaum, J. M. (1980) 'Evaluation and modification of exercise patterns in the natural environment.' *American Journal of Psychiatry*, 137: 1540–5.

Buonamano, R., Cei, A. and Missino, A. (1995) 'Participation motivation in Italian youth sport.' *The Sport Psychologist*, 9: 265–81.

Butler, C. C., Rollnick, S., Cohen, D., Bachmann, M., Russell, I. and Stott, N. (1999) 'Motivational consulting versus brief advice for smokers in general practice: A randomized trial.' *British Journal of General Practice*, 49: 611–16.

Buxton, K., Wyse, J. and Mercer, T. (1996) 'How applicable is the stages of change model to exercise behaviour? A review.' *Health Education Journal*, 55: 239–57.

Buxton, M. J., O'Hanlon, M. and Rushby, J. (1990) 'A new facility for the measurement of health-related quality of life.' *Health Policy*, 16: 199–208.

—— (1992) 'EuroQoL: A reply and reminder.' *Health Policy*, 20: 329–32.

Byrne, A. and Byrne, D. G. (1993) 'The effect of exercise on depression, anxiety and other mood states.' *Journal of Psychosomatic Research*, 37: 565–74.

Cacioppo, J. T., Gardner, W. and Berntson, G. G. (1999) 'The affect system has parallel and integrative processing components: Form follows function.' *Journal of Personality and Social Psychology*, 76: 839–55.

Calabrese, L. H. (1990) 'Exercise, immunity, cancer, and infection.' In C. Bouchard, R. J. Shephard, T. Stephens, J. R. Sutton and B. D. McPherson (eds), *Exercise, fitness and health* (pp. 567–79). Champaign, Ill.: Human Kinetics.

Calfas, K., Long, B., Sallis, J., Wooten, W., Pratt, M. and Patrick, K. (1996) 'A controlled trial of physician counseling to promote the adoption of physical activity.' *Preventive Medicine*, 25: 225–33.

Calfas, K. J., Sallis, J. F., Oldenburg, B. and Ffrench, M. (1997) 'Mediators of change in physical activity following an intervention in primary care: PACE.' *Preventive Medicine*, 26: 297–304.

Calfas, K. J. and Taylor, W. C. (1994) 'Effects of physical activity on psychological variables in adolescents.' *Pediatric Exercise Science*, 6: 406–23.

Camacho, T. C., Roberts, R. E., Lazarus, N. B., Kaplan, G. A. and Cohen, R. D. (1991) 'Physical activity and depression: Evidence from the Alameda county study.' *American Journal of Epidemiology*, 134: 220–31.

Cameron, J. and Pierce, D. (1994) 'Reinforcement, reward and intrinsic motivation: A meta-analysis.' *Review of Educational Research*, 64: 363–423.

Campbell, N., Grimshaw, J., Rawles, J. and Ritchie, L. (1994) 'Cardiac rehabilitation: The agenda set by post-myocardial infarction patients.' *Health Education Journal*, 53: 409–20.

Canada Fitness Survey (1983a) *Canadian youth and physical activity*. Ottawa: Canada Fitness Survey.

—— (1983b) *Fitness and lifestyle in Canada*. Ottawa: Canada Fitness Survey.

Cantu, R. C. (1982) *Diabetes and Exercise*. Ithaca, N.Y.: Mouvement.

Cardinal, B. J. and Sachs, M. L. (1995) 'Prospective analysis of stage-of-exercise movement following mail-delivered self-instructional exercise packets.' *American Journal of Health Promotion*, 9: 430–32.

Carmack, M. A. and Martens, R. (1979) 'Measuring commitment to running: A survey of runners' attitudes and mental states.' *Journal of Sport Psychology*, 1: 25–42.

Carpenter, D. M. and Nelson, B. W. (1999) 'Low back strengthening for the prevention and treatment of low back pain.' *Medicine and Science in Sports and Exercise*, 31: 18–24.

Carpenter, P. J., Scanlan, T. K., Simons, J. P. and Lobel, M. (1993) 'A test of the sport commitment model using structural equation modeling.' *Journal of Sport and Exercise Psychology*, 15, 119–33.

Carron, A. V. and Hausenblas, H. A. (1998) *Group dynamics in sport* (2nd edn). Morgantown, W. Va.: Fitness Information Technology.

Carron, A. V., Hausenblas, H. A. and Estabrooks, P. A. (1999) 'Social influence and exercise involvement.' In S. J. Bull (ed.), *Adherence issues in sport and exercise* (pp. 1–17). Chichester: Wiley.

Carron, A. V., Hausenblas, H. A. and Mack, D. (1996) 'Social influence and exercise: A meta-analysis.' *Journal of Sport and Exercise Psychology*, 18: 1–16.

Carron, A. V., Widmeyer, W. N. and Brawley, L. R. (1988) 'Group cohesion and individual adherence to physical activity.' *Journal of Sport and Exercise Psychology*, 10: 127–38.

Caspersen, C. J. (1989) 'Physical activity epidemiology: Concepts, methods, and applications to exercise science.' *Exercise and Sport Sciences Reviews*, 17: 423–73.

Caspersen, C. J., Merritt, R. K. and Stephens, T. (1994) 'International physical activity patterns: A methodological perspective.' In R. K. Dishman (ed.), *Advances in exercise adherence* (pp. 73–110). Champaign, Ill.: Human Kinetics.

Caspersen, C. J., Powell, K. E. and Christenson, G. M. (1985) 'Physical activity, exercise and physical fitness: Definitions and distinctions for health-related research.' *Public Health Reports*, 100: 126–31.

Cattell, R. B., Eber, H. W. and Tatsuoka, M. M. (1970) *Handbook of the 16PF questionnaire*. Champaign, Ill.: Institute of Personality and Ability Testing.

Centres for Disease Control and Prevention (1997) 'Guidelines for school and community programs to promote lifelong physical activity among young people.' *Morbidity and Mortality Weekly Report*, 46 (RR-6): 1–36.

Chaiken, S. (1980) 'Heuristic versus systematic information processing and the use of source versus message cues in persuasion.' *Journal of Personality and Social Psychology*, 39: 752–66.

Chamove, A. S. (1986) 'Positive short-term effects of activity on behaviour in chronic schizophrenic patients.' *British Journal of Clinical Psychology*, 25: 125–33.

Chaouloff, F. (1997) 'The serotonin hypothesis.' In W. P. Morgan (ed.), *Physical activity and mental health* (pp. 179–98). Washington, D.C.: Taylor and Francis.

Chatzisarantis, N. and Biddle, S. J. H. (1998) 'Functional significance of psychological variables that are included in the Theory of Planned Behaviour: A self-determination theory approach to the study of attitudes, subjective norms, perceptions of control, and intentions.' *European Journal of Social Psychology*, 28: 303–22.

—— (1999) 'A self-determination theory approach to the boundary conditions of the theories of reasoned action and planned behaviour in exercise and sport: Theoretical extensions using meta-analysis.' Manuscript in review.

Chatzisarantis, N., Biddle, S. J. H. and Meek, G. A. (1997) 'A self-determination theory approach to the study of intentions and the intention-behaviour relationship in children's physical activity.' *British Journal of Health Psychology*, 2: 343–60.

Chelladurai, P. (1993) 'Leadership.' In R. N. Singer, M. Murphey and L. K. Tennant (eds), *Handbook of research on sport psychology* (pp. 647–71). New York: Macmillan.

Chelladurai, P. and Saleh, S. (1980) 'Dimensions of leader behavior in sports: Development of a leadership scale.' *Journal of Sport Psychology*, 2: 34–45.

Choi, P. Y. L. and Salmon, P. (1995) 'Symptom changes across the menstrual cycle in competitive sportswomen, exercisers and sedentary women.' *British Journal of Clinical Psychology*, 34: 447–60.

Chow, R., Harrison, J. E. and Notarius, C. (1987) 'Effect of two randomized exercise programmes on bone mass of healthy postmenopausal women.' *British Medical Journal*, 295, 1441–4.

Cleary, J. (1996) *Safe routes to school project: Findings of schools survey*. Bristol: Sustrans.

Clore, G. L., Ortony, A. and Foss, M. A. (1987) 'The psychological foundations of the affective lexicon.' *Journal of Personaity and Social Psychology*, 53: 751–66.

Coakley, J. and White, A. (1992) 'Making decisions: Gender and sport participation among British adolescents.' *Sociology of Sport Journal*, 9: 20–35.

Coggins, A., Swanston, D. and Crombie, H. (1999) *Physical activity and inequalities: A briefing paper*. London: Health Education Authority.

Comella, C., Stebbins, G., Toms, N. and Goetz, C. (1994) 'Physical therapy and Parkinson's disease: A controlled clinical trial.' *Neurology*, 44: 376–8.

Conner, M. and Armitage, C. (1998) 'Extending the theory of planned behavior: A review and avenues for further research.' *Journal of Applied Social Psychology*, 28: 1429–64.

Conner, M. and Norman, P. (1994) 'Comparing the Health Belief Model and the Theory of Planned Behaviour in health screening.' In D. R. Rutter and L. Quine (eds), *Social psychology and health: European perspectives* (pp. 1–24). Aldershot: Avebury.

—— (eds) (1996) *Predicting health behaviour*. Buckingham: Open University Press.

Conner, M. and Sparks, P. (1996) 'The theory of planned behaviour and health behaviours.' In M. Conner and P. Norman (eds), *Predicting health behaviour* (pp. 121–62). Buckingham: Open University Press.

Corbin, C. B. (1984) 'Self confidence of females in sports and physical activity.' *Clinics in Sports Medicine*, 3: 895–908.

Corbin, C. B., Nielsen, A. B., Borsdorf, L. L. and Laurie, D. R. (1987) 'Commitment to physical activity.' *International Journal of Sport Psychology*, 18: 215–22.

Corbin, C. B., Whitehead, J. R. and Lovejoy, P. (1988) 'Youth physical fitness awards.' *Quest*, 40: 200–18.

Cowart, V. S. (1989) 'Can exercise help women with PMS?' *The Physician and Sportsmedicine*, 17(4): 169–78.

Cowles, E. (1898) 'Gymnastics in the treatment of inebriety.' *American Physical Education Review*, 3: 107–10.

Craft, L. L. and Landers, D. M. (1998) 'The effect of exercise on clinical depression and depression resulting from mental illness: A meta-analysis.' *Journal of Sport and Exercise Psychology*, 20: 339–57.

Crammer, S. R., Neiman, D. and Lee, J. (1991) 'The effects of moderate exercise training on psychological well-being and mood state in women.' *Journal of Psychosomatic Research*, 35: 437–49.

Crews, D. J. and Landers, D. M. (1987) 'A meta-analytic review of aerobic fitness and reactivity to psychosocial stressors.' *Medicine and Science in Sports and Exercise*, 19 (5: supplement): S114–S120.

Csikszentmihalyi, M. (1975) *Beyond boredom and anxiety*. San Francisco: Jossey-Bass.

Davies, D. G., Halliday, M. E., Mayes, M. and Pocok, R. L. (1997) *Attitudes to cycling – A qualitative and conceptual framework: Report 266, Transport Research Laboratory*. London: Crowthorne.

Davis, A. (1999) *Active transport: A guide to the development of local initiatives to promote walking and cycling*. London: Health Education Authority.

Davis, C., Brewer, H. and Ratusny, D. (1993) 'Behavioral frequency and psychological commitment: Necessary concepts in the study of excessive exercising.' *Journal of Behavioral Medicine*, 16: 611–28.

Davis, C., Kaptein, S., Kaplan, A. S., Olmsted, M. P. and Woodside, D. B. (1998) 'Obsessionality in anorexia nervosa: The moderating influence of exercise.' *Psychosomatic Medicine*, 60: 192–7.

De Bourdeauhuij, I. (1998) 'Behavioural factors associated with physical activity in young people.' In S. Biddle, J. Sallis and N. Cavill (eds), *Young and active? Young people and health-enhancing physical activity: Evidence and implications* (pp. 98–118). London: Health Education Authority.

De Bourdeaudhuij, I. and Van Oost, P. (1999) 'A cluster-analytical appoach toward physical activity and other health-related behaviors.' *Medicine and Science in Sports and Exercise*, 31: 605–12.

Dearing, R. (1994) *The National Curriculum and its assessment: Final report*. London: School Curriculum and Assessment Authority.

deCharms, R. (1968) *Personal causation*. New York: Academic Press.

Deci, E. (1992) 'On the nature and functions of motivation theories.' *Psychological Science*, 3: 167–71.

Deci, E., Eghrari, H., Patrick, B. C. and Leone, D. R. (1994) 'Facilitating internalisation: The Self-Determination Theory perspective.' *Journal of Personality*, 62, 119–42.

Deci, E. L. (1975) *Intrinsic motivation*. New York: Plenum.

Deci, E.L. and Flaste, R. (1995) *Why we do what we do: Understanding self-motivation*. New York: Penguin.

Deci, E. L., Koestner, R. and Ryan, R. M. (1999) 'A meta-analytic review of experiments examing the effects of extrinsic rewards on intrinsic motivation.' *Psychological Bulletin*, 125: 627–68.

Deci, E. L. and Ryan, R. M. (1985) *Intrinsic motivation and self-determination in human behavior*. New York: Plenum Press.

—— (1991) 'A motivational approach to self: Integration in personality.' In R. A. Dienstbier (ed.), *Nebraska symposium on motivation: Perspectives on motivation* (vol. 38, pp. 237–88) Lincoln, Nebr.: University of Nebraska Press.

Department of the Environment, Transport and the Regions (1998) *A new deal for transport – better for everyone: The Government's White Paper on the future of transport*. London: The Stationery Office.

Department of Health (1993a) *Better living, better life*. Henley: Knowledge House.

—— (1993b) *The Health of the Nation: A strategy for health for England*. London: HMSO.

—— (1995) *Obesity: Reversing the increasing problem of obesity in England*. London: Department of Health.

—— (1998) *Our healthier nation: A contract for health*. London: The Stationery Office.

Department of Health and Human Services (1980) *Promoting health/Preventing disease: Objectives for the nation*. Washington, D.C.: US Goverment Printing Office.

—— (1986) *Midcourse review: 1990 physical fitness and exercise objectives*. Washington, D.C.: US Government Printing Office.

—— (1991) *Healthy people 2000: National health promotion and disease prevention objectives* (DHHS Pub. No. PHS 91–50212) Washington, D.C.: US Government Printing Office.

—— (1996) *Physical activity and health: A report of the Surgeon General*. Atlanta, Ga.: Centres for Disease Control and Prevention.

—— (1997) 'Guidelines for school and community programs to promote lifelong physical activity among young people.' *Morbidity and Mortality Weekly Report*, 46 (7 March): 1–36.

—— (1999) *Promoting physical activity: A guide for community action*. Champaign, Ill.: Human Kinetics.

Derogatis, L. R., Lipman, R. S. and Covi, L. (1973) 'The SCL-90: An outpatient psychiatric rating scale.' *Psychopharmacology Bulletin*, 9: 13–28.

Desharnais, R., Bouillon, J. and Godin, G. (1986) 'Self-efficacy and outcome expectations as determinants of exercise adherence.' *Psychological Reports*, 59: 1155–9.

Diener, E. (1999) 'Introduction to the special section on the structure of emotion.' *Journal of Personality and Social Psychology*, 76: 803–4.

Dishman, R., Ickes, W. and Morgan, W. (1980) 'Self-motivation and adherence to habitual physical activity.' *Journal of Applied Social Psychology*, 10: 115–32.

Dishman, R., Oldenburg, B., O'Neal, H. and Shephard, R. J. (1998) 'Worksite physical activity interventions.' *American Journal of Preventive Medicine*, 15: 344–61.

Dishman, R. K. (1981) 'Biologic influences on exercise adherence.' *Research Quarterly for Exercise and Sport*, 52: 143–59.

—— (1982) 'Compliance/adherence in health-related exercise.' *Health Psychology*, 1: 237–67.

—— (1987) 'Exercise adherence and habitual physical activity.' In W. P. Morgan and S. E. Morgan (eds), *Exercise and mental health* (pp. 57–83). Washington: Hemisphere.

—— (1988a) 'Behavioral barriers to health-related physical fitness.' In L. K. Hall and G. C. Meyer (eds), *Epidemiology, behavior change, and intervention in chronic disease* (pp. 49–83). Champaign, Ill.: Life Enhancement Publications.

—— (ed.) (1988b) *Exercise adherence: Its impact on public health.* Champaign, Ill.: Human Kinetics.

—— (1990) 'Determinants of participation in physical activity.' In C. Bouchard, R. J. Shephard, T. Stephens, J. R. Sutton and B. D. McPherson (eds), *Exercise, fitness, and health* (pp. 75–101). Champaign, Ill.: Human Kinetics.

—— (1993) 'Exercise adherence.' In R. N. Singer, M. Murphey and L. K. Tennant (eds), *Handbook of research on sport psychology* (pp. 779–98). New York: Macmillan.

—— (1994a) 'Consensus, problems and prospects.' In R. K. Dishman (ed.), *Advances in exercise adherence* (pp. 1–27). Champaign, Ill.: Human Kinetics.

—— (1994b) 'The measurement conundrum in exercise adherence research.' *Medicine and Science in Sports and Exercise*, 26: 1382–90.

—— (1995) 'Physical activity and public health: Mental health.' *Quest*, 47: 362–85.

—— (1997) 'The norepinephrine hypothesis.' In W. P. Morgan (ed.), *Physical activity and mental health* (pp. 199–212). Washington, D.C.: Taylor and Francis.

Dishman, R. K. and Buckworth, J. (1996) 'Increasing physical activity: A quantitative synthesis.' *Medicine and Science in Sports and Exercise*, 28: 706–19.

—— (1997) 'Adherence to physical activity.' In W. P. Morgan (ed.), *Physical activity and mental health* (pp. 63–80). Washington, D.C.: Taylor and Francis.

Dishman, R. K. and Dunn, A. L. (1988) 'Exercise adherence in children and youth: Implications for adulthood.' In R. K. Dishman (ed.), *Exercise adherence: Its impact on public health* (pp. 155–200). Champaign, Ill.: Human Kinetics.

Dishman, R. K. and Gettman, L. (1980) 'Psychobiologic influences on exercise adherence.' *Journal of Sport Psychology*, 2: 295–310.

Dishman, R. K. and Ickes, W. (1981) 'Self-motivation and adherence to therapeutic exercise.' *Journal of Behavioral Medicine*, 4: 421–38.

Dishman, R. K. and Landy, F. J. (1988) 'Psychological factors and prolonged exercise.' In D. R. Lamb and R. Murray (eds), *Perspectives in exercise science and sports medicine: I. Prolonged exercise* (pp. 281–355). Indianapolis, Ind.: Benchmark Press.

Dishman, R. K. and Sallis, J. F. (1994) 'Determinants and interventions for physical activity and exercise.' In C. Bouchard, R. J. Shephard and T. Stephens (eds), *Physical activity, fitness, and health* (pp. 203–13). Champaign, Ill.: Human Kinetics.

Dishman, R. K., Sallis, J. F. and Orenstein, D. (1985) 'The determinants of physical activity and exercise.' *Public Health Reports*, 100: 158–71.

Dishman, R. K. and Steinhardt, M. (1990) 'Health locus of control predicts free-living, but not supervised physical activity: A test of exercise-specific control and outcome-expectancy hypotheses.' *Research Quarterly for Exercise and Sport*, 61: 383–94.

Dixon, P., Heaton, J., Long, A. and Warburton, A. (1994) 'Reviewing and applying the SF-36.' *Outcomes Briefing*, 4: 3–25.

Doan, R. E. and Scherman, A. (1987) 'The therapeutic effect of physical fitness on measures of personality: A literature review.' *Journal of Counselling and Development*, 66: 28–36.

Doganis, G. and Theodorakis, Y. (1995) 'The influence of attitude on exercise participation.' In S. J. H. Biddle (ed.), *European perspectives on exercise and sport psychology* (pp. 26–49). Champaign, Ill.: Human Kinetics.

Doganis, G., Theodorakis, Y. and Bagiatis, K. (1991) 'Self-esteem and locus of control in adult female fitness program participants.' *International Journal of Sport Psychology*, 22: 154–64.

Donaghy, M. and Mutrie, N. (1997) 'Physical self-perception of problem drinkers on entry to an alcohol rehabilitation programme.' *Physiotherapy*, 83(7): 358.

—— (1998) 'A randomized controlled study to investigate the effect of exercise on the physical self-perceptions of problem drinkers.' *Physiotherapy*, 84(4): 169.

Donaghy, M., Ralston, G. and Mutrie, N. (1991) 'Exercise as a therapeutic adjunct for problem drinkers' (abstract). *Journal of Sports Sciences*, 9: 440.

Dong, W. and Erins, B. (1997) *Scottish Health Survey 1995*. Edinburgh: The Stationery Office.

Donovan, R. J. and Owen, N. (1994) 'Social marketing and population interventions.' In R. K. Dishman (ed.), *Advances in Exercise Adherence* (pp. 249–90). Champaign, Ill.: Human Kinetics.

Doyne, E. J., Ossip-Klein, D. J., Bowman, E., Osborn, K. M., McDougall-Wilson, I. B. and Neimeyer, R. A. (1987) 'Running versus weightlifting in the treatment of depression.' *Journal of Consulting and Clinical Psychology*, 55: 748–54.

Drinkwater, B. L. (1994) 'Physical activity, fitness, and osteoporosis.' In C. Bouchard, R. J. Shephard and T. Stephens (eds), *Physical activity, fitness, and health* (pp. 724–36). Champaign, Ill.: Human Kinetics.

Duda, J. L. (1993) 'Goals: A social cognitive approach to the study of achievement motivation in sport.' In R. N. Singer, M. Murphey and L. K. Tennant (eds), *Handbook of research on sport psychology* (pp. 421–36). New York: Macmillan.

Duda, J. L. and Whitehead, J. (1998) 'Measurement of goal perspectives in the physical domain.' In J. L. Duda (ed.), *Advances in sport and exercise psychology measurement* (pp. 21–48). Morgantown, W. Va.: Fitness Information Technology.

Dugmore, D. (1992) 'Exercise and heart disease.' In K. Williams (ed.), *The community prevention of coronary heart disease* (pp. 43–58). London: HMSO.

Dummer, G., Rosen, L., Heusner, W., Roberts, P. and Counsilman, J. (1987) 'Pathogenic weight control behaviors of young competitive swimmers.' *The Physician and Sportsmedicine*, 15(5): 75–84.

Dunn, A., Marcus, B., Kampert, J., Garcia, M., Kohl, H. and Blair, S. (1999) 'Comparison of lifestyle and structured interventions to increase physical activity and cardiorespiratory fitness: a randomized trial.' *Journal of the American Medical Association*, 281(4): 327–34.

Dunn, A. L. (1996) 'Getting started: A review of physical activity adoption strategies.' *British Journal of Sports Medicine*, 30: 193–9.

Dunn, A. L. and Dishman, R. K. (1991) 'Exercise and the neurobiology of depression.' *Exercise and Sport Sciences Reviews*, 19: 41–98.

Dunn, A. L., Garcia, M. E., Marcus, B. H., Kampert, J. B., Kohl, H. W. and Blair, S. N. (1998) 'Six-month physical activity and fitness changes in Project Active, a randomized trial.' *Medicine and Science in Sports and Exercise*, 30: 1076–83.

Dunn, A. L., Marcus, B. H., Kampert, J. B., Garcia, M. E., Kohl, H. W. and Blair, S. N. (1997) 'Reduction in cardiovascular disease risk factors: 6-months results from Project Active.' *Preventive Medicine*, 26: 883–92.

Dunn, S. W. (1993) 'Psychological aspects of diabetes in adults.' In S. Maes, H. Leventhal and M. Johnston (eds), *International Review of Health Psychology* (vol. 2, pp. 175–97). London: John Wiley.

Durnin, J. V. G. A. (1990) 'Assessment of physical activity during leisure and work.' In C. Bouchard, R. J. Shephard, T. Stephens, J. R. Sutton and B. D. McPherson (eds), *Exercise, fitness, and health* (pp. 63–70). Champaign, Ill.: Human Kinetics.

Dweck, C. (1992) 'The study of goals in psychology.' *Psychological Science*, 3: 165–7.

—— (1996) 'Implicit theories as organizers of goals and behavior.' In P. Gollwitzer and J. Bargh (eds), *The Psychology of action* (pp. 69–90). New York: Guilford Press.

Dweck, C. S. (1980) 'Learned helplessness in sport.' In C. H. Nadeau, W. R. Halliwell, K. M. Newell and G. C. Roberts (eds), *Psychology of motor behavior and sport – 1979* (pp. 1–11). Champaign, Ill.: Human Kinetics.

—— (1999) *Self-theories: Their role in motivation, personality, and development*. Philadelphia, Pa.: Taylor and Francis.

Dweck, C. S., Chiu, C. Y. and Hong, Y. Y. (1995) 'Implicit theories and their role in judgments and reactions: A world from two perspectives.' *Psychological Inquiry*, 6: 267–85.

Dweck, C. S. and Leggett, E. (1988) 'A social-cognitive approach to motivation and personality.' *Psychological Review*, 95: 256–73.

Dwyer, T., Coonan, W. E., Leitch, D. R., Hetzel, B. S. and Baghurst, R. A. (1983) 'An investigation of the effects of daily physical activity on the health of primary school students in South Australia.' *International Journal of Epidemiology*, 12: 308–13.

Dzewaltowski, D. A. (1989) 'Toward a model of exercise motivation.' *Journal of Sport and Exercise Psychology*, 11: 251–69.

—— (1994) 'Physical activity determinants: A social cognitive approach.' *Medicine and Science in Sports and Exercise*, 26: 1395–9.

Dzewaltowski, D. A., Noble, J. M. and Shaw, J. M. (1990) 'Physical activity participation: Social cognitive theory versus the theories of reasoned action and planned behavior.' *Journal of Sport and Exercise Psychology*, 12: 388–405.

Eadie, D. R. and Leathar, D. S. (1988) *Concepts of fitness and health: An exploratory study*. Edinburgh: Scottish Sports Council.

Edwards, W. (1954) 'The theory of decision making.' *Psychological Bulletin*, 51: 380–417.

Eiser, J. R. (1986) *Social psychology*. Cambridge: Cambridge University Press.

—— (1994) *Attitudes, chaos and the connectionist mind*. Oxford: Blackwell.

Eiser, J. R. and van der Pligt, J. (1988) *Attitudes and decisions*. London: Routledge.

Ekkekakis, P. and Petruzzello, S. J. (1999) 'Acute aerobic exercise and affect: Current status, problems and prospects regarding dose-response.' *Sports Medicine*, 28: 337–74.

—— (in press-a) 'Analysis of the affect measurement conundrum in exercise psychology: I. Fundamental issues.' *Psychology of Sport and Exercise*, 1: 71–88.

—— (in press-b) 'Analysis of the affect measurement conundrum in exercise psychology: II. Conceptual and methodological critique of the Exercise-induced Feeling Inventory.' *Psychology of Sport and Exercise*.

—— (in press-b) 'Analysis of the affect measurement conundrum in exercise psychology: III. Conceptual and methodological critique of the Subjective Exercise Experiences Scale.' *Psychology of Sport and Exercise*.

Engstrom, L.-M. (1991) 'Exercise adherence in sport for all from youth to adulthood.' In P. Oja and R. Telama (eds), *Sport for all* (pp. 473–83). Amsterdam: Elsevier.

Epling, W. F. and Pierce, W. D. (1988) 'Activity-based anorexia: A biobehavioral perspective.' *International Journal of Eating Disorders*, 7: 475–85.

Epstein, L. H., Koeske, R. and Wing, R. R. (1984) 'Adherence to exercise in obese children.' *Journal of Cardiac Rehabilitation*, 4: 185–95.

Etnier, J. L., Salazar, W., Landers, D. M., Petruzzello, S. J., Han, M. and Nowell, P. (1997) 'The influence of physical fitness and exercise upon cognitive functioning: A meta-analysis.' *Journal of Sport and Exercise Psychology*, 19: 249–77.

Ewart, C. (1989) 'Psychological effects of resistive weight training: Implications for cardiac patients.' *Medicine and Science in Sports and Exercise*, 21: 683–88.

Ewart, C. E., Stewart, K. J., Gillilan, R. E. and Kelemen, M. H. (1986) 'Self-efficacy mediates strength gains during circuit weight training in men with coronary artery disease.' *Medicine and Science in Sports and Exercise*, 18: 531–40.

Ewart, C. E., Taylor, C. B., Reese, L. B. and DeBusk, R. F. (1983) 'Effects of early post myocardial infarction exercise testing on self perception and subsequent physical activity.' *American Journal of Cardiology*, 51: 1076–80.

Ewart, C. K. (1997) 'Role of physical self-efficacy in recovery from heart attack.' In R. Schwarzer (ed.), *Self-efficacy: Thought control of action* (pp. 287–304). Bristol, Pa.: Taylor and Francis.

Eysenck, H. J. and Eysenck, S. (1963) *Manual of the Eysenck Personality Inventory*. San Diego, Calif.: Educational and Industrial Testing Service.

Fagard, R. H. and Tipton, C. M. (1994) 'Physical activity, fitness, and hypertension.' In C. Bouchard, R. J. Shephard and T. Stephens (eds), *Physical activity, fitness, and health* (pp. 633–55). Champaign, Ill.: Human Kinetics.

Falloon, I. R. H. and Talbot, R. E. (1981) 'Persistent auditory hallucinations: Coping mechanisms and implications for management.' *Psychological Medicine*, 11: 329–39.

Farmer, M., Locke, B., Moscicki, E., Dannenberg, A., Larson, D. and Radloff, L. (1988) 'Physical activity and depressive symptoms: The NHANES-I epidemiological follow-up study.' *American Journal of Epidemiology*, 128, 1340–51.

Faulkner, G. and Biddle, S. (1999) 'Exercise as an adjunct treatment for schizophrenia: A review of literature.' *Journal of Mental Health*, 8: 441–57.

Faulkner, G. and Sparkes, A. (1999) 'Exercise as therapy for schizophrenia: An ethnographic study.' *Journal of Sport and Exercise Psychology*, 21:52–69.

Fehily, A. (1999) 'Epidemiology of obesity in the UK.' In British Nutrition Foundation (ed.), *Obesity* (pp. 23–36). Oxford: Blackwell Scientific.

Feltz, D. (1992) 'Understanding motivation in sport: A self-efficacy perspective.' In G. C. Roberts (ed.), *Motivation in Sport and Exercise* (pp. 93–105). Champaign, Ill.: Human Kinetics.

Feltz, D. L. (1988) 'Self-confidence and sports performance.' *Exercise and Sport Sciences Reviews*, 16: 423–57.

Fentem, P. H., Bassey, E. J. and Turnbull, N. B. (1988) *The new case of exercise*. London: Sports Council and Health Education Authority.

FEPSAC (1996) 'Position Statement of the European Federation of Sport Psychology: II. Children in sport.' *The Sport Psychologist*, 10: 224–6.

Fishbein, M. and Ajzen, I. (1975) *Belief, attitude, intention and behaviour: An introduction to theory and research*. Reading, Mass.: Addison-Wesley.

Fiske, S. T. and Taylor, S. E. (1991) *Social cognition*. New York: McGraw-Hill.

Flegal, K. M. (1999) 'The obesity epidemic in children and adults: Current evidence and research issues.' *Medicine and Science in Sports and Exercise*, 31(11: supplement), S509–S514.

Fletcher, G. F., Blair, S. N., Blumenthal, J., Caspersen, C., Chaitman, B., Epstein, S., Falls, H., Froelicher, S. S., Froelicher, V. F. and Pina, I. L. (1992) 'Statement of exercise: Benefits and recommendations for physical activity programs for all Americans.' *Circulation*, 86: 340–4.

Forsterling, F. (1988) *Attribution theory in clinical psychology*. Chichester: Wiley.

Fortier, M. S., Vallerand, R. J., Briere, N. M. and Provencher, P. J. (1995) 'Competitive and recreational sport structures and gender: A test of their relationship with sport motivation.' *International Journal of Sport Psychology*, 26: 24–39.

Fox, K., Biddle, S., Edmunds, L., Bowler, I. and Killoran, A. (1997) 'Physical activity promotion through primary health care in England.' *British Journal of General Practice*, 47: 367–9.

Fox, K., Goudas, M., Biddle, S., Duda, J. and Armstrong, N. (1994) 'Children's task and ego goal profiles in sport.' *British Journal of Educational Psychology*, 64: 253–61.

Fox, K. R. (1990) *The physical self-perception profile manual*. DeKalb, Ill.: Office of Health Promotion, Northern Illinois University.

—— (1992) 'A clinical approach to exercise in the severely obese.' In T. A. Wadden and T. B. Van Itallie (eds), *Treatment of severe obesity by diet and lifestyle modication* (pp. 354–82). New York: Guilford Press.

—— (1997a) 'The physical self and processes in self-esteem development.' In K. R. Fox (ed.), *The physical self: From motivation to well-being* (pp. 111–39). Champaign, Ill.: Human Kinetics.

—— (ed.) (1997b) *The physical self: From motivation to well-being*. Champaign, Ill.: Human Kinetics.

—— (1998) 'Advances in the measurement of the physical self.' In J. L. Duda (ed.), *Advances in sport and exercise psychology measurement* (pp. 295–310). Morgantown, W. Va.: Fitness Information Technology.

—— (1999a) 'Aetiology of obesity XI: Physical inactivity.' In British Nutrition Foundation (ed.), *Obesity* (pp. 116–31). Oxford: Blackwell Scientific.

—— (1999b) 'Treatment of obesity III: Physical activity and exercise.' In British Nutrition Foundation (ed.), *Obesity* (pp. 165–75). Oxford: Blackwell Scientific.

—— (2000) 'The effects of exercise on self-perceptions and self-esteem.' In S. J. H. Biddle, K. R. Fox and S. H. Boutcher (eds), *Physical activity and psychological well-being* (pp. 88–117). London: Routledge.

Fox, K. R. and Corbin, C. B. (1989) 'The Physical Self Perception Profile: Development and preliminary validation.' *Journal of Sport and Exercise Psychology*, 11: 408–30.

Frankel, A. and Murphy, J. (1974) 'Physical fitness and personality in alcoholism: Canonical analysis of measures before and after treatment.' *Quarterly Journal of Studies on Alcohol*, 35: 1271–8.

Franklin, B. (1988) 'Program factors that influence exercise adherence: Practical adherence skills for the clinical staff.' In R. K. Dishman (ed.), *Exercise adherence: Its impact on public health.* (pp. 237–58). Champaign, Ill.: Human Kinetics.

Fremont, J. and Craighead, L. W. (1987) 'Aerobic exercise and cognitive therapy in the treatment of dyshoric moods.' *Cognitive Therapy and Research*, 11: 241–51.

Friedenrich, C. M. and Courneya, K. S. (1996) 'Exercise as rehabilitation for cancer patients.' *Clinical Journal of Sports Medicine*, 6: 237–44.

Frost, H., Klaber-Moffett, J. A., Moser, J. S. and Fairbank, J. C. T. (1995) 'Randomized controlled trial for evaluation of a fitness programme for patients with chronic low back pain.' *British Medical Journal*, 310: 151–4.

Fruin, D., Pratt, C. and Owen, N. (1991) 'Protection motivation theory and adolescents' perceptions of exercise.' *Journal of Applied Social Psychology*, 22: 55–69.

Gannon, L. (1988) 'The potential role of exercise in the alleviation of menstrual disorders and menopausal symptoms: A theoretical synthesis of recent research.' *Women and Health*, 14(2): 105–27.

Gary, V. and Guthrie, D. (1972) 'The effects of jogging on physical fitness and self-concept in hospitalized alcoholics.' *Quarterly Journal of Studies on Alcoholism*, 33: 1073–8.

Gauvin, L. and Rejeski, W. J. (1993) 'The Exercise-Induced Feeling Inventory: Development and initial validation.' *Journal of Sport and Exercise Psychology*, 15: 403–23.

George, T. and Feltz, D. (1995) 'Motivation in sport from a collective efficacy perspective.' *International Journal of Sport Psychology*, 26: 98–116.

Gettman, L. R. (1996) 'Economic benefits of physical activity.' *The President's Council on Physical Fitness and Sports Physical Activity and Fitness Research Digest*, 2 (7): 1–6.

Giacca, A., Qing Shi, Z., Marliss, E. B., Zinman, B. and Vranic, M. (1994) 'Physical activity, fitness, and Type I diabetes.' In C. Bouchard, R. J. Shephard and T. Stephens (eds), *Physical activity, fitness, and health* (pp. 656–68). Champaign, Ill.: Human Kinetics.

Gibberd, F. B., Page, N. G. R., Spencer, K. M., Kinnear, E. and Hawksworth, J. B. (1981) 'Controlled trial of physiotherapy and occupational therapy for Parkinson's disease.' *British Medical Journal*, 282: 1196.

Gillies, F. C., Hughes, A. R., Kirk, A. F., Mutrie, N., McCann, G., Hillis, W. S. and MacIntyre, P. D. (2000) 'Exercise consultation: An intervention to improve adherence to phase IV cardiac rehabilitation?' *British Journal of Sports Medicine*, 34: 148.

Glasser, W. (1976) *Positive addiction*. New York: Harper and Row.

Gleser, J. and Mendelberg, H. (1990) 'Exercise and sport in mental health: A review of the literature.' *Israel Journal of Psychiatry and Related Sciences*, 27: 99–112.

Gloag, D. (1985) 'Rehabilitation of patients with cardiac conditions.' *British Medical Journal*, 290: 617–20.

Godin, G. (1993) 'The theories of reasoned action and planned behavior: Overview of findings, emerging research problems and usefulness for exercise promotion.' *Journal of Applied Sport Psychology*, 5: 141–57.

—— (1994) 'Social-cognitive models.' In R. K. Dishman (ed.), *Advances in exercise adherence* (pp. 113–36). Champaign, Ill.: Human Kinetics.

Godin, G. and Shephard, R. J. (1983) 'Physical fitness promotion programmes: Effectiveness in modifying exercise behaviour.' *Canadian Journal of Applied Sports Sciences*, 8: 104–13.

—— (1986a) 'Importance of type of attitude to the study of exercise behaviour.' *Psychological Reports*, 58: 991–1000.

—— (1986b) 'Psychosocial factors influencing intentions to exercise of young students from grades 7 to 9.' *Research Quarterly for Exercise and Sport*, 57: 41–52.

Godin, G., Valois, P., Shephard, R. J. and Desharnais, R. (1987) 'Prediction of leisure time exercise behaviour: A path analysis (LISREL V) model.' *Journal of Behavioral Medicine*, 10: 145–58.

Goldberg, D. P., Cooper, B., Eastwood, M. R., Kedward, H. B. and Shephard, M. (1970) 'A standardized psychiatric interview for use in community surveys.' *British Journal of Preventive and Social Medicine*, 24: 18–23.

Gordon, J. and Grant, G. (1997) *How we feel*. London: Jessica Kingsley.

Gordon, N. F. (1993a) *Arthritis: Your complete exercise guide*. Champaign, Ill.: Human Kinetics.

—— (1993b) *Breathing disorders: Your complete exercise guide*. Champaign, Ill.: Human Kinetics.

Goudas, M. and Biddle, S. (1994) 'Perceived motivational climate and intrinsic motivation in school physical education classes.' *European Journal of Psychology of Education*, 9: 241–50.

Goudas, M., Biddle, S. and Fox, K. (1994a) 'Achievement goal orientations and intrinsic motivation in physical fitness testing with children.' *Pediatric Exercise Science*, 6: 159–67.

—— (1994b) 'Perceved locus of causality, goal orientations, and perceived competence in school physical education classes.' *British Journal of Educational Psychology*, 64: 453–63.

Goudas, M., Biddle, S., Fox, K. and Underwood, M. (1995) 'It ain't what you do, it's the way that you do it! Teaching style affects children's motivation in track and field lessons.' *The Sport Psychologist*, 9: 254–64.

Gould, D. (1987) 'Understanding attrition in children's sport.' In D. Gould and M. Weiss (eds), *Advances in pediatric sport sciences: II. Behavioural issues* (pp. 61–85). Champaign, Ill.: Human Kinetics.

Gould, D. and Petlichkoff, L. (1988) 'Participation motivation and attrition in young athletes.' In F. L. Smoll, R. A. Magill and M. J. Ash (eds), *Children in sport* (pp. 161–78). Champaign, Ill.: Human Kinetics.

Gould, M. M., Thorogood, M., Iliffe, S. and Morris, J. N. (1995) 'Promoting physical activity in primary care: Measuring the knowledge gap.' *Health Education Journal*, 54: 304–11.

Grealy, M. A., Johnston, D. A. and Rushton, S. K. (1999) 'Improving cognitive functioning following brain injury: The use of exercise and virtual reality.' *Archives of Physical Medicine and Rahabilitation*, 80: 661–7.

Green, D. P., Salovey, P. and Truax, K. M. (1999) 'Static, dynamic, and causative bipolarity of affect.' *Journal of Personality and Social Psychology*, 76: 856–67.

Greene, J. G. (1991) *Guide to the Greene Climacteric Scale*. Glasgow: University of Glasgow.

Greist, J. H., Klein, M. H., Eischens, R. R., Faris, J. W., Gurman, A. S. and Morgan, W. P. (1979) 'Running as a treatment for depression.' *Comprehensive Psychiatry*, 20: 41–54.

—— (1981) 'Running through your mind.' In M. H. Sacks and M. L. Sachs (eds), *Psychology of running* (pp. 5–31). Champaign, Ill.: Human Kinetics.

Griffin, N. S. and Keogh, J. F. (1982) 'A model of movement confidence.' In J. A. S. Kelso and J. E. Clark (eds), *The development of movement control and co-ordination* (pp. 213–36). New York: Wiley.

Gruber, J. J. (1986) 'Physical activity and self-esteem development in children: A meta-analysis.' In G. A. Stull and H. M. Eckert (eds), *Effects of physical activity on children* (pp. 30–48). Champaign, Ill.: Human Kinetics.

Grundy, S. M., Blackburn, G., Higgins, M., Lauer, R., Perri, M. G. and Ryan, D. (1999) 'Physical activity in the prevention and treatment of obesity and its comorbidities.' *Medicine and Science in Sports and Exercise, 31* (11: supplement): S502–508.

Gudat, U., Berger, M. and Lefebvre, P. J. (1994) 'Physical activity, fitness, and non-insulin-dependent (Type II) diabetes mellitus.' In C. Bouchard, R. J. Shephard and T. Stephens (eds), *Physical activity, fitness and health* (pp. 669–83). Champaign, Ill.: Human Kinetics.

HMI. (1989) *Physical education from 5 to 16*. London: HMSO.

Hackfort, D. (1994) 'Health and wellness: A sport psychology perspective.' In S. Serpa, J. Alves and V. Pataco (eds), *International perspectives on sport and exercise psychology* (pp. 165–83). Morgantown, W. Va.: Fitness Information Technology.

Haisch, J., Rduch, G. and Haisch, I. (1985) 'Long-term effects of attribution therapy measures in the obese: Effects of attribution training on successful slimming and dropout rate in a 23-week weight reduction programme.' *Psychotherapy, Medicine and Psychology*, 35: 133–40.

Hale, A. S. (1997) 'ABC of mental disorders: Depression.' *British Medical Journal*, 315: 43–6.

Hall, D. C. and Kaufmann, D. A. (1987) 'Effects of aerobic and strength conditioning on pregnancy outcomes.' *American Journal of Obstetrics and Gynecology*, 157: 1199–1203.

Hamilton, M. (1960) 'A rating scale for depression.' *Journal of Neurosurgical Psychiatry*, 23: 56–61.

Hardy, C. J., Hall, E. G. and Prestholdt, P. H. (1986) 'The mediational role of social influence in the perception of exertion.' *Journal of Sport Psychology*, 8: 88–104.

Hardy, C. J. and Rejeski, W. J. (1989) 'Not what, but how one feels: The measurement of affect during exercise.' *Journal of Sport and Exercise Psychology*, 11: 304–17.

Harland, J., White, M., Drinkwater, C., Chinn, D., Farr, L. and Howel, D. (1999) 'The Newcastle exercise project: A randomized controlled trial of methods to promote physical activity in primary care.' *British Medical Journal*, 319: 828–32.

Harris, B., Rohaly, K. and Dailey, J. (1993) *Mid-life women and exercise: A qualitative study*. Paper presented at the 12th Congress of the International Association of Physical Education and Sport for Girls and Women, Melbourne, Australia.

Harris, D. V. (1973) *Involvement in sport: A somatopsychic rationale for physical activity*. Philadelphia: Lea and Febiger.

Harris, J. and Cale, L. (1997) 'How healthy is school PE? A review of the effectiveness of health-related physical education programmes in schools.' *Health Education Journal*, 56: 84–104.

Harrison, J. A., Mullen, P. D. and Green, L. W. (1992) 'A meta-analysis of studies of the Health Belief Model with adults.' *Health Education Research: Theory and Practice*, 7: 107–16.

Hart, E. A., Leary, M. R. and Rejeski, W. J. (1989) 'The measurement of social physique anxiety.' *Journal of Sport and Exercise Psychology*, 11: 94–104.

Harter, S. (1978) 'Effectance motivation reconsidered: Toward a developmental model.' *Human Development*, 21: 34–64.

—— (1985) *Manual for the self-perception profile for children*. Denver, Colo.: University of Denver.

Harter, S. and Connell, J. P. (1984) 'A model of children's achievement and related self perceptions of competence, control and motivational orientations.' In J. G. Nicholls (ed.), *Advances in motivation and achievement. III. The development of achievement motivation* (pp. 219–50). Greenwich, Conn.: JAI Press.

Harter, S. and Pike, R. (1983) *Procedural manual to accompany the Pictorial Scale of Perceived Competence and Social Acceptance for Young Children*. Denver, Colo.: University of Denver.

Hasler, T., Fisher, B. M., MacIntyre, P. D. and Mutrie, N. (1997) 'A counseling approach for increasing physical activity for patients attending a diabetic clinic.' *Diabetic Medicine*, 4: S3–4.

Hathaway, S. R. and McKinley, J. C. (1943) *Minnesota Multiphasic Personality Inventory*. New York: Psychological Corporation.

Hausenblas, H., Carron, A. V. and Mack, D. E. (1997) 'Application of the Theories of Reasoned Action and Planned Behavior to exercise behavior: A meta-analysis.' *Journal of Sport and Exercise Psychology*, 19: 36–51.

Health Education Authority (1995a) *Becoming more active: A guide for health professionals*. London: Health Education Authority.

—— (1995b) *Promoting physical activity: Guidance for commissioners, purchasers and providers*. London: Health Education Authority.

Health Education Authority and Sports Council (1988) *Children's exercise, health and fitness: Fact sheet*. London: Health Education Authority and Sports Council.

Heartbeat Wales (1987) *Exercise for health: Health-related fitness in Wales. Heartbeat report 23*. Cardiff: Heartbeat Wales.

Heather, N., Roberston, I. and Davies, P. (1985) *The misuse of alcohol: Crucial issues in dependance treatment and prevention*. London: Croom Helm.

Helmrick, S. P., Ragland, D. R., Leung, R. W. and Paffenbarger, R. S. (1991) 'Physical activity and reduced occurences of non-insulin-dependent diabetes mellitus.' *New England Journal of Medicine*, 325: 147–52.

Hendry, L. B., Shucksmith, J. and Cross, J. (1989) 'Young people's mental well-being in relation to leisure.' In Health Promotion Research Trust (ed.), *Fit for life* (pp. 129–53). Cambridge: Health Promotion Research Trust.

Higgins, M. W. (1989) 'Chronic airways disease in the United States: Trends and determinants.' *Chest*, 96: 328s–334s.

Hill, A. B. (1965) 'The environment and disease: Association or causation?' *Proceedings of the Royal Society of Medicine*, 58: 295–300.

Hill, J. O., Drougas, H. J. and Peters, J. C. (1994) 'Physical activity, fitness, and moderate obesity.' In C. Bouchard, R. J. Shephard and T. Stephens (eds), *Physical activity, fitness, and health* (pp. 684–95). Champaign, Ill.: Human Kinetics.

Hillsdon, M. and Thorogood, M. (1996) 'A systematic review of physical activity promotion strategies.' *British Journal of Sports Medicine*, 30: 84–9.

HMSO. (1992) *Scotland's Health – a challenge to us all: A policy statement*. Edinburgh: Scottish Office.

Hochstetler, S. A., Rejeski, W. J. and Best, D. L. (1985) 'The influence of sex-role orientation on ratings of preceived exertion.' *Sex Roles*, 12: 825–35.

Hoffmann, P. (1997) 'The endorphin hypothesis.' In W. P. Morgan (ed.), *Physical activity and mental health* (pp. 163–77). Washington, D.C.: Taylor and Francis.

Hofstetter, C. R., Hovell, M. F., Macera, C., Sallis, J. F., Spry, V., Barrington, E., Callender, L., Hackley, M. and Rauh, M. (1991) 'Illness, injury and correlates of aerobic exercise and walking: A community study.' *Reserach Quarterly for Exercise and Sport*, 62: 1–9.

Holgate, S. T. (1993) 'Asthma: Past, present, and future.' *European Respiratory Journal*, 6: 1507–20.

Holmes, D. S. (1993) 'Aerobic fitness and the response to psychosocial stress.' In P. Seraganian (ed.), *Exercise psychology: The influence of physical exercise on psychological processes* (pp. 39–63). New York: John Wiley.

Horne, J. A. (1981) 'The effects of exercise upon sleep: A critical review.' *Biological Psychology*, 12: 241–90.

Hospers, H. J., Kok, G. and Strecher, V. J. (1990) 'Attributions for previous failures and subsequent outcomes in a weight reduction program.' *Health Education Quarterly*, 17: 409–15.

Hovland, C. I. and Rosenberg, M. J. (eds) (1960) *Attitudes, organisation and change: An analysis of consistency among attitude components.* New Haven, Conn.: Yale University Press.

Hunt, S. M., McEwan, J. and McKenna, S. P. (1986) *Measuring health status.* London: Croom Helm.

Hunter, M., Battersby, R. and Whitehead, M. (1986) 'Relationships between psychological symptoms, somatic complaints and menopausal status.' *Maturitas*, 8: 217–88.

Hunter, M. and Whitehead, M. (1989) 'Psychological experience of the climacteric and post menopause.' *Progress in Clinical and Biological Research*, 320: 211–24.

Hyman, G. P. (1987) *The role of exercise in the treatment of substance abuse.* Unpublished MS thesis, Pennsylvania State University.

Iannos, M. and Tiggeman, M. (1997) 'Personality of the excessive exerciser.' *Personality and Individual Differences*, 22: 775–8.

Inger, F. and Dahl, H. A. (1979) 'Dropouts from an endurance training programme: Some histochemical and physiological aspects.' *Scandinavian Journal of Sports Sciences*, 1: 20–2.

Ingledew, D. K., Markland, D. and Medley, A. R. (1998) 'Exercise motives and stages of change.' *Journal of Health Psychology*, 3: 477–89.

Israel, R. G., Sutton, M. and O'Brien, K. F. (1985) 'Effects of aerobic training on primary dysmenorrhea symptomatology in college females.' *Journal of the Amercian College of Health*, 33: 241–4.

Iverson, D. C., Fielding, J. E., Crow, R. S. and Christenson, G. M. (1985) 'The promotion of physical activity in the United States population: The status of programs in medical, worksite, community, and school settings.' *Public Health Reports*, 100: 212–14.

Jankowski, L. W. and Sullivan, S. J. (1990) 'Aerobic and neuromuscular training: Effect on the capacity, efficiency, and fatigability of patients with traumatic brain injuries.' *Archives of Physical Medicine and Rehabilitation*, 71: 500–4.

Janz, N. K. and Becker, M. H. (1984) 'The Health Belief Model: A decade later.' *Health Education Quarterly*, 11: 1–47.

Jette, A. M., Smith, K., Haley, S. M. and Davis, K. D. (1994) 'Physical therapy episodes of care for patients with low back pain.' *Physical Therapy*, 74: 101–10.

Juneau, M., Rogers, F., DeSantos, V., Yee, M., Evans, A. and Bohn, A. (1987) 'Effectiveness of self-monitored, home-based, moderate intensity exercise training in middle-aged men and women.' *American Journal of Cardiology*, 60: 66–70.

Kaman, R. L. and Patton, R. W. (1994) 'Costs and benefits of an active versus an inactive society.' In C. Bouchard, R. J. Shephard and T. Stephens (eds), *Physical activity, fitness, and health* (pp. 134–44). Champaign, Ill.: Human Kinetics.

Kanis, J., Aaron, J., Thavarajah, M., McCluskey, E. V., O'Doherty, D., Hamdy, N. A. T. and Bickerstaff, D. (1990) 'Osteoporosis: Causes and therapeutic implications.' In R. Smith (ed.), *Osteoporosis* (pp. 45–56). London: Royal College of Physicians.

Kaplan, G. A., Roberts, R. E., Camacho, T. C. and Coyne, J. C. (1987) 'Psychosocial predictors of depression.' *American Journal of Epidemiology*, 125: 206–20.

Kaplan, R. M., Atkins, C. J. and Reinsch, S. (1984) 'Specific efficacy expectations mediate exercise compliance in patients with COPD.' *Health Psychology*, 3: 223–42.

Kasimatis, M., Miller, M. and Macussen, L. (1996) 'The effects of implicit theories on exercise motivation.' *Journal of Research in Personality*, 30: 510–16.

Kavale, K. and Mattson, P. D. (1983) '"One jumped off the balance beam": Meta-analysis of perceptual-motor training.' *Journal of Learning Disabilities*, 16: 165–73.

Kearney, J. M., de Graaf, C., Damkjaer, S. and Engstrom, L. M. (1999) 'Stages of change towards physical activity in a nationally representative sample in the European Union.' *Public Health Nutrition*, 2 (1a): 115–24.

Kelly, M. P. and Mutrie, N. (1997) 'Exercise and health promotion.' *Sport, Exercise and Injury*, 3: 76–9.

Kendzierski, D. (1988) 'Self-schemata and exercise.' *Basic and Applied Social Psychology*, 9: 45–59.

—— (1990a) 'Decision-making vs. decision implementation: An action control approach to exercise adoption and adherence.' *Journal of Applied Social Psychology*, 20: 27–45.

—— (1990b) 'Exercise self-schemata: Cognitive and behavioral correlates.' *Health Psychology*, 9: 69–82.

—— (1994) 'Schema Theory: An information processing focus.' In R. K. Dishman (ed.), *Advances in exercise adherence* (pp. 137–60). Champaign, Ill.: Human Kinetics.

Kendzierski, D. and DeCarlo, K. J. (1991) 'Physical activity enjoyment scale: Two validation studies.' *Journal of Sport and Exercise Psychology*, 13: 50–64.

Kendzierski, D. and LaMastro, V. (1988) 'Reconsidering the role of attitudes in exercise behaviour: A decision theoretic approach.' *Journal of Applied Social Psychology*, 18: 737–59.

Kenyon, G. S. (1968) 'Six scales for assessing atitudes toward physical activity.' *Reserach Quarterly*, 39: 566–74.

Kidane, F. (1995) 'South Africa: United by sport.' *Olympic Review*, 25 (4): 24–5; 27.

Killoran, A., Cavill, N. and Walker, A. (1994) 'Who needs to know what? An investigation of the -characteristics of the key target groups for the effective promotion of physical activity in England.' In A. Killoran, P. Fentem and C. Caspersen (eds), *Moving on: International perspectives on promoting physical activity* (pp. 149–69). London: Health Education Authority.

Kimiecik, J. (1992) 'Predicting vigorous physical activity of corporate employees: Comparing theories of reasoned action and planned behavior.' *Journal of Sport and Exercise Psychology*, 14: 192–206.

Kimiecik, J. C. and Harris, A. T. (1996) 'What is enjoyment? A conceptual/definitional analysis with implications for sport and exercise psychology.' *Journal of Sport and Exercise Psychology*, 18: 247–63.

Kimiecik, J. C. and Stein, G. L. (1992) 'Examining flow experiences in sport contexts: Conceptual issues and methodological concerns.' *Journal of Applied Sport Psychology*, 4: 144–60.

King, A. C. (1991) 'Community intervention for promotion of physical activity and fitness.' *Exercise and Sport Sciences Reviews*, 19: 211–59.

—— (1994) 'Are community-wide programmes likely to be effective in getting the message across? Lessons from abroad.' In A. J. Killoran, P. Fentem and C. Caspersen (eds), *Moving on: International perspectives on promoting physical activity* (pp. 170–93). London: Health Education Authority.

King, A. C., Blair, S. N., Bild, D. E., Dishman, R. K., Dubbert, P. M., Marcus, B. H., Oldridge, N. B., Paffenbarger, R. S., Powell, K. E. and Yeager, K. K. (1992) 'Determinants of physical activity and interventions in adults.' *Medicine and Science in Sports and Exercise*, 24 (6: supplement), S221–S236.

King, A. C. and Frederiksen, L. W. (1984) 'Low-cost strategies for increasing exercise behaviour: Relapse prevention training and social support.' *Behavior Modification*, 8: 3–21.

King, A. C., Sallis, J. F., Dunn, A. L., Simons-Morton, D. G., Albright, C. A., Cohen, S., Rejeski, W. J., Marcus, B. H. and Coday, M. C. (1998) 'Overview of activity counseling trial (ACT) intervention or promoting physical activity in primary health care settings.' *Medicine and Science in Sports and Exercise*, 30: 1086–96.

King, A. C., Taylor, C. B., Haskell, W. L. and DeBusk, R. F. (1989) 'Influence of regular aerobic exercise on psychological health: A randomized, controlled trial of healthy middle-aged adults.' *Health Psychology*, 8: 305–24.

King, A. J. C. and Coles, B. (1992) *The health of Canada's youth*. Canada: Ministry of Supply and Services.

King, J. B. (1982) 'The impact of patients' perceptions of high blood pressure on attendance at screening: An extension of the health belief model.' *Social Science and Medicine*, 16: 1079–91.

Kirk, A. F., Higgins, L., Hughes, A. R., Mutrie, N., Fisher, M., McLean, J. and MacIntyre, P. (2000) *The effectiveness of exercise consultation on promotion of physical activity in a group of type 2 diabetes patients: A pilot study. Medicine and Science in Sport and Exercise*, 32 (Supplement): 177.

Kirkendall, D. R. (1986) 'Effects of physical activity on intellectual development and academic performance.' In G. A. Stull and H. M. Eckert (eds), *Effects of physical activity on children* (pp. 49–63). Champaign, Ill.: Human Kinetics and American Academy of Physical Education.

Klaber Moffet, J., Torgerson, D., Bell-Syer, S., Jackson, D., Llewlyn-Phillips, H., Farrin, A. and Barber, J. (1999) 'Randomized control trial of exercise for low back pain: Clinical outcomes, costs, and preferences.' *British Medical Journal*, 319: 279–83.

Klaber Moffet, J. A., Richardson, G., Sheldon, T. A. and Maynard, A. (1995) *Back Pain: Its management and cost to society*. York: Centre for Health Economics.

Klein, M. J., Griest, J. H., Gurman, A. S., Neimeyer, R. A., Lesser, D. P., Bushnell, N. J. and Smith, R. E. (1985) 'A comparative outcome study of group psychotherapy vs. exercise treatments for depression.' *International Journal of Mental Health*, 13: 148–77.

Knapp, D. N. (1988) 'Behavioral management techniques and exercise promotion.' In R. K. Dishman (ed.), *Exercise adherence: Its impact on public health* (pp. 203–35). Champaign, Ill.: Human Kinetics.

Koltyn, K. F. (1997) 'The thermogenic hypothesis.' In W. P. Morgan (ed.), *Physical activity and mental health* (pp. 213–26). Washington, D.C.: Taylor and Francis.

Koplan, J. P., Siscovick, D. S. and Goldbaum, G. M. (1985) 'The risks of exercise: A public health view of injuries and hazards.' *Public Health Reports*, 100: 189–95.

Kraus, H. and Raab, W. (1961) *Hypokinetic disease*. Springfield, Ill.: C.C. Thomas.

Kriska, A. M., Bayles, C., Cauley, J. A., Laporte, R. E., Sandler, R. B. and Pambianco, G. (1986) 'A randomized exercise trial in older women: Increased activity over two years and the factors associated with compliance.' *Medicine and Science in Sports and Exercise*, 18: 557–62.

Kubitz, K. A. and Landers, D. M. (1993) 'The effects of aerobic training on cardiovascular responses to mental stress: An examination of underlying mechanisms.' *Journal of Sport and Exercise Psychology*, 15: 326–37.

Kubitz, K. A., Landers, D. M., Petruzzello, S. J. and Han, M. (1996) 'The effects of acute and chronic exercise on sleep: A meta-analytic review.' *Sports Medicine*, 21: 277–91.

Kugler, J., Seelbach, H. and Kruskemper, G. (1994) 'Effects of rehabilitation exercise programmes on anxiety and depression in coronary patients: A meta-analysis.' *British Journal of Clinical Psychology*, 33: 401–10.

Kuhl, J. (1985) 'Volitional mediators of cognition-behaviour consistency: Self-regulatory processes and action versus state orientation.' In J. Kuhl and J. Beckmann (eds), *Action control: From cognition to behaviour* (pp. 101–28). Berlin: Springer-Verlag.

Kuroda, K. K., Tatara, K., Takatorige, T. and Shinsho, F. (1992) 'Effect of physical exercise on mortality in patients with Parkinson's disease.' *Acta Neurologica Scandinavia*, 86: 55–9.

Kurtz, Z. (1992) *With health in mind*. London: Action for Sick Children.

La Forge, R. (1995) 'Exercise-associated mood alterations: A review of interactive neurobiological mechanisms.' *Medicine, Exercise, Nutrition and Health*, 4: 17–32.

Lacasse, Y., Wong, E., Guyat, G. H., King, D., Cook, D. J. and Goldstein, R. S. (1996) 'Meta-analysis of respiratory rehabilitation in chronic obstructive pulmonary disease.' *Lancet*, 348: 1115–19.

Laitakari, J. and Asikainen, T. (1998) 'How to promote physical activity through individual counselling: A proposal for a practical model of counselling on health-related physical activity.' *Patient Education and Counselling*, 33: S13–S24.

LaPerriere, A. R., Antoni, M. H., Schneiderman, N., Ironson, G., Klimas, N., Caralis, P. and Fletcher, M. (1990) 'Exercise intervention attenuates emotional distress and natural killer cell decrements following notification of positive serological status for HIV-1.' *Biofeedback and Self Regulation*, 15: 229–242.

LaPerriere, A. R., Fletcher, M. A., Antoni, M. H., Klimas, N. G., Ironson, G. and Schneiderman, N. (1991) 'Arobic exercise training in an AIDS risk group.' *International Journal of Sports Medicine*, 12 (1: supplement), S53–S57.

LaPorte, R. E., Montoye, H. J. and Caspersen, C. J. (1985) 'Assessment of physical activity in epidemiological research: Problems and prospects.' *Public Health Reports*, 100: 131–46.

Law, M. and Tang, J. L. (1995) 'An analysis of the effectiveness of interventions intended to help people stop smoking.' *Archives of Internal Medicine*: 155: 1933–41.

Lawless, D., Jackson, C. and Greenleave, J. (1995) 'Exercise and human imunodeficiency virus (HIV-1) infection.' *Sports Medicine*, 19: 235–9.

Lazarus, R. S. (1991) *Emotion and adaptation*. New York: Oxford University Press.

Leary, M., R. (1992) 'Self presentational processes in exercise and sport.' *Journal of Sport and Exercise Psychology*, 14: 339–51.

—— (1995) *Self-presentation: Impression management and interpersonal behavior*. Dubuque, Iowa: Wm C. Brown.

Leary, M. R., Tchividjian, L. R. and Kraxberger, B. E. (1994) 'Self-presentation can be hazardous to your health: Impression management and health risk.' *Health Psychology*, 13: 461–70.

Lee, I. M. (1994) 'Physical activity, fitness, and cancer.' In C. Bouchard, R. J. Shephard and T. Stephens (eds), *Physical activity, fitness and health* (pp. 814–31). Champaign, Ill.: Human Kinetics.

—— (1995) 'Exercise and physical health: Cancer and immune function.' *Research Quarterly for Exercise and Sport*, 66: 286–91.

Leith, L. (1994) *Foundations of exercise and mental health*. Morgantown, W. Va.: Fitness Information Technology.

Leith, L. and Taylor, A. H. (1990) 'Psychological aspects of exercise: A decade literature review.' *Journal of Sport Behavior*, 13, 219–39.

Lenney, E. (1977) 'Women's self-confidence in achievement situations.' *Psychological Bulletin*, 84: 1–13.

Leon, A. S. (ed.) (1997) *Physical activity and cardiovascular health*. Champaign, Ill.: Human Kinetics.

Lepper, M. R. and Greene, D. (1975) 'Turning play into work: Effects of adult surveillance and extrinsic rewards on children's intrinsic motivation.' *Journal of Personality and Social Psychology*, 31: 479–86.

Lepper, M. R., Greene, D. and Nisbett, R. E. (1973) 'Undermining children's intrinsic interest with extrinsic reward: A test of the "overjustification" hypothesis.' *Journal of Personality and Social Psychology*, 28: 129–37.

Levine, M. D., Marcus, M. D. and Moulton, P. (1996) 'Exercise in the treatment of binge eating disorders.' *International Journal of Eating Disorders*, 19: 171–7.

Levy, S. R., Stroessner, S. J. and Dweck, C. S. (1998) 'Stereotype formation and endorsement: The role of implicit theories.' *Journal of Personality and Social Psychology*, 74: 1421–36.

Lewis, F. M. and Daltroy, L. H. (1990) 'How causal explanations influence behavior: Attribution theory.' In K. Glanz, F. M. Lewis and B. K. Rimer (eds), *Health behavior and health education* (pp. 92–114). San Francisco, Calif.: Jossey-Bass.

Lindsay, R., Aitken, J. M., Anderson, J. B., Hart, D. M., MacDonald, E. B. and Clarke, A. (1976) 'Long term prevention of postmenopausal osteoporosis by oestrogen.' *Lancet*, 1 (7968): 1038–41.

Lindsay-Reid, E. and Osborn, R. W. (1980) 'Readiness for exercise adoption.' *Social Science and Medicine*, 14: 139–46.

Lirgg, C. (1991) 'Gender differences in self-confidence in physical activity: A meta-analysis of recent studies.' *Journal of Sport and Exercise Psychology*, 13: 294–310.

Liska, A. E. (1984) 'A critical examination of the causal structure of the Fishbein/Ajzen attitude-behaviour model.' *Social Psychology Quarterly*, 47: 61–74.

Lokey, E. A., Tran, Z. V., Wells, C. L., Myers, B. C. and Tran, A. C. (1991) 'Effects of exercise on pregnancy outcomes: A meta-analytic review.' *Medicine and Science in Sports and Exercise*, 23: 1234–9.

Long, B., Calfas, K. J., Wooten, W., Sallis, J. F., Patrick, K., Goldstein, M., Marcus, B. H., Schwenk, T. L., Chenoworth, J., Carter, R., Torres, T., Palinkas, L. A. and Heath, G. (1996) 'A multisite field test of the acceptibility of physical activity counseling in primary care: Project PACE.' *American Journal of Preventive Medicine*, 12 (2): 73–81.

Long, B. C. and Haney, C. J. (1986) 'Enhancing physical activity in sedentary women: Information locus of control and attitudes.' *Journal of Sport Psychology*, 8: 8–24.

Long, B. C. and van Stavel, R. (1995) 'Effects of exercise training on anxiety: A meta-analysis.' *Journal of Applied Sport Psychology*, 7: 167–89.

Lorr, M. and McNair, D. M. (1984) *Profile of Mood States, Bipolar Form*. San Diego, Calif.: Educational and Industrial Testing Service.

Lorr, M., Shi, A. Q. and Youniss, R. P. (1989) 'A bipolar multifactor conception of mood states.' *Personality and Individual Differences*, 10: 155–9.

Loughlan, C. and Mutrie, N. (1995) 'Conducting an exercise consultation: Guidelines for health professionals.' *Journal of the Institute of Health Education*, 33(3): 78–82.

——— (1997) 'A comparison of three interventions to promote physical activity: Fitness assessment, exercise counseling, and information provision.' *Health Education Journal*, 56: 154–65.

Lowery, B. J. and Jacobsen, B. S. (1985) 'Attributional analysis of chronic illness outcomes.' *Nursing Research*, 34: 82–8.

Lowther, M., Mutrie, N., Laughlan, C. and McFarlane, C. (1999a) 'Development of a Scottish physical activity questionnaire: A tool for use in physical activity interventions.' *British Journal of Sports Medicine*, 33: 244–9.

Lowther, M., Mutrie, N. and Scott, M. (1999b) 'Attracting the general public to physical activity interventions: A comparison of fitness assessment and exercise consultations' (abstract). *Journal of Sports Sciences*, 17: 62–3.

Lox, C. L., McAuley, E. and Tucker, R. S. (1995) 'Exercise as an intervention for enhancing subjective well-being in an HIV-1 population.' *Journal of Sport and Exercise Psychology*, 17: 345–62.

Lubin, B. (1965) 'Adjective checklists for measurement of depression.' *Archives of General Psychiatry*, 12: 57–62.

McArthur, R. D., Levine, S. D. and Berk, T. J. (1993) 'Supervised exercise training improves cardiopulmonary fitness in HIV infected persons.' *Medicine and Science in Sports and Exercise*, 25: 648–88.

McAuley, E. (1991) 'Efficacy, attributional,and affective responses to exercise participation.' *Journal of Sport and Exercise Psychology*, 13: 382–93.

——— (1992) 'Understanding exercise behavior: A self-efficacy perspective.' In G. C. Roberts (ed.), *Motivation in Sport and Exercise* (pp. 107–27). Champaign, Ill.: Human Kinetics.

McAuley, E. and Courneya, K. (1994) 'The Subjective Exercise Experiences Scale (SEES): Development and preliminary validation.' *Journal of Sport and Exercise Psychology*, 16: 163–77.

McAuley, E. and Courneya, K. S. (1993) 'Adherence to exercise and physical activity as health-promoting behaviors: Attitudinal and self-efficacy influences.' *Applied and Preventive Psychology*, 2: 65–77.

McAuley, E., Duncan, T. and Russell, D. (1992) 'Measuring causal attributions: The Revised Causal Dimension Scale (CDSII).' *Personality and Social Psychology Bulletin*, 18: 566–73.

McAuley, E. and Mihalko, S. L. (1998) 'Measuring exercise-related self-efficacy.' In J. L. Duda (ed.), *Advances in sport and exercise psychology measurement* (pp. 371–90). Morgantown, W. Va.: Fitness Information Technology.

McAuley, E., Poag, K., Gleason, A. and Wraith, S. (1990) 'Attrition from exercise programs: Attributional and affective perspectives.' *Journal of Social Behavior and Personality*, 5: 591–602.

McCann, I. L. and Holmes, D. S. (1984) 'Influence of aerobic exercise on depression.' *Journal of Personality and Social Psychology*, 46: 1142–7.

McCready, M. L. and Long, B. C. (1985) 'Locus of control, attitudes toward physical activity, and exercise adherence.' *Journal of Sport Psychology*, 7: 346–59.

McDonald, D. G. and Hodgdon, J. A. (1991) *Psychological effects of aerobic fitness training: Research and theory*. New York: Springer-Verlag.

McEntee, D. J. and Halgin, R. P. (1996) 'Therapist's attitudes about addressing the role of exercise in psychotherapy.' *Journal of Clinical Psychology*, 52: 48–60.

McGuire, W. J. (1969) 'The nature of attitudes and attitude change.' In G. Lindzey and E. Aronson (eds), *Handbook of social psychology: Vol III* (pp. 136–314). Reading, Mass.: Addison-Wesley.

McKenzie, T. L., Nader, P. R., Strikmiller, P. K., Yang, M., Stone, E. J., Perry, C. L., Taylor, W. C., Epping, J. N., Feldman, H. A., Luepker, R. V. and Kelder, S. H. (1996) 'School physical education: Effect of the Child and Adolescent Trial for Cardiovascular Health.' *Preventive Medicine*, 25: 423–31.

McKenzie, T. L., Sallis, J. F., Kolody, B. and Faucette, F. N. (1997) 'Long-term effects of a physical education curriculum and staff development program: SPARK.' *Research Quarterly for Exercise and Sport*, 68: 280–91.

Mackinnon, L. T. (1989) 'Exercise and natural killer cells: What is the relationship?' *Sports Medicine*, 7: 141–9.

MacMahon, J. R. and Gross, R. T. (1987) 'Physical and psychological effects of aerobic exercise in boys with learning difficulties.' *Developmental and Behavioral Pediatrics*, 8: 274–7.

McNair, D. M., Lorr, M. and Droppleman, L. F. (1971) *Profile of mood states manual*. San Diego, Calif.: Educational and Industrial Testing Service.

McSwegin, P. J., Pemberton, C. and Petray, C. (1989) 'An educational plan.' *Journal of Physical Education, Recreation and Dance*, 60 (1): 32–4.

Maddux, J. E. (1993) 'Social cognitive models of health and exercise behavior: An introduction and review of conceptual issues.' *Journal of Applied Sport Psychology*, 5: 99–115.

Maehr, M. L. and Braskamp, L. A. (1986) *The motivation factor: A theory of personal investment*. Lexington, Mass.: Lexington Books.

Maehr, M. L. and Nicholls, J. G. (1980) 'Culture and achievement motivation: A second look.' In N. Warren (ed.), *Studies in cross-cultural psychology* (vol. II, pp. 221–67). New York: Academic Press.

Magill, R. A. (1989) *Motor learning: Concepts and applications*. Dubuque, Iowa: Wm C. Brown.

Maibach, E. and Parrott, R. L. (eds) (1995) *Designing health messages*. Thousand Oaks, Calif.: Sage.

Malina, R. M. (1988) 'Physical activity in early and modern populations: An evolutionary view.' In R. M. Malina and H. M. Eckert (eds), *Physical activity in early and modern populations* (pp. 1–12). Champaign, Ill.: Human Kinetics and the American Academy of Physical Education.

Mandela, N. (1994) *Long walk to freedom*. London: Little, Brown.

Manson, J. E., Rimm, E. B. and Stampfer, M. J. (1991) 'Physical activity and incidence of non-insulin-dependent diabetes mellitus in women.' *The Lancet*, 338: 774–8.

Marcus, B., Goldstein, M. G., Jette, A., Simkin-Silverman, L., Pinto, B. M., Milan, F., Wahburn, R., Smith, K., Rakowski, W. and Dub, C. E. (1997) 'Training physicians to conduct physical activity counseling.' *Preventive Medicine*, 26: 382–8.

Marcus, B. and Owen, N. (1992) 'Motivational readiness, self-efficacy and decision making for exercise.' *Journal of Applied Social Psychology*, 22: 3–16.

Marcus, B., Owen, N., Forsyth, L. H., Cavill, N. and Fridinger, F. (1998) 'Physical activity interventions using mass media, print media, and information technology.' *American Journal of Preventive Medicine*, 15: 362–78.

Marcus, B. H., Banspach, S. W., Lefebvre, R. C., Rossi, J. S., Carleton, R. A. and Abrams, D. B. (1992a) 'Using the stages of change model to increase the adoption of physical activity among community participants.' *American Journal of Health Promotion*, 6: 424–9.

Marcus, B. H., Eaton, C. A., Rossi, J. S. and Harlow, L. L. (1994) 'Self-efficacy, decision-making and stages of change: An integrative model of physical exercise.' *Journal of Applied Social Psychology*, 24: 489–508.

Marcus, B. H., Rakowski, W. and Rossi, J. S. (1992) 'Assessing motivational readiness and decision making for exercise.' *Health Psychology*, 11: 257–61.

Marcus, B. H., Rossi, J. S., Selby, V. C., Niaura, R. S. and Abrams, D. B. (1992b) 'The stages and processes of exercise adoption and maintenance in a worksite sample.' *Health Psychology*, 11: 386–95.

Marcus, B. H., Selby, V. C., Niaura, R. S. and Rossi, J. S. (1992c) 'Self-efficacy and stages of exercise behavior change.' *Research Quarterly for Exercise and Sport*, 63: 60–6.

Marcus, B. H., Simkin, L. R. (1994) 'The transtheoretical model: Applications to exercise behavior.' *Medicine and Science in Sports and Exercise*, 26: 1400–4.

Marcus, R., Drinkwater, B., Dalsky, G., Dufek, J., Raab, D., Slemenda, C. and Snow-Harter, C. (1992d) 'Osteoporosis and exercise in women.' *Medicine and Science in Sports and Exercise*, 24 (6: supplement): S301–S307.

Markland, D. (1999) 'Self-determination moderates the effects of perceived competence on intrinsic motivation in an exercise setting.' *Journal of Sport and Exercise Psychology*, 21: 351–61.

Markland, D., Emberton, M. and Tallon, R. (1997) 'Confirmatory factor analysis of the Subjective Exercise Experiences Scale among children.' *Journal of Sport and Exercise Psychology*, 19: 418–33.

Markland, D. and Hardy, L. (1993) 'The Exercise Motivations Inventory: Preliminary development and validity of a measure of individuals' reasons for participation in regular physical exercise.' *Personality and Individual Differences*, 15: 289–96.

Marks, D. F. (1994) 'Psychology's role in the Health of the Nation.' *The Psychologist: Bulletin of the British Psychological Society*, 7 (3): 119–21.

Marks, D. F., Murray, M., Evans, B. and Willig, C. (2000) *Health psychology: Theory, research and practice*. London: Sage.

Marlatt, G. A. (1985) 'Relapse prevention: Theoretial rationale and overview of the model.' In G. A. Marlatt and J. R. Gordon (eds), *Relapse prevention: Maintenance strategies in the treatment of addictive behaviours* (pp. 3–70). New York: Guilford Press.

Marlatt, G. A. and Gordon, G. R. (1985) *Relapse prevention.* New York: Guilford Press.

Marsden, E. (1996) *The role of exercise in the well-being of people with insulin dependent diabetes mellitus: Perceptions of patients and health professionals.* Unpublished Ph.D. thesis, University of Glasgow.

—— (1999) 'Adoption and maintenace of a physical activity programme for people with diabetes.' In B. Burr and D. Nagi (eds), *Exercise and sport in diabetes* (pp. 137–57). London: John Wiley.

Marsh, H. W., Richards, G. E., Johnson, S., Roche, L. and Tremayne, P. (1994) 'Physical Self-Description Questionnaire: Psychometric properties and the multitrait-multimethod analysis of relations to existing instruments.' *Journal of Sport and Exercise Psychology*, 16: 270–305.

Marsh, H. W. and Sonstroem, R. J. (1995) 'Importance ratings and specific components of physical self concept: Relevance to predicting global components of self-concept and exercise.' *Journal of Sport and Exercise Psychology*, 17: 84–104.

Marshall, S. J. and Biddle, S. J. H. (2000) *The transtheoretical model of behavior change: A meta-analysis of applications to physical activity and exercise.* Unpublished manuscript, Loughborough University.

Martinsen, E. W. (1989) 'The role of aerobic exercise in the treatment of depression.' *Stress Medicine*, 3: 93–100.

—— (1990a) 'Benefits of exercise for the treatment of depression.' *Sports Medicine*, 9 (6): 380–9.

—— (1990b) 'Physical fitness, anxiety and depression.' *British Journal of Hospital Medicine*, 43: 194; 196; 199.

—— (1993) 'Therapeutic implications of exercise for clinically anxious and depressed patients.' *International Journal of Sport Psychology*, 24: 185–99.

—— (1994) 'Physical activity and depression: Clinical experience.' *Acta Psychiatrica Scandinavica*, 377: 23–7.

Martinsen, E. W., Hoffart, A. and Solberg, O. (1989a) 'Comparing aerobic and non-aerobic forms of exercise in the treatment of clinical depression: A randomized trial.' *Comprehensive Psychiatry*, 30: 324–31.

—— (1989b) 'Aerobic and non-aerobic forms of exercise in the treatment of anxiety disorders.' *Stress Medicine*, 5: 115–20.

Martinsen, E. W., Medhus, A. and Sandvik, L. (1985) 'Effects of aerobic exercise on depression: A controlled trial.' *British Medical Journal*, 291: 100.

Martinsen, E. W., Sandvik, I. and Kolbjornsrud, O. B. (1989c) 'Aerobic exercise in the treatment of non psychotic mental disorders: An exploratory study.' *Nordic Journal of Psychiatry*, 43: 411–15.

Martinsen, E. W., Strand, J., Paulson, G. and Kaggestad, J. (1989d) 'Physical fitness level in patients with anxiety and depressive disorders.' *International Journal of Sports Medicine*, 10: 58–61.

Mason, V. (1995) *Young people and sport in England, 1994.* London: Sports Council.

Massie, J. F. and Shephard, R. J. (1971) 'Physiological and psychological effects of training: A comparison of individual and gymnasium programs, with a characterisation of the exercise "dropout".' *Medicine and Science in Sports*, 3: 110–17.

Meltzer, H., Gill, B., Petticrew, M. and Hinds, K. (1995) *The prevalence of psychiatric morbidity among adults living in private households.* London: HMSO.

Messer, B. and Harter, S. (1986) *Manual for the Adult Self-Perception Profile.* Denver, Colo.: University of Denver.

Mihalik, B., O'Leary, J., Mcguire, F. and Dottavio, F. (1989) 'Sports involvement across the life span: Expansion and contraction of sports activities.' *Research Quarterly for Sport and Exercise*, 60: 396–98.

Miilunpalo, S. (1991) 'Exercise guidance in primary health care.' In P. Oja and R. Telama (eds), *Sport for all* (pp. 185–92). Amsterdam: Elsevier.

Milani, R. V., Lavie, C. J. and Cassidy, M. M. (1996) 'Effects of cardiac rehabilitation and exercise training on depression in patients after major coronary events.' *American Heart Journal*, 132: 726–32.

Miller, W. R. and Rollnick, S. (1991) *Motivational interviewing: Preparing people to change addictive behavior.* New York: Guilford Press.

Mitchell, S., Grant, S. and Aitchison, T. (1998) 'Physiological effects of exercise on post-menopausal osteoporotic women.' *Physiotherapy*, 84(4): 157–63.

Moore, G. E. (1997) Introduction. In *ACSM's exercise management for persons with chronic diseases and disabilities* (pp. 3–5). Champaign, Ill.: Human Kinetics.

Moreira, H., Sparkes, A. C. and Fox, K. R. (1995) 'Physical education teachers and job comitment: A preliminary analysis.' *European Physical Education Review*, 1: 122–36.

Morgan, W. P. (1968) 'Selected physiological and psychomotor correlates of depression in psychiatric patients.' *Research Quarterly*, 39: 1037–43.

—— (1969) 'A pilot investigation of physical working capacity in depressed and non-depressed psychiatric males.' *Research Quarterly*, 40: 859–61.

—— (1970a) 'Physical fitness correlates of psychiatric hospitalization.' In G. S. Kenyon (ed.), *Contemporary psychology of sport* (pp. 297–300). Chicago: Athletic Institute.

—— (1970b) 'Physical working capacity in depressed and non-depressed psychiatric females: A preliminary study.' *American Corrective Therapy Journal*, 24: 14–16.

—— (1979) 'Anxiety reduction following acute physical activity.' *Psychiatric Annals*, 9: 36–45.

—— (1985) 'Affective beneficence of vigorous physical activity.' *Medicine and Science in Sports and Exercise*, 17: 94–100.

—— (1994) 'Physical activity, fitness and depression.' In C. Bouchard, R. J. Shephard and T. Stephens (eds), *Physical activity, fitness and health* (pp. 851–67). Champaign, Ill.: Human Kinetics.

—— (ed.) (1997) *Physical activity and mental health*. Washington, D.C.: Taylor and Francis.

Morgan, W. P. and Goldston, S. E. (eds) (1987a) *Exercise and mental health*. Washington: Hemisphere.

—— (1987b) 'Summary.' In W. P. Morgan and S. E. Goldston (eds), *Exercise and mental health* (pp. 155–59). Washington: Hemisphere.

Morgan, W. P. and O'Connor, P. J. (1988) 'Exercise and mental health.' In R. K. Dishman (ed.), *Exercise adherence: Its impact on public health* (pp. 91–121). Champaign, Ill.: Human Kinetics.

Morris, J. N., Everett, M. G. and Semmence, A. M. (1987) 'Exercise and coronary heart disease.' In D. Macleod, R. Maughan, M. Nimmo, T. Reilly and C. Williams (eds), *Exercise: Benefits, limits and adaptation* (pp. 4–17). London: E. and F. N. Spon.

Morris, J. N., Heady, J. A., Raffle, P. A. B., Roberts, C. G. and Parks, J. W. (1953) 'Coronary heart disease and physical activity of work.' *The Lancet*, ii: 1053–7; 1111–20.

Morris, J. N., Kagan, A., Pattison, D. C., Gardner, M. and Raffle, P. A. B. (1966) 'Incidence and reduction of ischaemic heart disease in London busmen.' *The Lancet*, ii: 552–9.

Morris, M., Steinberg, H., Sykes, E. A. and Salmon, P. (1990) 'Effects of temporary withdrawal from regular running.' *Journal of Psychosomatic Research*, 34: 493–500.

Moses, J., Steptoe, A., Mathews, A. and Edwards, S. (1989) 'The effects of exercise training on mental well-being in the normal population: A controlled trial.' *Journal of Psychosomatic Research*, 33: 47–61.

Mueller, C. M. and Dweck, C. S. (1998) 'Praise for intelligence can undermine children's motivation and performance.' *Journal of Personality and Social Psychology*, 75: 33–52.

Muldoon, M. F., Barger, S. D., Flory, J. D. and Manuck, S. B. (1998) 'What are the quality of life measurements measuring?' *British Medical Journal*, 316: 542–5.

Mullan, E. and Markland, D. (1997) 'Variations in self-determination across the stages of change for exercise in adults.' *Motivation and Emotion*, 21: 349–62.

Mullan, E., Markland, D. and Ingledew, D. (1997) 'A graded conceptualisation of self-determination in the regulation of exercise behaviour: Development of a measure using confirmatory factor analytic procedures.' *Personality and Individual Differences*, 23: 745–52.

Mullen, P. D., Hersey, J. C. and Iverson, D. C. (1987) 'Health behaviour models compared.' *Social Science and Medicine*, 24: 973–81.

Murdoch, F. A. (1988) *Short term interventions for withdrawal from benzodiazepines: A comparative study of group therapy plus exercise vs group therapy*. Unpublished MBCHB thesis, University of Glasgow.

Murphy, T. J., Pagano, R. R. and Marlatt, G. A. (1986) 'Lifestyle modification with heavy alcohol drinkers: Effects of aerobic exercise and meditation.' *Addictive Behaviors*, 11: 175–86.

Musgrave, B. and Menell, Z. (1980) *Change and choice: Women and middle-age*. London: Peter Owen.

Mutrie, N. (1988) *Exercise as a treatment for moderate depression in the UK National Health Service*. Paper presented at the Sport, Health, Psychology and Exercise Symposium, London.

—— (2000) 'The relationship between physical activity and clinically defined depression.' In S. J. H.

Biddle, K. R. Fox and S. H. Boutcher (eds), *Physical activity and psychological well-being* (pp. 46–62). London: Routledge.

Mutrie, N., Carney, C., Blamey, A., Whitelaw, A., Crawford, F. and Aitchison, T. (1999) *The effects of a cognitive behavioural intervention on active commuting behaviour: 3-month results.* Paper presented at the 10th European Congress of Sport Psychology, Prague.

Mutrie, N. and Choi, P. Y. L. (1993) *Psychological benefits of physical activity for specific populations.* Paper presented at the 7th Conference of the European Health Psychology Society, Brussels.

Mutrie, N. and Knill-Jones, R. (1986) 'Psychological effects of running: 1985 survey of Glasgow People's Marathon.' In J. H. McGregor and J. A. Moncur (eds), *Sport and Medicine: Proceedings of VIII Commonwealth and International Conference on Sport, Physical Education, Dance, Recreation and Health* (pp. 186–90). London: E. and F. N. Spon.

Nachemson, A. L. (1990) 'Exercise fitness and back pain.' In C. Bouchard, R. J. Shephard, T. Stephens, J. R. Sutton and B. D. McPherson (eds), *Exercise, fitness, and health* (pp. 533–40). Champaign, Ill.: Human Kinetics.

Naughton, J. (1985) 'Role of physical activity as a secondary intervention for healed myocardial infarction.' *American Journal of Cardiology*, 55: 210–60.

Neeman, J. and Harter, S. (1986) *Manual for the Self-Perception Profile for college students.* Denver, Colo.: University of Denver.

Neuberger, G. B., Kasal, S., Smith, K. V. and Hassanein, R. (1994) 'Determinants of exercise and aerobic fitness in outpatients with arthritis.' *Nursing Research*, 43: 11–17.

Nicholls, J. G. (1989) *The competitive ethos and democratic education.* Cambridge, Mass.: Harvard University Press.

Nieman, D. C. (1994) 'Physical activity, fitness, and infection.' In C. Bouchard, R. J. Shephard and T. Stephens (eds), *Physical activity, fitness, and health* (pp. 796–813). Champaign, Ill.: Human Kinetics.

Nitsch, J. R. and Seiler, R. (eds) (1994) *Health sport – Movement therapy.* Sankt Augustin: Academia.

Noble, B. J. and Robertson, R. J. (1996) *Perceived exertion.* Champaign, Ill.: Human Kinetics.

Noland, M. and Feldman, R. (1984) 'Factors related to the leisure exercise behavior of "returning" women college students.' *Health Education*, March/April: 32–6.

—— (1985) 'An empirical investigation of leisure exercise behavior in adult women.' *Health Education*, October/November: 29–34.

Norstrom, J. (1988) 'Get fit while you sit: Exercise and fitness options for diabetics.' *Caring*, November: 52–8.

North, T. C., McCullagh, P. and Tran, Z. V. (1990) 'Effect of exercise on depression.' *Exercise and Sport Sciences Reviews*, 18: 379–415.

Ntoumanis, N. and Biddle, S. (1999a) 'A review of motivational climate in physical activity.' *Journal of Sports Sciences*, 17: 643–65.

—— (1999b) 'Affect and achievement goals in physical activity: A meta-analysis.' *Scandinavian Journal of Medicine and Science in Sports*, 9: 315–32.

Oatley, K. and Jenkins, J. M. (1996) *Understanding emotions.* Cambridge, Mass.: Blackwell Scientific.

O'Connell, J. and Price, J. (1982) 'Health locus of control of physical fitness program participants.' *Perceptual and Motor Skills*, 55: 925–6.

O'Connor, P. J., Aenchbacher, L. E. and Dishman, R. K. (1993) 'Physical activity and depression in the elderly.' *Journal of Aging and Physical Activity*, 1: 34–58.

O'Connor, P. J. and Cook, D. B. (1999) 'Exercise and pain: The neurobiology, measurement, and laboratory study of pain in relation to exercise in humans.' *Exercise and Sport Sciences Reviews*, 27: 119–66.

O'Connor, P. J. and Youngstedt, S. D. (1995) 'Influence of exercise on human sleep.' *Exercise and Sport Sciences Reviews*, 23: 105–34.

Ogden, J. (1996) *Health psychology: A textbook.* Buckingham: Open University Press.

Oja, P. (1995) 'Descriptive epidemiology of health-related physical activity and fitness.' *Reserach Quarterly for Exercise and Sport*, 66: 303–12.

Oja, P., Paronen, O., Manttari, A., Kukkonen-Harjula, K., Laukkanen, R., Vuori, I. and Pasanen, M. (1991) 'Occurrence, effects and promotion of walking and cycling as forms of transportation during work commuting: A Finnish experience.' In P. Oja and R. Telama (eds), *Sport for all* (pp. 233–8). Amsterdam: Elsevier.

Oja, P., Vuori, I. and Paronen, O. (1998) 'Daily walking and cycling to work: Their utility as health-enhancing physical activity.' *Patient Education and Counseling*, 33 (supplement 1): S87–S94.

Oldridge, N., Donner, A. and Buck, C. (1983) 'Predictors of dropout from cardiac exercise rehabilitation: Ontario Exercise Heart Collaborative Study.' *American Journal of Cardiology*, 51: 70–4.

Oldridge, N. B., Guyatt, G. H., Fischer, M. E. and Rimm, A. A. (1988) 'Cardiac rehabilitation after myocardial infarction: Combined experience of randomized clinical trials.' *Journal of the American Medicial Association*, 260: 945–50.

Olson, J. M. and Zanna, M. P. (1982) *Predicting adherence to a programme of physical exercise: An empirical study*. Toronto: Ontario Ministry of Tourism and Recreation.

—— (1993) 'Attitudes and attitude change.' *Annual Review of Psychology*, 44: 117–54.

Ommundsen, Y. and Vaglum, P. (1991) 'Soccer competition anxiety and enjoyment in young boy players: The influence of perceived competence and significant others' emotional involvement.' *International Journal of Sport Psychology*, 22: 35–49.

Opatz, J., Chenoweth, D. and Kaman, R. (1991) 'Economic impact of worksite health promotion programs.' Northbrook, Ill.: Association for Fitness in Business Publications.

Orwin, A. (1981) 'The running treatment: A preliminary communication on a new use for an old therapy (physical activity) in the agorophobic syndrome.' In M. H. Sacks and M. Sachs (eds), *Psychology of running* (pp. 32–9). Champaign: Human Kinetics.

Ossip-Klein, D. J., Doyne, E. J., Bowman, E. D., Osborn, K. M., McDougall-Wilson, I. B. and Neimeyer, R. A. (1989) 'Effects of running and weight lifting on self-concept in clinically depressed women.' *Journal of Consulting and Clinical Psychology*, 57: 158–61.

Owen, N. and Bauman, A. (1992) 'The descriptive epidemiology of a sedentary lifestyle in adult Australians.' *International Journal of Epidemiology*, 21: 305–10.

Owen, N. and Dwyer, T. (1988) 'Approaches to promoting more widespread participation in physical activity.' *Community Health Studies*, 12: 339–47.

Paffenbarger, R. S., Hyde, R. T., Wing, A. L. and Hsieh, C.-C. (1986) 'Physical activity, all-cause mortality, and longevity of college alumni.' *New England Journal of Medicine*, 314: 605–13.

Paffenbarger, R. S., Hyde, R. T., Wing, A. L., Lee, I.-M., Jung, D. L. and Kampert, J. B. (1993) 'The association of changes in physical activity level and other lifestyle characteristics with mortality among men.' *New England Journal of Medicine*, 328: 538–45.

Paffenbarger, R. S., Hyde, R. T., Wing, A. L., Lee, I.-M. and Kampert, J. B. (1994a) 'Some interrelations of physical activity, physiological fitness, health and longevity.' In C. Bouchard, R. J. Shephard and T. Stephens (eds), *Physical activity, fitness, and health* (pp. 119–33). Champaign, Ill.: Human Kinetics.

Paffenbarger, R. S., Lee, I. M. and Leung, R. (1994b) 'Physical activity and personal characteristics associated with depression and suicide in American college men.' *Acta Psychiatrica Scandinavia*, 89 (s377): 16–22.

Paffenbarger, R., S., Wing, A. L. and Hyde, R. T. (1978) 'Physical activity as an index of heart attack risk in college alumni.' *American Journal of Epidemiology*, 108: 161–75.

Palenzuela, D. L. (1988) 'Refining the theory and measurement of expectancy of internal versus external control of reinforcement.' *Personality and Individual Differences*, 9: 607–29.

Palmer, J., Vacc, N. and Epstein, J. (1988) 'Adult inpatient alcoholics: Physical exercise as a treatment intervention.' *Journal of Studies on Alcohol*, 49(5): 418–29.

Palmer, S. S., Mortimer, J. A., Webster, D. D., Bistevins, R. and Dickinson, G. L. (1986) 'Exercise therapy for Parkinson's disease.' *Archives of Physical Medicine and Rehabilitation*, 67: 741–5.

Papaioannou, A. (1994) 'Development of a questionnaire to measure achievement orientation in physical education.' *Research Quarterly for Exercise and Sport*, 65: 11–20.

—— (1995) 'Motivation and goal perspectives in children's physical education.' In S. J. H. Biddle (ed.), *European Perspectives on Sport and Exercise Psychology* (pp. 245–69). Champaign, Ill.: Human Kinetics.

Papaioannou, A. and Goudas, M. (1999) 'Motivational climate of the physical education class.' In Y. Vanden Auweele, F. Bakker, S. Biddle, M. Durand and R. Seiler (eds), *Psychology for physical educators* (pp. 51–68). Champaign, Ill.: Human Kinetics.

Parfitt, G., Markland, D. and Holmes, C. (1994) 'Response to physical exertion in active and inactive males and females.' *Journal of Sport and Exercise Psychology*, 16: 178–86.

Pate, R. R. (1988) 'The evolving definition of physical fitness.' *Quest*, 40: 174–9.

Pate, R. R., Baranowski, T., Dowda, M. and Trost, S. G. (1996) 'Tracking of physical activity in young children.' *Medicine and Science in Sports and Exercise*, 28: 92–6.

Pate, R. R. and Macera, C. A. (1994) 'Risks of exercising: Musculoskeletal injuries.' In C. Bouchard, R. J. Shephard and T. Stephens. (eds), *Physical activity, fitness, and health* (pp. 1008–18). Champaign, Ill.: Human Kinetics.

Pate, R. R., Pratt, M., Blair, S. N., Haskel, W. L., Macera, C. A., Bouchard, C., Buchner, D., Ettinger, W., Heath, G., King, A. C., Kriska, A., Leon, A., Marcus, B. H., Morris, J., Paffenbarger, R. S., Patrick, K., Pollock, M. L., Rippe, J. M., Sallis, J. F. and Wilmore, J. H. (1995) 'Physical activity and public health: A recommendation from the Centers for Disease Control and Prevention and the American College of Sports Medicine.' *Journal of the American Medicial Association*, 273: 402–7.

Paton, L. (1993) *Barriers and motivation to exercise in osteoporotic post-menopausal women.* Unpublished M.App. Sci. thesis, University of Glasgow.

Patrick, K., Sallis, J. F., Long, B. J., Calfas, K. J., Wooten, W. J. and Heath, G. (1994) 'PACE: Physician-based assessment and counseling for exercise, background and development.' *The Physician and Sportsmedicine*, 22: 245–55.

Patton, R. W., Corry, J. M., Gettman, L. R. and Graf, J. S. (1986) *Implementing health/fitness programs.* Champaign, Ill.: Human Kinetics.

Paykel, E. S. and Priest, R. G. (1992) 'Recognition and management of depression in general practice: A consensus statement.' *British Medical Journal*, 305: 1198–202.

Pedestrians' Association (1997) *Did you walk today?* London: Pedestrians' Association.

—— (1998) *Stepping out: Local Authority policies and provision for walking.* London: Pedestrians' Association.

Pelham, T. W. and Campagna, P. D. (1991) 'Benefits of exercise in psychiatric rehabilitation of persons with schizophrenia.' *Canadian Journal of Rehabilitation*, 4(3): 159–68.

Pelham, T. W., Campagna, P. D., Ritvo, P. G. and Birnie, W. A. (1993) 'The effects of exercise therapy on clients in a psychiatric rehabilitation programme.' *Psychosocial Rehabilitation Journal*, 16 (4): 75–84.

Pell, J., Pell, A., Morrison, C., Blatchford, O. and Dargie, H. (1996) 'Retrospective study of influence of deprivation on uptake of cardiac rehabilitation.' *British Medical Journal*, 313: 267–8.

Pelletier, L. G., Fortier, M. S., Vallerand, R. J., Tuson, K. M., Briere, N. M. and Blais, M. R. (1995) 'Toward a new measure of intrinsic motivation, extrinsic motivation, and amotivation in sports: The Sport Motivation Scale (SMS).' *Journal of Sport and Exercise Psychology*, 17: 35–53.

Pender, N. J., Sallis, J. F., Long, B. J. and Calfas, K. J. (1994) 'Health-care provider counseling to promote physical activity.' In R. K. Dishman (ed.), *Advances in exercise adherence* (pp. 213–35). Champaign, Ill.: Human Kinetics.

Peronnet, F. and Szabo, A. (1993) 'Sympathetic response to psychosocial stressors in humans: Linkage to physical exercise and training.' In P. Seraganian (ed.), *Exercise psychology: The influence of physical exercise on psychological processes* (pp. 172–217). New York: John Wiley.

Peterson, C., Maier, S. F. and Seligman, M. E. P. (1993) *Learned helplessness: A theory for the age of personal control.* New York: Oxford University Press.

Peterson, C. and Seligman, M. E. P. (1984) 'Causal explanations as a risk factor for depression: Theory and evidence.' *Psychological Review*, 91: 347–74.

Petruzzello, S. J. (1995) 'Does physical exercise reduce anxious emotions? A reply to W. Schlicht's meta-analysis.' *Anxiety, Stress and Coping*, 8: 353–6.

Petruzzello, S. J., Landers, D. M., Hatfield, B. D., Kubitz, K. A. and Salazar, W. (1991) 'A meta-analysis on the anxiety-reducing effects of acute and chronic exercise: Outcomes and mechanisms.' *Sports Medicine*, 11: 143–82.

Petty, R. E. and Cacioppo, J. T. (1986) 'The elaboration-likelihood model of persuasion.' In L. Berkowitz (ed.), *Advances in experimental social psychology* (vol. 19, pp. 123–205). San Diego, Calif.: Academic Press.

Petty, T. (1993) 'Pulmonary rehabilitation in perspective: Historical roots, present status and future projections.' *Thorax*, 48: 855–62.

Pierce, E. (1994) 'Exercise dependence syndrome in runners.' *Sports Medicine*, 18: 149–55.

Pieron, M., Cloes, M., Delfosse, C. and Ledent, M. (1996) 'An investigation of the effects of daily physical education in kindergarten and elementary school.' *European Physical Education Review*, 2: 116–32.

Pitts, F. N. and McClure, J. N. (1967) 'Lactate metabolism in anxiety neurosis.' *New England Journal of Medicine*, 277: 1329–36.

Plante, T. G. (1993) 'Aerobic exercise in prevention and treatment of psychopathology.' In P. Seraganian (ed.), *Exercise psychology. The influence of physical exercise on psychological processes* (pp. 358–79). New York: John Wiley.

Poag-DuCharme, K. A. and Brawley, L. R. (1993) 'Self-efficacy theory: Use in the prediction of exercise behavior in the community setting.' *Journal of Applied Sport Psychology*, 5: 178–94.

Polivy, J. (1994) 'Physical activity, fitness, and compulsive behaviors.' In C. Bouchard, R. J. Shephard and T. Stephens (eds), *Physical activity, fitness, and health* (pp. 883–97). Champaign, Ill.: Human Kinetics.

Pollatschek, J. L. and O'Hagan, F. J. (1989) 'An investigation of the psycho-physical influences of a quality daily physical education programme.' *Health Education Research: Theory and Practice*, 4: 341–50.

Potempa, K., Braun, L. T., Tinkell, T. and Popovich, J. (1996) 'Benefits of aerobic exercise after stroke.' *Sports Medicine*, 21: 337–46.

Powell, K. E. (1988) 'Habitual exercise and public health: An epidemiological view.' In R. K. Dishman (ed.), *Exercise adherence: Its impact on public health* (pp. 15–39). Champaign, Ill.: Human Kinetics.

Powell, K. E. and Blair, S. N. (1994) 'The public health burdens of sedentary living habits: Theoretical but realistic estimates.' *Medicine and Science in Sports and Exercise*, 26: 851–6.

Powell, K. E., Spain, K. S., Christenson, C. J. and Mollenkamp, M. P. (1986) 'The status of the 1990 objectives for physical fitness and exercise.' *Public Health Reports*, 101: 15–21.

Powell, K. E., Stephens, T., Marti, B., Heinemann, L. and Kreuter, M. (1991) 'Progress and problems in the promotion of physical activity.' In P. Oja and R. Telama (eds), *Sport for all* (pp. 55–73). Amsterdam: Elsevier.

Powell, K. E., Thompson, P. D., Caspersen, C. J. and Kendrick, J. S. (1987) 'Physical activity and the incidence of coronary heart disease.' *Annual Review of Public Health*, 8: 253–87.

Prentice, A. M. and Jebb, S. A. (1995) 'Obesity in Britain: Gluttony or sloth?' *British Medical Journal*, 311: 437–9.

Prentice-Dunn, S. and Rogers, R. (1986) 'Protection Motivation Theory and preventive health: Beyond the Health Belief Model.' *Health Education Research: Theory and Practice*, 1: 153–61.

Prior, J. C. and Vigna, Y. (1987) 'Conditioning exercise decreases premenstrual symptoms: A prospective, controlled 6-month trial.' *Fertility and Sterility*, 47: 402–8.

Prochaska, J. and Velicer, W. (1997) 'The transtheoretical model of health behavior change.' *American Journal of Health Promotion*, 12: 38–48.

Prochaska, J. O. (1994) 'Strong and weak principles for progressing from precontemplation to action on the basis of twelve problem behaviors.' *Health Psychology*, 13: 47–51.

Prochaska, J. O., DiClemente, C. C. and Norcross, J. C. (1992) 'In search of how people change: Applications to addictive behaviors.' *American Psychologist*, 47: 1102–14.

Prochaska, J. O. and Marcus, B. H. (1994) 'The transtheoretical model: Application to exercise.' In R. K. Dishman (ed.), *Advances in exercise adherence* (pp. 161–80). Champaign, Ill.: Human Kinetics.

Prochaska, J. O., Norcross, J. C. and DiClemente, C. C. (1994a) *Changing for good*. New York: Avon.

Prochaska, J. O., Velicer, W. F., Rossi, J. S., Goldstein, M. G., Marcus, B. H., Rakowski, W., Fiore, C., Harlow, L. L., Redding, C. A., Rosenbloom, D. and Rossi, S. R. (1994b) 'Stages of change and decision balance for 12 problem behaviors.' *Health Psychology*, 13: 39–46.

Prosser, G., Carson, P. and Phillips, R. (1985) 'Exercise after myocardial infarction: Long term rehabilitation effects.' *Journal of Psychosomatic Research*, 29: 535–40.

Quaglietti, S. and Froelicher, V. F. (1994) 'Physical activity and cardiac rehabilitation for patients with coronary heart disease.' In C. Bouchard, R. J. Shephard and T. Stephens (eds), *Physical activity, fitness and health* (pp. 591–608). Champaign, Ill.: Human Kinetics.

Quinney, H. A., Gauvin, L. and Wall, A. E. T. (eds) (1994) *Toward active living*. Champaign, Ill.: Human Kinetics.

Radloff, L. S. (1977) 'The CES-D scale: A self-report depression scale for research in the general population.' *Applied Psychological Measurement*, 1: 385–401.

Raglin, J. S. (1997) 'Anxiolytic effects of physical activity.' In W. P. Morgan (ed.), *Physical activity and mental health* (pp. 107–26). Washington, D.C.: Taylor and Francis.

Redman, S., Spencer, E. A. and Sanson-Fisher, R. W. (1990) 'The role of mass media in changing health-related behaviour: A critical appraisal of two models.' *Health Promotion International*, 5: 85–101.

Reed, B. D., Jensen, J. D. and Gorenflo, D. W. (1991) 'Physicians and exercise promotion.' *American Journal of Preventive Medicine*, 7: 410–15.

Reed, G. R. (1999) 'Adherence to exercise and the transtheoretical model of behaviour change.' In S. J. Bull (ed.), *Adherence issues in sport and exercise* (pp. 19–46). Chichester: Wiley.

Rejeski, W. J. (1981) 'The perception of exertion: A social psychophysiological integration.' *Journal of Sport Psychology*, 3: 305–20.

—— (1985) 'Perceived exertion: An active or passive process?' *Journal of Sport Psychology*, 7: 371–8.

—— (1992) 'Motivation for exercise behavior: A critique of theoretical directions.' In G. C. Roberts (ed.), *Motivation in sport and exercise* (pp. 129–57). Champaign, Ill.: Human Kinetics.

—— (1994) 'Dose-response issues from a psychosocial perspective.' In C. Bouchard, R. J. Shephard and T. Stephens (eds), *Physical activity, fitness, and health* (pp. 1040–55). Champaign, Ill.: Human Kinetics.

Rejeski, W. J. and Brawley, L. R. (1988) 'Defining the boundaries of sport psychology.' *The Sport Psychologist*, 2: 231–42.

Rejeski, W. J., Brawley, L. R. and Shumaker, S. A. (1996) 'Physical activity and health-related quality of life.' *Exercise and Sport Sciences Reviews*, 24: 71–108.

Rejeski, W. J. and Sanford, B. (1984) 'Feminine-typed females: The role of affective schema in the perception of exercise intensity.' *Journal of Sport Psychology*, 6: 197–207.

Rejeski, W. J. and Thompson, A. (1993) 'Historical and conceptual roots of exercise psychology.' In P. Seraganian (ed.), *Exercise psychology. The influence of physical exercise on psychological processes* (pp. 3–35). New York: John Wiley.

Research Quarterly for Exercise and Sport (1995) 'Physical Activity, Health and Well-Being.' *Research Quarterly for Exercise and Sport*, special issue: Proceedings of the International Scientific Consensus Conference, 66 (4): whole.

Reuter, I., Engelhardt, M., Stecker, K. and Baas, H. (1999) 'Therapeutic value of exercise training in Parkinson's disease.' *Medicine and Science in Sports and Exercise*, 31: 1544–9.

Rickabaugh, T. E. and Saltarelli, W. (1999) 'Knowledge and attitudes related to diabetes and exercise guidelines among selected diabetic children, their parents, and physical education teachers.' *Research Quarterly for Exercise and Sport*, 70: 389–94.

Rickli, R. E. and McManus, R. (1990) 'The effect of exercise on bone mineral content in post menopausal women.' *Research Quarterly for Exercise and Sport*, 61: 243–9.

Riddle, P. K. (1980) 'Attitudes, beliefs, behavioral intentions and behaviors of women and men toward regular jogging.' *Research Quarterly for Exercise and Sport*, 51: 663–74.

Riddoch, C. (1998) 'Relationships between physical activity and physical health in young people.' In S. Biddle, J. Sallis and N. Cavill (eds), *Young and active? Young people and health-enhancing physical activity: Evidence and implications* (pp. 17–48). London: Health Education Authority.

Riddoch, C., Puig-Ribera, A. and Cooper, A. (1998) *Effectiveness of physical activity promotion schemes in primary care: A review*. London: Health Education Authority.

Rigsby, L., Dishman, R. K., Jackson, W., McClean, G. S. and Rowen, P. B. (1992) 'Effects of exercise training on men seropositive for HIV–1.' *Medicine and Science in Sports and Exercise*, 24: 6–12.

Rippetoe, P. A. and Rogers, R. (1987) 'Effects of components of protection-motivation theory on adaptive and maladaptive coping with a health threat.' *Journal of Personality and Social Psychology*, 52: 596–604.

Roberts, G. C. (ed.) (1992) *Motivation in sport and exercise*. Champaign, Ill.: Human Kinetics.

Robertson, R. J. and Noble, B. J. (1997) 'Perception of physical exertion: Methods, mediators, and applications.' *Exercise and Sport Sciences Reviews*, 25: 407–52.

Rodgers, W. M. and Brawley, L. R. (1993) 'Using both the self-efficacy theory and the theory of planned behavior to discriminate adherers and dropouts from structured programmes.' *Journal of Applied Sport Psychology*, 5: 195–206.

Rogers, R. W. (1983) 'Cognitive and physiological processes in fear appeals and attitude change: A revised theory of protection motivation.' In J. R. Cacioppo and R. E. Petty (eds), *Social psychology: A sourcebook* (pp. 153–76). New York: Guilford Press.

Rollnick, S., Mason, P. and Butler, C. (1999) *Health behavior change: A guide for practitioners*. Edinburgh: Churchill Livingstone.

Rosenstock, I. M. (1974) 'Historical origins of the Health Belief Model.' *Health Education Monographs*, 2: 328–35.

—— (1990) 'The Health Belief Model: Explaining health behavior through expectancies.' In K. Glanz, F. M. Lewis and B. K. Rimer (eds), *Health behavior and health education: Theory, research, and practice* (pp. 39–62). San Fransisco: Jossey-Bass.

Rothman, A. J., Salovey, P., Turvey, C. and Fishkin, S. A. (1993) 'Attributions of responsibility and persuasion: Increasing mammography utilization among women over 40 with an internally oriented message.' *Health Psychology*, 12: 39–47.

Rotter, J. B. (1954) *Social learning and clinical psychology*. Englewood Cliffs, N.J.: Prentice-Hall.

—— (1966) 'Generalised expectancies for internal versus external control of reinforcement.' *Psychological Monographs*, 80 (whole no. 609): 1–28.

—— (1975) 'Some problems and misconceptions related to the construct of internal versus external control of reinforcement.' *Journal of Consulting and Clinical Psychology*, 43: 56–67.

Rovario, S., Holmes, D. and Holmsten, D. (1984) 'Influence of a cardiac rehabilitation program on the cardiovascular, psychological, and social functioning of cardiac patients.' *Journal of Behavioral Medicine*, 7: 61–81.

Rudolph, D. L. and McAuley, E. (1995) 'Self-efficacy and salivary cortisol responses to acute exercise in physically active and less active adults.' *Journal of Sport and Exercise Psychology*, 17: 206–13.

Rummel, A. and Feinberg, R. (1988) 'Cognitive evaluation theory: A meta-analytic review of the literature.' *Social Behavior and Personality*, 16: 147–64.

Rusbult, C. and Farrel, D. (1983) 'A longitudinal test of the investment model: The impact of job satisfaction, job commitment and turnover of variations in rewards, costs, alternatives and investments.' *Journal of Applied Psychology*, 68: 429–38.

Russell, J. A. (1980) 'A circumplex model of affect.' *Journal of Personality and Social Psychology*, 39: 1161–78.

Russell, J. A. and Barrett, L. F. (1999) 'Core affect, prototypical emotional episodes, and other things called emotion: Dissecting the elephant.' *Journal of Personality and Social Psychology*, 76: 805–19.

Ryan, R. and Connell, J. (1989) 'Perceived locus of causality and internalization: Examining reasons for acting in two domains.' *Journal of Personality and Social Psychology*, 57: 749–61.

Ryan, R. M., Connell, J. P. and Grolnick, W. S. (1992) 'When achievement is not intrinsically motivated: A theory of internalization and self-regulation in school.' In A. K. Boggiano and T. S. Pittman (eds), *Achievement and motivation: A social developmental perspective* (pp. 167–88). Cambridge: Cambridge University Press.

Ryckman, R. M., Robbins, M. A., Thornton, B. and Cantrell, P. (1982) 'Development and validation of a Physical Self-Efficacy Scale.' *Journal of Personality and Social Psychology*, 42: 891–900.

Sallis, J. (1998) 'Family and community interventions to promote physical activity in young people.' In S. Biddle, J. Sallis and N. Cavill (eds), *Young and Active? Young people and health-enhancing physical activity: Evidence and implications* (pp. 150–61). London: Health Education Authority.

Sallis, J. and Owen, N. (1996) 'Ecological models.' In K. Glanz, F. Lewis and B. Rimer (eds), *Health behavior and health education: Theory, research and practice* (pp. 403–24). San Francisco: Jossey-Bass.

Sallis, J. and Patrick, K. (1994) 'Physical activity guidelines for adolescents: Consensus statement.' *Pediatric Exercise Science*, 6: 302–14.

Sallis, J. F., Bauman, A. and Pratt, M. (1998) 'Environmental and policy interventions to promote physical activity.' *American Journal of Preventive Medicine*, 15: 379–97.

Sallis, J. F., Haskell, W., Fortmann, S., Vranizan, K., Taylor, C. B. and Solomon, D. (1986) 'Predictors of adoption and maintenance of physical activity in a community sample.' *Preventive Medicine*, 15: 331–41.

Sallis, J. F. and Hovell, M. (1990) 'Determinants of exercise behavior.' *Exercise and Sport Sciences Reviews*, 18: 307–30.

Sallis, J. F., Hovell, M. F., Hofstetter, C. R. and Barrington, E. (1992a) 'Explanation of vigorous physical activity during two years using social learning variables.' *Social Science and Medicine*, 34: 25–32.

Sallis, J. F., McKenzie, T. L., Alcaraz, J. E., Kolody, B., Faucette, N. and Hovell, M. F. (1997) 'The effects of a 2-year physical education program (SPARK) on physical activity and fitness in elementary school students.' *American Journal of Public Health*, 87: 1328–34.

Sallis, J. F. and Owen, N. (1999) *Physical activity and behavioral medicine*. Thousand Oaks, Calif.: Sage.

Sallis, J. F., Pinski, R. B., Grossman, R. M., Patterson, T. L. and Nader, P. R. (1988) 'The development of self-efficacy scales for health-related diet and exercise behaviors.' *Health Education Research: Theory and Practice*, 3: 283–92.

Sallis, J. F., Simons-Morton, B. G., Stone, E. J., Corbin, C. B., Epstein, L. H., Faucette, N., Iannotti, R. J., Killen, J. D., Klesges, R. C., Petray, C. K., Rowland, T. W. and Taylor, W. C. (1992b) 'Determinants of phyical activity and interventions in youth.' *Medicine and Science in Sports and Exercise*, 24 (6: supplement): S248–S257.

Salonen, J. T., Puska, P., Kottke, T. E., Tuomilehto, J. and Nissinen, A. (1983) 'Decline in mortality from coronary heart disease in Finland from 1969 to 1979.' *British Medical Journal*, 286: 1857–60.

Sarrazin, P., Biddle, S., Famose, J. P., Cury, F., Fox, K. and Durand, M. (1996) 'Goal orientations and conceptions of the nature of sport ability in children: A social cognitive approach.' *British Journal of Social Psychology*, 35: 399–414.

Scanlan, T. K., Carpenter, P. J., Schmidt, G. W., Simons, J. P. and Keeler, B. (1993) 'An introduction to the sport commitment model.' *Journal of Sport and Exercise Psychology*, 15: 1–15.

Scanlan, T. K. and Lewthwaite, R. (1986) 'Social psychological aspects of competition for male youth sport participants: IV. Predictors of enjoyment.' *Journal of Sport Psychology*, 8: 25–35.

Scanlan, T. K. and Simons, J. P. (1992) 'The construct of sport enjoyment.' In G. C. Roberts (ed.), *Motivation in sport and exercise* (pp. 199–215). Champaign, Ill.: Human Kinetics.

Schifter, D. E. and Ajzen, I. (1985) 'Intention, perceived control, and weight loss: An application of the Theory of Planned Behaviour.' *Journal of Personality and Social Psychology*, 49: 843–51.

Schlackmans. (1986) *Women's fitness and exercise classes. Vol. 1: Summary and conclusions*. London: Schlackmans.

Schlicht, W. (1994a) 'Does physical exercise reduce anxious emotions? A meta-analysis.' *Anxiety, Stress and Coping*, 6: 275–88.

—— (1994b) 'Sport und seelische Gesundheit: Eine meta-analyse' (Sport and mental health: A meta-analysis). In J. Nitsch and R. Seiler (eds), *Health sport – movement therapy: Proceedings of the 8th European Congress of Sport Psychology 1991* (vol. 4, pp. 57–63). Sankt Augustin, Germany: Academia Verlag.

—— (1995) 'Does physical exercise reduce anxious emotions? A retort to Steven J. Petruzzello.' *Anxiety, Stress and Coping*, 8: 357–9.

Schmidt, R. A. (1982) *Motor control and learning*. Champaign, Ill.: Human Kinetics.

Schoeneman, T. and Curry, S. (1990) 'Attributions for successful and unsuccessful health behaviour change.' *Basic and Applied Social Psychology*, 11: 421–31.

Schoeneman, T. J., Hollis, J. F., Stevens, V. J., Fischer, K. and Cheek, P. R. (1988a) 'Recovering stride versus letting it slide: Attributions for "slips" following smoking cessation treatment.' *Psychology and Health*, 2: 335–47.

Schoeneman, T. J., Stevens, V. J., Hollis, J. F., Cheek, P. R. and Fischer, K. (1988b) 'Attribution, affect and expectancy following smoking cessation treatment.' *Basic and Applied Social Psychology*, 9: 173–84.

Schutz, R. W., Smoll, F. L., Carre, F. A. and Mosher, R. E. (1985) 'Inventories and norms for children's attitudes toward physical activity.' *Research Quarterly for Exercise and Sport*, 56: 256–65.

Schwarz, L. and Kindermann, W. (1992) 'Changes in B–endorphin levels in response to aerobic and anaerobic exercise.' *Sports Medicine*, 13: 25–36.

Schwarzer, R. (1992) 'Self-efficacy in the adoption and maintenance of health behaviours: Theoretical approaches and a new model.' In R. Schwarzer (ed.), *Self-efficacy: Thought control of action* (pp. 217–43). Bristol, Pa.: Taylor and Francis.

Scott, J. (1996) 'Cognitive therapy of affective disorders: A review.' *Journal of Affective Disorders*, 37: 1–11.

Scottish Office (1999) *Towards a healthier Scotland: A White Paper on health*. Edinburgh: The Stationery Office.

Sechrist, K. R., Walker, S. N. and Pender, N. J. (1987) 'Development and psychometric evaluation of the exercise benefits/barriers scale.' *Research in Nursing and Health*, 10: 357–65.

Secord, P. F. and Jourard, S. M. (1953) 'The appraisal of body cathexis: Body-cathexis and the self.' *Journal of Consulting Pychology*, 17: 343–7.

Seifriz, J., Duda, J. L. and Chi, L. (1992) 'The relationship of perceived motivational climate to intrinsic motivation and beliefs about success in basketball.' *Journal of Sport and Exercise Psychology*, 14: 375–91.

Seligman, M. E. P. (1975) *Helplessness: On depression, development and death*. San Fransisco: Freeman.

Sexton, H., Maere, A. and Dahl, N. H. (1989) 'Exercise intensity and reduction in neurotic symptoms: A controlled follow-up study.' *Acta Psychiatrica Scandinavica*, 80: 231–5.

Sharratt, M. T. and Sharratt, J. K. (1994) 'Potential health benefits of active living for persons with chronic conditions.' In H. A. Quinney, L. Gauvin and A. E. T. Wall (eds), *Toward active living* (pp. 39–45). Champaign, Ill.: Human Kinetics.

Shavelson, R. J., Hubner, J. J. and Stanton, G. C. (1976) 'Self-concept: Validation of construct interpretations.' *Review of Educational Research*, 46: 407–41.

Sheeran, P. and Abraham, C. (1996) 'The Health Belief Model.' In M. Conner and P. Norman (eds), *Predicting health behaviour* (pp. 23–61). Buckingham: Open University Press.

Shephard, R. J. (1985) 'Motivation: The key to fitness compliance.' *The Physician and Sportmedicine*, 13(7): 88–101.

—— (1989) 'Current perspectives on the economics of fitness and sport with particular reference to worksite programmes.' *Sports Medicine*, 7: 286–309.

——(1992) 'A critical analysis of work-site fitness programs and their postulated economic benefits.' *Medicine and Science in Sports and Exercise*, 24: 354–70.

—— (1997) 'Curricular physical activity and academic performance.' *Pediatric Exercise Science*, 9: 113–26.

Sheppard, B. H., Hartwick, J. and Warshaw, P. R. (1988) 'The theory of reasoned action: A meta-analysis of past research with recommendations for modifications and future research.' *Journal of Consumer Research*, 15: 325–43.

Sherer, M., Maddux, J. E., Mercendante, B. and Prentice-Dunn, S. (1982) 'The Self-Efficacy Scale: Construction and validation.' *Psychological Reports*, 51: 663–71.

Sheridan, C. L. and Radmacher, S. A. (1992) *Health psychology: Challenging the biomedical model*. New York: Wiley.

Siafakis, M. (1999) *Exercise and HIV+*. Unpublished M.Sc. thesis, University of Glasgow.

Sidney, K. H., Niinimaa, V. and Shephard, R. J. (1983) 'Attitudes towards exercise and sports: Sex and age differences and changes with endurance training.' *Journal of Sports Sciences*, 1: 195–210.

Simkin, A. J., Ayalon, J. and Leichter, I. (1987) 'Increased trabecular bone density due to bone-loading exercises in postmenopausal osteoporotic women.' *Calcified Tissue International*, 40: 59–63.

Simon, H. B. (1990) 'Discussion: Exercise, immunity, cancer, and infection.' In C. Bouchard, R. J. Shephard, T. Stephens, J. R. Sutton and B. D. McPherson (eds), *Exercise, fitness and health* (pp. 581–8). Champaign, Ill.: Human Kinetics.

Simons-Morton, D. G., Calfas, K. J., Oldenburg, B. and Burton, N. W. (1998) 'Effects of interventions in health care settings on physical activity or cardiorespiratory fitness.' *American Journal of Preventive Medicine*, 15: 413–30.

Singer, R. N., Murphey, M. and Tennant, L. K. (eds) (1993) *Handbook of research on sport psychology*. New York: Macmillan.

Singh, N. A., Clements, K. M. and Fiatorone, M. A. (1997) 'A randomized controlled trial of progressive resistance in depressed elders.' *Journal of Gerontology*, 52A (1): M27–M35.

Sinyor, D., Brown, T., Rostant, L. and Seraganian, P. (1982) 'The role of physical exercise in the treatment of alcoholism.' *Journal of Studies on Alcohol*, 43: 380–6.

Siscovick, D. S. (1990) 'Risks of exercising: Sudden cardiac death and injuries.' In C. Bouchard, R. J. Shephard, T. Stephens, J. R. Sutton and B. D. McPherson (eds), *Exercise, fitness and health* (pp. 707–13). Champaign, Ill.: Human Kinetics.

Siscovick, D. S., Weiss, N. S., Fletcher, R. H. and Lasky, T. (1984) 'The incidence of primary cardiac arrest during vigorous physical exercise.' *New England Journal of Medicine*, 311: 874–7.

Skinner, E. (1995) *Perceived control, motivation, and coping*. Thousand Oaks, Calif.: Sage.

—— (1996) 'A guide to constructs of control.' *Journal of Personality and Social Psychology*, 71: 549–70.

Slavin, J. L., Lutter, J. M., Cushman, S. and Lee, V. (1988) 'Pregnancy and exercise.' In J. Puhl, C. H. Brown and R. O. Voy (eds), *Sport science perspectives for women* (pp. 151–60). Champaign, Ill.: Human Kinetics.

Smith, E. L. (1982) 'Exercise for the prevention of osteoporosis: A review.' *The Physician and Sports Medicine*, 10 (3): 72–83.

Smith, E. L., Smith, K. A. and Gilligan, C. (1990) 'Exercise, fitness, osteoarthritis, and osteoporosis.' In C. Bouchard, R. J. Shephard, T. Stephens, J. R. Sutton and B. D. McPherson (eds), *Exercise, fitness, and health* (pp. 517–28). Champaign, Ill.: Human Kinetics.

Smith, R. A. (1995) *Social psychological factors in exercise adherence in adults*. Unpublished Ph.D. thesis, University of Exeter.

Smith, R. A. and Biddle, S. J. H. (1990) *Exercise adherence in the commercial sector*. Paper presented at the European Health Psychology Society 4th annual conference, Oxford University, England.

—— (1995) 'Psychological factors in the promotion of physical activity.' In S. J. H. Biddle (ed.), *European perspectives on exercise and sport psychology* (pp. 85–108). Champaign, Il: Human Kinetics.

—— (1999) 'Attitudes and exercise adherence: Tests of the Theories of Reasoned Action and Planned Behaviour.' *Journal of Sports Sciences*, 17: 269–81.

Smith, R. E. and Smoll, F. L. (1996) *Way to go coach! A scientifically-proven approach to coaching effectiveness*. Portola Valley, Calif.: Warde Publishers.

Smith, R. E., Smoll, F. L. and Curtis, B. (1979) 'Coach effectiveness training: A cognitive-behavioral approach to enhancing relationship skills in youth sport coaches.' *Journal of Sport Psychology*, 1: 59–75.

Solomon, R. L. (1980) 'The opponent-process theory of acquired motivation.' *American Psychologist*, 35: 691–712.

Sonstroem, R. J. (1984) 'Exercise and self-esteem.' *Exercise and Sport Sciences Reviews*, 12: 123–55.

Sonstroem, R. J. (1988) 'Psychological models.' In R. K. Dishman (ed.), *Exercise adherence: Its impact on public health* (pp. 125–53). Champaign, Ill.: Human Kinetics.

—— (1997a) 'Physical activity and self-esteem.' In W. P. Morgan (ed.), *Physical activity and mental health* (pp. 127–43). Washington, D.C.: Taylor and Francis.

—— (1997b) 'The physical self-system: A mediator of exercise and self-esteem.' In K. R. Fox (ed.), *The physical self: From motivation to well-being* (pp. 3–26). Champaign, Ill.: Human Kinetics.

Sonstroem, R. J. and Morgan, W. P. (1989) 'Exercise and self-esteem: Rationale and model.' *Medicine and Science in Sports and Exercise*, 21: 329–37.

Sonstroem, R. J. and Walker, M. (1973) 'Relationship of attitudes and locus of control to exercise and physical fitness.' *Perceptual and Motor Skills*, 36: 1031–4.

Sparkes, A. C. (1997) 'Reflections on the socially constructed physical self.' In K. R. Fox (ed.), *The physical self: From motivation to well-being* (pp. 83–110). Champaign, Ill.: Human Kinetics.

Spielberger, C. D., Gorsuch, R. L. and Lushene, R. (1970) *State-trait anxiety inventory manual*. Palo Alto, Calif.: Consulting Psychologists Press.

Spitzer, R. L., Endicott, J. and Robins, E. (1978) 'Research diagnostic criteria.' *Archives of General Psychiatry*, 35: 773–82.

The Sports Council and Health Education Authority (1992) *Allied Dunbar National Fitness Survey: Main findings*. London: Sports Council and Health Education Authority.

Stanley, M. and Maddux, J. (1986) 'Cognitive processes in health enhancement: Investigation of a combined protection motivation and self-efficacy model.' *Basic and Applied Social Psychology*, 7: 101–13.

Steinhardt, M. A. and Dishman, R. K. (1989) 'Reliability and validity of expected outcomes and barriers for habitual physical activity.' *Journal of Occupational Medicine*, 31: 536–46.

Stenstrom, C. H. (1994) 'Therapeutic exercise in rheumatoid arthritis.' *Arthritis Care and Research*, 7 (4): 190–7.

Stephens, T. (1987) 'Secular trends in physical activity: Exercise boom or bust?' *Research Quarterly for Exercise and Sport*, 58: 94–105.

—— (1988) 'Physical activity and mental health in the United States and Canada: Evidence from four population surveys.' *Preventive Medicine*, 17: 35–47.

Stephens, T. and Caspersen, C. J. (1994) 'The demography of physical activity.' In C. Bouchard, R. J. Shephard and T. Stephens (eds), *Physical activity, fitness, and health* (pp. 204–13). Champaign, Ill.: Human Kinetics.

Stephens, T., Jacobs, D. R. and White, C. C. (1985) 'A descriptive epidemiology of leisure-time phyical activity.' *Public Health Reports*, 100: 147–58.

Steptoe, A. and Bolton, J. (1988) 'The short-term influence of high and low intensity physical exercise on mood.' *Psychology and Health*, 2: 91–106.

Steptoe, A. and Butler, N. (1996) 'Sports participation and emotional well-being in adolescents.' *The Lancet*, 347: 1789–92.

Steptoe, A. and Cox, S. (1988) 'Acute effects of aerobic exercise on mood.' *Health Psychology*, 7: 329–40.

Steptoe, A., Doherty, S., Rink, E., Kerry, S., Kendrick, T. and Hilton, S. (1999) 'Behavioural counseling in general practice for the promotion of health behaviour among adults at increased risks of coronary heart disease: Randomized trial.' *British Medical Journal*, 319: 943–8.

Steptoe, A., Edwards, S., Moses, J. and Mathews, A. (1989) 'The effects of exercise training on mood and perceived coping ability in anxious adults from the general population.' *Journal of Psychosomatic Research*, 33: 537–47.

Steptoe, A., Moses, J., Edwards, S. and Mathews, A. (1993) 'Exercise and responsivity to mental stress: Discrepancies between the subjective and physiological effects of aerobic training.' *International Journal of Sport Psychology*, 24: 110–29.

Stewart, A. L., Hays, R. D., Wells, K. B., Roger, W. H., Spritzer, K. L. and Greenfield, S. (1994) 'Long-term functioning and well-being outcomes associated with physical activity and exercise in patients with chronic conditions in the medical outcomes study.' *Journal of Clinical Epidemiology*, 47: 719–30.

Stone, E. J., McKenzie, T. L., Welk, G. J. and Booth, M. L. (1998) 'Effects of physical activity interventions in youth: Review and synthesis.' *American Journal of Preventive Medicine*, 15: 298–315.

Strang, V. R. and Sullivan, P. L. (1985) 'Body image attitudes during pregnancy and the postpartum period.' *Journal of Obstetric Gynecological Neonatal Nursing*, 14: 332–7.

Strecher, V. J., DeVellis, B. E., Becker, M. H. and Rosenstock, I. M. (1986) 'The role of self-efficacy in achieving health behaviour change.' *Health Education Quarterly*, 13: 73–92.

Strickland, B. (1978) 'Internal-external expectancies and health-related behaviors.' *Journal of Consulting and Clinical Psychology*, 46: 1192–211.

Stringer, W. W. (1999) 'HIV and aerobic exercise: Current recommendations.' *Sports Medicine*, 28: 389–95.

Stringer, W. W., Berezovskaya, M., O'Brien, W., Beck, C. K. and Casaburi, R. (1998) 'The effect of exercise training on aerobic fitness, immune indices, and quality of life in HIV+ patients.' *Medicine and Science in Sports and Exercise*, 30: 11–16.

Stroebe, W. and Stroebe, M. S. (1995) *Social psychology and health*. Buckingham: Open University Press.

Swift, C. S., Armstrong, J. E., Beerman, K. A., Campbell, R. K. and Pond-Smoth, D. (1995) 'Attitudes and beliefs about exercise among persons with non-insulin-dependent diabetes.' *The Diabetes Educator*, 21: 533–40.

Swinburn, B. A., Walter, L. G., Arrol, B., Tilyard, M. W. and Russell, D. G. (1997) 'Green prescriptions: attitudes and perceptions of general practitioners towards prescribing exercise.' *British Journal of General Practice*, 47: 567–9.

—— (1998) 'The green prescription study: A randomized controlled trial of written exercise advice in general practice.' *American Journal of Public Health*, 88(2): 228–91.

Szabo, A. (1995) 'The impact of exercise deprivation on well-being of habitual exercisers.' *Australian Journal of Science and Medicine in Sport*, 27(3): 68–75.

—— (2000) 'Physical activity as a source of psychological dysfunction.' In S. J. H. Biddle, K. R. Fox and S. H. Boutcher (eds), *Physical activity and psychological well-being* (pp. 130–53). London: Routledge.

Tai, S. S., Gould, M. and Iliffe, S. (1997) 'Promoting health exercise among older people in general practice: Issues in designing and evaluating therapeutic interventions.' *British Journal of General Practice*, 47: 119–22.

Tang, S. H. and Hall, V. C. (1995) 'The overjustification effect: A meta-analysis.' *Applied Cognitive Psychology*, 9: 365–404.

Taylor, A. (1999) 'Adherence in primary health care exercise promotion schemes.' In S. J. Bull (ed.), *Adherence issues in sport and exercise* (pp. 47–74). Chichester: John Wiley.

—— (2000) 'Physical activity, anxiety, and stress.' In S. J. H. Biddle, K. R. Fox and S. H. Boutcher (eds), *Physical activity and psychological well-being* (pp. 10–45). London: Routledge.

Taylor, A. H., Doust, J. and Webborn, N. (1998a) 'Randomised controlled trial to examine the effects of a GP exercise referral programme in Hailsham, East Sussex, on modifiable coronary heart disease risk factors.' *Journal of Epidemiology and Community Health*, 52: 595–601.

Taylor, W. C., Baranowski, T. and Sallis, J. F. (1994) 'Family determinants of childhood physical activity: A social cognitive model.' In R. K. Dishman (ed.), *Advances in Exercise Adherence* (pp. 319–42). Champaign, Ill.: Human Kinetics.

Taylor, W. C., Baranowski, T. and Young, D. R. (1998b) 'Physical activity interventions in low-income, ethnic minority, and populations with disability.' *American Journal of Preventive Medicine*, 15: 334–43.

Telama, R. and Silvennoinen, M. (1979) 'Structure and development of 11 to 19 year olds' motivation for physical activity.' *Scandinavian Journal of Sports Sciences*, 1: 23–31.

Tenenbaum, G. and Bar-Eli, M. (1995) 'Contemporary issues in exercise and sport psychology research.' In S. J. H. Biddle (ed.), *European perspectives on exercise and sport psychology* (pp. 292–323). Champaign, Ill.: Human Kinetics.

Terry, D. J. and O'Leary, J. E. (1995) 'The theory of planned behaviour: The effects of perceived behavioural control and self-efficacy.' *British Journal of Social Psychology*, 34: 199–220.

Terry, P. C., Biddle, S. J. H., Chatzisarantis, N. and Bell, R. D. (1997) 'Development of a test to assess the attitudes of older adults towards physical activity and exercise.' *Journal of Aging and Physical Activity*, 5: 111–25.

Thirlaway, K. and Benton, D. (1996) 'Exercise and mental health: The role of activity and fitness.' In J. Kerr, A. Griffiths and T. Cox (eds), *Workplace health, employee fitness and exercise* (pp. 69–82). London: Taylor and Francis.

Thompson, C. E. and Wankel, L. M. (1980) 'The effects of perceived activity choice upon frequency of exercise behaviour.' *Journal of Applied Social Psychology*, 10: 436–43.

Thompson, J. K. and Blanton, P. (1987) 'Energy conservation and exercise dependence: A sympathetic arousal hypothesis.' *Medicine and Science in Sports and Exercise*, 19: 91–7.

Thompson, J. K. and Pasman, L. (1991) 'The obligatory exercise questionnaire.' *Behavior Therapist*, 14: 137.

Timm, K. E. (1991) 'Management of chronic low back patient pain: A retrospective analysis of different treatment approaches.' *Isokinetics and Exercise Science*, 1: 44–8.

Tomporowski, P. D. and Ellis, N. R. (1986) 'Effects of exercise on cognitive processes: A review.' *Psychological Bulletin*, 99: 338–46.

Transport 2000 (no date) *Changing journeys to work: An employers' guide to green commuter plans.* London: Transport 2000.

Triandis, H. C. (1977) *Interpersonal behaviour.* Monterey, Calif.: Brooks/Cole.

Tsukue, I. and Shohoji, T. (1981) 'Movement therapy for alcoholic patients.' *Journal of Studies on Alcohol*, 42: 144–9.

Tunstall-Pedoe, H. and Smith, W. L. S. (1986) 'Level and trends of coronary heart disease mortality in Scotland compared to other countries.' *Health Bulletin*, 44: 153–61.

Ulrich, B. D. (1987) 'Perceptions of physical competence, motor competence and participation in organised sport: Their interrelationships in young children.' *Research Quarterly for Exercise and Sport*, 58: 57–67.

Urdan, T. C. and Maehr, M. L. (1995) 'Beyond a two-goal theory of motivation and achievement: A case for social goals.' *Review of Educational Research*, 65: 213–43.

Vallerand, R. J. (1997) 'Toward a hierarchical model of intrinsic and extrinsic motivation.' In M. P. Zanna (ed.), *Advances in experimental social psychology* (vol. 29, pp. 271–360). New York: Academic Press.

Vallerand, R. J. and Blanchard, C. M. (2000) 'The study of emotion in sport and exercise: Historical, definitional, and conceptual perspectives.' In Y. L. Hanin (ed.), *Emotions in sport* (pp. 3–37). Champaign, Ill.: Human Kinetics.

Vallerand, R. J. and Fortier, M. S. (1998) 'Measures of intrinsic and extrinsic motivation in sport and physical activity: A review and critique.' In J. L. Duda (ed.), *Advances in sport and exercise psychology measurement* (pp. 81–101). Morgantown, W. Va.: Fitness Information Technology.

Vallerand, R. J. and Losier, G. F. (1999) 'An integrative analysis of intrinsic and extrinsic motivation in sport.' *Journal of Applied Sport Psychology*, 11: 142–69.

Valois, P., Desharnais, R. and Godin, G. (1988) 'A comparison of the Fishbein and Ajzen and the Triandis attitudinal models for the prediction of exercise intention and behaviour.' *Journal of Behavioral Medicine*, 11: 459–72.

Van Wersch, A. (1997) 'Individual differences and intrinsic motivations for sport participation.' In J. Kremer, K. Trew and S. Ogle (eds), *Young people's involvement in sport* (pp. 57–77). London: Routledge.

Van Wersch, A., Trew, K. and Turner, I. (1992) 'Post-primary school pupils interest in physical education: Age and gender differences.' *British Journal of Educational Psychology*, 62: 56–72.

Vasterling, J. J., Sementilli, M. E. and Burish, T. G. (1988) 'The role of aerobic exercise in reducing stress in diabetic patients.' *Diabetic Education*, 14(3): 197–201.

Vaughn, C. C. (1976) 'Rehabilitation of post-menopausal osteoporosis.' *Israeli Journal of Medical Sciences*, 12: 652–9.

Veale, D. (1995) 'Does primary exercise dependence really exist?' In J. Annett, B. Cripps and H. Steinberg (eds), *Exercise addiction. Motivations for participation in sport and exercise* (p. 71). Leicester: British Psychological Society Sport and Exercise Psychology Section.

Veale, D. and Le Fevre, K. (1988) *A survey of exercise dependence.* Paper presented at the Sport, Health, Psychology and Exercise Symposium, Bisham Abbey National Sports Centre.

Veale, D., Le Fevre, K., Pantelis, C., de Souza, V., Mann, A. and Sargeant, A. (1992) 'Aerobic exercise in the adjunctive treatment of depression: A randomized controlled trial.' *Journal of the Royal Society of Medicine*, 85: 541–4.

Veale, D. M. W. (1987) 'Exercise dependence.' *British Journal of Addiction*, 82: 735–40.

Vealey, R. S. (1986) 'Conceptualisation of sport confidence and competitive orientation: Preliminary investigation and instrument development.' *Journal of Sport and Exercise Psychology*, 8: 221–53.

Vitale, A. E., Sullivan, S. J., Jankowski, L. W., Fleury, J., Lefrancois, C. and Lebouthillier, E. (1995) 'Screening of health risk factors prior to exercise or a fitness evaluation of adults with traumatic brain injury: A consensus by rehabilitation professionals.' *Brain Injury*, 10: 367–75.

Vlachopoulos, S., Biddle, S. and Fox, K. (1996) 'A social-cognitive investigation into the mechanisms of affect generation in children's physical activity.' *Journal of Sport and Exercise Psychology*, 18: 174–93.

Vlachopoulos, S. and Biddle, S. J. H. (1997) 'Modeling the relation of goal orientations to achievement-related affect in physical education: Does perceived ability matter?' *Journal of Sport and Exercise Psychology*, 19: 169–87.

Vranic, M. and Wasserman, D. (1990) 'Exercise, fitness, and diabetes.' In C. Bouchard, R. J. Shephard, T. Stephens, J. R. Sutton and B. D. McPherson (eds), *Exercise, fitness and health: A consensus of current knowledge* (pp. 467–90). Champaign, Ill.: Human Kinetics.

Vuori, I. (1995) 'Exercise and physical health: Musculoskeletal health and functional capabilities.' *Reserach Quarterly for Exercise and Sport*, 66: 276–85.

Vuori, I. M., Oja, P. and Paronen, O. (1994) 'Physically active commuting to work: Testing its potential for exercise promotion.' *Medicine and Science in Sports and Exercise*, 26: 844–50.

Waddell, G. (1992) 'Biopsychosocial analysis of low back pain.' *Balliere's Clinical Rheumatology*, 6: 523–57.

Wallace, A. M., Boyer, D. B., Dan, A. and Holm, K. (1986) 'Aerobic exercise, maternal self-esteem, and physical discomforts during pregnancy.' *Journal of Nurse-Midwifery*, 31: 255–62.

Wallston, B. and Wallston, K. (1978) 'Locus of control and health: A review of the literature.' *Health Education Monographs*, 6: 107–17.

Wallston, B. S. and Wallston, K. A. (1985) 'Social psychological models of health behaviour: An examination and integration.' In A. Baum, S. E. Taylor and J. E. Singer (eds), *Handbook of psychology and health: IV. Social psychological aspects of health* (pp. 23–53). Hillsdale, N.J.: Erlbaum.

Wallston, K. A., Wallston, B. S. and DeVellis, R. (1978) 'Development of the multidimensional health locus of control (MHLC) scales.' *Health Education Monographs*, 6: 160–70.

Walter, S. D. and Hart, L. E. (1990) 'Application of epidemiological methodology to sports and exercise science research.' *Exercise and Sport Sciences Reviews*, 18: 417–48.

Wankel, L. and Hills, C. (1994) 'A social marketing approach and stage of change perspective of interventions to enhance physical activity: The importance of PRs.' In H. A. Quinney, L. Gauvin and A. E. T. Wall (eds), *Toward active living* (pp. 115–22). Champaign, Ill.: Human Kinetics.

Wankel, L. M. (1997) '"Strawpersons", selective reporting, and inconsistent logic: A response to Kimiecik and Harris's analysis of enjoyment.' *Journal of Sport and Exercise Psychology*, 19: 98–109.

Wankel, L. M. and Kreisel, P. S. J. (1985) 'Factors underlying enjoyment of youth sports: Sport and age group comparisons.' *Journal of Sport Psychology*, 7: 51–74.

Wankel, L. M. and Mummery, K. W. (1993) 'Using national survey data incorporating the theory of planned behavior: Implications for social marketing strategies in physical activity.' *Journal of Applied Sport Psychology*, 5: 158–77.

Wankel, L. M. and Sefton, J. M. (1994) 'Physical activity and other lifestyle behaviors.' In C. Bouchard, R. J. Shephard and T. Stephens (eds), *Physical activity, fitness, and health* (pp. 531–50). Champaign, Ill.: Human Kinetics.

Wankel, L. M., Yardley, J. K. and Graham, J. (1985) 'The effects of motivational interventions upon the exercise adherence of high and low self-motivated adults.' *Canadian Journal of Applied Sports Sciences*, 10: 147–56.

Ward, A. and Morgan, W. P. (1984) 'Adherence patterns of healthy men and women enrolled in an adult exercise program.' *Journal of Cardiac Rehabilitation*, 4: 143–52.

Wardman, M., Hatfield, R. and Page, M. (1997) 'The UK national cycling strategy: Can improved facilities meet the targets?' *Crowthorne: Transport Policy*, 4(2): 123–33.

Ware, J., Snows, K. K., Kosinski, M. and Gandek, B. (1993) *SF36: Health survey manual and interpretation guide*. Boston: Nimrod Press.

Warner, K., Wickizer, T. M., Wolfe, R. A., Schildroth, J. E. and Samuelson, M. H. (1988) 'Economic implications of workplace health promotion programs: Review of the literature.' *Journal of Occupational Medicine*, 30: 106–12.

Watson, D., Clark, L. A. and Tellegen, A. (1988) 'Development and validation of brief measures of positive and negative affect: The PANAS scales.' *Journal of Personality and Social Psychology*, 54: 1063–70.

Watson, D., Wiese, D., Vaidya, J. and Tellegen, A. (1999) 'The two general activation systems of affect: Structural findings, evolutionary considerations, and psychobiological evidence.' *Journal of Personality and Social Psychology*, 76: 820–38.

Weber, J. and Wertheim, E. H. (1989) 'Relationships of self-monitoring, special attention, body fat percentage, and self-motivation to attendance at a community gymnasium.' *Journal of Sport and Exercise Psychology*, 11: 105–14.

Weinberg, R. S., Hughes, H. H., Critelli, J. W., England, R. and Jackson, A. (1984) 'Effects of pre-existing and manipulated self-efficacy on weight loss in a self-control programme.' *Journal of Research in Personality*, 18: 352–8.

Weiner, B. (1979) 'A theory of motivation for some classroom experiences.' *Journal of Educational Psychology*, 71: 3–25.

—— (1986) *An attributional theory of motivation and emotion*. New York: Springer-Verlag.

——(1992) *Human motivation*. Newbury Park, Calif.: Sage.

—— (1995) *Judgements of responsibility*. New York: Guilford Press.

Weinstein, N. (1988) 'The precaution adoption process.' *Health Psychology*, 7: 355–86.

—— (1993) 'Testing four competing theories of health-protective behavior.' *Health Psychology*, 12: 324–33.

Weinstein, N. D., Rothman, A. J. and Sutton, S. R. (1998) 'Stage theories of health behavior: Conceptual and methodological issues.' *Health Psychology*, 17: 290–9.

Weismann, M. M. and Klerman, G. L. (1992) 'Depression: Current understanding and changing trends.' *Annual Review Public Health*, 13: 319–39.

Weiss, M. R. (1986) 'A theoretical overview of competence motivation.' In M. R. Weiss and D. Gould (eds), *Sport for children and youths* (pp. 75–80). Champaign, Ill.: Human Kinetics.

Weiss, M. R., Bredemeier, B. J. and Shewchuk, R. M. (1985) 'An intrinsic/extrinsic motivation scale for the youth sport setting: A confirmatory factor analysis.' *Journal of Sport Psychology*, 7: 75–91.

—— (1986) 'The dynamics of perceived competence, perceived control, and motivational orientation in youth sport.' In M. R. Weiss and D. Gould (eds), *Sport for children and youths* (pp. 89–102). Champaign, Ill.: Human Kinetics.

Wells, N. (1985) *Back pain*. London: Office of Health Economics.

Weyerer, S. (1992) 'Physical inactivity and depression in the community: Evidence from the Upper Bavarian Field Study.' *Journal of Sports Medicine*, 13: 492–6.

White, R. W. (1959) 'Motivation reconsidered: The concept of competence.' *Psychological Review*, 66: 297–333.

Whitehead, J. R. (1993) 'Physical activity and intrinsic motivation.' *President's Council on Physical Fitness and Sports Physical Activity and Fitness Research Digest*, 1(2): 1–8.

—— (1995) 'A study of children's physical self-perceptions using an adapted physical self-perception profile questionnaire.' *Pediatric Exercise* Science, 7: 132–51.

Whitehead, J. R. and Corbin, C. B. (1988) 'Multidimensional scales for the measurement of locus of control of reinforcements for physical fitness behaviors.' *Research Quarterly for Exercise and Sport*, 59: 108–17.

—— (1991) 'Youth fitness testing: The effect of percentile-based evaluative feedback on intrinsic motivation.' *Research Quarterly for Exercise and Sport*, 62: 225–31.

Whitehead, J. R., Pemberton, C. L. and Corbin, C. B. (1990) 'Perspectives on the physical fitness testing of children: The case for a realistic educational approach.' *Pediatric Exercise Science*, 2: 111–23.

Widmeyer, W. N., Brawley, L. R. and Carron, A. V. (1985) *The measurement of cohesion in sport teams: The Group Environment Questionnaire*. London, Ontario: Sports Dynamics.

Widmeyer, W. N., Carron, A. V. and Brawley, L. R. (1993) 'Group cohesion in sport and exercise.' In R. Singer, M. Murphey and L. K. Tennant (eds), *Handbook of research on sport psychology* (pp. 672–92). New York: Macmillan.

Wiersma, U. J. (1992) 'The effects of extrinsic rewards in intrinsic motivation: A meta-analysis.' *Journal of Occupational and Organizational Psychology*, 65: 101–14.

Williams, H. G. (1986) 'The development of sensory-motor function in young children.' In V. Seefeldt (ed.), *Physical activity and well-being* (pp. 106–22). Reston, Va.: American Alliance for Health, Physical Education, Recreation, and Dance.

Williams, J. G. and Eston, R. G. (1989) 'Determination of the intensity dimension in vigorous exercise programmes with particular reference to the use of the Rating of Perceived Exertion.' *Sports Medicine*, 8: 177–89.

Williamson, D. F., Madans, J., Anda, R. F., Kleinman, J. C., Kahn, H. S. and Byers, T. (1993) 'Recreational physical activity and 10-year weight change in a US national cohort.' *International Journal of Obesity*, 17: 279–86.

Wimbush, E., Macgregor, A. and Fraser, E. (1997) 'Impacts of a mass media campaign on walking in Scotland.' *Health Promotion International*, 13: 45–53.

Wing, R. R., Epstein, L. H., Nowalk, M. P. and Lamparski, D. M. (1986) 'Behavioral self-regulation in the treatment of patients with diabetes mellitus.' *Psychological Bulletin*, 99: 78.

Wollman, R. L., Cornall, C., Fulcher, K. and Greenwood, R. (1994) 'Aerobic training in brain-injured patients.' *Clinical Rehabilitation*, 8: 253–7.

Woods, C., Mutrie, N. and Scott, M. (1999) 'More students, more active, more often: Exercise behaviour change in a student population' (abstract). *Journal of Sports Sciences*, 17: 75–6.

World Health Organization (1986) *Targets for Health for All*. Copenhagen: World Health Organization.

—— (1993) *The ICD–10 classification of mental and behavioral disorders: Diagnostic criteria for research*. Geneva: World Health Organization.

Wurtele, S. and Maddux, J. (1987) 'Relative contributions of protection motivation theory components in predicting exercise intentions and behaviour.' *Health Psychology*, 6: 453–66.

Wyse, J., Mercer, T., Ashford, B., Buxton, K. and Gleeson, N. (1995) 'Evidence for the validity and utility of the Stages of Exercise Behaviour Change scale in young adults.' *Health Education Research: Theory and Practice*, 10: 365–77.

Young, D. R. (1997) 'Community-based interventions for increasing physical activity.' In A. S. Leon (ed.), *Physical activity and cardiovascular health: A national consensus* (pp. 252–61). Champaign, Ill.: Human Kinetics.

Youngstedt, S. D., O'Connor, P. J. and Dishman, R. K. (1997) 'The effects of acute exercise on sleep: A quantitative synthesis.' *Sleep*, 20: 203–14.

Zaitz, D. (1989) 'Are you an exercise addict?' *Idea Today*, 7: 44.

Zuckerman, M. and Lubin, B. (1965) *Manual for the Multiple Affect Adjective Checklist.* San Diego, Calif.: Educational and Industrial Testing Service.

Zung, W. W. K. (1965) 'A self-rating depression scale.' *Archives of General Psychiatry*, 12: 63–70.

Zung, W. W. K., Richards, C. B. and Short, M. J. (1965) 'Self-rating depression scale in an outpatient clinic.' *Archives of General Psychiatry*, 13: 508–15.

Index